RESTITUTION AND
UNJUST ENRICHMENT

ASPEN CASEBOOK SERIES

RESTITUTION AND UNJUST ENRICHMENT

Cases and Notes

Andrew Kull

Distinguished Senior Lecturer
The University of Texas School of Law

Ward Farnsworth

Dean and John Jeffers Research Chair in Law
The University of Texas School of Law

 Wolters Kluwer

Published by Wolters Kluwer in New York.

Wolters Kluwer Legal & Regulatory U.S. serves customers worldwide with CCH, Aspen Publishers, and Kluwer Law International products. (www.WKLegaledu.com)

To contact Customer Service, e-mail customer.service@wolterskluwer.com, call 1-800-234-1660, fax 1-800-901-9075, or mail correspondence to:

    Wolters Kluwer
    Attn: Order Department
    PO Box 990
    Frederick, MD 21705

Printed in the United States of America.

2 3 4 5 6 7 8 9 0

ISBN 978-1-5438-0090-6

Library of Congress Cataloging-in-Publication Data

Names: Kull, Andrew (Law teacher), author. | Farnsworth, Ward, 1967- author.
Title: Restitution and unjust enrichment : cases and notes / Andrew Kull, Distinguished Senior Lecturer, The University of Texas School of Law; Ward Farnsworth, Dean and John Jeffers Research Chair in Law, The University of Texas School of Law.
Description: New York : Wolters Kluwer, 2018. | Series: Aspen casebook series
Identifiers: LCCN 2018023672 | ISBN 9781543800906
Subjects: LCSH: Unjust enrichment—United States. | Restitution—United States. | LCGFT: Casebooks (Law).
Classification: LCC KF1244 .K85 2018 | DDC 346.7302/9—dc23
LC record available at https://lccn.loc.gov/2018023672

About Wolters Kluwer Legal & Regulatory U.S.

Wolters Kluwer Legal & Regulatory U.S. delivers expert content and solutions in the areas of law, corporate compliance, health compliance, reimbursement, and legal education. Its practical solutions help customers successfully navigate the demands of a changing environment to drive their daily activities, enhance decision quality and inspire confident outcomes.

Serving customers worldwide, its legal and regulatory portfolio includes products under the Aspen Publishers, CCH Incorporated, Kluwer Law International, ftwilliam.com and MediRegs names. They are regarded as exceptional and trusted resources for general legal and practice-specific knowledge, compliance and risk management, dynamic workflow solutions, and expert commentary.

SUMMARY OF CONTENTS

TABLE OF CONTENTS

PREFACE

Restitution is a body of law that has immense practical value and wide application to disputes of all sorts. Simply put, it is the set of rules that govern recovery of gains that a party should not keep—or "unjust enrichment," as it is formally called; and unjust enrichment occurs every day in both private and commercial transactions. Restitution has the dual distinction of being one of the most useful of all bodies of law and the one most often overlooked. It is overlooked because several generations of modern lawyers never heard about the subject in law school. The development of this field into a coherent subject of study occurred in a manner and at a time that kept it from gaining a secure foothold in the standard curriculum. Never having learned it as students, few of today's law professors went forth to teach it. Ignorance of the law of restitution has been growing with compound interest.

The neglect of restitution has become nearly complete in recent years, with the absence of a single casebook in print. It has thus become nearly impossible to teach restitution law even if one wants to do it. This book seeks to fill that void. It presents the law of restitution—its substance, its remedies, its history—in a manner meant to be consistently practical and interesting. Students who persevere will end up in possession of tools that are of great and regular value in the practice of law, and they will have the advantage of understanding things that their adversaries probably will not. They also will have the pleasure of learning a new way of thinking about many familiar kinds of conflicts. The conditioned reflex of the modern American lawyer is to view nearly every dispute as an occasion to seek damages. What happens when we look at those disputes instead as an occasion to reverse the defendant's gains? The answers are found in cases that possess all the same charm and instruction as the classic cases in the common-law fields that every student encounters early in law school. Indeed, we suggest that this is the right spirit in which to approach the study of restitution: to see it as the forgotten member of the great family of first-year subjects.

Caveat Lector

The basic organization of this book follows the various headings of liability in restitution: mistakes; other instances of defective consent, such as fraud and duress; unrequested intervention; and so forth. At the end of the book come three important chapters cutting across the liabilities: recapitulations of remedies, defenses, and priorities in restitution. These are topics that invite a separate review, though it is naturally impossible to read even two or three cases without encountering them all in one way or another. Liabilities, defenses, and remedies are mixed up throughout the book, just as they are in real life, and the reader, like the lawyer, must be prepared to take them as they come.

Most of what follows has been copied from somewhere else — usually judicial opinions, sometimes books or articles. Quoted material is presented here in a manner designed to promote the convenience of the reader and the editors. That means, in particular, that we do not indicate the omission of text, citations, or footnotes, by ellipsis or otherwise — except when we feel like it, in which case we do. Minor variations in wording have occasionally been incorporated, sometimes with brackets and sometimes without, to preserve the continuity of the edited text. On the other hand, we are scrupulous about any citations that do appear, to the point of expanding or otherwise improving those given by our sources.

The idea is that the book should be as readable as possible, and that it should provide an infallible guide to finding the original authorities. But our edited materials must not be quoted as if they matched their sources.

Andrew Kull
Ward Farnsworth

Austin
August 2018

ACKNOWLEDGMENTS

Douglas Laycock was a mainstay of the American Law Institute's *Restatement Third, Restitution and Unjust Enrichment*. Without his support for that project, it would not have been undertaken; without his active participation, it would not have succeeded. When R3RUE was finally completed, Doug was an early and eloquent advocate of the next step to be taken toward the rehabilitation of the subject:

> For restitution and unjust enrichment to be once again firmly planted in the legal consciousness, it has to be restored to the curriculum. Some students would take the course, more would hear about the course from friends, and nearly all would see its title on the list of courses. They would know that restitution and unjust enrichment is a body of law.
>
> For that to happen on more than a scattered or occasional basis, someone must produce a casebook. . . . If he builds it, they will come.*

May these words prove as prescient as they were encouraging!

We are grateful to Sam Bray, Ralph Brubaker, Bruce Frier, and Henry Smith, all of whom used tentative versions of this book in their classrooms and shared their comments, suggestions, and corrections. Among the many students at Boston University and the University of Texas who learned about Restitution from a slowly-evolving casebook, we particularly thank Francesco DeLuca, Adam Foldes, and Norman Walczak for their memorable contributions.

For their assistance in locating illustrations that appear in this book, we are grateful to the staff of the Los Angeles Public Library (History & Genealogy

---

* Laycock, *Restoring Restitution to the Canon,* 110 Mich. L. Rev. 929, 951 (2012).

Department) and the David M. Rubenstein Rare Book and Manuscript Library at Duke University.

RESTITUTION AND
UNJUST ENRICHMENT

Chapter 1

Introduction

A. WHAT IS "RESTITUTION," ANYWAY?

As used in this book, "restitution" means liability based on unjust enrichment. (The standard vocabulary of the subject is both unsatisfactory and controversial. Fortunately it is easier to recognize what this part of the law is doing than to agree about definitions.)

The reader is likely familiar with the law of tort. That body of law awards damages to victims of wrongs to compensate them for their losses. The law of restitution takes the opposite approach. It is focused on gain-based recovery—that is, on lawsuits in which the plaintiff seeks to take away gains that the defendant should not have made, rather than obtaining compensation for losses that the plaintiff should not have suffered. Sometimes restitution can be used to address the same problems that tort law does. If a swindler takes $10,000 from a victim, invests it, and ends up with $1,000,000, a tort claim would usually provide the victim with $10,000 in damages. Recovery in restitution produces a recovery of $1,000,000. But there are also many important situations in which a suit to take away a defendant's gains can solve problems that are not reached by any other body of law at all. If a donor mistakenly gives assets to A that were meant for B, the only way the donor (or B) can get the assets back from A is by a claim for restitution. There is no tort or contract claim in sight. That is a simple example; there are many others, often highly significant, as we shall see.

The word "restitution" is used in various ways in law, and this sometimes causes confusion. First, many lawyers mistakenly think of restitution only as a species of remedy. They might recall that in an action for breach of contract, the plaintiff can sometimes seek "restitution for breach" instead of the usual expectation damages, and they imagine that restitution is just one variety of the damages that a plaintiff might seek at the end of other lawsuits as well. But restitution isn't just a remedy. It is the name of a theory of liability, or cause of action—again, analogous to tort—that a plaintiff can assert in many cases where no other kind of claim helps. The theory of the suit is not that the plaintiff has been wronged. It is that the defendant has been unjustly enriched.

Second, the word "restitution" suggests, as a matter of English, "restoration" or "giving back." This sometimes causes lawyers to imagine that restitution always involves an effort to make a defendant return something the plaintiff once had. Sometimes a restitution claim does work that way, but sometimes not. A claim for restitution can arise any time a defendant has been unjustly enriched, whether or not the "enrichment" amounts to possession of some-thing that ever belonged to the plaintiff. In the case of mistake described a moment ago, the donor's claim against A seeks the return of property that the donor once owned. But a restitution claim against A by B (in other words, a suit by the person who was supposed to receive the property, brought against the person who received it by mistake) is an effort to take gains away from A that B never owned, but to which B has better rights.

Beginning in the 1970s, lawyers have also used the word "restitution" in a very different way: to refer to payments that convicted criminals may be ordered to make to their victims as part of the sentencing process. Statutes that authorize payments of this kind sometimes call them "victim restitution." But the payments amount to an award of damages—they force the defendant to make the victim whole, not to turn over profits from the crime. So-called restitution of that kind is not gain-based recovery, and it has nothing to do with our subject in this book.

Once the principles of unjust enrichment have become recognizable and familiar, these problems of terminology usually fall away. But a lawyer approaching the subject for the first time needs some initial patience with an unfamiliar vocabulary.

B. SOME LEGAL HISTORY, AND AN IMPORTANT CASE

Courts of law and courts of equity used to be separate. They had their own rules and vocabularies. The body of law we now call "restitution" has origins in both of those systems. On rare occasions it still can matter whether some particular feature of restitution law has its roots in law or in equity, as when a statute entitles a plaintiff to "appropriate equitable relief," or when a plain-tiff's request for a jury trial depends on whether the claim is considered legal or equitable. But the modern use of restitution law does not usually require much worry about these distinctions.

At the same time, however, the law of restitution does use some concepts and vocabulary that were developed in equity courts and that can seem unfamiliar and puzzling to lawyers who are accustomed to the language of contract and tort. Terms such as "constructive trust" and "subrogation," for example, are common and important in restitution cases, but they never arise during the first year of law school and are impossible to understand without help. A brief discussion of some of the "law v. equity" background of our subject will make it easier to understand those terms and much else that follows.

(1) Restitution at law: the fictitious promise

Some parts of restitution law began as efforts to stretch contract law to solve problems that didn't have much to do with contracts. Suppose that A takes room and board at B's inn, then refuses to pay the bill—but never explicitly promised to pay it. Modern analysis would see this as a simple example of a contract "implied in fact," or (better) an "implied contract"—meaning that an agreement can be inferred even though a promise was never made. Early decisions reached the same result by letting B recover for breach of a fictitious promise. B's pleading was that "A promised he would pay for the room at the usual rate, then refused to perform his promise." Liability based on promises that had never been made was a versatile tool, and it was easily turned to other uses as well. Suppose that A owed B £5 and paid the debt twice by mistake. A asked B to return the overpayment; B refused. Obviously A should be entitled to recover the money, but it was not clear what legal theory was available to produce that result. Some lawyer for A eventually had the idea that a fictitious promise might work in this context as well. So A pleaded that "when I paid B twice by mistake, B promised to repay the extra £5 but then refused to perform." Courts went along with it.

For a modern lawyer, the first of these two scenarios is a case of implied contract; the second is a case of restitution. So long as legal claims were organized by the rules of pleading, however, there was no reason to distinguish the two cases. Both were called cases of "implied contract" or "assumpsit" (meaning "he promised"). The first came to be called a contract "implied in fact," while the second was called a contract "implied in law." Additional synonyms were used to describe this second form of liability, notably "constructive contract" and "quasi-contract." These terms made many restitution cases appear to be a species of contract—though a strange one, since it was usually evident that the defendant had never made any promise. It therefore was a helpful breakthrough when scholars of the 1890s began to say that liability in such cases was based not on the defendant's promise, but on the defendant's unjust enrichment at the expense of the plaintiff—a separate theory of liability we now identify with the law of restitution.

References to "quasi-contract" or to "contracts implied in law" still appear in the cases, and it is important to understand that liability under such headings has nothing to do with an enforceable promise. The old association between restitution and fictitious contracts persists elsewhere as well. Statutes of limitations in many jurisdictions have been interpreted to cover restitution claims within a provision governing "contracts not in writing"—or some similar category—because of the history just mentioned, and because the legislatures did not put them anywhere else.

(2) Restitution at law: the idea of unjust enrichment

When 19th-century writers like James Barr Ames and Samuel Williston insisted that a liability in "quasi-contract" was actually based on unjust enrichment, they were not advancing a novel theory. They were embracing an idea that had been expounded in a number of 18th-century decisions by Lord Mansfield, as Chief Justice of the Court of King's Bench. Like some other notable suggestions by the great English judge—such as the decisions by which he attempted to eliminate the doctrine of consideration from the law of contracts—the proposition that the common law embodied a largely equitable concern with unjust enrichment proved too radical for his contemporaries. After Lord Mansfield's retirement from the bench, his statements about unjust enrichment as a principle of liability at common law tended to be either ignored or explained away as rhetorical excess.

But to this day, the fountainhead of the idea of unjust enrichment as a basis of liability in our legal system can be pinpointed in some profoundly influential statements by Lord Mansfield, notably in his opinion in Moses v. Macferlan, 2 Burr. 1005, 97 Eng. Rep. 676 (K.B. 1760). The facts of the case were convoluted: they involved an effort by Moses to get back money that Macferlan had won from him in an earlier lawsuit that Moses claimed was improperly brought. To plead such an action, Moses could not (yet) say, "Macferlan has been unjustly enriched at my expense," because no one had yet recognized that this was a basis of liability at common law. Instead Moses had to plead his case the old, formal way, based on one of the fictitious promises—this one called "money had and received"—to the effect that "Macferlan got money from me by improper means, he promised to return it, and he broke his promise."

Moses won the case, but its importance doesn't arise from the result (indeed, the result has since been questioned). The opinion is important, rather, because Lord Mansfield took this occasion to explain what the well-established fictitious pleadings were actually aiming at:

> Money may be recovered by a right and legal judgment; and yet the iniquity of keeping that money may be manifest, upon grounds which could not be used by way of defence against the judgment. Suppose an indorsee of a promissory note, having received payment from the drawer (or maker) of it, sues and recovers the same money from the indorser who knew nothing of such payment. Suppose a man recovers upon a policy for a ship presumed to be lost, which afterwards comes home;—or upon the life of a man presumed to be dead, who afterwards appears;—or upon a representation of a risque deemed to be fair,

which comes out afterwards to be grossly fraudulent. [2 Burr. at 1010, 97 Eng. Rep. at 679.]

This kind of equitable action, to recover back money, which ought not in justice to be kept, is very beneficial, and therefore much encouraged. It lies only for money which, *ex aequo et bono*, the defendant ought to refund: it does not lie for money paid by the plaintiff, which is claimed of him as payable in point of honor and honesty, although it could not have been recovered from him by any course of law; as in payment of a debt barred by the Statute of Limitations, or contracted during his infancy, or to the extent of principal and legal interest upon an usurious contract, or, for money fairly lost at play: because in all these cases, the defendant may retain it with a safe conscience, though by positive law he was barred from recovering. But it lies for money paid by mistake; or upon a consideration which happens to fail; or for money got through imposition, (express, or implied;) or extortion; or oppression; or an undue advantage taken of the plaintiff's situation, contrary to laws made for the protection of persons under those circumstances. In one word, the gist of this kind of action is, that the defendant, upon the circumstances of the case, is obliged by the ties of natural justice and equity to refund the money. [*Id.* at 1012, 97 Eng. Rep. at 681.]

Lord Mansfield's reasoning sounds less remarkable to modern ears than it did at the time because many of his observations are now so well accepted. References to obligations based on "natural justice and equity" were shockingly out of place in explaining a legal (as opposed to an equitable) liability, but the radical nature of this departure is scarcely recognizable for lawyers today; they might be hard put to explain the difference between these formerly separate legal systems. The more lasting significance of Lord Mansfield's judgment was his innovative and accurate insight about the nature of the obligations being enforced in the guise of fictitious promises. These cases had nothing to do with contracts, implied or otherwise. They were about what we now call unjust enrichment.

(3) Restitution in equity

Equity supplied the underlying rationale, in Lord Mansfield's version, for the *legal* side of restitution. "Natural justice" and "*ex aequo et bono*" reflect the language and thinking of the equity courts—as does the idea of "unjust enrichment"—so we could conclude that equity is the glue that holds this body of law together.

In addition to explaining why people should be able to recover for unjust enrichment at all, principles of equity made important contributions to the remedial side of restitution. Their importance is again best seen by contrast to other areas of law. A plaintiff who wins a tort claim usually obtains a judgment for damages against the defendant. Now the defendant owes the plaintiff money, which the plaintiff can try to collect in the same way as anyone else owed money by the defendant. Sometimes the plaintiff in a restitution case seeks (and gets) the same thing: a simple judgment for money. But courts of equity offered powerful additional remedies to a plaintiff who could show that the defendant's unjust enrichment took the form of identifiable assets; the plaintiff in such a case might want ownership of those assets (or a lien on them) rather than a judgment against the defendant personally. The same remedies are available today, under their traditional names, which courts usually do not stop to explain. We will encounter these equitable remedies frequently in the materials that follow, and even when they are not explicitly invoked they may be not far offstage. A detailed understanding will emerge from the cases, but here is a brief list by way of introduction:

(a) *Constructive trust* is the most important equitable remedy in restitution and the most frequently encountered. Suppose the defendant embezzled $1 million from the plaintiff. A court can say that the defendant holds the money in "constructive trust" for the plaintiff. That declaration means that the plaintiff still owns the money and is entitled to the delivery of it. This might sound the same as giving the plaintiff a judgment against the defendant for $1 million, but there is an important difference. If the defendant is insolvent—in other words, if the defendant does not have enough money to pay every creditor—the plaintiff who holds a money judgment gets into the queue with everyone else and collects some number of pennies on the dollar. The constructive trust prevents the assets from being divided in that way. They belong entirely to the plaintiff. This result can have great practical significance. When the law catches up to defendants who have embezzled money or committed other wrongs, they usually do not have enough money to satisfy all the claims against them.

The expression "constructive trust" is often a source of puzzlement. The device has that name because it began as a supplement to the liability of a trustee under a real trust to account for (real) trust assets. Suppose Uncle creates a trust fund for the benefit of Niece, and appoints Trustee to administer the fund for Niece's benefit. Trustee misappropriates $10,000 of funds from the trust and uses it to buy shares of stock in his own name. On discovery of the facts, Niece would have a claim against the trustee to recover the missing $10,000. (One way to characterize such a claim is restitution, though she may have other options as well.) But the beneficiary might prefer to have the stock itself. (Why?) Early chancellors in equity reached this result by announcing that the faithless trustee would be made a "constructive" trustee of the asset he had acquired with trust funds. In 19th-century American law, the constructive trust became far more flexible when courts began to employ it in situations where there was no previous trust relationship between the parties—as in the case of embezzlement described a moment ago.

Once this last step had been taken, it became commonplace for U.S. lawyers to repeat that a constructive trust is "not a real trust, only a remedy." At least most of the time it is a remedy for unjust enrichment.

(b) Equitable lien. Suppose that Embezzler used Claimant's $10,000 to make improvements to Blackacre (which Embezzler already owned). Claimant is not entitled to the whole property, only to one part of it—but to a part of it that cannot be severed from the rest. Yet Claimant's property (the $10,000) has clearly been incorporated within Embezzler's property and used to augment it. Claimant might still prefer a property-based remedy, giving him a claim on Blackacre, to a simple money judgment against Embezzler. (Why?) The traditional way to achieve this is to declare that Blackacre is subject to an "equitable lien" securing Claimant's right to recover the $10,000. (The lien is "equitable" because it is imposed by judicial decree—as opposed to a "consensual lien" created by the parties' agreement.) Now if Embezzler does not pay the $10,000 to redeem his property, Claimant can foreclose the equitable lien—with the result that Blackacre will be sold, and Claimant paid his $10,000 out of the proceeds.

(c) Following property into its product. Another equitable remedy of vital importance is implicit in the hypotheticals just considered. Restitution to the trust beneficiary (or the embezzlement victim) need not take the form of ownership of the original $10,000. That money is probably gone. Instead, the claimant wants to be the owner of the property that the trustee (or embezzler) acquired with the missing money. The equitable side of property law allows a wrongfully dispossessed owner to "follow" his property through changes in form and to assert ownership of the substitute. Since the defendant will have legal title to the substitute property—the shares of stock, or whatever the defendant bought—the remedy normally involves two steps: (i) identify the stock as the product of the stolen money, then (ii) ask the court to declare that the wrongdoer is a "constructive trustee" of the stock. Again, this remedy has much practical importance. A defendant's unjust enrichment usually starts as money, but the money is soon spent on other things. Restitution allows a plaintiff to claim those things, if he can show that the defendant acquired them with the plaintiff's money.

(d) Subrogation. Instead of following his property into the acquisition of another asset, the dispossessed owner might be able to follow it into the payment of a debt. Subrogation (meaning "substitution") is the name of the remedy that permits a claimant to do this. In the previous hypothetical, Embezzler might have taken $10,000 of Claimant's funds and used the money to pay a debt owed by Embezzler to Bank. Claimant would like to get the money back from Bank, but—so long as Bank did not realize it was being paid in stolen money—this is not going to be possible. As a second-best solution, subrogation allows Claimant to step into Bank's shoes and assert Bank's claim against Embezzler—or rather, the claim that Bank would have had, if Embezzler's debt to Bank had not yet been paid. This approach might be attractive to Claimant if Bank had powerful rights against Embezzler, such as a security interest in Embezzler's property that can now be enforced. Those rights of Bank now become rights of Claimant.

C. A LITTLE MORE LEGAL HISTORY

The fact that the law of unjust enrichment combined legal and equitable principles made the concept heretical and delayed its recognition as a coherent set of rules and a subject around which the law might be organized, comparable to the fields of Contract and Tort. Restitution was thus a latecomer to the law school curriculum and to the library shelf, and the effects of its late arrival are still felt. Contracts and Torts were creations of the mid-19th-century treatise writers, making them more recent discoveries than might generally be supposed. But they were already on the scene when the law schools formalized their courses of study, and when the West Publishing Company drew up its "Key Number" indexing system. Restitution had not yet been described in that way, so it was left out. It has lagged ever since in the understanding of the bench and bar, and has often been overlooked in cases where it would provide more useful solutions or larger recoveries than other types of claims.

> By the usual account, the common law of unjust enrichment received its earliest modern description in the work of the American Law Institute. The occasion was the publication, in 1937, of the original *Restatement of Restitution*. According to Douglas Laycock, a leading American authority, "The Restatement legitimated three insights: that a seemingly great variety of specific rules serve a common purpose, that these rules can be thought of as a single body of law under the name 'restitution,' and that these rules support a general principle that unjust enrichment must be disgorged. This was a major accomplishment; it created the field." English commentators have been no less generous. In the first edition of their treatise, Robert Goff and Gareth Jones were scrupulous to acknowledge a primary debt to Warren A. Seavey and Austin W. Scott, the two professors at the Harvard Law School who served as Reporters for the ALI's project on *Restitution and Unjust Enrichment* (as it was originally called). Surveying the few positive references within the common-law tradition to what they called "the substantive principle of unjust enrichment"—amid a host of skeptical and disparaging judicial comments—Goff and Jones juxtaposed Lord Mansfield with the 1937 *Restatement of Restitution*, putting virtually nothing in between. Professor Peter Birks began his last book on unjust enrichment by observing that "The law of restitution is better known than the law of unjust enrichment because it was under that name, starting in America in the 1930s, that the first serious attempts were made to overcome the problems of misclassification which deprived unjust enrichment of its own place on the map of the law." Many less eminent writers on either side of the Atlantic—the present author among them—might be quoted to the same effect. While some have looked further into this history than others, the prevailing attitude

toward the modern sources of restitution has been to take the claims made for the Restatement essentially on faith.

It has never been supposed, of course, that Seavey and Scott cut the law of restitution out of the whole cloth. Scholars are aware that William A. Keener—former Harvard professor, later Dean of the Columbia Law School—published in 1893 a *Treatise on the Law of Quasi-Contracts*. Keener's treatise collected and analyzed a wide range of cases imposing a liability at law—ostensibly on the old fictions of implied contract—that was based in reality, as Keener unhesitatingly asserted, "upon the doctrine that a man shall not be allowed to enrich himself unjustly at the expense of another." Keener's work is still cited, as is a second such treatise—differing in a few details, but proceeding from the same premises—that was published by Frederic C. Woodward, a professor at Stanford, in 1913. Anyone who tracks down Keener and Woodward in the library might also discover that two excellent casebooks on the topic had been brought out by major U.S. law-book publishers as early as 1905. Both referred to their subject as "quasi-contracts," while explaining in unqualified terms that the source of liability was not contract but unjust enrichment. The books supplied a growing market. A survey of the American law-school curriculum in the year 1907-1908 reported that a separate course in Quasi-Contracts was being offered at 30 of 49 "Leading Law Schools," typically as a one-semester course for two hours a week. The "leading law schools" surveyed ran the gamut from such institutions as Harvard and Columbia (both of which offered the course) to the Cincinnati Y.M.C.A. (which regrettably did not).

The awkward name "quasi-contract" always hindered professional acceptance. Still, the treatises and casebooks that were widely available in the United States (and evidently being used) a hundred years ago show that most of the legal side of what we recognize as the modern law of restitution had already been discovered. . . . It seems fair to say that as regards the legal side of restitution, or the part that originated in the action of implied assumpsit, the achievement of the Restatement was to summarize, for the use of the legal profession, a doctrine and a set of authorities that had been worked out in the law schools over the preceding 40 years; and (scarcely less important) to get rid of that troublesome name.

This is why the usual claim for the originality of the Restatement is somewhat different: namely, that the ALI Reporters were the first to take the practical step of unifying the legal and equitable sides of the body of law they named restitution. The language and the avowed objects of equity made it easy to observe—once it was pointed out—that a significant function of equitable remedies in many circumstances was the prevention of unjust enrichment. Yet after centuries of legal history in which law and equity had developed as competing legal systems, it required a significant insight and a boldly innovative step to describe the corresponding features of law and equity as parallel responses to the same problem.

Kull, *James Barr Ames and the Early Modern History of Unjust Enrichment*, 25 Oxford J.L.S. 297, 297-299, 303-304 (2005) (footnotes omitted).

———————————

Chapter 2

Mistake

A. DIRECT PAYMENTS

Pilot Life Ins. Co. v. Cudd
208 S.C. 6, 36 S.E.2d 860 (1945)

Mr. Associate Justice Taylor delivered the unanimous Opinion of the Court.

Plaintiff seeks to recover on the ground of alleged mistake, as alleged in the complaint, the sum of $1,013.36, paid to defendant as beneficiary under a policy on the life of her nephew and foster son, Lewis Edward Cudd, of which the sum of $1,000.00 was death benefit and $13.36 was premium refund.

Defendant answered, admitting the payment, denying mistake, and alleging that the payment was voluntary and was in the nature of a compromise settlement by plaintiff, as set forth in the answer. [The trial court directed a verdict for the plaintiff insurance company, and defendant appealed.]

The respondent, Pilot Life Insurance Company, issued its policy, dated April 12, 1936, for $1,000.00 on the life of Lewis Edward Cudd, naming the insured's aunt and adopted mother as beneficiary; on or about November 18, 1942, the insured sailed from Ceylon as a member of the Merchant Marine aboard the American Export Lines vessel, Swaokla; on January 16, 1943, Elizabeth Blackwell Cudd who was married to the insured in April, 1942, received the following letter from the War Shipping Administration:

WAR SHIPPING ADMINISTRATION
99 John Street
New York, N. Y.
January 15th, 1943

Mrs. Elizabeth Cudd
111 West 16th Str.
New York City
Re: SA—Lewis E. Cudd
Dear Madam:

This letter will advise you that the above-named member of the crew of the indicated vessel has been reported missing as a result of enemy action.

There was war risk insurance effective upon his life. This office is in possession of documentary evidence that you were designated as the beneficiary of this insurance. In order to facilitate the payment thereof, if and when it is determined to be due and payable, a questionnaire is herewith enclosed for your completion and return to this office with the documents checked on page 5 thereof. A certified copy of an English translation should, if necessary, accompany the documents requested.

Your prompt attention to this matter will be appreciated.

Yours very truly,
(s) E. A. Bloomquist
Chief Adjuster
Division of Wartime Insurance

On January 21, 1943, she received the following telegram from the Navy Department:

The Navy Department deeply regrets to inform you that your husband, Lewis Edward Cudd, is missing and presumed lost following action in the performance of his duty and in the service of his country. The Coast Guard appreciates your great anxiety and will furnish you further information promptly when received. To prevent possible aid to our enemies please do not divulge the name of his ship.

Vice-Admiral R. R. Waesche, Commandant,
U. S. Coast Guard.

On February 9, 1943, the Maritime War Emergency Board issued the following Certificate of Presumptive Death:

Maritime War Emergency Board
Washington, D. C.
Certificate of Presumptive Death
Form A

I hereby certify that the Maritime War Emergency Board has found that Lewis Edward Cudd with the rating of 2nd Cook and Baker is presumed to have died on or about November 28, 1942, as a result of a cause specified in the applicable Decisions of the Maritime War Emergency Board; and that under date of February 9, 1943, the Maritime Emergency Board duly made and entered its Order declaring said person presumptively dead in accordance with the provisions of its applicable Decisions and authorized the Secretary of the Board to issue a Certificate of Presumptive Death of said person.

(s) Erich Nielsen, Secretary

At the request of appellant the American Export Lines wrote her under date of February 26, 1943, as follows:

Your letter of February 10th has been referred to the writer for answer. We are extremely sorry that we must report that there is very little information which we can give you in respect to the above mentioned vessel.

Your son signed the articles of this vessel in the capacity of Second Cook and Baker. The vessel left Colombo, Ceylon, about November 18th and has not been heard from since As she was overdue, the U.S. Coast Guard sent notices to the next of kin. Mr. Cudd gave as his next of kin at the time he signed the articles his wife, Elizabeth, of 111 West 16th Street, New York City.

We wish we were in a position to advise you something more definite, but under the circumstances, and owing to the lack of information, it is impossible for us to do so.

We have asked the Maritime War Emergency Board to forward to us an individual certificate of presumptive death and upon receipt of same we will have it photostated, forwarding the original and the photostat to Mrs. Cudd in order to enable her to collect whatever insurance Mr. Cudd might have carried.

Some time during the Spring of 1943, appellant communicated this information to the local agent of the respondent, and he in turn gave such information as he had to the home office . . . . Thereupon respondent communicated with the Maritime War Emergency Board stating that it had been advised of the death of the insured and requested "a copy of the original Certificate of Presumptive Death" and received same under date of May 8, 1943, which was based on the original order of the Board dated February 9, 1943, together with their letter advising "We believe this will be sufficient for you to pay the beneficiary the amount of the policy carried by you on the deceased." As a result of this death, claims were signed and filed by the appellant. Respondent then issued its check for $1,013.36 covering the face amount of the policy plus a premium payment of $13.36 which had been paid after the date of presumptive death. This check was delivered to the beneficiary who endorsed it and received payment therefor, June 7, 1943, respondent having at the time of delivery of the check taken up the original policy.

On August 20, 1943, the U.S. Coast Guard wrote the wife, Mrs. Elizabeth Cudd, said letter being signed by Lieutenant of the Coast Guard, title "Chief, Merchant Marine Personnel Records and Welfare Section" as follows:

> You are advised that this office is in receipt of an official report from the Prisoner of War Information Bureau, through the International Red Cross, that your husband, Lewis Edward Cudd, is a prisoner of War of Japan. He is interned in the Hakodate Prisoner of War Camp located on Hokkaido Island, Japan.
>
> All prisoner of war communications are subject to censorship; it is, therefore, suggested that all such communications deal only with personal matters. To facilitate clearance in the Far East, communication should be either typed or hand-printed in capital letters and the envelope containing any communication to your husband should be addressed as follows:
>
> Postage Free
> Civilian Internee
> Mr. Lewis Edward Cudd
> American Civilian Internee Held by Japan in Hakodate Camp,
> Det. 1, Hokkaido Island, Japan
> c/o Japanese Red Cross, Tokyo, Japan, Via New York, New York

On October 8, 1945, respondent received from the Maritime War Emergency Board a certificate correcting the Certificate of Presumptive Death. Thereupon respondent's agent called upon the appellant and informed her of same and asked that she refund the money and reinstate the policy, no definite answer being given, respondent wrote and asked that this be done. Later attorneys for respondent visited the beneficiary for the purpose of getting a restoration of the status which has been refused by the appellant.

That the insured is alive and back in the United States at this time is undisputed.

"It is a firmly established general rule that money paid to another under the influence of a mistake of fact, that is, on the mistaken supposition of the existence of a specific fact which would entitle the other to the money, which would not have been paid if it had been known to the payor that the fact was otherwise, may be recovered, provided the payment has not caused such a change in the position of the payee that it would be unjust to require a refund. The ground on which the rule rests is that money paid through misapprehension of facts belongs, in equity and good conscience to the person who paid it."

Both parties to this action had been advised that the insured had sailed from Ceylon and that his ship and all aboard had been unheard from and were presumed lost as a result of enemy action. Both parties exhausted their sources of information and all accepted the death of the insured as a fact. The U.S. Government also thought and so certified as a result of which appellant filed her claim and accepted the payment of the policy by respondent. It is obvious that both parties accepted as a fact that the insured had died shortly after sailing from Ceylon. There is no evidence of fraud, therefore, the question resolves itself into whether or not there was a mutual mistake. Appellant contends that there was no mutual mistake but rather a mistake or error of judgment on the part of the insurer. That settlement was made under the realization of an uncertainty and that the settlement was a compromise of a doubtful liability.

All of the facts available to one of the parties was available to, and known by, both and their reactions thereto were the same. The acceptance of the death of the insured as a fact was a mutual mistake of fact equally concurred in by both parties. The whole situation having arisen because of the acceptance by the parties as a fact that the insured came to his death shortly after he sailed from Ceylon, when such fact did not exist. To follow appellant's line of argument would be to allow the beneficiary to be enriched to the amount of $1,013.36 for which the essential prerequisite was the death of the insured when in fact he is still alive. A mistake of fact having existed the proposition is elementary that repayment to the insurers could be compelled.

Appellant argues strenuously and at length that what occurred in the payment of the face of the policy was voluntary and made in compromise, and, therefore, is not the subject of rescission.

"That cannot be said with propriety to be voluntarily done, where a formal assent thereto is induced by *mistake* as to facts material to control the operation of the will therein, any more than where such formal assent is extorted by the application of a *force* which fetters and obstructs its free working." Kenneth v. South Carolina Railway Co., 15 Rich. 284, 294 (S.C. Ct. App. 1868).

A compromise, as shown by the principal authority cited by appellant (Taylor v. Insurance Company, 196 S.C. 195, 12 S.E.2d 708 (1940)), involves the essential element of a dispute or a controversy. The *Taylor* settlement was upheld because there was a bona fide basis for dispute between the parties as to whether the insured had committed suicide. But here there was no dispute, nor claim for double indemnity nor controversy between the parties. Both parties had substantially the same information and proceeded upon the same mistake of fact.

Appellant does not argue the question of whether or not the Court erred by impressing a trust upon "Any bonds, money or other property into which defendant had invested the moneys paid her by plaintiff," therefore, under the rules of this Court it is deemed abandoned and the Court intimates no opinion thereon.

This Court is of the opinion that all exceptions should be dismissed and it is so ordered. Judgment affirmed.

Mistake or compromise?

1. In an omitted passage from the opinion in *Pilot Life*, the South Carolina court referred to an earlier case of life-insurance mistake:

> In Riegel v. American Life Ins. Co., [140 Pa. 193, 21 A. 392 (1891)], we find the reverse of the position of the parties in this case. The plaintiff-beneficiary held a policy for $6,000.00 on the life of a debtor, Leisenring, who had not been heard from for about thirteen years. The beneficiary was paying premiums on this policy in an annual amount of $153.90, which premiums were burdensome to her, and an arrangement was worked out whereby she surrendered the $6,000.00 policy and accepted a new policy, paid up, for $2,500.00 and was thereupon relieved from the payment of premiums. This, of course, was based upon the assumption of fact by both parties that the insured was alive. A short time later it was discovered that Leisenring, the insured, had died some time prior to the arrangements between the beneficiary and the insurer, and thereupon the beneficiary brought action against the company for recovery on the original policy of $6,000.00.

How should this "reverse position" be resolved?

2. Charles R. Baumgrass was a member of the Ancient Order of United Workmen, a fraternal organization. Sears v. Grand Lodge A.O.U.W., 163 N.Y. 374, 57 N.E. 618 (1900). Lodge membership included life insurance in the amount of $2,000, payable to the member's wife as beneficiary. Baumgrass disappeared in September 1886; his wife waited nine years, then applied for payment of the death benefit. When the lodge refused to pay, she brought suit to enforce the insurance contract. In March 1896 the parties reached a settlement: Mrs. Baumgrass agreed to discontinue her lawsuit, and the lodge agreed to pay her "the sum of $666 in cash promptly," which amount was "not to be returned in any event." The lodge further agreed to put $1,334 into the hands of a trustee,

> to be held by him until July 1, 1897, subject to the condition that if before that time the defendant should produce reasonable proof that the insured was alive the money so deposited was to be returned to it, but failing in such proof it was to be paid to the beneficiary, and, in the language of the agreement, "she shall take full title to the same."
>
> Twenty days after the execution of this agreement, and before the defendant had made the absolute payment of $666 as agreed, the insured was proved to be alive. Thereupon the beneficiary demanded payment of the $666, which was refused, and she assigned her claim under the agreement of compromise to the plaintiff. The facts are undisputed. The special term rendered judgment for plaintiff, which was reversed by the appellate division with a divided court.

What do you suppose was the theory of the defendant—apparently adopted by the Appellate Division? How would the case be different if the lodge had already paid the $666?

3. In New York Life Ins. Co. v. Chittenden & Eastmen, 134 Iowa 613, 112 N.W. 96 (1907), New York Life had issued a policy on the life of a man named Jarvis. Jarvis vanished and was not heard from for seven years. An administrator was appointed for Jarvis's estate, and he filed a claim with New York Life seeking to collect the policy benefits. The claim included these assertions:

> (7) Date of death: During Christmas week, 1894.
> (8) Place of death: The assured disappeared, and since that date he has not been heard from. There was nothing in his family or business relations to explain his absence. His brother at the time of his disappearance was a resident of Burlington, Iowa, and has ever since continued to reside there and the most pleasant relations existed between them.

As the court recounted the subsequent facts:

> Negotiations were had between attorneys representing the administrator and an agent of the insurance company in which it was insisted for the administrator that the insurance money was due and payable, and that, unless it was paid, suit would be instituted on the policies. Subsequently two drafts for the amount specified in the policies, payable jointly to Chittenden & Eastmen, assignees, and C. W. Waldeck, administrator, were tendered to the attorneys for the administrator by the agent of the plaintiff, with the condition that the administrator and assignees should give a bond of indemnity to the company for the return of the money in case it should be subsequently discovered that Jarvis was not dead at the time of this settlement. The attorneys for the administrator refused in behalf of their client to furnish such bond, and thereupon the drafts were delivered without further insistence upon this condition.

Jarvis then reappeared alive and well. New York Life sued to recover the payments it had made. The court held for the defendants. Why?

4. As a further variation on the theme, consider Grand Trunk Western R. Co. v. Lahiff, 218 Wis. 457, 261 N.W. 11 (1935). The ferry *Milwaukee*, which shuttled railroad cars across Lake Michigan, was lost in a storm in October 1929. "Wm. Lahiff had married the defendant, Selma Lahiff, some fourteen years prior to the trial, but the parties had separated, and defendant had not heard from him for seven years prior to the sinking of the car ferry." Lahiff sometimes used the name Leahy; a man named Leahy was on the list of crew members lost in the disaster. When dependents of the victims brought an action for damages against the Grand Trunk, Selma sued as Leahy's widow. The railroad investigated Selma's claim and agreed to a $4,000 settlement. After the money had been paid in exchange for a release, the railroad heard

from Leahy's real widow in Ireland. William Lahiff had never been on board the *Milwaukee* and was probably still alive. The railroad sued Selma to recover the $4,000.

Selma's lawyers could point to numerous authorities (such as the last two cases mentioned) holding that a payment made to settle a disputed claim is *not* subject to restitution merely because it turns out that the paying party might have refused to settle (and avoided any liability) if it had only known the true facts. Selma prevailed at trial on grounds like these, and the railroad appealed. The Wisconsin Supreme Court declared itself "satisfied that the payment in question was made as the consideration for a compromise of the pending suit in federal court. This, however, does not solve the difficulty."

> [W]hile a compromise may be set aside for mistake of fact, the mistake must not relate to one of the uncertainties of which the parties were conscious and which it was the purpose of the contract to resolve and put at rest.
>
> [But] it is our conclusion that there was such a mistake of fact as will entitle plaintiff to recover. A consideration of the record indicates that neither of the parties was "in a mental state of conscious want of knowledge." Each assumed that Lahiff had lost his life in the disaster, and neither approached the settlement with the consciousness of ignorance or doubt as to the existence of this fact. It is clear that no controversy ever existed between the parties as to the identity of the deceased employee, and that no payment would have been made had the facts in this respect been known. The amount paid was not in any way modified or affected by recognition of any uncertainty on this point.

What change in the facts would have made the payment irrecoverable?

5. In Tarrant v. Monson, 619 P.2d 1210 (Nev. 1980), the facts were stated as follows:

> Appellant delivered a diamond engagement ring to respondent jeweler for repairs. Respondent stated that the ring would be fixed within two weeks. Appellant returned to respondent's store on several occasions but respondent was unable to deliver the ring. After several months, respondent admitted that he could not find the ring and offered to replace it. Appellant traveled to Salt Lake City, Utah and chose a replacement wedding set. Respondent asserted that the replacement set was worth approximately $450 more than appellant's original ring. However, respondent did agree that appellant could have the set of her choice as a replacement.
>
> Six months later, respondent found appellant's ring in his safe. Respondent discovered that he had mislabeled the envelope in which the ring had been stored. Upon his discovery, respondent informed appellant and offered to exchange the rings. Appellant stated that she would exchange the rings if respondent would also give her a pair of

diamond earrings. Respondent refused and later commenced a suit in equity to rescind the replacement agreement and to recover the repair cost.

What is the theory of the jeweler's lawsuit? Should it succeed?

Farnsworth, *Restitution* 18-19 (2014):

Sometimes the allocation of risk when making a contested payment is not so clear. Some prominent close cases of this type involve decisions by insurance companies to pay uncertain claims [comparing *Pilot Life Ins. Co. v. Cudd* and *New York Life Ins. Co. v. Chittenden & Eastmen*].

These two insurance cases reflect the alternative ways of interpreting a payment that its maker would not have made if better informed: it can be viewed as a mistake or as a calculated risk. Deciding which pattern a case follows can be difficult in practice. If the assumptions behind a payment are not made explicit, the court has to consider whether the party making it stood in conscious ignorance of some feature of the facts. A more recent application of the principle is furnished by *Tarrant v. Monson*. A jeweler lost a customer's ring and so offered to let her choose a replacement from his collection. Later the jeweler found the original ring; the customer preferred to keep the replacement, which was more valuable; the jeweler sued and lost. His replacement of the ring was viewed not as a mistake but as the settlement of what otherwise would have been a dispute: "Since respondent at time of agreement knew that the ring might later be found, respondent bargained with conscious uncertainty and not under a mistaken belief."

Whatever its difficulties in practice, the theory of this "voluntary payment" rule is easy to understand. If the parties are aware that the premise behind a payment may be wrong, the size of the payment will reflect the payor's judgment about that possibility, his willingness to risk litigation by holding out until the unknowns are cleared up, and his assessment of other such uncertainties. He is consenting to a particular allocation of risks, and presumably knows better than anyone else how he values them. If a court were to undo that allocation later by awarding restitution, payors in the same position would not be able to credibly commit themselves in the future. A defendant would offer a plaintiff a certain sum to settle a case; the plaintiff would be distrustful, worrying that if facts were to later turn out the defendant's way, the defendant could claim the plaintiff had been unjustly enriched by the earlier payment. So the plaintiff would refuse the offer. The result would be litigation that neither side wanted.

Bank of Naperville v. Catalano
86 Ill. App. 3d 1005, 408 N.E.2d 441 (1980)

LINDBERG, Justice:

Defendants, Robert and Beth J. Catalano, appeal from a judgment of the Circuit Court of DuPage County ordering them to make restitution to plaintiff, the Bank of Naperville. The bank cross-appeals the trial court's denial of its claim for interest and attorney's fees.

On September 13, 1975, Mrs. Catalano took out a $4,000 loan from the bank, secured by a note on which Mr. Catalano was guarantor. The note was renewed seven times and was due following the last renewal on July 5, 1977. As of August 3, 1977, the note was approximately 30 days past due, and Mrs. Catalano's checking account was overdrawn in the amount of $35.95. Mr. Stearns, the bank's president, determined that the loan was a "troublesome credit" which had been renewed too many times and that there was considerable difficulty with the checking account. Accordingly, he instructed that the checking account be closed and that the loan be paid off.

On August 4, 1977, Mr. Catalano went to the bank's drive-in window to make a deposit. The teller asked him to step inside, at which time an employee told him that his deposit could not be accepted and that his account had been closed. The employee tendered to Mr. Catalano a group of documents, including a paid-up loan statement, a cashier's check drawn on the bank for $1,825.45 and the documents which had accompanied the attempted deposit. Mr. Catalano refused to accept these papers and asked to see the bank president. He was shown into Mr. Stearns' office shortly thereafter. Mr. Stearns testified that he told Mr. Catalano that the bank would charge his savings account for the principal and interest due on the note and for the overdraft, with the balance being returned to him in the form of a cashier's check. Mr. Catalano admitted at one point that Stearns had said the money came from a savings account, but elsewhere denied having been so informed. Mr. Catalano stated that his money was "scattered all over," implying that he was uncertain as to which accounts had been used by the bank to produce the cashier's check.

Mr. Stearns testified that Catalano had thereafter made a telephone call from the bank lobby and cashed the check. According to Mr. Stearns, Catalano then threatened Stearns' life and Stearns called the police. Following arrival of the police, Catalano left the premises. Mr. Catalano, on the other hand, denied threatening Stearns' life. Catalano testified that Stearns had said that the bank did not choose to do business with people of Catalano's character, and that Stearns had called the police when he had refused to accept the various papers given to him. The police advised Catalano to accept the documents, so Catalano, not trusting the bank, had cashed the cashier's check and departed.

Subsequent to these events, it was discovered that defendants did not maintain a savings account at the Bank of Naperville, and that the money which the bank had applied to the overdraft, the loan and the cashier's check had been inadvertently taken from the savings account of a third party who coincidentally was also named Robert Catalano. Mr. Stearns admitted that preparation of the cashier's check had been done in "a less than careful manner."

This lawsuit followed.

As a general rule, where money is paid under a mistake of fact, and payment would not have been made had the facts been known to the payor, such money may be recovered. The fact that the person to whom the money was paid under a mistake of fact was not guilty of deceit or unfairness, and acted in good faith, does not prevent recovery of the sum paid, nor does the negligence of the payor preclude recovery.

The Catalanos, citing Central Bank & Trust Co. v. General Finance Corp. (5th Cir. 1961), 297 F.2d 126, argue that special rules of restitution apply in the case of commercial banks, and that the amount paid by a bank on its customer's check under a mistaken belief that the customer had sufficient funds to his credit to cover the checks is not recoverable in an action for restitution where there is no showing of fraud, misrepresentation or overreaching. The Catalanos also contend that inasmuch as a bank has a duty to know the state of its depositors' accounts, it must abide by the consequences of any mistakes it makes in administering those accounts. (See Citizen's Bank of Norfolk v. Schwarzschild & Sulzberger Co. (1909), 109 Va. 539, 64 S.E. 954).

[But] the situation in *Central Bank and Trust* and *Citizen's Bank* is distinguishable from the case at bar. Mr. Catalano was not simply a holder of an instrument presenting it for payment. Rather, he was informed that the cashier's check represented the proceeds of an account which he had previously maintained in the bank and which was being closed. The bank president testified that he informed Mr. Catalano that the funds being given to him purportedly came from his savings account, and even if defendant did not understand the reference to a savings account specifically, he apparently understood that the money was supposedly from funds that he had previously had on deposit. Mr. Catalano was therefore in a different position from a holder in due course of an instrument who in good faith presents it for payment.

The next question presented is whether the payment to the Catalanos was actually made in consequence of a mistake of fact. The Catalanos reply in the negative, contending that there can be no recognized mistake of fact where facts were readily ascertainable, where the channels of information were open, where there was a failure to investigate known facts or where there was carelessness, indifference or inattention. They cite John J. Calnan Co. v. Talsma Builders, Inc. (1977), 67 Ill.2d 213, 367 N.E.2d 695 and Steinmeyer v. Schroeppel (1907), 226 Ill. 9, 80 N.E. 564, for the proposition that a mistake of fact must not be due to negligence, but both of those cases involved discussions of the conditions necessary before a contract will be rescinded for a mistake by one of the parties. While it has been held that a court of equity will not relieve a party from a mistake which was the result of his own negligence when the channels of information are open to him and no fraud or deception is practiced upon him (National Union Fire Ins. Co. v. John Spry Lumber Co. (1908), 235 Ill. 98, 85 N.E. 256), that holding came in the course of an action by certain insurance companies to reform their policies because of mistakes made in the descriptions of the location of the property intending to be covered, such actions coming after the property was destroyed. These cases do not stand for the proposition that a party erroneously receiving money may keep it simply because the payment was negligently made.

The Catalanos contend that inasmuch as the bank knows what its agents know, the instant plaintiff had actual knowledge that its payment was in error. This overlooks that, despite apparent negligence, there is no evidence that any of the bank's agents actually knew of the error. In our view, the bank's good faith misidentification of its depositor is a mistake of fact, entitling the bank to restitution of amounts erroneously paid to the erroneously identified party. The Catalanos characterize the bank's conduct as reckless and vengeful, but the record does not reveal any deliberate misconduct on its part. The bank may have been negligent in debiting the wrong account. However, as noted above, restitution will generally not be precluded because an overpayment was made negligently.

The Catalanos, referring to the trial court's citation of the Restatement of Restitution §59 (1937) [*cf.* R3RUE §65], further contend that restitution may not be ordered in the instant case because they have made a change of position in reliance on the mistaken payment, thereby defeating the bank's claim. The change of position to which defendants refer was their alleged failure to bring suit against the bank for wrongfully paying an $8,400 check over defendant's stop payment order.

It is true that when one party is misled by the representations or conduct of another and acts on these representations to his injury, the party making the representation may be "estopped" from asserting a legal right. However, in the instant case, there is no evidence that the Catalanos changed their position or suffered any permanent injury as a result of their alleged failure to sue the bank on their unrelated claim. We can see no reason why this failure to stop payment claim could not have been brought as a counterclaim in the instant action. Also, there has been no allegation that this claim has been barred by any statute of limitations and thus we must assume that it could be prosecuted in the future. In sum, we find that even if the Catalanos had deferred bringing suit against the bank as some sort of extrajudicial set-off, such a deferral was not a change of position under §59 of the Restatement of Restitution. Accordingly, the trial court's award of restitution is affirmed.

Bank error in your favor

1. A favorite card in "Monopoly" (from the yellow "Community Chest" pile) reads, "Bank Error in Your Favor, Collect $200." What happens the next day, when the bank discovers the error?

2. The "special rules of restitution in the case of commercial banks" have nothing to do with this case, though they are interesting and significant in the law of payments. Certain mistakes about a customer's account might lead

a bank to pay a check that it should properly have dishonored. For example, the check might be a forgery; the account might be closed or overdrawn; or the customer might have ordered the bank to stop payment. A very old rule at common law, announced by Lord Mansfield in Price v. Neal, 3 Burr. 1354, 97 Eng. Rep. 871 (K.B. 1762), bars restitution to the bank from the payee of the check in cases like these—even though the payee had no right to payment from the bank—so long as the payee took the check in payment of a valid debt, then received payment of the check without notice of the bank's mistake. In the modern U.S. law of negotiable instruments, the rule of Price v. Neal is incorporated in U.C.C. §3-418 (rev. 1990); in the modern U.S. law of restitution, it is one strand of the broader defense allowed to a "creditor/ payee" (a topic for Chapter 9). While the rule itself is clear, its rationale has been the subject of debate for the last 250 years. What reasons justify letting the payee keep the money? (Whatever they are, they are scarcely applicable to the Catalanos, as the court points out.) Might the bank that pays a check by mistake have a restitution claim against its own customer?

3. In Employers Ins. of Wausau v. Titan Int'l, Inc., 400 F.3d 486 (7th Cir. 2005), a computer error led Wausau to miscalculate Titan's insurance premiums. Instead of sending Titan a bill for the $3,987 balance actually due, Wausau sent them a check for a $239,132 refund. Wausau discovered the mistake and asked for its money back. Titan refused to pay, and Wausau sued. Affirming a grant of summary judgment for the insurer, Judge Posner made these observations:

> Wausau has an alternative theory of entitlement to the return of the $239,132 that it sent the defendants in error: restitution for money paid by mistake. Illinois Graphics Co. v. Nickum, 159 Ill. 2d 469, 639 N.E.2d 1282, 1293 (1994); Allstate Life Ins. Co. v. Yurgil, 259 Ill. App. 3d 375, 632 N.E.2d 282, 285 (1994); Bank of Naperville v. Catalano, 86 Ill. App. 3d 1005, 408 N.E.2d 441, 444 (1980). The defendants argue that it was a careless mistake and therefore restitution should be denied. There is no "therefore." Probably the mistake *was* careless; but the law does not permit a person to keep money that he has received by mistake, just because the mistake is careless. Such a rule would make people too careful, penalizing them for mistakes that caused nobody any harm and so should not be penalized at all—the defendants do not argue that having to return their windfall will cause them harm beyond the natural disappointment that one is bound to feel at having to cough up money to someone else, for whatever reason. The law is not finders keepers, unless the property found has been abandoned, which is to say deliberately relinquished, not merely lost or misplaced. It would be absurd to suppose that if Wausau owed the defendants $1 and by the careless mistake of one of its clerks issued them a check for $1 million, they could keep the $1 million because the mistake was a careless one. But that is their argument.

Id. at 490-491.

Glover v. Metropolitan Life Ins. Co.
664 F.2d 1101 (8th Cir. 1981)

RICHARD ARNOLD, Circuit Judge.

This case was brought to determine who owns the proceeds of a policy of insurance on the life of Robert Woods. Mr. Woods, an employee of Interco, Inc., took out a policy of group life insurance and originally designated his wife, Jeanne B. Woods, now Mrs. Glover, as the beneficiary. After Mr. Woods and his first wife, who is the plaintiff in this case, were divorced, Mr. Woods married again, this time to Roberta R. Woods, one of the defendants. When Mr. Woods died, the insurer, Metropolitan Life Insurance Company, the other defendant in this case, paid the policy proceeds to Mrs. Woods, the second wife. Mrs. Glover then brought this action, claiming that she was entitled to the insurance proceeds by reason of a property settlement agreement entered into at the time of the divorce. The District Court, interpreting the property settlement agreement, held for Mrs. Glover against Metropolitan. The Court found it unnecessary to discuss Mrs. Glover's alternative claim that Mrs. Woods should turn over to her the money previously received by Mrs. Woods from Metropolitan.

In the meantime, Metropolitan had filed a cross-claim against Mrs. Woods, asserting that, if it should be held liable to Mrs. Glover, it should be reimbursed by Mrs. Woods in the amount that had been paid over to her, some $116,000. The District Court held that the payment had been made under a mistake of law, rather than a mistake of fact, and dismissed Metropolitan's cross-claim. As a result, Metropolitan has in effect paid the sum due under this policy of insurance twice. Metropolitan appeals, asking this Court either to hold that Mrs. Glover was not entitled to the money, or to enter judgment directing Mrs. Woods to return the payment that Metropolitan has made to her.

We affirm the District Court's decision that Mrs. Glover was the true beneficiary, but reverse the dismissal of Metropolitan's cross-claim against Mrs. Woods.

I.

Mr. Woods was employed by Interco, formerly known as International Shoe Co., from August 15, 1964, until his death on February 2, 1978. On October 26, 1964, he enrolled in a group life-insurance plan which his company had with Metropolitan. The Insurance Department of Interco administered the plan and kept all pertinent records. Mr. Woods designated his then wife, the present Mrs. Glover, as beneficiary.

Mr. Woods and Mrs. Glover were divorced on October 29, 1971. Their property settlement agreement, as construed by the District Court, provided that Mrs. Glover would remain the designated beneficiary of the life-insurance policy, and that if Interco changed the plan or issued a substitute policy, Mrs. Glover would also be the beneficiary of that substitute policy. Interco knew of the provisions of the settlement agreement, and the District Court found that

Metropolitan had notice of it through Interco, which was held to be its agent for this purpose.

Mr. Woods remarried on November 8, 1971. On October 31, 1975, in violation of the agreement, he purported to designate the new Mrs. Woods as the sole beneficiary of the life-insurance policy.

Mr. Woods died on February 2, 1978, and Mrs. Woods subsequently filed a claim with Interco. Rosemarie Glueck, at the time an Interco clerk, processed the relevant documents. On February 17, 1978, she sent Metropolitan the death certificate, the group insurance certificate, the enrollment card, the 1975 beneficiary designation, and Mrs. Woods's claim form. She did not know Mr. Woods had been previously married. On February 28, 1978, acting through an agent without personal knowledge of the property settlement, Metropolitan Life sent Interco a check payable to Mrs. Woods. Interco forwarded the check to Mrs. Woods on March 2, 1978. Mrs. Woods invested the money, and the funds remain intact.

II.

The District Court held that in accordance with the divorce decree and the property settlement agreement, Mrs. Glover was entitled to recover from Metropolitan. The court held that the agreement gave Mrs. Glover an indefeasible contractual right to the policy proceeds. Although another construction of the agreement is possible, we agree with the District Court and affirm this portion of its ruling for the reasons stated in its opinion.

III.

As noted above, Metropolitan filed a cross-claim for restitution against Mrs. Woods for an amount equal to the judgment rendered against it, if any, in favor of Mrs. Glover. Metropolitan claimed that it should not have to pay both Mrs. Woods and Mrs. Glover, and that if it had mistakenly paid Mrs. Woods, it was entitled to recover from her. The District Court focused on the question whether Metropolitan's mistaken payment to Mrs. Woods was a "mistake of law" or a "mistake of fact." "Metropolitan and its agent, Interco," the District Court said, "had in their possession information that the plaintiff (Mrs. Glover) was the beneficiary of the policy under a divorce settlement agreement." Metropolitan's mistake, therefore, was held to be a mistake of law (presumably a misinterpretation of the ambiguous property settlement agreement), against which, under Missouri law, no relief by way of restitution is available. We normally defer to the district courts on such questions. In this case, however, our reading of the Missouri cases has led us to the firm conviction that the courts of Missouri would not subject Metropolitan to double liability in the circumstances shown here.

There is language in the books that the courts will not grant relief against a mistake of law. The Missouri courts have indicated, however, that the rule is harsh and should be abandoned when independent equitable considerations warrant. See State Farm Mutual Automobile Insurance Co. v. Sabourin, 574 S.W.2d 8 (Mo. App. 1978); Handly v. Lyons, 475 S.W.2d 451 (Mo. App. 1971). *Handly* noted that in cases of this kind "'It is better to yield to the force of truth and con-science, than to any reverence for maxims.'" *Handly*, 475 S.W.2d at 462, quoting Northrop's Executors v. Graves, 19 Conn. 548, 554 (1849). It criticized the rule denying relief from mistakes of law, stating that "[w]hatever may be the status of the general rule, it is universally acknowledged that *equity always relieves against a mistake of law when the surrounding facts raise an independent equity*, as where the mistake is induced, or is accompanied by inequitable conduct of the other party" (emphasis added). 475 S.W.2d at 462-63. *Sabourin* indicated that "[t]he trend in Missouri is to give greater weight to the competing equities of a dispute even in situations when the mistake is clearly one of law." 574 S.W.2d at 10.

The Missouri courts, when weighing the equities of a case, lay great empha-sis on whether or not the payee has relied on retention of the payment received.

In the case at hand equity favors a holding for Metropolitan and against Mrs. Woods; a holding otherwise would grant Mrs. Woods a windfall. Mrs. Woods was not entitled to the proceeds of the insurance policy. Nor has she in any way relied upon it, so far as this record shows. The full amount has been invested by Mrs. Woods, and the fund remains intact.

The District Court took the view that Metropolitan's mistake of law could be relieved against only if the other party, here Mrs. Woods, had herself induced the mistaken payment by some inequitable conduct. No one contends that Mrs. Woods acted unfairly. She has been innocent throughout, and honestly believed, because of what her husband told her before his death, that she was the true and lawful beneficiary of the policy. The District Court relied on the passage in *Handly* quoted above, to the effect that "equity always relieves against a mistake of law when the surrounding facts raise an independent equity, as where the mistake is induced, or is accompanied by inequitable conduct of the other party." With deference, we believe this reading of *Handly* is too restrictive. In context, the opinion seems to us to mean, not that a mistake of law will be relieved against only when the other party has behaved inequitably, but that inequitable behavior on the part of the payee is one ground for relief against a mistake of law, among many possible grounds. The *Handly* opin-ion's copious quotations with approval from Pomeroy, Williston, and Corbin, among other authorities, convince us that, in Missouri, "the important ques-tion is not whether the mistake was one of law or of fact, but is whether the case falls within the fundamental principle of equity that no person shall be unjustly enriched at the expense of another." 475 S.W.2d at 462.

We conclude that under the law of Missouri Mrs. Woods must return the money to Metropolitan. It is now plain that Mrs. Glover is the lawful benefi-ciary of the policy. Mrs. Woods has not spent the money, and she now knows, if she did not before, that the money does not, in equity and good conscience, belong to her. To make Metropolitan pay twice is tantamount to a forfeiture, which, we are told by the text writers, equity abhors. The difficulty was cre-ated in the first place, not by any act on the part of Metropolitan, but by Mr. Woods's attempt to break his agreement with Mrs. Glover. And if the employee of Metropolitan who directed the payment of Mrs. Woods's claim had person-ally known all the facts, obviously the payment would never have been made.

In all the circumstances, it would be unjust, in our view, for Mrs. Woods to keep the money. This result disappoints an expectation on her part that she had every reason to believe, at one time, to be legitimate, but to decide otherwise would be intolerably unfair to Metropolitan.

The judgment for Mrs. Glover against Metropolitan is affirmed. The judgment for Mrs. Woods against Metropolitan is reversed, and the cause is remanded for the entry of judgment in favor of Metropolitan on its cross-claim. Each party will bear her or its own costs on this appeal.

Ignorance of the law

1. Judge Arnold was at considerable pains to repudiate the arbitrary distinction between "mistake of fact" and "mistake of law," precisely because a rule denying restitution for "mistake of law" has long been recognized, if not always followed, in many jurisdictions. Although R3RUE §5 flatly rejects any such distinction, the original Restatement of Restitution approached the topic much more gingerly (see Restatement of Restitution Chapter 2, Topic 3, Introductory Note (1937)), and it has still not been completely eliminated from U.S. law. Why should it make any difference whether Metropolitan's payment to the second wife was a mistake of fact or of law—assuming we can tell such mistakes apart? How did such an idea ever get into the law of mistaken payments?

2. If the facts of *Glover v. Metropolitan Life* are adjusted slightly—or just interpreted differently—the 1975 beneficiary designation by Mr. Woods becomes effective, with the result that the insurance proceeds were properly paid by Metropolitan to the second Mrs. Woods. Such a case is no longer about mistake: it is about a double-cross (and breach of contract) by Mr. Woods, who had promised his first wife that the insurance would be left in her name. Cases like this are common. They take the form of the claim that the court here found unnecessary to discuss: "Mrs. Glover's alternative claim that Mrs. Woods should turn over to her the money previously received by Mrs. Woods from Metropolitan."

Such a claim rests on a theory of unjust enrichment, which R3RUE classifies under this heading:

§48. PAYMENT TO DEFENDANT TO WHICH CLAIMANT HAS A BETTER RIGHT

If a third person makes a payment to the defendant to which (as between claimant and defendant) the claimant has a better legal or equitable right, the claimant is entitled to restitution from the defendant as necessary to prevent unjust enrichment.

Assuming a claim on this basis by Mrs. Glover (first wife) against Mrs. Woods (second wife), a court would typically find that the first wife did indeed have "a better legal or equitable right" to the insurance proceeds. Is this merely an application of "first in time, first in right," or is something else going on?

3. In Amoco Prod. Co. v. Smith, 946 S.W.2d 162 (Tex. Ct. App. 1997), the parties stipulated to the facts as follows:

> Both Herbert W. Smith and Huling W. Smith owned oil and gas interests and received royalty payments from Amoco. Both men were listed in Amoco's records as H.W. Smith. In 1985, Amoco mistakenly started sending Herbert W. Smith payments for both his and Huling W. Smith's properties. Herbert W. Smith died in August 1987 and Amoco then paid the revenue checks to his estate. Following July of 1989, the revenue payments were split between appellees, as equal devisees under Herbert W. Smith's will. Amoco realized its error in late 1992 and stopped the erroneous payments.

Who should be able to recover from Herbert W. Smith's devisees: (a) Amoco, (b) Huling W. Smith, (c) either, or (d) neither?

Restatement Third, Restitution and Unjust Enrichment

§5. Invalidating mistake

(1) A transfer induced by invalidating mistake is subject to rescission and restitution. The transferee is liable in restitution as necessary to avoid unjust enrichment.

(2) An invalidating mistake may be a misapprehension of either fact or law. There is invalidating mistake only when

(a) but for the mistake the transaction in question would not have taken place; and

(b) the claimant does not bear the risk of the mistake.

(3) A claimant bears the risk of a mistake when

(a) the risk is allocated to the claimant by agreement of the parties;

(b) the claimant has consciously assumed the risk by deciding to act in the face of a recognized uncertainty; or

(c) allocation to the claimant of the risk in question accords with the common understanding of the transaction concerned.

(4) A claimant does not bear the risk of a mistake merely because the mistake results from the claimant's negligence.

Illustrations:

6. Intending to give her nephew a life interest in Blackacre, Aunt executes a deed in which (by mistake of the conveyancer) she conveys a fee simple. The conveyance of a larger interest than Aunt intended is the result of an invalidating mistake as defined in this section. Aunt has a claim in restitution to recover what was not intended to be conveyed (§11).

7. Assuming that her nephew would make good use of the property, Aunt makes him a gift of Blackacre. Nephew proves to be an unworthy and ungrateful recipient, causing Aunt intense regret. The risk of nephew's misconduct is one that is assigned to Aunt as a matter of law. Aunt's conveyance to Nephew was a terrible mistake—in common parlance—but it was not the result of an invalidating mistake as defined in this section.

---

§6. Payment of money not due

Payment by mistake gives the payor a claim in restitution against the recipient to the extent payment was not due.

B. INDIRECT PAYMENTS

Partipilo v. Hallman
156 Ill. App. 3d 806, 510 N.E.2d 8 (1987)

Justice Jiganti delivered the opinion of the court:

The facts are not in dispute Partipilo was the owner of a parcel of real estate in the City of Chicago adjoining Hallman's property. For the tax years 1977, 1978 and 1979, the Cook County Assessor's office mistakenly included a building, portions of a driveway and a fence in its assessment of the Partipilo property when these improvements were in fact located on the Hallman property. As a result, the Partipilo property was overassessed and the Hallman property underassessed by the same amount, $26,467.10. Partipilo paid the taxes for those years and judgment was subsequently entered in favor of Partipilo and against Hallman for that amount.

In arguing that he had a right to recover the amount of the overassessment, Partipilo relies upon the general proposition that a person shall not enrich himself at another's expense. This proposition is contained in the Restatement of Restitution, which states that "[a] person who has been unjustly enriched at the expense of another is required to make restitution to the other." (Restatement of Restitution sec. 1, at 12 (1937).) In this vein, section 43 of the Restatement of Restitution states as follows:

§43. Performance of Another's Duty or Discharge of Lien Against His Property.

(1) A person who, by payment to a third person, has discharged the duty of another or has released another's property from an adverse interest, doing so unintentionally or acting because of an erroneous belief induced by a mistake of fact that he was thereby discharging a duty of his own or releasing property of his own from a lien, is entitled to restitution from such other of the value of the benefit conferred up to the value of what was given, unless the other disclaims the transaction." (Restatement of Restitution sec. 43, at 172 (1937); [*cf.* R3RUE §8].)

To illustrate this proposition, the Restatement of Restitution includes the following example, which appears pertinent to the issue in the case at bar:

A receives from the collector of taxes a notification of taxes due, describing lot X which is owned by B. Believing that it describes lot Y owned by him, A pays the tax. A is entitled to restitution from B. (Restatement of Restitution sec. 43, at 176 (1937).)

See also 1 A. Corbin, Contracts sec. 19, at 47 (1963).

In order to achieve the result suggested in the Restatement of Restitution, Illinois courts have implied a contract in law based upon the defendant's receipt of a benefit which would be unjust for him to retain without paying for it. [T]hese cases stand for the general proposition that a person shall not enrich himself at another's expense and thus appear to support the action of the trial court in allowing Partipilo to recover.

Hallman, however, raises a number of arguments in support of his contention that the relief requested by Partipilo is barred. First, he claims that the plaintiff's theory of unjust enrichment is equitable in nature and as an equitable claim it is unavailable where there exists a full and adequate remedy at law. The alleged adequate remedy at law is the relief afforded by the Illinois Revenue Act. Hallman is in error in this contention. The theory on which the plaintiff in this suit seeks money damages, unjust enrichment, sometimes referred to as restitution, a contract implied in law, quasi-contract, or an action in *assumpsit*, is the product of a long tradition in law, and is an action at law. See Restatement of Restitution, Introductory Note (1937); 1 Palmer, Restitution sec. 1.2 (1978); 1 A. Corbin, Contracts, sections 19, 20 (1 vol. ed. 1952); Dobbs, Remedies sec. 4.2, at 232 (1976); [R3RUE §4].) The confusion with equity emanates from the decision of the King's Bench in 1760 in the case of *Moses v. Macferlan,* 2 Burr. 1005, 97 Eng. Rep. 676, where Lord Mansfield stated that the defendant's obligation came "from the ties of natural justice" founded in "the equity of the plaintiff's case." As Palmer explains, the statement concerning the action of quasi-contract being equitable has been repeated many times, but merely refers to the way in which a claim should be approached "since it is clear that the action is at law and the relief given is a simple money judgment." Consequently, Hallman's equitable defense based upon an adequate remedy at law is unavailable since this is an action at law for a monetary recovery.

Hallman next makes a number of contentions suggesting that the plaintiff was at fault and that there was no fault on the part of Hallman. A cause of action based on unjust enrichment, however, does not require fault on the part of the defendant. Instead the essence of the cause of action is that one party is enriched and it would be unjust for that party to retain the enrichment.

Hallman further contends that any enrichment in the case at bar has not been at the expense of the plaintiff. He argues that he neither took nor received any benefit from Partipilo. Obviously, Hallman received a benefit in the form of lower taxes. His innocence in receiving the benefit does not mean that his retention of that benefit without payment is just.

Hallman does make two arguments concerning the amount of the recovery that we believe are meritorious. First, Hallman claims that he has been deprived of his right to object to the assessed evaluation of his improvements. Where Hallman is no more at fault than Partipilo, he has no duty to pay more than the amount of the tax he would have had to pay if the improvements were assessed as part of his property. Thus, Hallman was not enriched to the extent that his taxes would have been lowered had he filed an objection to the assessment. It is a question of fact, of course, whether the assessment would have been reduced. This question of fact precludes the entry of summary judgment, and the cause must therefore be remanded to the trial court.

Hallman's second contention is that he was not allowed to and can no longer take deductions on his Federal income taxes for the real estate taxes in question. For the same reasons concerning the objections to the amount of the assessment, we believe that Hallman was not enriched to the extent that he may have overpaid his Federal incomes taxes. Any overpayment should be borne by Partipilo, and the amount of such overpayment is a question of fact to be resolved by the trial court.

Hallman's final contention is that this action is barred by the statute of limitations and by laches. As discussed earlier, this is a legal action and laches is not an appropriate defense to a legal action. As to the statute of limitations, we believe that Hallman's point is well taken. The 1977 general taxes and the first installment of the 1978 taxes were paid more than five years prior to the filing of the lawsuit and consequently are barred by the statute of limitations. On remand, the judgment is to be reduced by the amount which Partipilo paid more than five years preceding the filing of this lawsuit.

The cause is reversed and remanded for proceedings not inconsistent with the views expressed in this opinion.

Who is enriched?

1. Why didn't Partipilo seek restitution of his excess payments from Cook County? The county would reply that it took the money in satisfaction of a valid tax obligation (Hallman's), and that it accordingly qualified as a bona fide payee (R3RUE §67)—in other words, a bona fide purchaser of the money. Affirmative defenses along these lines are reviewed in Chapter 9.

2. In Sykeston Township v. Wells County, 356 N.W.2d 136 (N.D. 1984), four of the Townships within Wells County were under the impression, shared by Wells County, that the townships were responsible for the maintenance of a gravel road. The parties were mistaken about the provisions of North Dakota law on this point, by which maintenance of the road was the sole responsibility of the county. The townships sued the county to recover $25,000 that they had spent on gravel at the county's direction. What result? In view of the fact that the townships are all political subdivisions of Wells County—which comprises 36 townships in all—who was unjustly enriched, at whose expense, as a result of the parties' mistake?

3. In Upton-on-Severn Rural District Council v. Powell, 1 All E.R. 220 (Ct. App. 1942), the facts were stated as follows:

> The appellant [Mr. Powell] lives at Strensham, and in Nov., 1939 a fire broke out in his Dutch barn; he thereupon telephoned to the police inspector at the Upton police office and told him that there was a fire and asked for the fire brigade to be sent. The police inspector telephoned a garage near to the fire station at Upton, which itself had no telephone, the Upton brigade was informed and immediately went to the fire, where it remained for a long time engaged in putting it out. It so happens that, although the appellant's farm is in the Upton police district, it is not in the Upton fire district. It is in the Pershore fire district, and the appellant was entitled to have the services of the Pershore fire brigade without payment. The Upton fire brigade, on the other hand, was entitled to go to a fire outside its area and, if it did so, quite apart from its statutory rights, it could make a contract that it would be entitled to repayment of its expenses.
>
> It appears that some 6 hours after the arrival of the Upton fire brigade, the officer of the Pershore brigade arrived on the scene, but without his brigade; he pointed out to the Upton officer that it was a Pershore fire, and not an Upton fire, but the Upton fire brigade continued rendering services until the next day when the Pershore fire brigade arrived and took over.

Upton sued Powell, claiming the amount it would charge for contractual firefighting services outside the Upton district. Judgment for Upton against Powell was upheld in the Court of Appeal on a theory of implied contract: the objection that Powell did not intend to pay, and that Upton did not (initially) intend to charge him, was brushed aside by the court.

Upton v. Powell is a famous case: first for its facts, and second because nobody who reads it (or scarcely anyone) agrees that Powell made an implied contract with Upton. Would Upton have a better claim on a restitution theory? Against whom, and in what amount?

Mistaken discharge of obligation or lien

1. The facts of Ex parte AmSouth Mortgage Company, 679 So. 2d 251 (Ala. 1996), were summarized as follows:

> In August 1992, Madelaine Stewart bought a house for the use and benefit of her daughter, Linda Stewart Sanders, who was going through divorce proceedings. Madelaine paid an equity amount of $6,786 and assumed an existing mortgage in favor of Wachovia Mortgage Company. Linda lived in the house and made the monthly mortgage payments to Wachovia.
>
> In the spring of 1993, Linda applied for a loan from AmSouth Mortgage Company to refinance the mortgage indebtedness at a lower interest rate. Linda told the AmSouth loan officer that the title to the house was in her mother's name. The loan officer informed Linda that the property would need to be deeded into Linda's name in order to refinance it and pay off her mother's mortgage.
>
> In May 1993, Madelaine executed a warranty deed conveying title to herself and her daughter "for and during their joint lives and upon the death of either of them, then to the survivor of them in fee simple." The deed was properly recorded on May 18, 1993. Linda gave the loan officer a copy of the deed.
>
> In June 1993, Madelaine and Linda went to the office of AmSouth's lawyer to close the loan. The lawyer explained to Madelaine that the proceeds of the AmSouth loan would be used to pay off Madelaine's mortgage to Wachovia. Madelaine reviewed all the documents and asked AmSouth's lawyer if there were any papers for her to sign. The lawyer told her that she did not need to sign anything. Linda alone signed the note and mortgage.
>
> Less than one month after the closing, Linda died.

Where did this leave AmSouth? Who (if anyone) has been enriched as a result of AmSouth's mistake? Three Alabama courts ruled on the case, and each saw the problem differently:

(a) The trial court ruled that Madelaine was the sole owner of the property, subject to a mortgage in favor of AmSouth. It determined that "AmSouth, by virtue of paying in full the first mortgage [to Wachovia], was subrogated to all the rights and privileges of the holder of the first mortgage [to the extent of its payment of $84,201.71, plus interest]." Madelaine appealed.

(b) The Court of Civil Appeals pointed out an important factor the trial court had ignored. In most jurisdictions, Alabama among them, a mortgage of real property by only one of two joint tenants effects a severance of the joint tenancy. Severance, followed by Linda's untimely death, made AmSouth's path to recovery more complicated though not impossible. The Court of Civil Appeals was not interested. It reversed the judgment in favor of AmSouth, stating that "the equitable doctrines that might, under other circumstances, afford relief are unavailable here because of AmSouth's culpable neglect and Madelaine's freedom from fault."

(c) The Alabama Supreme Court rejected this harsh proposition about the bank's negligence. "If all persons who negligently confer an economic benefit upon another are disqualified from equitable relief because of their negligence, then the law of restitution, which was conceived in order to prevent unjust enrichment, would be of little or no value." The case was remanded for another try at deciding who held what interests in the house.

2. *AmSouth* contains, among other things, our first judicial reference to the remedy of *subrogation,* an old synonym for "substitution." If A by mistake pays B's debt to C, A presumably has a direct claim against B on a theory of unjust enrichment. But sometimes A would prefer to step into C's shoes and assert against B the claim that A's payment has discharged. The most common reason to do this would be that C's claim against B benefited from some form of security, priority, or other advantage.

The trial court's version of *AmSouth*—which ignored the severance issue—illustrates the subrogation remedy in a typical setting. (With no severance, Linda's death means that the house belongs to Madelaine again.) By mistake, AmSouth has discharged Madelaine's debt to Wachovia without obtaining either the contractual obligation (Madelaine's promise to pay) or the security it expected (a mortgage on Madelaine's interest in the house) for its new loan. Even without a promissory note, AmSouth should have a simple restitution claim against Madelaine (to recover the money it paid by mistake on her behalf). But AmSouth would much prefer to have a *secured* claim. (Madelaine may have other creditors, and it would be better anyway to have a mortgage already in place, without worrying about enforcing a judgment lien.) This is why AmSouth asks to be subrogated to the position of Madelaine's former creditor, Wachovia. Subrogation allows AmSouth to assert Wachovia's rights against Madelaine under the promissory note and mortgage that AmSouth's funds were used to discharge, precisely as those rights would stand today if the Wachovia loan had not been paid off.

3. The case is more difficult if we accept that the bank's mistake effected a severance of the joint tenancy. Consider the problem at two stages. Who owns what on the day after the closing—given the underlying principle that Linda can only convey (*i.e.*, mortgage) what she has? Then who owns what when Linda dies? Let's assume that Madelaine inherits from Linda. What does she inherit, and what does AmSouth say to her now?

4. In Decatur Fed. Sav. & Loan v. Gibson, 268 Ga. 362, 489 S.E.2d 820 (1997), the facts were stated as follows:

> In May 1989, defendants John W. and Paula Taggart Gibson borrowed $129,000 from plaintiff Decatur Federal to purchase a home. They executed a promissory note in favor of Decatur Federal as well as a security deed to the property [*i.e.*, a mortgage]. In September 1994, the Bank erroneously marked the note "paid in full" and returned the original to the Gibsons. It is undisputed that the Gibsons had not paid the outstanding balance and were not entitled to cancellation. Nevertheless, they made no further payments on the debt and have repeatedly demanded cancellation of the security deed.
>
> The Bank filed a complaint for declaratory judgment and equitable action to reform the note to reflect that the underlying debt has not been paid. The Gibsons counterclaimed for damages and attorney fees based on allegations that the Bank maliciously refused to cancel the mortgage and maliciously reported false information to its credit reporting agencies.

Has the Gibsons' debt to the Bank been discharged or not? Does it matter?

Restatement Third, Restitution and Unjust Enrichment

§8. MISTAKEN DISCHARGE OF OBLIGATION OR LIEN

(1) Mistaken discharge by an obligee of an obligation or the security therefor gives the obligee a claim in restitution by reinstatement of the rights mistakenly surrendered.

(2) If the use of the claimant's funds to discharge a lien confers an unintended benefit on another person as the result of the claimant's mistake about title to the encumbered property, the existence of intervening liens, or other relevant circumstances, the claimant is entitled to restitution via subrogation to the discharged lien (§57(1)(a)) as necessary to prevent unjust enrichment.

Farnsworth, *Restitution* 32-33 (2014):

The mistaken payment of an obligation owed by someone else can raise a special difficulty. I mistakenly pay X the money that you owed him—or that you seemed to owe him; but actually you *deny* owing him the money. And maybe you have a good argument. Perhaps I inadvertently paid your tax bill, and now you tell me that you thought the bill was erroneous and that you had planned to contest it. Do you owe me the full amount that I paid? Not necessarily. You are free to argue that the tax bill was wrong. I, in turn, will argue that the bill was valid. It might seem odd that I end up arguing the government's position in the lawsuit between us, but that is what can happen when one party pays an obligation owed by another. To state the point more generally, the beneficiary of a mistaken payment to a creditor has all the same defenses against the plaintiff that he would have had against the creditor who was mistakenly paid. And now suppose those defenses succeed, so you don't have to repay me. Do *I* now have a claim against the town for reimbursement? So it might seem. After all, I paid money to the town that a court has said was not due. But the town fairly can claim that it hasn't had its own day in court yet. It can't be bound by the finding in my lawsuit against you, because it did not participate—a necessary condition of collateral estoppel. So I will have to bring a fresh lawsuit against the town, arguing that the tax bill it sent you was wrong—after I just finished, in my suit against you, arguing that the bill was right. What fun!

C. BENEFITS OTHER THAN MONEY

Michigan Central Railroad v. State
85 Ind. App. 557, 155 N.E. 50 (1927)

REMY, J.

On June 10, 1920, the State of Indiana contracted for a year's supply of coal for the Indiana State Prison, a penal institution located at Michigan City, the contract price for the coal being $3.40 per ton, delivered. On October 22, 1920, while the contract was in force, appellant railway company had in its possession for interstate transportation a carload of coal of the same kind and quality as that contracted for by the state, which coal, by mutual mistake of the carrier and agents of the state, was delivered to the Indiana State Prison and there consumed. This carload of coal at the time and place of its delivery was of the market value of $6.85 per ton. Upon learning of the misdelivery of the coal and its consumption, appellant paid to the consignee of the coal the market value thereof, and demanded of the state that it be reimbursed for the amount so paid. With this demand the state refused to comply. Whereupon appellant commenced this action against the state to recover the market value of the coal. The cause was submitted to the court upon an agreed statement of facts, the substance of which is as above set forth. The court found against the state, but limited recovery to $3.40 per ton.

Claiming that the amount of the recovery should have been $6.85 per ton, the market value of the coal, and was therefore too small, the railroad company prosecutes this appeal. The state not having assigned cross-errors, the only question for determination by this court is whether, under the facts stipulated, the measure of recovery is the market value of the coal at the time and place of the misdelivery; or, as held by the trial court, the price at which the state had purchased the year's supply. A decision of the question will require a consideration of the nature and character of the action.

The facts in this case are unusual, as is the legal proceeding. By reason of a mistake of fact, the state received the coal from the carrier, and before the mistake was discovered, the coal had been consumed. Recognizing its liability for the conversion of the coal, the carrier paid to the consignee the market value thereof, and by this action seeks indemnity from the state. That a carrier may recover for a consignment of goods delivered to the wrong person by mistake, in an action against the person who received and retained the goods, is not questioned by appellees, nor can it be; nor do appellees question the right of appellant to sue the state in an action of this character. The state's obligation which forms the basis of this action is what is termed quasi contractual. Though frequently referred to by the courts as equitable in character, it is a legal obligation on the part of the obligor to make restitution in value, that is, to pay the equivalent of the benefit received and unjustly enjoyed. Woodward, Law of Quasi Contracts, §3; Quasi-Contractual Obligations, 21 Yale Law J. 533; Grossbier v. Chicago, etc., R. Co. (1921), 173 Wis. 503, 181 N.W. 746.

The legal obligation of the state in this action is to pay to appellant a sum equal to the benefit to the state which resulted from the misdelivery. The benefit is not fixed by any agreement, for there had been no agreement by the state as to this carload of coal; and since this is not an action in tort, the rules governing the measure of damages in actions *ex delicto* are not controlling. In actions to enforce quasi contractual obligations, the general rule is that the measure of recovery is the value of the benefit received by the defendant (Bowen v. Detroit Union Railway [1920], 212 Mich. 432, 180 N.W. 495; Moore v. Richardson [1902], 68 N.J.L. 305, 53 A. 1032); but it cannot be said that to this rule there are no exceptions. If, for example, the carrier has settled with the owner of a consignment of goods which had been misdelivered, the settlement being for a sum less than the market value, it would not be contended that the carrier could recover the market value in an action against the person who had received the goods. It is unnecessary, however, to discuss the exceptions to the general rule.

The obligation forming the basis of the action is essentially an obligation to restore a benefit received by the defendant, and not to compensate the plaintiff for damages sustained. The obligation rests upon the principle that the defendant—the state in this case—cannot be allowed, in equity and good conscience, to keep what it has obtained. But affirmatively, the state must restore what in good conscience it cannot retain. The state having contracted, in the way provided by the statute, for a year's supply of coal for its penal institution, at the price of $3.40 per ton, the state's representatives could not, by their mistake in receiving from a common carrier coal of a like quality, but which had been sold and consigned to another, obligate the state to pay the carrier for the coal a price in excess of the state's contract price, the carrier having been a party to the mistake. It would be contrary to sound public policy to require the state to pay more for coal delivered and received by mistake than it would be required to pay under a contract resulting from competitive bids. We hold that the measure of recovery is the state's contract price, and not the market value of the coal at the time and place of the misdelivery.

Continental Forest Products, Inc. v. Chandler Supply Co.
95 Idaho 739, 518 P.2d 1201 (1974)

BAKES, Justice.

Continental Forest Products, Inc., the plaintiff-respondent, is an Oregon corporate lumber broker. As plaintiff, it instituted this action against Chandler Supply Company, also a corporation, the defendant-appellant, seeking recovery of $10,231.45, plus interest for two carloads of plywood allegedly sold defendant in the summer of 1969. Following trial without a jury, the court entered findings of fact and conclusions of law in favor of the plaintiff (hereinafter referred to as Continental), and entered judgment in conformity with its findings and conclusions. The defendant-appellant (hereinafter referred to as Chandler) appeals from this judgment.

The appellant Chandler is a wholesale lumber distributor at Boise and has done business, both buying and selling of lumber products, with a company known as North America Millwork, Inc., of Tacoma, Washington. On June 26, 1969, Larry Williams, an employee of Chandler, phoned North America Millwork, Inc., for quotations on plywood prices, advising North America it was in the market for a carload of 1/2-inch plywood and a carload of 5/8-inch plywood. Williams spoke with Ed Barker, an employee of North America, giving him the necessary data. Later on the same day, Barker advised Williams of the quoted prices for plywood, and Williams ordered the two carloads of plywood from North America Millwork, giving Barker the Chandler purchase order numbers 3246 and 3247. On the same day, Williams prepared two separate Chandler purchase orders covering the two carloads of plywood fixing the delivery date as two weeks or sooner, f. o. b. mill, with the quoted prices. These two purchase orders, one numbered 3246 and the other numbered 3247, were mailed by Chandler to North America Millwork on the same day.

This was Chandler's first order for plywood from North America Millwork, although it had transacted a considerable volume of other lumber business with North America Millwork between December 1968, and July 1969. In prior transactions when Chandler had purchased from North America, North America had sent its own written acknowledgments of Chandler's purchase orders placed with it and later had submitted invoices upon shipments being made. In this instance, North America neither confirmed nor rejected the June 26, 1969, Chandler purchase orders by written acknowledgment nor did it send its invoices to Chandler.

However, on July 2, 1969, Chandler received two acknowledgements of the orders for plywood from Continental, both dated June 27, 1969, one for a carload of 1/2-inch plywood, and the other for a carload of 5/8-inch plywood. The specifications, prices and terms for the plywood as recited in the acknowledgements were substantially the same as the orders placed by Chandler with North America on June 26. The acknowledgments also referred to the Chandler purchase orders 3246 and 3247 which had been sent to North America Millwork. It is not entirely clear how Continental received Chandler's orders sent to North America. Apparently Ed Barker left his employment with North America and commenced brokering for Continental and gave the orders to Continental.

On July 7, 1969, the Monday following the Fourth of July holiday, Earl Chandler, the president of appellant company, in his own handwriting, wrote on each duplicate copy of the acknowledgments of orders received from Continental, "Purchased from North America Millwork. Earl Chandler 7-7-69" and directed that they be mailed to Continental. Earl Chandler testified that in writing this notation he assumed that Continental was making the shipments for North America. Mrs. Hebein, Earl Chandler's secretary, testified that she mailed these copies of the acknowledgments of orders, addressed to Continental, by regular mail. Witnesses for Continental testified that even though they searched through their files for these copies of the acknowledgements, they could not be found. Chandler kept copies of these acknowledgments with his handwritten note on them, and they were introduced into evidence.

Chandler received the first carload of plywood on July 24, 1969, and received an invoice from Continental for this carload. The second carload of plywood arrived August 6, 1969, and the invoice from Continental arrived on August 15. Chandler took delivery of both of these carloads, and at no time offered to return the plywood.

The terms of the orders provided for a 2% discount if paid for within five days after arrival of the invoice. On August 11, 1969, Chandler made a check for $3,636.36 payable to both Continental and North America Millwork and returned it to North America Millwork in payment of these two carloads of plywood. In calculating the amount of the payment, Chandler first deducted the 2% discount for the two carloads of plywood and also deducted a $6,212.95 trade debt owing from North America to Chandler.[1]

North America returned Chandler's check and denied that Chandler owed it money for the shipment of plywood. Chandler sent the payment to North America a second time, but it was again returned. Through a series of letters and telephone calls Chandler attempted to induce North America to accept payment. During this time, Ed Barker (who was then acting as an independent lumber broker, having left employment with North America on June 30, 1969), sent a letter to Williams (employee of Chandler) indicating that

---

1. During the summer of 1969 North America Millwork began experiencing financial difficulties. Eventually, in December, 1969, North America Millwork made a common law assignment of assets to its creditors in an effort to liquidate its trade obligations. Through a letter of July 17, 1969, North America Millwork advised Chandler of its financial problems. At this time there was a balance due from North America to Chandler on other transactions in the amount of $6,212.95.

Continental was the actual supplier of the plywood. Chandler's attempt to pay North America failed, and Chandler refused to tender payment to Continental without deducting North America's trade debt.

Not having received payment for the two carloads, Continental brought this action for the quoted price of the plywood plus interest. Continental subsequently filed its supplemental complaint alleging a second claim against Chandler on the theory of unjust enrichment on the part of Chandler and seeking as damages $10,231.45.

Appellant Chandler answered the complaint and supplemental complaint, denying that it owed Continental any money or that Continental had sold it any goods. Chandler alleged that it had a contract only with North America to whom it had tendered payment. Following trial to the court on the issues framed by the pleadings, the trial court rendered its memorandum opinion in favor of Continental. Thereafter findings of fact, conclusions of law and judgment for $11,559.93 were entered, to which appellant objected. The district court denied these objections, and this appeal was taken.

Appellant first assigned as error the trial court's failure to find that Continental's claim was subject to Chandler's right of set off against North America.

In the trial court's memorandum opinion, rendered on May 26, 1971, the court discussed the relationship between Continental and Chandler and found that "the very least we have was an implied agreement or quasi contract."

Basically the courts have recognized three types of contractual arrangements. First is the express contract wherein the parties expressly agree regarding a transaction. Secondly, there is the implied in fact contract wherein there is no express agreement but the conduct of the parties implies an agreement from which an obligation in contract exists. The third category is called an implied in law contract, or quasi contract. However, a contract implied in law is not a contract at all, but an obligation imposed by law for the purpose of bringing about justice and equity without reference to the intent or the agreement of the parties and, in some cases, in spite of an agreement between the parties. It is a non-contractual obligation that is to be treated procedurally as if it were a contract, and is often referred to as quasi contract, unjust enrichment, implied in law contract or restitution.

In this case it is clear that there is neither an express nor an implied in fact contract since there was an express rejection by Chandler of any intention to enter into a contract with Continental as evidenced by the notation made on the acknowledgments and Chandler's subsequent attempts to pay North America Millwork for the carloads of plywood. However, we agree with the trial court that under the peculiar circumstances of this case, the third type of contract, implied in law or quasi contract, exists obligating Chandler to pay for the materials which he received. However, the problem which arises is determining the amount of recovery to which Continental is entitled.

As the essence of a contract implied in law lies in the fact that the defendant has received a benefit which it would be inequitable for him to retain, it necessarily follows that the measure of recovery in a quasi-contractual action is not the actual amount of the enrichment, but the amount of the enrichment which, as between the two parties it would be unjust for one party to retain. In the instant case we feel that the enrichment which Chandler "unjustly received" was the value of the plywood shipped less the trade set-off which Chandler had against North America Millwork and which he would have been entitled to take had the transaction been completed the way Chandler had intended and attempted to complete it. Chandler had a right to deal exclusively with North America and use his trade set-off as part of the purchase price. Chandler should not be deprived of this set-off in view of the way that Continental became involved in this transaction.

The foregoing conclusions necessarily follow as a matter of law from the salient facts found in the record. Those facts are that Chandler had placed the orders initially with North America Millwork, knowing that he had a trade set off; that the North America Millwork employee Ed Barker left his employment with North America Millwork and apparently took the Chandler orders with him, and that the orders subsequently wound up in the Continental organization; that Continental, without notifying Chandler that Barker had terminated his employment with North America and was now brokering for Continental, mailed its acknowledgments of the two orders which Chandler had placed with North America Millwork, referring to them by Chandler purchase order numbers which were sent to North America Millwork; that Chandler wrote on those acknowledgments that he had purchased the plywood from North America Millwork and mailed the acknowledgments back to Continental; and that Chandler attempted to make payment for the plywood to North America Millwork. If any party was responsible for the situation present in this case, it was Continental. Although it is not entirely clear from the record, it would appear that Barker breached the fiduciary duty which he owed to his employer North America Millwork by taking the Chandler purchase orders to Continental. Continental then, wittingly or unwittingly, took advantage of that breach of a fiduciary relationship and filled the orders, apparently without inquiry concerning the status of North America Millwork, the existence of a trade debt, the situation behind Barker's taking the purchase orders to Continental, or notifying Chandler that it was attempting to take over the North America transactions. Under these circumstances we feel that it would not be unjust to require Chandler to pay only that amount which he would have had to pay to North America had the transaction gone the way Chandler had intended and attempted to have it go.

Since the resolution of the quasi-contractual issue is dispositive in this case it is unnecessary to become embroiled in a discussion of the presumption of receipt of a letter duly mailed versus the weight to be given to testimony on non-receipt, as did the trial court in deciding the case and as did the parties on appeal.

Judgment should be entered for Continental against Chandler in the amount of the principal claim less the amount of the North America Millwork trade debt which Chandler had. The matter should be remanded to the trial court to make the necessary computations including adjustments for interest on account.

Judgment reversed and remanded. Costs awarded to appellant.

———————————

Measuring the benefit

1. In *Michigan Central R.R.*, how would the outcome be affected if the mistakenly delivered coal were sitting untouched in the prison's coal yard? What if it had been delivered by mistake to another customer down the line—maybe a steel mill—that was buying its coal on the spot market?

2. The railroad lost out because—as luck would have it—the mistaken delivery went to a recipient that was getting all the coal it needed at a below-market rate. Could the railroad recover the missing $3.45/ton by an action in restitution against the coal mine? R3RUE appears to accommodate such a claim:

§7. MISTAKEN PERFORMANCE OF ANOTHER'S OBLIGATION

Mistaken performance of another's obligation gives the performing party a claim in restitution against the obligor to the extent of the benefit mistakenly conferred on the obligor.

3. In *Continental Forest Products*, why did the trial court "become embroiled in a discussion of the presumption of receipt of a letter duly mailed versus the weight to be given to testimony on non-receipt"? What change in the facts would have led the Idaho Supreme Court to affirm judgment for Continental in the amount of $11,559.93? Conversely, what change in the facts would have led the Supreme Court to deny Continental's claim altogether? Finally, what change in the facts would have made the case not worth litigating?

4. The *Restatement* offers a rule (with comments) to acknowledge that benefits in the form of goods and services present special difficulties. If we apply the test stated in R3RUE §9—which follows—is there a viable restitution claim in the cases given as Illustrations 13 and 21 to that section? What is the amount of recovery (if any) in either case?

Restatement Third, Restitution and Unjust Enrichment

§9. BENEFITS OTHER THAN MONEY

A person who confers on another, by mistake, a benefit other than money has a claim in restitution as necessary to prevent the unjust enrichment of the recipient. Such a transaction ordinarily results in the unjust enrichment of the recipient only to the extent that:

(a) specific restitution is feasible;

(b) the benefit is subsequently realized in money or its equivalent;

(c) the recipient has revealed a willingness to pay for the benefit; or

(d) the recipient has been spared an otherwise necessary expense.

b. Valuation and liquidity. The conclusion that a recipient has been unjustly enriched by the receipt of an unrequested, nonreturnable benefit is hindered by problems of both *valuation* and *liquidity*.

The value to a given recipient of land, goods, or services can be determined with confidence only by the price that the recipient has willingly offered to pay. Neither market value nor cost to the provider reveals the value to the recipient when the transfer is nonconsensual. Even where value may be established with confidence, the illiquidity of a given benefit—in other words, the relative difficulty of exchanging it for money—means that a liability to pay that value in money is potentially prejudicial to the recipient. In a case where services have been provided by mistake, for example, the fact that their value to the recipient is objectively measured at $5,000 will not in itself support a restitutionary liability in that amount. If the recipient lacks the resources to purchase the services at that price—or if the recipient simply would not have chosen to make that particular expenditure—imposing a liability in restitution to pay $5,000 subjects the recipient to a forced exchange that is objectively fair but nevertheless disadvantageous.

The significance of the various circumstances identified in §9 is that they resolve the problems of valuation and liquidity that threaten to make a liability in restitution prejudicial to an innocent recipient. Thus the recipient's ability to return a benefit *in specie* solves both problems at once. . . .

Illustrations:

13. Mason agrees to construct a brick wall of specified dimensions on Owner's land for $5,000. Mason orders 10,000 bricks from Brickyard at 10 cents apiece. Unknown to Mason or Owner, Brickyard delivers 12,000 bricks by mistake. Mason's workmen use all the bricks delivered to the job site. The finished wall is larger, stronger, and handsomer than the wall Owner was promised. . . .

21. A undertakes to plow a 160-acre field belonging to B at a price of $10 per acre. A deals with C, an employee of B, but in fact C has neither actual nor apparent authority to contract on behalf of B. B discovers the facts and orders A to stop after A has plowed 40 acres. B thereupon engages D to plow the remainder of the field at a price of $5 per acre; D would have plowed the whole field at the same price per acre. B proceeds to cultivate the entire 160 acres. . . .

D. MISTAKEN IMPROVEMENTS

Somerville v. Jacobs
153 W. Va. 613, 170 S.E.2d 805 (1969)

[The Somervilles built a warehouse on a lot they thought was theirs, but that in fact belonged to Jacobs. Jacobs claimed ownership of the building, and Somerville brought this suit. It was found that the Somervilles reasonably relied on an incorrect survey, and that Jacobs had been unaware of the construction until it was complete: in other words, both sides were innocent. The trial court ordered Jacobs to choose between keeping the building and paying Somerville for the market value that the building added to the lot ($17,500), or selling the lot to Somerville for the market value it had before it was improved ($2,000). This appeal followed.]

HAYMOND, President [after stating the facts]:

Though the precise question here involved has not been considered and determined in any prior decision of this Court, the question has been considered by appellate courts in other jurisdictions. Though the cases are conflicting, the decisions in some jurisdictions, upon particular facts, recognize and sustain the jurisdiction of a court of equity to award compensation to the improver to prevent unjust enrichment to the owner and in the alternative to require the owner to convey the land to the improver upon his payment to the owner of the fair value of the land less the improvements.

In the early case of Bright v. Boyd, 4 Fed. Cas. 127 (No. 1875) (C.C. D. Me. 1841), a Federal trial court held in an opinion by Justice Story that an improving occupant could institute and maintain a suit in equity to secure compensation for his improvements on land of the owner and that as a doctrine of equity an innocent purchaser for valuable consideration, without notice of any infirmity in his title, who by his improvements added to the permanent value of the owner is entitled to compensation for the value of the improvements and to a lien upon the land which its owner must discharge before he can be restored to his original rights in the land.

In McKelway v. Armour, 10 N.J. Eq. (2 Stock.) 115 (Ch. 1854), the plaintiff by mistake built a valuable dwelling-house upon the defendant's adjoining lot instead of his own. [Both parties had acquired their lots from one Redmond, who possibly started the trouble by giving Armour a deed to the wrong lot. Excerpts from the *McKelway* decision are inserted here:]

> But it is proved, beyond all doubt, that the complainant erected his improvements on this lot *by mistake:* he supposed that it was the lot next that belonged to Armour. Armour labored under the same mistake. He lived in the vicinity; he saw the complainant progressing, from day to day, with these improvements. If he knew this to be his lot, his silence was a fraud upon the complainant; but this is not pretended. He admits that he did not suspect the erections to be upon his lot, until some time after their erection, when by actual measurement, to his surprise, he discovered the mistake. Under such circumstances, it would be most unjust to permit

Armour to take these improvements, and to send the complainant away remediless.

It is very true, as was urged upon the argument, the complainant is the most to blame in this matter. A diligent examination of the deed to Armour, and an actual measurement of the land, would have decided the difficulty. But it was a vacant lot of land, plotted out upon a map only, and the mistake was one which might occur to the most careful and diligent man. The fact of Armour's standing by, and participating in the mistake, is an important feature in the case.

In adjusting the equities of the parties, a decree should be made, which, while it relieves the complainant, must put Armour to as little inconvenience as possible.

I have concluded, therefore, to offer Armour the privilege of taking the improvements at a value to be ascertained upon equitable principles by a master; or, if he prefers it, to order a reference to a master to ascertain the value of the lot, and to decree a release to the complainant upon his paying the valuation. Twenty days will be allowed Armour to make his selection of these offers, if he desires it. Should he decline selecting either of them within the time limited, I shall order a decree to the following effect: that Redmond convey to Armour lot No. 32 free and clear of all encumbrances, and that Armour release to complainant lot No. 34. As between the complainant and Armour, this will be just and equitable, for it appears, by the evidence, that lot 32 is more valuable than lot 34. As to Redmond, he admits this to be correct, and agreeable to his original intention, and tenders himself ready to do this.

In Voss v. Forgue, 84 So.2d 563 (Fla. 1956), the court held that where a landowner mistakenly constructed a dwelling on a lot adjacent to one he owned and the two adjoining lots were substantially the same in value and the landowner was innocent of wrongdoing and the adjacent landowner was not shown to have been harmed, equity at the suit of the first landowner compelled both landowners to exchange deeds to their respective lots, upon payment by the first landowner of a certain sum and court costs.

In the recent case of Beacon Homes, Inc. v. Holt, 266 N.C. 467, 146 S.E.2d 434 (1966), the court said in the opinion: "It is as contrary to equity and good conscience for one to retain a house which he has received as the result of a bona fide and reasonable mistake of fact as it is for him to retain money so received. We, therefore, hold that where through a reasonable mistake of fact one builds a house upon the land of another, the landowner, electing to retain the house upon his property, must pay therefor the amount by which the value of his property has been so increased."

It is clear that the defendants claim the ownership of the building. Under the common law doctrine of annexation, the improvements passed to them as part of the land. The record does not disclose any express request by the plaintiffs for permission to remove the building from the premises if that could be done without its destruction, which is extremely doubtful as the building was constructed of solid concrete blocks on a concrete slab, but it is reasonably clear, from the claim of the defendants of their ownership of the building and their insistence that certain fixtures which have been removed from the building be replaced, that the defendants will not consent to the removal of the building even if that could be done.

In that situation if the defendants retain the building and refuse to pay any sum as compensation to the plaintiff W. J. Somerville they will be unjustly enriched in the amount of $17,500.00, the agreed value of the building, which is more than eight and one-half times the agreed $2,000.00 value of the lot of the defendants on which it is located, and by the retention of the building by the defendants the plaintiff W. J. Somerville will suffer a total loss of the amount of the value of the building.

To prevent such unjust enrichment of the defendants, and to do equity between the parties, this Court holds that an improver of land owned by another, who through a reasonable mistake of fact and in good faith erects a building entirely upon the land of the owner, with reasonable belief that such land was owned by the improver, is entitled to recover the value of the improvements from the landowner and to a lien upon such property which may be sold to enforce the payment of such lien, or, in the alternative, to purchase the land so improved upon payment to the landowner of the value of the land less the improvements and such landowner, even though free from any inequitable conduct in connection with the construction of the building upon his land, who, however, retains but refuses to pay for the improvements, must, within a reasonable time, either pay the improver the amount by which the value of his land has been improved or convey such land to the improver upon the payment by the improver to the landowner of the value of the land without the improvements.

CAPLAN, Judge, dissenting:

Respectfully, but firmly, I dissent from the decision of the majority in this case. Although the majority expresses a view which it says would result in equitable treatment for both parties, I am of the opinion that such view is clearly contrary to law and to the principles of equity and that such holding, if carried into effect, will establish a dangerous precedent.

I am aware of the apparent alarmist posture of my statements asserting that the adoption of the majority view will establish a dangerous precedent. Nonetheless, I believe just that and feel that my apprehension is justified. On the basis of unjust enrichment and equity, the majority has decided that the errant party who, without improper design, has encroached upon an innocent owner's property is entitled to equitable treatment. That is, that he should be made whole. How is this accomplished? It is accomplished by requiring the owner of the property to buy the building erroneously constructed on his property or by forcing (by court edict) such owner to sell his property for an amount to be determined by the court.

What of the property owner's right? The solution offered by the majority is designed to favor the plaintiff, the only party who had a duty to determine which lot was the proper one and who made a mistake. The defendants in this case, the owners of the property, had no duty to perform and were not parties to the mistake. Does equity protect only the errant and ignore the faultless? Certainly not.

It is not unusual for a property owner to have long range plans for his property. He should be permitted to feel secure in the ownership of such property by virtue of placing his deed therefor on record. He should be permitted to feel secure in his future plans for such property. However, if the decision expressed in the majority opinion is effectuated then security of ownership in property becomes a fleeting thing. It is very likely that a property owner in the circumstances of the instant case either cannot readily afford the building mistakenly built on his land or that such building does not suit his purpose. Having been entirely without fault, he should not be forced to purchase the building.

In my opinion for the court to permit the plaintiff to force the defendants to sell their property contrary to their wishes is unthinkable and unpardonable. This is nothing less than condemnation of private property by private parties for private use. Condemnation of property (eminent domain) is reserved for government or such entities as may be designated by the legislature. Under no theory of law or equity should an individual be permitted to acquire property by condemnation. The majority would allow just that.

I am aware of the doctrine that equity frowns on unjust enrichment. However, contrary to the view expressed by the majority, I am of the opinion that the circumstances of this case do not warrant the application of such doctrine. It clearly is the accepted law that as between two parties in the circumstances of this case he who made the mistake must suffer the hardship rather than he who was without fault.

I would reverse the judgment of the Circuit Court of Wood County and remand the case to that court with directions that the trial court give the defendant, Jacobs, the party without fault, the election of purchasing the building, of selling the property, or of requiring the plaintiff to remove the building from defendant's property.

Forced exchange?

1. Ever since Justice Story's influential decision in *Bright v. Boyd* (1841), the consistent tendency of U.S. law has been toward more liberal relief for the mistaken improver. The doctrinal watershed was the point at which the improver was allowed *affirmative relief*—by an action that seeks to recover the unjust enrichment conferred by the improver's mistake—as opposed to the strictly defensive measures permitted by earlier law. Previously, if an owner sought ejectment plus damages for the trespass (alias "mesne profits," alias "use and occupation"), the improver was entitled to a set-off based on the value added by the improvement; but a set-off would yield no recovery to the improver. Moving beyond this limited relief required a big step, and it is easy to see why the common law hesitated to take it. Restitution to the improver for unjust enrichment typically imposes a "forced exchange" on the owner, who is obliged to pay for

something he did not ask for or (alternatively) to sell property he did not choose to sell. In doing so, the law violates what is normally one of its cardinal limitations. According to R3RUE §2(4), "Liability in restitution may not subject an innocent recipient to a forced exchange: in other words, an obligation to pay for a benefit that the recipient should have been free to refuse."

Cases of mistaken improvement sometimes persuade courts to relax this principle, but in doing so they remain acutely sensitive to the relative "equities" of owner and improver. These include the context of the transaction; the extent of enrichment on one side and hardship on the other; and the individual factors (notice and fault on either side, or the absence thereof) that make a given resolution appear just in a particular case. The statement by the New Jersey court in *McKelway v. Armour*—"In adjusting the equities of the parties, a decree should be made, which, while it relieves the complainant, must put Armour to as little inconvenience as possible"—describes the instinctive reaction of equity to such situations.

2. In Pearl Township v. Thorp, 17 S.D. 288, 96 N.W. 99 (1903), the township wanted to sink an artesian well. It acquired a two-acre tract for this purpose, carved out of an unimproved quarter-section (160 acres) owned by defendant Nelson. The state engineer for irrigation came onto this tract and marked the exact spot for the well by driving a "substantial stake" into the ground. Thereafter "some unknown person" removed the stake and placed it on the adjoining land of Nelson, "at a point 2 rods [11 yards], 4 feet, and 6 inches west of its original location, and 19 feet west of the west line of the [township's] two-acre tract."

> At the time the well machinery was brought upon the ground and placed in position, immediately over the spot where the stake was found, appellant Thorp was present, and during the progress of the work was a frequent visitor there, until the flow of water was struck, and was present upon that occasion. Immediately after the completion of the well, and for the sum of $600, he purchased of Andrew Nelson the unimproved quarter section above described, with the exception of the two-acre tract previously deeded to the respondent township for artesian well purposes. As soon as respondent's officials ascertained that the well in controversy was not upon the 2-acre tract, but upon the 158-acre tract purchased by Thorp from Nelson, they made every reasonable effort to purchase the one-half acre of land upon which the well is situated, and which joins such 2-acre tract on the west, but Thorp declined all negotiations, and said, "We have got the well; we have got a good thing, and we propose to keep it."

What remedy would you grant on these facts?

3. The facts of Lawson v. O'Kelley, 81 Ga. App. 883, 60 S.E.2d 380 (1950), were stated as follows:

> During June and July, 1947, Fred W. O'Kelley owned the Bee Hive Market Building in Gainesville, Hall County, Georgia, and some time

during this period, apparently during the latter part of June, on a Sunday, two tenants, Toy Minor and George Convil, went to O'Kelley, complaining about the roof of the building, which was leaking badly and needed replacing, and suggested that N. E. Lawson be authorized to do the work. O'Kelley refused to authorize them to get Lawson to do the work, thinking some one else would do the work cheaper than Lawson, and told them he would see about it the following week. Thereafter Minor and Convil went to Lawson and discussed the matter with him, and finally Convil, without any authority from O'Kelley, told Lawson to go ahead and do the work. Lawson purchased shingles at the Parris Dunlap Hardware Store and proceeded to replace the roof. O'Kelley first learned that Lawson was replacing the roof when he went to the same hardware store to inquire about the price of shingles and was informed by one of the owners, James Dunlap, upon stating the reason for the inquiry, that Lawson had already bought some shingles and was replacing the roof. O'Kelley left the hardware store and went by the building on his way home. He noticed that two men were working on the roof, and that the work on the new roof was practically completed. Lawson was not present. O'Kelley said nothing to the two men, and subsequently refused to pay Lawson for the work. A short time thereafter, in July, 1947, O'Kelley sold the building to Ralph Cleveland. During the negotiations O'Kelley tried to impress Cleveland with the fact that the building had a new roof on it, but Cleveland did not increase his offer, as he wanted the land and intended tearing down the building. During the short time that O'Kelley owned the building after the new roof was placed on it he did not increase his charges for rent, but after Cleveland acquired the building he changed his mind about tearing it down, and increased the rent and painted the building. Lawson testified that the cost of the labor and material and the reasonable value thereof was $318.25, and Cleveland testified that the value of the building was increased by this amount on account of the new roof. O'Kelley admitted that the value of the building was increased on account of the new roof.

How should the case be decided?

4. In Ochoa v. Rogers, 234 S.W. 693 (Tex. Civ. App. 1921), the facts were stated as follows:

On Christmas Eve, 1918, a 6-cylinder Studebaker passenger automobile was stolen from its owner, Miguel Ochoa, in San Antonio. In some unaccountable way it got into the possession of the United States government, and on November 12, 1919, the government sold it to Henry A. Rogers, at an auction sale at Camp Travis, at which a large number of dismantled cars called "junk" were likewise disposed of. At the time it was so purchased by Rogers no part of the car was intact. It had no top except a part of the frame thereof; its steering rod was without a wheel; it had no tires, no rims, no cushions, no battery; the motor was out of the car, but included in the junk, as was also the radiator; one headlight was entirely gone, the other was useless; part of the gears were out and one wheel was gone, as was one axle; the fenders were partly gone, and had to be entirely replaced; the differential was beyond repair, and the frame, or chassis, was there, but broken. It was no longer an automobile, but a pile of broken and dismantled parts of what was once Ochoa's car. It was "junk." Rogers paid the government $85 for this junk at the auction sale, which was its market value at the time. Having purchased these parts, Rogers used them in the construction of a delivery truck, at an expense of approximately $800. When the truck was completed, he put it in use in his furniture business. This was late in 1919. On August 7, 1920, Ochoa, passing Rogers' place of business recognized the machine from a mark on the hood and another on the radiator, and completed the identification by checking the serial and engine numbers, which tallied accurately with similar numbers on the car he had owned. The identification being complete and satisfactory to himself and other witnesses, Ochoa demanded the property of Rogers, who refused to surrender it, whereupon Ochoa brought this suit to recover possession of the property, or, in the alternative, for the value thereof at the time of the suit, which he alleged to be $1000, and for the value of the use of the car at the rate of $5 per day from the time Rogers purchased it from the government.

Does either party have a claim against the other? If so, for what?

———————————

Restatement Third, Restitution and Unjust Enrichment

§10. MISTAKEN IMPROVEMENTS

A person who improves the real or personal property of another, acting by mistake, has a claim in restitution as necessary to prevent unjust enrichment. A remedy for mistaken improvement that subjects the owner to a forced exchange will be qualified or limited to avoid undue prejudice to the owner.

a. General principles. Restitution for mistaken improvement requires an accommodation between powerful competing principles. The prima facie showing of unjust enrichment in such a case may be very strong, particularly where the value of the improvements greatly exceeds the value of the unimproved property. Because improvements normally constitute nonreturnable benefits, however, effective relief to the improver may require subjecting the landowner to an involuntary exchange. Any remedy that requires the owner to pay for an unrequested improvement, to sell improved property to the improver at a court-determined price, or to exchange a mistakenly improved tract for an unimproved substitute, is open to objection on this ground. The reason for the common law's traditional reluctance to relieve the mistaken improver is not that a mistaken improver is less deserving of restitution than any other restitution claimant, but that effective relief to the improver may in some circumstances impose unjustified hardship on the owner.

b. Betterment acts. Statutes enacted in most U.S. jurisdictions, commonly known as "betterment acts" or "occupying claimant acts," afford limited relief to mistaken improvers of real property under specified circumstances. . . .

In a few states, the statutory remedy merely codifies the improver's common-law right to a set-off against liability to the owner for wrongful occupancy. More frequently, however, the betterment acts afford a radical form of restitutionary relief in favor of a limited class of mistaken improvers. At an earlier stage of American land development, when both title to land and the land itself remained largely to be settled, a contest between competing land titles might be resolved in favor of an absentee owner against an original settler who—believing in the validity of his title—had reduced a former wilderness to cultivation. The gross inequity of dispossessing a good-faith occupant in favor of a passive investor, allowing the defendant only a set-off against liability for mesne profits, inspired the striking remedy that is the most common feature of the betterment acts, appearing in the majority of the statutes. This is the "buy/sell election," giving the owner a choice between paying the value of the improvements and selling the land to the improver at its unimproved value. . . .

h. Measure of recovery. Except where the owner is responsible for the improver's mistake (see §52), the claim allowed by this section will limit any monetary recovery in favor of mistaken improvers to the cost to the improver or the value realized by the owner, whichever is less. Because a mistaken improvement is almost never economically efficient, the usual effect of such a rule is that a money judgment in restitution will represent only partial compensation to the improver for the expense incurred in making the improvement. The reason for this outcome is not that restitution favors owners over improvers, but that the theory of liability in restitution is payment for benefits received by the defendant, not compensation for losses incurred by the plaintiff.

Farnsworth, *Restitution* 26-28 (2014):

Large-scale improvements are of particular theoretical interest because the equities of them put pressure on the usual principles of restitution and sometimes cause them to buckle a bit. We again can start with stylized facts. A builder mistakenly erects a house on someone else's vacant lot. He was confused about which lot he owned, or he bought the lot from someone he mistakenly thought had authority to sell but didn't, or he had a deed but the deed was defective. The owner of the lot discovers this, moves into the new house, and posts a guard dog outside to prevent Builder from trespassing. Builder brings a restitution claim against the owner. What is the result?

Under the principles seen so far, the outlook for the builder seems grim. Assume the owner hadn't previously planned to build a house on his property but has no plans to sell the house now that it exists. On those facts it will likely be impossible to prove how much the owner values the house. The fact that he chooses to live there is interesting, and might suggest that he should at least pay some sort of amount for the pleasure—maybe something like its rental value each month. But this would force a transaction on him that he might not have wanted. Maybe he only likes living in the house because it is free. Of course the builder is likely to be allowed whatever specific restitution he can get without violating our second principle: if the house can be removed without damaging the owner's land, the builder will likely be allowed to come take it away. (Sneaking onto the property to destroy the improvement is a very different thing, and may result in an award of damages against the destroyer.) But often it will not be movable and Builder will be able to salvage only a bit of his work. So he seems likely to receive nothing or close to it. If the builder is entitled to demolish and remove the house, perhaps the result will be a negotiation in which he agrees not to do that in return for some small amount— anything more than what the builder would net from the wreckage after he carts it away.

The result—a blundering builder puts up a house, perhaps at enormous cost, and receives nothing in return for it—is very harsh, and intolerably harsh in the view of most courts today. Not that the courts set rules about when the harshness becomes too much to bear; they just look at each case and try to come up with solutions that seem reasonable on all the facts, constrained only by the idea that the remedy must not impose undue prejudice on the recipient—a standard that provides much flexibility and a long menu of solutions to consider. Those possible solutions include forcing an owner to choose between buying the house from the builder or selling the underlying land to him, in either case at a market rate. Or it can give the builder an equitable lien on the house, perhaps in a conditional form that allows the value of the improvement to be collected from rental payments produced by the property or by a later rather than immediate sale of it. Or the court can order a simple payment of the value of the house or other improvements to the builder. Or it can always follow the older rules and just let the builder remove whatever parts of the house he can carry away, with nothing more.

All these options are available in principle. Whether a court is willing to use them in practice will depend on the equities of the situation. First, of course, there is the simple question of good faith. The builder who knew he was outside his rights—an unusual character, but not unheard of—will be out of luck entirely; he probably does not belong in this chapter, since strictly speaking he did not commit a mistake. Likewise, the owner who knew of the builder's mistake but kept silent will not be heard to complain later when the builder is granted liberal relief. Then comes related matters of negligence. We saw earlier that a claimant's negligence usually is not relevant to whether a defendant is found to have been unjustly enriched; it becomes very relevant, however, at the remedial stage of a case. A builder who was negligent about where to build will be entitled to less solicitude than one who did all that could be asked but was the victim of a bad surveyor. From an economic standpoint, the general idea is to preserve good incentives by denying some benefits to anyone who had a chance to avoid the fiasco but didn't.

Finally, a court choosing a remedy will be interested in the relationships between the parties and their properties. If an innocent owner lives on the land that was mistakenly improved, the costs of a forced sale are at their highest. No court will oust him. At the other end of the spectrum, where unoccupied property is held just for the sake of investment, a court is more likely to be creative in fashioning relief. The old example was wooded property on the frontier. A more modern version is *Voss v. Forgue*, [84 So. 2d 563 (Fla. 1956)]. The parties owned different plots in a subdivision that was under construction. One of them mistakenly put up a house on the square of land owned by the other. After finding that the two squares of property had the same value and no intrinsic advantages relative to one another, the court simply ordered the parties to trade lots. The remedy didn't really cost anybody anything, and it probably increased the overall value in the situation because the house the builder had created was no doubt more valuable to him than it was to the owner of the underlying land (who presumably had a slightly different design of his own in mind). And the solution still leaves the mistaken builder with plenty of incentive to be careful, since he can't count on being so lucky next time: the law's usual presumption is that every parcel of land is unique, meaning the owner attaches special value to whichever one he has, so a forced trade of the kind used in *Voss* is rarely going to be an attractive remedy.

E. MISTAKEN GIFTS

Massicotte v. Matuzas
143 N.H. 711, 738 A.2d 1260 (1999)

THAYER, J.

The defendant, Anthony James Matuzas, appeals from a Superior Court (Murphy, J.) decision imposing a constructive trust on his interest in certain real property in favor of the plaintiff, Josephine B. Massicotte. We vacate and remand.

After a trial on the merits, the court found the following facts. The property at issue is located in Nashua and was purchased in 1965 by the plaintiff and her then husband, Peter K. Matuzas, Sr. In 1974, by divorce decree, the plaintiff was awarded exclusive title to the property. The plaintiff has three children from the marriage, including the defendant. In 1978, she married Henry Massicotte, the father of two children from a prior marriage. After their marriage, the plaintiff and Massicotte resided at the Nashua property. In 1981, the plaintiff asked her attorney to draw up a deed placing the property in the names of herself and Massicotte, and providing that upon their deaths her three children would receive title. The deed was drafted by the attorney, signed by the plaintiff and Massicotte without either having read it, and recorded. As drafted, the deed conveyed title to Massicotte, the plaintiff, and her three children, all as joint tenants with rights of survivorship.

In 1989, the defendant informed the plaintiff that he was aware that he had an interest in the Nashua property and that he intended to "get what was coming to [him]" when the Nashua house was sold. It was not until 1993 that the plaintiff examined the deed and learned that it provided a grant of a present interest to her children. In an attempt to correct the deed, the plaintiff had a quitclaim deed prepared for each of her children conveying their interest back to the plaintiff and Massicotte. While two of her children signed the quitclaim deeds, the defendant did not. Consequently, the plaintiff brought a petition seeking a court order requiring the defendant to reconvey his interest to the plaintiff, or alternatively, declaring the property free and clear of any interest the defendant has in it. The trial court found in the plaintiff's favor and ordered the defendant to execute and deliver to the plaintiff a quitclaim deed conveying all rights, title, and interest he has in the property. The trial court denied the defendant's motion for reconsideration, and this appeal followed.

The defendant argues that the trial court's order should have conformed with the plaintiff's intent at the time she executed the 1981 deed. Therefore, the court erred by imposing a constructive trust on all of his interest in the property, rather than reforming the deed and conveyance to preserve for the defendant a remainder interest in the property. We agree.

In imposing a constructive trust, a trial court is not bound by rigid requirements; rather, "a court may impose such a trust to prevent the enrichment of one who acquires title to property through a mistake." Dubois v. Dubois, 122 N.H. 532, 535, 446 A.2d 1181, 1182-83 (1982). "Thus a constructive trust arises where the title to property is acquired through a mistake." Lamkin v. Hill, 120 N.H. 547, 551, 419 A.2d 1077, 1080 (1980). "It is old and well-established law that equity, at the instance of a grantor . . . will reform a voluntary conveyance, where, by mistake of law or fact, a larger estate or more land has been granted than was intended to be conveyed . . . ." Archer v. Dow, 126 N.H. 24, 28-29, 489 A.2d 574, 578 (1985).

The trial court found that instead of the remainder interest she intended, the plaintiff mistakenly conveyed a present interest to her three children. The court specifically found that the plaintiff asked that "the property be placed in the names of herself and her husband, and upon their death to her three children." Once the court determined that the defendant would be unjustly enriched by the plaintiff's mistake, and therefore the circumstances warranted reforming the conveyance, established principles of equity should have controlled the reformation. Thus, because the plaintiff made a voluntary conveyance, she was entitled to have the court reform the conveyance to correct the mistake and grant that which she intended to convey. Instead of reforming the deed to reflect the plaintiff's intent at the time of the conveyance, however, the court canceled the conveyance in its entirety. In doing so, the trial court erred.

Therefore, we vacate the court's order with respect to the relief granted and remand for further proceedings consistent with this opinion.

———————————

Gratuitous unjust enrichment

1. Recipients of mistaken gifts are "unjustly enriched" by comparison to what? To judge from *Massicotte* and many cases like it, the benchmark is evidently not their just deserts. In Soberanes v. Soberanes, 97 Cal. 140, 144-45, 31 P. 910, 911-12 (1893), an elderly mother—once wealthy, now destitute and incapacitated—asked the court to help her recover some of the extensive property she had rashly conveyed to the defendant, one of her sons. Finding no fraud or undue influence, the court delivered a lecture about the consequences of this kind of mistake:

> Transactions of the kind in question should be thoroughly sifted, but a voluntary deed, free from any imputation of undue influence, executed by a mother with her eyes open, cannot be set aside merely upon the ground that an honorable man would not accept a gift which strips his mother of all her property and leaves her dependent upon the charity of others. A person in possession of all his faculties has a right to dispose of his property as he sees fit, upon the principle stated by Lord Nottingham, that if he will improvidently bind himself up by a voluntary deed, he need not expect the court to break the fetters put upon himself by his own folly.

2. The court in *Massicotte* decided that particular interests in property had come by mistake into the wrong hands. The opinion suggests an extensive list of remedies that might be employed to rectify such a situation. The mother's remedy against the opportunistic son (as sought and obtained at trial) is successively described as "imposing a constructive trust," "requiring the defendant to reconvey his interest," "declaring the property free and clear of any interest the defendant has in it," "ordering the defendant to execute and deliver a quitclaim deed," and finally "cancellation of the conveyance in its entirety." These are all things a court of equity has the power to do, and in the context the expressions are nearly synonymous. The argument on appeal was that the proper remedy was instead "reforming the deed and conveyance." What is the difference on these facts?

3. In Hutson v. Hutson, 168 Md. 182, 177 A. 177 (1935), Mr. & Mrs. H. believed they were married. Intending to provide for his widow in the event of his death, Mr. H. conveyed property that he already owned "to Mr. & Mrs. H. as joint tenants with right of survivorship." The parties then discovered to their surprise that they were not married after all, because Mrs. H. was still

married to someone else. (She had heard that her first husband was dead, but he turned out to be alive.) Mr. H. sued the former Mrs. H., asking the court to cancel the conveyance. The court held for Mr. H., finding it "evident that the gift was predicated upon the theory that he was, at the time of the execution of the deeds, legally married to the appellant." Does this mean that Mrs. H. was unjustly enriched? Does it matter?

4. In Mott v. Iossa, 119 N.J. Eq. 185, 181 A. 689 (1935), the plaintiff married a woman, one Filomena, without realizing that she was also married to someone else. He lived with Filomena and her son for ten years; the son referred to the plaintiff as his father. The plaintiff made a gift of land to the son, then discovered that his marriage was invalid. He sought to rescind the gift. The court held for the defendant, concluding that "the cause of the gift was [the plaintiff's] affection for the boy himself and not his belief that Filomena was his lawful wife." Is that the real difference between *Hutson v. Hutson* and *Mott v. Iossa?*

5. Lady Hood of Avalon v. Mackinnon, [1909] 1 Ch. 476 (Ch. D.), is paraphrased by the *Restatement* as follows:

> Donor has two children, A and B. Intending to match an earlier gift to A, Donor gives $50,000 to B. In fact Donor has already made a $50,000 gift to each child, but has forgotten the earlier gift to B. Donor can recover the second $50,000 from B.

R3RUE §11, Illustration 13. What if Donor learned about the mistake but died without bringing the action? (The suit in that case would be *Estate of Donor v. B.*) Does Estate have a viable claim?

6. The facts of Larisa's Home Care, LLC v. Nichols-Shields, 362 Or. 115, 404 P.3d 912 (2017), were introduced as follows:

> Plaintiff owns two adult foster homes for the elderly. Prichard, an elderly woman who suffered from cognitive difficulties and dementia, became one of plaintiff's patients in June 2007. Prichard then resided and received care in one of plaintiff's adult foster homes until her death in November 2008. Because Prichard had been approved to receive Medicaid benefits, plaintiff charged Prichard the rate for Medicaid-qualified patients: approximately $2,000 per month, with approximately $1,200 of that being paid by the [Oregon Department of Human Services].
>
> Plaintiff's Medicaid rates were substantially below the rates paid by plaintiff's non-Medicaid patients, or "private pay" patients. For private pay patients, the rate varied depending on the level of care. During Prichard's stay, plaintiff charged private pay patients $4,000 per month for Level 2 care; for more intensive Level 3 care, plaintiff charged private pay patients $5,700 per month. Prichard received Level 2 and

Level 3 care during her stay in plaintiff's facility. If Prichard had not been approved for Medicaid benefits and had instead been a private pay patient, she would have paid plaintiff over $48,000 more for her care.

Following Prichard's death, it transpired that her approval for Medicaid benefits had been procured by her son's fraudulent misrepresentations to the Oregon DHS about his mother's financial circumstances. The son was attempting to conceal the fact that in recent years he had siphoned away most of his mother's assets into his own bank accounts. (Prichard herself was unaware of the facts and innocent of any misrepresentation.)

Prichard's son has been convicted of a crime and required to repay the embezzled funds to his mother's estate. Now Larisa's Home Care is suing the estate. What is the theory of their claim, and what can they recover?

———————————————

Chapter 3

Defective Consent

A. FRAUD AND MISREPRESENTATION

Earl v. Saks & Co.
36 Cal. 2d 602, 226 P.2d 340 (1951)

SCHAUER, J.

A. K. Barbee appeals from judgments, in consolidated actions hereinafter described, that respondent Mrs. Richard Earl is the owner of a certain mink coat and that Barbee owes respondent Saks and Company $3,981.25. He contends that an asserted sale of the coat to him by Saks, and an asserted gift of the coat by him to Mrs. Earl, were voidable, and were rescinded by him, because his consent thereto was induced by fraud of Mrs. Earl and Saks. We have concluded that these contentions are tenable.

On April 4, 1947, Barbee and Mrs. Earl went to the fur salon of Saks. A representative of Saks showed them a mink coat and told them its price was $5,000. Barbee told Saks that he would like to buy the coat for Mrs. Earl but that he would pay no more than $4,000 for it. Saks rejected repeated offers of Barbee to purchase the coat for $4,000. Unknown to Barbee, Mrs. Earl then asked Saks to pretend to sell the coat to him for $4,000, and stated that she would pay the difference between $4,000 and the price of the coat. Saks agreed to this. It told Barbee that it would sell the coat to him for $3,981.25, made out a sales slip for that amount, and Barbee signed it in the belief that that was the full price of the coat. Saks then delivered the coat to Barbee; he in turn delivered it to Mrs. Earl and said that he gave it to her. Mrs. Earl, wearing the coat, left the store with Barbee.

The next day, April 5, Mrs. Earl returned the coat to Saks to be monogrammed and paid Saks the balance of its price, $916.30. Later the same day Barbee told Saks that he had revoked the gift to Mrs. Earl, that he was the owner of the coat (which he thought he had purchased for $3,981.25), that he would pay the agreed price ($3,981.25) only if Saks would deliver the coat to him, and that it was not to deliver the coat to Mrs. Earl. Thereafter Mrs. Earl demanded that Saks deliver the coat to her; Saks refused and attempted to return her $916.30; but she refused to accept the money; Saks retained (and still retains) possession of the coat.

Mrs. Earl then sued Saks, alleging conversion of the coat. Saks answered, denying the conversion, and at the same time filed a pleading which it denominated "Cross-Complaint in Interpleader," which, however, not only named Mrs. Earl and Barbee as asserted interpleader cross-defendants but also implicitly and necessarily, in the light of the circumstances, required, if Saks was to prevail, the granting of affirmative adversary relief against Barbee or Mrs. Earl or both of them. Saks alleged that it sold the coat to Barbee for $3,981.25; that Mrs. Earl, "as additional consideration . . . to induce" Saks to make the sale to Barbee, agreed to pay Saks $916.30 and later paid Saks that sum; that Saks is indifferent between the claims of the cross-defendants and is willing to deliver the coat to either cross-defendant as the court may direct (but, it is implicit from Saks' several pleadings read together, only upon condition that it recover from Barbee or from Mrs. Earl or from both of them the full price of the coat); it asked that the cross-defendants be required to "litigate between themselves their claims to said mink coat"; it did not offer to relinquish its asserted claim for any part of the full price of approximately $4,900. Mrs. Earl's answer to the cross-complaint admitted that she paid Saks $916.30 and alleged that at that time title to the coat "was transferred to her as is more fully alleged in her complaint." The complaint, however, contains no allegations as to transfer of title. Barbee in answer to the cross-complaint admitted that he told Saks he would pay the price discussed between Saks and Barbee if and only if Saks "would sell and deliver the coat to him at and for [such] price," and alleged that Mrs. Earl's agreement to pay Saks $916.30 was fraudulently concealed from him by Saks and Mrs. Earl; that they represented to him that the full price of the coat was $3,981.25; and that if he had known of the secret agreement he would not have agreed to buy the coat.

From what has been stated it appears that Saks, because of its duplicitous compact with Mrs. Earl, finds itself in this position: It knowingly and purposefully caused Barbee to believe that it was selling him—and him only—a certain fur coat for the full price of $3,981.25. It wants to collect the $3,981.25 from Barbee but it cannot (or will not) deliver the coat to him—fully paid, for $3,981.25 or otherwise—because, although it has possession of the coat, it has already collected $916.30 for the same coat from Mrs. Earl, and she claims to own the coat and refuses to release her claim to it (or for damages for its alleged conversion) as against either Saks or Barbee. Mrs. Earl further claims the coat as against both Saks and Barbee on the theory of an asserted gift from Barbee. But the gift is, necessarily, dependent upon Barbee's having purchased the coat from Saks and that purchase, it is obvious, was induced by the joint fraud of Mrs. Earl and Saks. Saks and Mrs. Earl—both guilty of express fraud—are seeking the aid of the court to recover that which they are entitled to, if at all, only because of their fraud.

Rescission of gift

While, as indicated above, the pleadings do not specifically allege, or suggest the theory of, the origin of Mrs. Earl's claim of title to the coat, the trial proceeded on the theory that the issues were whether there was a sale by Saks to Barbee and a gift by Barbee to Mrs. Earl, and whether the two transactions were voidable by Barbee because of the secret agreement and misrepresentation. Barbee testified that he would not have bought the coat if he had known that the price was more than $4,000. Every element of the transaction and all the circumstances shown appear to support this position; no evidence is inconsistent with it. At the trial Barbee's counsel restated the position which Barbee had announced to Saks before the actions were instituted: "we are perfectly willing to accept the coat and pay . . . the price that we agreed to pay for it [$3,981.25] . . . but we certainly are under the circumstances disclosed here already in this evidence [the secret agreement] . . . not willing to let this coat be handed over to this young lady." Counsel for Barbee also offered to prove that the gift was made in reliance on Mrs. Earl's representations that she would "reciprocate his affection and would give up running around with other men" and that Barbee rescinded the gift when he learned that those representations were false. The offered proof on the latter theory was properly rejected, for no such issue was raised by the pleadings.

[Nevertheless, Barbee] could not have made the gift unless he made the purchase, and it is indisputably established that the purchase was induced by the express fraud of both Mrs. Earl and Saks. The facts that Barbee at the trial, by correctly rejected offers of proof, sought to show another fraudulent representation which also was an inducement to his making the gift, and that he announced rescission before he learned of the secret agreement, do not prevent him from now basing his defense on such secret agreement. "One may justify an asserted rescission by proving that at the time there was an adequate cause although it did not become known to him until later. One cannot waive or acquiesce in a wrong while ignorant thereof" (12 Am. Jur. 1027, §445).

A gift can be rescinded if it was induced by fraud or material misrepresentation (whether of the donee or a third person) or by mistake as to a "basic fact." (Rest., Restitution, §§26, 39 [R3RUE §§11, 13]; see Murdock v. Murdock (1920), 49 Cal. App. 775, 783-785 [194 P. 762] [fraud of donee]; In re Clark's Estate (1931), 233 App. Div. 487 [253 N.Y.S. 524, 527], noted 45 Harv. L. Rev. 750, 80 Pa. L. Rev. 747 [innocent misrepresentation of third party]; Rest., Contracts, §477, comment a.) "A failure by the donee to reveal material facts when he knows that the donor is mistaken as to them is fraudulent nondisclosure." (Rest., Restitution, §26, comment c.) "A mistake which entails the substantial frustration of the donor's purpose entitles him to restitution. No more definite general statement can be made as to what constitutes a basic mistake in the making of a gift. The donor is entitled to restitution if he was mistaken as to the . . . identity or essential characteristics of the gift." (Rest., Restitution, §26, comment *c*; [R3RUE §11, comment *b*].)

Since Barbee was not merely mistaken but was actively misled as to a material element in the purchase and as to an essential characteristic of the gift—he believed that the coat was purchased entirely by him so that it could be given in its entirety as a gift—he was entitled to, as he did, rescind the gift.

Rescission of contract

It appears from the findings of probative facts that Saks did more than merely fail to disclose its agreement with Mrs. Earl. In the circumstances, implicit in the finding that Barbee "was informed by Saks and Company's representatives that they would sell said mink coat to him for the sum of $3,981.25" is a finding that Saks actively misrepresented that the price had been reduced and that $3,981.25 was the full price. It is completely unreasonable to deny that a representation by a clerk in a reputable store that an article has a certain price, followed by the clerk's preparation and the customer's signing of a sales check showing purchase of the article for that price, amounts to a representation by the store that the *total* price and the *entire* sales transaction are as represented. This misrepresentation, it appears from the undisputed evidence, was made by Saks with knowledge that Barbee insisted on a reduction in price; from this it follows that such misrepresentation must have been made with intent to deceive Barbee and to induce him to buy the coat.

Saks relies on California cases which say that "fraud which has produced and will produce no injury will not justify a rescission." (Spreckels v. Gorrill (1907), 152 Cal. 383, 388 [92 P. 1011]; Munson v. Fishburn (1920), 183 Cal. 206, 216 [190 P. 808]; Darrow v. Houlihan (1928), 205 Cal. 771, 774 [272 P. 1049].) It asserts that a person is not injured by being induced to buy a $5,000 coat for $4,000. But the coat was neither sold nor bought for $4,000. Saks was selling the coat for the full price, and a person other than seller Saks and buyer Barbee paid a substantial part—approximately one fifth-of the full price. Furthermore, this "no injury, no rescission" formula is not very helpful, because of disagreement in the authorities as to what is meant by "injury." In a sense, anyone who is fraudulently induced to enter into a contract is "injured"; his "interest in making a free choice and in exercising his own best judgment in making decisions with respect to economic transactions and enterprises has been interfered with." (See McCleary, Damage as a Requisite to Rescission for Misrepresentation, 36 Mich. L. Rev. 1, 227, 245.)

Saks says that Barbee bargained for and expected to get a certain coat for a cost to him of not more than $4,000, and this is what he got. In the present situation, however, where the motives of Barbee were clearly noneconomic, the general social interest in stability of transactions is overridden by the interest in not having a seller make intentional misrepresentations which mislead a would-be donor into the erroneous belief that he alone is purchasing and that his donee is to receive from him a fully paid for gift, when the seller is fully aware of the effect which the misrepresentations may have and intends that they should have that effect. Again, it is important, the element of a complete gift by donor to donee is being destroyed through the misrepresentation and concealment.

Saks contends that Barbee has not rescinded, and cannot rescind, the sale because he has stated that he was willing to carry out the objectively manifested bargain to purchase the coat for $3,981.25. But at no time since Barbee's announced willingness to stand on the transaction which he believed he had entered into with Saks, did Saks offer to comply with the transaction and give Barbee what he bargained for: a coat for which he was paying in full, without Mrs. Earl, a stranger to the Saks-Barbee transaction, paying a portion of the price. Indeed, Saks, at the time of the rescission and mentioned offer by Barbee, was apparently unable to sell Barbee the coat in question as a fully paid for coat for $3,981.25 because Mrs. Earl refused to take back the $916.30 which she paid for the coat and which Saks had previously accepted. Barbee's counsel, at the trial, made clear his position; after the secret agreement, misrepresentation and payment of $916.30 were in evidence he said, "under the circumstances of this case we shouldn't be required to pay Saks and Company anything . . . [W]hen he [Barbee] learned all the facts he never would have approved that transaction and your Honor knows it . . . [He] would do anything that could be done to repudiate that transaction and say it never was a real transaction." We are satisfied that the contract of purchase and the gift were voidable and were properly rescinded.

For the reasons above stated, the judgments are reversed.

TRAYNOR, J. (dissenting)

Barbee received what he bargained for. The mink coat that he examined and agreed to pay $3,981.25 for, was the one he received and gave to Mrs. Earl. He concedes that the fair value of the coat was $5,000. It was not unreasonable for the trial court to conclude that, since the coat Barbee received was actually worth more than he agreed to pay, he would not have rejected it because Mrs. Earl arranged to pay the difference. It was under no compulsion to believe his statement that he would have rejected it.

It was for the trial court to determine whether Barbee was a man of such temperament that he would have preferred having Mrs. Earl get along without the fur coat to accepting her contribution toward its purchase. He declared his love for her, expressing the sentiment several times that he wanted to give her a fur coat. She was "very much in love with the coat and wanted it badly." It was important to him that the woman he loved possess the coat; it was important to her to possess it. Her contribution enabled him to fulfill his wish and hers at a price he was willing to pay. Since they were both fur-coat-minded, it is a reasonable inference that he would not have risked disturbing the relationship between them by depriving her of the coat because she was willing to contribute toward its purchase.

2 ²* Los Angeles Times
Part I—WED., AUGUST 11, 1948

WANTS COAT — Janice Earl says fur garment was a gift from soft drink man.

Times photo

GIFT, SHE SAYS

Actress Sues for Return of Mink Coat

Janice Earl, copper-haired screen actress, went to court yesterday in the hope of retrieving a $5000 mink coat she said was given her by A. K. Barbee, wealthy soft drink distributor.

Mrs. Earl, the wife of Richard Earl, film editor, brought her suit in Superior Judge Charles E. Haas' court against a Beverly Hills store which originally sold the coat April 4, 1917.

Deal Arranged

The store admitted that the coat was sold to Barbee for $3981.25 with Mrs. Earl agreeing to pay an additional $916.30. Barbee's account, according to the suit, was charged with his share.

The store contends that two weeks later Mrs. Earl returned the coat to have a monogram embroidered on the garment and that while the coat was again in the store's possession, Barbee served notice that the coat was his property and should not be given back to Mrs. Earl.

In three-cornered litigation, the store asks that Barbee be forced to meet the obligation and that the court determine who is to receive the fur piece.

Deposition Offered

In support of its position, the store offered the deposition of the head of its fur department, Edward J. O'Hanion, who testified that when the sale was made both Barbee and Mrs. Earl were present and that Barbee informed him the coat was a present for her. O'Hanion also recalled that Barbee had attempted to get the price reduced to $4000 and that at one point of the discussion he excused himself and returned a few minutes later with a sales contract written on tissue paper, which O'Hanion refused to accept.

Mrs. Earl is represented by Atty. Thomas D. Mercola. The hearing will be resumed today.

ACTRESS WINS

Barbee Must Pay for That Gift Mink Coat

Actress Janice Earl is ahead one mink coat, worth $5000, by ruling of Superior Judge Thomas J. Cunningham.

A. K. (Al) Barbee, soft drink distributor, "victim of his own generous heart," must pay a Beverly Hills store $3981.25 for the coat he changed his mind about giving Mrs. Earl in April, 1917.

Barbee's attorney, Charles Nichols, pleaded with the court that his client was "innocent as new-driven snow," and a victim of a woman who made "a heroic effort to take advantage of her opportunities."

They Object

He mentioned "chicanery and machinations," but was stopped by Atty. Thomas D. Mercola, counsel for the actress, and by Hershel B. Green, representing the store.

Love crept into the hearing for a short time, but the Judge ruled it out as soon as possible. However, that was not before Mrs. Earl admitted Barbee purchased the wrap for her because he "liked" her and told her he loved her.

It was not before Barbee testified that he had been "quite interested in Mrs. Earl for about three weeks." Nor was it before Nichols said his client was serious about the actress and had "honorable intentions."

Gets Sympathy

The Judge was sympathetic toward Barbee and scored the store for its arrangement of a "side transaction" under which the actress paid $916.30 on her own gift coat. However, he termed the present "irrevocable," and said he could not permit Barbee to turn "Indian giver."

Nichols was granted 10 days' stay of execution on his statement he would seek a new trial, so Mrs. Earl will not get the mink coat just yet.

MUST PAY—A. K. Barbee adjudged loser in court row over payment for mink coat.

Times photo

Los Angeles Examiner ** Thurs., Aug. 12, 1948   Part I—5

Fur Flies as Actress Testifies on Gift Coat

What does an actress say when a friend buys her a mink coat?

"I said 'thanks,'" Janice Earl testified in Superior Court yesterday.

She was telling how she accepted a fur from A. K. Barbee, soft drink manufacturer, a year ago.

The actress told Judge Thomas J. Cunningham that Barbee agreed to buy her coat at the Beverly Hills store.

IT'S YOURS

"He draped it around my shoulders and asked if I liked it. I said 'yes,' and he said, 'it's yours,'" she related.

The coat was not entirely gratis, Miss Earl told the court. She testified Barbee boggled at paying more than $3981. She said that she agreed to make up the difference of $916.

As court opened Barbee's attorney said the manufacturer knew nothing of this arrangement. He amended answers to two suits, accusing the store and Miss Earl of collusion.

The actress is suing for return

of the coat or its value.
or its value.

She charges that the establishment refused to deliver the fur to her after she returned it to be monogrammed.

The store is suing Barbee for the $3981 he supposedly agreed to pay.

The Beverly Hills firm charges that it was on Barbee's order that the coat was denied Miss Earl.

The actress was estranged from her husband, Film Editor Richard Earl, at the time she was given the coat, according to her attorney, Thomas D. Mercola. The couple have since become reconciled.

Los Angeles Herald-Express G *   Friday, August 12, 1948   A-9

Court Orders Barbee to Pay For Blonde Beauty's Fur Coat

A. K. "Al" Barbee, soft drink maker, today had been ordered to pay Saks & Co. $3981.25 due on a $5000 mink coat which he gave Actress Janice Earl as an admitted love token last year.

That was the ruling of Superior Judge Thomas J. Cunningham after the blonde beauty testified that the donor had tried to renege. Mrs. Earl, who was and is still married, told the court Barbee made the gift while she was estranged from her husband, with whom she has since reconciled.

"Because he liked me," she answered when Barbee's attorney asked why she had been given the expensive fur, and added that Barbee had told her he loved her.

She was accused of practicing duplicity and breaking her promise to the wealthy donor by going out with other men. Barbee testified he understood the beauty was "unattached" when he became enamored of her.

Attorney Charles L. Nichols, representing Barbee, told the court his client was "deceived, to his undying chagrin, when he

wanted to be generous and gallant."

Mrs. Earl agreed to pay the store the almost $1000 difference in the cost of the coat over the $3981.25 Barbee assumed, she said.

Indian Giving Void— She Keeps Mink Coat

He took the actress into a Wilshire boulevard shop to buy her a pair of nylons—and by the time they got out, he had bought her a $5000 mink coat!

And by a ruling, yesterday, of Superior Judge Thomas J. Cunningham, married film actress Janice Earl still has the coat.

And Al K. Barbee, vice president of a national soft drink concern, has to pay the shop the $3981 still due on it.

". . . because he is not entitled, in the eyes of this court, to be 'an Indian giver,'" ruled the judge.

3-DAY TRIAL

It was the culmination of the three-day trial of a complicated suit to settle ownership and payment for the coat. The garment had been "held" by the store when the actress sent it in to be monogrammed.

Mrs. Earl herself (who after a

reconciliation is living with her husband at Malibu) testified about the deal.

"He told me he would give me a fur coat," she said.

"Why?" asked a lawyer.

"He liked me," she smiled.

"Did he tell you he loved you?"

"Yes, sir—right out of a clear sky. I think I gave him a polite answer," she said.

Barbee testified, too.

He said he understood Mrs. Earl was unattached when he became enamoured of her. She had told the court she was married, but separated at the time.

"My intentions were honorable and serious," said Barbee. "I wanted to be generous and gallant, but Mrs. Earl turned the coat deal into a commercial transaction."

He explained he meant that she and the store had a side deal, of which he was unaware. By it, he thought she paid an additional amount above the price he said he had "bargained" for.

Barbee told of the visit to the store:

"It was to buy some hose for Mrs. Earl. When we had the stockings, she went into the fur department to see about renovating a coat, she said."

BUYS COAT

It wound up with his purchase of the mink.

A store executive testified Barbee had asked Mrs. Earl be allowed to wear the coat overnight "on approval," but the store refused.

Then, the store man testified, Barbee went into a rest room, came out with a piece of tissue paper inscribed:

"$4000; charge to A. K. Barbee, Vice President . . ."—and named his soft-drink company.

The tissue paper, inscribed in ink, was introduced in evidence.

Then the judge handed down the "Indian giver" ruling, ordered the store to deliver the coat without ado to Mrs. Earl, and gave Barbee ten days to pay the store $3981.

Counsel at the trial made it clear that Barbee sought rescission of the sale because Mrs. Earl failed to live up to his expectations.[1] This failure can in no way be attributed to Saks and Company. Its coat was of sound quality and came up to Mrs. Earl's expectations. The court properly rejected Barbee's offer of proof of his expectations and disappointment. Not only were they no concern of Saks and Company, but no issue was raised in the pleadings regarding his arrangements with Mrs. Earl. I would therefore affirm the judgments.

Harmless fraud?

1. Since everyone agrees the coat was worth $5,000, has Saks & Co. been unjustly enriched? How about Mrs. Earl? Cases in which the defendant's fraud is invoked as the reason *to set aside a transaction* do not depend on a showing of unjust enrichment, and some fraud cases (possibly including *Earl v. Saks*) are thus examples of "restitution without enrichment." (The expression comes from a controversial article by John Dawson, *Restitution Without Enrichment*, 61 B.U. L. Rev. 563 (1981).)

2. Who has the coat at the end of the story? Where does the California Supreme Court leave matters between Mrs. Earl and Saks & Co.?

3. In Gray v. Baker, 485 So. 2d 306 (Miss. 1986), Baker approached Gray about selling a piece of land to Faith Presbyterian Church. Gray eventually sold to the Church at his asking price. Thirty days later, the Church resold half the land to Roussel—a despised neighbor to whom Gray would not have sold under any circumstances. Alleging that the two-step transaction had been made by prearrangement, Gray asked the court to cancel his deed to the Church and the Church's deed to Roussel. What result? (Assume that the Church paid Gray the fair market value of the land.) What will Gray have to show about what the other parties knew, and when they knew it?

4. In Seneca Wire & Mfg. Co. v. A.B. Leach & Co., 247 N.Y. 1, 159 N.E. 700 (1928), Leach offered to sell to Seneca some corporate bonds issued by

---

1. "Mr. Barbee did entertain real affections for this young lady and in bestowing these gifts he was perfectly willing to do so as long as she showed him due feeling, respect, and verity . . . ."

"[W]e were perfectly willing if the understanding between these parties was carried out, we were perfectly willing that she should have the coat . . . ."

"[W]hen Mr. Barbee that very day finds out that the pretenses that this girl has been showing him were not genuine, they were false and just insubstantial as they could be, Mr. Barbee concluded and he did,—the witness says she never was with him again,—that he was off on the wrong tangent and that he wasn't going to give a gift of a coat or anything else to a person that was treating him in that fashion."

"Mr. Barbee had grown very fond of this girl, that he did express affection for her and he told her in effect that if she wanted to reciprocate his affection and would give up running around with other men and give them a chance to see whether or not they might be able to mature their affection, he would be very pleased to give her suitable gifts, a token of his esteem and regard. Now that is all that I meant to say, and I think that is all I did say, and we expect further to attempt to show your Honor that on the very evening of this gift that Mr. Barbee became confronted with the reality that the young lady wasn't telling him the truth about things, she wasn't keeping appointments and on the contrary was misleading him about her plans and intentions and when that realization came upon him he felt that he wanted to interrupt the giving of the gift."

Island Oil. Seneca replied that it would buy the securities only if they were listed on the New York Stock Exchange. Leach assured Seneca that the bonds were going to be listed; Seneca bought them in reliance on those assurances. Shortly after the sale, Island Oil became insolvent, and its bonds lost most of their value. Seneca then discovered that the bonds had not been listed on the New York Stock Exchange and that Leach had no basis for saying they would be. Seneca immediately demanded that Leach take back the bonds and return the original purchase price. (The Exchange would have been happy to list the bonds if Island had paid the fee; Island's insolvency, and the decline in the value of its securities, had nothing to do with the bonds' not being listed.) The court held that Leach's misrepresentation was *material*, meaning that it had induced Seneca's decision to purchase the bonds: this allowed Seneca to rescind its deal with Leach, return the bonds, and get all of its money back. Can this result be justified? If Leach's misrepresentation was merely negligent, not fraudulent, are the consequences of rescission overly harsh? What would Seneca recover if they sued Leach for breach of warranty?

Porreco v. Porreco
571 Pa. 61, 811 A.2d 566 (2002)

Justice NEWMAN.

In this case we must decide whether a misstatement by one party to a prenuptial agreement of the assets of the other party constitutes fraud such that the prenuptial agreement is voidable. We find that there is no justifiable reliance by the party claiming fraud with respect to this representation and, accordingly, we reverse the Superior Court on that issue. We also remand this case to the Superior Court to review the determination by the trial court that a confidential relationship existed between the parties.

Factual and Procedural Background

Appellant Louis Porreco was forty-five years old, and previously married, when he met Appellee Susan Porreco, who was seventeen years old, in high school, living with her parents, and working part-time at a ski shop. The parties dated for over two years, during which time Louis provided Susan with an apartment, an automobile, insurance, a weekly allowance, access to one of his credit cards as a secondary card holder, and a gas charge account at his car dealership's fueling station.

When the parties engaged to be married, Louis presented Susan with an engagement ring. The parties dispute whether Susan knew at the time Louis gave her the ring that it was not a genuine diamond but, instead, a cubic zirconium. The trial court credited Susan's testimony that she believed the engagement ring contained a real diamond and did not discover that it was fake until the parties separated many years later. However, prior to giving her the engagement ring, Louis had given Susan other rings that contained genuine stones.

In July of 1984, Louis presented Susan with the first draft of a prenuptial agreement. Louis did not discuss the agreement with Susan, other than to say that it was a standard agreement with the provisions left blank, and that Susan should seek legal counsel. This first draft of the agreement made no provision for Susan, other than that she was to retain her separate property in the event of a divorce. Louis later presented Susan with a second version of the agreement, which provided that, in the event of divorce, Susan was to receive $3500 for each year of marriage in lieu of alimony, alimony *pendente lite*, and spousal support. Also pursuant to this agreement, Louis would provide Susan with an automobile and health insurance for one year. In all other respects, the agreement provided that the parties would retain their separate property, including all increase in value thereof.

Prior to the execution of the final version of the agreement, Louis prepared, in his own handwriting, a personal financial statement that listed Susan's assets. Included in this list was an entry for the engagement ring, with the value listed at $21,000. Although the financial statement described the ring as an engagement ring, it did not state that the ring contained a diamond, or any other kind of stone. The final version of the agreement contained a typed personal financial statement of Susan's assets, which also stated a value of $21,000 for the engagement ring. Based on this financial statement, the net worth of Susan's assets appeared to be $46,592.00. Louis' personal financial statement—the accuracy of which is not in dispute—listed his net worth at $3,317,666. Susan testified that she understood that, as a consequence of signing the prenuptial agreement, she would only receive, in the event of a divorce, the lump sum payment of $3,500 per year of marriage, an automobile, insurance, and whatever individual assets she possessed. An attorney reviewed the agreement on Susan's behalf, although he conducted no negotiations for her.

When the parties separated more than ten years later, Susan took the ring to a jeweler in South Carolina, who informed her that it was not a diamond. Subsequently in the divorce proceedings, Susan filed a Petition for Special Relief to set aside the prenuptial agreement. Susan alleged three grounds for invalidation of the prenuptial agreement: (1) that Louis fraudulently induced her to enter the prenuptial agreement by misrepresenting the value of the ring; (2) that Louis breached a confidential relationship with her; and (3) that Louis violated his duty, pursuant to our decision in Simeone v. Simeone, 525 Pa. 392, 581 A.2d 162 (1990), of a full and fair disclosure.

The trial court invalidated the prenuptial agreement. The court concluded that a confidential relationship existed between Louis and Susan, due to the difference in the parties' age, sophistication, wealth and status, and Susan's dependence on Louis for her material and social well-being. Louis breached this confidential relationship, according to the trial court, by having a prenuptial agreement drafted that was lopsided in his favor. Additionally, the court found that Louis misrepresented the nature and value of the ring in order to induce Susan to sign the prenuptial agreement, which she signed in reliance on Louis' representation as to the ring's value, and that this misrepresentation was material to her decision to sign the agreement. The court found credible Susan's testimony that if she knew that Louis had given her a fake ring and lied about it, she would not have signed the prenuptial agreement and "would not have married the man." Finally, the court declined to address Susan's claim that Louis violated his duty to provide her with a full and fair disclosure, pursuant to *Simeone*.

The Superior Court affirmed in a 2-1 unpublished decision. The majority determined that Susan had proven, by clear and convincing evidence, that Louis fraudulently induced her to enter the prenuptial agreement by misrepresenting the value of the ring. Because the majority agreed with the trial court that the prenuptial agreement was voidable due to Louis' fraud, they did not address the merits of the determination by the trial court that Louis breached a confidential relationship with Susan. Judge Kelly dissented. In Judge Kelly's view, the remedy of invalidating the entire prenuptial agreement was too harsh. Instead, Judge Kelly would have required Louis to pay Susan $21,000 to compensate her for the value of the ring as stated in the prenuptial agreement, but would otherwise have enforced the agreement.

Discussion

The starting point for assessing the merit of any challenge to the validity of a prenuptial agreement is our decision in *Simeone*. In that opinion, we reevaluated our criteria for enforcing prenuptial agreements and rejected the paternalistic assumption in our caselaw that courts must scrutinize these agreements and refuse to enforce those that failed to make a reasonable provision for the other spouse. As we stated in *Simeone*, "[s]uch decisions rested upon a belief that spouses are of unequal status and that women are not knowledgeable enough to understand the nature of contracts that they enter." 525 Pa. at 399, 581 A.2d at 165. Instead, we placed prenuptial agreements on the same general footing as other contracts, to be enforced pursuant to the well-settled principles of contract law.

In reorienting our standards for enforcing prenuptial agreements to the traditional principles of contract law, however, we did not lose sight of the fact that parties to these agreements do not necessarily deal with each other at arm's length. Accordingly, we reaffirmed "the longstanding principle that a full and fair disclosure of the financial positions of the parties is required. Absent this disclosure, a material misrepresentation in the inducement for entering a prenuptial agreement may be asserted." Thus, despite the prevailing theme in *Simeone* that the provisions of prenuptial agreements should be subject to no greater scrutiny than ordinary business contracts, we nevertheless continued the principle from our previous decisions that these agreements will only be enforced where the parties make a "full and fair" disclosure. In addition to preserving this vestige of our common-law caution towards the enforcement of prenuptial agreements, we affirmed that these agreements may be invalidated when fraudulently procured. "If an agreement provides that full disclosure has been made, a presumption of full disclosure arises. If a spouse attempts to rebut this presumption through an assertion of fraud or misrepresentation then this presumption can be rebutted if it is proven by clear and convincing evidence." *Id.* at 403, 581 A.2d at 167. Thus, in *Simeone*, we recognized two alternate bases for invalidating a prenuptial agreement: (1) any ground for voiding a contract under the common law (such as fraud); and (2) where a party fails to make "full and fair" disclosure of his or her own assets prior to entering the agreement.

Presently, we are not asked to decide the extent of the "full and fair" disclosure rule of *Simeone*; neither the trial court nor the Superior Court relied on this rule to invalidate the prenuptial agreement. Rather, we must consider whether the trial court properly concluded that Louis fraudulently induced Susan to sign the prenuptial agreement by misrepresenting the value of the engagement ring on the list of her individual assets, which he prepared as part of the prenuptial agreement.

The elements of fraudulent misrepresentation are well settled. In order to void a contract due to a fraudulent misrepresentation, the party alleging fraud must prove, by clear and convincing evidence: (1) a representation; (2) which is material to the transaction at hand; (3) made falsely, with knowledge of its falsity or recklessness as to whether it is true or false; (4) with the intent of misleading another into relying on it; (5) justifiable reliance on the misrepresentation; and (6) resulting injury proximately caused by the reliance. Bortz v. Noon, 556 Pa. 489, 499, 729 A.2d 555, 560 (1999); Gibbs v. Ernst, 538 Pa. 193, 207, 647 A.2d 882, 889 (1994). All of these elements must be present to warrant the extreme sanction of voiding the contract.

To be justifiable, reliance upon the representation of another must be reasonable. See Restatement (Second) of Contracts §164, Comment d ("A misrepresentation, even if relied upon, has no legal effect unless the recipient's reliance on it is justified"). While the nature of the relationship between the parties may affect the reasonableness of one's reliance, we hesitate to find reliance justified where the party claiming reliance had an adequate opportunity to verify the allegedly fraudulent statements. In Moore v. Steinman Hardware Co., 319 Pa. 430, 179 A. 565 (1935), a case in which the plaintiff alleged fraud in connection with the sale of corporate stock, we stated, "It has many times been pointed out that a buyer or seller is not entitled to rely on such statements where he has an equal opportunity to ascertain the facts affecting the value of the thing to be sold." Since *Simeone*, we have moved towards treating parties to a prenuptial agreement the same as parties to other contracts, with the attendant duties of investigation and due care for their bargain. We will, accordingly, judge the reasonableness of a party's reliance.

In the present case, although we are bound by the factual conclusions of the trial court, we cannot agree that Susan's alleged reliance on Louis' misrepresentation of the value of the ring on the schedule of her assets was justifiable. Susan had possession of the ring and was not impeded from doing what she ultimately did when the parties separated: obtain an appraisal of the ring. She had sufficient opportunity to inform herself fully of the nature and extent of her own assets, rather than rely on Louis' statements concerning the valuation of her holdings. We find her failure to do this simple investigation to be unreasonable. Although we do not excuse Louis' actions, we will not sanction the avoidance of an entire prenuptial agreement—the consequences of which Susan admittedly understood—on the basis of fraud in these circumstances.

Because the Superior Court never reviewed the determination by the trial court that a confidential relationship existed between Louis and Susan, however, we will reverse and remand for consideration of that issue.

Chief Justice ZAPPALA, concurring.

I join Justice Newman's opinion. I write separately to address my grave concern that the filing of an opinion that expresses itself in rhyme reflects poorly on the Supreme Court of Pennsylvania. . . .

Justice CAPPY, concurring.

I write because I too am genuinely concerned with the point raised by the learned Chief Justice in his concurring opinion. . . .

Justice SAYLOR, dissenting.

As I would not impose a duty to investigate upon Appellee, I respectfully dissent. Preliminarily, in the context of fraud or misrepresentation, the elements necessary to avoid a contract correspond with those required to establish tort liability. See generally Restatement (Second) of Contracts (Topic 1. Misrepresentation, Introductory Note) (1979) (explaining that the rules applicable in the contractual context conform to those provided for in tort, although because "tort law imposes liability in damages for misrepresentation, while contract law does not, the requirements imposed by contract law are in some instances less stringent"). In either context, a recipient's reliance need only be justifiable. See Restatement (Second) of Contracts §164(1); Restatement (Second) of Torts §525. Justifiable reliance represents an intermediate level of dependence, falling between reasonable reliance and mere or bare reliance. See generally Field v. Mans, 516 U.S. 59, 72-75, 116 S.Ct. 437, 444, 446, 133 L.Ed.2d 351 (1995) (collecting cases discussing the required level of reliance for common law fraud). Although whether one's reliance is justified depends upon the facts and circumstances surrounding the representation, as a general rule, there is no duty to investigate. See Restatement (Second) of Contracts §172 (stating that "a recipient's fault in not knowing or discovering the facts before making the contract does not make his reliance unjustified unless it amounts to a failure to act in good faith and in accordance with reasonable standards of fair dealing").

Justice NIGRO joins this dissenting opinion.

Justice EAKIN, dissenting.

> A groom must expect matrimonial pandemonium
> when his spouse finds he's given her a cubic zirconium
> instead of a diamond in her engagement band,
> the one he said was worth twenty-one grand.
>
> Our deceiver would claim that when his bride relied
> on his claim of value, she was not justified
> for she should have appraised it; and surely she could have,
> but the question is whether a bride-to-be *would* have.
>
> The realities of the parties control the equation,
> and here they're not comparable in sophistication;
> the reasonableness of her reliance we just cannot gauge
> with a yardstick of equal experience and age.
>
> This must be remembered when applying the test
> by which the "reasonable fiancée" is assessed.
> She was 19, he was nearly 30 years older;
> was it unreasonable for her to believe what he told her?
>
> Love, not suspicion, is the underlying foundation
> of parties entering the marital relation;
> mistrust is not required, and should not be made a priority.
> Accordingly, I must depart from the reasoning of the majority.

———————————

Cubic zirconium

1. The surprising ground of decision adopted by the *Porreco* majority—that Susan was not justified in relying on Louis' concededly fraudulent misstatement of the value of her engagement ring—is not itself a reliable proposition about the availability of rescission for fraud. According to Restatement Second, Contracts §164, Comment *d* (reading a little further in the passage quoted by the court), those instances in which someone is *not* justified in relying on a misrepresentation typically involve statements of opinion, or matters "as to which the maker's assertion would not be expected to be taken seriously." To the same effect, "an affirmation merely of the value of the goods or a statement purporting to be merely the seller's opinion or commendation of the goods does not create a warranty." UCC §2-313(2).

2. Consider the Porrecos' situation in light of the following, more traditional statement:

> In order for a misrepresentation to support a suit for rescission of a contract, it must have been made with the intent of inducing the other party

to act in the transaction in reliance thereon and must have been relied on, and, unless it was intentionally false, it must have been material in the sense that reliance thereon was reasonable.

If the misrepresentation is an intentional misstatement of fact, it defeats the contract if the other party actually relied upon it. It is not required that such reliance was reasonable. One who intentionally deceives another cannot claim the benefits of the transaction merely because the other did not exercise reasonable care to prevent the success of the strategem.

McClintock, Principles of Equity §81, at 217-18 (2d ed. 1948).

Houston v. Mentelos
318 So. 2d 427 (Fla. Dist. Ct. App. 1975)

HAVERFIELD, Judge.

Plaintiff in the trial court appeals that portion of a final judgment determining defendant Henry Gordon to be a bona fide mortgagee for value, and finding that he held a lien to the amount of $70,253 in the property owned by the plaintiff.

Marie Houston, appellant herein, acquired title to the real property which is the subject matter of this litigation in April 1954, and in March 1972 was the record owner thereof when she was approached by the defendant Thomas E. Mentelos, who represented that he was an agent of Paramount Studios and expressed the desire to lease her property for use in filming a motion picture. Subsequently, plaintiff and Mentelos orally agreed that the premises were to be leased for several months for $42,000.

On or about April 26, 1972 Mentelos presented to the plaintiff documents for her to sign and misrepresented that these documents embodied the terms of the oral lease agreement. Thereupon, plaintiff signed these two documents, one ultimately styled "Sale of Property Agreement" and the other styled "Warranty Deed" which described the subject realty, named plaintiff as grantor and designated defendant Mentelos as a grantee. On May 2, 1972 the deed was recorded in the public records of Dade County, Florida. In addition, defendant caused the document styled "Sale of Property Agreement" to be altered by the addition of language which made the document to read like a contract to convey the subject real property rather than a lease agreement. As of May 30, 1972 Mentelos had paid Marie Houston a total of $8,543.65 which she utilized to satisfy an existing second mortgage on her property and the 1971 real property taxes.

On May 16, 1972 Thomas Mentelos executed and delivered to the defendant Henry Gordon, appellee herein, and his wife a promissory note in the amount of $55,000. To secure said indebtedness Mentelos also executed and delivered to Gordon a mortgage deed on the subject realty. This mortgage was recorded on May 24, 1972. Prior to disbursing the [balance of the] $55,000 to

Mentelos, Henry Gordon paid the following: (1) $16,186.07 to First Federal Savings & Loan Association in satisfaction of plaintiff's mortgage with that institution, (2) $3,151.08 to Evia L. Maxwell in satisfaction of a 1971 judgment rendered against plaintiff Marie Houston, and (3) $1,609.57 in payment of the sanitary sewer liens filed against the subject realty by the City of Miami.

At all times, plaintiff-appellant continued to reside on the subject realty and prior to the execution and delivery of the May 16, 1972 mortgage, defendant-appellee Gordon was informed of plaintiff's occupation of the premises by Mentelos. Nevertheless, Gordon made no inquiry of plaintiff as to her interest therein. Subsequently, in July 1972 Marie Houston discovered the fraud and thereupon filed a complaint against Mentelos, Gordon and others and prayed therein that the trial court rescind the "Sale of Property Agreement," cancel the "Warranty Deed" and the May 1972 mortgage to Henry Gordon, and award both compensatory and punitive damages against the defendants for slander of title. In response thereto, defendant Mentelos answered generally denying the allegations of fraud in plaintiff's complaint and then counterclaimed against plaintiff for slander of title. This counterclaim upon proper motion of plaintiff was dismissed. Defendant Gordon upon proper motion succeeded in having plaintiff's claim for punitive damages against him stricken. He then filed his answer denying that he participated in the fraud and alleging that even if the deed had been procured by fraud, it was voidable rather than void and, therefore, his mortgage was a valid lien on the property. Gordon also filed a cross-claim against defendant Mentelos and claimed therein that if his mortgage was set aside, he was entitled to judgment against Mentelos in the amount thereof. Defendant Gordon then filed a counterclaim against the plaintiff and alleged that he had expended certain sums of money in satisfaction of liens and encumbrances on the property and prayed for an equitable lien therefor against the subject property. Plaintiff filed an answer denying that Gordon had a right to an equitable lien on her property.

In September 1972 Mentelos defaulted under the terms of the promissory note and mortgage delivered to Henry Gordon by failing to make the monthly payments due thereunder, and thereafter defendant Gordon filed an amended cross-claim against Mentelos and an amended counterclaim against Marie Houston seeking to foreclose the mortgage. Defendant Mentelos then filed an amended counterclaim against the plaintiff for impairment to and slander of his title. Plaintiff answered and denied the allegations thereof.

In this posture the case came on for trial without jury. After the conclusion of the trial, the judge entered his final judgment reciting extensive findings of fact and concluding as follows:

Conclusions of Law

1. The document ultimately styled "Sale of Property Agreement," having been fraudulently obtained and having been materially altered after Plaintiff signed it, is voidable at the instance of the Plaintiff.

2. The Plaintiff's signature on the "Warranty Deed" was obtained through the fraud of the Defendant, THOMAS E. MENTELOS, and [the deed] is voidable in equity at the instance of the Plaintiff. Said fraud was perpetrated by the Defendant, THOMAS E. MENTELOS, upon the Plaintiff without the knowledge or participation of the Defendant, HENRY GORDON.

3. The act of the Defendant, THOMAS E. MENTELOS, in causing the "Warranty Deed" to be recorded constitutes the tort of slander of title, and the Defendant, THOMAS E. MENTELOS, is therefore liable to Plaintiff in damages.

4. The Defendant HENRY GORDON is a bona fide mortgagee for value, and as such was an innocent mortgagee, and had the right to rely on record title in making the mortgage loan in question.

Based upon the foregoing, the trial judge ordered and adjudged: (1) that the mortgage deed executed by Thomas Mentelos to Henry Gordon is a valid first mortgage on the subject real property of the plaintiff Marie Houston; (2) that the Warranty Deed executed by the plaintiff to defendant Mentelos be avoided and cancelled, and title to the subject realty be revested in Marie Houston subject to the first mortgage of defendant Henry Gordon; (3) that the "Sale of Property Agreement" be rescinded; (4) that defendant Thomas Mentelos is indebted to the defendant Henry Gordon in the sum of $55,000 plus interest and attorney's fees for a total of $70,253; (5) that defendant Henry Gordon holds a lien for the said above amount superior to any claim or estate of the plaintiff Marie Houston or the defendant Thomas Mentelos on the subject real property; (4) that if the total sum with interest at the rate prescribed by law and all costs of this action accruing subsequent to the judgment were not paid within three days from the date thereof, then the property was to be sold at public sale; (5) that plaintiff recover $110,776.23 as compensatory damages against the defendant Thomas Mentelos and that plaintiff Marie Houston take nothing by this action from defendants Mentelos Electric Company, William Talbot and Henry Gordon.

Plaintiff Marie Houston appeals therefrom.

The issue central to this appeal is whether the warranty deed from Marie Houston to Thomas Mentelos is void as appellant Houston argues or voidable as the trial judge concluded.

Long ago our Supreme Court in Houston v. Adams et al., 85 Fla. 291, 95 So. 859 (1923), in effect held that in the absence of negligence on the part of a grantor, that if by trick or fraud an instrument other than the one which the grantor intended to sign is substituted and signed by the grantor, the instrument is void at law for there is a failure of delivery upon which a deed takes effect. See also Houston v. Forman, 92 Fla. 1, 109 So. 297 (1926); 23 Am.Jur.2d Deeds s 142 (1965) and Annot., 11 A.L.R.3rd 1074 (1967).

In the case before us, the trial judge reached the conclusion, which is supported in the record by competent substantial evidence that plaintiff's signature on the "Warranty Deed" was obtained through the fraud of the defendant Thomas E.

Mentelos who misrepresented that the documents which plaintiff signed embodied the oral lease agreement. Implicit in that conclusion was the finding that there was no negligence or inattention on the part of the plaintiff-appellant. Hence, the deed is void and the fraudulent procurement thereof by Thomas Mentelos, the grantee named therein, did not operate to pass the title to the subject real property and, therefore, defendant-appellant acquired no lien thereon for the amount of the mortgage executed and delivered to him by defendant Mentelos.

Nevertheless, defendant-appellee Gordon having expended $20,936.72 to satisfy liens and/or encumbrances on the subject realty, we hold that appellee Henry Gordon is entitled to an equitable lien for said amount on plaintiff's property.

Those aspects of the judgment pertaining to the defendant Thomas E. Mentelos are affirmed. Accordingly, the judgment herein appealed is affirmed in part, reversed in part and remanded to the trial court with directions to enter an amended judgment consistent with the holdings hereinabove.

Affirmed in part, reversed in part and remanded with directions.

PEARSON, Judge (concurring specially).

I concur in the result reached but I would question the applicability of the "void-voidable" rule to the claim of the mortgagee. The distinction seems artificial. The real question is whether the mortgagee had a right to rely upon the public records showing a deed perfectly valid on its face. I would hold that the mortgagee did have a right to rely on the record title, but that he lost that right when he was put on notice that the former owner was in possession. See Carolina Portland Cement Co. v. Roper, 1914, 68 Fla. 299, 67 So. 115 at 116, where the rule is stated:

> One who acquires title to or a judgment lien on land with constructive notice of the actual possession and occupancy of the land by one other than the vendor or judgment debtor takes subject to such rights as proper inquiry will disclose the occupant of the land actually has therein. Possession, in order to be constructive notice of a claim of title to the land occupied, must be open, visible, and exclusive; and such occupancy may be shown by any use of the land that indicates an intention to appropriate it for the benefit of the possessor. Such use may be any to which the land is adapted, and is calculated to apprise the world that the property is occupied under a claim of right therein.

"Void or voidable" and the bona fide purchaser

1. The distinction between "void and voidable" title, which the concurring judge here calls "artificial," is both well established and highly significant to this part of the law of restitution. Fraud as a basis for rescission and

restitution comes in two strengths: regular and "high test." Regular "fraud in the inducement" involves persuading someone to enter into a transaction by misrepresenting relevant facts—the price of the coat in *Earl v. Saks & Co.* or the value of the ring in *Porreco v. Porreco. Houston v. Mentelos* would be a case of ordinary fraud if Mentelos had merely lied about being an agent for Paramount Pictures. Instead (according to the decision on appeal) it involved the kind of high-test fraud known as "fraud in the factum"—whereby a victim is persuaded to sign a document (typically a deed or a promissory note) in the belief that it is something else entirely. (Cases of fraud in the factum sometimes involve plaintiffs who are blind or illiterate.) The proposition is that a signature obtained under such circumstances—barring negligence by the fraud victim—has no more legal effect than if the signature were forged. It follows that a transfer obtained by "high-test" fraud is altogether ineffective or "void": the transferee (like a thief) acquires nothing and has nothing to convey.

By contrast, a transfer that results from everyday "fraud on the inducement" is *partially* effective. The fraudulent transferee obtains legal title, but that title is naturally subject to the victim's restitution claim—thus making it "voidable"—so long as the victim can find the transferee with the property still in his hands. Still, the transfer is partially effective because of the doctrine of bona fide purchase, which allows the fraudulent transferee to convey a good title—one free of the victim's restitution claim—to a subsequent purchaser who takes for "value" and without notice of the fraud.

To summarize, the distinction between void and voidable title—or between the two species of fraud—is of no significance to the immediate parties. Marie Houston is entitled to rescission and restitution of her property from Thomas Mentelos on either view of the transaction. But as soon as the effective contest is between the fraud victim (Houston) and a subsequent purchaser from Mentelos (Gordon), the distinction will decide the outcome. If the transaction was merely a case of fraud in the inducement, plaintiff recovers her property—but subject to the Gordon mortgage. If there was "fraud in the factum," Mentelos has nothing to convey—so the mortgage to Gordon was a nullity.

2. Notice that the Court of Appeal gives limited relief to Gordon in the form of an equitable lien. What is the theory of the restitution counterclaim (by Gordon against Houston) to which this remedy responds? Could Gordon obtain the same relief on a theory of subrogation? *Cf.* R3RUE §8 (at page 35).

3. The affirmative defense of bona fide purchase will get further attention in Chapter 9, but its essential elements are all visible in this case. The person asserting the defense must show that he acquired an interest in the property by a voluntary transaction, in other words by "purchase." The mortgage to Gordon is a "purchase" for this purpose. The relevant definition is the one given by UCC §1-201(29):

> "Purchase" means taking by sale, lease, discount, negotiation, mortgage, pledge, lien, security interest, issue or reissue, gift, or any other voluntary transaction creating an interest in property.

The purchaser must take the property "for value" (not as a gift) and *without notice* of the facts underlying the restitution claim. (In this context, the "good faith" or *bona fides* that is required to be a "bona fide purchaser" means nothing more or less than the absence of notice.)

The issue of whether or not the purchaser had notice is usually a matter of inference from the circumstances. Here the concurring judge would have held that Mentelos acquired "voidable title," but that Gordon did *not* qualify as a bona fide purchaser—because of the "constructive notice" afforded by Houston's continued possession.

––––––––––––––

Restatement Third, Restitution and Unjust Enrichment

§13. FRAUD AND MISREPRESENTATION

(1) A transfer induced by fraud or material misrepresentation is subject to rescission and restitution. The transferee is liable in restitution as necessary to avoid unjust enrichment.

(2) A transfer induced by fraud is void if the transferor had neither knowledge of, nor reasonable opportunity to learn, the character of the resulting transfer or its essential terms. Otherwise the transferee obtains voidable title.

Illustrations:

5. Father conveys Blackacre to Son, induced by Son's fraudulent misrepresentation of his personal circumstances. Son thereafter borrows money on the security of Blackacre, giving a mortgage to Bank. On discovery of the fraud, Father is entitled to rescind the transfer to Son. The mortgage is not subject to avoidance, however, if Bank establishes that it took the mortgage as a bona fide purchaser (§66). The outcome is that title to Blackacre is revested in Father, subject to the mortgage in favor of Bank.

6. Same facts as Illustration 5, except that Father has no ability to read or write English; Son procures Father's signature on the deed by representing the document to be a will. Discovering the fraud, Father is entitled to rescind the transfer to Son. The mortgage to Bank is likewise invalid, Son's title to Blackacre being void and not merely voidable, although the purported mortgage (if valid) would have made Bank a bona fide purchaser.

––––––––––––––

Farnsworth, *Restitution* 84-85 (2014):

Compare a restitution claim based on fraud to actions of other kinds that may lie on similar facts. Suppose you enter into a contract on the basis of

fraud and therefore receive less than full value for your money; the house
you bought is a disaster. There are options available to you under contract,
tort, and restitution law. If the fraudulent statement that caused you to buy
the house amounted to a warranty—that is, to a guarantee about properties of
the house—then you can sue to enforce that warranty like any other promise
and seek damages to put you in the financial position you would have had
if the contract had been performed. Or you can bring a tort suit and collect
damages to restore you to the financial position you had before the transaction was made. Punitive damages may be a possibility as well. Or—of greatest
interest to us here—you can bring a restitution claim that seeks to rescind the
contract and recover whatever you might have given the other side by way of
performance.

At first that final option might seem less attractive than the first one and
maybe less attractive than the second. Why just seek to unwind the transaction
when you could sue for the gains you expected to receive from it? One answer
is that those gains may be hard to prove, whereas reversing the transaction, and
getting back whatever was passed to the other side, may be simple. Second,
your expectations from the contract may have turned out to be negative. You
were defrauded, but the deal—if honestly made and carried out—would have
lost money for you. So you don't want to be put into the position you would
have had in that case, and you may have no tort damages, either. You would
rather just reverse the transaction and get your money or goods back, or recover
the market value of the goods if the original deal called for something less than
that. A restitution claim founded on fraud thus can allow a plaintiff to escape
the consequences of a losing contract.

An example is furnished by *Farnsworth v. Feller*, 471 P.2d 792 (Or. 1970).
The plaintiffs bought a sand and gravel concern from the defendants. The
sale was based on a fraudulent appraisal that overstated the value of the
business. The plaintiffs successfully rescinded the transaction and got their
money back. The defendants protested that the plaintiffs' "real reasons" for
wanting rescission involved the money the business had been losing since
the plaintiffs acquired it, but the court wasn't interested: "Whatever may be
[the plaintiffs'] ulterior motive in escaping from what had probably proved
an unprofitable venture, it cannot affect their equitable right to rescind on
the ground of the misrepresentation." In a situation of this kind, both sides
may have behaved in less than commendable ways—the defendant by lying
and the plaintiff, perhaps, by showing bad business judgment. Letting the
plaintiff recover might give him a kind of windfall, since he is freed from
the consequences of his bad judgment by the defendant's lie (and there may
have been no causal connection between the lie and the judgment). But
this seems better than the alternative, which is to inadequately deter the
defrauder by letting him use the plaintiff's misjudgment as a way to avoid
responsibility for his wrong. These points are similar to the tort rules that
generally forbid contributory negligence to be used as a defense against a
claim of intentional tort and that say tortfeasors take their victims as they
find them.

There is another strong and common reason—by now familiar—to prefer restitution to a claim sounding in contract or tort. A winning suit for tort or contract damages makes the plaintiff a creditor of the defendant. He is simply owed as much money as the court awards. If the defendant is insolvent, the plaintiff will have to get in line with all of his other creditors and receive something less than full payment. But a restitution claim brought against a defrauder can have different consequences. It always begins with rescission of the parties' agreement, and this equitable step does not make the plaintiff a creditor of the defendant; [instead it can make] the plaintiff the *owner* of whatever was transferred on account of the fraud. So long as he can still find it, or its product, he takes it back directly—whether the "it" consists of goods or money—and ahead of the defrauder's ordinary creditors, through the imposition of a constructive trust or similar remedy.

B. DURESS

Rubinstein v. Rubinstein
20 N.J. 359, 120 A.2d (1956)

HEHER, J.

The gravamen of the complaint is that plaintiff, while "in fear of his safety and under duress" practiced by his defendant wife, by a deed of conveyance in which she joined, conveyed to her wholly-owned corporation, Natalie's Realty Co., Inc., all his right, title and interest in a farm of 126-1/2 acres containing a 14-room dwelling house and several farm buildings, situate on the Freehold-Matawan Road in Marlboro Township, Monmouth County, known as the "Marlboro Manor Farm," of the value of $90,000, and a plot of ground and a factory building on Dowd Avenue in Farmingdale, Monmouth County, of the value of $12,000, both tracts then being held by plaintiff and his wife in a tenancy by the entirety. The intervener-respondent was made a party defendant as the purchaser of 110 acres of the farm property for $23,000 by contract made with Natalie and her corporate codefendant, a price said to be "far below its present market value."

The complaint charges that by the conveyances thus made plaintiff "has divested himself of all his real property and all his assets"; that "when he made the said conveyances and thereafter" Natalie "promised and agreed that she would support" their two infant children, Leon, 5-1/2 years of age, and Norman Thomas, 2-1/2 years old, "out of the incomes" of these properties; that the farm land which Natalie "proposes to sell has been under lease," yielding $2500 annually; and that the farm property, "if properly managed, would produce sufficient revenues to provide for the support, maintenance and education of the infant children," but if 110 acres be sold at the stated price "the property will be so depreciated in value that the interest of the infants will be seriously jeopardized."

The relief sought is a reconveyance of an undivided half interest in the properties or, in the alternative, the transfer to plaintiff of shares of the capital stock of the defendant corporation equal to one-half of the capital stock outstanding or, by an amendment of the prayer made some four months after the filing of the complaint, the imposition of a trust upon the land "in favor of the infant children of the marriage."

[The trial court dismissed the complaint at the close of the plaintiff's case, finding that his testimony "does not spell out what, under the cases, is required to prove duress, a course of action which leaves the person at whom it is directed bereft of free will and his own mind." The Appellate Division concurred in the view of the trial judge that "it did not clearly appear that the threats and other conduct of Mrs. Rubinstein in the surrounding circumstances actually subjugated the mind and will of the plaintiff and constituted the efficient cause of his execution of the deed of conveyance."]

If these conveyances were procured by means of duress, they are inoperative and voidable. Actual violence is not an essential element of duress of the person, even at common law, because consent is the very essence of a contract and, if there be compulsion, there is no actual consent. And moral compulsion, such as that produced by threats to take life or to inflict great bodily harm, as well as that produced by imprisonment, came to be regarded everywhere as sufficient in law to destroy free agency, indispensable to the consent without which there can be no contract. Duress in its more extended sense means that degree of constraint or danger, either actually inflicted or threatened and impending, sufficient in severity or in apprehension to overcome the mind or will of a person of ordinary firmness, according to the earlier rule, but now, by the weight of modern authority, such as in fact works control of the will.

There are two categories under the common law: duress *per minas* and duress of imprisonment. Duress *per minas* at common law "is where the party enters into a contract (1) For fear of loss of life; (2) For fear of loss of limb; (3) For fear of mayhem; (4) For fear of imprisonment"; and some of the later English cases confine the rule within these limits, while the American rule is more liberal and contracts procured by threats of battery to the person, or the destruction of property, were early held to be voidable on the ground of duress, "because in such a case there is nothing but the form of a contract, without the substance." Brown v. Pierce, 7 Wall. 205 (1869). In many cases it was found to be enough that there was moral compulsion "sufficient to overcome the mind and will of a person entirely competent, in all other respects, to contract," for "it is clear that a contract made under such circumstances is as utterly without the voluntary consent of the party menaced as if he were induced to sign it by actual violence." United States v. Huckabee, 16 Wall. 414, (1873).

It would seem to be basic to the legal concept of duress, proceeding as it does from the unreality of the apparent consent, that the controlling factor be the condition at the time of the mind of the person subjected to the coercive measures, rather than the means by which the given state of mind was induced, and thus the test is essentially subjective.

> The test of duress is not so much the means by which the party was compelled to execute the contract as it is the state of mind induced by the means employed—the fear which made it impossible for him to exercise his own free will. The threat must be of such a nature and made under such circumstances as to constitute a reasonable and adequate cause to control the will of the threatened person, and must have that effect; and the act sought to be avoided must be performed by such person while in such condition.

Fountain v. Bigham, 235 Pa. 35, 84 A. 131 (Sup. Ct. 1912).

In the modern view, moral compulsion or psychological pressure may constitute duress if, thereby, the subject of the pressure is overborne and he is deprived of the exercise of his free will. It was said in the early books that there could not be duress by threats unless the threats were such as "to put a brave man in fear"; then came the qualified standard of something sufficient to overcome the will of a person of "ordinary firmness"; but the tendency of the more recent cases, and the rule comporting with reason and principle, is that any "unlawful threats" which do "in fact overcome the will of the person threatened, and induce him to do an act which he would not otherwise have done, and which he was not bound to do, constitute duress. The age, sex, capacity, relation of the parties and all the attendant circumstances must be considered." Williston on Contracts, §1605.

But the pressure must be wrongful, and not all pressure is wrongful. Means in themselves lawful must not be so oppressively used as to constitute, e.g., an abuse of legal remedies. The act or conduct complained of need not be "unlawful" in the technical sense of the term; it suffices if it is "wrongful in the sense that it is so oppressive under given circumstances as to constrain one to do what his free will would refuse." First State Bank v. Federal Reserve Bank, 174 Minn. 535, 219 N.W. 908 (1928).

We come now to the case made by plaintiff which fell before the motion to dismiss. All was serene, apparently, in the domestic relation until the older boy developed a mental condition diagnosed in the Fall of 1952 as "childhood schizophrenia," a disclosure that no doubt had an emotional impact accounting in the main for the later occurrences now the subject of controversy here. In all seeming, it did not make for sympathetic understanding and dedication of the parents as one to the care and protection of the stricken child, but rather led to sharp differences of opinion, e.g., as to the mode of treatment of the child, and eventually to an estrangement attended by the wife's insistent demands for the transfer of the husband's entire interest in the properties at issue, practically the whole of his possessions.

There is no occasion now to set down the plaintiff's evidence in detail. It suffices to say that he gave a circumstantial account of threats of gangster violence, arsenic poisoning, and a course of action designed to overcome his will, he affirms, culminating in his arrest for desertion and nonsupport. The arsenic threat, he said, had a background that filled him with an overpowering sense of foreboding and dread. His wife's father was then serving a life sentence in a Pennsylvania prison for murder committed while he was identified with an "arsenic ring" engaged in killings to defraud life insurers. The threats were first made in December 1952. The demand for the conveyances came in April 1953, and was refused. It was repeated at intervals until the following July, when the arsenic threat was made. He was seized with a great fear for his life and, so conditioned, he agreed the following day to make the conveyance. But he reconsidered and concluded, as a means of his own safety, to leave the farm where they resided. This he did forthwith, going to New York to visit his sister. The following day he went to his parents' home at Farmingdale, about 12-1/2 miles from the farm. He had left his wife with $200 in bank and $300 in checks. Two or three days later, he returned home to see the children. He told his wife to take the income from the farm "apartments and use it for living expenses." She made no demand for money. The same was true of two later visits; but on August 6, when he again called to see the children, he was placed under arrest, and his wife said as he was led away, "Now you can have time to think." He was held for action by the grand jury, and released on bail. When he called again to see the children, three days later, the demand for the conveyances was renewed, and again refused. Defendant then said she would "prosecute to the hilt"; the threats of physical violence were repeated, then and later; and she declared, "I'd be better off if you were dead." She was not in need, plaintiff testified; she had money in bank and had the farm rents to support herself and the children; and he offered to provide a weekly allowance for their support, but this she refused, insisting upon a conveyance of the properties. Shortly before October 5, 1953, after continued threats, she told him that the complaint for desertion and nonsupport was about to be heard by the grand jury "and could not be postponed"; and, in fear for his safety, he said, the threats continuing meanwhile, he finally yielded. A witness, Anna Kamish, testified that defendant told her: "He must give me the property, otherwise I will arrest him again."

The trial judge said of the plaintiff: "I saw a witness who in many ways, in the way he testified, by voice, by his answers to direct questions and so on, who to me is possessed of an insecurity from within," one who "in life hasn't faced up to reality frontally and boldly. He has in life tended to avoid important problems, and marriage was one." These findings suggest psychologic factors bearing on the subjective standard of free will.

The inquiry now is whether, in this posture of the proofs, it was proper to dismiss the complaint without hearing the defense. There was a prima facie showing here of a compulsive yielding to the demand for the conveyances, rather than the volitional act of a free mind, which called for a full disclosure by the defendant wife; and so it was error to entertain the motion to dismiss at the close of the plaintiff's case. The testimony of plaintiff stood unchallenged. Stress is laid upon the advantage of personal observation of the plaintiff witness in the assessment of his testimony; but this is peculiarly a case for explanation by the defendant under the same scrutiny, in particular as to dominance of will. Duress is a species of fraud, although unlike fraud, duress does not necessarily depend on the intent of the person exercising it.

The judgment is reversed; and the cause is remanded for further proceedings in conformity with this opinion.

An elusive category

1. The core cases of duress are hard to miss. If A induces B to pay money (or to make a contract) by wrongful imprisonment of B personally, or by wrongful detention of B's goods, B can recover the money or avoid the contract. Threats of "loss of life or mayhem or loss of limb" are further examples of duress that are likewise centuries old. But the concept of duress became incomparably broader, and correspondingly more difficult to define, when it expanded to include various forms of "wrongful" coercion. The expansion reflected the influence of 19th century purists for whom the validity of a legal act depended on the unqualified autonomy of the actor. As Holmes once expressed it, "the ground upon which a contract is voidable for duress is the same as in the case of fraud; and is, that, whether it springs from a fear or from a belief, the party has been subjected to an improper motive for action." Fairbanks v. Snow, 145 Mass. 153, 154, 13 N.E. 596, 598 (1887).

2. Modern law readily accepts the idea of "economic duress," in which a threat to impose an economic loss can be as wrongful as (if less dire than) a threat of bodily injury. But the expansion of duress beyond the old categories of wrongful detention and threats of violence has made it necessary to explain the difference between the unacceptable methods of bargaining and those forms of pressure—every bit as coercive in their effects—that follow from ordinary freedom of contract. "Take it or leave it" can be as much a source of coercion as a gun to the head, but without more it can hardly be "an improper motive for action." Compare the following observations:

> (a) [Railroad paid Commission a fee to obtain the issuance of a certificate. It challenged the fee as illegal, arguing that it had paid under duress. Commission responded that Railroad had paid the fee "voluntarily."] "On the facts we can have no doubt that the application for a certificate and the acceptance of it were made under duress. The certificate was a commercial necessity for the issue of the bonds. The statutes, if applicable, purported to invalidate the bonds and threatened grave penalties if the certificate was not obtained. The Railroad Company and its officials were not bound to take the risk of these threats being verified. Of course, it was for the interest of the Company to get the certificate. It always is for the interest of a party under duress to choose the lesser of two evils. But the fact that a choice was made according to interest does not exclude duress. It is the characteristic of duress properly so called." Union Pacific R. Co. v. Public Service Comm'n, 248 U.S. 67, 70 (1918) (Holmes, J.).

(b) "'Agreement' does not even today carry any necessary connotation of real willingness. Acquiescence in the lesser evil is all that need be understood. The problem of 'reality of consent' is essentially one of determining what types of pressure or other stimuli are sufficiently out of line with our general presuppositions of dealing to open the expression of agreement to attack." Llewellyn, *What Price Contract?—An Essay in Perspective*, 40 Yale L.J. 704, 728 n.49 (1931).

3. The *Restatement* suggests that the recurrent forms of impermissible coercion tend to fall into four categories. The first three, relatively straightforward, are those in which (i) the defendant's threatened conduct is independently tortious; (ii) a threat is employed to enforce a bad-faith demand; or (iii) a threat induces the overpayment of a subsisting obligation. For examples of each, see R3RUE §14, Illustrations 7-16. A final category of wrongful coercion, probably comprising the most interesting cases, is said to arise when

> the stronger party exploits the other's vulnerability in a manner that passes the bounds of legitimate self-interest. Legitimate self-interest (and lawful coercion) encompasses the usual freedom to deal with another on one's own terms or not at all. So long as the stronger party is not responsible for the other's vulnerability, driving a hard bargain does not constitute duress. But the exploitation of a superior bargaining position will predictably be found wrongful when the stronger party seeks additional leverage by exploiting a vulnerability to which the weaker party (in dealing with the stronger) is not properly subject.

R3RUE §14, Comment g. The *Restatement* proposes the following illustrations, all based on well-known cases:

> 17. The fur department of Department Store is operated by Lessee. Lessee receives customers' furs for storage; this service is provided by Warehouse under contract with Lessee. Lessee becomes insolvent. Winter approaches, and Store's customers demand the return of their furs. Warehouse refuses to deliver the furs unless Store pays $5000 in current storage charges (for which Warehouse has a valid lien on the furs), plus $10,000 in debts of Lessee to Warehouse from previous transactions (for which Warehouse has no lien and Store is not responsible). The parties negotiate unsuccessfully as the weather grows colder. Finally Store pays Warehouse $15,000 to obtain the release of the furs; Store then sues Warehouse in restitution to recover the payment.

> 19. Landlord declines to renew a lease of commercial property in which Tenant has made substantial investment, but expresses a willingness to lease to a buyer of the business acceptable to Landlord. Tenant locates Buyer, whom Landlord pronounces acceptable. On the eve of the scheduled closing, Landlord informs Tenant that he will decline to lease to Buyer unless Tenant pays Landlord half the price received from Buyer

for Tenant's business. In order to consummate the sale to Buyer, Tenant submits to Landlord's demand. Tenant then sues Landlord in restitution.

21. Corporation threatens to dismiss Employee, employed under a contract at will, unless Employee accepts Corporation's tender offer for the shares of its stock owned by Employee. Employee transfers the shares and continues in the employ of Corporation until his death shortly thereafter. Employee's personal representative sues Corporation to rescind the transfer.

R3RUE §14, Comment g, Illustrations 17, 19, and 21. Should the claimants in these cases be permitted to accede to a demand that they intend to repudiate?

4. In Wilbur v. Blanchard, 22 Idaho 517, 126 P. 1069 (1912), Wilbur had stolen $150 from Blanchard. By threats of criminal prosecution, Blanchard persuaded Wilbur to pay him $2,150. Wilbur sued Blanchard for restitution on the basis of duress. How should the case be decided? Let's make the facts even simpler. Wilbur had stolen $150 from Blanchard; Blanchard compels Wilbur to repay $150 at gunpoint. Now what?

5. In Murphy v. Brilliant Co., 323 Mass. 526, 83 N.E.2d 166 (1948), defendant boatyard agreed to put owner's boat "into shape" for "a low of $5,000 and a top of $6,000." Boatyard's invoices for progress payments quickly exceeded the high estimate. When Owner protested that "the thing was running completely out of line," Boatyard informed him: "There isn't anything we can do about it. You'll have to pay for it. Your boat is here, and you can't take it out until these things are paid, and if you don't make this payment, work will stop. No other yard would take the boat as long as we have got a claim against it." Owner eventually paid some $14,000 in response to these demands, recovered his boat, then brought an action in restitution to recover the overcharge. What result? Does it matter that Owner had various alternatives to recover his property (by legal process) without paying more than he owed?

"Voluntary payment" and duress by civil litigation

1. In Shockley v. Wickliffe, 150 S.C. 476, 148 S.E. 476 (1929), Wickliffe demanded payment of $400 on two promissory notes given by Shockley to Wickliffe's deceased father, threatening a lawsuit if payment was not forthcoming. Shockley had already paid the debt to the father, but he was unable to prove it. "Realizing he had no defense," Shockley paid Wickliffe another $400, "making said payment under protest, and knowing full well at the time that he had already paid the same." Six years later, Shockley found the receipt for the first $400 and sued Wickliffe in restitution to recover the second $400. Was this a case of payment made by mistake? Under duress? No, because payment was held to be "voluntary." According to the court:

the threat of a lawsuit does not constitute coercion or oppression. It is the business of the courts to settle disputes between litigants, and to hold that a threat of bringing suit for collection of a note is oppression would be to defeat the very purposes for which the courts were established.

150 S.C. at 480, 148 S.E. at 477.

2. Consider the following observations about "voluntary payment" in this context:

> (a) "[P]ayment would be an idle ceremony if the only effect thereof were to reverse the position of the parties as plaintiff and defendant." Keener, Law of Quasi-Contracts 411 (1893).

> (b) "The reason of the rule, and its propriety, are quite obvious, when applied to a case of payment upon a mere demand of money, unaccompanied with any power or authority to enforce such demand except by a suit at law. In such case, if the party would resist an unjust demand, he must do so at the threshold. The parties treat with each other on equal terms, and if litigation is intended by the party of whom the money is demanded, it should precede payment. If it were not so, the effect would be to leave the party, who pays the money, the privilege of selecting his own time and convenience for litigation; delaying it, as the case may be, until the evidence, which the other party would have relied upon to sustain his claim, may be lost by the lapse of time and the various casualties to which human affairs are exposed." Boston & Sandwich Glass Co. v. City of Boston, 41 Mass. 181, 188 (1842).

3. The fact that payment in a case like *Shockley v. Wickliffe* could ever be called "voluntary" reflects a highly significant proviso to the idea of duress — namely, that neither the threat of civil litigation (nor its actual commencement) constitutes wrongful coercion, so long as legal process is threatened or employed to support a good-faith demand:

> A threat of litigation is ordinarily employed to compel the discharge of what is asserted to be a subsisting obligation. Comparison to other forms of lawful coercion might suggest that the threat of litigation should be impermissible to the extent that it induces an overpayment, or a transfer not due the recipient, as measured by the real underlying obligation. Two important considerations preclude any unqualified rule in such terms. The first is the fact that a payment in response to threatened litigation will often be made pursuant to an enforceable accord, even if the payment exceeds the amount of the original underlying obligation [referring to cases such as *Sears v. Grand Lodge* in Chapter 2]. The second is a policy against disturbing the procedural balance between the parties, traditionally expressed by the statement that a person on whom a demand is made in good faith must meet it "at the threshold." This means that the

(alleged) debtor may not switch places with the (alleged) creditor by the simple expedient of acceding to the demand, then trying the same case in reverse—as plaintiff in a restitution action, rather than as defendant on the original claim. If the rule were otherwise, the original claimant would be denied the choice of time and place for suit. Moreover, the policy of the statute of limitations would be undermined if the period of limitations might be started anew by a payment that recast the underlying dispute as a claim for restitution.

R3RUE §14, Comment *h*.

Texas Association of Counties v. Matagorda County
52 S.W.3d 128 (Tex. 2000)

Justice O'NEILL delivered the opinion of the Court.

In this case, we decide whether the Texas Association of Counties County Government Risk Management Pool (TAC) may obtain reimbursement from its insured, Matagorda County, for an amount that TAC paid to settle a claim that was later determined to be excluded from coverage. The trial court ruled that TAC was entitled to reimbursement, but the court of appeals reversed. 975 S.W.2d 782. Because TAC established neither an implied-in-fact nor an implied-in-law right to reimbursement, we affirm the court of appeals judgment.

I

Since the late 1980s, TAC has provided law-enforcement-liability insurance to Matagorda County. Because Matagorda County's jail fell out of compliance with the minimum requirements of the Texas Commission on Jail Standards, in 1991 TAC began including an endorsement to its policy excluding coverage for any claim "arising out of jail."

In 1993, inmates armed with razor blades physically and sexually assaulted three other prisoners ("the *Coseboon* plaintiffs"). The *Coseboon* plaintiffs sued Matagorda County and its sheriff, Keith Kilgore (collectively "the County"), both of whom demanded that TAC defend and indemnify them under the law-enforcement-liability insurance policy. TAC initially denied coverage because of the jail exclusion. But after negotiations with the County, TAC agreed to pay the defense costs of the counsel that the County had retained to represent it in the *Coseboon* suit, subject to a reservation of rights to continue to deny coverage. Also, TAC filed this suit seeking a declaratory judgment that the claims were not covered. The County asserted that the claims were covered, and filed several counterclaims against TAC.

In 1995, the *Coseboon* plaintiffs offered to settle their lawsuit for $300,000. This demand was within the policy limits. The County's lawyer advised TAC that the proposed settlement was reasonable and prudent, given the facts and circumstances of the case. The Matagorda county judge, the chief administrative officer for the County, was advised of the proposed settlement and the County was asked to fund the settlement. The County, however, continued to insist that the claim was covered, and advised TAC that it would not contribute to the settlement.

TAC then issued a second reservation-of-rights letter to the County, this time reserving its rights to continue to deny coverage and to seek reimbursement of the settlement funds from the County if the declaratory-judgment action established that the *Coseboon* suit was not covered. The letter stated:

> 1. we have advised you of ongoing settlement discussions with Coseboon's counsel;
>
> 2. you have chosen not to contribute to the funding of the settlement;
>
> 3. Jim Ludlum, your counsel, agrees with [TAC] that a $300,000 settlement of the *Coseboon* matter is not only *not* unreasonable, but prudent given the facts and circumstances;
>
> 4. [TAC is not] waiving any of its rights to pursue full recovery of this settlement amount from the County . . . in the declaratory judgment action;
>
> 5. the funding of this settlement by [TAC and its reinsurers] is based solely upon the recognition of the exposure inherent in the *Coseboon* litigation and their desire to avoid having this opportunity to settle fall through, possibly resulting in a jury verdict far in excess of the $300,000 settlement;
>
> 6. this funding should not be construed by anyone as a voluntary payment and is specifically made without prejudice to the rights of [TAC] to recover up to the entire amount as determined in [the declaratory-judgment action].

The letter concluded: If you have any question that the intent of [TAC] is anything other than funding settlement of the *Coseboon* matter and proceeding with the declaratory judgment action to recover the full amount of the funding, please advise me immediately.

The County did not respond to the letter.

The insurance agreement between the County and TAC allowed TAC to settle any claim at its own discretion, and without the County's consent. TAC settled the *Coseboon* litigation for $300,000, and the *Coseboon* plaintiffs dismissed their lawsuit. The settlement agreement released the County and its employees from any and all claims, and released any claims against TAC. The County did not object to the settlement. After the settlement, TAC amended its declaratory-judgment action to request reimbursement of the settlement funds. The County stipulated that it "does not dispute the reasonableness of TAC's settlement of the *Coseboon* litigation."

The case proceeded to trial on the coverage dispute. The trial court ruled that the jail exclusion was not ambiguous, and a jury resolved the remaining issues in TAC's favor. The trial court rendered a declaratory judgment for TAC and awarded recovery of its $300,000 settlement payment, together with interest, attorneys' fees, and costs. The court of appeals concluded that no equitable remedy allowed TAC to recover the settlement funds, and that there was no indication that the County agreed either to be bound by the settlement or to reimburse TAC. 975 S.W.2d 782. Accordingly, the court of appeals reversed and rendered judgment that TAC take nothing.

II

It is undisputed that the insurance policy that defines the parties' rights and obligations does not provide TAC a right of reimbursement; TAC first asserted such a right in its reservation-of-rights letter. It is similarly undisputed that the County did not otherwise expressly agree to reimburse TAC for the *Coseboon* settlement. We must decide whether the County's consent to reimburse TAC may be implied from this record, or whether the circumstances presented warrant imposing, in law, an equitable reimbursement obligation. We consider first the implied-consent issue.

A. IMPLIED CONSENT TO REIMBURSE

TAC contends that the County's silence in response to its reservation-of-rights letter, together with the County's stipulation acknowledging no dispute as to the settlement's reasonableness, establishes an implied-in-fact contractual obligation for the County to provide reimbursement. For a number of reasons, we disagree.

First, a unilateral reservation-of-rights letter cannot create rights not contained in the insurance policy. See Shoshone First Bank v. Pac. Employers Ins. Co., 2 P.3d 510, 515-16 (Wyo. 2000) (rejecting the notion that the insurer could base a right to recover defense costs on a reservation letter and stating "we will not permit the contract to be amended or altered by a reservation of rights letter"). The insurance policy at issue allows TAC to settle a case against its insured without the insured's consent. It would have been a simple matter for TAC to also state in the policy that it could seek reimbursement for those settlement funds if it is later determined that the policy does not provide coverage.[2] If TAC had done so, its reservation letter would in fact be reserving contractual rights. But TAC's "reservation" letter was simply a unilateral offer to append a reimbursement provision to the insurance contract. That

---

2. TAC does not contend that it could not have included a reimbursement clause in its policy.

provision is binding only if the County accepted it. [Further discussion of this point omitted.]

B. EQUITABLE RIGHTS TO REIMBURSEMENT

TAC argues that we should apply the doctrine of equitable subrogation to support its reimbursement claim. Typically, an insurer paying a claim under a policy is equitably subrogated to any claim the insured may have against a third party responsible for the insured's injury. . . .

As the court of appeals recognized, allowing an insurer to unilaterally settle claims and then step into the shoes of the claimant could potentially foster conflict and distrust in the relationship between an insurer and its insured. Allowing subrogation of an insurer against its insured has been widely rejected in this context. Accordingly, we hold that TAC is not entitled to reimbursement on an equitable subrogation theory.

Finally, TAC argues that it is entitled to recover under the intertwined quasi-contractual theories of quantum meruit and unjust enrichment. We agree with the court of appeals that these equitable theories do not apply in the circumstances presented. Otherwise, the insured is forced to choose between rejecting a settlement within policy limits or accepting a possible financial obligation to pay an amount that may be beyond its means, at a time when the insured is most vulnerable. Rather than place the insured in this position, we hold that, when coverage is disputed and the insurer is presented with a reasonable settlement demand within policy limits, the insurer may fund the settlement and seek reimbursement only if it obtains the insured's clear and unequivocal consent to the settlement and the insurer's right to seek reimbursement.

III

TAC contends that denying a reimbursement right places insurers faced with a reasonable settlement offer within policy limits in an untenable position. We recognize that, however the issue is resolved, either insurers or insureds will face a difficult choice when coverage is questioned. But an insurer in such a situation that cannot obtain the insured's consent may, among other options, seek prompt resolution of the coverage dispute in a declaratory judgment action, a step we have encouraged insurers in TAC's position to take. TAC's position [would reduce] reducing insurers' incentive to seek early resolution of coverage disputes.[3]

Requiring the insurer, rather than the insured, to choose a course of action is appropriate because the insurer is in the business of analyzing and allocating

3. We note that in this case, almost two years elapsed between the time TAC filed its declaratory-judgment action and the date it settled the Coseboon suit. The record reflects no effort by TAC during that time to resolve the coverage dispute.

risk and is in the best position to assess the viability of its coverage dispute. See *Shoshone*, 2 P.3d at 516 (stating "[t]he question as to whether there is a duty to defend an insured is a difficult one, but because that is the business of an insurance carrier, it is the insurance carrier's duty to make that decision"); *Gonzalez v. Mission Am. Ins. Co.*, 795 S.W.2d 734, 737 (Tex. 1990)(observing that, if a policy provision is vague or ambiguous, the fault lies with the insurer as the policy's drafter). On balance, insurers are better positioned to handle this risk, either by drafting policies to specifically provide for reimbursement or by accounting for the possibility that they may occasionally pay uncovered claims in their rate structure.

We hold that the County's consent to reimburse TAC's settlement costs cannot be implied from this record, and no equitable remedy will support a right of reimbursement under the circumstances presented. Accordingly, we affirm the court of appeals' judgment.

Justice OWEN, joined by Justice HECHT, dissenting.

Matagorda County has been unjustly enriched in this case. It acknowledges that the amount that the Texas Association of Counties paid to settle serious claims against it was reasonable. And Matagorda County must now concede that those claims were not covered by its agreement with the Association. The County should be required to bear responsibility for its own liabilities. Because the Court does not require it to do so, I dissent.

I would hold that when an insurer reserves its right to contest coverage and there has been a settlement demand within policy limits that the insured agrees is reasonable, the insurer may settle the claim and recover settlement costs based on an obligation that is implied in law. In order to prevent unjust enrichment, obligations are implied in law even when there is no agreement, either express or implied.

An obligation of reimbursement should be imposed when an insured pays an amount that the insured agrees is reasonable to settle a claim that is not covered. This rule of law would preserve the respective rights and obligations of parties to an insurance contract. An insured would be responsible for liabilities it incurs that are not covered by the policy of insurance. In this case, there is no principled basis for requiring the Association rather than Matagorda County to bear the cost of settling the *Coseboon* litigation. There is no dispute that the amount the Association paid to settle the matter was reasonable. Matagorda County is receiving a benefit for which it did not bargain—payment of a claim that was not covered under its agreement with the Association. Matagorda County has been unjustly enriched because it paid nothing to settle a serious claim against it. The Association has paid an obligation that was Matagorda County's alone.

The Court says that an insured should not be required "to choose between rejecting a settlement within policy limits or accepting a possible financial obligation to pay an amount that may be beyond its means, at a time when the insured is most vulnerable." Certainly, an insured who has no coverage for claims brought against it may be in a "vulnerable" position. But that is not due to anything that the insurance carrier has done. It is a consequence of the insured's choice not to obtain full coverage. The Court's statement is also irrational. A reasonable settlement offer is one that the insured, acting as a person of ordinary care and prudence, would accept. In situations like the one before us, when there was a coverage dispute, an insured's knowledge that it ultimately may have to fund a settlement offer will cause the insured to make a fair evaluation of whether the settlement offer is in fact a reasonable one. But regardless of the size of a claim that is not covered, the financial obligation to pay that claim remains with the insured. An insured's lack of financial resources does not change that fact.

_____

"Voluntary payment" and reservation of rights

1. In Still v. Equitable Life Assurance Soc'y of N.Y., 165 Tenn. 224, 54 S.W.2d 947 (1932), Still's insurance policy provided for monthly payments and a waiver of premiums in the event of "total and permanent disability," effective upon receipt of "due proof" by Equitable. Still submitted proof of disability which Equitable rejected. An extended controversy ensued, during which Still paid two more annual premiums "to prevent the defendant from declaring a forfeiture of said policy." Still eventually sued Equitable (i) to enforce the contract for the monthly payments, and (ii) for restitution of the annual premiums paid under duress. The claim for disability payments was settled by the parties—leading the court to infer that Still really *was* disabled. Nevertheless, Equitable went to trial on the restitution claim, arguing that "complainant paid said premiums voluntarily and with full knowledge of the facts."

A conclusion that payment was "voluntary" is normally fatal to a restitution claim. Frequently, as in this case, an argument about duress is the claimant's way of saying, "I did not make this payment voluntarily." But the underlying problem is not really the claimant's mental state. Payment followed by restitution may be a more reasonable resolution, and one that is less expensive overall, than adamant refusal followed by risky litigation. The opinion in *Still v. Equitable* anticipates the kind of payment "under protest" that was attempted in *Texas Association of Counties*:

> We think the case presented is one in which the parties were each acting in good faith, complainant claiming that his disability was total and permanent, and defendant asserting the contrary. Under these circumstances, defendant declined to waive the two premiums and complainant paid them.
>
> The complainant was confronted with the alternative of paying the premiums when due, or by not doing so, assuming the risk of losing his right to continue his insurance in force until its maturity at his death, if he should be unsuccessful in proving his disability to be both total and

permanent. That this was a real hazard, with the outcome uncertain, is inherently obvious in the nature of the issue in controversy. The defendant, after months of investigation, had declined to recognize liability, first in January 1931, and again in January 1932, and the question of the totality and permanency of the disability was one to be determined upon probabilities, not capable of ascertainment with exact certainty. This uncertainty, created by defendant's refusal to concede the disability and waive the premiums, was the compulsion which prompted and impelled the complainant to pay the two premiums, rather than risk his right to continue the insurance on the waiver contracted for.

We are strongly inclined to the view that, under the facts and circumstances of this case as herein set out, a person of ordinary business sense and prudence would have weighed the consequences with the same result as did the complainant. The compulsion under which the payments were made is apparent to any one who appreciates the value of a life insurance contract. The complainant was so situated that, if he failed to establish the permanency of his disability, he could not hope to obtain other insurance. Decision could not be postponed and time was of the essence of the matter. The payments were necessary to preserve valuable rights, and, under the authorities cited, we hold they were not voluntary. This holding is, we think, in accord with the rules of law and equity.

2. Why would the insurer in *Texas Association of Counties* ever pay to settle a claim that the "unambiguous" terms of its policy excluded from coverage? The coercion implicit in a coverage dispute of this kind is an artifact of insurance law, combined with certain facts of life in civil litigation:

(a) An insurer that declines to settle a claim for which there is later determined to be coverage under the policy will be liable to indemnify its insured against any resulting judgment, *without regard to policy limits*. Exposure of this kind is generally called "bad faith" liability, after the kinds of cases in which the doctrine originated. If the insurer's obligation is reasonably clear, but foot-dragging (and consequent refusal to settle within policy limits) leaves its policyholder facing an uninsured judgment, an understandable judicial reaction holds the insurer liable for the consequences. In modern insurance law, however, an insurer could not avoid "bad faith" liability by proving that it was acting reasonably (in good faith) in refusing to settle. Liability for refusal to settle within policy limits has thus become strict—always assuming that the claim is ultimately determined to be within the scope of the coverage. In short, if the holder of a $300,000 liability policy faces viable claims for damages in the millions—claims which the plaintiff's attorney will eventually offer to settle for $300,000—the insurer's dilemma is clear. Even an insurer that is very confident of its legal position cannot entirely exclude "judicial risk"—here, the chance that the policy will be misconstrued.

(b) An insurer that tries diligently to obtain a judicial resolution of its coverage dispute—normally by a suit for declaratory judgment—will not necessarily have an answer by the time its policyholder must respond to the settlement demand. The majority in *Texas Association of Counties* notes that "almost two years elapsed between the time TAC filed its declaratory-judgment action and the date it settled the *Coseboon* suit," and moreover that "the record reflects no effort by TAC during that time to resolve the coverage dispute." What are we supposed to make of that?

3. Whether to allow restitution in a case like *Texas Association of Counties* is a much disputed, somewhat politicized question of insurance law. Yet even the courts that deny restitution based on an insurer's "unilateral reservation of rights" agree that there would be no objection if the terms of the policy provided for reimbursement to the insurer of the cost of defending or settling non-covered claims. Of course, if the question of reimbursement is addressed by the policy, the policyholder's liability to reimburse becomes a matter of contract rather than unjust enrichment. Why might courts prefer to enforce a contractual rather than an enrichment-based liability in these cases? Why might insurers neglect to include such a provision in their policy language? The same questions arise in the area of insurance subrogation, as will be seen in Chapter 5.

4. What is called "unilateral reservation of rights" in the context of insurance is merely one example of "payment under protest"—an announcement by the person making a payment that he disputes the asserted liability and will try to get the money back. The significance of such "protest" to the availability of a restitution claim depends very much on the setting of the dispute.

(a) There are circumstances in which the possibility of a payment "under protest" or "with reservation of rights" is explicitly favored as a practical way to minimize the eventual costs of the parties' dispute. Thus the Uniform Commercial Code states as a general proposition:

> A party that with explicit reservation of rights performs or prom-
> ises performance or assents to performance in a manner demanded
> or offered by the other party does not thereby prejudice the rights
> reserved. Such words as "without prejudice," "under protest," or the
> like are sufficient.

UCC §1-308(a). The rule makes the most sense in a case where insisting on an immediate test of the parties' legal positions would cause disruption and expense that might be avoided if a resolution could be postponed.

(b) Conversely, there are settings in which an attempted "protest" will predictably be ignored. So long as the only pressure being brought to bear is the threat of civil litigation, a debtor who is asked to pay more than he owes must normally resist the creditor's demand "at the threshold," as a defendant in a contract case, rather than submit to the claim and seek restitution afterwards, as a plaintiff in a restitution case. This is the idea behind the rule of "voluntary payment" in its true application.

(c) Payment is not voluntary when it is made under duress. Still paid his insurance premiums under threat of cancellation, and TAC paid the County's claim under threat of "bad faith" liability exceeding the amount in dispute. In cases of this kind, part of the function of "protest" is to serve as contemporaneous evidence of the compulsion to which the paying party will assert he was subject—thereby refuting the contention that payment was "voluntary."

(d) Finally, there are settings in which the function of "protest" is supposedly to protect the payee against a prejudicial change of position. Statutes authorizing refunds of taxes improperly collected often require that the payment have been made "under protest"; courts that enforce a protest requirement in this context tend to reason that the taxing authority needs to know in advance how much of its revenues it is free to spend. But where a taxpayer (or any other claimant) is justifiably unaware of the grounds for restitution until after a payment has been made, a requirement of contemporaneous protest would have the perverse effect of precluding restitution altogether.

Restatement Third, Restitution and Unjust Enrichment

§35. PERFORMANCE OF DISPUTED OBLIGATION

(1) If one party to a contract demands from the other a performance that is not in fact due by the terms of their agreement, under circumstances making it reasonable to accede to the demand rather than to insist on an immediate test of the disputed obligation, the party on whom the demand is made may render such performance under protest or with reservation of rights, preserving a claim in restitution to recover the value of the benefit conferred in excess of the recipient's contractual entitlement.

(2) The claim described in subsection (1) is available only to a party acting in good faith and in the reasonable protection of its own interests. It is not available where there has been an accord and satisfaction, or where a performance with reservation of rights is inadequate to discharge the claimant's obligation to the recipient.

a. General principles. Where a valid contract defines the scope of the parties' respective performance obligations, a performance in excess of contractual requirements—neither gratuitous, nor pursuant to compromise—results in the unjustified enrichment of the recipient and a prima facie claim in restitution. "Restitution in such a case does not require that the contract be set aside; instead, it is a means of enforcing adherence to the contract, through ordering repayment of a sum to which the recipient was not entitled under the contract." 3 Palmer, Law of Restitution §14.1 (1978).

Performance in [the cases within this section] is not the result of mistake, because the claimant has consciously and justifiably resisted a demand for a performance that was not in fact due. Nor is performance necessarily induced by duress, as commonly defined, because the recipient—in demanding a performance believed to be due under the contract—may have exerted no pressure that can be characterized as wrongful. Faced with the impossibility, in many circumstances, of obtaining a determination of the parties' rights and obligations before the claimed performance is due, and failing a compromise, a contracting party may be compelled by circumstances to render a performance to which the other is not entitled. Compulsion frequently lies in the fact that the alternative course of action—rejecting the other party's demand before the requirements of the contract can be judicially determined—would expose the claimant to a risk of loss or liability whose expected value exceeds the amount in controversy.

Disputes over contractual requirements commonly arise in the midst of the undertaking, rather than at its outset or conclusion. The cost of interruption is then at its highest; the risk of consequential harms (which must ultimately be borne by one party or the other) leverages the stakes beyond the amount initially in dispute. If the party on whom a questionable demand is made can protect its position only by refusing performance, the costs of resolution are magnified accordingly. Performance with reservation of rights can reduce these costs by deferring dispute resolution to a point at which the risk of consequential harm is lower.

C.   UNDUE INFLUENCE

Eldridge v. May
129 Me. 112, 150 A. 378 (1930)

STURGIS, J.

Action by the plaintiff as administratrix of the estate of her husband, Amos L. Eldridge, late of Ossipee, N. H., to recover moneys in the possession of his sister, the defendant, claimed to have been paid her by the deceased under an agreement for his support and maintenance. At the trial below, the case turned on the validity of this contract. The moneys in question admittedly came into the defendant's possession. Her rights under this contract are her only defense to this suit. The contract reads:

> This memorandum of an agreement made and entered into this sixth day of November, A. D. 1928, by and between Amos L. Eldridge, formerly of Ossipee in the State of New Hampshire, now of Island Falls in the County of Aroostook in the State of Maine, and Annie B. May of said Island Falls, *Witnesseth:*

That whereas the said Eldridge has this day assigned, transferred, granted, set-over, and delivered to the said May all of his personal estate and chattels of any and every name and nature, whatsoever, in the State of Maine, including all deposits of money in any banking institution in said States of Maine and New Hampshire belonging to said Eldridge, to have and to hold to her, the said Annie B. May, her heirs, executors, administrators, and assigns, forever.

Now, therefore, the said Annie B. May, for and in consideration of the aforesaid grant to her by the said Eldridge, does hereby agree with the said Eldridge, that she and her heirs, executors, administrators, and assigns, will well and truly support and maintain him, the said Eldridge, in some suitable and proper place to be designated by her, for and during the term of his natural life, and him provide with food, drink, lodging, and clothing, suited to his degree and station in life, also with proper medicine, medical attendance, and nursing whenever required; and that she will treat him at all times with courtesy, kindness, and consideration, and at his death cause him to be decently interred in the cemetery at said Ossipee where his father and mother are buried.

This action for money had and received is equitable in spirit and purpose. It lies for money obtained through fraud, duress, extortion, imposition, or any other taking of undue advantage of the situation of the plaintiff's intestate. If the defendant is proved to have in her possession money which in equity and good conscience she ought to refund, the law will conclusively presume that she has promised to do so. As a general rule, any set of facts which would, in a court of equity, entitle the plaintiff to a decree for the money here in question, if that were the specific relief sought, will entitle her to recover it in an action for money had and received. This action is governed by equitable principles.

Fraud in equity includes all willful or intentional acts, omissions, and concealments which involve a breach of either legal or equitable duty, a trust or confidence, and are injurious to another, or by which an undue or unconscientious advantage is taken over another. 2 Pomeroy's Eq. Jur. (3d ed.) §873; 1 Story's Eq. Jur. §187.

Undue influence is a species of constructive fraud, and the doctrine of equity concerning it is very broad. Whenever two persons have come into such a relation that confidence is necessarily reposed by one, and the influence which naturally grows out of that confidence is possessed by the other, and this confidence is abused, or the influence is exerted to obtain an advantage at the expense of the confiding party, the person so availing himself of his position will not be permitted to retain the advantage, although the transaction could not have been impeached, if no such confidential relation had existed. The principle extends to every possible case in which a fiduciary relation exists as a fact, in which there is confidence reposed on one side and a resulting superiority or influence on the other.

The term "fiduciary or confidential relation," as used in the law relative to undue influence, is a very broad one. It embraces both technical fiduciary relations and those informal relations which exist whenever one man trusts in and relies upon another. The relations and duties involved in it need not be legal, but may be moral, social, domestic, or merely personal.

And the rule seems to be that, whenever a fiduciary or confidential relation exists between the parties to a deed, gift, contract, or the like, the law implies a condition of superiority held by one of the parties over the other, so that in every transaction between them, by which the superior party obtains a possible benefit, equity raises a presumption of undue influence, and casts upon that party the burden of proof to show affirmatively his compliance with equitable requisites and of entire fairness on his part and freedom of the other from undue influence.

This rule has been often applied to transactions between brothers and sisters, brothers and brothers, and sisters and sisters. Their relations may be of such reciprocal confidence as to cast upon either the burden of proof to show the exact fairness of a transaction between them by which either is benefited. In such cases where this burden has not been sustained, equity has set the transaction aside.

Even a summary of the evidence must be unduly long. . . . We have read and considered the evidence with care, and are of opinion that the jury were warranted in the following conclusions:

Amos L. Eldridge, the plaintiff's husband and intestate, in 1928, lived with her at Ossipee, N. H. He owned his home, but, outside of that, the moneys here in question represented his entire life's savings. He was 73 years of age, broken in health, and somewhat enfeebled in mind. He had valvular disease of the heart and kidney trouble. Dropsy had set in, and his legs had become swollen and ulcerated. He was at times helpless, and at all times in a serious condition. His physician testifies that it was uncertain whether he would live for a day or for months, and says that he had become childish and fretty, and there was a degeneration of his mental faculties.

The defendant was a younger sister who formerly had lived with her brother at their old home in Ossipee. In those years she was in her brother's closest confidence, writing his letters, handling his moneys, and making his deposits in the bank. They both had married, she moving to Island Falls, Me., to live with her husband, Levi H. May, and he staying in Ossipee with his wife in a new home which he had acquired.

In August, 1928, Mrs. May visited her brother in Ossipee, and, unbeknown to his wife, invited him to come to Maine and live with her, although she was advised by his physician that such a removal was risky and would be detrimental to him. She was then advised as to his condition and the uncertainty of his life.

In October, 1928, Mrs. May secretly arranged a meeting with Mr. Eldridge at the home of an older sister, Julia Wormwood, who lived in Rochester, N. H. Mr. Eldridge was brought to Rochester on October 24th by a neighbor, stating to his wife as he left home that he was going down to his sister Julia's to stay over Sunday, and leaving her uninformed of Mrs. May's arrival in Rochester and his proposed meeting with her.

The next day Mr. Eldridge was taken home by Mrs. Wormwood's husband. He got a cleaning rod from the garage, said he was going to a rifle shoot that afternoon, and, unbeknown to his wife, gathered up all his bank books, and left for Rochester again without waiting for dinner.

The next day, October 26th, Mr. Eldridge accompanied Mrs. May to Island Falls, Me. No one appears, outside of Mrs. May, who admits knowledge that the trip was planned. Mrs. Eldridge did not know that her husband had gone to Maine with Mrs. May until nearly a week had passed, assuming all the time that he was in Rochester with Mrs. Wormwood. Frank A. Eldridge, an older brother who lived in Ossipee and was on most friendly terms with Mr. Eldridge, was apparently also kept in ignorance. What Mrs. Wormwood, the older sister, knew, does not appear. Her deposition might have shed valuable light upon the events which took place in her home. We are impressed with the view that Mrs. May's dealings with her brother at Rochester, prior thereto and thereafter, were intended to be secret, and were effectually kept so.

When Mr. Eldridge arrived at Island Falls, he was still in a most serious condition. The local physician there, called by Mrs. May as early as November 2, found him in bed still suffering from the complication of diseases already described. This doctor called again November 5th and again on the 7th and 10th. At all times, he says, Mr. Eldridge was in bed and in distress. We think the evidence fairly indicates that, from the day of his arrival at Island Falls, Mr. Eldridge progressively grew weaker, and it was evident that he could live but a short time.

As already stated, Mr. Eldridge arrived at Island Falls on Friday, October 26th.Examining the testimony of Mrs. May, we find that she admits that on the Sunday following, his sister was talking with him about turning over all his property to her in consideration of an agreement for life support. [The court here describes in detail how, within the space of 10 days, Brother's money was withdrawn from five banks in New Hampshire and deposited in Sister's bank account in Maine, and the parties executed the agreement for support already quoted. Brother executed the necessary documents (and endorsed the checks from the New Hampshire banks) by mark ("X"). An attorney summoned by his Sister held the pen for him.]

All this time no word had been sent by Mrs. May to Mrs. Eldridge, nor does it appear that relatives in New Hampshire had been informed of Mr. Eldridge's condition. No one but the Mays, the attorney in Houlton, and the notary knew of Mr. Eldridge's attempted contract and conveyance. The transaction was kept secret until Mr. Eldridge died, four days later, on November 11th. An examination of his effects at Ossipee then disclosed that the bank books were missing. Inquiry at the banks disclosed the withdrawals.

The defendant's claim is that she received the money in suit from her brother in good faith and without fraud on her part. She testified before the jury that Mr. Eldridge came to her home of his own volition and without her solicitation. She asserts that his home life in Ossipee was unhappy and he was ill treated by his wife. She told the jury that the transfer of his moneys and lands to her were suggested by him, and purely voluntary and in no way influenced by her. The jury were not convinced by her story. They did not find in the evidence before them proof of her good faith and fair dealing in this transaction.

The secrecy surrounding Mr. Eldridge's departure to Maine, his stay with Mrs. May, and the execution of his contract and conveyance was sufficient to arouse suspicion in the minds of fair-minded men. Evidently it did not appeal to reason that a man, without causes more cogent than the evidence discloses, would of his own volition, and uninfluenced by the defendant, strip himself of all earthly possessions, pauperize his wife, and disinherit his other heirs for a consideration so uncertain and in all probability so inadequate. Mrs. May had been advised by her brother's physician in Ossipee that his span of life might be a day or longer, or, to use her own words, that he "was liable to pass out any time." The jury might well have concluded that Mr. Eldridge's early demise was apparent to any one who saw him, and that even in permitting him, unadvised by impartial and disinterested counsel, to enter into the contract in question, she took an unconscionable and unfair advantage of him which in equity cannot be allowed to stand.

We think the jury were justified in going further and, from all of the evidence in the case, drawing the inference that it was through the influence and persuasion of the defendant that Mr. Eldridge was induced to transfer his moneys and property to her and execute the contract of November 6th. We are convinced also that a finding that the influence was undue is not error.

Under the equitable principles stated, the plaintiff was entitled to recover the moneys in the possession of the defendant in this action of general assumpsit.

The undue influence amalgam

1. The story of *Eldridge v. May* makes it almost too obvious as an illustration of undue influence, but it combines a number of ideas that are predictable legal themes of this class of cases. Typically, the evidence relied on to establish undue influence points simultaneously to a set of intertwined transactional defects: fraud, duress, and breach of confidence on the part of the defendant, as well as incapacity on the part of the victim—where the direct evidence of any of these elements, taken singly, might not suffice to justify recovery.

As is nearly always the case, the critical conversations and dealings between Brother and Sister have taken place off stage. Brother is not around to give his version of events—assuming he would be competent to do so. Instead of direct evidence of what the courts sometimes call "overpersuasion," the case for undue influence rests on inferences and legal presumptions.

Notice the way the evidence for the jury in *Eldridge*—though it might seem overwhelming—is entirely a matter of inference. Facts about Brother's declining physical condition take us right to the edge of the conclusion that he was mentally incapacitated, though of course there could be no such finding. The outrageous terms of the contract for lifetime support—when Brother's life expectancy, as the court implies, was a matter of weeks or days—make it an example of what equity used to call "constructive fraud." We cannot know whether threats were made, but the way in which Brother was spirited off to Island Falls—a tiny village in the remotest region of northern Maine—make us suspect the worst. The secrecy with which Sister managed the entire affair strongly supports the inference that the facts, if known, would be discreditable to her. Under the circumstances disclosed, the jury's common-sense conclusion is that these transactions must have been Sister's idea, not Brother's.

2. The available inferences from circumstantial evidence were stronger in *Eldridge* than in many cases of undue influence, where liability more clearly depends on legal *presumptions*. In most jurisdictions, the standard definition of "undue influence" begins with the necessary relationship of the parties—often described as "a relation of trust and confidence" or "a relationship of dominance on one side and subservience on the other." Such a relationship is presumed to exist, as a matter of law, in established fiduciary settings: between lawyer and client, doctor and patient, guardian and ward. It may be shown to exist, as a matter of fact, in any other relationship where one person reposes a particular trust in another—for example, between brother and sister or parent and child, particularly if one relies on the other for the management of financial affairs.

In a case that depends more clearly on these legal presumptions, the analysis is what we see initially sketched in *Eldridge*. Once the necessary relationship has been established, a transaction that benefits the trusted party at the expense of the trusting party is *presumed* to be the result of undue influence—shifting to the trusted party "the burden of proof to show affirmatively his compliance with equitable requisites and of entire fairness on his part and freedom of the other from undue influence."

Notwithstanding this textbook introduction, the decision in *Eldridge* does not appear to depend very much on this kind of burden-shifting—simply because the inferences of Sister's misconduct were so strong. But it explains the reasoning by which gifts to lawyers from clients, or to doctors from patients, may be held to be the result of undue influence—unless the recipient can make the affirmative showing to which the *Eldridge* court refers. Evidence that a challenged transfer was the subject of independent consultation and advice is probably the strongest source of justification in such cases; while evidence suggesting that the transfer was kept secret from those who might have dissuaded the transferor is particularly damning.

3. Does the First Amendment leave any room for finding undue influence on the part of religious leaders and spiritual advisers? In Roberts-Douglas v. Meares, 624 A.2d 405 (D.C. 1992), church parishioners claimed that their donations to a building fund had been induced by overbearing threats:

> They were told by church leaders that Bishop Meares represented the "voice of God," and that what he said should not be questioned. Claiming divine inspiration for his statements, Bishop Meares announced that God required each parishioner who was gainfully employed to give $5,000 to the building

fund within five months. Bishop Meares threatened that if they did not do so, God would curse them, kill them, or "turn His back" on them.

According to the plaintiffs, parishioners who had not given enough money to the building funds were publicly identified by name during church services and were made to stand and to walk a gantlet in disgrace between two lines of deacons. Those parishioners who had met their pledges were directed to "lay hands" upon those who had not as the latter passed through the gantlet, and each delinquent member was required, when he or she reached the end of the line, to make a public pledge to give the amount demanded. Anyone who declined to do so would be ordered to leave the church, in disgrace, by the front door.

Id. at 411-412. One of the plaintiffs, "a divorced mother of two teenaged daughters" with an annual income of less than $10,000, testified that:

> Every Sunday they would always preach money, money, money, and that was a pressure that I couldn't take any more of, money, money, money, preached every Sunday that I know of. Then, when Pastor Meares stated that if we didn't give the $5,000 that God would put a curse on us, or he would turn his back on us, that is what made me very uncomfortable, and being forced to do something that I knew I couldn't do, and that I had to do it so that God wouldn't put a curse on me.
>
> The reason that I am here now is if I couldn't give them the $5,000 that they wanted and only gave what I could and God would put a curse on me, I would rather take my money back and let God do whatever.

Id. at 427. With the exception of two parishioners who were subject to additional "one-on-one" pressure—a church deacon visited their home and "urged them to sell it, indicating that this was God's will"—the court affirmed summary judgment in favor of the defendants. As to the remaining plaintiffs, the court observed that "any coercion . . . came from the pulpit to the congregation at large." If the one-on-one pressure might constitute undue influence, why not "coercion from the pulpit"?

D. INCAPACITY

Pettit v. Liston
97 Or. 464, 191 P. 660 (1920)

Plaintiff, a minor, brings this action by his guardian to recover $125 paid by him upon the purchase price of a certain motorcycle purchased from the defendants.

The defendants in the case were engaged in the selling of motorcycles and attachments. The plaintiff purchased from them a motorcycle at the agreed price of $325. He paid $125 down, and was to pay $25 per month upon the purchase price until the payments were completed. He took and used the motorcycle for a little over a month and finally returned the same to the defendants and demanded the return of his money. The defendants answer and allege that plaintiff used the machine, and in so doing damaged it to the amount of $156.65. Plaintiff's demurrer to this answer was overruled, and the case was dismissed.

BENNETT, J. (after stating the facts as above).

The amount involved in this proceeding is not large, but the question of law presented is a very important one, and one which has been much disputed in the courts, and about which there is a great and irreconcilable conflict in the authorities, and we have therefore given the matter careful attention.

The courts, in an attempt to protect the minor upon the one hand, and to prevent wrong or injustice to persons who have dealt fairly and reasonably with such minor upon the other, have indulged in many fine distinctions and recognized various slight shades of difference.

The result has been that there are not only two general lines of decisions directly upon the question involved, but there are many others, which diverge more or less from the main line, and make particular cases turn upon real or fancied differences and distinctions, depending upon whether the contract was executory or partly or wholly executed, whether it was for necessaries, whether it was beneficial to the minor, whether it was fair and reasonable, whether the minor still had the property purchased in his possession, whether he had received any beneficial use of the same, etc.

Many courts have held broadly that a minor may so purchase property and keep it for an indefinite time, if he chooses, until it is worn out and destroyed, and then recover the payments made on the purchase price, without allowing the seller anything whatever for the use and depreciation of the property.

Many other authorities hold that where the transaction is fair and reasonable, and the minor was not overcharged or taken advantage of in any way, and he takes and keeps the property and uses or destroys it, he cannot recover the payments made on the purchase price, without allowing the seller for the wear and tear and depreciation of the article while in his hands.

The plaintiff contends for the former rule, and supports his contention with citations from the courts of last resort of Maine, Connecticut, Indiana, Massachusetts, Vermont, Nebraska, Virginia, Iowa, Mississippi, and West Virginia, most of which (although not all) support his contention. On the contrary, the courts of New York, Maryland, Montana, Illinois, Kentucky, New Hampshire, and Minnesota, with some others, support the latter rule, which seems to be also the English rule.

We find the decisions rather equally balanced, both in number and respectability. Our attention has not been called to any Oregon case bearing upon the question, and as far as our investigation has disclosed, there is none. In this condition of the authorities, we feel that we are in a position to pass upon the question as one of first impression, and announce the rule which seems to us to be the better one, upon considerations of principle and public policy.

We think, where the minor has not been overreached in any way, and there has been no undue influence, and the contract is a fair and reasonable one, and the minor has actually paid money on the purchase price, and taken and used the article, that he ought not to be permitted to recover the amount actually paid, without allowing the vendor of the goods the reasonable compensation for the use and depreciation of the article, while in his hands.

Of course, if there has been any fraud or imposition on the part of the seller, or if the contract is unfair, or any unfair advantage has been taken of the minor in inducing him to make the purchase, then a different rule would apply. And whether there had been such an overreaching on the part of the seller would always, in case of a jury trial, be a question for the jury.

We think this rule will fully and fairly protect the minor against injustice or imposition, and at the same time it will be fair to the business man who has dealt with such minor in good faith. This rule is best adapted to modern conditions, and especially to the conditions in our Far Western states.

Here, minors are permitted to and do in fact transact a great deal of business for themselves, long before they have reached the age of legal majority. Most young men have their own time long before reaching that age. They work and earn money and collect it and spend it oftentimes without any oversight or restriction.

No business man questions their right to buy, if they have the money to pay for their purchases. They not only buy for themselves, but they often are intrusted with the making of purchases for their parents and guardians. It would be intolerably burdensome for every one concerned if merchants and other business men could not deal with them safely, in a fair and reasonable way, in cash transactions of this kind.

Again, it will not exert any good moral influence upon boys and young men, and will not tend to encourage honesty and integrity, or lead them to a good and useful business future, if they are taught that they can make purchases with their own money, for their own benefit, and after paying for them in this way, and using them until they are worn out and destroyed, go back and compel the business man to return to them what they have paid upon the purchase price. Such a doctrine, as it seems to us, can only lead to the corruption of young men's principles and encourage them in habits of trickery and dishonesty.

We must not be understood as deciding at this time what would be the rule where the vendor is seeking to enforce an executory contract against the minor, which is a different question not necessarily involved in this case.

It follows that the judgment of the court below should be affirmed.

Shield or sword?

1. One consequence of reducing the age of majority from 21 to 18 has been largely to eliminate a rich vein of cases in which 18- and 19-year-olds would buy cars, trucks, and motorcycles, wreck them, then ask for their money back. Purchasers in these cases asserted a right of rescission and restitution on the ground of incapacity. The proper consequences of the remedy in these circumstances were much debated. If the question of law was "very important," as the court in *Pettit* suggests, it was because it presents a thumbnail version of some larger issues.

2. Because a contract is not enforceable against a person without legal capacity, whether for nonage or another reason, a minor can generally walk away from an *executory* obligation without legal consequences. (The enforceability of a minor's debt for "necessaries" is not so much an exception to this rule as an instance of liability in restitution—do you see why?) When the minor's contracts were said to be "voidable" rather than "void," this meant voidable at the election of the incapacitated party—in order to preserve for the minor the option of enforcing a contract that might be advantageous. So far the results are fairly straightforward. The minor will not be required to pay any amounts he has not yet paid (or to do anything else he does not want to do). The interesting problems arise when the minor repudiates the unenforceable agreement after paying all or part of the price.

3. Obviously, the purpose of rules defining legal capacity is to protect the incapacitated person against the consequences of imprudence. Pettit will not be required to perform his imprudent contract to pay $325 for the motorcycle: he can change his mind and walk away with no obligation. But does the same protective policy require that we permit Pettit to ride the bike for year or two—maybe until the day before his 21st birthday—then return it for a full refund? (If he keeps it beyond the age of 21, he will probably be found to have "ratified" the contract.) What if he rides it imprudently for a week or two, then destroys it in a wreck? The traditional response of equity is that we must try to accommodate two conflicting objectives: to protect the minor against his imprudence, and to protect the honest merchant against the minor's opportunism. Two statements are quoted especially often:

> A third rule deducible from the nature of the privilege, which is given as a shield, and not as a sword, is that it never shall be turned into an offensive weapon of fraud or injustice.

Zouch v. Parsons, 3 Burr. 1794, 1802, 97 Eng. Rep. 1103, 1107 (K.B. 1765) (Mansfield, C.J.).

The privilege of infancy is to be used as a shield and not as a sword. He cannot have the benefit of the contract on one side, without returning the equivalent on the other.

2 Kent, Commentaries on American Law *240 (2d ed. 1832).

4. Martin Johnson—aged 17 at the time—purchased $1,000 of life insurance. Premiums of $23.29 were payable every six months.

He made eight semiannual payments amounting to the total sum of $186.32, and immediately thereafter plaintiff attained his majority, or full age of 21 years; and thereupon, on the 21st day of December, 1892, he duly served upon [defendant insurer] his notice in writing that he had arrived at his majority, and that he elected to avoid the contract of insurance between the defendant and himself, and offered to return said policy to the defendant, and demanded of the defendant that it return to him the moneys which he had paid to said company, amounting to the sum above named, which the defendant refused to do, whereupon he brought this action to recover of the defendant the amount so paid, upon the ground that he was an infant at the time of the execution of the said contract and during the times when he made the semiannual payments as herein stated.

Johnson v. Northwestern Mut. Life Ins. Co., 56 Minn. 365, 57 N.W. 934, *modified on reh'g*, 59 N.W. 992 (1894). The terms of policy provided that Johnson's $1,000 policy would be fully "paid up" after premiums had been paid for 20 years. This entitlement was pro ratable, so that after four years of premium payments, the "surrender value" of Johnson's policy was paid up insurance in the face amount of $200. It was agreed that Johnson was entitled to rescind the policy, subject to the usual requirement of rescission that he account for anything of value received from the other party. In its initial decision, the court held that Johnson was entitled to restitution of $186.32, because "he retains nothing either of actual value or any right. In no way has he appropriated any of the fruits of the contract to his own advantage, nor does he seek to do so." What do you suppose was the court's decision on rehearing?

Chapter 4

Transfers Under Legal Compulsion

A. JUDGMENT SUBSEQUENTLY REVERSED

Miga v. Jensen
299 S.W.3d 98 (Tex. 2009)

Chief Justice JEFFERSON delivered the opinion of the Court.

A judgment debtor is entitled to supersede the judgment while pursuing an appeal; this defers payment until the matter is resolved but does not halt the accumulation of interest on the judgment. If the debtor rejects the supersedeas option and does not otherwise suspend enforcement, the creditor may execute on the judgment by seizing bank accounts or other property. To avoid seizure, the debtor may pay the judgment outright, which stops the accumulation of post-judgment interest. But these alternatives to suspending enforcement put at risk the judgment debtor's ability to recoup the seized assets or payment when the appeal is successful. The judgment debtor in this case, under an agreement with the judgment creditor, made a payment toward satisfying the judgment and subsequently won the appeal. The question is whether the creditor may nevertheless keep the money because equitable principles of restitution do not apply. Because we reject the creditor's approach, we affirm the court of appeals' judgment.

Background

This case stems from Ronald Jensen's breach of an option agreement with Dennis Miga, under which Miga would have been entitled to buy stock in a privately held corporation. The facts and the parties are well known to us. See Miga v. Jensen ("*Miga I* "), 96 S.W.3d 207, 209 (Tex. 2002). In the initial round of litigation, a jury found for Miga on all issues, and the trial court rendered judgment in his favor for almost $19 million, plus more than $4 million in prejudgment interest. To suspend execution during his appeal, Jensen posted a supersedeas bond in the amount of $25,496,623.39, which subsequent riders increased to $29,500,000. The court of appeals largely affirmed the trial court's judgment.

Despite the bond, postjudgment interest continued to mount. Shortly after the court of appeals' decision, the parties entered into an Agreed Order under which Jensen made "an unconditional tender [to Miga] . . . of the sum of $23,439,532.78 . . . toward satisfaction of the Judgment in order to terminate the accrual of post-judgment interest on that sum." Jensen then filed a petition for review with this Court. Miga moved to dismiss Jensen's petition, arguing that Jensen's tender mooted the appeal. We rejected that argument. On the merits, we held that Miga's contract damages should have been measured by the value of the option at the time of breach, rather than at the time of trial. We reversed the court of appeals' judgment on that issue and rendered judgment for Miga for $1,034,400.

Jensen then sought restitution of $21,560,150.67, the difference between the amount paid to Miga—$23,439,532.78—and the amount owed under the modified judgment. When Miga refused to tender that amount, Jensen filed this suit. The trial court granted Jensen's and denied Miga's motion for summary judgment A divided court of appeals affirmed. 214 S.W.3d 81. We granted the petition for review.

Restitution After Reversal

Restitution after reversal has long been the rule in Texas and elsewhere. See, *e.g.*, Bank of U.S. v. Bank of Wash., 31 U.S. 8, 17 (1832) ("On the reversal of the judgment, the law raises an obligation in the party to the record, who has received the benefit of the erroneous judgment, to make restitution to the other party for what he has lost."); Cleveland v. Tufts, 69 Tex. 580, 583, 7 S.W. 72 (1888) ("It is settled that money paid upon a judgment afterward reversed may be recovered by the party making the payment."); see also Restatement of the Law of Restitution ("Restatement") §74; [R3RUE §18;] Peticolas v. Carpenter, 53 Tex. 23, 29 (1880) ("Where a judgment for debt is reversed after it has been enforced by execution, and the case is finally decided in favor of defendant, he is certainly entitled to restitution"). The question here is whether this case presents an exception to that rule. Miga contends that it does, for three reasons.

A. DOES THE PARTIES' CONTRACT PRECLUDE RESTITUTION?

Miga first argues that because the parties' agreement made Jensen's $23,439,532.78 tender "unconditional," the restitution remedy is unavailable. See Restatement §74 (requiring restitution upon reversal unless it "would be inequitable or the parties contract that payment is to be final"). While it is true that "when a valid, express contract covers the subject matter of the parties' dispute, there can be no recovery under a quasi-contract theory," Fortune Prod. Co. v. Conoco, Inc., 52 S.W.3d 671, 684 (Tex. 2000), here both sides agree that the Agreed Order is silent on restitution.

Miga contends that he and Jensen contracted for the payment to be final, but if that were so, we would not have held that Jensen's appeal—despite the payment—was viable. We concluded, instead, that the parties agreed to disagree: "While Miga may have believed that Jensen's payment mooted the appeal, he could not have had any reasonable doubt that Jensen believed it did not, or that Jensen intended to pursue the appeal if legally allowed to do so." We agree with the court of appeals that "implicit in reserving a right to appeal is the right to a refund of the money in the event that the judgment is later modified or reversed." 214 S.W.3d at 89. The situation would be no different had Miga executed on a non-superseded judgment. In that instance, there would be no "agreement" that Jensen could seek restitution and no agreement that he could not, but the right to recover the funds upon reversal of the judgment would nevertheless be established as a matter of law. Because the parties' agreement is silent on this point, it does not displace the restitution-after-reversal rule.

B. WAS JENSEN'S PAYMENT VOLUNTARY?

Second, Miga argues that the voluntary payment rule precludes restitution. This common law principle provides that "money voluntarily paid on a claim of right, with full knowledge of all the facts, in the absence of fraud, duress, or compulsion, cannot be recovered back merely because the party at the time of payment was ignorant of or mistook the law as to his liability." Pennell v. United Ins. Co., 150 Tex. 541, 243 S.W.2d 572, 576 (1951) (quoting 40 Am. Jur. §205 (1942)). It is a defense to a restitution claim. BMG Direct Mktg., Inc. v. Peake, 178 S.W.3d 763, 768–69 (Tex. 2005) (citing Restatement (Third) §6 cmt. e (Tentative Draft No. 1, 2001)) ("The restitution claim to recover a payment in excess of an underlying liability . . . meets an important limitation in the so-called voluntary payment rule").

The voluntary payment rule precludes a party from "pay[ing] out his money, leading the other party to act as though the matter were closed, and then be in the position to change his mind and invoke the aid of the courts to get it back." Peake, 178 S.W.3d at 768–69. In Miga I, we rejected the notion that the voluntary payment rule mooted Jensen's appeal. As we made clear, Jensen never led Miga to believe that the matter was closed. His pursuit of an appeal—and stated intent to seek restitution if that appeal was successful—removed any reasonable doubt to the contrary.

In one of only two cases in which we have affirmatively applied the voluntary payment rule in the last forty years, we held that a services fee paid by community college students fell within the rule: "In light of the choices retained and [the students'] right to request a waiver of the fees or otherwise protest the imposition of the fee, any coercion that existed was not actual and imminent and did not constitute duress as a matter of law," making the payment voluntary. Dallas County Cmty. College Dist. v. Bolton, 185 S.W.3d 868, 883 (Tex. 2005). We recognized that certain financial incentives or disincentives, like the fee, do not "transform a choice into coercion."

In contrast, Jensen faced not only mounting post-judgment interest, but the coercive power of the judgment. In Highland Church of Christ v. Powell, 640 S.W.2d 235, 237 (Tex. 1982), we hinted at this notion, determining that the voluntary payment rule was inapplicable when a church paid a judgment but made clear its intent to pursue an appeal. We held that the church's payment was made under "implied duress," caused by accruing penalties and interest, as well as the embarrassment the Church would have faced had execution issued against it. The *Third Restatement* explains it more fully:

> Nor is the restitution claim of the judgment debtor barred by the doctrine of "voluntary payment" if the debtor elects to pay a judgment that he regards as invalid, without waiting for the issuance or levy of execution. On the contrary, any payment made in response to a judgment is treated as a payment made under compulsion, at least for the purpose of permitting the judgment debtor to avoid the consequences that would flow from regarding the payment as "voluntary."

Restatement (Third), §18, cmt. c; see also *id.* ch. 2, Introductory Note (Tentative Draft No. 1, 2001) (referring to a payment made in compliance with a judgment as a "transfer . . . made under legal compulsion"); Restatement §74, cmt. b (noting coercive effect of judgment).

The court of appeals held that the voluntary payment rule did not apply because "Jensen signed the Agreed Order under economic duress." 214 S.W.3d at 92 (noting that "interest on the judgment was accruing at a rate of ten percent, compounded annually"). Miga complains that, under *Bolton*, the mere running of interest on a judgment is insufficient to constitute duress, and Jensen's ability to supersede the judgment eliminated any compulsion. But, as outlined above, it is not just the interest but the judgment's coercive effect that make the payment involuntary, regardless of the judgment debtor's means. To avoid execution pending appeal, Jensen could either pay the judgment or make arrangements to suspend its enforcement. See Tex. R. App. P.24.1. His ability to secure a supersedeas bond does not make his payment voluntary. See Restatement §74, cmt. b (noting that, upon reversal of a judgment, amounts paid can be recovered "although no execution was issued, and although the payor could have obtained a supersedeas or stay of execution"); Restatement (Third) §18, cmt. a (noting that "a party is under no obligation to postpone compliance with a judgment that he seeks to overturn"). When, as here, payment on a judgment is coupled with an expressed intent to appeal when appellate relief is attainable, the voluntary payment rule will not preclude restitution if the judgment is later reversed.

Voluntary payment yet again

1. It should not require this much discussion to demonstrate that the satisfaction of an adverse judgment for $24 million is hardly a "voluntary payment" in any meaningful sense—particularly when the judgment debtor is pursuing an ultimately successful appeal. (The full opinion of the Texas Supreme Court devotes even more space to this contention.) *Miga v. Jensen* illustrates the pernicious influence and hypnotic power of the expression "voluntary payment" in another important context, beyond the cases of mistake in which it was previously encountered.

2. Reading between the lines, what was the nature of the dispute in *Dallas County Cmty. College Dist. v. Bolton?* Could the students' payment of the challenged fees have been "voluntary" in any meaningful sense? Why would the Texas courts have said that they were?

3. Compare the following illustrations from the *Restatement*:

(a) A owes B $5,000, but (unknown to either party) the debt is no longer enforceable because the statute of limitations has run. A pays B, then learns that his payment could not have been legally compelled. A has a prima facie claim to restitution of the mistaken payment (§6), but B is not unjustly enriched by A's payment of a valid but unenforceable debt. B is not liable to A in restitution. [R3RUE §62, Illustration 1.]

(b) B sues A to enforce a $5,000 debt. A defends on the basis of the statute of limitations. The trial court holds that the statute does not bar the action, and B obtains a judgment that A satisfies. B's judgment is reversed on appeal, on the ground that the action was time-barred. It is conceded that A's underlying debt to B was legal and valid, and that it would have been enforceable were it not for the statute of limitations. B is liable to A in restitution nevertheless. [R3RUE §18, Illustration 8.]

Both illustrations are supported by authority. Can the outcomes be reconciled?

B.   RESTITUTION OF TAX PAYMENTS

Brookside Memorials, Inc. v. Barre City
167 Vt. 558, 702 A.2d 47 (1997)

Before AMESTOY, C.J., and GIBSON, DOOLEY, MORSE and JOHNSON, JJ.

[Most residents of Barre are billed for sewer service based on metered water use. Granite manufacturers, such as Brookside, are charged a flat rate based on their number of employees, because the large volume of water they use in the manufacturing process is discharged into sludge pits or lagoons rather than the city sewer system. From 1982 to 1994, the City billed plaintiff for sewer disposal at the metered rate, which often exceeded $3,500 per year, rather than the flat rate, which would have been only about $100 per year. Before the mistake was discovered, Brookside had paid over $40,000 more than it was obligated to pay for sewage disposal.

[The City agreed to apply the lower rate in the future and offered to give Brookside a refund for overpayments made during the most recent year, but refused to refund all overpayments made during the previous six years—the general limitations period for civil actions. Brookside sued the City under theories of breach of contract and unjust enrichment.]

The superior court granted the City summary judgment, ruling that plaintiff bore the responsibility but failed to ascertain whether its sewer bills were reflective of and consistent with the use of its premises. According to the court, regardless of whether the City knew that plaintiff was operating as a granite shed, plaintiff was not entitled to a refund because it had paid the sewer bills voluntarily without protest and could have discovered the problem through reasonable diligence, including examining the bills.

On appeal, plaintiff contends that the law and facts of the case require the City to refund the overpayments. The City concedes that plaintiff was entitled to pay the flat rate, and does not contend that the metered rate was reasonable or equitable as applied to plaintiff. Rather, the City argues that plaintiff was in the best position to discover that it was being billed under the wrong rate, and thus bore the responsibility for informing the City of the mistake.

Under a quasi-contract theory of unjust enrichment, the law implies a promise to pay when a party receives a benefit and retention of the benefit would be inequitable. This theory may be applied in an action seeking a refund from a municipality: "If money is paid to a municipality which, in justice and in good conscience it ought to return, it is generally liable for repayment on an implied contract." 17 McQuillin, The Law of Municipal Corporations §49.62, at 425 (3d ed. 1993). Generally, *voluntary* payments made to a municipality, including payments made to obtain water or sewer services, are not recoverable. *Id.* This voluntary payment rule is based on public policy concerns that governmental bodies must be able to rely on the presumptive validity of their laws in planning their budgets. Nevertheless, "in the absence of fraud, imposition, undue influence and the like, money paid to a municipality with a full knowledge of the facts, but under a mistake of the law, cannot be recovered."*Id.*

The City argues that the court properly applied the voluntary payment rule in this instance because plaintiff's failure to discover the existence of the flat rate to which it was entitled was a mistake of law that precludes recovery of the overpayments. According to the City, plaintiff should have learned of the correct rate by discussing the matter with its peers in the granite industry or by inquiring at the Water and Sewer Department. We conclude that the voluntary payment rule does not apply under the circumstances of this particular case because plaintiff made the payments without a full knowledge of the facts, and the City, not plaintiff, was in a better position to discover and correct the error. See Getto v. City of Chicago, 86 Ill. 2d 39, 426 N.E.2d 844, 849–50 (1981) (voluntary payment rule does not apply unless it is shown that plaintiff had knowledge of facts upon which to frame protest).

The overpayments in this case arose out of the parties' mutual mistake as to the correct sewer rate to apply to plaintiff. The City's mistake was one of fact — failing to recognize that plaintiff was a granite manufacturing business entitled to the flat rate. Although plaintiff's "mistake" — failing to become aware of the existence of the City's flat rate for businesses such as itself — could be characterized as a mistake of law, it was not a typical mistake of law involving a failure to appreciate the effect or consequences of a recognized law. Cf. New Jersey Hospital v. Fishman, 283 N.J. Super. 253, 661 A.2d 842, 849 (App. Div. 1995) (payment of taxes under commissioner's misinterpretation of statute was mistake of law); G. Heileman Brewing Co. v. City of La Crosse, 105 Wis. 2d 152, 312 N.W.2d 875, 880 (App. 1981) (plaintiff's failure to recognize difficult and innovative reason why it need not pay taxes was mistake of law). Indeed, courts faced with fact patterns analogous to the instant case have treated the "mistake" as one of fact and declined to apply the voluntary payment rule. See, e.g., United States v. C.J. Tower & Sons of Buffalo, Inc., 499 F.2d 1277, 1282 (C.C.P.A. 1974) (importer of aircraft fuel cells seeking refund of ad valorem tax on ground that he was unaware that fuel cells were considered emergency defense purchases made mistake of fact rather than law and thus had no reason to protest imposition of tax); San Antonio Indep. Sch. Dist. v. National Bank of Commerce, 626 S.W.2d 794, 797 (Tex. Ct. App. 1981) (voluntary payment rule did not apply where city erred in computing ad valorem tax and plaintiff erred in not recognizing that it was paying taxes on valuation different from figure it had submitted to taxing agency).

The instant case is an equitable action, not an action based on a refund statute. See American Tierra Corp. v. City of West Jordan, 840 P.2d 757, 760 (Utah 1992) (action to recover unlawful charges for city services is equitable in nature). Equity affords relief against mutual mistakes as long as the mistake is not wholly one of law. See MacGowan v. Gaines, 127 Vt. 477, 481, 253 A.2d 121, 124 (1969); In re Estate of Watkins, 114 Vt. 109, 137, 41 A.2d 180, 196 (1945). In determining whether a quasi-contract should be implied under an equitable theory of unjust enrichment, the inquiry is whether, in light of the totality of the circumstances, equity and good conscience demand that the defendant return that which the plaintiff seeks to recover. Legault v. Legault, 142 Vt. 525, 531, 459 A.2d 980, 984 (1983) (whether there has been unjust enrichment must be realistic determination based on broad view of human setting involved).

Given the undisputed facts and circumstances of this case, equity demands a refund.Cf. Knutson Hotel Corp. v. City of Moorhead, 250 Minn. 392, 84 N.W.2d 626, 629 (1957) (where city charged hotel for disposal of sewage that never entered city system, city was required to make restitution because it took money that it had no right in equity or good conscience to retain).

Reversed, plaintiff's motion for summary judgment is granted, and the case is remanded for computation of damages.

Notes on restitution of tax payments

1. Payment of taxes or rates that have been erroneously or illegally assessed would seem to present an obvious case for restitution, but state and local governments (and the state courts in which they must be sued) tend to reject any obligation to give the money back. *Brookside Memorials* reaches a liberal, pro-restitution outcome after canvassing a number of objections that might still derail the taxpayer's claim in many jurisdictions. Notice in this connection:

- *The hackneyed assertion that payment was "voluntary."* While it might seem self-evident that no one pays excessive or illegal taxes voluntarily, the "voluntary payment rule" is still the most frequent objection to restitution of overpaid taxes. As seen in Chapter 3, the word "voluntary" in this context has the semi-technical meaning of "not under duress."

- *The relevance of "protest."* A taxpayer who can show that he was coerced into the payment of excessive or illegal taxes has a strong claim to restitution on the basis of duress, without the need of other theories (such as mistake or illegality). Here the City objected, among other things, that the plaintiff had paid its taxes "without protest"—the idea being that "no one was forcing it to pay." Taxpayers tend to respond that they have no way to protest an improper tax assessment before they know it is improper.

- *Mistake of law.* Cases mentioned by the court in *Brookside Memorials* show that restitution of tax payments may still depend, ostensibly at least, on whether the taxpayer is found to have made a mistake of fact as opposed to a mistake of law. That discredited distinction is artificial to begin with—particularly in any context, such as payment of taxes, where a mistake is so likely to combine factual and legal elements. "Mistake of law" persists as a formulaic way to deny restitution, sometimes avoiding a discussion of the reasons for denial.

- *Affirmative defenses.* Taxing authorities, like the recipients of mistaken payments generally, may have a defense to restitution based on change of position. (See the further discussion in Chapter 9.) What facts would suffice in a particular case to establish that restitution of excess tax payments would be inequitable? (Who bears the burden of restitution in tax cases, and who is unjustly enriched if restitution is denied?)

2. Consider the following judicial observations regarding restitution of tax payments:

> It is too well settled in this state to need the citation of authority, that if money be paid through a clear mistake of law or fact, essentially affecting the rights of the parties, and which in law or conscience was not payable,

and should not be retained by the party receiving it, it may be recovered. Both law and sound morality so dictate. Especially should this be the rule as to illegal taxation. The taxpayer has no voice in the imposition of the burden. He has the right to presume that the taxing power has been lawfully exercised. He should not be required to know more than those in authority over him, nor should he suffer loss by complying with what he *bona fide* believes to be his duty as a good citizen. Upon the contrary, he should be prompted to its ready performance by refunding to him any illegal exaction, paid by him in ignorance of its illegality; and certainly in such a case, if he be subject to a penalty for non-payment, his compliance under a belief of its legality, and without awaiting a resort to judicial proceedings, should not be regarded in law as so far voluntary as to affect his right of recovery.

City of Newport v. Ringo's Ex'x, 87 Ky. 635, 636, 10 S.W. 2, 3 (1888).

It seems anomalous, if not inequitable, that a State which makes laws requiring other persons to return ill-gotten gains may itself retain property which it has received but to which it was not entitled. But the law as to retention of taxes voluntarily paid has been in effect since Territorial days and we decline to change it now.

William Clairmont, Inc. v. State, 261 N.W.2d 780, 786 (N.D. 1977).

The requirement of resistance to or involuntary payment of a tax is one of public policy: government has an interest in allocating its resources. It is desirable that government know when it contemplates spending public funds that those funds are either available or subject to loss through tax refund. The requirement that one who seeks repayment of illegally assessed taxes notify the governmental unit [by contemporaneous protest] that he wants them returned is not onerous. The inequity of paying illegally collected taxes is outweighed by the requirement that government know what amount of income it has available.

G. Heileman Brewing Co. v. City of La Crosse, 105 Wis. 2d 152, 161-62, 312 N.W.2d 875, 880 (Ct. App. 1981).

3. The extensive and somewhat convoluted law governing restitution of tax payments is almost exclusively concerned with state and municipal (not federal) taxes. The federal rule is that a tax "erroneously or illegally assessed or collected" is subject to recovery in restitution, "whether or not such tax, penalty, or sum has been paid under protest or duress." 26 U.S.C. §7422. As explained by Justice Cardozo:

the government was unjustly enriched at the expense of the taxpayer when it held on to moneys that had been illegally collected, whether with protest or without. So at least the lawmakers believed, and gave expression to that belief, not only in the statute, but in Congressional reports. . . . A high-minded government renounced an advantage that was felt to be ignoble, and set up a new standard of equity and conscience.

George Moore Ice Cream Co. v. Rose, 289 U.S. 373, 378-79 (1933). Although statutes in all the states permit recovery of tax payments in specified circumstances of mistake or illegality, their provisions vary widely; they are rarely comprehensive; and (as suggested in Note 1) they are often subject to narrow judicial construction. See R3RUE §19, Comment *i*, and the accompanying Statutory Note.

Wayne County Produce Co. v. Duffy-Mott Co.
244 N.Y. 351, 155 N.E. 669 (1927)

CARDOZO, Ch. J.

Plaintiff bought from the defendant large quantities of sweet cider. The price was to be 14½ cents per gallon subject to a stated discount, plus the manufacturer's war tax of 10 per cent, which was to be paid in full without discount. For 157,210 gallons bought between November 8, 1920, and August 13, 1921, the payment was $27,514.55, of which $2,501.33 was for the tax. Defendant, the manufacturer, after collecting the amount of the tax from the plaintiff, paid it over to the Federal government. In 1922 came a ruling of the courts that sales of sweet cider were not subject to any tax whatever (Monroe Cider Vinegar & Fruit Co. v. Riordan, 280 Fed. Rep. 624; Casey v. Sterling Cider Co., 294 Fed. Rep. 426). The Treasury Department and manufacturers generally had misconstrued an act of Congress whereby a tax of ten per cent was levied upon sales of unfermented grape juice and "other soft drinks." Defendant demanded and obtained a refund of the taxes thus unlawfully collected. The question is whether the money thus refunded by the government is held by the defendant to its own use or to the use of the plaintiff who is suing to get the money back.

We think the plaintiff must prevail. This is not a case where the item of the tax is absorbed in a total or composite price to be paid at all events. In such a case the buyer is without remedy, though the annulment of the tax may increase the profit to the seller (Moore v. Des Arts, 1 N.Y. 359 [1848]). This is a case where the promise of the buyer is to pay a stated price, and to put the seller in funds for the payment of a tax besides. In such a case the failure of the tax reduces to an equivalent extent the obligation of the promise. The form of the transaction was not thoughtless or accidental. It was deliberate and purposed. The end to be served is conceded in the briefs of counsel. If a sum equal to 10 per cent of the quoted price per gallon had been added to the price as something to be paid at all events, a tax would have been due upon the sum so added as well as upon the residue. A form was adopted whereby the manufacturer was in a position to account to the government at the quoted rate per gallon, and to pay the tax with the excess. The defendant had the benefit of the transaction as thus moulded in its dealings with the government. It is now attempting to set upon the transaction the impress of another quality in its dealings with the plaintiff. We find no evidence in the record to justify the change of front. The quality impressed at the beginning persists until the end.

The contract, therefore, in effect was this and nothing more, that whatever moneys were necessary for the payment of a tax would be furnished by the buyer. Annulment of the tax after the sale and the delivery of an invoice, but before the payment of the price, would have extinguished the seller's right to exact payment from its customer of the added 10 per cent. Payment, if then exacted, would have been no longer payment for a tax, but payment for something else. By the same token, annulment at a later date, when followed by the refund of the tax and the undoing of the whole transaction between the seller and the government, leaves the money applicable to the same use as if the invalidity of the impost had been declared at the beginning.

We think the judgment for the plaintiff is well sustained by the decisions. There have been rulings to the contrary (Heckman & Co. v. Dawes & Son Co., 12 F.2d 154 (D.C. Cir. 1926); Kastner v. Duffy-Mott Co., 125 Misc. 886, 213 N.Y.S. 128 (App. Term 1925).) They have their origin, it would seem, in a misconception of the contract. The distinction is unimportant, at least for present purposes, between mistakes of fact and those of law. The quality of the mistake did not prevent the defendant from recovering the money from the government. It cannot absolve from the duty of disposing of the money thus recovered as good conscience shall dictate.

The documents and the course of dealing establish so clearly the nature of the transaction that there remains nothing to be tried. The judgment should be affirmed with costs.

"Passing on"

1. In Roxborough v. Rothmans of Pall Mall Australia Ltd., [2001] H.C.A. 68, a group of tobacco retailers had paid their wholesaler's invoices which separately itemized (i) the price of the goods sold and (ii) an *ad valorem* "tobacco license fee" to which the retailers were thought to be subject. After the license fee was held in a separate action to be unconstitutional, the retailers sued to recover fees paid to the wholesaler and not yet remitted by the wholesaler to the taxing authority. What result? Would the result be the same if it had been the wholesaler, rather than the retailers, that was subject to the tax?

2. Decisions in this area uniformly emphasize a distinction between (i) a tax itemized separately and (ii) a tax forming one component of a seller's composite price. Why does this minor question of presentation seem to make so much difference?

3. Sales, use, and excise taxes are typically assessed on and payable by sellers but "passed on" by the taxpayers/sellers to the sellers' customers. If restitution in tax cases is based on principles of unjust enrichment, what happens to the taxpayer's claim for a refund if the economic burden of the tax in question was actually borne by someone else? Consider that the statutory scheme permitting a refund may only accommodate a claim by the taxpayer, not by a third party such as the taxpayer's customer.

When the taxing authority resists a claim to restitution of improper taxes and fees it has collected in such circumstances, it may interpose the defense known as "passing on." Conceding for the sake of argument that a tax was illegal, the restitution defendant (the taxing authority) argues that it has not been unjustly enriched *at the expense of the plaintiff* (typically a seller), because its enrichment was at the expense of a third party (the seller's customers). In U.S. law, a defense in these terms is broadly accepted. As summarized by the *Restatement*, "Between the claimant who has lost nothing and the innocent recipient of an undeserved gain, American law sees equal equities and applies a rule of inertia."

> There is no doubt that if the tax authority retains a payment to which it was not entitled it has been unjustly enriched. It has not been enriched at the taxpayer's expense, however, if he has shifted the economic burden of the tax to others. *Unless restitution for their benefit can be worked out,* it seems preferable to leave the enrichment with the tax authority instead of putting the judicial machinery in motion for the purpose of shifting the same enrichment to the taxpayer.

Palmer, Law of Restitution §14.20(a) (1978 & Supp.) (emphasis added), quoted in R3RUE §64, Comment *b*, Reporter's Note.

4. Does this "rule of inertia" for tax cases contradict the principle of *jus tertii* from property law? If A seeks to recover property misappropriated by B, it is normally no defense for B to argue that some third person (C) has a better claim to the property than A. Recall the case of the chimneysweep's boy who sued to recover the jewel stolen from him by the goldsmith's apprentice. Because the plaintiff had merely "found" the jewel, he was not the true owner—someone else had lost it—but the superior rights of C are irrelevant to the contest between A and B. Armory v. Delamirie, 1 Strange 505, 93 Eng. Rep. 664 (K.B. 1722).

5. Whatever its merits between the parties to the litigation, the logic of the "passing on" defense is largely restricted to a case in which restitution would result in a windfall to the taxpayer—because the parties who bore the economic burden of the tax (the taxpayer's customers) will not receive the benefit of the refund. This reasoning melts away if the circumstances suggest that restitution to the taxpayer would facilitate restitution to the customers.

How far a court may want to get involved in unwinding the improper tax collection is another question. In Decorative Carpets, Inc. v. State Board of

Equalization, 58 Cal. 2d 252, 373 P.2d 637 (1962), a seller of carpet charged sales tax to its customers on the price of both carpet and installation. The result was an overpayment of taxes, because sales tax was not due on the cost of installation. Seller sued to recover the tax, though it admitted that it had no plans to refund any sales tax to its customers. The California Supreme Court reversed a judgment awarding restitution:

> To allow plaintiff a refund without requiring it to repay its customers the amounts erroneously collected from them would sanction a misuse of the sales tax by a retailer for his private gain. . . . The judgment is reversed and the cause remanded to the trial court with directions to enter judgment for plaintiff only if it submits proof satisfactory to the court that the refund will be returned to plaintiff's customers from whom the excess payments were erroneously collected.

Id. at 255, 256, 373 P.2d at 638, 639 (Traynor, J.).

6. Assuming that an improper cider tax or sales tax has been separately invoiced and in that way "passed on" by the taxpayer to its customers, does it necessarily follow that the "economic burden" of the tax has been borne by the customers? Dissenting from the judgment in Indian Motorcycle Co. v. United States, 283 U.S. 570 (1931)—a case about intergovernmental immunity from taxation—Stone and Brandeis, JJ., pointed to extensive authority among contemporary economics and tax theorists to the effect that "whether the burden of any tax paid by the seller is actually passed on to the buyer depends upon considerations so various and complex as to preclude the assumption *a priori* that any particular tax at any particular time is passed on." *Id.* at 581 (citations omitted). What are some of the considerations the theorists had in mind?

———————

Chapter 5

Unrequested Intervention: Conferrings

Under normal circumstances, if A has an idea for a mutually beneficial trans-action with B—one in which A confers benefits that he wants B to pay for—A must obtain B's agreement ahead of time. Conduct by which one party per-forms first, then asks to be paid—like washing car windshields at a stoplight, without being asked—is objectionable on so many grounds as to be essentially antisocial. Contract law will not tolerate such a thing, nor will restitution—as a starting proposition. (Restitution traditionally deals with such transactions by calling the claimant a "volunteer," which is one way of saying that restitution will be denied.)

At the same time, the law of restitution recognizes an extensive set of cir-cumstances in which A may in fact recover for benefits intentionally conferred on B, without any request by B and even (in some cases) in the face of B's express refusal to pay. We might think of this part of the subject as a list of exceptions to the usual rule of "contract first."

Restatement Third, Restitution and Unjust Enrichment

§2. LIMITING PRINCIPLES

(1) The fact that a recipient has obtained a benefit without paying for it does not of itself establish that the recipient has been unjustly enriched.

(2) A valid contract defines the obligations of the parties as to matters within its scope, displacing to that extent any inquiry into unjust enrichment.

(3) There is no liability in restitution for an unrequested benefit vol-untarily conferred, unless the circumstances of the transaction justify the claimant's intervention in the absence of contract.

(4) Liability in restitution may not subject an innocent recipient to a forced exchange: in other words, an obligation to pay for a benefit that the recipient should have been free to refuse.

d. Benefits voluntarily conferred. Instead of proposing a bargain, the restitution claimant first confers a benefit, then seeks payment for its value. When this manner of proceeding is unacceptable—as it usually is, if the claimant neglects an opportunity to contract—a claim based on unjust enrichment will be denied.

The limitation of §2(3) is traditionally expressed by denying restitution to a claimant characterized as "officious," an "intermeddler," or a "volunteer." This section states the same rule, substituting a functional explanation for the familiar epithets. Because contract is strongly preferred over restitution as a basis for private obligations, restitution is not usually available to a claimant who has neglected a suitable opportunity to make a contract beforehand.

There are cases in which a claimant may indeed recover compensation for unrequested benefits intentionally conferred—because the claimant's intervention was justified under the circumstances, and because a liability in restitution will not prejudice the recipient. . . .

Volunteers

1. "One cleans another's shoes; what can the other do but put them on?" Taylor v. Laird, (1856) 25 L.J. Ex. 329, 332 (Pollock, C.B.).

2. Ideas that courts once expressed by referring to claimants as "volunteers" or "officious intermeddlers" have been given an economic cast by some more recent decisions:

> One who voluntarily confers a benefit on another, which is to say in the absence of a contractual obligation to do so, ordinarily has no legal claim to be compensated. If while you are sitting on your porch sipping Margaritas a trio of itinerant musicians serenades you with mandolin, lute, and hautboy, you have no obligation, in the absence of a contract, to pay them for their performance no matter how much you enjoyed it; and likewise if they were gardeners whom you had hired and on a break from their gardening they took up their musical instruments to serenade you. When voluntary transactions are feasible (in economic parlance, when transaction costs are low), it is better and cheaper to require the parties to make their own terms than for a court to try to fix them—better and cheaper that the musicians should negotiate a price with you in advance than for them to go running to court for a judicial determination of the just price for their performance.

Indiana Lumbermens Mut. Ins. Co. v. Reinsurance Results, Inc., 513 F.3d 652, 656-57 (7th Cir. 2008) (Posner, J.).

3. In Liggett & Myers Tobacco Co. v. Meyer, 101 Ind. App. 420, 194 N.E. 206 (1935), defendants were the makers of Chesterfield cigarettes. The plaintiff sent the defendants an unsolicited idea for an advertisement. His letter, mailed in December 1925, read as follows:

I am submitting for your approval an original advertising scheme to be used in the way of billboard advertising. The idea consists of this: Two gentlemen, well groomed, in working clothes or in hunting togs apparently engaged in conversation, one extending to the other a package of cigarettes saying, "Have one of these," the other replying, "No thanks; I smoke Chesterfields."

I trust that this idea will be of sufficient value as to merit a reasonable charge therefor. Awaiting your reply, I remain. . . .

The defendants did not reply. In July 1928, the defendants published a set of new advertisements in national magazines and newspapers featuring a picture of two men and a caddy with golf clubs. The plaintiff claimed that publication of these advertisements amounted to acceptance of the offer he had made in his letter, and sued to collect a "reasonable charge" under the contract thus formed.

Does the plaintiff have a viable claim in contract? In tort? In restitution?

A. EMERGENCIES

Cotnam v. Wisdom
83 Ark. 601, 104 S.W. 164 (1907)

F. L. Wisdom and George C. Abel presented a claim against the estate of A. M. Harrison, deceased, of which T. T. Cotnam is administrator, for $2,000 on account of surgical attention to the deceased, who was killed by being thrown from a streetcar. The probate court allowed the account in the sum of $400, and the administrator appealed to the circuit court.

The evidence showed that deceased received fatal injuries in a streetcar wreck; that while he was unconscious some person summoned Dr. Wisdom to attend him; that Dr. Wisdom called in Dr. Abel, an experienced surgeon, to assist him; that they found that the patient was suffering from a fracture of the temporal and parietal bones, and that it was necessary to perform the operation of trephining; that the patient lived only a short time after the operation, and never recovered consciousness.

Dr. Abel testified, over defendant's objection, that the charge of $2,000 was based on the result of inquiry as to the financial condition of deceased's estate. It was further proved, over defendant's objection that deceased was a bachelor, and that his estate, which amounted to about $18,500, including $10,000 of insurance, would go to collateral heirs. Various physicians testified as to the customary fees of doctors in similar cases, and fixed the amount at various sums ranging from $100 to $2,000. There was also evidence that the ability of the patient to pay is usually taken into consideration by surgeons in fixing their fee.

At the plaintiffs' request the court charged the jury as follows:

> 1. If you find from the evidence that plaintiffs rendered professional ser-
> vices as physicians and surgeons to the deceased, A. M. Harrison, in a sud-
> den emergency following the deceased's injury in a streetcar wreck, in an
> endeavor to save his life, then you are instructed that plaintiffs are entitled to
> recover from the estate of the said A. M. Harrison such sum as you may find
> from the evidence is a reasonable compensation for the services rendered.

> 2. The character and importance of the operation, the responsibility rest-
> ing upon the surgeon performing the operation, his experience and pro-
> fessional training, and the ability to pay of the person operated upon, are
> elements to be considered by you in determining what is a reasonable
> charge for the services performed by plaintiffs in the particular case.

In his opening statement to the jury, counsel for claimants stated that "Harrison
was worth $8,000, and had insurance, and his estate was left to collateral heirs,
that is, to nephews and nieces." Counsel for defendant objected to such argument, but the court overruled the objection; and the defendant saved his
exceptions.

Verdict for $650 was returned in plaintiffs' favor. Defendant has appealed.

HILL, C.J.

Mr. Harrison, appellant's intestate, was thrown from a street car, receiving
serious injuries which rendered him unconscious, and while in that condition
the appellees were notified of the accident and summoned to his assistance by
some spectator, and performed a difficult operation in an effort to save his life,
but they were unsuccessful, and he died without regaining consciousness. The
appellant says: "Harrison was never conscious after his head struck the pave-
ment. He did not and could not, expressly or impliedly, assent to the action of
the appellees. He was without knowledge or will power. However merciful or
benevolent may have been the intention of the appellees, a new rule of law, of
contract by implication of law, will have to be established by this court in order
to sustain the recovery." Appellant is right in arguing that the recovery must be
sustained by a contract by implication of law, but is not right in saying that it
is a new rule of law, for such contracts are almost as old as the English system
of jurisprudence. They are usually called "implied contracts." More properly
they should be called "quasi contracts" or "constructive contracts."

The following excerpts from Sceva v. True, 53 N.H. 627, are peculiarly
applicable here:

> We regard it as well settled by the cases referred to in the briefs of
> counsel, many of which have been commented on at length by Mr.
> Shirley for the defendant, that an insane person, an idiot, or a per-
> son utterly bereft of all sense and reason by the sudden stroke of an
> accident or disease may be held liable, in assumpsit, for necessaries

furnished to him in good faith while in that unfortunate and helpless condition. And the reasons upon which this rest are too broad, as well as too sensible and humane, to be overborne by any deductions which a refined logic may make from the circumstances that in such cases there can be no contract or promise, in fact, no meeting of the minds of the parties. The cases put it on the ground of an implied contract and by this is not meant, as the defendant's counsel seems to suppose, an actual contract—that is, an actual meeting of the minds of the parties, an actual, mutual understanding, to be inferred from language, acts, and circumstances by the jury—but a contract and promise, said to be implied by the law, where, in point of fact, there was no contract, no mutual understanding, and so no promise. The defendant's counsel says it is usurpation for the court to hold, as a matter of law, that there is a contract and a promise, when all the evidence in the case shows that there was not a contract, nor the semblance of one. It is doubtless a legal fiction, invented and used for the sake of the remedy. If it was originally usurpation, certainly it has now become very inveterate, and firmly fixed in the body of the law.

Illustrations might be multiplied, but enough has been said to show that when a contract or promise implied by law is spoken of, a very different thing is meant from a contract in fact, whether express or tacit. The evidence of an actual contract is generally to be found either in some writing made by the parties, or in verbal communications which passed between them, or in their acts and conduct considered in the light of the circumstances of each particular case. A contract implied by law, on the contrary, rests upon no evidence. It has no actual existence. It is simply a mythical creation of the law. The law says it shall be taken that there was a promise, when in point of fact, there was none. Of course this is not good logic, for the obvious and sufficient reason that it is not true. It is a legal fiction, resting wholly for its support on a plain legal obligation, and a plain legal right.

In its practical application [this body of law] sustains recovery for physicians and nurses who render services for infants, insane persons, and drunkards. 2 Page on Contracts, §§867, 807, 806. And services rendered by physicians to persons unconscious or helpless by reason of injury or sickness are in the same situation as those rendered to persons incapable of contracting, such as the classes above described. The court was therefore right in giving the instruction in question.

2. The defendant sought to require the plaintiff to prove, in addition to the value of the services, the benefit, if any, derived by the deceased from the operation, and alleges error in the court refusing to so instruct the jury. The court was right in refusing to place this burden upon the physicians. The same question was considered in Ladd v. Witte, 116 Wis. 35, 92 N.W. 365 (1902), where the court said: "That is not at all the test. So that a surgical operation be conceived and performed with due skill and care, the price to be paid therefor

does not depend upon the result. The event so generally lies with the forces of nature that all intelligent men know and understand that the surgeon is not responsible therefor. In absence of express agreement, the surgeon, who brings to such a service due skill and care, earns the reasonable and customary price therefor, whether the outcome be beneficial to the patient or the reverse."

3. The court permitted to go to the jury the fact that Mr. Harrison was a bachelor, and that his estate would go to his collateral relatives, and also permitted proof to be made of the value of the estate, which amounted to about $18,500, including $10,000 from accident and life insurance policies.

There is a conflict in the authorities as to whether it is proper to prove the value of the estate of a person for whom medical services were rendered, or the financial condition of the person receiving such services. In Robinson v. Campbell, 47 Iowa 625 (1878), it was said: "There is no more reason why this charge should be enhanced on account of the ability of the defendants to pay than that the merchant should charge them more for a yard of cloth, or the druggist for filling a prescription, or a laborer for a day's work." On the other hand, see Haley's Succession, 50 La. Ann. 840; and Lange v. Kearney, 4 N.Y. Supp. 14, *aff'd*, 127 N.Y. 676, holding that the financial condition of the patient may be considered.

Whatever may be the true principle governing this matter in contracts, the court is of the opinion that the financial condition of a patient cannot be considered where there is no contract and recovery is sustained on a legal fiction which raises a contract in order to afford a remedy which the justice of the case requires.

Evidence in this case proving that it was customary for physicians to graduate their charges by the ability of the patient to pay [would be relevant if this were a true case of implied contract], because the custom would render the financial condition of the patient a factor to be contemplated by both parties when the services were rendered and accepted.

This could not apply to a physician called in an emergency by some bystander to attend a stricken man whom he never saw or heard of before; and certainly the unconscious patient could not, in fact or in law, be held to have contemplated what charges the physician might properly bring against him. While the law may admit such evidence as throwing light upon the contract and indicating what was really in contemplation when it was made, yet a different question is presented when there is no contract to be ascertained or construed, but a mere fiction of law creating a contract where none existed in order that there might be a remedy for a right. This fiction merely requires a reasonable compensation for the services rendered. The services are the same be the patient prince or pauper, and for them the surgeon is entitled to fair compensation for his time, service, and skill. It was therefore error to admit this evidence, and to instruct the jury in the second instruction that in determining what was a reasonable charge they could consider the "ability to pay of the person operated upon."

It was improper to let it go to the jury that Mr. Harrison was a bachelor and that his estate was left to nieces and nephews. This was relevant to no issue in the case, and its effect might well have been prejudicial. While this verdict is no higher than some of the evidence would justify, yet it is much higher than some of the other evidence would justify, and hence it is impossible to say that this was a harmless error.

Judgment is reversed, and cause remanded.

BATTLE and WOOD, JJ., concur in sustaining the recovery, and in holding that it was error to permit the jury to consider the fact that his estate would go to collateral heirs; but they do not concur in holding that it was error to admit evidence of the value of the estate, and instructing that it might be considered in fixing the charge.

———————

Preservation of life and health

1. The fact that Mr. Harrison never recovered consciousness not only repels any inference of implied contract, but—on the assumption that recovery is necessarily in restitution—it invites speculation about the nature and the amount of benefit conferred. Was Mr. Harrison (or his estate) unjustly enriched by the claimants' intervention? If so, how and in what amount? What is the reasoning by which the trial court allowed the jury to hear evidence about the size of Harrison's estate?

2. What if surgery on the unconscious patient had been miraculously successful? According to a more recent decision:

> the plaintiff [in such a case] is entitled to the market value of his services rather than to the benefit that he conferred on the defendant, which might be much greater—for example if the plaintiff physician had saved the defendant's life. The court tries to simulate a competitive market; and in such a market, price is based on the cost to the seller rather than on the subjective value to the buyer, which often is much greater.

ConFold Pacific, Inc. v. Polaris Indus., Inc., 433 F.3d 952 (7th Cir. 2006) (Posner, J.). Is "cost to the seller" the real standard in case like this?

3. In Meriter Hospital, Inc. v. Lester, 1991 WL 236508 (Wis. Ct. App.), the case on appeal was stated as follows:

> On August 25, 1986, Lester was involved a bicycle accident. His front bicycle wheel fell off and Lester crashed to the pavement and was rendered unconscious. Lester was conveyed to the emergency clinic at Meriter, where he was examined by a physician. Lester was semi-conscious during the examination.

The physician recommended that numerous x-rays be taken. While en route to the x-ray room on a gurney, Lester awoke and requested that he be discharged. Over Lester's objections, the x-rays were administered.

After Lester refused to pay his medical bill, Meriter commenced a small claims action. At trial, Lester conceded that he was obligated to Meriter for $96.59, the cost of all non-x-ray related medical services.

The trial court found that Lester was obligated under an implied contract to pay for the x-ray services. Lester appeals.

The hospital had introduced evidence at trial to show that "during the examination Lester was 'confused,' 'asking what happened,' did not know the date or the day of the week, and could not recall his telephone number." What result on appeal?

4. In the famous contracts case of Webb v. McGowin, 27 Ala. App. 82, 168 So. 196 (1935), Webb performed a heroic rescue of McGowin—jumping from an upper story of the lumber mill where he worked to divert a 75-pound pine block that was about to fall on his employer. McGowin was saved from harm, but Webb was crippled for life. To show his gratitude, McGowin promised Webb a lifetime pension of $15 every two weeks. Payments were made faithfully for more than 8 years thereafter, but—3 weeks after McGowin's death—his executors repudiated the obligation and refused to pay Webb anything more.

Suppose that McGowin had made no payments and no promise. Does Webb have a restitution claim against McGowin on the analogy of *Cotnam v. Wisdom*? Why or why not?

Quantum meruit and the "common counts"

Besides introducing the subject of restitution for unrequested services, *Cotnam v. Wisdom* focuses attention on a cause of action in restitution called *quantum meruit*. Recall from Chapter 1 that the legal side of restitution originated when the courts began to allow plaintiffs to plead—and to recover on the basis of—*fictitious promises*: promises that the defendants had never made (and that everyone knew the defendants had never made), but which furnished a basis for liabilities the courts considered appropriate. The fictitious-promise pleadings that were most often used, because they fit recurring factual scenarios, came to be called "the common counts." Lawyers no longer refer to "the common counts" in the aggregate, but the individual causes of action comprised within this description are still sometimes referred to by their traditional names. The best-known of these are probably the following:

Shorthand name	Meaning
Quantum meruit	Plaintiff performed services for defendant [this much was real], *for which defendant promised to pay what the services were worth* [the promise was fictitious].
Money had and received	Defendant received money from plaintiff, or money from a third party to which plaintiff was entitled [real], *which defendant promised to repay or pay over to plaintiff* [fiction].
Money paid	Plaintiff paid money to a third person for defendant's benefit [real], *for which defendant promised to reimburse plaintiff* [fiction].
Quantum valebant	Plaintiff delivered goods at defendant's request [real], *for which defendant promised to pay plaintiff what the goods were worth* [fiction].

As previously mentioned, part of the problem with these fictitious-promise pleadings is that they invited confusion between transactions that subsequent generations of lawyers would view as analytically distinct: what we call "implied contracts," on the one hand, and what we view as enrichment-based (not promissory) liability, on the other. *Quantum meruit*—the most popular of all the common counts, and a term in common professional use today—has been particularly susceptible to this confusion. On the one hand, if A goes to work for B under circumstances where A would reasonably expect to be paid, yet the parties never discuss payment, modern contract law makes it easy to conclude that A and B have formed an implied contract. If A does the work and B refuses to pay, B is in breach of this contract. In such a case, A's lawsuit against B is likely to be styled an "action in *quantum meruit*"—by which everyone understands that A is claiming the reasonable value of the work done at B's request. Yet A's claim on these facts is *not* a claim in restitution, because it is clearly based on an enforceable contract. *Cotnam v. Wisdom* is the classic illustration of the converse case. The doctors' claim will also be styled *quantum meruit* (if anyone gives it a label), and they are still seeking the reasonable value of their services; but this form of *quantum meruit* has to be a claim in restitution, because for one reason or another—here, the unconscious patient—it is impossible to explain it as a liability in contract.

So *quantum meruit* remains the accepted name for two fundamentally different kinds of liability. This equivocation causes significant confusion in the case law, because statements that might be true about one kind of *quantum meruit* case are often applied unthinkingly to the other kind—by judges as well as lawyers. It is rare that the distinction between the two kinds of *quantum meruit* is correctly drawn, but it can be done:

> This conclusion might be stated thus: The claimants are entitled to recover on a quantum meruit basis. But "quantum meruit" is ambiguous;

it may mean (1) that there is a contract "implied in fact" to pay the reasonable value of the services, or (2) that, to prevent unjust enrichment, the claimant may recover on a quasi-contract (an "as if" contract) for that reasonable value. It has been suggested that the latter is a rule-of-thumb measure of damages adopted in quasi contract cases where the actual unjust enrichment or benefit to the defendant is too difficult to prove; see Costigan, *Implied-In-Fact Contracts*, 33 Harv. Law Rev. [1920] 376, 387.

The confusion involved in the use of the old phrase "implied contracts" to label both those "implied in fact" and those "implied in law" (now called "quasi contracts") has not been entirely obliterated. Nor is it easy to eradicate. . . .

Martin v. Campanaro, 156 F.2d 127, 130 n.5 (2d Cir. 1946) (Frank, J.).

Preservation of property

1. In Chase v. Corcoran, 106 Mass. 286 (1871), the facts were stated as follows:

> The plaintiff, while engaged with his own boats in the Mystic River, within the ebb and flow of the tide, found the defendant's boat adrift, with holes in the bottom and the keel nearly demolished, and in danger of sinking or being crushed between the plaintiff's boats and the piles of a bridge, unless the plaintiff had saved it. The plaintiff secured the boat, attached a rope to it, towed it ashore, fastened it to a post, and, after putting up notices in public places in the nearest town, and making other inquiries, and no owner appearing, took it to his own barn, stowed it there for two winters, and during the intervening summer made repairs (which were necessary to preserve the boat) and for its better preservation put it in the water, fastened to a wharf, and directed the wharfinger to deliver it to any one who should prove ownership and pay the plaintiff's expenses about it. The defendant afterwards claimed the boat; the plaintiff refused to deliver it unless the defendant paid him the expenses of taking care of it; and the defendant then took the boat by a writ of replevin, without paying the plaintiff anything. This action is brought to recover money paid by the plaintiff for moving and repairing the boat, and compensation for his own care and trouble in keeping and repairing the same, amounting to twenty-six dollars in all.
>
> The plaintiff testified, without objection, that the boat, when found by him, was worth five dollars.

Plaintiff was allowed to recover. What if the present value of the boat had been less than $26?

2. Compare Glenn v. Savage, 14 Or. 567, 13 P. 442 (1887), as summarized by the *Restatement*:

> Observing in Owner's absence that property of Owner is threatened by an approaching flood, Neighbor supplies labor and equipment to move Owner's goods to higher ground. Neighbor's services have a reasonable value of $2,000, and Owner is thereby spared a loss of $20,000. Six months later, following a business dispute, Owner sues Neighbor for $5,000 on a promissory note. Neighbor asserts a counterclaim for services rendered in the earlier emergency. The trier of fact determines that Neighbor had no intention to charge for his services at the time and that he decided to seek compensation only in reaction to Owner's later demands. Because Neighbor intended to act gratuitously, Neighbor has no claim in restitution.

R3RUE §21, Illustration 8. According to the court, "The law will never permit a friendly act, or such as was intended to be an act of kindness or benevolence, to be afterwards converted into a pecuniary demand." 14 Or. at 577, 13 P. at 448. Is this an appropriate limitation on restitution for rescues?

3. The law of sales recognizes various circumstances in which one party is under a duty to care for another's property, in the absence of any contract to specify who pays for what. When a "merchant buyer" rightfully rejects a shipment of goods, the buyer may be under an affirmative duty to care for them (and eventually to sell them) for the seller's account. Such a buyer "has a security interest"—in other words, the buyer is given an equitable lien—for expenses reasonably incurred in the "care and custody" (and subsequent sale) of the rejected goods. See UCC §§2-603, 2-711(3). Remember that Buyer and Seller are already involved in a dispute about the conformity of the goods to the contract, with the result that Seller is almost certainly not requesting the rejecting Buyer to look after the goods, nor is Seller promising to reimburse Buyer for his expenditures. The effect of the U.C.C. is that Buyer's unrequested services in preserving and disposing of Seller's property are a benefit that Seller cannot refuse. What explains the law's relatively sympathetic attitude to the restitution claim of a rejecting "merchant buyer"?

A rightfully rejecting buyer who resells the seller's goods for more than the amount of the buyer's security interest—*i.e.*, the amount of the buyer's restitution claim—"must account [to the seller] for any excess." U.C.C. §2-706(6). Assume however that the problem is the other way around: the buyer *wrongfully* rejects the goods (in other words, repudiates the contract), and the seller resells them to another buyer—but at a higher price. In that event, "The seller is not liable to the buyer for any profit made on any resale." *Id.* What accounts for the difference?

4. "On land the person who rushes in to save another's property from damage is an officious intermeddler . . . At sea the person who saves property receives a reward which is generously computed in light of 'the fundamental

public policy at the basis of awards of salvage—the encouragement of seamen to render prompt service in future emergencies.'" Gilmore & Black, *The Law of Admiralty* § 8-1, at 521 (2nd ed. 1975) (quoting Kimes v. United States, 207 F.2d 60, 63 (2d Cir. 1953)). The comparison is overdrawn (see *Chase v. Corcoran, supra*), but it contains more than a grain of truth. What might account for the law's more generous attitude toward unrequested intervention to protect property at sea than on land?

5. Suppose that effective intervention by quick-thinking Bystander prevents harm to some property insured against casualty loss by Insurer. Might Bystander have a claim in restitution for the benefit thereby conferred on Insurer? The *Restatement* offers the following rather tentative illustration:

> Contractor is performing excavation for a building project. Subcontractor is working on an unrelated part of the job. Insurer is Contractor's liability insurer. Observing Contractor at work on a hillside, Subcontractor notices that adjoining property is in danger of immediate collapse unless shored up by emergency means. Acting with minutes to spare, Subcontractor places his own heavy trucks where they will support the earthwork. Subcontractor's trucks are destroyed, but the threatened buildings are preserved. Subcontractor claims reimbursement from Insurer on a theory of restitution. The court finds that Subcontractor's emergency action prevented damage to adjoining property; that Contractor would have been liable to the property owners for the resulting damage; and that the loss would have been covered by Insurer's policy. The value of Subcontractor's trucks was $50,000; the covered loss would have been at least $500,000. Given the court's reconstruction of the sequence of events avoided by Subcontractor's intervention, Subcontractor has a claim against Insurer for $50,000. If this reasoning is rejected as overly speculative, Subcontractor's restitution claim fails.

R3RUE §21, Illustration 9. Actual authority, though, is sparse or nonexistent. What if the person whose heroic and effective intervention prevents damage to property is the owner of the property and the policyholder? These questions are explored in Levmore, *Obligation or Restitution for Best Efforts*, 67 S. Cal. L. Rev. 1411 (1994).

———————

Farnsworth, *Restitution* 44-49 (2014):

[In a case like *Cotnam v. Wisdom*] allowing a doctor to recover at his market rate is sensible enough, but what if the provider of the emergency services has no market rate? Suppose he was a passerby who does not normally provide medical treatment to anyone and for whose services no market would exist. Valuation of such treatment is difficult and prone to error, and the law deals with these problems by simply denying any recovery to the nonprofessional rescuer. The result is sometimes defended as well by saying it is unclear whether amateur efforts at rescue generally do more good than harm (sometimes such attempts endanger both parties), so the law is reluctant to push for them. When viewed that way, the rule in restitution is like the tort doctrine that refuses to impose a duty on people to rescue strangers from distress, even if they seem able to do it easily.

Acts to save property in an emergency, as when I make heroic efforts to save your boat rather than your life, are governed by the same general principles just shown, but their application is a bit more complicated. As ever, the first question is whether the facts excuse the plaintiff's failure to obtain consent in advance. When property is at stake, the justification for bypassing the owner often involves a transaction cost that may be hard to prove: it is not feasible to identify the owner of the property or to contact him. When it's simply the owner of a house who is out of town, that element may be easy enough to satisfy. But property takes various forms, and sometimes the feasibility of approaching its owner can become controversial.

Thus in *Trott v. Dean Witter & Co.*, 438 F. Supp. 842 (S.D.N.Y. 1977), an employee of Dean Witter invited Trott to join a scheme to defraud the firm. Trott did not report the matter to Dean Witter because he worried that he would not be believed (he did not work there himself) and because he feared reprisals from the employee, whom he thought was involved in organized crime. Instead Trott went along with the scheme until he had solid evidence of a crime, *then* reported it to Dean Witter and to the government. The corrupt employee went to prison; Trott went into a witness protection program with a notably reduced income. Trott brought a restitution claim against Dean Witter. It failed. The problem was not that Trott was an amateur rescuer. As noted a moment ago, courts are willing to allow recovery by amateurs who rescue property (in many such cases there may be no relevant professionals to whom one can defer). Nor was there any doubt that Trott had saved Dean Witter a great deal of money—had in fact "rescued" the firm's property. But the court held that Trott did not have a satisfactory excuse for failing to talk to Dean Witter before undertaking to collect the evidence. Since Trott had a chance to proceed consensually but didn't, he was simply a volunteer.

Rescues of property can also lead to restitution claims of a different kind. My boat runs into yours, which begins to sink. A rescuer arrives and tows your boat to safety. The rescuer has a good restitution claim against me because he reduced my liability to you; if your boat had sunk, my exposure to damages would have been much greater. Claims of this kind are rare but interesting. An example is *McNeilab, Inc. v. North River Ins. Co.*, 645 F. Supp. 5525 (D.N.J. 1986), where the claimant was a pharmaceutical company that recalled one of its products at great expense. Had it not done so, it would have been subject to tort liabilities that its insurer would have been obliged to cover. Should the insurer therefore be liable in restitution for the expense of the recall? This case, like most others of its type, turned largely on interpretation of the contract between the insurer and the insured. Contracts of that kind naturally impose certain duties on the insured to avoid running up costs that the insurer will have to pay. One question in the pharmaceutical case was whether the efforts taken were within that duty or beyond it. Yet even if they were beyond the requirements of the contract, the court was not inclined to award any recovery to the insured. The plaintiff here, like the plaintiff in the Dean Witter case, had plenty of time to discuss its course of action with the beneficiary of its "rescue"—the insurance company—before going through with it. Those chances for a voluntary deal scotch the claim for collection when the plaintiff proceeds involuntarily.

B.   PERFORMANCE OF ANOTHER'S DUTY

Greenspan v. Slate
12 N.J. 426, 97 A.2d 390 (1953)

VANDERBILT, C.J.

I.   *The Facts and the Issue.*

Barbara Slate, the 17-year-old daughter of the defendants, injured a foot while playing basketball at high school. Within two or three days it became exceedingly swollen and conspicuously discolored so that she could walk on it only with the greatest difficulty and pain. Her parents, thinking it nothing more than a sprain, declined to provide her with medical aid. The plaintiff, Garfield, a member of the bar of this State, discovered her plight by chance, when she was on a visit to his home in company with Berkley Badgett, his housekeeper's son, who was courting her.

Mr. Garfield promptly sent young Badgett, his mother and Barbara to the nearby office of the plaintiff, Dr. Sidney Greenspan, who discovered from X-ray plates he made that a bone of Barbara's foot had been fractured. He applied a cast which Barbara wore for about a month until it was removed by Dr. Greenspan. Meantime she used crutches. Barbara lived at home with her parents and the presence of the cast and her use of crutches were thus known to them. Clearly the broken bone that was causing much swelling, high discoloration and great pain necessitating the taking of X-ray plates, the application of a cast for a month and the use of crutches did present an emergency. The testimony of Dr. Greenspan that permanent injury would have ensued if there had not been proper medical care and attention at the time is uncontradicted.

On the completion of his services Dr. Greenspan rendered a bill to the parents of $45, which they have refused to pay. Mr. Garfield thereupon brought suit against them on behalf of Dr. Greenspan or himself in the alternative. At the end of the plaintiffs' case the trial court granted the defendants' motion to dismiss on the ground that Dr. Greenspan had acted without any express authorization from the defendants and that the proofs were insufficient in the circumstances to establish an implied authorization by them. On appeal the Appellate Division of the Superior Court, considering itself bound by earlier decisions in our courts, reluctantly affirmed the judgment below. Because of the public importance of the question presented, we granted certification.

The question before us is whether or not the parents of an infant child are liable, in the absence of a contract, express or implied in fact, for necessaries furnished their child in an emergency.

II.   *The Conflicting Views at Law and in Equity.*

According to Blackstone, "the duty of parents to provide for the maintenance of their children is a principle of natural law." 1 Bl.Comm. 447. Blackstone waxes eloquent over this principle of "natural law" and quite properly so when the relations of parent and child are normal, but unconvincingly in the only cases with which the law should be concerned, i.e., when the parent fails to perform his natural duty. Neither the child nor any third party who ventured to supply the child with his necessaries had any cause of action against the parents to enforce the duty of support which Blackstone termed "a principle of natural law." The utter inadequacy of the common law in this stage of its development is especially manifest in meeting emergencies involving the life or limb of a child.

A child's need in these circumstances is quite as great as that of a neglected wife, but his rights and remedies are far less effective than hers, for she has an absolute right to pledge her husband's credit for necessaries, even though there is no agency in fact existing such as the common law required in the case of a child to permit recovery. The law imposes the obligation on her husband for the benefit of the deserted wife without regard to whether or not there was any agency in fact, Strawbridge & Clothier v. Sigle, 73 N.J.L. 419, 63 A. 865 (1906). The quasi-contractual nature of the husband's duty to a neglected wife is demonstrated by the fact that at common law it survives her death so as to include her funeral expenses, Mondock v. Gennrich, 19 N.J. Misc. 499, 21 A.2d 611 (Dist. Ct. 1941).

The impact of these shortcomings of the common law remedy with respect to the maintenance of a child in comparison with that available to a neglected wife inevitably led the law courts to hold, in an effort to achieve a measure of justice, that "the authority of an infant to bind the father for necessaries may be inferred from *slight* evidence." Freeman v. Robinson, 38 N.J.L. 383, 384 (1876). But any such artificial basis for a fundamental doctrine as "inferences from slight evidence" is not only unsound in principle but ineffective in operation, because it does not reach the cases where no express promise exists and where there is no "slight evidence" from which to infer a promise, and the cases not so reached are the ones where in simple justice a legal right and an adequate remedy are most needed. There is quite as great necessity for the imposition of a quasi-contractual obligation by operation of law in favor of a neglected child as there is in the case of a neglected wife.

The Court of Chancery within the limit of its jurisdiction was not content to regard the father's duty as a mere principle of natural law, but it has sought to enforce it as a matter of equity. [Chief Justice Vanderbilt proceeds to a lengthy examination of the existing New Jersey authorities—legal, equitable, and statutory—on the issue of a parent's duty to furnish a child with "necessaries." His most surprising conclusion, for a reader today, is that as recently as 1953 the question had not received a definitive answer.]

III.   *The Preferable Rule.*

As we have seen, there are no precedents in our courts of last resort so we are free to choose between the common law rule and the Chancery principle in deciding the instant case. Normal instincts of humanity and plain common honesty as well as the substantial weight of judicial decisions in this country, the uniform rule of the civil law in European countries, and the unanimous views of the text writers and the Restatement of the Law all combine to demonstrate the superiority of the equitable rule. It shocks one's sensibilities to think that the common law would permit a wealthy parent to do no more than respond to the minimum demands of the Poor Law, while he himself is living in affluence. It reflects a point of view which is utterly inconsistent with the common feelings of humanity, and which fortunately is found in relatively few instances of unnatural conduct, yet it is against those instances that the law must safeguard the offspring of an abnormal human being.

The principles governing the application of the rule are set forth in three sections of the Restatement of the Law of Restitution (1937):

§112. A person who without mistake, coercion or request has unconditionally conferred a benefit upon another is not entitled to restitution, except where the benefit was conferred under circumstances making such action necessary for the protection of the interests of the other or of third persons.

§113. A person who has performed the noncontractual duty of another by supplying a third person with necessaries which in violation of such duty the other had failed to supply, although acting without the other's knowledge or consent, is entitled to restitution therefor from the other if he acted unofficiously and with intent to charge therefor.

§114. A person who has performed the duty of another by supplying a third person with necessaries, although acting without the other's knowledge or consent, is entitled to restitution from the other therefor if (a) he acted unofficiously and with intent to charge therefor, and (b) the things or services supplied were immediately necessary to prevent serious bodily harm to or suffering by such person.

IV. *Services Rendered in an Emergency.*

There can be no doubt that the physician plaintiff comes within the terms of sections 113 and 114 of the Restatement of the Law of Restitution above quoted. The defendants were under an obligation as part of their duty to support and educate their daughter, to provide her with medical services both under normal circumstances and in emergencies.

The evidence is uncontradicted that an emergency existed. The parents had refused to provide their child with medical attention with the result that permanent injury would have ensued but for the immediate treatment rendered by the physician plaintiff. Clearly they knew that the services were necessary and that a physician would expect payment for his services. Here the defendants permitted their daughter not only to use the cast and crutches for a month, but to return to the doctor at the end of the month to have the cast removed. Having retained the benefit of the physician plaintiff's services and permitted their daughter to return to him for further services, they are in no position in the circumstances of the case to complain that he acted without notice to them. He did not act officiously, and as a physician in practice of his profession he naturally intended to charge for his services. All the necessary elements are present to impose on the defendants the legal obligation to pay for medical expenses rendered to their child in an emergency.

The judgment below is reversed. Judgment will be entered here in favor of the plaintiff, Dr. Sidney Greenspan, for $45.

For reversal: Chief Justice VANDERBILT, and Justices OLIPHANT, BURLING, JACOBS and BRENNAN — 5.

For affirmance: Justices HEHER and WACHENFELD — 2.

Is defendant under a duty?

1. It is startling to think that a New Jersey parent's obligation to support a minor child could be seriously questioned in 1953. Do you suppose that Justices Heher and Wachenfeld disagreed with this part of the court's opinion? What would be the gist of their dissenting opinion, if they had written one?

2. In Gulley v. Gulley, 570 P.2d 127 (Utah 1977), the facts were stated as follows:

> Plaintiff Leora M. Gulley and the defendant were divorced in August 1967. The decree awarded custody of four children to the plaintiff, together with $50 per month support for each child and $50 per month as alimony. Defendant made regular support payments until September 1970. At that time he entered into a contract with his ex-wife Leora M. Gulley whereby he agreed to pay her $10,000, which was to be prepayment of all of his obligations under the decree, in return for her release of those obligations.

A little over two years later, in November 1972, Leora appears to have become financially distressed. She then applied to the plaintiff Department of Social Services and she was approved for and has received public assistance for the support of herself and the four children since that time. In June 1976, the State of Utah initiated this action under the provisions of Section 78-45-9, U.C.A., 1953, seeking reimbursement from the defendant for assistance it had provided to the extent defendant had been ordered to pay such support under the decree. As a defense, the defendant pleaded performance of the above-mentioned agreement as a release of his obligations.

The court held that, although Guy's obligation to Leora to pay alimony could be liquidated by contract, a father could not be released by contract from the obligation to support his minor children.

Guy Gulley insisted—and some dissenting judges agreed—that his $10,000 represented a *prepayment* of several years' future obligations under the divorce decree, not a liquidation and settlement. Even if the purported contract was ineffective to liquidate his child-support obligation, doesn't his payment of $10,000 count for anything? (Is he entitled to any credit against his liability to the Department of Social Services?)

3. In Sommers v. Putnam County Bd. of Educ., 113 Ohio St. 177, 148 N.E. 682 (1925), a school board was required by statute to provide transportation to the nearest high school for any qualified student living more than four miles away. Father requested that school board provide transportation for his children; school board refused; father drove them himself and sent school board a bill. Restitution was granted:

An act of beneficial intervention in the discharge of another's legal obligation, which results in a quasi contractual obligation, must contain the following elements: The obligation must be of such a nature that actual and prompt performance thereof is of grave public concern; the person upon whom the obligation rests must have failed or refused with knowledge of the facts to perform the obligation; or it must reasonably appear that it is impossible to perform it; and the person who intervenes must, under the circumstances, be not a mere intermeddler but a proper person to perform the duty. Woodward, Law of Quasi Contracts, p. 310; Forsyth v. Ganson, 5 Wend. (N. Y.) 558; Rundell v. Bentley, 53 Hun (N. Y.) 272.

It is plain that the actual performance of this duty of making high school branches accessible to children is a matter of grave public concern. It is of the utmost importance that the coming race receive school training. The moral sense of the community requires that this obligation be actually performed, and the school boards, upon whom the obligation rested, failed to perform the duty.

Passing to the question of the appropriateness of the intervention of the parent, the father was surely the proper person to perform the obligation.

It is his obligation to see that his children attend school, and the fact that the transportation has not been supplied cannot be pleaded as an excuse for his failure to send such children to school, or as an excuse for the failure of the children to attend school.

Id. at 184-185, at 148 N.E. at 684.

Compare the facts of Hurdis Realty, Inc. v. Town of N. Providence, 121 R.I. 275, 397 A.2d 896 (1979), where a backed-up sewer line threatened to damage Owner's property. Maintaining the sewer was Town's legal responsibility. Town's sewer inspector was unable to see any problem, and Town—relying on the inspector's report—refused to do anything. Owner hired his own contractor to locate the blockage and make the necessary repairs, which required excavating a public street 100 feet beyond Owner's property line. Town refused to pay the bill, but Owner recovered in restitution.

4. Modern disputes about status-based obligations sometimes reflect concerns with health-care finance. The case Jersey Shore Medical Center v. Estate of Baum, 84 N.J. 137, 417 A.2d 1003 (1980), presented typical facts:

Sidney Baum, defendant's late husband, died at the hospital after a long illness which exhausted his Medicaid benefits and left a balance due the hospital of $25,709.50. He owned no assets at the time of his death, except his interest as tenant by the entirety with Mrs. Baum in their home, and, presumably, miscellaneous personal assets of minimal value. His estate was insolvent. Mrs. Baum owns no assets of any value other than her home, which is assessed at $25,200. She never agreed to pay her husband's hospital bill.

Hospital sued Mrs. Baum to recover payment of its bill. Mrs. Baum was not liable in contract, because she never promised to pay; nor was she liable in restitution, because at common law—and in New Jersey until this case was decided—while husbands had an obligation to support their wives, wives were under no corresponding duty to support their husbands. Considering this distinction antiquated and indefensible, the court announced that each spouse was henceforth under a duty to support the other—although the new rule would be applied prospectively, so that Mrs. Baum was not liable.

Courts in most states have likewise decided that the common-law duty of support—often referred to as the "doctrine of necessaries"—should be extended to work both ways. Others resist the implications of such a rule, at least where the issue is a hospital's claim in restitution against a surviving spouse. In Medical Center Hospital of Vermont v. Lorrain, 165 Vt. 12, 675 A.2d 1326 (1996), the court avoided imposing liability on a widow for her husband's medical care by announcing that—from that day forward—neither spouse in Vermont was under a common-law duty to support the other:

In truth, extension of the doctrine serves creditors' rights, not spousal support rights.

. . . Virtually all of the necessaries doctrine cases concern hospitals or clinics seeking to collect debts resulting from medical services rendered to spouses, often during a last illness. The public policy issues surrounding these circumstances are complex, and are best taken up by the Legislature in family-expense statutes, creditors' rights laws, or even comprehensive health care legislation. The Legislature, not this Court, is better equipped to assemble the facts and determine the appropriate remedies in an arena fraught with social policy involving the law of property, the institution of marriage, and the distribution of the costs of health care expenses.

Id. at 15-16, 675 A.2d at 1329.

5. In St. Barnabas Medical Center v. County of Essex, 111 N.J. 67, 543 A.2d 34 (1988), the facts were stated as follow:

On July 13, 1982, Jessie Williams was committed to the Essex County Jail Annex, located in Caldwell, to begin serving a fifteen-day sentence. On July 16, Williams set himself on fire and required emergency treatment. Corrections officers transported Williams to Saint Barnabas because of its specialized burn unit. The officers apparently told the hospital staff that they had brought Williams from the Essex County Jail, and gave them a phone number to call for information. However, there is no evidence of any discussion concerning responsibility for his medical bills.

Three days later, on July 19, 1982, Ray Grimm of Saint Barnabas phoned Elizabeth Neff in the Jail Annex's business office to confirm Williams' status as an inmate and to ascertain whether the County would be responsible for the treatment costs. Earlier that day, on the County's motion, the remaining eight days of Williams' sentence had been vacated by the Newark Municipal Court. Accordingly, Neff informed Grimm that Williams was being "released," but acknowledged that the County would pay for the hospitalization costs incurred thus far, from Williams' admission to the hospital on the sixteenth through the end of the day.

After roughly seven weeks of treatment, Williams was released from the hospital on September 2, 1982; the total cost of his treatment and hospitalization came to $53,725.59, and an invoice in that amount was forwarded to the County. Consistent with its stated position, the County refused to acknowledge liability except for the first four days of Williams' treatment, an amount stipulated to be $5,401.

Saint Barnabas commenced this action against Williams and Essex County for the total cost of treatment. Williams was never served, and the case against him was subsequently dismissed without prejudice.

Jailers are under a duty to provide medical care to their prisoners. What was the extent of County's liability in restitution to Saint Barnabas? (It appears that Williams was "released" from the last 8 days of his 15-day term, with that portion of the sentence being "vacated," only because he would be hospitalized for the period in question.)

6. Liability for "clean-up costs" incurred by public agencies or other intervenors in environmental emergencies such as train wrecks or oil spills, in cases not governed by statute, has an obvious basis in unjust enrichment. Claims for "emergency services" become controversial, by contrast, when the defendant—although concededly involved with the situation that requires remediation—could not have been held legally responsible at the time the intervention takes place. The reason this situation might arise is normally that a "clean up" takes place after the limitations period applicable to defendant's tort has already expired.

Thus while it is understandable that New York City (for instance) would seek reimbursement for its costs incurred in remediating hazardous conditions in public schools and city-owned housing—and equally understandable that the New York courts would want to accommodate such a claim—the desired outcome has been difficult to square with any acknowledged basis of liability. For example, in City of New York v. Keene Corp., 132 Misc. 2d 745, 505 N.Y.S.2d 782 (Sup. Ct. 1986), the court approved the City's restitution claim to recover the costs of removing asbestos from school buildings, citing a further section of the 1937 *Restatement* (following the sequence we saw quoted in *Greenspan v. Slate*):

> §115. A person who has performed the duty of another, by supplying things or services, although acting without the other's knowledge or consent, is entitled to restitution from the other if (a) he acted unofficiously and with intent to charge therefor, and (b) the things or services supplied were immediately necessary to satisfy the requirements of public decency, health, or safety.

[*Cf.* R3RUE §22.] The court assumed that asbestos abatement was "immediately necessary" in the required sense, and that "in equity the manufacturer has the duty to remove asbestos if proven hazardous." But is there a "duty" that will support a restitution claim if a direct action against the manufacturer would be barred by the statute of limitations? (Does the court's reference to "equity" take care of this difficulty?) Much of the asbestos in New York school buildings had been sold and installed decades earlier. The same point arises when the restitution claim is characterized as one for "indemnity," as we see in the following section.

C.   INDEMNITY AND CONTRIBUTION

Yellow Cab of D.C., Inc. v. Dreslin
181 F.2d 626 (D.C. Cir. 1950)

PROCTOR, Circuit Judge.

The question here concerns contribution between tort-feasors where the judgment creditor is the wife of the tort-feasor against whom contribution is sought.

A taxicab of appellant (hereinafter called "Cab Co."), driven by its agent, and an automobile, driven by appellee (hereafter called "Dreslin"), collided. Dreslin's wife and others in his car were injured. They sued the Cab Co. for damages. Dreslin joined with them, claiming for loss of consortium, medical expenses for Mrs. Dreslin and damages to his automobile. Among its defenses, the Cab Co. pleaded contributory negligence of Dreslin. It also cross-claimed against him for damages to the taxicab and for contribution for any sums recovered by the other plaintiffs against it. The jury's verdict established the collision to have been caused by concurrent negligent operation of the two cars. Accordingly judgments for varying amounts were entered in favor of all plaintiffs except Dreslin. In addition a declaratory judgment was entered allowing the Cab Co. contribution against Dreslin upon the several judgments except that of Mrs. Dreslin. This was disallowed because, as the Court held, "the right to contribution arises from a joint liability," and as Dreslin was not liable in tort to his wife, there was no joint liability between him and the Cab Co. as to her. This appeal is confined to that single question.

We agree with the conclusion of the trial court. Neither husband nor wife is liable for tortious acts by one against the other. That is the common law rule. It prevails today in the District of Columbia, unaffected by 30 D.C. Code (1940) § 208.

The right of contribution arises out of a common liability. The rule "hinges on the doctrine that general principles of justice require that in the case of a common obligation, the discharge of it by one of the obligors without proportionate payment from the other, gives the latter an advantage to which he is not equitably entitled." George's Radio, Inc., v. Capital Transit Co., 1942, 75 U.S. App. D.C. 187, 189, 126 F.2d 219, 221. Contribution, then, depends upon joint liability. An injured party plaintiff in the suit from which a right of contribution develops must have had a cause of action against the party from whom contribution is sought. Here there was no liability by Dreslin to his wife, — no right to action against him and the Cab Co. [jointly], hence nothing to which a right of contribution could attach.

The argument that it would be inequitable to allow Mrs. Dreslin to be "enriched" at the sole expense of the Cab Co., permitting her husband, equally at fault, to escape any of the burden, overlooks the fact that preservation of domestic peace and felicity is the policy upon which the rule of immunity between husband and wife is based. Koontz v. Messer, 1935, 320 Pa. 487, 181 A. 792. The judgment is Affirmed.

Obligations between joint obligors

1. Obligations of indemnity or contribution arise when two parties (A and B) are jointly and severally liable to a third (C), and one of the two (A or B) discharges more than his share of the common liability. Calculating the "share" for this purpose requires an analysis of the relation between A and B and of the circumstances leading to their joint liability to C. For example, if A's liability to C is purely vicarious—as where A, a non-negligent employer, is held liable for the torts of B, a negligent employee—A would be entitled to "indemnification" from B: in other words, to have B reimburse the entire amount that A has been obliged to pay C. By contrast, if A and B are joint tortfeasors whose responsibility for C's damages is assessed at 50/50, and A is required to satisfy 100% of C's judgment, A would be entitled to "contribution" from B in the amount of 50% of what A has been required to pay C. As these simple examples suggest, the difference between indemnity and contribution is the difference between liability for the whole of an obligation and liability for a proportionate share.

2. Claims for indemnity or contribution are familiar in a variety of contexts, and lawyers do not often stop to analyze what the basis of such a liability (*i.e.*, between A and B) might be. The question is complicated by the fact that the A/B claim might in some cases be based on a contract between them, express or implied, or even on a tort—to be distinguished from the tort for which both A and B are jointly liable to C. Still, the more frequent basis of the A/B liability is unjust enrichment: "I was compelled to perform [what was in reality] your obligation, therefore you should reimburse me." But such a claim is not coherent except to the extent that B was actually obligated, as the *Restatement* is at pains to emphasize:

Restatement Third, Restitution and Unjust Enrichment

§23. PERFORMANCE OF A JOINT OBLIGATION (INDEMNITY AND CONTRIBUTION)

(1) If the claimant renders to a third person a performance for which claimant and defendant are jointly and severally liable, the claimant is entitled to restitution from the defendant as necessary to prevent unjust enrichment.

(2) There is unjust enrichment in such a case to the extent that

(a) the effect of the claimant's intervention is to reduce an enforceable obligation of the defendant to the third person, and

(b) as between the claimant and the defendant, the obligation discharged (or the part thereof for which the claimant seeks restitution) was primarily the responsibility of the defendant.

---

3. The traditional interspousal tort immunity that blocked contribution in *Yellow Cab v. Dreslin* is a thing of the past, having been limited or abrogated in most jurisdictions, including D.C. (For a comprehensive survey of this development see Bozman v. Bozman, 376 Md. 461, 830 A.2d 450 (2003).) But the case nicely illustrates one of the basic limits to an action for indemnity or contribution based on unjust enrichment. The idea is sometimes summarized in the expression, "No indemnity (or no contribution) without liability." We can assume that A and B are joint tortfeasors who have injured third-party C. Payment by A to C confers no benefit on B if B (for whatever reason) was under no enforceable obligation to C. An interspousal immunity between B and C is only one of the reasons why B might escape liability, as the following notes will illustrate.

4. The case of Western Steamship Lines, Inc. v. San Pedro Peninsula Hospital, 8 Cal. 4th 100, 876 P.2d 1062 (1994), can be summarized (and simplified) as follows:

Employer and Hospital are found jointly and severally liable to Employee for $5 million in noneconomic damages suffered as the result of an industrial accident, exacerbated by inappropriate medical care. The defendants' proportionate liability is fixed at 20 percent for Employer and 80 percent for Hospital. Employer pays the judgment and seeks contribution from Hospital in the amount of $4 million. By statute, a healthcare provider's liability to an injured person for noneconomic damages cannot exceed $250,000.

R3RUE §23, Illustration 11. What is the extent of Hospital's contribution liability to Employer?

5. Consistent with the logic of the claim in restitution, a cause of action for indemnity or contribution does not accrue (for limitations purposes) until A pays to C the first dollar that exceeds A's share of the parties' joint liability. What if A pays C at a time when C's direct action against B would be barred by the applicable statute of limitations?

After it discovered the health hazards associated with lead-based paint, the City of New York incurred massive costs in removing old paint from city-owned

apartment buildings, many of which it had acquired when the building owners stopped paying their property taxes. With no other defendants available, the
City sought reimbursement from the paint manufacturers. Applicable statutes
of limitations would have barred a direct suit against the manufacturers by anyone—such as paint buyers, building owners, or tenants—based on warranty or on
product liability in tort. That being the case, the manufacturers argued that they
could not be liable to the City on a theory of indemnity. The courts disagreed:

> [I]t is the breach by defendant of an underlying *duty* owed to a third party,
> even if an action based thereon by that party against defendant is time
> barred, that is critical to a plaintiff's right to bring an indemnity action
> to recover the damages which plaintiff was caused to pay as a result of
> defendant's breach of its duty to the third party.

City of New York v. Lead Industries Ass'n, Inc., 222 App. Div. 2d 119, 127, 644
N.Y.S.2d 919, 924 (1996). The idea seems to be that B's liability to indemnify
A is based on B's indirect *injury* to A, rather than (as in the orthodox view) B's
indirect enrichment at A's expense. The New York Court of Appeals had previously explained that:

> Often, the absence of direct liability to plaintiff [on the part of the party from
> whom contribution is sought] is merely the result of a special defense, such
> as the Statute of Limitations or the exclusivity of workers' compensation,
> and not because defendant was free of fault. In such cases, we have held
> that codefendants may seek contribution from the joint wrongdoer, despite
> the wrongdoer's own defense to plaintiff's claim. This principle is fully in
> accord with the rationale of [contribution between joint tortfeasors], which
> promotes equitable distribution of the loss in proportion to actual fault.

Sommer v. Federal Signal Corp., 79 N.Y.2d 540, 558, 593 N.E.2d 1365,
1373 (1992). Does this reasoning avoid the difficulty posed by the statute of
limitations? Have the New York courts created a new form of delayed-action,
third-party tort liability? See Kull, *The Source of Liability in Indemnity and
Contribution*, 36 Loy. L.A. L. Rev. 927 (2003).

6. Another form of immunity stands in the way of achieving a perfect "equitable distribution of loss in proportion to actual fault." It is the universal rule
that a defendant who settles with the plaintiff cannot thereafter be liable in
contribution or indemnity to a nonsettling codefendant. In the paradigm case,
plaintiff alleges that defendants A and B are jointly liable for damages in the
amount of $100,000. Plaintiff eventually reaches a settlement with A, who
pays $25,000 in exchange for an unconditional release of plaintiff's claims
against him. B refuses to settle and goes to trial. The jury determines that (i)
plaintiff's damages are $80,000, and (ii) A and B are jointly responsible on a
50/50 basis. How much should plaintiff recover from B?

A rule of "pro tanto credit" allows plaintiff to recover $55,000 from B, while the competing rule of "comparative-share credit" caps B's liability at $40,000. If the first approach adheres more closely to the idea of joint and several liability for multiple tortfeasors, the second is more faithful to the idea of liability in proportion to fault:

> The major advantage of a pro tanto credit system is that it encourages early partial settlements, because the plaintiff is assured that all damages can be recovered from the remaining tortfeasors if the plaintiff prevails at trial. Early settlement is especially attractive to a plaintiff who needs financing for his suit or who needs funds promptly to pay for medical rehabilitation or to replace lost income. . . .
>
> A pro tanto credit has the disadvantage of imposing any inadequacy in a partial settlement between the plaintiff and a settling tortfeasor on nonsettling tortfeasors against whom the plaintiff prevails at trial. . . . In effect, the plaintiff and settling tortfeasor can externalize a portion of the settling tortfeasor's responsibility to a nonsettling tortfeasor, which results in an inequitable apportionment of liability.
>
> By contrast, a comparative-share credit tends to produce a fairer ultimate allocation of responsibility among all parties—plaintiff, settling tortfeasors, and nonsettling tortfeasors. A nonsettling tortfeasor's liability is not dependent on the outcome of negotiations between other parties to the suit, negotiations that exclude the nonsettling tortfeasor.

Restatement Third, Torts (Apportionment of Liability) §16, Comment *c*. The torts *Restatement* favors the comparative-share credit as the better approach on balance, while recognizing that the question is very much a matter of local law.

D. EQUITABLE SUBROGATION

American National Bank & Trust Co. of Chicago v. Weyerhaeuser Co.
692 F.2d 455 (7th Cir. 1982)

CUDAHY, Circuit Judge.

I.

On August 9, 1978, Weyerhaeuser issued a written offer to purchase up to 3,500,000 shares of its common stock at $32.00 per share, provided that the stock was tendered by August 22, 1978. Under the terms of Weyerhaeuser's offer, if more than 3,500,000 shares were tendered, Weyerhaeuser would purchase shares on a pro rata basis from shareholders tendering 100 or more shares each. The offer also allowed shareholders to condition the tender of their shares upon Weyerhaeuser's acceptance of a designated minimum number of shares if the offer was oversubscribed and proration was undertaken. A shareholder could conditionally tender his shares simply by writing the minimum number of shares that Weyerhaeuser must accept in a box captioned "Conditional Tender" appearing on the letter of transmittal which accompanied the tendered share certificates. First Jersey, pursuant to a contract with Weyerhaeuser, was designated as the depositary for the tender offer.

Bivest & Co. was the nominee of American to hold title to securities on behalf of the beneficial owners whose trust accounts were managed by American. In this case, Bivest held title to 40,000 shares of Weyerhaeuser common stock beneficially owned by American's customer, the Illinois State Board of Investment (the "Board"). By letter received by American during the afternoon of August 18, the Board authorized American to tender its 40,000 shares of Weyerhaeuser common stock registered in the name of Bivest.

Later that afternoon, a teller in American's securities division prepared a letter of transmittal on behalf of Bivest as the registered owner of the Board's 40,000 shares of Weyerhaeuser stock. The teller then sent both the letter and the share certificates to First Jersey, and First Jersey received the letter and certificates before the expiration of Weyerhaeuser's tender offer. Several days after the August 22 expiration date, Weyerhaeuser announced that more than 3,500,000 shares had been tendered. Because the offer was oversubscribed, Weyerhaeuser invoked the proration provisions of the offer to purchase, agreeing to buy 61% of the shares tendered by any tenderor. The offer, however, precluded acceptance of those shares that were defectively tendered and those shares that were conditionally tendered by any tenderor where the minimum number entered in the "Conditional Tender" box exceeded 61% of the total shares tendered by that tenderor.

By letter dated September 1, 1978, and received by American no later than September 6, First Jersey returned to American all of the Board's shares of Weyerhaeuser stock, together with a photocopy of the letter of transmittal. First Jersey informed American that the tender was rejected because the letter of transmittal's "Conditional Tender" box was marked "40,000," and this number was in excess of 61% of the total shares tendered. The parties to this appeal dispute as a factual matter who was responsible for entering the number "40,000" in the "Conditional Tender" box. American contends that it desired to tender the 40,000 shares unconditionally (without requiring Weyerhaeuser to accept all 40,000) and, thus, none of its employees wrote that figure in the box. First Jersey, on the other hand, contends that none of its employees entered the "40,000" figure in the box; according to First Jersey, the letter of transmittal it received from American contained the "40,000" figure entered in the "Conditional Tender" box.

If the tender had been accepted, Weyerhaeuser would have purchased 24,400 shares (61% of 40,000) at $32.00 per share for a total price of $780,800.00. On September 7, 1978, one day after receiving the rejection letter from First

Jersey, American purchased 24,400 shares of Weyerhaeuser stock at $32.00 per share from the Board for a total price of $780,800.00. Although the market price of Weyerhaeuser stock was actually less than $32.00 at this time of purchase, American paid the higher tender offer price in order to make the Board whole for its loss.

[For about three weeks, representatives of American, First Jersey, and Weyerhaeuser discussed whether Weyerhaeuser might be persuaded to accept the Board's tender after all. Meanwhile, the market price of Weyerhaeuser's stock continued to decline slowly. American received notice of Weyerhaeuser's definite refusal on September 20.] The next day, September 21, 1978, American sold on the open market the 24,400 shares of Weyerhaeuser stock it had purchased from the Board. Because the market price of Weyerhaeuser stock at this time was more than two dollars per share lower than the tender offer price of $32.00 per share (as well as being about $1.50 below the market price on September 7), American received only $710,887.75 for its shares, compared to the $780,000.00 it paid the Board for these shares.

American filed this suit for breach of contract on January 30, 1979, against Weyerhaeuser and First Jersey seeking to recover $69,912.25 (the difference between the price American paid the Board for the Weyerhaeuser stock on September 7, 1978, and the price at which American sold the stock on September 21). Shortly thereafter, Weyerhaeuser filed a third-party complaint against First Jersey, claiming that First Jersey was obligated to indemnify Weyerhaeuser for any liability it might incur. Weyerhaeuser then moved for summary judgment, joined by First Jersey, asserting that under the undisputed facts, American could not state any claim for alleged breach of the offer to purchase the tendered shares since American was not the real party in interest.

In response to Weyerhaeuser's assertion that it lacked standing as the real party in interest, American argued that it might maintain this action as (1) the assignee of Bivest's claims; (2) as the assignee of the Board's claims; (3) as the principal of its agent, Bivest; (4) as the agent of its undisclosed principal, the Board; and (5) as the subrogee of the Board. The district court, however, rejected all of these theories. The court concluded that since Bivest and the Board assigned their claims *after* American had made the Board whole for the rejected stock tender, the assignments were, in effect, legal nullities since neither Bivest nor the Board possessed any assignable rights when the purported assignments were made. The court relied on the same reasoning to deny American's claims based on agency principles. The court found that, since the parties (Bivest and the Board) whose rights American claimed to assert as principal or agent, respectively, possessed no rights after they had been fully compensated for their losses (as title holder and beneficiary, respectively), American could not derivatively assert their rights. Finally, the court rejected American's claim that it was subrogated to the rights of the Board because American acted as a "volunteer" when it paid the Board for its 24,400 shares at the tender offer price, and such a volunteer cannot claim rights to subrogation. Summary judgment was therefore entered for Weyerhaeuser and First Jersey, and American appealed.

II.

"Legal" subrogation is an equitable right which arises by operation of law and not by contract. "Where property of one person is used in discharging an obligation owed by another. . . under such circumstances that the other would be unjustly enriched by the retention of the benefit thus conferred, the former is entitled to be subrogated to the position of the obligee." Restatement of Restitution §162 (1937) [*cf.* R3RUE §24]; *accord*, 4 Pomeroy's Equity Jurisprudence §1419 (5th ed. 1941). Illinois courts have stated that "[t]he doctrine of subrogation is broad enough to include every instance in which one person, not a mere volunteer, pays a debt for which another is primarily liable and which in equity and good conscience should have been discharged by the latter." Indeed, the Illinois Supreme Court has admonished us that "the policy of this court [is] to apply the expanding doctrine of subrogation, which originated in equity, and is now an integral part of the common law, in all cases where its essential elements are present, and where it effectuates a just resolution of the rights of the parties, irrespective of whether the doctrine has previously been invoked in the particular situation." Dworak v. Tempel, 17 Ill. 2d 181, 161 N.E.2d 258, 263 (1959).

Notwithstanding the Illinois policy favoring a liberal application of subrogation principles, there are several requirements a potential subrogee (in this case, American) must satisfy before it may assert a right of subrogation. . . . The subrogee must have paid a claim or debt for which a third party—not the subrogee—is primarily liable either in law or equity. It is, of course, a matter of dispute whether the putative subrogee, American, or the third parties, Weyerhaeuser and First Jersey, are responsible for entering the figure "40,000" in the "Conditional Tender" box. Since the parties have stipulated that this is a contested issue of fact, summary judgment based on a right of subrogation could not now be entered on the ultimate merits of American's claim. But if this factual question is resolved against the third parties, then the requirement that the claim paid was one for which a third party was primarily liable would be met.

[Moreover,] the subrogor must possess a right which he could enforce against a third party and which the subrogee seeks to enforce. This requirement is based upon the principle that the subrogee's rights are derived from and dependent upon the rights of the subrogor. Illinois courts commonly express this needed element by saying that the subrogee must step into the shoes of, or be substituted for, the subrogor. See, e.g., London & Lancashire Indemnity Co. v. Tindall, 377 Ill. 308, 36 N.E.2d 334, 337 (1941); Dunlap v. Peirce, 336 Ill. 178, 168 N.E. 277, 282 (1929). For the purpose of determining whether subrogation rights may be asserted by American, we need only conclude that either Bivest or the Board could have, in the absence of the satisfaction of their claim by American, stated a claim for relief against First Jersey or Weyerhaeuser. Under the equitable doctrine of subrogation, that claim is saved for the benefit of the party (in this case, American) that made the Board whole. We conclude that both Bivest and the Board, in the *absence* of satisfaction by American, could have stated claims for relief against Weyerhaeuser and First Jersey, and that, since instead there *has* been satisfaction by American, *American* can now state these claims for relief.

A final, and crucial, requirement for exercising the right of subrogation, which the district court found dispositive here, is that the potential subrogee must not have acted as a "volunteer" in paying a claim of the subrogor properly lying against a third party. Although Illinois courts have formulated this requirement in various ways, it may be succinctly stated as follows:

> It is well settled that a mere stranger or volunteer can not, by paying a debt for which another is bound, be subrogated to the creditor's rights in respect to the security given by the real debtor. But if the person who pays the debt is compelled to pay for the protection of his own interest and rights, then the substitution should be made . . . In [Bennett v. Chandler, 199 Ill. 97, 64 N.E. 1052 (1902),] it was said that "a stranger within the meaning of this rule is not necessarily one who has had nothing to do with the transaction out of which the debt grew. Any one who is under no legal obligation or liability to pay the debt, is a stranger, and, if he pays the debt, a mere volunteer."

Ohio National Life Insurance Co. v. Board of Education, 387 Ill. 159, 55 N.E.2d 163, 171 (1944). The district court concluded that American "was under no legal obligation to either Bivest or to the Illinois Board to purchase the Weyerhaeuser shares, but did so without compulsion and as a mere volunteer."

But this is an overly narrow interpretation of the term "legal obligation" and ignores the agency relationship between American and the Board, under which American was legally obligated to the Board. One can be subrogated to the rights of another even if the debt in question is not paid pursuant to an unconditional or fully choate requirement of law, such as might be represented by a provision of a binding contract or by a final judgment. Both the Illinois courts and federal courts applying Illinois law have not required for subrogation compulsion similar to that of a final judgment or of an enforceable contract; rather, the *potential* for legal liability to the subrogor, as well as the disruption of normal relations and the frustration of reasonable expectations can, in many cases, supply sufficient compulsion to support subrogation. Indeed, to require an unconditional or fully choate legal liability is, to a degree, inconsistent with the nature of legal subrogation, which is *not* dependent upon a contract, statute or judgment but instead arises out of equitable principles as a matter of law. Rather then emphasizing the form of the legal compulsion, Illinois decisions involving rights of subrogation demand careful analysis of the nature of the relationship between the putative subrogee (American) and the subrogor (either Bivest or the Board) to determine whether the subrogee paid the debt "'pursuant to a legal liability.'" Because American as either an agent or a trustee could be reasonably charged with legal liability to the Board for the improper tender of the Board's Weyerhaeuser stock, we believe that American purchased the Board's stock under "compulsion" and under a "legal obligation," entitling American to exercise rights of subrogation.

It would serve no purpose to deny standing to American in this case. First, a loss was suffered by the Board because the tender of its stock was rejected. But the Board is not responsible for that loss. Rather, it appears that the loss was caused by one or more of several other parties—American, First Jersey, or Weyerhaeuser—each or all of whom could be sued by the Board for the loss. Under the facts of this case, it makes sense that the innocent party be made whole now for its losses by the one of the potential wrongdoers who was its agent; subsequently this reimbursing party should be authorized to institute suit to determine who, among the three potential wrongdoers, should in equity be required ultimately to bear the loss. To frustrate this result by invocation of the "volunteer" doctrine may result in the one clearly innocent party (here the Board) needlessly bearing the heavy costs and enduring the uncertainties of litigation.

The case is remanded to the district court with directions to enter an order granting partial summary judgment to American and for further proceedings consistent with this opinion.

Obligations between independent obligors

1. The topic of subrogation lies behind a thicket of confusing terminology, but the essential meaning is fairly clear. "Subrogation" means "substitution." If A pays B's debt to C, one possible response is to subrogate A to C's claim— substituting A for C, thereby allowing A to enforce against B the claim that A's payment has satisfied. As the court indicates in *American National Bank*, a reference to "legal subrogation" (the term more often used is "equitable subrogation") describes a form of substitution that occurs by operation of law; the point is to distinguish it from "conventional subrogation," designating subrogation by agreement of the parties. (The typical example of *conventional* subrogation would be a provision in a policy of casualty insurance by which the policyholder assigns to the insurer his right of recourse against a third party, such as a tortfeasor, who might be liable to the policyholder for an injury constituting an insured loss.)

2. Another synonym for "equitable subrogation" is "equitable assignment." Notice one of the ways American's lawyers tried to prepare for this litigation, and how the trial court responded: "You purport to sue as the assignee of your customer, the Board. The Board might have had a claim against these defendants—and one which they could have assigned to you—but you paid

them first, then arranged this purported 'assignment.' You did this backwards, because by this point they had no more claim to assign." By contrast, the equitable idea is that the just outcome in the case is the same, whether there was a formal assignment or not. If subrogation is called "equitable assignment," it is because the effect is like that of an "equitable lien." To serve the interests of justice in either case, the court grants a status (that of lienor or assignee) that might have been acquired by contract but was not.

3. Still on these questions of terminology, notice that *subrogation* in cases of this kind identifies a particular kind of unjust enrichment claim, while *subrogation* in other cases refers not to the claim but to the remedy. If fraud or mistake causes a claimant to pay money that discharges a defendant's secured debt (in a case like *Ex parte AmSouth Mortgage* or *Houston v. Mentelos*), the claimant might seek the *remedy* of subrogation—the power to step into the shoes of the former secured creditor—when it affords more effective relief than a simple judgment for money. But the unjust enrichment in such cases is the result of fraud or mistake, not of paying someone else's debt. In *American National Bank*, by contrast, the term "equitable subrogation" identifies the basis of the claim: the fact that in discharging my own (potential) obligation to a third party, I have discharged yours as well. Besides, the equitable *remedy* of subrogation would be entirely superfluous where a defendant (like Weyerhaeuser) has more than enough money to pay any judgment.

4. The most common instances of independent and unrelated obligations involve insurance. Company insures Victim against loss; Victim suffers loss from a casualty for which Tortfeasor is to blame. Company and Tortfeasor now have independent and overlapping obligations to Victim for the same loss, but obligations entirely different in character: Company's arises from the insurance contract, while Tortfeasor's arises from the tort. Company pays Victim, then seeks reimbursement from Tortfeasor via subrogation. This is "conventional subrogation" if the policy provides for it in advance, and "equitable subrogation" if the policy is silent; but Company's rights against Tortfeasor should be the same either way.

In the latter case, is it appropriate to give Company (in effect) an assignment of Victim's tort claim if Company has not bothered to include in its policy a provision for "conventional subrogation"? Consider the alternatives: (i) Tortfeasor has to be liable to someone, or else he gets the benefit of the insurance that Victim has paid for. (ii) If Victim retains his claim against Tortfeasor, he recovers twice for the same injury. It is almost inconceivable that the insurance contract should be interpreted to permit this result. (iii) By contrast, if Company is subrogated to Victim's claim, there is one liability, one recovery, and the cost of the insurance is minimized.

5. The epithet "volunteer" constitutes the traditional objection to subrogation whenever a claimant has paid a debt he was not legally obligated to pay. How great is the danger that A will pay B's debt to C without a legitimate reason to do so? In *American National Bank*, the Bank's theory was that it

had intervened to protect the Board even though the Bank might not have been responsible for the Board's predicament—the question that remains to be decided. The case represents the liberalizing tendency of modern subrogation law, because the court holds that intervention may be justified when the claimant acts reasonably to protect its own interests.

———————————

Restatement Third, Restitution and Unjust Enrichment

§24. PERFORMANCE OF AN INDEPENDENT OBLIGATION (EQUITABLE SUBROGATION)

(1) If the claimant renders to a third person a performance for which the defendant would have been independently liable to the third person, the claimant is entitled to restitution from the defendant as necessary to prevent unjust enrichment.

(2) There is unjust enrichment in such a case to the extent that

(a) the claimant acts in the performance of the claimant's independent obligation to the third person, or otherwise in the reasonable protection of the claimant's own interests; and

(b) as between the claimant and the defendant, the performance in question (or the part thereof for which the claimant seeks restitution) is primarily the obligation of the defendant.

———————————

State Farm Fire & Casualty Co. v. East Bay Municipal Utility Dist.
53 Cal. App. 4th 769, 62 Cal. Rptr. 2d 72 (1997)

ANDERSON, P. J.

Today we consider whether an insurer that promptly pays the claim of its insured is barred from subrogation from the actual tortfeasor because the insurer could have legitimately denied the claim as excluded. From time to time and in a variety of situations, the "volunteer" rule has been invoked to curtail an insurer's ability to pursue equitable subrogation against a tortfeasor who caused damage to its insured. As a general rule equitable subrogation has not been awarded to one who has officiously, and as a mere interloper, paid the debt of another without any moral or legal duty to do so.

We hold that an insurer does not necessarily act as a mere volunteer when it pays its insured under a valid homeowners policy and where the loss falls under the general grant of coverage, even though coverage in all likelihood is precluded under policy exclusions. This is especially true when, as here, the tortfeasor delays accepting responsibility while the insureds are rendered homeless and are faced with an imminent need for shelter and repairs. This, together with the recent intense scrutiny of claims handling practices of California homeowners insurers, convinces us that appellant insurer did *not* act as a mere volunteer in paying its insureds' claim and *is* therefore entitled to equitable subrogation against the tortfeasor. Accordingly, we reverse summary judgment in favor of respondent tortfeasor.

I. Facts

A. THE ACCIDENT AND CLAIM

Effective November 14, 1992, through November 15, 1993, appellant State Farm Fire and Casualty Company (State Farm) insured the home of Harold and Kathleen Anthony under a "Homeowner's Extra Policy" of insurance. The policy provided coverage for "accidental direct physical loss" to the property, except as excluded under the "Losses Not Insured" provisions. On or about January 15, 1993, a water pipe owned, installed and maintained by respondent East Bay Municipal Utility District (EBMUD) burst in the vicinity of the Anthonys' Walnut Creek home, causing flooding on the premises. As a result of this event, the clay soils underlying the Anthonys' foundation became saturated, causing damage to the foundation. The Anthonys did not become aware of noticeable signs of distress to their home until that August.

The Anthonys lodged a claim with State Farm for their losses. EBMUD became involved in determining causation and reviewing damages. As of the middle of 1994, State Farm's internal files indicated its understanding that "EBMUD has accepted liability."

The engineer who evaluated the distress to the Anthonys' home, at the request of EBMUD's handling adjuster, concluded that "the flooding of the foundation soils around the house south and west sides probably did contribute substantially to the current house cosmetic distress." This engineer considered a few of the proposed items of repair to be "upgrades" and EBMUD expressed to State Farm its disagreement with State Farm's valuation of the claim.

State Farm paid the Anthonys $117,906.12 to repair the foundation, relevel the home, replace damaged patios and walkways, replace the sub-drain system, repaint and repatch the interior and exterior, and perform other items of repair. Additionally, State Farm paid over $10,000 for living expenses while the Anthonys relocated pending repairs.

b.   LITIGATION

State Farm and EBMUD engaged in settlement negotiations. In May 1995 EBMUD's insurance adjuster offered State Farm $17,554. State Farm rejected that offer and filed suit in October 1995. EBMUD moved for summary judgment on grounds that State Farm voluntarily paid the Anthonys' claim and, therefore, was not entitled to seek equitable subrogation.

EBMUD argued that the Anthonys' property damage claim was excluded from coverage under relevant policy exclusions and the recent case of Waldsmith v. State Farm Fire & Casualty Co., (1991) 232 Cal. App. 3d 693, and, thus, State Farm had no obligation to pay. EBMUD relied on several exclusions under the "Losses Not Insured" section of the policy [defining and excluding, *inter alia*, losses from "earth movement" and "water damage"].

The trial court granted summary judgment in favor of EBMUD. It found that the damage was caused by earth movement and flooding due to rupture of an EBMUD water pipe, and coverage for such harm was excluded under the insureds' policy. The trial court pointed out that in the factually similar *Waldsmith* case, the Court of Appeal had determined there was no coverage under the same policy exclusions as were present in the Anthonys' policy. The trial court concluded State Farm acted as a volunteer and could not take advantage of the equitable remedy of subrogation. This appeal followed.

II.   Analysis

Equitable subrogation allows one who has been required to pay a loss created by a third party to "step into the shoes" of the party suffering the loss and recover from the wrongdoer. The insurer's cause of action for equitable subrogation has these elements: (1) the insured has suffered a loss for which the party to be charged is liable, through act or omission or legal responsibility; (2) the insurer has compensated the insured for that loss; (3) the insured has an existing, assignable cause of action against the party to be charged, which the insured could have pursued absent compensation by the insurer; (4) the insurer has suffered damages caused by the act or omission which triggers the liability of the party to be charged; (5) justice requires that the loss should be shifted entirely from insurer to the party to be charged; and (6) the insurer's damages are in a stated sum, usually the amount paid to the insured, "assuming the payment was not voluntary and was reasonable."

Over the years, courts have liberalized their interpretation of the "interest" that must be at stake to avoid being dubbed a volunteer. . . .

The Anthonys submitted a claim under their policy to State Farm. The policy was in effect, and provided coverage for "accidental direct physical loss to property." Once, as here, the insured shows that an event comes within the scope of basic coverage under the policy, the burden shifts to the insurer to prove that a claim is otherwise excluded. This is not to say, as EBMUD points out, that good faith performance on the part of the insurer means the insurer has to pay every claim presented to it. Of course not.

But certainly an insurer cannot be held to act in anything except *good faith* when it pays a claim that comes, on first glance, within the scope of basic coverage. The question becomes whether such payment is *unreasonable* in light of a recent appellate decision finding no coverage under similar facts and near-identical policy exclusions. EBMUD takes the position that *it is* unreasonable when "decisions definitively declare that a particular claim is not covered," [the role of *Waldsmith* in the present case].

[We consider it more important that] the defendant is the tortfeasor attempting to escape liability by asserting a technical defense based on its reading of an insurance contract to which it is not even a party. EBMUD suggests that State Farm has some duty to evaluate a claim for possible exclusions but, again, State Farm does not owe that—or any other duty—to EBMUD.

Public policy favors prompt payment to the insured for losses occurring during the policy period. EBMUD, although it accepted responsibility, disputed what was needed to make the Anthonys whole. Meanwhile, State Farm, probably erroneously, decided the loss was covered under the Anthonys' policy and chose to proceed in a timely fashion to satisfy its insureds' claim.

If, as EBMUD maintains and *Waldsmith* suggests, State Farm was wrong in its conclusion, does that mean it was a volunteer and, therefore, cannot recover from the tortfeasor? We think not. "A subrogation action by an insurer is not a suit on the insurance contract, but an independent action in which equitable principles are applied to shift a loss for which the insurer has compensated its insured to one who caused the loss . . . *and whose equitable position is inferior to the insurer's.*"

The equities clearly favor State Farm. We hold that in the context of payment by an insurer to its first party insured, where the loss is covered under the basic grant of coverage, without regard to policy exclusions, the insurer is not necessarily a volunteer even in the face of authority suggesting that policy exclusions would have precluded coverage. More is at stake than proving applicability of policy exclusions.

Here, there was an existing contractual relationship between insureds and insurer, and an expectation on the part of the insured tendering the claim that the basic grant of coverage would compensate the loss. The tortfeasor had not accepted its responsibility on as timely a basis as had the insurer; rather, the tortfeasor was waiting, reviewing, reestimating—and all the while the insureds were living with the loss and the need, literally and figuratively, to right their home. Under these circumstances the insurer acted in a reasonable and morally responsible manner by timely paying the claim and *then* seeking subrogation.

For all these reasons we conclude that equity will not countenance the trumping of State Farm's right of subrogation by the volunteer doctrine; therefore, we reverse the judgment. EBMUD is to pay costs on appeal.

Benton v. Gaudry
230 Ga. App. 373, 496 S.E.2d 507 (1998)

RUFFIN, Judge.

Harriet Conneff Gaudry, individually and as executrix of the will of William T. Gaudry, sold certain real property to John Haupt on November 23, 1987. Prior to the sale, attorney Rebecca Benton, who was hired by Haupt to conduct a title search, located no outstanding liens or taxes on the property. After the sale, Benton learned that Chatham County had a notice of levy against the property for unpaid 1986 taxes. Benton voluntarily paid the taxes and then sued Gaudry for unjust enrichment and breach of warranty of title. The trial court granted Gaudry summary judgment, concluding that there was no evidence to support Benton's unjust enrichment claim and that Benton lacked standing to bring the breach of warranty claim. Benton appealed, and for the following reasons, we affirm.

The evidence reveals that on November 13, 1987, Haupt entered into a sales contract for the purchase of the property from Gaudry. Benton performed the title search, locating no outstanding liens or taxes. By general warranty deed, Gaudry conveyed the property to Haupt. The deed provided that Gaudry "does warrant and will forever defend the right and title to the [property] unto [Haupt], his successors and assigns, against the lawful claims of all persons whomsoever." Also, in an Owner's Affidavit, Gaudry averred "that there [were] no pending suits, proceedings, judgments, bankruptcies, liens or executions against said owner either in [Chatham County] or any other county in the State of Georgia." Haupt purchased the property on November 23, 1987, and on that same day, sold it by general warranty deed to George and Marie Backus.

On August 5, 1988, Chatham County's notice of levy regarding the 1986 delinquent taxes was sent to the Backuses. Benton learned of the overdue taxes and contacted Gaudry and her attorney requesting that Gaudry pay the taxes. When Gaudry declined to pay, Benton inexplicably paid the taxes on August 29, 1989.

Subsequently, on August 23, 1993, Benton sued Gaudry for breach of warranty of title, unjust enrichment, and attorney fees. On November 3, 1993, Haupt assigned "his claim for breach of warranty and all his rights, title, privileges and powers" in the property to Benton. Benton amended her complaint to include a claim based on the assignment. Benton, however, did not obtain an assignment of the property's current owners' interest in the breach of warranty claim until February 27, 1997, after the pretrial order in the case had been filed. According to the trial court, Benton never moved to amend the pretrial order or the complaint to incorporate this latter assignment from the Backuses.

Benton and Gaudry filed cross-motions for summary judgment. In granting summary judgment to Gaudry, the trial court ruled that the unjust enrichment claim failed because Benton "was never the owner of the property, and she has shown no evidence whatsoever that she was compelled in any way to pay the debt of the defendant." As for the breach of warranty claim, the court found that because Benton never owned the property, she had no standing. Furthermore, the court said, when she amended her complaint to add Haupt's assignment, Haupt no longer owned the property and thus had no interest to assign to her. Accordingly, because "at the time of filing, at the time of the amended complaint, and at the time of the pretrial order [Benton] did not have standing," the trial court also granted summary judgment to Gaudry on Benton's breach of warranty claim.

1. Initially we note that although Benton claimed she paid the taxes "under coercion and threat of power of government and figuratively speaking 'gun at head' by employees of the Tax Assessors office," we know of no statute, rule, regulation or duty that required her to pay someone else's delinquent taxes. While Haupt, who apparently employed her to perform the title search, might have a viable action against her for negligence or malpractice, Benton had no obligation to pay the taxes for the benefit of Haupt, the Backuses, or Gaudry.

2. Turning to the breach of warranty claim, we first note that it is possible for an assignee of a purchaser of property to pursue a breach of warranty claim against the seller. See Northside Title & Abstract Company, Inc. v. Simmons, 200 Ga. App. 892 (409 S.E.2d 885) (1991). However, it is imperative that the assignor have a viable interest to assign.

In the instant case, the evidence shows Gaudry's general warranty deed and owner's affidavit amounted to a general warranty of title against all persons, which included "covenants of a right to sell, of quiet enjoyment, and of freedom from encumbrances." OCGA §44-5-62. Chatham County's notice of levy against the property for outstanding 1986 taxes was clearly an encumbrance on the title. Accordingly, Haupt would have had the right to pursue a breach of warranty claim against Gaudry, had he not conveyed his interest in the property to the Backuses. In Haupt's general warranty deed to the Backuses, he conveyed to them the "property, together with all and singular the rights, members, hereditaments, improvements, easements, and appurtenances." Furthermore, under OCGA §44-5-60 (a), "the purchaser of lands obtains with the title . . . all the rights which any former owner of the land under whom he claims may have had by virtue of any covenants of warranty of title, of quiet enjoyment, or of freedom from encumbrances contained in the conveyance from any former grantor unless the transmission of such covenants with the land is expressly prohibited in the covenant itself." Thus, by selling the property to the Backuses, Haupt conveyed to them any interest he had in pursuing a claim for breach of warranty of title. Accordingly, Haupt's assignment of his right to pursue the breach of warranty claim was of no value to Benton.

Instead, the Backuses, as current owners of the property responsible for payment of the delinquent taxes, had the right to sue for breach of warranty, and they could have sued either Haupt or Gaudry. However, in this case the record does not show that the Backuses sued either Haupt or Gaudry. Rather, Benton, with an assignment of Haupt's interest, sued Gaudry for breach of the warranty. Benton never owned the property and thus could only pursue a claim through an assignment of another's interest who had a viable right of action.

Haupt, by selling the property, no longer had the right to sue for breach of warranty, and thus his assignment provided no avenue by which Benton could pursue the breach of warranty claim.

Over three years after Benton filed suit and six months after the pretrial order was filed, she finally obtained an assignment from the Backuses. However, as the trial court pointed out, Benton never sought to amend her complaint to include a claim based on the assignment or to add herself in the capacity of an assignee of the Backuses. Thus, at the time the trial court ruled on the parties' motions for summary judgment, Benton had no standing to sue for breach of warranty. Accordingly, summary judgment to Gaudry was appropriate.

3. Benton's unjust enrichment claim fails as well. "'Where money is paid on the debt of another by a person who is under no legal or moral obligation to pay the debt, and he does not do so at the instance, request, or consent of the debtor, and the debtor does not ratify his act as one done in his behalf, or does not otherwise become liable therefor, it is a voluntary payment, and the person making the payment cannot recover from the debtor.' [Cits.]" Ginsberg v. Termotto, 175 Ga. App. 265, 267 (1) (333 S.E.2d 120) (1985).

There is no evidence that Gaudry asked Benton to pay the taxes or consented to Benton's payment. There is further no indication that Gaudry ratified Benton's payment as one done on Gaudry's behalf. Finally, and most importantly, as we pointed out in Division 1, we find no evidence that Benton was under any legal or moral obligation to pay the debt. She paid the taxes voluntarily, and thus cannot recover from Gaudry. Judgment affirmed.

Wilder Corp. of Delaware v. Thompson Drainage & Levee District
658 F.3d 802 (7th Cir. 2011)

POSNER, Circuit Judge.

This appeal from the grant of summary judgment to the defendant in a diversity suit governed by Illinois law tests the outer limits of the common law doctrine of indemnity.

The word "indemnity" is from a Latin word that means "security from damage." The most common form of indemnity in modern life is an insurance contract: A is harmed by conduct covered by an insurance contract issued by insurance company B; the contract secures A from the harm by shifting its cost to B. But indemnity is not limited to insurance contracts—or, more to the point, to contracts, period. For there is a tort doctrine of indemnity, which shifts the burden of liability from a blameless tortfeasor (which sounds like an oxymoron, but we're about to see that it isn't) to a blameworthy one. Restatement (Second) of Torts §886B (1979). The tort doctrine is sometimes called "implied indemnity" to distinguish it from contractual indemnity, but a clearer term is "noncontractual indemnity."

To illustrate: an employee, acting within the scope of his employment (whether or not with the authorization, or to the benefit, of his employer) negligently injures a person. The victim sues the employer, the employer being strictly liable for the employee's tort under the doctrine of respondeat superior. After paying a judgment to, or settling with, the victim, the employer, being itself blameless (respondeat superior is as we just said a doctrine of strict liability) turns around and sues the employee to recover the cost of the judgment or settlement, the employee being liable to the employer for that cost under the doctrine of noncontractual indemnity. This may seem a roundabout alternative to a rule that only the employee is liable. But it is more than that. The employee often will be judgment-proof. In that event the employer won't be able to shift its liability to him, and so the employee will be underdeterred, to the detriment of the employer, whom respondeat superior will stick with liability for the employee's tort. This prospect gives an employer an incentive to try to prevent its employees from committing torts. The employer may screen applicants for employment more carefully, or monitor their performance at work more carefully, than it would do had it no back-up liability for its employees' torts. Or it might try to reduce the number of negligent injuries inflicted by its employees by reducing the scale or scope of its activity; a reduction in output is one way of reducing potential tort liability.

The twist in this case is that the party seeking indemnity (the plaintiff, Wilder) is trying to shift liability not for a tort but for a breach of contract.

Wilder owned 6,600 acres of farmland, on which it grazed cattle, in Fulton County, southwest of Peoria; Fulton is a rural county bounded by the Illinois River. In 2000 Wilder sold the land for $16.35 million to The Nature Conservancy, the well-known environmental organization, which wanted to restore Wilder's land to its pre-twentieth century condition as an ecologically functional floodplain (that is, land adjacent to a body of water, in this case the Illinois River, that overflows from time to time, soaking the land, creating wetlands that preserve biodiversity). The Conservancy claims that its restoration project is one of the largest such projects in the United States. (What had been Wilder's land now constitutes more than half of Emiquon Natural Wildlife Refuge.)

Wilder expressly warranted in the contract of sale that there was no contamination of the land by petroleum. But the land *was* contaminated by petroleum, though there is no indication that Wilder knew this and we'll assume it didn't.

Six years later the Conservancy, having discovered the contamination, sued Wilder in an Illinois state court for breach of warranty. The federal district court to which Wilder removed the case (the parties being of diverse citizenship) gave judgment for the Conservancy, awarding it some $800,000 in damages.

Wilder appealed the judgment, unsuccessfully. See Nature Conservancy v. Wilder Corp. of Delaware, 656 F.3d 646 (7th Cir. 2011). It had already brought the present suit, a companion suit, against the local drainage district. To facilitate the drainage of excess water, the district had long ago obtained a right of way on the land later bought by Wilder and had built a pump house on the land to pump excess surface waters into the Illinois River. To have at hand fuel for the pumps, the drainage district stored petroleum both in storage tanks that it owned in the vicinity, of which at least one was on or under the land Wilder sold to The Nature Conservancy, and in the pump house itself. (The Conservancy, wanting to restore the land as wetlands, turned off the pumps.)

Wilder asks that the drainage district be ordered to indemnify it for the money it's had to pay the Conservancy as damages for its breach of warranty. It claims to be entitled to indemnity because, it argues, negligent maintenance by the drainage district of the pump house and the storage tanks was the sole cause of the contamination of the Conservancy's (formerly Wilder's) land. It argues that it should have been allowed to conduct discovery to try to prove that it was indeed blameless and the district at fault.

The Nature Conservancy's suit against Wilder was a contract suit rather than a tort suit. The warranty on which the suit was based was, as we noted, imposed in the contract of sale, not by law, as in the case of implied warranties. Granted, Wilder's denial that it contributed to the petroleum contamination is not inconsistent with its having lost the suit brought by the Conservancy, because liability for breach of contract is strict. As Holmes explained in *The Common Law* 300 (1881), "in the case of a binding promise that it shall rain tomorrow, the immediate legal effect of what the promisor does is, that he takes the risk of the event, within certain defined limits, as between himself and the promisee. He does no more when he promises to deliver a bale of cotton." But the blameless contract breaker ("blameless" in the sense that his breach was involuntary) cannot invoke noncontractual indemnity to shift the risk that he assumed in the contract.

The reasons are several. One is to head off the avalanche of litigation that might be triggered if an involuntary contract breaker could sue anyone for indemnity who a court might find had contributed to the breach. Suppose through negligence a livery service had failed to deliver Wilder's lawyer to a key negotiating session with The Nature Conservancy, and as a result the lawyer had been unable to review the warranty against petroleum contamination that the Conservancy wanted included in the contract of sale; had he been able to do so he would have persuaded Wilder not to agree to it. Could Wilder obtain a judgment against the livery service for indemnity?

It could not. The harm caused by the livery service's negligence would be deemed, as in such cases as Edwards v. Honeywell, Inc., 50 F.3d 484, 489–91 (7th Cir. 1995), to have been unforeseeable. For how could the livery service have known what the consequences might be of failing to get the lawyer to his appointment in time? . . .

The present suit is barred as well by the economic-loss doctrine, which is also based (though only in part) on concern with liability for unforeseeable consequences, and which bars most negligence suits for purely financial loss (that is, a loss unaccompanied by personal injury or property damage), other than suits for fraud. . . .

To impose noncontractual indemnity in this case would have the further, perverse consequence of making the drainage district an insurer of Wilder's contract with The Nature Conservancy. One generally can't insure against a breach of contract, because of moral hazard (the tendency of an insured to be less careful about preventing the harm insured against than if it were not insured). Krueger Int'l, Inc. v. Royal Indemnity Co., 481 F.3d 993, 996 (7th Cir. 2007). Yet Wilder seeks to make the drainage district the insurer of Wilder's breach of contract—and an involuntary insurer at that, as the district couldn't have prevented Wilder from warranting that the land it was selling to the Conservancy was uncontaminated, though it might have been able to intervene in the Conservancy's suit against Wilder to protect its interests.

We acknowledge that as between Wilder and the drainage district, the latter was in a better, and probably the only, position to prevent the contamination. And so Wilder can appeal to the principle, which underlies the tort doctrine of indemnity along with many other tort doctrines, that liability for inflicting a harm should come to rest on the party that could, at the lowest cost, have prevented the harm in the first place. The pump house, and the petroleum-storage tank or tanks on the property, were outside Wilder's control. It had no right to oversee their maintenance. It might therefore seem to have a compelling argument for shifting liability for the contamination from its own shoulders to those of the district.

Had Wilder refused to give The Nature Conservancy a warranty against petroleum contamination, the Conservancy would doubtless have sued the drainage district for committing the tort of nuisance (it could not have sued Wilder for creating the nuisance—even if, as is doubtful, Philadelphia Electric Co. v. Hercules, Inc., 762 F.2d 303, 312–16 (3d Cir. 1985), a buyer of land can ever sue his seller for creating a nuisance—because Wilder had no control over the storage of petroleum by the drainage district). And then liability would have come to rest ultimately on the least-cost avoider. It was Wilder's choice to shoulder the risk of liability for petroleum contamination, and it would have been compensated in advance by getting a higher price for the land—it wouldn't have given such a dangerously broad warranty for nothing. One cannot be heard to complain when a risk materializes if one took it voluntarily because paid one's price for taking it.

Alternatively, Wilder could have insisted on the inclusion in its contract with The Nature Conservancy of a subrogation clause, whereby if forced to make good on its warranty Wilder would step into the Conservancy's shoes as plaintiff in a nuisance suit against the district. In Cutting v. Jerome Foods, Inc., 993 F.2d 1293 (7th Cir.1993), for example, a clause in the company's ERISA plan subrogated to the plan any claims by a beneficiary against a third party. The beneficiary was injured in an automobile accident, and the plan paid her medical expenses and by virtue of doing so acquired her tort claim against the injurer under the subrogation clause. By its warranty Wilder insured the Conservancy against petroleum contamination of the land Wilder was selling, and a subrogation clause would have authorized Wilder to sue the drainage district after making good on its warranty to the Conservancy; so again the ultimate liability would have come to rest on the least-cost avoider of the contamination—and again Wilder failed to take steps to accomplish this.

Subrogation is imposed usually by contract and sometimes by statute, but shouldn't be available automatically to every seller who provides his buyer with a warranty. For then it would swallow the doctrine of indemnity: unable to obtain indemnity because the doctrine cannot be used to shift the cost of a breach of contract from the contract breaker to a tortfeasor who contributed to the breach, the contract breaker would call his claim against the tortfeasor a subrogee's claim instead of a claim for indemnity.

The spectre of automatic subrogation, divorced from a contractual or statutory grant of subrogation rights and potentially overlapping with indemnity and contribution (partial indemnity, from a joint tortfeasor that is not entirely blameless), is presented by the doctrine of "equitable subrogation" (which the Illinois courts also refer to as "legal subrogation," though a more accurate term would be "common law subrogation"): the provider to a person of a benefit that was the primary obligation of a third person may obtain restitution from that person if necessary to prevent that person's being unjustly enriched, even if no right of subrogation is conferred by contract or statute. Restatement (Third) of Restitution and Unjust Enrichment §24 (2011); American Nat'l Bank & Trust Co. v. Weyerhaeuser Co., 692 F.2d 455, 460–61 (7th Cir. 1982) (Illinois law).

Equitable subrogation is a troublesomely vague doctrine: "There is no general rule which can be laid down to determine whether a right of [equitable] subrogation exists since this right depends upon the equities of each particular case." Dix Mutual Ins. Co. v. LaFramboise, 149 Ill.2d 314, 597 N.E.2d 622, 624 (1992). So when, as in this case, contractual subrogation is feasible, it should be encouraged, rather than bypassed by appeal to equitable subrogation; for when it is feasible for parties to arrange their affairs by contract, they should have to do so rather than be allowed to make a court do it for them. Wilder could have protected itself against the drainage district's negligence by a subrogation clause in its contract with The Nature Conservancy, failed to, and has only itself to blame for that failure. It cannot invoke contractual subrogation, having failed to obtain a subrogation clause, and it has not invoked equitable subrogation—the scope of which under Illinois law we therefore need not try to determine. Affirmed.

Subrogation: "equitable" or "conventional"?

1. *Wilder Corp.* makes a striking illustration of the way modern judges sometimes reinvent wheels in the area of restitution, not always on the pattern of the originals. Where doctrine is relatively unfamiliar, there is an understandable tendency to substitute analytical tools with which a judge feels more at home. Judge Posner's reasons for refusing to allow Wilder to recover from Drainage District may or may not be persuasive, but his account of the legal rules in this area is idiosyncratic and potentially misleading. Most fundamentally, you should remember that indemnity (or "noncontractual indemnity")

is not a "tort doctrine," and that a liability to indemnify—the liability that Wilder was seeking to impose on the Drainage District—is not a liability in tort. Remember, also, that a liability in indemnity or contribution can only arise between parties who are *jointly and severally liable* to a third. (This is the simpler explanation of why "the doctrine cannot be used to shift the cost of a breach of contract from the contract breaker to a tortfeasor who contributed to the breach.") Because their overlapping liabilities to the Conservancy were independent and distinct—one in contract, one in tort—Wilder's complaint against the Drainage District should have been pleaded as equitable subrogation from the outset, omitting the reference to indemnity which may have thrown the court off the track.

2. For the definition of indemnity, compare R3RUE §23 (set forth at pages 144-145, *supra*) with Restatement (Second) of Torts §886B(1):

> (1) If two persons are liable in tort to a third person for the same harm and one of them discharges the liability of both, he is entitled to indemnity from the other if the other would be unjustly enriched at his expense by the discharge of the liability.

"The basis for indemnity is restitution, and the concept that one person is unjustly enriched at the expense of another when the other discharges liability that it should be his responsibility to pay." *Id.*, Comment *c*.

3. Why do you suppose the contract between Wilder and the Conservancy did not contain a "subrogation clause," assigning (to Wilder) the Conservancy's rights against any third party who might be found responsible for a hypothetical petroleum contamination? What difference does it make to the Drainage District whether such a clause is included?

4. By contrast, the casualty policy at issue in *State Farm v. EBMUD* almost certainly contained a boilerplate subrogation cause, assigning to State Farm the homeowner's rights against any third party responsible for a covered injury. Why was that case all about "volunteers" and not about "conventional subrogation"?

Farnsworth, *Restitution* 49-50, 52-53 (2014):

The most straightforward cases for recovery are those where the claimant has performed a duty that he shared with the defendant. Suppose you and I are joint tortfeasors, having both contributed to an accident that injured someone else. Our obligations are evenly shared. The doctrine of joint and several liability allows the tort plaintiff to collect all of his damages from either of us—and he decides to collect them all from me. Now I have a good claim for restitution against you, though the claim also can go by other more specific names. It may be called a claim for "indemnity" if you are obliged to reimburse me in full, or a claim for "contribution" if you just need to reimburse me in part. Or suppose you and I jointly guarantee payment of a note by someone else; when he defaults, I end up paying the entire amount, either because I step forward to do so or because the creditor makes me the target of his collection efforts. My subsequent claim against you would arise from a combination of restitution and contract law (or restitution and tort law in the case of the accident). The contract and tort rules, or rules from suretyship or whatever other body of underlying law may be involved, set the terms on which we share responsibility and the extent of my right to collect restitution from you after I have paid for both of us.

Now suppose that two parties have overlapping legal obligations to a third, but the obligations are not the same. I am your insurer. You are hit by a car. The driver now has a duty to compensate you and so, let us suppose, do I. But the driver's obligation seems greater; he is the one who did the actual damage, whereas my duty arises just because we have an insurance contract. So if I pay your bills, I now have a right to seek restitution from the driver. To state the reasoning more formally, we say that the driver and I both had obligations to you, but that the driver's obligation was primary. So he was unjustly enriched by my payment of it, and I can collect it from him in a restitution suit.

Restitution of this kind is often called "equitable subrogation." "Subrogation" generally means "substitution." The "equitable" part of the term refers, historically, to the origins of the device in courts of equity. As a more practical matter it refers to the result the suit seeks, which has been aptly described as "securing the ultimate discharge of a debt by the person who in equity and good conscience ought to pay it." In equity and good conscience, the driver of the car, not your insurance company, should have the ultimate responsibility to pay for the damage inflicted on you. And the word "equitable" has still another significance. It means that my right to sue in this way arises not from contract but from law. I may also have rights of subrogation under our insurance contract; that would be "conventional" subrogation rather than the equitable variety. My rights then would be defined by whatever the contract says, though principles of restitution law may be used to fill in gaps.

———————

E. SELF-INTERESTED INTERVENTION

Ulmer v. Farnsworth
80 Me. 500, 15 A. 65 (1888)

O. G. Hall, for plaintiffs: When one stands by in silence and sees valuable services rendered for his benefit, such silence, accompanied with knowledge on his part that the party rendering the service expects payment therefor, may fairly be treated as evidence of an acceptance of the service, and as showing an agreement to pay for such services. Day v. Caton, 119 Mass. 513 (1876).

Robinson and Rowell, for the defendants.

DANFORTH, J.

The plaintiffs are the owners of a lime quarry in which they have a pump used for the purpose of draining their quarry from such water as may accumulate therein, whether coming from sources within its own limits or outside. The defendant owns another quarry adjacent to, but not adjoining the plaintiffs', there being one quarry between them. It is alleged that water accumulates in the defendant's quarry, and running through the one intervening, comes upon that of the plaintiffs and is pumped up by them. It is to recover compensation for this service that this action is brought, the plaintiffs alleging that the defendant receives benefit from it, as it prevents the injurious accumulation of water in his own quarry.

The action is assumpsit and must therefore be maintained, if at all, upon proof of a promise, express or implied. The case shows no sufficient proof of an express promise.

Nor will the facts proved, independent of the alleged custom or usage relied upon by the plaintiffs, raise an implied promise. The pump by which the service was performed was situated in the plaintiffs' quarry, put there primarily for the purpose of draining their own premises. The running of the water from the defendant's quarry to the plaintiffs', was the result of the plaintiffs' own act in digging theirs deeper than the other. The benefit accruing to the defendant, if any, was merely incidental, with no legal right to interfere with the operation of the pump, and hence under no obligation to give notice of a denial of liability. These circumstances could not raise an implied promise on the part of the defendant, certainly not if he was guilty of no wrong in permitting the water to run as it did, and if he was guilty the remedy would be in another form of action. And when we add to this the unqualified and uncontradicted denial of the defendant that any contract was made, we must come to the conclusion that the testimony not only fails to sustain a promise, but that in fact none, either express or implied, ever existed.

But the plaintiffs rely upon an alleged custom or usage in that neighborhood by which under like circumstances the parties receiving this incidental benefit, have recognized a liability to pay a certain specified sum, one cent for each cask of lime burned from the rock taken out of the quarry thus drained. It is claimed that this usage of itself raises an implied promise on the part of the defendant.

It requires the citation of no authorities to show that to give a custom the force of law, among other things, it must be universal and its origin in point of time so far back "that the memory of man runneth not to the contrary." This custom is at best but a local one and is confined to "a particular business or employment," and so recent in its origin that its beginning is within the memory of some of the witnesses. But as a local and limited usage the evidence fails to show its uniformity or certainty. On the other hand, it appears that the price paid was not the same in all cases, and in many instances both the price paid and the liability was the result of a contract. Nor does it clearly appear that this was not true in all cases; while in the constantly varying circumstances attending each case, the application must be difficult and uncertain.

But assuming the evidence to be plenary and to establish all that is claimed for it, still, as a local and limited usage, and it can be no other, while it may be received to modify a contract, to explain the intention of the parties to it in case of an ambiguity, or the meaning of certain words used, or control to some extent the modes of dealing between parties in like business, as well as the manner of performing their contracts, many illustrations of which may be found in the usages of banks and merchants, but "it cannot be received to establish a liability, or to prove the origin of the relation by which the parties became responsible to each other." Such a usage may have an application to a contract previously existing, but cannot of itself create one. Nor can it be received to change an express contract, or in violation of an established principle of law. If this alleged usage is allowed to prevail in this case, it imposes a contract liability upon this defendant in direct opposition to the established principle of law requiring assent to a binding contract. This action must therefore fail, whatever remedy may be open to the plaintiffs in a process of a different form.

Judgment for defendant.

Proximity

1. *Ulmer v. Farnsworth* is the classic American citation for the proposition that restitution will not subject an innocent defendant to what the Restatement calls "a forced exchange: in other words, an obligation to pay for a benefit that the recipient should have been free to refuse." R3RUE §2(4). Litigated cases frequently involve controversies between neighbors over improvements, because the fact of physical proximity can make it impossible for A to pursue his own legitimate objectives without simultaneously benefiting B.

Ulmer raises more difficult questions than Baron Pollock's famous rhetorical question ("One cleans another's shoes; what can the other do but put them on?"), because it is easy to see that A's initiative may be socially desirable, and that B's refusal to pay may be unreasonable, strategic, and opportunistic. (If A is discouraged by B's attitude, so that neither quarry is drained, the result may be inefficient as well.) The law of restitution is prepared to live with these consequences, so long as the benefit conferred by A is one that B has a right to refuse. From this vantage point, the set of instances in which the law *will* require the defendant to pay for the claimant's unrequested intervention can be seen as a list of unrequested benefits that a defendant, for one reason or another, has no right to refuse.

2. In Hollifield v. Monte Vista Biblical Gardens, Inc., 251 Ga. App. 124, 553 S.E.2d 662 (2001), Hollifield made improvements to his neighbors' land, initially in the expectation that he would one day be able to buy it. The neighbors refused to sell and eventually sued Hollifield for trespass and ejectment. Hollifield counter-claimed in restitution:

> Hollifield undertook to clean up and beautify the plaintiffs' land to benefit his own land and for future purchase by him. "I was just cleaning it up because it was an eyesore and I wanted my side to look good as well as his side. I wanted to make a change for the entire community as well as myself." Hollifield claimed to have put $50,000 worth of flowers, trees, and shrubs on the land after his failure to purchase the property, because
>
>> it was one of the most ugly pieces of property in the state of Georgia, number one. It was an eyesore to the entire community and it didn't represent me because what I was living next door to I just didn't want that next door to me. That was my number one reason to clean it up, to make it look decent because wouldn't nobody come to see me with that over there, water, trees and everything all in the place. It was a mess.

Id. at 128, 553 S.E.2d at 668. Assume that $50,000 worth of beautification increased the value of the neighbors' property by $10,000. What result?

3. Where neighbors are required to bargain with each other, co-owners ("co-tenants" in property law) are not. An owner who makes necessary expenditures to preserve common property—the usual categories being mortgage payments, taxes and "necessary repairs"—can compel fellow-owners to contribute to the expense, even if he proceeds in the face of their prior refusal. By contrast, there is no right to compel contribution to expenditures regarded as discretionary—typically, "improvements" as opposed to "repairs." Then again, the improving co-tenant may be given credit for any value added by improvements in the event of a subsequent partition. These general consequences (along with more detailed ramifications) are a familiar topic of that of part of real property law relating to co-ownership. From the standpoint of restitution they can be summarized by the following rule and illustrations:

Restatement Third, Restitution and Unjust Enrichment

§26. PROTECTION OF CLAIMANT'S PROPERTY

If the claimant incurs necessary expense to protect an interest in property and in so doing confers an economic benefit on another person in consequence of the other's interest in the same property, the claimant is entitled to restitution from the other as necessary to prevent unjust enrichment.

Illustrations:

1. A and B are co-tenants of Blackacre. The property is subject to a pre-existing mortgage. A is in possession; B has not been ousted but chooses to live elsewhere. A makes payments on the mortgage note, and pays for taxes, insurance, and necessary repairs. A asks B to share the cost of all these expenditures, but B refuses. By the rule of this section, B is liable in restitution for B's proportionate share of A's expenditures, all of which protect their common property. So long as the co-tenancy continues, A's remedy will be limited to enforcement of an equitable lien on B's interest in Blackacre. (In other words, B's liability in restitution cannot exceed the value of B's interest.)

2. Same facts as Illustration 1, except that A makes valuable improvements to Blackacre and seeks to compel B to share the cost. A is not entitled to restitution in respect of improvements so long as the co-tenancy continues. If the property is later sold, A's share of the proceeds will reflect (i) the value added by A's improvements, or (ii) the cost of those improvements to A, whichever is less (§50(4)). If Blackacre is physically partitioned, the court may be able to avoid unjust enrichment by allocating to A the part of the property that A has improved.

The logic supporting restitution for necessary expenditures between tenants in common applies equally well to *successive* interests in the same property, such as leasehold/reversion or life estate/remainder. Compare two more illustrations from R3RUE §26:

3. After Lessee fails to do so, Lessor pays taxes assessed against Blackacre and carries out repairs ordered by the building commissioner. Construing the lease, the court determines that taxes are the liability of Lessee, while necessary repairs are within Lessor's covenant of habitability. Lessor has a claim against Lessee under this section for the taxes but not the repairs, enforceable (if need be) by subrogation to the claim of the tax authority. . . .

5. A is the life tenant of Blackacre; B owns the remainder in fee. Municipality levies assessment on Blackacre for street and sewer improvements. A pays the assessment after B refuses to share the cost. A is entitled to an equitable lien on B's remainder securing payment of B's allocable share of the cost.

---

4. Restitution on this pattern almost always involves interrelated interests in real property, but there is nothing in the logic of of the claim that limits it to such cases. The facts of In re Montgomery's Estate, 299 Pa. 452, 149 A. 705 (1930), were stated as follows:

In 1912, two brothers, Marshall Montgomery and Henry S. Montgomery, procured from a life insurance company a joint life policy for an insurance of $20,000, payable to the survivor of either. The yearly premium was $1,540.80, less earned dividends. From 1912 to 1919 the premiums were regularly met by each of the coinsured paying one-half of the amount. Upon the premium for 1919 falling due, Henry refused to pay his one-half, and thereafter paid no portion of the assessments. From that year until his death in 1927, the entire premiums were paid by Marshall, to whom, as the survivor, the company paid the whole of the $20,000 insurance money. At the audit of the estate of Henry, the survivor claimed repayment of one-half of the entire amount paid by him as premiums from 1919 to 1926, inclusive, with interest on these payments.

Id. at 454-455, 149 A. at 706. What result? What if Henry were the survivor, and the same action were brought against Henry by Marshall's estate? Perhaps Henry stopped paying in 1919 because he was in poor health and concluded (correctly, as it turned out) that he would not survive his brother. What should Henry have done?

Robinson v. Robinson
100 Ill. App. 3d 437, 429 N.E.2d 183 (1981)

UNVERZAGT, Justice:

This action was brought by the plaintiff, Ann M. Robinson, to obtain a dissolution of marriage from Wylie Robinson, and against his parents, Earl J. and Alice M. Robinson, to establish her rights in certain property owned by them, known as the Johnson Road property. As the principal parties of this action have the same surnames, to save time and space we will refer to them usually by their given names.

The novel question presented by this appeal is whether one who improves real property which she knows to be owned by others, who neither request nor encourage the improvement but merely give their permission for the improvement, is entitled to restitution.

After hearing all of the evidence, the able and experienced trial judge made a finding that all issues of credibility are found against Earl and Wylie, based upon the many inconsistencies in their testimony. The trial court entered judgment for dissolution of marriage finding that both husband and wife are self-supporting, in good health, and have sufficient income and assets that neither was entitled to maintenance. The trial court gave custody of the two minor children to Ann and required Wylie to pay child support, and found that he was then $980 in arrearage. The trial court determined that Wylie's Teacher's Retirement Pension Fund was a marital asset and awarded Ann one-half of its current value and also awarded Ann $3,000 in legal fees. The judgment also assigned to the parties various items of furniture, furnishings, other personal property, automobiles, bank accounts and insurance policies.

The judgment further determined that Ann and Wylie each had a one-half interest in the house constructed on the land owned by Earl and Alice and known as the Johnson Road property. The court valued the house and improvements at $71,000 and determined that there was a construction loan for the house amounting to $15,000 and that the value of the lot upon which the house was constructed was $12,000.

The judgment went on to provide for the disposition of the Johnson Road property by two alternate methods to be determined by the election of Earl and Alice. The first method was that the house and lot be sold, sale expenses be paid, the construction loan be paid, then Earl and Alice be paid the value of the land and the remaining sale proceeds be divided between Ann and Wylie. A lien was imposed on Wylie's one-half in favor of Ann in an amount equal to the court's determination of the amount owed her for child support arrearages, attorney's fees and her one-half interest in Wylie's Teacher's Retirement Pension Fund.

Alternatively, the judgment provided that if Earl and Alice do not elect to have the house and lot sold then they are to pay Ann $28,000 representing her one-half interest in the house, and pay the bank $7,500 representing one-half of the amount due on the construction loan and, further, Wylie was required to hold Ann harmless and indemnify her as to any liability on the other $7,500 due on that loan. This alternative also provided that Ann would have a lien on Wylie's one-half interest in the house in the amount he was required to pay her for child support arrearages, attorney's fees and one-half of the Teacher's Retirement fund. Upon receipt of the above-described funds, Ann was to quit-claim her interest in the property to Earl and Alice. They, however, rejected both alternatives. The trial court appointed a receiver for the property, but the receiver declined appointment. All of the parties then took this appeal.

To determine the principal issues in this case, it is necessary to recite the facts in some detail to determine the relationship of the parties and the rights and obligations flowing therefrom.

Wylie grew up on a farm in Kendall County. He is the only child of Earl and Alice. They owned the farm upon which they lived and, in addition, owned another farm of 160 acres some five miles away known as the Johnson Road property which is the focus of the controversy here.

Wylie and Ann were married in 1966. Ann was a registered nurse and Wylie was attending college and graduated in 1968. Soon thereafter they moved to Aurora where Ann worked as a nurse and Wylie was employed as a school teacher. They lived off of Wylie's salary and saved Ann's salary to build a home. Wylie wanted to move back to the country.

Early in the spring of 1969, Wylie had a conversation with his father, Earl, in which Wylie asked his father if he and Ann could build their home on the Johnson Road property. Earl agreed. Earl told his wife, Alice, that Wylie had asked if he and Ann could build their home on the Johnson Road property. Earl told Alice that he was agreeable and Alice also consented. Wylie told Ann that his father had agreed to let them build their home on the Johnson Road property. Earl and Alice were pleased because Wylie would be more available to help them with work on the farm.

Wylie testified he selected the site for the house. Earl advised him that down at the end of the lane near Johnson Road was an appropriate place to build. Wylie drew the plans for the house. He surveyed and staked out the site. A registered land surveyor testified that the landscaped site upon which the house is built is exactly one acre, although Wylie testified he did not stake out any particular size site.

Wylie and Ann had saved $4,000. They borrowed $18,000 from the local bank as a construction loan and told the president of the bank that when they completed the home the land would be theirs and a regular mortgage would be placed on the property for purposes of security. The note was renewed on a yearly basis and monthly payments reduced the debt to $15,000.

Wylie and Ann began construction of the house in the spring of 1969 and occupied it in 1970. The construction work was done mainly by Wylie with substantial help from friends and family including Earl, Alice, and Ann's father. Ann sanded and finished woodwork and cabinets. After the home was occupied, additional improvements in the amount of $5,000 were made. These included carpeting, drapes, kitchen cabinets, linoleum and paint.

All of the parties knew that the house was Wylie's and Ann's home and treated it as such. They did all of the landscaping and planted shrubbery. They repaired it and maintained it. They made all of the loan payments and treated the interest thereon as a deduction on tax returns. They insured the house with a homeowner's policy. They had the only keys to the house and never paid or were asked for rent on it. The one connection Earl and Alice had with the house was that it was included on the farm tax bill since the lot was not subdivided. Earl and Alice paid the real estate tax bill. In exchange for that payment, Wylie worked additional time for his parents on their farm.

The bank president drove to the property and inquired if the house was completed so that Wylie and Ann could obtain a conventional mortgage. Wylie, thereafter, obtained an estimate of the cost of a survey which was several hundred dollars. He and Ann did not have those funds and the matter was dropped.

There was no written agreement between the young and older Robinsons as to a transfer of title to the property. However, Wylie and his parents had many oral dealings over the years. They were very close. Wylie borrowed money from his parents by oral agreement. He not only had access to his parents' checkbook, but the right to sign checks. He could charge items to his parents' accounts and then repay them. The younger Robinsons and the older Robinsons exchanged services and assistance in the old fashioned country manner. Wylie worked for his parents on their farm each year and received a share of the farm income. Over the years he contributed a substantial amount of his time and knowledge to the construction of various farm improvements on his parents' farm.

Marital discord arose in 1977, and Wylie moved to his parents' home where he resided at the time of the hearing. From the relationship of the parties it can thus be seen that the younger Robinsons would have every expectation of eventual ownership of the home they constructed. However, the testimony was in strong disagreement on this point.

Ann testified that she and Wylie had conversations with Earl and Alice with respect to transferring the lot to her and Wylie. She said the matter was discussed in general terms on more than one occasion. According to Ann, it was made understood to Wylie and her that the house was sitting on property that would be theirs. She testified that Earl said they would sign it over to them.

Wylie testified that his father did not promise to transfer the house or sell it to him. His mother never promised anything, and neither parent ever said he would inherit all their property. Wylie acknowledged that the agreement was that he could live in the house.

Earl testified that he never had a conversation with Wylie and Ann about transferring the property to them. He never promised to transfer title or give Wylie the property and he never told Wylie he was going to leave him the property by will or inheritance.

Alice testified that her husband gave Wylie and Ann permission to build a building, but that there were no representations that they were going to transfer an interest in the property to the younger Robinsons.

The trial judge put the following questions to Earl:

> "Q   All right. Mr. Robinson, when you allowed Ann and Wylie to put this $23,000 in the house, did you think they were making a gift to you of $23,000?
> A   No, I didn't.
> Q   What did you think they were doing with the $23,000?
> A   I don't know. But anybody builds on anything they don't have its title it's their own hard luck.
> Q   When Wylie asked you could he build a house, whom did you understand he was building the house for?
> A   Building it for himself was the understanding. It was the second farm house."

The following questions were put to Alice:

> "Q   Now, Mrs. Robinson, you were aware of the fact that your husband had given Wylie and Ann permission to build a building?
> A   Yes.
> Q   Okay. Did you think they were making a gift of this building to you?
> A   No.
> Q   Then why were they putting this money into your property as far as you were concerned?
> A   For a house for them."

The trial judge concluded that it would unjustly enrich Earl and Alice to gain the house without compensation to Ann.

After hearing all of the evidence in this case, the trial court determined that Ann had an interest in the improvements made on the Johnson Road property. The court's rationale for the decision was that the evidence established that Earl and Alice had been unjustly enriched by the improvements made on the Johnson Road property. In making this decision, the court stated that it was based on theories that are available to the court in equity.

Earl and Alice argue that the evidence at trial did not establish recovery under a theory of unjust enrichment. They argue that as a general rule, improvements of a permanent character, made upon real estate, and attached thereto, without consent of the owner of the fee, by one having no title or interest, become a part of the realty and vest in the owner of the fee. But, as the supreme court pointed out years ago:

> "(C)ourts of equity have not hesitated to soften the harshness and rigor of the rule of law, when the circumstances of the case and the relation of the parties required it to be done to meet the ends of justice." Cable v. Ellis (1887), 120 Ill. 136, 152, 11 N.E. 188.

In Olin v. Reinecke (1929), 336 Ill. 530, 534, 168 N.E. 676, the court said:

> In equity, however, if the owner stands by and permits another to expend money in improving his land he may be compelled to surrender his rights to the land upon receiving compensation therefor, or he may be compelled to pay for the improvements. In such cases there is always some ingredient which would make it a fraud in the owner to insist upon his legal rights. Such an ingredient may consist in the owner encouraging the stranger to proceed with the improvement, or where one party acts ignorantly and without the means of better information and the other remains silent when it is in his power to prevent the expenditure of the money under a delusion. It has been held in such cases that to permit one to take advantage of the mistake of another would be revolting to every sentiment of justice. The exercise of such a judicial power, however, unless based upon some actual or implied culpability on the part of the party subjected to it, is a violation of constitutional rights.

In Pope v. Speiser (1955), 7 Ill. 2d 231, 240, 130 N.E.2d 507, where the plaintiff placed valuable improvements on the defendant's farm with the knowledge and consent of the defendant and after repeated statements by the defendant that the farm would belong to the plaintiff upon the defendant's death, the court granted plaintiff an equitable lien in the land, after the defendant attempted to sell the farm to a third person.

These cases support the trial court's ruling granting Ann an interest in the Johnson Road property. The improvements were made with the knowledge, co-operation and approval of Earl and Alice. They were the major investment a young couple would ever be expected to make. The relationship of the parties and their dealings would lead one to believe that the home that was constructed would be a permanent home for Wylie and Ann. The court did not err in granting Ann an interest in the property.

We determine that while he did not denominate it as such, the interest awarded to Ann in the Johnson Road property by the trial judge was an equitable lien. As this court stated in Calacurcio v. Levson (1966), 68 Ill. App. 2d 260, 263, 215 N.E.2d 839:

> The trend of modern decisions is to hold that in the absence of an express contract, a lien based upon the fundamental maxims of equity may be implied and declared by a court of equity out of general considerations of right and justice as applied to the relationship of the parties and the circumstances of their dealing. An equitable lien is the right to have property subjected in a court of equity to payment of a claim. It is neither a debt nor a right of property, but a remedy for a debt.

The next question posed by this case is the extent or amount of the equitable lien. The trial court ruled that Ann was entitled to one-half of the appraised value of the improvements less the value of the land after making provision for payment of the construction loan.

Earl and Alice argue that if Ann is entitled to restitution her recovery should be measured by the subjective value to them or the value of the labor and materials that went into the house, and not the increased value of the land resulting from the addition of the house. [The court found that the increased value of the property was the proper measure of restitution in this case. Should the defendants refuse to pay, the trial court might order the property sold to foreclose Ann's equitable lien.]

Ann asserts that the trial court erred in not finding that Earl and Alice had either made an irrevocable gift of the Johnson Road lot to Wylie and Ann or had promised to make a gift of the lot and were estopped from refusing to complete the gift. In reviewing the evidence in this case we find it insufficient to establish the existence of a gift of the lot. The trial court was correct in its rulings in this regard.

Earl and Alice next assert that the trial court erred in attaching a lien for Wylie's debts on the Johnson Road property. The trial court placed a lien on one-half of the property for Ann's attorney's fees, child support arrearage and one-half interest in the Teacher's Retirement Plan. We agree that this was erroneous because an equitable lien is a remedy and not a property right.

We have found no case in which a lien was imposed on an equitable lien under such circumstances, as if the latter were a piece of property. Wylie has disclaimed any interest in the Johnson Road property. No matter how obstinate or intractable the trial court may have felt his action was in disclaiming the interest, the trial court cannot create a lien upon an equitable lien where none is sought. That portion of the judgment is reversed.

In sum, we affirm the circuit court of Kendall County's disposition of every issue raised on appeal by all parties, except that relating to the attachment of a lien on Wylie Robinson's interest in the Johnson Road improvements which we reverse. The cause is remanded for further proceedings as may be necessary to conclude this matter.

AFFIRMED IN PART; REVERSED IN PART AND REMANDED.

Disappointed expectations; equitable liens

1. The facts of *Robinson* could almost support recovery in contract on a theory of promissory estoppel (per Restatement Second, Contracts §90)—except that the courts were unable to find that Earl and Alice had made any promise regarding ownership of the land. Even so, the general idea of estoppel obviously lies close to the surface in the finding of unjust enrichment.

2. The *Restatement* includes a rule designed to accommodate cases like *Robinson* (in which no promises were made) as well as cases in which a property transaction goes off the rails after the would-be purchaser has made improvements. See R3RUE §27 with sample illustrations below.

3. *Robinson* provides a further introduction to the remedy of *equitable lien*. The opinion paraphrases the idea when it refers to the trial court's finding that Ann acquired "an interest in the Johnson Road property." What sort of an interest? Not ownership: property law does not permit separate ownership of an improvement (the house Ann and Wylie built) and the land beneath it. Instead, Ann is given a lien (in this context, a mortgage) on the Johnson Road property to secure her claim against Earl and Alice for unjust enrichment. The court's discussion about "what is the amount of the equitable lien" is actually about "what is the amount by which Earl and Alice have been unjustly enriched at Ann's expense?" Note that the court could have stopped there, awarding Ann a simple money judgment against Earl and Alice in that amount. The remedy of equitable lien in restitution cases incorporates almost tacitly a further, supplemental idea: that it would be inequitable for the defendants to enjoy unencumbered ownership of the property in question (in this case, the piece of land that now has a house on it) without discharging their liability in restitution.

The result is achieved by an order subjecting the defendant's property to an equitable lien in the amount of the defendant's unjust enrichment. The lien is "equitable" because it is imposed by the court—as distinct from a lien (or mortgage) imposed on property by agreement of the parties. An equitable lien acts essentially like a consensual lien, meaning that the lienor (here Ann) can foreclose the lien if the underlying debt is not paid. A court that imposes an equitable lien can give further instructions about the manner or the circumstances in which the lien may be enforced. This is what the trial court was doing when it ordered "the disposition of the Johnson Road property by two alternate methods to be determined by the election of Earl and Alice."

4. *Robinson* is harder to follow when it explains why the trial court should not have imposed a further equitable lien on Wylie's one-half share of the value of the improvement—this one securing "the amount owed [Ann] for child support arrearages, attorney's fees and her one-half interest in Wylie's Teacher's Retirement Pension Fund." Wylie has apparently disclaimed any interest in the Johnson Road property: an equitable lien to secure Wylie's obligations cannot be imposed on something Wylie does not own.

But isn't Wylie committing some sort of wrong (to Ann) in disclaiming his interest? The trial court found his behavior "obstinate and intractable." If Wylie's motive in disclaiming was an "actual intent to hinder, delay, or defraud" Ann as his creditor, his disclaimer of rights constitutes a fraudulent transfer which Ann, as his defrauded creditor, has the right to avoid. See Uniform Fraudulent Transfer Act §§4, 7.

The trial court's idea seems to have been that (i) the property would be sold somehow, whereupon (ii) the sale proceeds would be applied to satisfy all of Ann's claims—against Earl and Alice for unjust enrichment, and against Wylie for child support—before anything was paid out to Earl, Alice, or Wylie. The result can be achieved once Wylie's disclaimer is avoided, because the court can then give Ann "an attachment, or other provisional remedy" that prevents Wylie from otherwise disposing of his share of the proceeds from the sale of the house. See UFTA §7(a)(2).

Restatement Third, Restitution and Unjust Enrichment

§27. CLAIMANT'S EXPECTATION OF OWNERSHIP

If the claimant makes expenditures to maintain, improve, or add value to property that the claimant reasonably expects to retain or to acquire, and (because such expectation is frustrated) another person becomes the unintended beneficiary of the claimant's expenditure, the claimant is entitled to restitution from the other as necessary to prevent unjust enrichment.

Illustrations:

3. Vendor sells Purchaser a large tract of desert land that Purchaser intends to develop for commercial jojoba production. The contract is negotiated on the erroneous assumption, shared by both parties, that the property has sufficient water resources to support its projected use. After spending $250,000 on the improvement of the tract, Purchaser sues to avoid the contract. The court decrees rescission and restitution on the basis of mutual mistake. Purchaser's claim to recover the purchase price, upon reconveyance of the property, is within [the rules governing rescission for mutual mistake]. Purchaser's improvements increase the value of the property by $100,000. Purchaser has a claim against Vendor under

this section to recover $100,000 of its $250,000 expenditure. (Renner v. Kehl, 150 Ariz. 94, 722 P.2d 262 (1986).) . . .

6. Farmer and Rancher complete what both believe is a binding contract for the sale of Blackacre to Farmer. Farmer prepares the land for cultivation by incorporating a substantial layer of manure at a cost of $10,000. This expenditure increases the value of Blackacre by a like amount, but only if Blackacre is used for agriculture. Disagreements arise, and the parties sue each other for breach of contract. The court determines that neither party is liable for breach because (contrary to their supposition) no agreement was ever reached. Rancher resumes possession with no further plans to sell the property. Rancher uses Blackacre as pasture, not cropland, and the amendment of the soil brings Rancher no appreciable benefit. Because Farmer's enrichment of Blackacre has not enriched Rancher, Farmer is not entitled to restitution. (Estok v. Heguy, 40 D.L.R. (2d) 88 (B.C. Sup. Ct. 1963).) . . .

19. Wife is named as beneficiary in Husband's life insurance policy. Husband is the owner of the policy with the right to revoke the beneficiary designation. Wife pays the premiums after Husband ceases to do so, intending to keep the policy alive for her own benefit. Without informing Wife, Husband revokes the beneficiary designation; at his death, the proceeds are payable to Husband's Estate. Wife has a claim against Estate under this section to recover the premiums paid by her, with interest from the date of each payment. (Multiple authorities.)

Cox v. Wooten Brothers Farms, Inc.
271 Ark. 735, 610 S.W.2d 278 (Ct. App. 1981)

GLAZE, Judge.

The appellant, Cox, appeals an adverse chancery court decision and argues one issue for reversal. The sole issue to be decided is whether the trial court erred in applying the equitable doctrine of subrogation so as to entitle the appellee, Wooten, to the rights of the Federal Land Bank of St. Louis on its note and mortgage executed by Cox and other named heirs who acquired an interest in certain property under a family settlement agreement. Whether or not the trial court correctly applied the doctrine directly depends upon the facts before the court and the facts are not in dispute.

On February 27, 1967, Clinton Hickingbottom, Nola Hickingbottom, his wife (now Cox, appellant), and Jerry Hickingbottom, Mildred Hickingbottom, Shirley Baker and Jane Dare (all children of Clinton Hickingbottom by a former marriage) executed a promissory note and mortgage to the Federal Land Bank of St. Louis in the sum of $89,475. Clinton Hickingbottom owned land situated in Phillips County which secured the promissory note. Clinton

Hickingbottom died, and after his death the widow, Cox, and the heirs, the deceased's four children, entered into a family agreement. The agreement limited each family member's liability on the Federal Land Bank note. First, 100 acres of the encumbered land was assigned to Cox as her dower interest [a life estate], and the remaining 267 acres were assigned to the heirs. By this same agreement, the note payment to Federal Land Bank was prorated between Cox and the heirs so that each was to pay their share when the note payment came due. This agreement became a part of a probate court order.

Sometime after the family agreement, Hickingbottom's heirs (children) agreed to sell their assigned property to Wooten. Wooten agreed, among other things, to assume the heirs' total obligation on the note to the Federal Land Bank. Wooten received credit on the purchase price paid in the amount the heirs were to pay on the note, *i.e.*, 71.2% of the entire debt. Wooten also required the heirs to give it a mortgage on their remainder interest in the lands assigned to Cox in case Wooten was ever called upon to pay her pro rata share (28.2%) of the debt owned on the Federal Land Bank loan.

All went well for four years until Wooten found it necessary to refinance its operation and obtain an additional loan from the Federal Land Bank. Before Wooten could be approved for additional funds, Wooten was required to pay off the entire mortgage indebtedness, including the pro rata obligation of Cox. Cox was unaware that Wooten had paid the entire Federal Land Bank note until she was advised that the pro rata payments she had continued to pay were being placed in Wooten's account and not on the Federal Land Bank note. Cox then refused to make her 1980 payment and any further payments, contending Wooten was a volunteer when it liquidated the Bank note, and she no longer was obligated to pay Wooten or the Federal Land Bank. Wooten filed action against Cox in lower court seeking the 1980 payment which was past due and an order compelling her to make all further payments to Wooten on her pro rata share of the original debt to the bank. The trial court granted Wooten the relief it sought and it is this adverse decision from which Cox appeals.

Our Supreme Court has considered the doctrine of subrogation and its application on many occasions, and most of the relevant Arkansas cases are set forth in the parties' briefs. The doctrine is no better set forth and explained than in the case of Baker, Adm'r v. Leigh, 238 Ark. 918, 385 S.W.2d 790 (1965), wherein the Court, citing Southern Cotton Oil Company v. Napoleon Hill Company, 108 Ark. 555, 158 S.W. 1082 (1913), adopted the following discussion and guidelines in determining when subrogation should be applied:

> The doctrine of subrogation is an equitable one, having for its basis the doing of complete and perfect justice between the parties without regard to form, and its purpose and object is the prevention of injustice. Cyc. also says, "And generally, where it is equitable that a person, not a mere stranger, intermeddler, or volunteer, furnishing money to pay a debt, should be substituted for or in place of the creditor, such person will be so substituted."

It rests upon the maxim that no one shall be enriched by another's loss, and may be invoked wherever justice and good conscience demand its application in opposition to the technical rules of law, which liberate securities with the extinguishment of the original debt. *This equity arises when one not primarily bound to pay a debt, or remove an incumbrance, nevertheless does so; either from his legal obligation, as in case of a surety, or to protect his own secondary right; or upon the request of the original debtor, and upon the faith that, as against the debtor, the person paying will have the same sureties for reimbursement as the creditor had for payment.* And this equity need not rest upon any formal contract or written instrument. Like the vendor's lien for purchase money, it is a creation of a court of equity from the circumstances.

The theory of equitable assignment, as laid down by Pomeroy is: "In general, when any person having a subsequent interest in the premises, and who is therefore entitled to redeem for the purpose of protecting such interest, and who is not the principal debtor, primarily and absolutely liable for the mortgage debt, pays off the mortgage, he thereby becomes an equitable assignee thereof, and may keep alive and enforce the lien so far as may be necessary in equity for his own benefit."

From a review of the record and undisputed facts of the case at bar, we can conceive of no more appropriate set of facts and circumstances to which the equitable doctrine of subrogation should apply. Of course, Wooten was not originally and primarily indebted to the Federal Land Bank; Cox and the four children (the heirs) were. Cox continued to be obligated to the Bank even after Wooten purchased the heirs' land and assumed the debt in question. It was not until Wooten was compelled to pay the entire note by the Federal Land Bank when Cox decided she was no longer indebted to anyone, the Bank or Wooten. Wooten was protecting a legitimate interest when it paid the entire debt to the bank, and Cox should not be permitted to be unjustly enriched merely because Wooten was required to pay off a loan for which both Wooten and Cox had an obligation to pay. It is difficult to perceive how Wooten can be called a volunteer under the circumstances described when it purchased land that is a part of the Hickingbottom family agreement, and in doing so also assumed a note obligation to the Federal Land Bank albeit to be paid apart but in conjunction with Cox, who had a continuing pro rata responsibility on the same note.

After a careful review of the record, it is clear that Wooten was required to and in good faith did liquidate the debt owing to the Federal Land Bank, including Cox's pro rata share. We further hold that Wooten was in no sense of the word a volunteer, and therefore, Wooten is entitled to equitable subrogation rights against the appellant, Cox.

AFFIRMED.

———————————

Self-serving claimants

1. *Cox v. Wooten Bros.* uses the word "subrogation," but does the claim qualify by the test of (for instance) *American National Bank v. Weyerhaeuser?* (Is it true that Wooten "was *required* to liquidate the debt," as the court concludes—or was it just convenient for Wooten to do so?) On the other hand, the consequences of restitution in this case are fairly painless—as compared, for example, with *Ulmer v. Farnsworth.* The defendant quarry owner was being asked to put his hand in his pocket and pay for something he did not want. But Mrs. Cox was already indebted to the Land Bank, and restitution will not require her to do anything but resume her preexisting obligation.

2. What if interest rates have fallen since the Federal Land Bank made the original loan to Clinton Hickingbottom?

3. As the Arkansas opinion points out, "equitable subrogation" is sometimes called "equitable assignment." Should the availability of this kind of restitution claim correspond to the *assignability* of the defendant's underlying obligation (meaning the one that the claimant has satisfied)? As a general proposition, an obligation to pay money represents the ultimate in assignability, because it is normally hard to see how the obligor is prejudiced by substituting one creditor for another.

Presumably the Federal Land Bank could have sold (assigned) to Wooten Bros. its claim against Mrs. Cox. Assuming that the transaction would have been unobjectionable had it taken the form of an express assignment, should that be enough to justify restitution (alias "equitable assignment") when Wooten simply went ahead—omitting the form of an assignment that no one seems to have cared about? Bear in mind that if the underlying obligation (such as Mrs. Cox's debt to the Federal Land Bank) is freely assignable, an assignment by the Bank (to Wooten Bros. or anyone else) does not require the consent of the obligor (Mrs. Cox)—or even that the obligor be informed.

F.   FORMER COHABITANTS

Sharp v. Kosmalski
40 N.Y.2d 119, 351 N.E.2d 721 (1976)

GABRIELLI, J.

Plaintiff commenced this action to impose a constructive trust upon property transferred to defendant on the ground that the retention of the property and the subsequent ejection of the plaintiff therefrom was in violation of a relationship of trust and confidence and constituted unjust enrichment. The

Trial Judge dismissed plaintiff's complaint and his decision was affirmed without opinion by the Appellate Division.

Upon the death of his wife of 32 years, plaintiff, a 56-year-old dairy farmer whose education did not go beyond the eighth grade, developed a very close relationship with defendant, a school teacher and a woman 16 years his junior. Defendant assisted plaintiff in disposing of his wife's belongings, performed certain domestic tasks for him such as ironing his shirts and was a frequent companion of the plaintiff. Plaintiff came to depend upon defendant's companionship and, eventually, declared his love for her, proposing marriage to her. Notwithstanding her refusal of his proposal of marriage, defendant continued her association with plaintiff and permitted him to shower her with many gifts, fanning his hope that he could induce defendant to alter her decision concerning his marriage proposal. Defendant was given access to plaintiff's bank account, from which it is not denied that she withdrew substantial amounts of money. Eventually, plaintiff made a will naming defendant as his sole beneficiary and executed a deed naming her a joint owner of his farm. The record reveals that numerous alterations in the way of modernization were made to plaintiff's farmhouse in alleged furtherance of "domestic plans" made by plaintiff and defendant.

In September, 1971, while the renovations were still in progress, plaintiff transferred his remaining joint interest to defendant. In February, 1973, the liaison between the parties was abruptly severed as defendant ordered plaintiff to move out of his home and vacate the farm. Defendant took possession of the home, the farm and all the equipment thereon, leaving plaintiff with assets of $300.

Generally, a constructive trust may be imposed "[w]hen property has been acquired in such circumstances that the holder of the legal title may not in good conscience retain the beneficial interest" (Beatty v. Guggenheim Exploration Co., 225 NY 380, 386; 1 Scott, Trusts [3d ed], §44.2, p 337; 4 Pomeroy's Equity Jurisprudence [5th ed], §1053, p 119). Most frequently, it is the existence of a confidential relationship which triggers the equitable considerations leading to the imposition of a constructive trust. Although no marital or other family relationship is present in this case, such is not essential for the existence of a confidential relation. The record in this case clearly indicates that a relationship of trust and confidence did exist between the parties and, hence, the defendant must be charged with an obligation not to abuse the trust and confidence placed in her by the plaintiff. The disparity in education between the plaintiff and defendant highlights the degree of dependence of the plaintiff upon the trust and honor of the defendant.

Unquestionably, there is a transfer of property here, but the Trial Judge found that the transfer was made "without a promise or understanding of any kind." Even without an express promise, however, courts of equity have imposed a constructive trust upon property transferred in reliance upon a confidential relationship. In such a situation, a promise may be implied or inferred from the very transaction itself. As Judge Cardozo so eloquently observed: "Though a promise in words was lacking, the whole transaction, it might be found, was 'instinct with an obligation' imperfectly expressed" (Wood v. Duff-Gordon, 222 N. Y. 88, 91). In deciding that a formal writing or express promise was not essential to the application of the doctrine of constructive trust, Judge Cardozo further observed in language that is most fitting in the instant case:

> Here was a man transferring to his sister the only property he had in the world. He was doing this, as she admits, in reliance upon her honor. Even if we were to accept her statement that there was no distinct promise to hold for his benefit, the exaction of such a promise, in view of the relation, might well have seemed to be superfluous. Sinclair v Purdy, 235 NY 245, 254.

More recently, in Farano v. Stephanelli (7 AD2d 420, 425), Chief Judge Breitel, then writing for the Appellate Division, First Department, followed the *Sinclair* approach stating that the decision to invoke the remedy of constructive trust "need not be determined exclusively by whether or not the defendant daughters expressed in so many words a promise to reconvey the properties to the father if he should ask." Indeed, in the case before us, it is inconceivable that plaintiff would convey all of his interest in property which was not only his abode but the very means of his livelihood without at least tacit consent upon the part of the defendant that she would permit him to continue to live on and operate the farm. I would therefore reject the Trial Judge's conclusion, erroneously termed a finding of fact, that no agreement or limitation may, as a matter of law, be implied from the circumstances surrounding the transfer of plaintiff's farm.

The salutary purpose of the constructive trust remedy is to prevent unjust enrichment and it is to this requirement that I now turn. The Trial Judge in his findings of fact, concluded that the transfer did not constitute unjust enrichment. In this instance also, a legal conclusion was mistakenly labeled a finding of fact. A person may be deemed to be unjustly enriched if he (or she) has received a benefit, the retention of which would be unjust (Restatement, Restitution, §1, Comment *a*). A conclusion that one has been unjustly enriched is essentially a legal inference drawn from the circumstances surrounding the transfer of property and the relationship of the parties. It is a conclusion reached through the application of principles of equity. Having determined that the relationship between plaintiff and defendant in this case is of such a nature as to invoke consideration of the equitable remedy of constructive trust, it remains to be determined whether defendant's conduct following the transfer of plaintiff's farm was in violation of that relationship and, consequently, resulted in the unjust enrichment of the defendant. This must be determined from the circumstances of the transfer since there is no express promise concerning plaintiff's continued use of the land. Therefore, the case should be remitted to the Appellate Division for a review of the facts. In so doing I would emphasize that the conveyance herein should be interpreted "not literally or irrespective of its setting, but sensibly and broadly with all its human implications" (Sinclair v. Purdy, 235 NY 245, 254). This case seems to present the classic example of a situation where equity should intervene to scrutinize a transaction pregnant with opportunity for abuse and unfairness. It was for just this type of case that there evolved equitable principles and remedies to prevent injustices. Equity still lives. To suffer the hands of equity to be bound by misnamed "findings of fact" which are actually conclusions of law and legal inferences drawn from the facts is to ignore and render impotent the rich and vital impact of equity on the common law and, perforce, permit injustice. Universality of law requires equity.

Accordingly, the order of the Appellate Division should be reversed and the case remitted to that court for a review of the facts, or, if it be so advised, in its discretion, to order a new trial in the interests of justice.

Chief Judge Breitel and Judges Wachtler and Fuchsberg concur with Judge Gabrielli; Judges Jasen, Jones and Cooke dissent and vote to affirm in the following memorandum: In view of the affirmed findings of fact that the appellant knowingly and voluntarily conveyed his property without agreement or condition of any kind, express or implied, and with full knowledge of their legal effect, it cannot be said that a constructive trust should be imposed as a matter of law. Although we are sympathetic to the appellant who has been doubly aggrieved by the loss of his wife and property, we are limited to consideration of questions of law and, therefore, in light of the factual findings, would affirm.

Salzman v. Bachrach
996 P.2d 1263 (Colo. 2000)

Justice KOURLIS delivered the Opinion of the Court.

We granted certiorari to review the court of appeals' decision in Bachrach v. Salzman, 981 P.2d 219 (Colo. App. 1999). We conclude that the Respondent, Erwin Bachrach, established a claim of unjust enrichment and is entitled to restitution of at least some of his contributions to the residence titled in the name of Petitioner Roberta F. Salzman. Accordingly, we affirm the court of appeals and remand this case to the trial court for a determination of the amount of restitution based upon the principles set out in this opinion.

I.

Bachrach and Salzman met in 1986 when Salzman, a divorcee, responded to a personal advertisement in the *Vail Trail* newspaper placed by Bachrach, a widower. Bachrach and Salzman enjoyed a relationship that included dining, travel, and visiting with family and friends. The two maintained separate residences during the first several years of their relationship. Bachrach lived in a one-bedroom condominium that he owned, and Salzman resided in a townhouse. Salzman disliked her townhouse because of its small size, poor winter access, and because she had difficulty climbing the stairs.

In 1993, Bachrach and Salzman agreed to build a home together. Bachrach placed the condominium that he owned on the market late that year, and sold it in February 1994. Bachrach netted roughly $100,000 from the sale. On March 31, 1994, Bachrach and Salzman purchased a lot in Eagle, Colorado for $49,000, and titled it in both of their names. They contributed approximately equally to the price.

Bachrach, a designer and drafter of residential properties for fifty years, designed the new home. Initially, he estimated a total construction cost of $370,000. The construction crew broke ground on July 19, 1994 and substantially completed construction by April 1995, when the two moved into the home together. The home ultimately cost $520,876.50 to build. Bachrach contributed $167,528.86, and Salzman paid $353,347.64 of the total cost. In March 1995, the residence appraised for $445,000; in November 1996, it appraised for $584,000.

On April 18, 1995, Bachrach quitclaimed his interest in the property to Salzman, and Salzman closed on the sale of her townhouse. Bachrach's delivery of the deed to Salzman at that time served two functions. It facilitated Salzman's ability to obtain a favorable mortgage on the home, and offered tax advantages to Salzman. However, there was a third purpose that came to light approximately six months later.

In November 1995, Salzman's ex-husband notified her that he intended to terminate his monthly maintenance payment of $1,800 because of her alleged marriage to Bachrach, cohabitation, and joint homeownership. Bachrach replied to Salzman's ex-husband in writing that they were not married, but lived together for convenience and companionship; that they maintained separate financial accounts; that she alone owned the home; and that his contribution was in exchange for an indefinite period of free rent. After receiving the letter, Salzman's ex-spouse did not further pursue termination of maintenance. Hence, in a written document, Bachrach disavowed any interest in the home—equitable or otherwise.

During their cohabitation in the new home, Salzman made all of the mortgage payments and Bachrach paid only for some utilities and food. He did not pay rent. Initially, the parties shared a bedroom, but after about a year, they found one another intolerable and Bachrach moved into a separate bedroom. In August 1996, Salzman asked Bachrach to move out, and he refused. On January 15, 1997, Salzman changed the locks and posted a No Trespassing sign on the property, with the added phrase "This means you Erwin." Bachrach has not lived in the home since that day.

On January 17, 1997, Bachrach filed suit in the District Court in the County of Eagle, Colorado against Salzman, seeking a partition of the property under the theory that the two were joint venturers in the construction of the home. Salzman asserted counterclaims that Bachrach negligently designed the home, poorly managed its construction, misrepresented himself as an architect, and miscalculated the cost of the home, among others. The parties tried the case before the District Court in November 1997. The court denied both parties the relief that they sought.

The court of appeals reversed the order of the trial court, holding that Salzman would be unjustly enriched were she allowed to keep Bachrach's contributions to the home. The court of appeals opined, however, that on remand, in determining the amount owed Bachrach, the trial court could consider the reasonable rental value Bachrach received while he resided in the house.

II.

We begin our analysis by addressing Bachrach's argument that Salzman should reimburse him for his design work, construction management services, and his $170,000 contribution on principles of unjust enrichment. The Restatement of Restitution states "[a] person who has been unjustly enriched at the expense of another is required to make restitution to the other." Restatement of Restitution § 1 (1937). "A person obtains restitution when he is restored to the position he formerly occupied either by the return of something which he formerly had or by the receipt of its monetary equivalent." *Id.* §1 cmt. a.

In Colorado, a plaintiff seeking recovery for unjust enrichment must prove: (1) at plaintiff's expense (2) defendant received a benefit (3) under circumstances that would make it unjust for defendant to retain the benefit without paying. See DCB Constr. Co. v. Central City Dev. Co., 965 P.2d 115, 119-20 (Colo. 1998). Absent some countervailing consideration, it would be unjust to allow Salzman to keep Bachrach's entire contribution to the home.

IIIA.

Salzman argues that Bachrach is without a remedy because he delivered the funds to her in exchange for a cohabitation agreement. She contends that public policy disapproves of such an arrangement and any decision in favor of Bachrach would operate to defeat that policy, citing three cases. See Houlton v. Prosser, 118 Colo. 304, 194 P.2d 911 (1948); Baker v. Sockwell, 80 Colo. 309, 251 P. 543 (1926); Baker v. Couch, 74 Colo. 380, 221 P. 1089 (1923).

In *Baker v. Couch*, this court declined to order the return of thirty-five promissory notes to the plaintiff, Paul Couch. Couch, a twenty-three year old man, and Alma Baker, a woman in her early thirties, lived together, in an intimate relationship. Couch had been married and divorced previously, and Baker had been married three times. Couch argued that Baker obtained the notes through undue influence, and Baker contended they were a gift. The parties did execute a contract, which Couch argued was without consideration. The contract closed with the following language: "Party to the first part [Baker] agrees to permit the party of the second part [Couch] to call at her home at reasonable hours and to continue the friendship already begun, until such time as the parties hereto agree to terminate this agreement." The court concluded that past, present, and future sexual relations were the sole consideration for the original delivery of the promissory notes and the "so-called written contract." Thus, the court held, because the contract was immoral, "neither law nor equity will aid either to enforce, revoke or rescind."

In *Houlton*, a single man and a married woman cohabited as husband and wife during a five-year period in the 1940s. Houlton purchased a home and the two took title as joint tenants. When the relationship soured, Houlton sought to have the court order his female cohabitant, Prosser, to convey to him any interest she held in the home. The court noted that Houlton knew that Prosser was married during most of their relationship and that he admitted that they lived together in an intimate relationship. The court reasoned that even though Houlton maintained that the sexual relationship was not in consideration of the deed, he was "not in a position to invoke the aid of a court of equity in his effort to obtain a conveyance of [Prosser's] interest in the property to himself."

Bachrach distinguishes the above cases because he contributed to the construction project in the expectation that he would live there indefinitely. Although Bachrach highly valued Salzman's companionship, he asserts that sexual relations constituted no part of the exchange. We find Bachrach's argument persuasive.

The facts present here are distinguishable from the *Baker v. Couch* line of cases. The facts in *Couch* and *Sockwell* exhibited clearer evidence than present here that the sole consideration for the monetary conveyance was sexual relations. Perhaps due to the era of the decisions, the court provided very little information to suggest that Baker offered Couch anything other than an intimate relationship. In essence, the contract mirrored a contract for prostitution. Contrarily, in this case, Salzman's agreement to allow Bachrach to live in the home constituted substantial consideration for his contribution.

Although a closer case, *Houlton* can also be distinguished because one of the cohabitants was married during the majority of the parties' relationship. This adulterous component made Houlton considerably more culpable than Bachrach.

IIIB.

Even were we unable to distinguish the above line of cases, we would decline to follow them under the facts present here. Although we find the rule of law in these earlier cases persuasive to some degree, social norms and behaviors have changed to such an extent that we now join the majority of courts in other states in holding that nonmarried cohabiting couples may legally contract with each other so long as sexual relations are merely incidental to the agreement. Furthermore, such couples may ask a court for assistance, in law or in equity, to enforce such agreements.

The frequency of nonmarital cohabitation has substantially increased since the 1940s. See Bureau of the Census, *Marital Status and Living Arrangements: March 1993*, VII-VIII, tbl. D (May 1994) (indicating that from 1970 to 1993 alone, the number of unmarried-couple households in the U.S. increased 571%, from 523,000 to 3,510,000). As a result, courts throughout the country now face with increasing regularity the controversies arising out of the breakup of these relationships. Litigants have asked courts to establish the appropriate balance between the public policy favoring marriage, old cases explicitly disapproving any intimate contact outside of marriage, and accepted modern mores. The majority of courts have held in favor of the ability of nonmarried couples to contract with one another and to enforce those contracts in court.

In many jurisdictions, courts have examined the factual circumstances underlying unmarried cohabiting relationships, and have regularly enforced express and implied contracts between nonmarried cohabitants and provided equitable remedies. See Marvin v. Marvin, 18 Cal. 3d 660, 557 P.2d 106 (1976) (holding, in this landmark case, that California courts must enforce express and implied agreements unless based wholly on sexual relations, and allowing the application of equitable remedies); Boland v. Catalano, 202 Conn. 333, 521 A.2d 142 (1987) (concluding that the existence of a sexual relationship between nonmarried cohabitants did not preclude enforcement of an express agreement to share equally in the assets accumulated while living together as long as the agreement was not founded upon their sexual relationship); Mason v. Rostad, 476 A.2d 662 (D.C. 1984) (finding that a man could recover the reasonable value of the work contributed toward the renovation of another's house reduced by the benefits he received from the arrangement despite the fact they were unmarried and living together); Spafford v. Coats, 118 Ill. App. 3d 566, 455 N.E.2d 241 (1983) (finding that a female unmarried cohabitant who furnished most of the money for several vehicles purchased during a cohabiting relationship was not barred by their cohabitation from bringing an unjust enrichment claim against the other cohabitant who retained control over the vehicles); Collins v. Davis, 68 N.C. App. 588, 315 S.E.2d 759 (1984) (reasoning that a married man living with a single woman was not barred from bringing a suit in equity for unjust enrichment when he contributed to the purchase of a house titled in the woman's name, if the agreement was not based exclusively on sexual intercourse); Wilbur v. DeLapp, 119 Or. App. 348, 850 P.2d 1151 (1993) (holding that the unmarried parties who lived together intended that the female cohabitant have a one-half interest in property held in the male partner's name); Lawlis v. Thompson, 137 Wis. 2d 490, 405 N.W.2d 317 (1987) (holding that nonmarital cohabitation alone would not preclude a cohabitant from bringing an unjust enrichment claim against the other cohabitant). But see Long v. Marino, 212 Ga. App. 113, 441 S.E.2d 475 (1994) (suggesting that the law will not support a contract founded on the immoral consideration of unmarried cohabitation); Hewitt v. Hewitt, 77 Ill. 2d 49, 394 N.E.2d 1204 (1979) (refusing to grant to a cohabitant one-half of the assets acquired during the cohabitation, reasoning that enforcing the contracts would grant a legal status to cohabitation); Schwegmann v. Schwegmann, 441 So. 2d 316 (La. Ct. App. 1983) (concluding that unmarried cohabitation does not give rise to property rights analogous to those arising from marriage, and that claims in equity are barred when sexual relations are interwoven with other tendered benefits); In re Estate of Alexander, 445 So. 2d 836 (Miss. 1984) (deciding that the legislature was better suited to handle unmarried cohabitation policies and expressing concern that extending equitable principles would resurrect the abolished common-law marriage doctrine).

We find these authorities persuasive and agree that cohabitation and sexual relations alone do not suspend contract and equity principles. We do caution, however, that mere cohabitation does not trigger any marital rights. A court should not decline to provide relief to parties in dispute merely because their dispute arose in relationship to cohabitation. Rather, the court should determine—as with any other parties—whether general contract laws and equitable rules apply.

In this case, the evidence supports Bachrach's claim that sexual relations with Salzman were not the sole motivation for his contributions toward the construction of the home. He sold his condominium and placed all of the proceeds and other funds directly into the home in which he expected to live for the balance of his life. Both Salzman and Bachrach took title to the land on which the home was built, and according to undisputed testimony, Bachrach quitclaimed his entire interest in the home largely for the benefit of Salzman.

In consideration for Bachrach's contributions he obtained a much larger, more luxurious home in which to live and work, a cohabitant for whom he cared, and reduced living expenses. As we see it, sexual relations with Salzman constituted only a portion of the benefits received by Bachrach, and definitely were not the sole consideration. While the home purchase related to their intimate relationship because they both lived in the home, Bachrach's cause of action does not depend on their sexual relations. Thus, their cohabitation does not bar this suit in equity.

IV.

Salzman also argues that Bachrach comes to the court with unclean hands because he agreed in writing that he had no ownership interest in the house and overtly structured the ownership of the home and other aspects of their relationship to avoid the negative effect a common-law marriage might have had on her receipt of maintenance payments. In her view, this wrongdoing should prevent Bachrach from his pursuit of an equitable remedy.

Generally, "[o]ne who comes into equity must come with clean hands." Dan B. Dobbs, *Law of Remedies* §2.4(2) (2d ed. 1993). The principal derives from the concept that one who seeks equity must do equity. Many different forms of improper conduct may bar a plaintiff's equitable claim, and the conduct need not be illegal. Generally, courts apply this doctrine only when a plaintiff's improper conduct relates in some significant way to the claim he now asserts. Otherwise, only those leading pristine and blameless lives would ever be entitled to equitable relief.

In Colorado, the clean hands maxim dictates that one who has engaged in improper conduct regarding the subject matter of the cause of action may, as a result, lose entitlement to an equitable remedy. The clean hands doctrine is one of public policy, devised to protect the integrity of the court.

Upon remand, the trial court should address whether the doctrine of unclean hands should limit Bachrach's claim for relief. Specifically, we note that Bachrach stated in writing that he held no interest in the house for the express purpose of deceiving Salzman's ex-husband and a court in Florida. On the other hand, the trial court may conclude that Bachrach did so at Salzman's urging and that, ultimately, she benefited far more from the deception than did Bachrach.

V.

Having determined that Bachrach's claim is not barred by the parties' cohabitation, we must now remand the case to the court of appeals to be returned to the trial court for further factual determinations. Several financial issues remain to be sorted out by the trial court. For example, the trial court must determine the exact worth of Bachrach's contribution to date, and the reasonable rental value for the periods Bachrach lived in the house. As set forth above, we also direct the trial court to determine whether the unclean hands doctrine should bar any portion of Bachrach's recovery.

Conditional gifts?

1. The opinion in *Salzman v. Bachrach* sketches the rapid evolution of economic claims between former cohabitants. As can be seen from the older Colorado cases, even an express contract formed in such a relationship—possibly involving a promise to provide support or to convey an interest in property—was formerly regarded as "meretricious," illegal, and therefore unenforceable. This traditional attitude was permanently disrupted in *Marvin v. Marvin*, the famous "palimony" decision by the California Supreme Court in 1976. Forty years later, it is a safe assumption that contracts (express or implied) formed by unmarried couples will not encounter objections to enforceability based on the parties' domestic relations. Restitution, rather than contract, becomes the predominant theory of property readjustments in those cases where no promises about compensation or property division were ever made.

2. What exactly is the reasoning by which uncompensated benefits between former cohabitants come to be seen—in retrospect—as a source of unjust enrichment? If no contract can be found, these transactions tend to look gratuitous. But so long as a gift is valid when made—being unaffected by fraud,

mistake, undue influence, and the like—the donor normally cannot recover in restitution by proving that the gift was a bad idea: for instance, that the donor could not afford it, that the result was unfair, or that the donee was an unworthy recipient.

3. Part of the court's opinion in *Sharp v. Kosmalski* relies on the idea that the parties occupied a confidential relationship, alias "a relation of trust and confidence." Such a relationship is a near relative of fiduciary obligation, and it imposes an equivalent duty to act in the interests of the other party. The transaction at issue in *Sinclair v. Purdy*, quoted by the court—a transfer between brother and sister—is typical of the circumstances in which courts sometimes find that a relation of trust and confidence has been violated. By contrast, a rule that unmarried cohabitants *ipso facto* occupy a relation of trust and confidence toward each other would quickly lead to unwieldy consequences, and most decisions on the rights of former cohabitants make no such suggestion.

4. The original Restatement of Restitution (1937) included the following rule:

§58. Gifts made in reliance on a relation.

A person who has conferred a benefit upon another, manifesting that he does not expect compensation therefor, is not entitled to restitution merely because his expectation that an existing relation will continue or that a future relation will come into existence is not realized, unless the conferring of the benefit is conditioned thereon.

Naturally, the 1937 *Restatement* did not make any reference to unmarried cohabitants: the illustrations to this section all involved "a husband or wife who makes gifts to the other spouse in the expectation that the relation will continue," or "a man or woman who makes gifts to a person with whom promises to marry have been exchanged." Gifts might of course be made expressly conditional, and "justice may require the creation of a condition although the donor had no such condition in mind." Restitution was also allowed if "the donee obtained the gift fraudulently or if the gift was made for a purpose which could be achieved only by the marriage." Consider this sample of 1937 illustrations:

4. A, seeking to gain the affection of B, makes valuable gifts to her. When he finally asks her to marry him, she refuses him. A is not entitled to restitution.

5. A promises to marry B, the daughter of C. In anticipation of a honeymoon motor trip by A and B, C gives to A a motor car. Thereafter by mutual agreement A and B terminate their contract. C is entitled to the return of the motor car.

7. A makes gifts of money and of family heirlooms to B who has promised to marry him. B spends the money for living expenses as was expected

but retains the jewelry. Later B comes to the conclusion that she does not wish to marry A and refuses to do so. A is not entitled to restitution of the money but is entitled to the return of the heirlooms.

5. Leaving aside cases of fraud by the donee (too easy), who is entitled to an engagement ring if the anticipated marriage does not take place? Does it matter why the engagement is broken, or by whom? According to Restatement §58 (1937), "Gifts made in anticipation of marriage are not ordinarily expressed to be conditional and . . . if the marriage fails to occur *without the fault of the donee*, normally the gift cannot be recovered"(emphasis added).

The traditional rule was tested in Lindh v. Surman, 560 Pa. 1, 742 A.2d 643 (1999), where the facts were stated as follows:

> The facts of this case depict a tumultuous engagement between Rodger Lindh (Rodger), a divorced, middle-aged man, and Janis Surman (Janis), the object of Rodger's inconstant affections. In August of 1993, Rodger proposed marriage to Janis. To that purpose, he presented her with a diamond engagement ring that he purchased for $17,400. Rodger testified that the price was less than the ring's market value because he was a "good customer" of the jeweler's, having previously purchased a $4,000 ring for his ex-wife and other expensive jewelry for his children. Janis, who had never been married, accepted his marriage proposal and the ring. Discord developed in the relationship between Rodger and Janis, and in October of 1993 Rodger broke the engagement and asked for the return of the ring. At that time, Janis obliged and gave Rodger the ring. Rodger and Janis attempted to reconcile. They succeeded, and Rodger again proposed marriage, and offered the ring, to Janis. For a second time, Janis accepted. In March of 1994, however, Rodger called off the engagement. He asked for the return of the ring, which Janis refused, and this litigation ensued.

The parties agreed that a gift of an engagement ring was impliedly "conditional" in Pennsylvania, but they disagreed on the substance of the implied condition. Janis (like the 1937 *Restatement*) agreed that a donee who broke off the engagement would be obliged to return the ring. This much follows pretty easily from the traditional idea of an engagement as a contract. But here it was Rodger, the donor of the ring, who had (twice) broken the engagement. According to the court, this presented "a novel question of Pennsylvania law." From this we can infer that—until Rodger sued Janis for conversion in 1994— no man in the history of Pennsylvania had ever presented his fiancée with an engagement ring, then repudiated his engagement, then sued his former fiancée to recover the gift.

Is Rodger entitled to restitution of the ring? (The Pennsylvania court held 4-3 that he was.) If so, why? Does Rodger's claim have any basis in contract? In unjust enrichment? Is there a possible analogy to restitution between former cohabitants?

Maglica v. Maglica

66 Cal. App. 4th 442, 78 Cal. Rptr. 2d 101 (1998)

Sills, P. J.

I.   Introduction

This case forces us to confront the legal doctrine known as "quantum meruit" in the context of a case about an unmarried couple who lived together and worked in a business solely owned by one of them. Quantum meruit is a Latin phrase, meaning "as much as he deserves," and is based on the idea that someone should get paid for beneficial goods or services which he or she bestows on another.

The trial judge instructed the jury that the reasonable value of the plaintiff's services was either the value of what it would have cost the defendant to obtain those services from someone else or the "value by which" he had "benefited as a result" of those services. The instruction allowed the jury to reach a whopping number in favor of the plaintiff—$84 million—because of the tremendous growth in the *value* of the business over the years.

As we explain later, the finding that the couple had no contract in the first place is itself somewhat suspect because certain jury instructions did not accurately convey the law concerning implied-in-fact contracts. However, assuming that there was indeed no contract, the quantum meruit award cannot stand. The legal test for recovery in quantum meruit is not the value of the benefit, but value of the services (assuming, of course, that the services were beneficial to the recipient in the first place). In this case the failure to appreciate that fine distinction meant a big difference. People who work for businesses for a period of years and then walk away with $84 million do so because they have acquired some *equity* in the business, not because $84 million is the going rate for the services of even the most workaholic manager. In substance, the court was allowing the jury to value the plaintiff's services as if she had made a sweetheart stock option deal—yet such a deal was precisely what the jury found she did not make. So the $84 million judgment cannot stand.

On the other hand, plaintiff was hindered in her ability to prove the existence of an implied-in-fact contract by a series of jury instructions which may have misled the jury about certain of the factors which bear on such contracts. The instructions were insufficiently qualified. They told the jury flat out that such facts as a couple's living together or holding themselves out as husband and wife or sharing a common surname did not mean that they had any agreement to share assets. That is not *exactly* correct. Such factors can, indeed, when taken together with other facts and in context, show the existence of an implied-in-fact contract. At most the jury instructions should have said that such factors do not *by themselves necessarily* show an implied-in-fact contract. Accordingly, when the case is retried, the plaintiff will have another chance to prove that she indeed had a deal for a share of equity in the defendant's business.

II. *Facts*

The important facts in this case may be briefly stated. Anthony Maglica, a Croatian immigrant, founded his own machine shop business, Mag Instrument, in 1955. He got divorced in 1971 and kept the business. That year he met Claire Halasz, an interior designer. They got on famously, and lived together, holding themselves out as man and wife—hence Claire began using the name Claire Maglica—but never actually got married. And, while they worked side by side building the business, Anthony never agreed—or at least the jury found Anthony never agreed—to give Claire a share of the business. When the business was incorporated in 1974 all shares went into Anthony's name. Anthony was the president and Claire was the secretary. They were paid equal salaries from the business after incorporation. In 1978 the business began manufacturing flashlights, and, thanks in part to some great ideas and hard work on Claire's part (e.g., coming out with a purse-sized flashlight in colors), the business boomed. Mag Instrument, Inc., is now worth hundreds of millions of dollars.

In 1992 Claire discovered that Anthony was trying to transfer stock to his children but not her, and the couple split up in October. In June 1993 Claire sued Anthony for, among other things, breach of contract, breach of partnership agreement, fraud, breach of fiduciary duty and quantum meruit. The case came to trial in the spring of 1994. The jury awarded $84 million for the breach of fiduciary duty and quantum meruit causes of action, finding that $84 million was the reasonable value of Claire's services.

III. *Discussion*

A. THE JURY'S FINDING THAT THERE WAS NO AGREEMENT TO HOLD PROPERTY FOR ONE ANOTHER MEANT THERE WAS NO BREACH OF FIDUCIARY DUTY

California specifically abolished the idea of a "common law marriage" in 1895 (see Elden v. Sheldon (1988) 46 Cal. 3d 267, 275) and that, if it is not too harsh to say it, was clearly the *substance* of Claire and Anthony's relationship. They had a common law marriage.

As our Supreme Court said in *Elden*, "[f]ormally married couples are granted significant rights and bear important responsibilities toward one another which are not shared by those who cohabit without marriage." The court noted, in that context, that a variety of statutes impose rights and obligations on married people. One set of such imposed rights and obligations, for example, is Family Code sections 1100 through 1103, which both establish a fiduciary duty between spouses with regard to the management and control of community assets and provide for remedies for a breach of that duty.

It would be contrary to what our Supreme Court said in *Elden* and to the evident policy of the law to promote formal (as distinct from common law) marriage to impose fiduciary duties based on a common law marriage. . . .

That leaves contract, and the jury found there was no contract. Claire, despite the closeness of their relationship, never entrusted her *property* to Anthony; she only rendered services. And without entrustment of property, or an oral agreement to purchase property together, there can be no fiduciary relationship no matter how "confidential" a relationship between an unmarried, cohabiting couple. (Toney v. Nolder (1985) 173 Cal. App. 3d 791, 796.)

B. QUANTUM MERUIT ALLOWS RECOVERY FOR THE VALUE OF
  BENEFICIAL SERVICES, NOT THE VALUE BY WHICH SOMEONE
  BENEFITS FROM THOSE SERVICES

The absence of a contract between Claire and Anthony, however, would not preclude her recovery in quantum meruit: As every first year law student knows or should know, recovery in quantum meruit does not require a contract.

The classic formulation concerning the measure of recovery in quantum meruit is found in Palmer v. Gregg, (1967) 65 Cal. 2d 657, 660. Justice Mosk, writing for the court, said: "The measure of recovery in *quantum meruit* is the reasonable value of the services rendered *provided* they were of direct benefit to the defendant."

The underlying idea behind quantum meruit is the law's distaste for unjust enrichment. If one has received a benefit which one may not justly retain, one should "restore the aggrieved party to his [or her] former position by return of the *thing* or its *equivalent* in money." (1 Witkin, Summary of Cal. Law, Contracts, §91, p. 122.)

But the threshold requirement that there be a benefit from the services can lead to confusion, as it did in the case before us. It is one thing to require that the defendant be benefited by services, it is quite another to *measure* the reasonable value of those *services* by the value by which the defendant was "benefited" as a *result* of them. Contract price and the reasonable value of services rendered are two separate things; sometimes the reasonable value of services exceeds a contract price. And sometimes it does not.

The jury instruction given here allows the value of services to depend on their *impact* on a defendant's business rather than their reasonable value. True, the services must be of benefit if there is to be any recovery at all; even so, the benefit is not necessarily related to the reasonable value of a particular set of services. Sometimes luck, sometimes the impact of others makes the difference. Some enterprises are successful; others less so. Allowing recovery based on *resulting* benefit would mean the law imposes an exchange of equity for services, and that can result in a windfall—as in the present case—or a serious shortfall in others. Equity-for-service compensation packages are extraordinary in the labor market, and always the result of specific bargaining. To impose such a measure of recovery would make a deal for the parties that they did not make themselves.

Telling the jury that it could measure the value of Claire's services by "[t]he value by which Defendant has benefited as a result of [her] services" was error. It allowed the jury to value Claire's services as having bought her a de facto ownership interest in a business whose owner never agreed to give her an interest. On remand, that part of the jury instruction must be dropped.

C.   CLAIRE'S QUANTUM MERUIT CLAIM IS NOT BARRED BY THE STATUTE OF LIMITATIONS

The statute of limitations for quantum meruit claims is two years (see Code Civ. Proc., §339 [action upon an "obligation" not founded upon an instrument of writing]), but Claire seeks payment for services rendered since 1971. Anthony contends that her claim for all but the last two years' worth of services must necessarily fail in light of that fact; Claire argues that the statute of limitations only began to run with the termination of her services. . . . On reflection, Claire has the better part of this argument, as illustrated by Lazzarevich v. Lazzarevich, (1948) 88 Cal. App. 2d 708. While the fact that Claire had a "common law marriage" is fatal to her fiduciary duty claims, *Lazzarevich* demonstrates why any expectation of compensation for her efforts would be at the termination of the relationship.

In *Lazzarevich*, a couple got married, then the husband filed for a divorce, but there was a reconciliation. However, without the husband's knowledge a final decree of divorce was entered. When the couple finally did split up, the wife sought recovery for the reasonable value of the services she rendered her husband during the period she lived with him under the mistaken belief that they were still married. The trial court awarded her only the last two years, but the appellate court modified the judgment to increase her recovery fourfold. The core of the court's reasoning was that because the plaintiff had rendered her services under the mistaken belief that her marriage was valid, it was "obvious" that any cause of action could not have accrued until she discovered her marriage was invalid. The fictitious implied promise to pay for the services inherent in the relationship entailed another fictitious implied promise to pay at termination of the services.

Lazzarevich reflects the contours of Claire and Anthony's own relationship here.They might not have been married, but they certainly acted married. While the special solicitude the law shows for formal marriage and putative relationships (i.e., where a person believes, in good faith, that he or she is married) means that Claire did not acquire the same substantive rights as a married person, the "common law marriage" nature of her relationship with Anthony certainly shows that, *like a married person*, any need to sue to assert whatever rights she did have would be expected to accrue at the termination of the relationship, not when some hypothetical paycheck might ordinarily come due.

Any other result simply does not accord with the reality of the situation as the parties experienced it. Accordingly, on remand, the statute of limitations will not limit Claire's quantum meruit claim.

[Reversed and remanded.]

Measuring enrichment between cohabitants

1. *Maglica v. Maglica* probably reaches the correct result in orthodox restitution terms (at least the *Restatement* says it does), but it is not hard to see why some observers find the court's approach unsatisfactory. See Candace Kovacic-Fleischer, *Cohabitation and the Restatement (Third) of Restitution and Unjust Enrichment*, 68 Wash. & Lee L. Rev. 1407 (2011). Restitution between cohabitants tends to focus on contributions of quantifiable assets such as cash or houses—as in *Sharp v. Kosmalski* and *Salzman v. Bachrach*. It tends to downplay or ignore contributions in the form of domestic services, usually on the view that it is impossible to value or account for the everyday give-and-take between people who choose to live together.

Claire Maglica's services were performed in a business setting, and the court is ready to recognize the usual *quantum meruit* claim for remuneration at fair market value. Notice, however, that this leaves her in the position of an employee who walked in off the street and worked for 20 years in Anthony's flashlight business without (somehow) ever making an express contract on the question of salary. Such an employee has an implied contract for wages at the going rate, but—as the court correctly says—no right to a share in the business.

If the Maglicas had been married and then divorced, the property division between them, in any jurisdiction, would have been much more favorable to Claire. (Compare the case of the Meyers, described in the following note.) If we feel that Claire has been unjustly treated, isn't it because justice in this case requires treating the Maglicas as if they had been married? This was the solution proposed by the American Law Institute's Principles of the Law of Family Dissolution: Analysis and Recommendations, ch. 6 (2002). Do the radically altered social norms in this area mean that "common law marriage," abolished by 19th-century legislatures, has been revived as a practical matter?

2. The facts of Meyer v. Meyer, 239 Wis. 2d 731, 620 N.W.2d 382 (2000), included the following elements:

> The Meyers met and began dating in 1985. In the spring of 1986 they began living together at her apartment in Green Bay. At that time, the petitioner was working as a nurse, and the respondent was pursuing his undergraduate education at the University of Wisconsin-Green Bay.
>
> During the time the parties lived together in Green Bay, the petitioner financially supported the household, and the respondent focused on his

education. While she remained fully employed, first as a nurse and then as an insurance claims examiner, his employment was limited to irregular work and summer jobs. He funded his education primarily with student loans. In addition to her financial role, the petitioner also performed homemaking duties and assisted the respondent with his schooling by typing some of his college papers.

According to the petitioner's testimony, in late 1986 the respondent gave her a "promise ring" to symbolize the parties' commitment to one another. However, the parties did not become engaged to marry until 1989. Their engagement coincided with the couple's move to Milwaukee. In the autumn of 1989, respondent began his studies at the Medical College of Wisconsin.

During their four-year engagement, the petitioner continued to work while the respondent attended school. In the spring of 1994, the respondent graduated from medical school. Following graduation the couple moved again, this time to La Crosse where the respondent began his residency program.

In La Crosse, the respondent worked to complete his residency, and the petitioner continued to work in the insurance industry. The respondent completed his residency in mid-1997. He then began practicing as a physician at a La Crosse clinic. At that time his monthly salary was $10,400 while hers was around $2,000.

In real life, the Meyers were finally married in 1994, but "in June 1997, just as the respondent was beginning his new career, the petitioner filed for divorce." This meant that questions of property division or alimony would be governed by Wisconsin statutes on marriage dissolution—not common-law restitution. Part of the petitioner's case, however, was that Dr. Meyer would be "unjustly enriched" unless petitioner received "compensation for the support given to the respondent during their period of premarital cohabitation." The trial court agreed, finding that petitioner had made "very significant and substantial" contributions to the respondent's "current status" and earning capacity, both before and during the marriage:

> The Respondent wanted to go to school, and the Petitioner made it easy for the Respondent to do that. She typed his papers and was there for him to do his laundry and make a home for him. It was a relationship that the Respondent clearly benefitted from, and which enabled him to obtain his current education and resulting earning capacity as a practicing physician. The Petitioner shared her bed, home, and income with the Respondent with the expectation that some day she would be a doctor's wife . . . .

Suppose instead that the Meyers had never married. When Dr. Meyer completed his residency in 1997, he took back his "promise ring" and ended the relationship. Is he liable in restitution? If so, for how much?

3. Consider the following illustration from R3RUE §28:

> 12. A and B, unmarried cohabitants, purchase a condominium for $100,000, taking title in B's name to facilitate obtaining a mortgage loan. Each of them contributes $10,000 to the $20,000 down payment; principal and interest on the $80,000 loan are thereafter paid from a joint bank account to which both parties deposit their current earnings. The parties separate two years later, and B sells the condo. The selling price is $120,000 and the outstanding balance of the loan is $76,000, yielding net proceeds of $44,000. B offers A $10,000 plus interest, which B characterizes as repayment of A's loan to him.

Our intuition is that A must be entitled to $22,000. How do we explain the result without relying on intuition?

———————————

Restatement Third, Restitution and Unjust Enrichment

§28. Unmarried Cohabitants

(1) If two persons have formerly lived together in a relationship resembling marriage, and if one of them owns a specific asset to which the other has made substantial, uncompensated contributions in the form of property or services, the person making such contributions has a claim in restitution against the owner as necessary to prevent unjust enrichment upon the dissolution of the relationship.

c. Unjust enrichment. Claimants within §28 assert a right to restitution for benefits conferred in transactions that are essentially voluntary, unaffected by fraud or mistake, between parties who have—in most cases—consciously forgone both contract and the legal regime (marriage) that would substitute for contract in specifying their economic obligations. (The last point must obviously be qualified, in most jurisdictions, in the case of same-sex partners.) The claimants' motives in conferring these benefits are presumably complex, but they might often be characterized, even in retrospect, as essentially gratuitous—had the parties' subsequent relationship only turned out differently. In theory, at least, the factors so far mentioned should weigh against the availability of restitution. The fact that some transactions between cohabitants appear nevertheless to result in manifest unjust enrichment—and that such unjust enrichment becomes visible only after the termination of the parties' relationship—shows that the propriety of the claim is explained by other features of the parties' relationship.

While a few of the cases within this section might lend themselves to an analysis in terms of undue influence (§15) or breach of confidential relation (§43), a more general explanation of unjust enrichment in this setting refers simply to the claimant's frustrated expectations. Recovery is allowed for benefits that the claimant would not have conferred, except in the expectation that the parties' subsequent relationship would be something other than it proved to be in the event. This is why the unjust enrichment in these cases can be demonstrated only in retrospect.

Even when a transfer between cohabitants is essentially gratuitous, it may be made in the expectation that the donor will share, directly or indirectly, in the resulting benefits. Decisions allowing restitution under §28 involve an implicit determination that the contributions at issue were made on that basis—thereby distinguishing them from ordinary gifts—and that the claimant's expectation was justifiable. They rest, moreover, on an implicit determination that the claimant should not be held to have assumed the risk that things would turn out as they did (compare §27, Comment g); in short, that the transaction is not one that the parties should have regulated by contract (§2(3)).

Farnsworth, *Restitution* 34-36 (2014):

The cases just discussed involved "mistakes" about what the future would hold. A similar logic is one way to understand restitution claims between unmarried former cohabitants—couples who were engaged but then called off the marriage, for example, or couples who lived as though they were married without ever tying the knot, or same-sex partners who lived together in a state that would not recognize their marriage and then separated. Sometimes one party to such an arrangement will sue the other to recover for benefits conferred while they were together. Perhaps one of them always paid the rent during the relationship, or one paid the other's tuition expenses, or one spent money to improve the house where they lived, which increased its resale value later on. Or in an extreme case one of them might simply have deeded property to the other. In any of these cases the parties might separate, with a claim for restitution then made by the party who paid against the party who did not.

These cases are an awkward fit to usual principles of restitution law because at the time the payments are made they typically are meant to be gratuitous. Neither side expected them to ever create any legal obligations. In most other settings, as when similar arrangements occur between family members or friends, this would spoil any possible restitution claim made later. The payments would just be considered either gifts or subjects of implied contracts. There would be no room between those options to squeeze in a restitution claim, because there would be nothing to excuse the claimant's failure to make a contract if he wanted legal obligations to arise from his payments. But the law of restitution handles unmarried cohabitants a little differently. It often lets the claimant collect if the benefits can be clearly proven and quantified.

The reason the law sometimes honors these claims can be viewed as analogous to its reasons for allowing recovery in cases where a party improves property with the reasonable expectation that he owns it, or soon will, but turns out to be mistaken. The unmarried cohabitants in a restitution case likewise had an expectation that their lives would continue in a certain way. In some of these cases one might question how reasonable that expectation really was, but let that point pass. The parties committed a temporal mistake. Nobody is likely to blame them for failing to make a contract for the benefits involved, because it was reasonable for them to suppose that no contract was needed. Enrichment that seemed just at the time it occurred thus comes to seem unjust in retrospect.

The most common case of successful recovery for unjust enrichment involves a clear trade of benefits that never gets completed or is lopsided in some other obvious way. Suppose a claimant pays $100,000 in tuition bills so that the defendant can go to medical school while they are living together. They expect that the defendant will go on to a lucrative career as a doctor and support them both in high style. And the defendant does begin a lucrative career, but then the parties end their relationship. Now what? Assuming liability for restitution is established, the claimant might seek a share of the income that the medical degree will entitle the claimant's former partner to earn. After all, both parties had expected those earnings to be enjoyed by both of them. Wouldn't allowing the graduate to keep all the earnings now amount to unjust enrichment? Probably not; the *Restatement* would limit recovery, in cases of this type that succeed, to the actual amount spent on tuition. The larger amount the claimant seeks—not just compensation for the services rendered, but a piece of their "traceable product"—is commonly awarded only against defendants who are guilty of wrongdoing. The defendant who went to medical school and then broke off the relationship is regarded as the beneficiary of a noncontractual transfer, and perhaps the beneficiary of a mistake, but not as a wrongdoer (at least not without more facts). The wrongdoer—especially the conscious wrongdoer—needs a stronger deterrent, and gets it in the form of a more generous measure of his enrichment.

G. COMMON FUND

Felton v. Finley
69 Idaho 381, 209 P.2d 899 (1949)

GIVENS, Justice.

March 1944, Seigle Finley and W. E. or William Finley, two of the three surviving nephews of Seigle Coleman, who died testate December 4, 1943, employed respondent to contest the deceased Coleman's will, which was successfully done. In re Coleman's Estate, 66 Idaho 567, 163 P.2d 847. At that time respondent told Seigle and William Finley that he would accept the employment only on condition that the other nephew and brother, Orval Finley, and the three sisters, Ida Davis, Nan Holder, and Rose Finley Nichles, likewise employ respondent as their attorney and that all six of the heirs participate in the contest.

Respondent requested Seigle and William Finley to contact their brother and sisters and secure signed contracts of employment similar to the ones which Seigle and William signed; namely, on a 50% contingent basis. Respondent likewise wrote the other four heirs requesting their execution of such contracts. Such heirs never replied to respondent's initial letter or to subsequent letters written by him continuing to request their execution of such contracts of employment and advising them as to the course of the litigation.

Seigle and William Finley contacted two sisters, Nan Holder and Ida Davis in Pilot Rock, Oregon, with reference to their joining in the employment of respondent and related that:

> they said they would have nothing to do with it. My oldest sister, Ida Davis, is very religious and she said she didn't feel like protesting. She said, "What you boys do is your business, but I will have nothing to do with it."

> Q.   Did they, the two sisters, make any statement that they would not oppose the contest?
> A.   The only statement they made was they would have nothing to do with it one way or the other.

Testifying further that they (Seigle and William Finley) attempted to get the three sisters and the other brother to join with them—that is, in the employment of respondent in the prosecution of the contest, stating further:

> A.   I had quite a time contacting my brother (Orval). He was in Alaska part of the time and I called him in St. Paul, Minnesota, that's his home, and he said, "I am having nothing whatever to do with a dead man's money."

and that he (Orval)

> would have nothing to do one way or the other, what I did was my business, to forget about him.

and about the same as to Rose Finley Nichles:

> She said she would have nothing to do with the estate. She said, "If you and Bill sign, that's your business. I am not going to. There is no use sending the contract." I read it to her over the phone and she said, "No."

Respondent testified he understood from Seigle and William, that while the other brother and sisters said they would have nothing to do with it, they would

leave the further handling of the matter to Seigle and William and he prosecuted the action on that basis, though Seigle testified he told respondent: "I
told him I couldn't get in touch with them and they wouldn't sign and would
have nothing to do with it."

William Finley testified with regard to the conference with the two sisters
as follows:

A.   When they came we talked about the contract and breaking the
will and my sisters were very much opposed to breaking the will
or having anything to do with it, and we talked quite a while and
I finally asked them if they would not fight us if we went ahead.

Q.   Not fight you?

A.   That's right, and they said they wouldn't oppose us, but would
have nothing to do with breaking the will. One of my sisters thinks
it is a terrible sin.

Q.   Did you have copies of the contract for the signature of Nan
Holder and Ida Davis? A. We did.

Q.   Were you able to get them to sign them?

A.   They would not.

Q.   You advised Mr. Felton that you were unable to get those contracts signed?

A.   Yes, sir.

Mrs. Holder testified that when she was in Missouri, she followed the case in
the Moscow newspapers and knew respondent was representing Seigle and
William and admitted she had received one letter from respondent, but not
the others. The other sisters and brother did not testify.

At the conclusion of the contest action, distributive checks were made
out to each one of the six heirs jointly with respondent for their respective
shares, which the three sisters and Orval refused to accept, taking the position
they had never employed respondent and were not obligated to pay him any
fee and subsequent conferences between respondent and Mrs. Holder were
unavailing.

The present suit to establish the implied contract and to enforce the
attorney's lien, resulted with findings, conclusions and decree there was an
implied contract of employment, from which decree the present appeal was
taken.

By stipulation, the appellants have been paid their distributive shares less
the portion thereof claimed by respondent and decreed to him as his fee from
them.

These facts are established by the record without dispute: that respondent
wrote the appellants to the effect he had been employed by their two brothers
and he desired their co-employment; that he wrote them of the progress of the
litigation and that they refused to sign the contracts and did not answer his
letters; that at least one of them had actual notice of the progress of the litigation and being a matter of public record, and they being parties to the Probate

proceedings, regardless of the contest because they were devisees under the will, they all had constructive notice of the proceedings; and that they did not repudiate respondent's appearing for them; that though appellants did not affirmatively participate in the contest, they did not resist and immediately upon the contest being successfully concluded, claimed the additional shares in their Uncle's estate which had been made available to them by the prosecution of the suit and respondent's services in connection therewith, which resulted in benefits to the appellants, together with the two brothers who did actually employ him.

"It is an elementary rule that, whenever services are rendered and received, a contract of hiring or an obligation to pay what they are reasonably worth will generally be presumed." Hartley v. Bohrer, 52 Idaho 72, 75, 11 P.2d 616, 617. The rule applicable to the above situation has been recently declared in a Washington case to be as follows:

> The rule is well established that the acceptance of the services rendered by an attorney may raise an implied promise to pay therefor, which will supply the place of a contract of employment. If an attorney renders valuable services, as in the case at bar, to one who has received the benefit thereof, a promise to pay the reasonable value of such services is presumed unless the circumstances establish the fact that such services were intended to be gratuitous. (McKevitt v. Golden Age Breweries, 14 Wash. 2d 50, 126 P.2d 1077, 1081.)

The record herein affirmatively and positively shows the respondent was not undertaking the services herein for anyone gratuitously. It is also held the acceptance of benefits must be voluntary. The acceptance and receipt by appellants of their share of their enhanced inheritance were entirely voluntary, because there is no law which required them to accept the greater amount; they could have taken only the $500.00 which the will initially gave them and refused the additional sum. Whatever scruples or feelings they had about not signing contracts, taking a dead man's money or interfering with his will, had thus evidently disappeared when the money was made available to them, even though without their active participation. Nevertheless, it was solely through respondent's efforts and successful prosecution of the contest case which procured this additional money for them and which, when thus secured to them by respondent's services, they promptly demanded and have pocketed.

Such course of conduct on their part amounts to such ratification and recognition of respondent's actions as to create in law an implied contract of employment and fully justified the decree in respondent's favor.

There is no conflict in the evidence as to the reasonableness of respondent's fee. The decree is, therefore, affirmed. Costs awarded to respondent.

HOLDEN, Chief Justice (dissenting).

It is urged in the case at bar that where one permits another to perform services for him, the law raises an implied promise to pay the reasonable value of the services. But respondent does not bring himself within the rule. Here, appellants, notwithstanding several efforts were made to induce them to employ respondent, refused to do so. It is true respondent performed services in contesting the will, but the services were performed for "S. P. Finley [Seigle]" and William Finley under the terms of a written contract. He was thus obligated to perform all the services he performed. He could not repudiate his solemn contract without committing a breach. Nor was respondent expected by those who thus employed him to perform such or any services gratuitously. The contract which respondent himself drew provided for the payment of the compensation which he thought his services were worth. The benefits which came to appellants were the result of the performance of the terms of the written contract entered into by respondent with Seigle and William Finley, not the result of any contract with appellants, because they refused to employ him. And, further, the services respondent performed in contesting the will were performed with knowledge appellants would not employ him. In fact, appellants were opposed to the contest and would not, and did not, have anything to do with it. No case has been cited and none can be found holding an implied promise or implied contract to pay for services under such facts and circumstances.

But it is argued the acceptance of accruing benefits created an implied contract to pay respondent. In resolving that question the above stated facts of this case should be kept in mind. The courts are unanimous in holding an acceptance of benefits does not create an implied contract to pay.

In O'Doherty & Yonts et al. v. Bickel et al., 166 Ky. 708, 179 S.W. 848, a case quite similar in its facts to the case at bar, the court held:

> As a general rule, an attorney cannot recover fees for his services from one who has not employed him or authorized his employment, although the services may have been beneficial to such person.

To the same effect: Rives et al. v. Patty et al., 74 Miss. 381, 384, 20 So. 862; Pepper v. Pepper, 98 S.W. 1039, 30 Ky. Law Rep. 460; In re Faling's Estate, 113 Or. 6, 228 P. 821, 231 P. 148.

The judgment should be reversed and the cause remanded with directions to dismiss the action.

On Rehearing

HOLDEN, Chief Justice.

A rehearing was had at Lewiston at our May, 1949, term. Since such rehearing the various contentions of the respective parties have been fully and carefully re-examined. We conclude, as a result of such re-examination, that the decree appealed from in the case at bar should be, and it is hereby, reversed and the cause remanded with directions to dismiss the action, in accordance with the views expressed in the foregoing dissenting opinion of Chief Justice Holden. Costs awarded to appellants.

GIVENS, Justice (dissenting on rehearing) (omitted).

The original case of "common fund"

The lawyer's claim in *Felton v. Finley* is one recognizable version of the pattern of restitution known as "common fund," but the basic theory of common fund is easier to see in a case of the kind for which it was originally developed by 19th-century decisions of the U.S. Supreme Court. The *Restatement* refers to the first of these decisions, Trustees v. Greenough, 105 U.S. 527 (1881), as "the wellspring of 'common fund' in American law," calling it "a perfect case from the restitution viewpoint." R3RUE §29, Reporter's Note to Comment *d*. The facts of that perfect case are summarized as follows:

> Bondholder holds defaulted mortgage bonds issued under a trust indenture. In the belief that mortgage collateral has been misappropriated by the indenture trustee, Bondholder brings suit to enforce the trust. In ten years of litigation, Bondholder incurs $1 million in reasonable and necessary legal expenses. He obtains a judgment recovering $50 million for the trust. The other bondholders have not participated in the litigation; nor can they be readily identified, as the bonds in question are payable to bearer. Bondholder is entitled to reimbursement of $1 million from the additional funds now in the hands of the successor trustee.

R3RUE §29, Illustration 3. What are the differences that make Bondholder's claim in *Trustees v. Greenough* so much stronger than lawyer Felton's claim in *Felton v. Finley*? Approached from another direction, what differences explain why Bondholder can recover his legal expenditures from his fellow bondholders, whereas Ulmer was not entitled to recover from Farnsworth for the expense of draining the limestone quarry?

Kerr v. Killian
191 Ariz. 293, 955 P.2d 49 (Tax Ct. 1998)

CATES, Judge.

The underlying case was brought by four named plaintiffs, former and current employees of various federal government agencies, who undertook to represent all similarly situated federal employees subject to Arizona's state income tax on federal retirement contributions. During the tax years 1985 through 1990, the State of Arizona, as directed by the Arizona Department of Revenue, imposed state income taxes upon the federal employees' mandatory federal retirement contributions. Although Arizona state and local employees pay mandatory state retirement contributions, the State did not tax these contributions.

The complaint in *Kerr* alleged that federal employees had been discriminated against with respect to the taxation of their mandatory retirement contributions in violation of the federal constitutional doctrine of intergovernmental tax immunity, codified in 4 U.S.C. §111, because state and local employees were not taxed similarly. Years of litigation and administrative action, in which the plaintiff class was represented by the two law firms who now seek fees, resulted in a Court of Appeals decision which concluded that Arizona's taxation of federal employees' mandatory retirement contributions was illegal and in violation of federal law. These efforts also resulted in a Board of Tax Appeals decision that the federal employees were entitled to a refund of the illegally collected taxes, which created a fund in the amount of approximately $28 million.

In the present action, plaintiffs' attorneys' motion for partial summary judgment argues that they are entitled to an award of reasonable attorneys' fees under the "common fund doctrine." They assert that because the $28 million fund was created through their efforts, allowing nearly 42,000 federal employees to receive tax refunds and interest, an award of attorneys' fees is necessary to prevent unjust enrichment. Defendant's cross-motion for summary judgment argues that plaintiffs' attorneys are not entitled to attorneys' fees for the following reasons: (1) such fees are available only pursuant to statute in tax cases, (2) there is no common fund against which their fees can be claimed, and (3) an award would violate the taxpayers' right to a full refund.

The common fund doctrine was articulated by the United States Supreme Court over a century ago in Trustees of the Internal Improvement Fund v. Greenough, 105 U.S. 527 (1881). The doctrine provides that "a litigant or a lawyer who recovers a common fund for the benefit of persons other than himself or his client is entitled to a reasonable attorney's fee from the fund as a whole." Boeing Co. v. Van Gemert, 444 U.S. 472, 478 (1980). A common fund case usually arises where a successful suit, brought by an individual or representative plaintiff, results in the creation of a monetary fund that benefits a limited and identifiable group situated similarly to the plaintiff. Therefore, it is the creation of the fund that triggers the common fund doctrine.

The purpose of the common fund doctrine is to "avoid the unjust enrichment of those who benefit from the fund that is created, protected, or increased by the litigation and who otherwise would bear none of the litigation costs." Court Awarded Attorney Fees, 108 F.R.D. 237, 250 (1985). Put another way, the common fund doctrine is a fee spreading device which avoids inequitable results by spreading the costs of litigation amongst those benefitted by the efforts and expenses incurred by the representative plaintiff and his counsel. *Id.* An attorney's right to recover fees in a common fund case derives from principles of equity and fairness. Attorneys who undertake collection suits such as the current case, and whose efforts result in the creation of a common fund, do not provide their services to the absentee plaintiffs as a gift. *Id.* (citing

Charles Silver, A *Restitutionary Theory of Attorneys' Fees in Class Actions*, 76 Cornell L. Rev. 656 (1991)). Accordingly, in order to prevent unjust enrichment of common fund beneficiaries, the attorneys responsible for its creation must be compensated for the reasonable value of their services.

The United States Supreme Court has set forth the following criteria for the application of the common fund doctrine: (1) the class of beneficiaries is sufficiently identifiable, (2) the benefits can be accurately traced, and (3) the fee can be shifted with some exactitude to those benefitting. Alyeska Pipeline Serv. v. Wilderness Soc'y, 421 U.S. 240, 261–64 n.39 (1975); Boeing v. Van Gemert, 444 U.S. at 478–79 (1980). These criteria are satisfied when each member of the certified class "has an undisputed and mathematically ascertainable claim to part of a lump-sum judgment recovered on his behalf." *Boeing*, 444 U.S. at 47. In the present case, the class of beneficiaries has already been identified and notified of its right to a refund of the illegally collected taxes. The precise value of each member's claim has been determined, and refunds of the illegally collected taxes have been secured. The fee can be shifted to those benefitting from the creation of the fund by taking the same percentage from each beneficiary to cover the reasonable attorneys' fees established. Therefore, the common fund doctrine applies to this case.

This court has read the numerous letters sent by federal employees entitled to the tax refunds. The theme of the letters is that those who are entitled to a refund did not retain, nor consent to representation by these two law firms. Therefore, they argue, the attorneys should not be entitled to a percentage of their refunds as a fee. While the court understands the position of the federal employees, the law cited above requires that the attorneys be compensated for the reasonable value of the services they rendered. The attorneys have worked on this case for more than eight years, putting in over 4,000 hours for which they have not been compensated. Because of the efforts of plaintiffs' counsel, the statute which mandated the tax at issue was declared unconstitutional and federal employees were put on notice of their right to a refund. This court concludes that the labor of plaintiffs' counsel in both the *Kerr* litigation and the Board of Tax Appeals decision resulted in the creation of the common fund from which the federal employees will receive their refunds. Absent counsel's efforts, it is unlikely that these federal employees would have received any refund.

Fairness dictates that those persons benefitting from the labor of the representative plaintiffs and their counsel pay their proportionate share of the reasonable attorneys' fees to be established by the court. The size of the fee to be deducted from each beneficiary's refund check will be minor compared to the cost of filing an individual suit to recover the illegally collected tax, both in terms of court expenses and time. This court wishes to stress that this ruling in no way constitutes an acceptance of the twenty per cent (20%) fee proposed by the attorneys. The recovery will be determined following a hearing to set the amount of the award, this hearing being scheduled by separate order.

Unrequested legal services

1. *Kerr v. Killian* makes a simple example of a garden-variety class action in which attorneys for a certified plaintiff class recover fees on the basis of common fund. At the very end of the opinion is a brief reminder that the truly contentious part of a common-fund case is often the problem of deciding what the attorneys' services are worth. A vast case law is devoted to this nearly unanswerable question. It originates primarily in statutory "fee-shifting" provisions, which encourage the assertion of certain kinds of claims by providing that successful plaintiffs shall be entitled to recover attorneys' fees in addition to damages. Fixing the amount of a reasonable fee is particularly difficult in class actions, where the attorneys for the class have not been hired by the persons they represent.

2. The facts of Kamilewicz v. Bank of Boston Corp., 100 F.3d 1348 (7th Cir. 1996), were stated as follows:

> A class action contending that the Bank of Boston did not promptly post interest to real estate escrow accounts was filed in Alabama by a Chicago law firm. *Hoffman v. BancBoston Mortgage Corp.*, No. CV-91-1880 (Mobile Cty. Cir. Ct.). Settlement ensued, and the class members learned only what the notice told them. Few opted out or objected, because the maximum award to any class member was less than $9. Any recovery, however small, seemed preferable to initiating a separate suit or even bearing the costs of protesting the settlement's terms. After the state judge approved the pact, the Bank carried out its part: it disbursed more than $8 million to the class attorneys in legal fees and credited most accounts with paltry sums. Problem: the fees, equal to 5.32 percent of the balance in each account, were debited to the accounts. For many accounts the debit exceeded the credit. Dexter J. Kamilewicz, for example, received a credit of $2.19 and a debit of $91.33, for a loss of $89.14.

What part of the theory of common fund did the Alabama judge misunderstand?

3. "Common fund" is what justifies a recovery from corporate assets in favor of a shareholder who has obtained benefits for other shareholders by a derivative suit brought in the name of the corporation. The rationale is easy to see when a derivative suit puts cash into the corporate treasury. Who confers what benefit on whom in the following two cases?

> Shareholders bring suit against Corporation, alleging that proxy materials soliciting approval of corporate action are materially misleading in violation of federal law. The court finds that Shareholders have demonstrated a violation by Corporation, entitling them to monetary or equitable relief (to be determined in subsequent proceedings) and to reimbursement of their legal expenses from the assets of Corporation.

R3RUE §29, Illustration 15 (based on Mills v. Electric Auto-Lite Co., 396 U.S. 375 (1970)).

Shareholders of ABC Corp. commence a derivative suit against its directors, alleging that their opposition to a tender offer by XYZ Corp. at $8 per share constitutes a breach of duty. XYZ eventually raises its offer to $11 and purchases all the shares of ABC at that price. After the acquisition has been completed, Shareholders' attorneys seek fees from ABC—now 100% owned by XYZ—for their services in causing XYZ to pay an additional $3 per share.

R3RUE §29, Illustration 16 (based on O'Neill v. Church's Fried Chicken, 910 F.2d 263 (5th Cir. 1990)).

4. The facts of Wolff v. Ampacet Corp., 284 Ill. App. 3d 824, 673 N.E.2d 745 (1996), were stated as follows:

In September of 1984, Fesco Plastics Corporation filed for protection under Chapter 11 of the Federal Bankruptcy Code. In its petition, Fesco listed Ampacet, Wolff, and a number of other creditors, all of whom were considered "deemed-filed" under the Code. As such, these creditors were not required to take any further action to present their claims in the bankruptcy court.

In October of 1985, however, the Fesco bankruptcy was converted into a Chapter 7 liquidation proceeding, and a deadline of February 6, 1986, was set for the filing of claims against the bankrupt estate. Many of the deemed-filed creditors took no action, believing that their prior status carried over into the liquidation proceeding. Among this group were Wolff and Ampacet. In April of 1987, the bankruptcy court upheld the trustee's request to bar the claims of all deemed-filed creditors who had missed the February 6 filing date. This decision would have barred Ampacet's claim permanently if no further action were taken.

Ampacet did not appeal the bankruptcy court's determination. Wolff and three other creditors (represented now by Wolff) did opt to appeal, however. Ampacet's claim was valued at $103,450.30; the claims of Wolff and the three creditors he represented ("the Lisk creditors") aggregated approximately $95,000. The Lisk creditors entered into a contingent fee agreement with Wolff, under which his fee would be a percentage of any recovery obtained by his client/creditors if he successfully revived their claims. On July 30, 1990, the U.S. Court of Appeals for the Seventh Circuit reversed the bankruptcy court and the District Court, holding that the Lisk creditors' claims were to be considered timely filed for Chapter 7 purposes (In Re Fesco Plastics (7th Cir. 1990),908 F.2d 240). In all of these appellate proceedings, Wolff had no direct contact with Ampacet and did not purport to represent it.

Based on the Seventh Circuit's decision, in August of 1991, the trustee reversed himself, honoring the claims of all the deemed-filed creditors of the estate, including Ampacet, Wolff and the Lisk creditors. Wolff's claim was accordingly paid in conformity with the Code, as were the claims of the Lisk creditors, and Wolff received the negotiated contingent fee from those creditors.

Ampacet had relocated during the period in which Wolff was prosecuting the appeal, however, and did not learn of the results until contacted by him. Ampacet thereafter, through attorneys it had retained, re-instituted its claim and recouped approximately $65,000 of its $103,450 claim. Wolff attempted to collect an attorneys' fee from Ampacet, as well as from [some] other non-Lisk creditors whose claims had been revived. [Footnote by the court: According to the Seventh Circuit, there were "hundreds of deemed-filed creditors" who had claims restored as a result of Wolff's efforts. This suit was initially filed against only Ampacet and GE Capital Mortgage Services, another of the deemed-filed creditors of Fesco. Wolff settled with GE, which is not a party to this appeal. The record does not indicate what efforts, if any, were made against the remaining hundreds of creditors.]

Wolff's claims were rebuffed, first by Ampacet and later by the bankruptcy court. Wolff appealed the denial of his fee request through to the U.S. Court of Appeals for the Seventh Circuit, which upheld the decision on a technical ground: because the Code does not confer the power to adjudicate fee disputes between creditors, the bankruptcy court lacked authority over the claim. Wolff then filed this action in the circuit court of Cook County.

Wolff's common-fund theory *must* be wrong—but why?

———————————

Maynard v. Parker
54 Ill. App. 3d 141, 369 N.E.2d 352 (1977)

STENGEL, Presiding Justice.

After he was injured in an automobile accident, plaintiff Russell Maynard retained attorney Louis E. Olivero who filed a personal injury suit in the Circuit Court of Bureau County. Pursuant to the Hospital Lien Act (Ill. Rev. Stat. 1975, ch. 82, par. 97 et seq.), the Sisters of the Third Order of St. Francis, who are the corporate owners and operators of St. Francis Hospital in Peoria, perfected a hospital lien for $11,028 against plaintiff's personal injury claim. The lien was for the unpaid balance of the hospital bill for treatment rendered to plaintiff. Attorney Olivero negotiated a settlement of plaintiff's claim for $37,500. In connection with the settlement, a check for $11,028 was issued payable to Russell A. Maynard, Estelle A. Maynard, Louis E. Olivero, and St. Francis Hospital.

Plaintiff filed a petition requesting, *inter alia*, that the hospital be ordered to pay a portion of plaintiff's attorneys' fees equal to 50% of costs and 50% of the value of its claim for medical services. The trial court found that plaintiff's counsel, through his efforts, created the settlement fund of $37,500, that plaintiff incurred expenses of $616.46, and that in equity plaintiff's counsel should be allowed compensation from all who directly benefit from the fund. The court then ordered that Olivero recover one-third of the costs and one-third of the lien claim, amounting to a total of $3,881, payable out of the check for $11,028, leaving $7,147 for the hospital. The hospital has appealed from that order.

The primary question presented by this appeal is whether plaintiff is entitled to have the hospital pay a proportionate share of plaintiff's attorneys' fees. As a general rule, the right of an attorney to recover for professional services must rest on the terms of a contract of employment, either express or implied, with the person sought to be charged, and cannot be based on a benefit derived by a third party from the services rendered by the attorney. Also, the client who engaged the attorney and paid his fees is not entitled to recover a proportionate share of the attorneys' fees from those who receive a benefit from the services. 7 Am. Jur 2d, Attorneys at Law §205.

Courts of equity have created several exceptions to these general rules. . . . The common fund doctrine has been described as "based on the equitable concept that an attorney who performs services in creating a fund should in equity and good conscience be allowed compensation out of the whole fund from all those who seek to benefit from it." Baier v. State Farm Ins. Co. (1977), 66 Ill. 2d 119, 124, 361 N.E.2d 1100, 1102. The common fund doctrine is most often applied in class action suits but is not limited to such cases. In *Baier* the supreme court ruled that, where a fund has been created as the result of legal services performed by an attorney for his client, and a subrogee of the client, who has done nothing to aid in creating the fund, seeks to benefit therefrom, the attorney is entitled to a fee from the subrogee in proportion to the benefit received by the subrogee.

In the trial court here, plaintiff successfully argued that the decision in *Baier* is controlling, and that the hospital should be required to pay to Olivero an amount equal to one-third of its lien claim because his efforts produced the settlement fund from which the lien would be satisfied.

The hospital contends that the *Baier* decision should be limited to cases involving funds recovered by subrogees, and points out that the court expressly declined to extend its ruling beyond a subrogation situation. The court said:

> Defendant contends next that if, under the circumstances of this case, it is required to pay an attorney fee, a physician or hospital who had rendered medical services to a claimant might also be required to pay proportionate share of the attorney fee. This record presents no such question, and the contention need not be further discussed. (66 Ill.2d at 127, 361 N.E.2d at 1103.)

In a case with facts nearly identical to the case at bar, the Supreme Court of Montana ruled that the benefit received by the hospital was an incidental benefit and did not create an implied contract by the hospital to pay for the services of plaintiff's attorney. Sisters of Charity v. Nichols (Mont. 1971), 483 P.2d 279. The Montana court distinguished subrogation cases as follows:

The attorneys and their client additionally contend, however, that the hospital here is obligated to share in the attorneys' fees and costs of collection on the same basis that a subrogated insurer is obligated to share attorneys' fees and costs with its insured in recovery against a third party. This analogy is inapt and the principle inapplicable here. The obligation of the subrogated insurer to share in the costs of recovery from a third party wrongdoer arises because the insurer occupies the position of the insured with coextensive rights and liabilities and no creditor-debtor relationship [exists] between them. But here, unlike that situation, the hospital's claim and lien is based upon a debt owed the hospital by its patient in whose shoes it does not stand for any purpose, the debt being owed to it by its patient irrespective of the patient's rights against a third party wrongdoer. Because the substitution principle does not apply here, no obligation arises on the part of the hospital to share in the costs of recovery against a third party, and the attempted analogy fails. (483 P.2d at 283.)

Furthermore, to permit this plaintiff to recover part of his attorneys' fees from the hospital could logically lead future plaintiffs to seek a similar contribution for fees from other creditors merely because the funds to pay debts were obtained through the efforts of the plaintiff's attorney. We cannot justify extending the common fund doctrine to require a mortgagee or a furniture store or any other creditor of a plaintiff to contribute to the fees of the plaintiff's attorney if the funds recovered by litigation are used to satisfy the plaintiff's obligations.

The allowance of counsel fees from a fund is capable of great abuse, and should be exercised with the most jealous caution in regard to the rights of creditors. In cases such as this it is better to leave those concerned to contract for the compensation to be paid for the services rendered or received.

For the reasons given, we conclude that the trial court erred when it ordered the hospital to pay $3,881 to plaintiff for attorneys' fees and costs. The order of the Circuit Court of Bureau County is reversed.

Fees from subrogated insurers

Maynard v. Parker contrasts the common-fund claim of a lawyer against the client's creditor with the claim of a lawyer against the client's subrogee — typically an insurance company. As might be imagined, a restitution claim on this pattern is sometimes vigorously resisted by the subrogated insurer, particularly if the insurer believes it would have obtained the same recovery without the lawyer's assistance. The question is addressed by the *Restatement* in the following comment:

Subrogees. Resolution of a tort claim by judgment or settlement often creates a fund—typically, a payment by the defendant's insurer—to be divided between the tort plaintiff and the *plaintiff's* insurer. The plaintiff's insurer in such a case, having paid some portion of the loss, has been subrogated to the plaintiff's claim against the defendant—whether by the rule of §24, by the provisions of the policy, or otherwise. Claims for all compensable injuries, including those that were covered by the plaintiff's insurance, are often asserted together by an attorney retained by the plaintiff insured, usually on the basis of a contingent fee. When settlement results in payment to the subrogated insurer, the plaintiff's attorney seeks a comparable (but noncontractual) fee from the insurer—frequently on the theory of common fund.

Claims on this pattern, while very frequent, occupy an uncomfortable position at the margin of the common-fund rule. They differ from the usual model because the beneficiaries of the fund—here, the tort plaintiff and the subrogated insurer—have interests that are not naturally aligned. The plaintiff asserts the subrogee's claim against the tortfeasor because procedural and strategic considerations make it unavoidable as a practical matter; but the interests of subrogor and subrogee are usually in competition. Unlike the relation between common-fund beneficiaries in the standard illustrations, it is only rarely the case that the addition of each dollar to the common fund will benefit the tort plaintiff and the subrogated insurer *pari passu*. Their claims to the fund, while arising from the same occurrence and asserted against the same defendant, relate to different elements of damage. Significantly, the insurer's claim is liquidated, while the plaintiff's claim for general damages is not. The steps necessary to obtain payment of these divergent claims will often be different, and professional services in obtaining payment will be differently valued by the two beneficiaries.

The law will often accommodate the attorney's claim despite its theoretical and practical difficulties. The reason is the perceived injustice of a regime in which the plaintiff, who has paid for *indemnity*, may be compelled as a practical matter to collect the subrogated insurer's claim along with his own, without contribution to the expense of doing so. But restitution remains a doubtful vehicle, at best, for imposing an obligation to pay for services that the recipient—were it free to do so—would often prefer to do without. One response to the difficulty of fitting the claim within the standard common-fund model is the existence in a number of jurisdictions of statutes requiring that the subrogee contribute to the expense of litigation. Alternatively, the subrogee's obligation to share in the cost of third-party recoveries may be located within the provisions of the insurance policy, whether express or implied. Either approach tends to make this contentious issue a matter of insurance law rather than unjust enrichment.

R3RUE §29 ("Common fund"), Comment *h.*

Farnsworth, *Restitution* 39-41(2014):

Suppose, for example, that I sue the state where I live, claiming it collected a tax that was illegal in some way. (My suit might be a class action, but not necessarily.) I win the case or settle it favorably; the state is found to have unlawfully collected a big pot of money from its taxpayers, including me. The court might order that the pot be distributed in the form of refunds to everyone who paid the bad tax. But the court also might order that some reasonable share of the pot be set aside to compensate me and my lawyer for the costs of bringing the suit. That order would be a form of restitution. Notice how the basic elements of recovery are satisfied. First, I had a good excuse for not making contracts with everyone who benefited from the suit. Getting consent from all of them would likely have been impossible. Second, it is obvious that they did benefit and to what extent: they all are receiving cash, which everybody likes, and after paying me they still will have more than they did before I brought the suit. A possible objection to recovery is that my action preempted a suit by others that would have produced even better results. If not, though, the main hard question will involve the fee my lawyer should get. Unless resolved by statute, that issue will be resolved by judicial discretion without much help from the law of restitution.

There are other constraints on common-fund recovery. The interests of the claimant and the other beneficiaries have to be closely aligned. Suppose we both are shareholders in a corporation. I bring a suit against the corporation that challenges a bad practice by its directors. I win my suit, and this saves the corporation a lot of money. A bit of that money can be diverted to me to cover my expenses of suit. The rules governing such recovery are likely to be settled now by statute, but otherwise they can still be viewed as matters for the law of restitution. From that perspective we would say the "common fund" is the corporation itself, the value of which has been preserved or increased by my efforts. The restitution obtained comes, in effect, from you and the other shareholders. So far, so good—but now notice that my victory might also be good news for the corporation's creditors. Maybe some of them were nervous about getting paid, but now the corporation can cover its debts with no trouble. Yet I can't collect any restitution from them. Recovery from a common fund is limited to cases where the claimant and the beneficiaries all have parallel interests in the pot that has been recovered, probably because the benefits to other, less similar parties too quickly become speculative.

Chapter 6

Failed Trades:
Restitution and Contract

The vocabulary of restitution and unjust enrichment is treacherous at every point. Confusion is especially severe in the contested region at the border of restitution and contract law. To avoid talking past each other, lawyers who want to make a point about "restitution and contract" must take a lot of care in defining their terms.

Restatement Third, Restitution and Unjust Enrichment divides this area as follows:

A. *Undoing or correcting the parties' mistakes* (R3RUE §§12, 34). Cases in this section are frequently part of a standard Contracts syllabus. Certainly it is possible to conclude that their primary concern is with the integrity of the parties' agreement, rather than with the unjust enrichment that will result if the requested remedy is denied. At the same time, this category of cases comprises indispensable examples of "restitution" in the sense of "restoration," and it includes important remedies that may not be encountered elsewhere.

B. *Restitution to a performing party with no claim on the contract* (R3RUE §§31-36). Here the source of liability in unjust enrichment is relatively clear. One party has rendered a valuable performance under a contract that for some reason the performing party cannot enforce. The contract might be unenforceable because it fails to satisfy a formal test, such as the Statute of Frauds or its modern analogues; because it is illegal; or because the recipient of a requested performance lacked the capacity to make a binding promise to pay for it. A contract initially valid might have been avoided after part performance, in light of a subsequently discovered mistake or a supervening change of circumstances. Or the performing party might have no claim to enforce a partly-performed contract simply because the performer himself is the party in breach. In all such cases it is generally accepted that the basis of restitution (and the extent of recovery) must be the unjust enrichment of the defendant at the expense of the plaintiff—if only because the defendant's liability on the contract has been excluded *ex hypothesi*.

C. *Alternative remedies for breach of an enforceable contract* (R3RUE §§37-38). A list of the remedies for breach of an enforceable contract often includes something called "restitution," and lawyers in contract cases speak of "restitution" as a possible alternative to damages. Here the confusion of terminology is at its worst. Rules that allow "restitution for breach" long antedate publication of the original Restatement of Restitution (1937), in which the word "restitution" was hastily chosen to designate "liability based on unjust enrichment." By contrast, books on contract law that refer to "restitution for breach" usually employ the term to mean something like this: "a remedy for a material breach of contract, neither expectation damages nor specific performance, that requires the defendant to restore what has been received from the plaintiff, either in specie or in value." R3RUE asserts emphatically that contract remedies of this kind have no necessary connection with the unjust enrichment of the breaching party.

This last point invites a reasonable objection. If these "restitutionary" contract remedies are independent of unjust enrichment, what are they doing in a *Restatement*—or a casebook, for that matter—devoted to the topic of liability for unjust enrichment? The answer lies in the tortured history of the term "restitution." To come up with any intelligible classification, we must accept that there are remedies for breach that pursue "restitution" in the sense of "giving back" without reference to unjust enrichment, just as there are remedies that require the surrender of unjust enrichment without any "giving back"—as when a defendant is forced to surrender wrongful gains that the plaintiff never possessed. There is also the fact that modern Contracts books do little or nothing to elucidate this awkward topic, making it that much harder for a work on "restitution" to ignore.

Getting past this initial hurdle, we discover that "restitution for breach" comes in two relatively familiar forms. They are fundamentally different, however, and it is essential to keep them separate. "Rescission and restitution" (or simply "rescission") is a two-way restoration of performance, returning both parties to the *status quo ante* by requiring them to go backwards instead of forwards: to unwind or reverse their partly-completed exchange instead of forcing it to completion, as expectation damages or specific performance would do. The second version of "restitution for breach" does not reverse the transaction at all: it awards damages, but by an alternative measure, to plaintiffs whose contractual expectation cannot be determined. Instead of "expectation damages" as a substitute for what the defendant promised the plaintiff, "performance-based damages" give the plaintiff either the cost or the value of the performance the plaintiff has rendered to the defaulting defendant. Damages measured this way are thus another means of "restitution," but only in the sense that they put the plaintiff back where he started.

D. *Disgorgement of profit from opportunistic breach* (R3RUE §39). The third and final set of cases within the area of "restitution for breach," entirely different from the first two, imposes an enrichment-based liability as an alternative to enforcement of the bargained-for exchange. In limited circumstances, a plaintiff with an enforceable claim to contract damages may elect instead to hold defendant liable to disgorge the gains realized from a wrongful and profitable breach. The topic is included in Chapter 6 as the final component of "Restitution and Contract," although in some respects it resembles the more familiar examples of a disgorgement liability—which typically strip a defendant of gains from tortious conduct—that are the subject of Chapter 7 on "Restitution for Wrongs."

A. UNDOING OR CORRECTING THE PARTIES' MISTAKES

(1) Mutual mistake

Yellow diamonds, fertile cows

1. In Wood v. Boynton, 64 Wis. 265, 25 N.W. 42 (1885), Mrs. Wood took a broken pin to be repaired by Mr. Boynton, the jeweler. The pin was in a pill-box with a small earring, a broken sleeve-button, and a yellow stone "about the size of a canary bird's egg." As Mrs. Wood told the story:

> I thought I would ask him what the stone was, and I took it out of the box and asked him to please tell me what that was. He took it in his hand and seemed some time looking at it. I told him I had been told it was a topaz, and he said it might be. He says, "I would buy this; would you sell it?" I told him I did not know but what I would. What would it be worth? And he said he did not know; he would give me a dollar and keep it as a specimen, and I told him I would not sell it; and it was certainly pretty to look at. . . . Afterwards, and about the twenty-eighth of December, I needed money pretty badly, and thought every dollar would help, and I took it back to Mr. Boynton and told him I had brought back the topaz, and he says, "Well, yes; what did I offer you for it?" and I says, "One dollar"; and he stepped to the change drawer and gave me the dollar, and I went out.

Not long after the sale, it transpired that the supposed topaz was actually an uncut yellow diamond worth upwards of $700. Mrs. Wood attempted to rescind the transaction: "she tendered the defendants $1.10 and demanded the return of the stone, which they refused." Her subsequent lawsuit met with no more success. Rescission would have been ordered if she could show fraudulent inducement; it is natural to wonder whether Boynton, the jeweler, had better information as to the identity of the yellow stone. The court found unequivocally that he did not:

We can find nothing in the evidence from which it could be justly inferred that Mr. Boynton, at the time he offered the plaintiff one dollar for the stone, had any knowledge of the real value of the stone, or that he entertained even a belief that the stone was a diamond. It cannot, therefore, be said that there was a suppression of knowledge on the part of the defendant as to the value of the stone which a court of equity might seize upon to avoid the sale. The cases show that, in the absence of fraud or warranty, the value of the property sold, as compared with the price paid, is no ground for a rescission of the sale. . . .

However unfortunate the plaintiff may have been in selling this valuable stone for a mere nominal sum, she has failed entirely to make out a case either of fraud or mistake in the sale such as will entitle her to a rescission of such sale so as to recover the property sold in an action at law.

2. In Sherwood v. Walker, 66 Mich. 568, 33 N.W. 919 (1887), Sherwood (a banker and gentleman farmer) bought a purebred cow, "Rose 2d of Aberlone," from Hiram Walker (a whisky distiller and cattle breeder). Rose was sold at 5-1/2¢ per pound—her value as beef—because both parties believed her to be barren. [This was the view of the facts expressed by the court majority. The dissenting judge reasoned, more logically, that the only reason Sherwood bought Rose was that he thought there was still a chance she might breed. While almost certainly correct, the superior analysis of the dissenting opinion destroys *Sherwood* as an example of "mutual mistake."] After the contract was formed, but before delivery to Sherwood, Rose was discovered to be with calf. As a breeding animal she was worth at least 10 times the contract price. Walker repudiated his obligation, and Sherwood sued to enforce the contract. The court held that Walker had a right to rescind on the ground of mutual mistake:

> It is true she is now the identical animal that they thought her to be when the contract was made; there is no mistake as to the identity of the creature. Yet the mistake was not of the mere quality of the animal, but went to the very nature of the thing. A barren cow is substantially a different creature than a breeding one. There is as much difference between them for all purposes of use as there is between an ox and a cow that is capable of breeding and giving milk. She was not in fact the animal, or the kind of animal, the defendants intended to sell or the plaintiff to buy. She was not a barren cow, and, if this fact had been known, there would have been no contract. The thing sold and bought had in fact no existence. She was sold as a beef creature would be sold; she is in fact a breeding cow, and a valuable one.

3. Contracts-class discussion of the yellow diamond and Rose 2d of Aberlone rarely considers what their juxtaposition might tell us about "restitution and contract." It tells quite a lot. Observe, first, that while *Wood v. Boynton* involves

a restitution claim, *Sherwood v. Walker* does not. Mrs. Wood seeks rescission and restitution of the topaz/diamond transaction, unwinding the deal after it has already been performed on both sides. By contrast, Sherwood wants the cow that Walker has refused to deliver: he is trying to enforce an executory contract, not unwind a completed one. If we see the mistakes in the two cases as substantially identical, this difference offers the easiest way to explain the apparently different results in the two cases. In short: the same significant, nonfraudulent, mutual mistake about quality and value that would suffice as a defense to the enforcement of an executory contract may not support a claim to rescission and restitution once the transaction has been completed. Is there a principled reason for the distinction, or it just a matter of convenience?

4. If you have any doubt that the distinction exists, try this thought experiment: Imagine what would have happened (a) if Mrs. Wood had discovered her mistake before delivering the stone to Mr. Boynton, or (b) if Rose's fertility had only become apparent the following spring, six months after her delivery to Sherwood's farm.

5. What would the result be in *Wood v. Boynton* if the court had been persuaded that Boynton knew what he was buying and suppressed that information?

6. Assuming (as the Wisconsin court found) that both parties were innocently mistaken, was Mr. Boynton unjustly enriched by his purchase of Mrs. Wood's diamond at a price of $1.00?

———————————

Farhat v. Rassey
295 Mich. 349, 294 N.W. 707 (1940)

BUTZEL, Justice.

Plaintiff filed a bill for the dissolution of a partnership and for an accounting. The case was submitted on the proofs in December 1939, and on January 18, 1940, at about 9 o'clock in the morning, the trial court filed a written opinion in which he found that plaintiff was entitled to $3,933.33 as his share of the assets of the co-partnership which totaled $11,297.68. On the same morning the attorney for defendants called plaintiff's attorney and suggested that defendants would pay $1,400 to settle the case if an agreement could be effected that day. Plaintiff's attorney went to Flint, arriving there about 4 o'clock in the afternoon, and a settlement was made, reduced to writing, signed by the parties, and a check for the agreed amount of $1,400 was delivered to plaintiff's attorney. Immediately upon receiving the opinion of the trial court, plaintiff's attorney filed a motion to repudiate the settlement and for a decree on the findings of the trial court. The trial court declined to abide by the settlement, and a decree was entered in accordance with his opinion.

It is conceded that at the time the settlement was actually made, the trial court had already filed his opinion. It appears that defendants' attorney stated that the case had not yet been decided, which statement was in fact untrue; his good faith is unchallenged. We accept as true the statement in his affidavit that he had no knowledge of the decision at the time the settlement was consummated, and we shall assume that such knowledge on the part of defendants and their counsel was likewise wanting.

The trial court was correct in holding that plaintiff may avoid the settlement. The basic assumptions upon which the settlement rested were wrong in fact. The state of mind of all the parties was not in accord with the facts (Restatement, Restitution, §6). The parties assumed that the case had not yet been determined and believed that a decision would not be forthcoming for several weeks. There can be no question but that these fundamental facts induced the compromise, and their absolute nonexistence was the starting point of the settlement contract. Having contracted on the faith of these assumptions not believed to have been doubtful, but which were in fact erroneous, the parties are to be relieved from their bargain. Williston on Contracts (Rev. Ed.), §1543, p.4332; Restatement, Contracts §502; Restatement, Restitution, §11 Comment c; Sherwood v. Walker, 66 Mich. 568, 33 N.W. 919; Richardson Lumber Co. v. Hoey, 219 Mich. 643, 189 N.W. 923; Grymes v. Sanders, 93 U.S. 55. The situation before us is to be distinguished from cases where there is a mistake as to a doubtful, disputed, unassumed fact leading to the compromise. "With respect to any matter not made a basic assumption of the contract the parties take their chances." Williston on Contracts, §1543, p. 4332. In Restatement, Restitution, §11(1), it is said: "A person is not entitled to rescind a transaction with another if, by way of compromise or otherwise, he agreed with the other to assume, or intended to assume, the risk of a mistake for which otherwise he would be entitled to rescission and consequent restitution."

In the instant case, while the parties may have assumed the risk of any mistake in connection with the anticipated outcome of the proceeding on its merits and the time in the future when the decision would be rendered, they were acting under a basic mutual mistake in assuming that the case had not been decided at the time they negotiated and consummated their settlement. All mistakenly felt certain that the case had not yet been determined, and all joined in the belief that it would be several weeks before a decision would be rendered. They cannot be held to have assumed, or to have intended to assume by their compromise, the risk of being mistaken in these basic regards. For such mistake, the settlement, like any other contract, may be rescinded. Restatement, Restitution, §11, Comment c; Williston on Contracts (Rev. Ed.) §1543, pp.4332, 4333. Knowledge that the case had already been determined would have put their negotiations on a different footing, if negotiations there would have been at all.

The decree is affirmed. Costs to plaintiff.

More mutual mistakes

1. Perhaps the quick work by the judge in *Farhat v. Rassey* carried some implication about how he saw the case—but perhaps not. Can there be a

"mutual mistake about basic assumptions" that is irrelevant to the terms of the parties' exchange? Is there any reason to rescind for such a mistake?

2. In a famous chapter of his memoir *North Toward Home* (1967), Willie Morris describes a boyhood exploit in Yazoo City, Mississippi. Twelve-year-old Willie would occasionally join a group of men who spent their afternoons sitting around the corner grocery store, listening to the ballgame on the radio. As was common at the time—though many listeners were unaware of it—the baseball broadcast heard in small towns was not live but "recreated." A radio announcer received the play-by-play information by telegraph, then described the game as if he were watching it from the press box—making up imaginary balls and strikes, and using sound effects for the crack of the bat and the roar of the crowd.

Playing with a short-wave radio at home, Willie discovered that it was sometimes possible to pick up the live broadcast of the same game—and thus to learn what was happening 30 minutes or so before the news reached the grocery store. The book describes how Willie listened to a few innings of the game at home, then headed down to the store, where he experienced a miraculous vision of what each batter would do before he did it.

Leaving precocious Willie out of it, let's suppose that two of the grocery store regulars make a serious wager on the outcome of a tie game in the 8th inning. Later they learn for the first time that the radio broadcast was "recreated"—and that when they made their wager, the game (unknown to either of them) was already over. Should the loser be able to get his money back—or avoid paying—on the authority of *Farhat v. Rassey?*

3. The appendicitis of King Edward VII forced the postponement of festivities planned for his coronation on June 26, 1902 and disrupted numerous contracts that had been made in the preceding weeks for the hire of "rooms to see the procession." Some would-be spectators had paid the whole of the agreed rent in advance; others had paid part of the price, with the balance due at some later date. The principal holding of "The Coronation Cases"—the best-known being Chandler v. Webster, [1904] 1 K.B. 493 (Ct. App.)—was that these contracts were valid until the procession was canceled, at which point they were "frustrated" (or prospectively discharged) as regards further performance. This meant that "losses would lie where they fell": there would be no restitution of money previously paid, but no obligation either (i) to make payments falling due after the cancellation, or (ii) to furnish a view of a nonexistent procession.

One of the "Coronation Cases" appears at first to be an outlier. In Griffith v. Brymer, 19 Times L. Rep. 434 (K.B. 1903), the contract for "rooms to see the procession" had been made at 11 A.M. on June 24, and the plaintiff had paid the full price of £100 on the spot. Unknown to either party, the decision to perform the royal appendectomy had been made at 10 A.M that same morning. The plaintiff recovered his £100, why?

4. In Strickland v. Turner, 7 Exch. 208, 155 Eng. Rep. 919 (1852), a Mr. Lane, living in Sydney, Australia, became entitled to a lifetime annuity of £100 yearly. Deciding he would rather have a lump sum, Lane prepared to sell his annuity. He appointed an agent to negotiate with a buyer in London. The parties eventually agreed on a price of £973. After the assignment had been formalized and the money paid in full, they learned that Lane had died about three weeks earlier. The buyer recovered his £973.

Compare Aldrich v. Travelers Ins. Co., 317 Mass. 86, 56 N.E.2d 888 (1944), in which a 67-year-old woman paid $5,000 for a single-payment annuity entitling her to $31.70 monthly for life. Unknown to the parties, the annuitant was already suffering from a fatal disease, and she died one year later. Her executor sued the insurance company to rescind the annuity for mutual mistake (and unconscionability, for good measure).

> [The trial court found] that both parties to the contract "assumed the existence of a certain fact, that being that the condition of [the testatrix's] health was such as to warrant a reasonable expectancy of life, while in fact she was suffering from an incurable disease"; and that "there was a mistake as to a matter that vitally affected the basis upon which the parties contracted." He entered a decree rescinding the contract and ordering the defendant to pay to the plaintiff the sum of $4,587.90, which seems to have been intended to represent the difference between the single premium of $5,000 and the sums paid monthly by the defendant to the testatrix in the period a little over a year in which she remained alive after the making of the contract.

Id. at 87-88, 56 N.E.2d at 888. This judgment was reversed on appeal. How do we distinguish *Strickland v. Turner*?

5. When Mary Cleghorn came of age, she inherited two fractional interests in the northwest quarter of section 11, township 18 north, range 6 west, Mount Diablo meridian—one from her father, one from her mother. Mary's lawyer told her that her inheritance was two undivided tenths of the quarter-section, making an undivided one-fifth. "The court finds that this—the one-fifth interest—is what she and the defendant both supposed she owned, when in November, 1887, she being then of lawful age, defendant agreed with her to purchase her interest in the tract, and pay her five hundred dollars therefor, which price the court finds was the value of an undivided one fifth of the tract." Cleghorn v. Zumwalt, 83 Cal. 155, 157, 23 P. 294 (1890). Mary had been misinformed about the effect of her Mother's will: in reality, Mary owned an undivided three-fifths. "The deed was in a form that conveyed all her interest, whatever it might be. The relief sought is to so reform the deed that it shall convey an undivided one fifth, as both parties expected it would and intended it should, at the time the bargain was made for it and the price was fixed." *Id.*

Zumwalt argues that before the date of the conveyance he had learned the true extent of Mary's ownership—without telling her—so that the case was not one of "mutual mistake." Does Zumwalt's subsequent information help his position?

Simkin v. Blank

19 N.Y.3d 46, 968 N.E.2d 459 (2012)

GRAFFEO, J.

Plaintiff Steven Simkin (husband) and defendant Laura Blank (wife) married in 1973 and have two children. Husband is a partner at a New York law firm and wife, also an attorney, is employed by a university. After almost 30 years of marriage, the parties separated in 2002 and stipulated in 2004 that the cut-off date for determining the value of marital assets would be September 1, 2004. The parties, represented by counsel, spent two years negotiating a detailed 22-page settlement agreement, executed in June 2006. In August 2006, the settlement agreement was incorporated, but not merged, into the parties' final judgment of divorce.

The settlement agreement set forth a comprehensive division of marital property. Husband agreed to pay wife $6,250,000 "as and for an equitable distribution of property . . . and in satisfaction of the Wife's support and marital property rights." In addition, wife retained title to a Manhattan apartment (subject to a $370,000 mortgage), an automobile, her retirement accounts and any "bank, brokerage and similar financial accounts in her name." Upon receipt of her distributive payment, wife agreed to convey her interest in the Scarsdale marital residence to husband. Husband received title to three automobiles and kept his retirement accounts, less $368,000 to equalize the value of the parties' retirement accounts. Husband further retained "bank, brokerage and similar financial accounts" that were in his name, two of which were specifically referenced—his capital account as a partner at the law firm and a Citibank account.

The agreement also contained a number of mutual releases between the parties. Each party waived any interest in the other's law license and released or discharged any debts or further claims against the other. Although the agreement acknowledged that the property division was "fair and reasonable," it did not state that the parties intended an equal distribution or other designated percentage division of the marital estate. The only provision that explicitly contemplated an equal division was the reference to equalizing the values of the parties' retirement accounts.

At the time the parties entered into the settlement, one of husband's unspecified brokerage accounts was maintained by Bernard L. Madoff Investment Securities. According to husband, the parties believed the account was valued at $5.4 million as of September 1, 2004, the valuation date for marital assets. Husband withdrew funds from this account to pay a portion of his distributive payment owed wife in 2006, and continued to invest in the account subsequent to the divorce. In December 2008, Bernard Madoff's colossal Ponzi scheme was publicly exposed and Madoff later pleaded guilty to federal securities fraud and related offenses.

As a result of the disclosure of Madoff's fraud, in February 2009—about 2½ years after the divorce was finalized—husband commenced this action against wife alleging two causes of action: (1) reformation of the settlement agreement predicated on a mutual mistake and (2) unjust enrichment. The amended complaint asserts that the settlement agreement was intended to accomplish an "approximately equal division of [the couple's] marital assets," including a 50/50 division of the Madoff account. To that end, the amended complaint states that $2,700,000 of wife's $6,250,000 distributive payment represented her "share" of the Madoff account. Husband alleges that the parties' intention to equally divide the marital estate was frustrated because both parties operated under the "mistake" or misconception as to the existence of a legitimate investment account with Madoff which, in fact, was revealed to be part of a fraudulent Ponzi scheme. The amended complaint admits, however, that funds were previously "withdrawn" from the "Account" by husband and applied to his obligation to pay wife.

In his claim for reformation, husband requests that the court "determine the couple's true assets with respect to the Madoff account" and alter the settlement terms to reflect an equal division of the actual value of the Madoff account. The second cause of action seeks restitution from wife "in an amount to be determined at trial" based on her unjust enrichment arising from husband's payment of what the parties mistakenly believed to be wife's share of the Madoff account. Wife moved to dismiss the amended complaint on several grounds. Supreme Court granted wife's motion and dismissed the amended complaint. The Appellate Division, with two Justices dissenting, reversed and reinstated the action (80 A.D.3d 401, 915 N.Y.S.2d 47 [1st Dept. 2011]). We now reverse and reinstate Supreme Court's order of dismissal.

Wife argues that the Appellate Division erred in reinstating the amended complaint because the allegations, even if true, fail to appropriately establish the existence of a mutual mistake at the time the parties entered into their settlement agreement. Rather, she claims that, at most, the parties may have been mistaken as to the value of the Madoff account, but not its existence. Wife also contends that allowing husband's claims to go forward years after the division of property and issuance of a divorce decree would undermine policy concerns regarding finality in divorce cases. Husband responds that the amended complaint states a viable claim because the parties were both unaware and misled as to the legitimacy of the Madoff account, which, in husband's view, "did not in fact ever exist" due to the fraud occasioned on investors.

Marital settlement agreements are judicially favored and are not to be easily set aside. Nevertheless, in the proper case, an agreement may be subject to rescission or reformation based on a mutual mistake by the parties. Similarly, a release of claims may be avoided due to mutual mistake. Based on these contract principles, the parties here agree that this appeal turns on whether husband's amended complaint states a claim for relief under a theory of mutual mistake.

We have explained that "[t]he mutual mistake must exist at the time the contract is entered into and must be substantial." Put differently, the mistake must be "so material that . . . it goes to the foundation of the agreement." The premise underlying the doctrine of mutual mistake is that "the agreement as expressed, in some material respect, does not represent the meeting of the minds of the parties."

Husband relies on True v. True, 63 A.D.3d 1145, 1146, 882 N.Y.S.2d 261 (2d Dept. 2009), where a settlement agreement provided that the husband's stock awards from his employer would be "divided 50/50 in kind" and recited that 3,655 shares were available for division between the parties. After the wife redeemed her half of the shares, the husband learned that only 150 shares remained and brought an action to reform the agreement, arguing that the parties mistakenly specified the gross number of shares (3,655) rather than the net number that was actually available for distribution. The Second Department agreed and reformed the agreement to effectuate the parties' intent to divide the shares equally, holding that the husband had established "that the parties' use of 3,655 gross shares was a mutual mistake because it undermined their intent to divide the *net* shares available for division, 50/50 in kind."

Wife in turn points to appellate cases denying a spouse's request to reopen a marital settlement agreement where the final value of an asset was not what the parties believed at the time of the divorce (see Greenwald v. Greenwald, 164 A.D.2d 706, 721 [1st Dept. 1991] [stating that "posttrial changes in value may not be used to reallocate the distribution of marital assets"]). In Kojovic v. Goldman, 35 A.D.3d 65 (2006), for example, the First Department dismissed the wife's reformation and rescission claims where the husband unexpectedly sold his interest in a company for $18 million after the divorce. And in Etzion v. Etzion, 62 A.D.3d 646 (2009), the Second Department rejected the wife's mutual mistake claim where the market value of the husband's warehouse property substantially increased in value after the city adopted a rezoning plan subsequent to the parties' settlement.

Applying these legal principles, we are of the view that the amended complaint fails to adequately state a cause of action based on mutual mistake. As an initial matter, husband's claim that the alleged mutual mistake undermined the foundation of the settlement agreement, a precondition to relief under our precedents, is belied by the terms of the agreement itself. Unlike the settlement agreement in *True* that expressly incorporated a "50/50" division of a stated number of stock shares, the settlement agreement here, on its face, does not mention the Madoff account, much less evince an intent to divide the account in equal or other proportionate shares. To the contrary, the agreement provides that the $6,250,000 payment to wife was "in satisfaction of [her] support and marital property rights," along with her release of various claims and inheritance rights. Despite the fact that the agreement permitted husband to retain title to his "bank, brokerage and similar financial accounts" and enumerated two such accounts, his alleged $5.4 million Madoff investment account is neither identified nor valued. Given the extensive and carefully negotiated nature of the settlement agreement, we do not believe that this presents one of those "exceptional situations" warranting reformation or rescission of a divorce settlement after all marital assets have been distributed.

Even putting the language of the agreement aside, the core allegation underpinning husband's mutual mistake claim—that the Madoff account was "nonexistent" when the parties executed their settlement agreement in June 2006—does not amount to a "material" mistake of fact as required by our case law. The premise of husband's argument is that the parties mistakenly believed that they had an investment account with Bernard Madoff when, in fact, no account ever existed. In husband's view, this case is no different from one in which parties are under a misimpression that they own a piece of real or personal property but later discover that they never obtained rightful ownership, such that a distribution would not have been possible at the time of the agreement. But that analogy is not apt here. Husband does not dispute that, until the Ponzi scheme began to unravel in late 2008—more than two years after the property division was completed—it would have been possible for him to redeem all or part of the investment. In fact, the amended complaint contains an admission that husband was able to withdraw funds (the amount is undisclosed) from the account in 2006 to partially pay his distributive payment to wife. Given that the mutual mistake must have existed at the time the agreement was executed in 2006, the fact that husband could no longer withdraw funds years later is not determinative.

This situation, however sympathetic, is more akin to a marital asset that unexpectedly loses value after dissolution of a marriage; the asset had value at the time of the settlement but the purported value did not remain consistent. Viewed from a different perspective, had the Madoff account or other asset retained by husband substantially increased in worth after the divorce, should wife be able to claim entitlement to a portion of the enhanced value? The answer is obviously no. Consequently, we find this case analogous to the Appellate Division precedents denying a spouse's attempt to reopen a settlement agreement based on post-divorce changes in asset valuation.

Finally, husband's unjust enrichment claim likewise fails to state a cause of action. It is well settled that, "[w]here the parties executed a valid and enforceable written contract governing a particular subject matter, recovery on a theory of unjust enrichment for events arising out of that subject matter is ordinarily precluded" (IDT Corp. v. Morgan Stanley Dean Witter & Co., 12 N.Y.3d 132, 142 [2009]).

Accordingly, the order of the Appellate Division should be reversed, with costs, the order of Supreme Court reinstated, and the certified question answered in the negative.

The vanishing brokerage account

1. Exactly why—according to the court—was there no unjust enrichment in *Simkin v. Blank*? Do they say there can be no unjust enrichment because

the parties had a written contract? Statements like the one quoted in the concluding paragraph of the opinion must be applied very cautiously.

2. What would you propose as the best analogy for the vanishing Madoff account? The court's preferred analogy is "a marital asset that unexpectedly loses value after dissolution of a marriage." This treats the Madoff account as if it were an account at Merrill, Lynch that was unwisely invested. Do you see a distinction?

3. The court thought the Madoff account was real enough at the time of the settlement, because husband took money out to pay wife's share of the property division. Does the fact that husband was able to withdraw funds mean that the account was an asset to be counted at face value, like the other ones the parties were dividing?

---

(2) Unilateral mistake

M. F. Kemper Construction Co. v. City of Los Angeles
37 Cal. 2d 696, 235 P.2d 7 (1951)

GIBSON, C. J.

M. F. Kemper Construction Company brought this action against the city of Los Angeles to cancel a bid it had submitted on public construction work and to obtain discharge of its bid bond. The city cross-complained for forfeiture of the bond and for damages. The trial court cancelled the bid, discharged the bond, and allowed appellant city nothing on its cross-complaint. The sole issue is whether the company is entitled to relief on the ground of unilateral mistake.

On July 28, 1948, the city Board of Public Works published a notice inviting bids for the construction of the general piping system for the Hyperion sewer project. Pursuant to the city charter, the notice provided that each bid must be accompanied by a certified check or surety bond for an amount not less than 10 per cent of the sum of the bid "as a guarantee that the bidder will enter into the proposed contract if it is awarded to him," and that the bond or check and the proceeds thereof "will become the property of the city of Los Angeles, if the bidder fails or refuses to execute the required contract." The charter provides: "After bids have been opened and declared, except with the consent of the officer, board or City Council having jurisdiction over the bidding, no bid shall be withdrawn, but the same shall be subject to acceptance by the city for a period of three months." The notice inviting bids reserved to the board the right to reject any and all bids, and both it and the official bid form stated that bidders "will not be released on account of errors."

Respondent company learned of the invitation for bids on August 17 and immediately began to prepare its proposal. Over a thousand different items were involved in the estimates. The actual computations were performed by three men, each of whom calculated the costs of different parts of the work, and in order to complete their estimates, they all worked until 2 o'clock on the morning of the day the bids were to be opened. Their final effort required the addition and transposition of the figures arrived at by each man for his portion of the work from his "work sheet" to a "final accumulation sheet" from which the total amount of the bid was taken. One item estimated on a work sheet in the amount of $301,769 was inadvertently omitted from the final accumulation sheet and was overlooked in computing the total amount of the bid. The error was caused by the fact that the men were exhausted after working long hours under pressure. When the bids were opened on August 25, it was found that respondent company's bid was $780,305 and the bids of the other three contractors were $1,049,592, $1,183,000 and $1,278,895.

The company discovered its error several hours after the bids were opened and immediately notified a member of the board of its mistake in omitting one item while preparing the final accumulation of figures for its bid. On August 27 the company explained its mistake to the board and withdrew its bid. A few days later, at the board's invitation, it submitted evidence which showed the unintentional omission of the $301,769 item. The board, however, passed a resolution accepting the erroneous bid of $780,305, and the company refused to enter into a written contract at that figure. On October 15, 1948, without readvertising, the board awarded the contract to the next lowest bidder. The city then demanded forfeiture of the Kemper Company's bond, and the company commenced the present action to cancel its bid and obtain discharge of the bond.

The trial court found that the bid had been submitted as the result of an excusable and honest mistake of a material and fundamental character, that the company had not been negligent in preparing the proposal, that it had acted promptly to notify the board of the mistake and to rescind the bid, and that the board had accepted the bid with knowledge of the error. The court further found and concluded that it would be unconscionable to require the company to perform for the amount of the bid, that no intervening rights had accrued, and that the city had suffered no damage or prejudice.

Once opened and declared, the company's bid was in the nature of an irrevocable option, a contract right of which the city could not be deprived without its consent unless the requirements for rescission were satisfied. The company seeks to enforce rescission of its bid on the ground of mistake. The city contends that a party is entitled to relief on that ground only where the mistake is mutual, and it points to the fact that the mistake in the bid submitted was wholly unilateral. However, the city had actual notice of the error in the estimates before it attempted to accept the bid, and knowledge by one party that the other is acting under mistake is treated as equivalent to mutual mistake for purposes of rescission. Relief from mistaken bids is consistently allowed where one party knows or has reason to know of the other's error and the requirements for rescission are fulfilled. Rescission may be had for mistake of fact if the mistake is material to the contract and was not the result of neglect of a legal duty, if enforcement of the contract as made would be unconscionable, and if the other party can be placed *in statu quo*. In addition, the party seeking relief must give prompt notice of his election to rescind and must restore or offer to restore to the other party everything of value which he has received under the contract.

The evidence clearly supports the conclusion that it would be unconscionable to hold the company to its bid at the mistaken figure. The city had knowledge before the bid was accepted that the company had made a clerical error which resulted in the omission of an item amounting to nearly one third of the amount intended to be bid, and, under all the circumstances, it appears that it would be unjust and unfair to permit the city to take advantage of the company's mistake. There is no reason for denying relief on the ground that the city cannot be restored to status quo. It had ample time in which to award the contract without readvertising, the contract was actually awarded to the next lowest bidder, and the city will not be heard to complain that it cannot be placed *in statu quo* because it will not have the benefit of an inequitable bargain. Finally, the company gave notice promptly upon discovering the facts entitling it to rescind, and no offer of restoration was necessary because it had received nothing of value which it could restore. We are satisfied that all the requirements for rescission have been met.

The city nevertheless contends that the company is precluded from relief because of the statement in the invitation and in the official bid form that bidders "will not be released on account of errors," and that this language required all contractors to warrant the accuracy of their bids and to waive all rights to seek relief for clerical mistake. There is a difference between mere mechanical or clerical errors made in tabulating or transcribing figures and errors of judgment, as, for example, underestimating the cost of labor or materials. The distinction between the two types of error is recognized in the cases allowing rescission and in the procedures provided by the state and federal governments for relieving contractors from mistakes in bids on public work. Generally, relief is refused for error in judgment and allowed only for clerical or mathematical mistakes. Where a person is denied relief because of an error in judgment, the agreement which is enforced is the one he intended to make, whereas if he is denied relief from a clerical error, he is forced to perform an agreement he had no intention of making. The statement in the bid form in the present case can be given effect by interpreting it as relating to errors of judgment as distinguished from clerical mistakes. If we were to give the language the sweeping construction contended for by the city, it would mean holding that the contractor intended to assume the risk of a clerical error no matter in what circumstances it might occur or how serious it might be. Such interpretation is contrary to common sense and ordinary business understanding and would result in the loss of heretofore well-established equitable rights to relief from certain types of mistake.

The city also argues that public interest precludes any right to rescind for mistake, and in this connection it asserts that a literal interpretation should be given to the provision in section 386(d) of the charter that "After bids have been opened and declared, except with the consent of the officer, board or

City Council having jurisdiction over the bidding, no bid shall be withdrawn." In Moffett, Hodgkins & Clarke Co. v. Rochester, 178 U.S. 373 (1900), the city of Rochester urged that a construction of a charter provision similar to one involved here prevented a bidder from rescinding, and the court in rejecting the argument, said:

> If the [city is] correct in [its] contention there is absolutely no redress for a bidder for public work, no matter how aggravated or palpable his blunder. The moment his proposal is opened by the executive board he is held as in a grasp of steel. There is no remedy, no escape. If, through an error of his clerk, he has agreed to do work worth one million dollars for ten dollars, he must be held to the strict letter of his contract, while equity stands by with folded hands and sees him driven into bankruptcy. The [city's] position admits of no compromise, no exception, no middle ground.

Most of the authorities from other jurisdictions heretofore cited as allowing rescission for mistake and relief from forfeiture involved public construction contracts, and in many of them there were express contract or charter provisions making the bids irrevocable. (See, also, cases collected in 59 A.L.R. 809, 824; 80 A.L.R. 586; 107 A.L.R. 1451.) The California cases uniformly refuse to apply special rules of law simply because a governmental body is a party to a contract.

The judgment is affirmed. Shenk, J., Edmonds, J., Traynor, J., and Schauer, J., concurred.

CARTER, J.

I dissent. The majority opinion is based upon two grounds: (1) that a bidder on a public construction job may rescind his bid for unilateral mistake after it is opened and thus escape the forfeiture provided by statute; (2) that the clause in the invitation for bids and the bid, that bidders "will not be released on account of errors," does not apply to clerical errors, and, therefore, is not applicable in the instant case. I do not agree with either premise.

The first violates one of the obvious and fundamental principles of the law of rescission for unilateral mistake, that is, that the one against whom rescission is sought *must have had knowledge of the mistake before a binding contract is made.* This question is glossed over in the majority opinion by a tacit assumption that the contract being rescinded is the contract for the performance of the work rather than the irrevocable and binding offer—the bid. Yet the action is one to cancel the bid—to permit its withdrawal—and throughout the opinion, the binding effect of the *bid* is the thing considered. Indeed, there is no contract to perform the work, for the bidder refused to enter into it. The contract to be rescinded is a contract to make a contract to perform the work, that is, the irrevocable bid, the performance of which is guaranteed by the bid bond. At the time the bids were opened the city had no knowledge and had no means of knowing that the bidder had made a mistake. There is nothing left therefore but a naked unilateral mistake which is not ground for rescission. As it is said: "A mistake of only one party that forms the basis on which he enters into a transaction does not of itself render the transaction voidable." (Rest. Contracts, §503.) If that rule is not applied to bidding contracts there is nothing left of the supposedly binding bid and forfeiture provision, for the bidder may always avoid it by claiming mistake. The proof of whether or not he has made such a mistake is so completely within his control and power that the public body is helpless to refute it. Charter provisions, invitation for bids, and the forfeiture provisions, such as those here involved, are made wholly meaningless, for in practically every case the reason the bidder wants to withdraw is because he has made a mistake. The important considerations of public policy behind those provisions will be completely destroyed.

In addition to the foregoing, the bidder here was advised by words printed in capital letters in the invitation for bids and also in the bid itself that *he would not be released for errors*. Nothing could be more explicit. There is no room left for claiming mistake. Yet the majority say that the "errors" to which reference is made in the above mentioned documents, are of judgment, not in computation. The term "error" has a broad meaning and is not confined to those of judgment. It means the same as mistake. To narrow its meaning is to alter the contract of the parties. The phrase was used to avoid the precise claim now made by the bidder. It was contemplated by the parties that the risk of any mistakes was to be borne by the bidder.

To limit the errors of the bidder for which he is responsible to those of judgment, is to strike at the very purpose of the clause in question and the bid bond. The clause and bond are there to assure certainty of contract and to preserve the integrity of the bidding system in letting public contracts. In the majority of cases that purpose will be defeated by the limitation. From the standpoint of the bidder, his mistake is far more inexcusable when it is in computation rather than judgment. There is no reason why he cannot have his arithmetic correct. School boys have been disciplined for stupidity in that field. It is entirely within his control, unaffected by any extraneous uncertain factors such as are involved in judgment as to the amount of materials and labor required, complicated by the fluctuation in their value, the physical conditions encountered, etc.

Thus we have: The charter provisions requiring competitive bidding; that the bidder's bid be irrevocable and binding; and that security must be posted to assure that the bidder will execute the contract, which security will be forfeited if he does not do so. The bidding papers expressly state that the bidder will not be excused for any mistakes he makes. Nevertheless, the majority opinion holds by dubious reasoning that all of those circumstances mean nothing.

I would, therefore, reverse the judgment.

Known to the other party

1. When a contracting party seeks rescission for unilateral mistake, the first question is usually whether the other party had notice that a mistake was being

made—in other words, whether the mistake was what is called "transparent" or "palpable." According to the dissenting opinion, "At the time the bids were opened the city had no knowledge and had no means of knowing that the bidder had made a mistake." Do you agree? How would the dissenting judge decide this case if Kemper's clerical error had involved misplacing a decimal point, resulting in a bid of $108,207.40?

2. The dissent properly draws our attention to the two-step process of offer and acceptance in this case, and to a possible ambiguity about what exactly is being rescinded. Statute law provided that Kemper's erroneous bid, once opened, was "in the nature of an irrevocable option," subject to withdrawal only on forfeiture of the bid bond—meaning, in this case, a penalty of approximately $78,000. The majority emphasizes that (i) at the time the City purported to accept Kemper's offer, it knew that the offer was based on a serious clerical error; and (ii) by accepting the lowest nonmistaken bid, without any delay or need to readvertise, the City was left *in statu quo*—in exactly the position it would have occupied if no mistake had been made by anyone. May an offeree form a contract on the basis of an offer that it knows to be erroneous and unintentional? Does the answer change if the unintended offer is stated to be "firm" or otherwise irrevocable?

3. *The Baseball Card Case*

> Twelve-year-old card collector Bryan Wrzesinski, owner of some 40,000 baseball cards, spotted a 1968 Nolan Ryan/Jerry Koosman rookie card at the Ball-Mart, a newly-opened baseball card store in Itasca, Illinois. The price of the card was marked as "1200/." An inexperienced sales clerk interpreted this figure to mean $12.00 and accepted that amount in exchange for the card. The proprietor of the Ball-Mart, Joe Irmen, claimed that the card had been offered for sale at $1,200 (a price in line with its market value) and asked for it back. Wrzesinski refused to reverse the transaction. After two days of trial on Irmen's suit for replevin or money damages, and moments before the judge was to issue her decision, the parties announced a settlement: the card would be sold at auction and the proceeds given to charity.

Kull, *Unilateral Mistake: The Baseball Card Case*, 70 Wash. U.L.Q. 57 (1992) (describing Irmen v. Wrzesinski, No. 90 SC 5362 (Ill. Cir. Ct. DuPage County [Small Claims Div.], filed June 29, 1990)). The settlement suggests that neither party was sure of his legal position, but how hard should this case have been to decide?

4. In Amlie Strand Hardware Co. v. Moose, 176 Minn. 598, 224 N.W. 158 (1929), a store held a promotion in which customers who bought merchandise (or paid their bills) were given votes that they could cast in favor of various contestants. The winning contestants would receive prizes: first prize was a Ford coupé. When the votes were counted, the car was awarded to Mrs. Moose,

who drove it away. The next day the contest judges discovered that their adding machine had malfunctioned. They ordered a recount, and this time Mrs. Moose came in second. When Mrs. Moose refused to return the prize car, the store sued to recover it. What result?

———————————

(3) Reformation

Mutual Life Insurance Co. of Baltimore v. Metzger
167 Md. 27, 172 A. 610 (1934)

BOND, Chief Judge.

The suit is one for reformation of a policy of life insurance, on the ground that by a clerk's mistake it was made out for an amount greater than that applied for and agreed upon, and the complainant appeals from a decree denying the relief.

The policy was issued upon an application signed by the insured, Mrs. Julia A. Lomax, and her daughter, Augusta Metzger, the appellee, was named as beneficiary. After the death of Mrs. Lomax, the beneficiary, according to her testimony, found the policy made out for $500. She knew nothing of the taking out of the policy, assumed that it was correctly made out as it appeared, and, relying on the availability of so much money, incurred and paid a bill of $400 for funeral expenses. The insurer, however, contends that a policy of only $50 was applied for, that the premium specified in the application, and subsequently paid, was the premium for a $50 policy, but that a clerk in writing the policy from the specifications in the application of the deceased mistook the $50 for $500. [The court explains in some detail how this happened.] It was testified for the company that the premium specified and paid was, as stated, the regular premium for a $50 policy. The deceased had two other policies in the same company, one for $120 and one for $55, and there is no dispute on these.

The controlling principles are plain. "If parties enter into an agreement, and through an error in the reduction of it to writing, the written agreement fails to express their real intentions or contains terms or stipulations contrary to their common intention, a court of equity will correct and reform the instrument so as to make it conform to the intention of the parties." The occurrence of the mistake, and the fact of agreement of both parties as contended, must be made clear beyond reasonable controversy. This we think has been done in the present case. The insured signed an application for a policy of $50 and paid premiums for so much insurance, yet the policy as drafted appears to give insurance in the amount of $500, and the condition of the writing which would lead to the error has been shown.

A year elapsed between the issuing of the policy and the death of the insured, and the objection on the ground of mistake was not made until the policy was brought back to the company after the death; and a question of laches is raised in defense to the application for reformation. But, of course, the mistake could not have been discovered earlier by any reasonable effort, and the lapse of time which might serve as a defense on this ground does not begin to run until the discovery.

In the making of the error in the office of the insurer there would seem to have been no such negligence as defeats an application for reformation. There could hardly be a less negligent error, and the existence of negligence in even the slightest degree does not prevent reformation. If it did, there would have been much less reformation by courts of equity in the past. In many, if not most, of the instances of correction of scriveners' errors, the scrivener has been the agent of the complainant alone. "The fact, however, that the defective instrument may have been drawn up by the party seeking relief is immaterial, if a proper case be made out." Kerr, Fraud and Mistake (6th Ed.) 611. "It is not every negligence that will stay the hand of the court. The conclusion from the best authorities seems to be, that the neglect must amount to the violation of a positive legal duty." Pomeroy, Equity Jurisprudence, §856; cases reviewed, 45 A.L.R. 700.

The principle that mistake of one party alone, not a mutual or common mistake, will not be corrected by reformation, cannot prevent relief in this instance, for the mistake was a common one within the meaning of that rule. It is not meant by it that the error in drafting by the agent of one party cannot be relieved. Insurance policies are always drafted by agents of the company, but that fact does not interfere with correction of mistakes in the drafting. The mistake common to both parties which supports reformation in these cases is in the supposition of both that their final writing states their agreement correctly. As Chief Judge Alvey put it in Stiles v. Willis, 66 Md. 552, 555, 8 A. 353, 354: "The proof must establish, incontrovertibly, that the error or mistake alleged was common to both parties; in other words, it must be conclusively established that both parties understood the contract as it is alleged it ought to have been expressed, and as in fact it was, but for the mistake alleged in reducing it to writing."

It is obvious that the effect of reformation if granted must influence the action of the court of equity on the application for it. In Philpott v. Elliott, 4 Md. Ch. 273, reformation of a lease to correct a mistake in a boundary line was denied after the defendant had built over the correct line. In Mullen v. Cronan, 90 N. J. Eq. 392, 107 A. 793, the court denied reformation of an assignment of shares of stock after money derived from a sale of them had been expended by the assignee and the executor of his will in the erection of a new building. The defense is more frequently met with, and its applications illustrated, in the equitable action for money had and received after payment by mistake. Cases reviewed, L.R.A. 1917E, 350, and 25 A.L.R. 129; Standish v. Ross, 3 Ex. 527; Baylis v. Bishop of London (1913) 1 Ch. 127; Holt v. Markham (1923) 1 K. B. 504, 514; Jones v. Waring & Gillow, [1926] A. C. 670; Kerr, Fraud & Mistake (6th Ed.) 635. Generally, repayment is not obtainable in so far as it may fail to leave the defendant *in statu quo*, or in a position to avoid detriment by some readjustment on his side. This raises a question of fact which is, of course, to be determined in each case from its circumstances.

The defendant here testifies that she was induced, by the apparent avail-ability of $500 of insurance payable to her on this policy, to contract and pay a funeral bill of $400. We are hardly permitted to suppose that she would have contracted a bill of only $50 if the policy had correctly stated the amount. It is more reasonable to suppose that she would even then have provided a more costly funeral, in expectation of paying for it from her other resources, the uncontested insurance for $175, and the still further resources she appears to have had at least temporarily available. Her testimony is that with all her resources she could not afford to pay $400 for the funeral, and she evidently made some part of the expenditure from the money expected from this policy over and above the amount of $50. For exactly what part she relied on this policy it is not possible to determine from the testimony given. She could not now estimate it except by conjecture, because when she contracted for the funeral the problem arising from a reduced amount of insurance was not actu-ally presented to her and decided. And it is the opinion of this court that in the exercise of its duty, in granting reformation, to avoid detriment to an innocent defendant whose position has altered, an estimate must be made by the court to protect the defendant from loss to the best of the court's ability in view of all the evidence. To this end it is held that reformation should be granted as prayed in the bill of complaint, and the policy held paid and canceled, upon the complainant's paying to the defendant the sum of $200.

Notes on reformation

1. "In an action for reformation the cause of complaint is not that a mistake has been made, but rather that a writing to which the parties are subject does not adequately express their true wishes. Equity is asked to relieve a condition, not a state of mind." Malone, *The Reformation of Writings for Mutual Mistake of Fact*, 24 Geo. L.J. 613, 618 (1936).

> If, in this kind of case, talk of "mutuality" of mistake is unnecessary, much confusion can be avoided. Invariably, two mistakes are involved. There is a natural tendency to concentrate on the making of the clerical error in the writing as the critical mistake involved, when the true crucial error is mistaken belief of the parties about the correctness of the written instrument.

Travelers Ins. Co. v. Bailey, 124 Vt. 114, 120, 197 A.2d 813, 817 (1964).

2. The possibility of reformation of a written contract to reflect the parties' agreement is (or should be) familiar from Contracts class. Unjust enrichment as the reason for the remedy becomes prominent, in cases like *Mutual Life Ins. Co. v. Metzger*, where there has already been a performance exceeding what was due under the real agreement. As in other cases of mistaken payment,

the characteristic defense to restitution is change of position on the part of an innocent payee.

Reformation is likewise available to correct mistakes in the terms of other instruments, typically deeds to real property or promissory notes. Given their different consequences, the important defense to reformation in such cases is usually bona fide purchase rather than change of position.

3. In Frederic E. Rose (London), Ltd. v. William H. Pim, Jr. & Co., Ltd., [1953] 2 Q.B. 450 (Ct. App.), the plaintiffs' Egyptian representatives cabled that they had a buyer for "up to five hundred tons Moroccan horsebeans described here feveroles. Please offer c.i.f. Port Said." Because plaintiffs' London personnel did not know what "feveroles" were, they asked defendant—another London merchant having "an extensive connexion with North African suppliers and shippers of local products." Defendant investigated and reported "that feveroles meant horsebeans and that these could be obtained from Algeria, Tunisia, or Morocco." Plaintiffs eventually purchased from defendant "500 tons Tunisian horsebeans, fair average quality," which they supplied to the Egyptian customer who wanted feveroles. It turned out that feveroles were not the same thing as Tunisian horsebeans, nor as valuable, and that plaintiffs were liable to their customer in Port Said for breach of contract. Back in London, plaintiffs sued defendant seeking (1) to reform the contract between them to read "horsebeans (feveroles)," then (2) to enforce the reformed feverole contract by an action for damages. Is this a case for reformation? What other remedy would you suggest for plaintiffs on these facts?

4. The facts of Prudential Ins. Co. of America v. S.S. American Lancer, 870 F.2d 867 (2d Cir. 1989), known as "the case of the missing zeros," have been recounted as follows:

> On April 14, 1986, as lawyers assembled closing documents for a refinancing of some outstanding debt of United States Lines (USL), a secretary working on something called "Amendment No. 1 to the First Preferred Ship Mortgage" omitted three zeros from the number representing the balance of USL's outstanding indebtedness to Prudential [the mortgagee]. The erroneous figure—"$92,885.00" instead of "$92,885,000.00"—was subsequently copied in dozens of other documents. Although lawyers from five or six different law firms and in-house legal departments were presumably reviewing the documents as they prepared for the closing, nobody noticed the error. The papers were filed and forgotten—until November of that year, when USL defaulted on the notes secured by the amended mortgage.
>
> Nobody with an interest in the matter was ever mistaken about the amount of Prudential's first mortgage. No creditor asserted that it had relied on erroneous information about the amount of USL's existing debt. The lender that tried most aggressively to profit from the situation—General Electric Capital Corp. (GECC), formerly GE Credit—had been intimately involved in USL's financing for some years and knew as much about the Prudential mortgage as Prudential itself.

When Prudential tried to foreclose its $92,885,000 first mortgage, USL's bankruptcy trustee objected that the mortgage should be limited to $92,885. The trustee eventually agreed to withdraw his opposition to the Prudential mortgage (and to help Prudential defend its first mortgage against the attacks of the junior lienors) in exchange for 17.5 percent of the net proceeds to Prudential from the sale of the mortgaged vessels. Because the sale realized something over $65 million, this payment amounted to more than $11 million.

Next, GECC, which (along with Prudential) held USL notes secured by a second mortgage on the same vessels, brought suit in admiralty for a declaration that Prudential's first mortgage was valid only to the extent of $92,885. Both in the Southern District of New York and on appeal to the Second Circuit, GECC lost. Finally, Prudential sued the various law firms involved in the refinancing, alleging that the expenses of settlement, legal fees and delay resulting from the typographical error had cost it $31 million.

This version of the story comes from Andrew Kull, *Zero-based Morality*, Business Law Today (July/August 1992), at 11-14. How much should it have cost — ideally — to correct the $92 million typo? Why did it cost so much more? Changing some of the facts of the "missing zeros" case would make it more difficult to correct the lawyers' mistake. What different facts would cause the most trouble?

B. RESTITUTION TO A PERFORMING PARTY WITH NO CLAIM ON THE CONTRACT

(1) Unenforceable contract

Boone v. Coe
153 Ky. 233, 154 S.W. 900 (1913)

CLAY, C.

Plaintiffs, W. H. Boone and J. T. Coe, brought this action against defendant, J. F. Coe, to recover certain damages, alleged to have resulted from defendant's breach of a parol contract of lease for one year to commence at a future date. It appears from the petition that the defendant was the owner of a large and valuable farm in Ford County, Tex. Plaintiffs were farmers, and were living with their families in Monroe County, Ky. In the fall of 1909 defendant made a verbal contract with plaintiffs, whereby he rented to them his farm in Texas for a period of 12 months, to commence from the date of plaintiffs' arrival at defendant's farm. Defendant agreed that if plaintiffs would leave their said homes and businesses in Kentucky, and with their families, horses, and wagons, move to defendant's farm in Texas, and take charge of, manage, and cultivate same in wheat, corn, and cotton for the 12 months next following plaintiffs' arrival at said farm, the defendant would have a dwelling completed on said farm and ready for occupancy upon their arrival, which dwelling plaintiffs would occupy as a residence during the period of said tenancy. Defendant also agreed that he would furnish necessary material at a convenient place on said farm out of which to erect a good and commodious stock and grain barn, to be used by plaintiffs. The petition further alleges that plaintiffs were to cultivate certain portions of the farm, and were to receive certain portions of the crops raised, and that plaintiffs, in conformity with their said agreement, did move from Kentucky to the farm in Texas, and carried with them their families, wagons, horses, and camping outfit, and in going to Texas they traveled for a period of 55 days. It is also charged that defendant broke his contract, in that he failed to have ready and completed on the farm a dwelling house in which plaintiffs and their families could move, and also failed to furnish the necessary material for the erection of a suitable barn; that on December 6th defendant refused to permit plaintiffs to occupy the house and premises, and failed and refused to permit them to cultivate the land or any part thereof; that on the ___ day of December, 1909, they started for their home in Kentucky, and arrived there after traveling for a period of 4 days. It is charged that plaintiffs spent in going to Texas, in cash, the sum of $150; that the loss of time to plaintiffs and their teams in making the trip to Texas was reasonably worth $8 a day for a period of 55 days, or the sum of $440; that the loss of time to them and their teams during the period they remained in Texas was $8 a day for 22 days, or $176; that they paid out in actual cash for transportation for themselves, families, and teams from Texas to Kentucky the sum of $211.80; that the loss of time to them and their teams in making the last-named trip was reasonably worth the sum of $100; that in abandoning and giving up their homes and businesses in Kentucky they had been damaged in the sum of $150, making a total damage of $1,387.80, for which judgment was asked. Defendant's demurrer to the petition was sustained and the petition dismissed. Plaintiffs appeal.

The statute of frauds provides as follows: "No action shall be brought to charge any person: 6. Upon any contract for the sale of real estate, or any lease thereof, for longer term than one year; nor 7. Upon any agreement which is not to be performed within one year from the making thereof, unless the promise, contract, agreement, representation, assurance, or ratification, or some memorandum or note thereof, be in writing, and signed by the party to be charged therewith, or by his authorized agent; but the consideration need not be expressed in the writing; it may be proved when necessary, or disproved by parol or other evidence." A parol lease of land for one year, to commence at a future date, is within the statute. The question sharply presented is: May plaintiffs recover for expenses incurred and time lost on the faith of a contract that is unenforceable under the statute of frauds?

It is the general rule that damages cannot be recovered for violation of a contract within the statute of frauds. To this general rule there are certain well-recognized exceptions. Thus in a number of cases, it has been held that, where services have been rendered during the life of another, on the promise that the person rendering the service should receive at the death of the person served a legacy, and the contract so made is within the statute of frauds, a reasonable compensation may be recovered for the services actually rendered. It has also been held that the vendee of land under a parol contract is entitled to recover any portion of the purchase money he may have paid, and is also entitled to compensation for improvements. And under a contract for personal services within the statute an action may be maintained on a quantum meruit.

The doctrine of these cases proceeds upon the theory that the defendant has actually received some benefits from the acts of part performance; and the law therefore implies a promise to pay. In 29 Am. & Eng. Ency. 836, the rule is thus stated: "Although part performance by one of the parties to a contract within the statute of frauds will not, at law, entitle such party to recover upon the contract itself, he may nevertheless recover for money paid by him, or property delivered, or services rendered in accordance with and upon the faith of the contract. The law will raise an implied promise on the part of the other party to pay for what has been done in the way of part performance. But this right of recovery is not absolute. The plaintiff is entitled to compensation only under such circumstances as would warrant a recovery in case there was no express contract; and hence it must appear that the defendant has actually received, or will receive, some benefit from the acts of part performance. It is immaterial that the plaintiff may have suffered a loss because he is unable to enforce his contract."

In the case under consideration the plaintiffs merely sustained a loss. Defendant received no benefit. Had he received a benefit, the law would imply an obligation to pay therefor. Having received no benefit, no obligation to pay is implied. The statute says that the contract of defendant made with plaintiffs is unenforceable. Defendant therefore had the legal right to decline to carry it out. To require him to pay plaintiffs for losses and expenses incurred on the faith of the contract, without any benefit accruing to him, would, in effect, uphold a contract upon which the statute expressly declares no action shall be brought. The statute was enacted for the purpose of preventing frauds and perjuries. That it is a valuable statute is shown by the fact that similar statutes are in force in practically all, if not all, of the states of the Union. Being a valuable statute, the purpose of the lawmakers in its enactment should not be defeated by permitting recoveries in cases to which its provisions were intended to apply.

The contrary rule was announced by this court in the case of McDaniel v. Hutcherson, 136 Ky. 412, 124 S. W. 384. There the plaintiff lived in the state of Illinois. The defendant owned a farm in Mercer County, Ky. The defendant agreed with plaintiff that if plaintiff and his family would come to Kentucky and live with defendant, the defendant would furnish the plaintiff a home during defendant's life, and upon his death would give plaintiff his farm. It was held that, although the contract was within the statute of frauds, plaintiff could recover his reasonable expenses in moving to Kentucky, and reasonable compensation for loss sustained in giving up his business elsewhere.

Upon reconsideration of the question involved, we conclude that the doctrine announced in that case is not in accord with the weight of authority, and should be no longer adhered to. It is therefore overruled.

Judgment affirmed.

Pelletier v. Johnson

188 Ariz. 478, 937 P.2d 668 (Ct. App. 1996)

PELANDER, Presiding Judge.

The primary issue in this case is whether a seller whose contract is covered by and fails to comply with Arizona's Home Solicitations and Referral Sales Act (the Act) may, under proper circumstances, recover equitable, restitutionary damages from the consumer/buyer based on unjust enrichment principles. Ruling in the affirmative, the trial court entered judgment for the seller and awarded it damages and attorney's fees. For the reasons set forth below, we affirm.

Pursuant to a written contract, defendants/appellants agreed to purchase and plaintiff/appellee G & B Design Builders (G & B), an Arizona licensed contractor, agreed to install vinyl siding on defendants' home for $5,475. Although the contract provided that defendants could cancel the transaction within three business days, they never attempted to do so. G & B installed the siding approximately one week after the contract was executed. When defendants refused to pay, G & B sued them for breach of contract and later added claims for *quantum meruit* and unjust enrichment.

After a bench trial, on appeal from arbitration, the trial court entered findings of fact and dismissed G & B's contract claim, concluding that the parties' transaction constituted a "home solicitation sale" within the meaning of Ariz. Rev. Stat. §44-5001(1) and that the parties' contract was "ineffective" because it lacked language required by §44-5004(B). The court also ruled, however, that G & B was entitled to recover the reasonable value of the improvements (siding and installation) in the amount of $5,475 based on unjust enrichment. The court entered judgment for G & B in that amount and awarded $7,800 of the $11,160 G & B had requested in attorney's fees plus taxable costs. This appeal followed.

Defendants contend G & B should have been precluded from recovering any unjust enrichment damages because its violation of §44-5004 rendered the contract invalid and constituted a class 3 misdemeanor under §44-5008. According to defendants, the trial court's judgment "effectively eviscerated the statutory mandate" of the Act and thwarted its underlying public policy.

The Act was originally passed in 1970 and has been amended several times since then. Section 44-5004(B) provides in part that "No agreement of the buyer in a home solicitation sale shall be effective unless it is dated, signed by the buyer and contains a conspicuous notice" to the buyer containing language set forth in that subsection, including a provision that the buyer "may cancel this agreement any time prior to midnight of the third business day after the date of this transaction." Similarly, §44-5004(C) provides in part that "No agreement of the buyer in a home solicitation sale shall be effective" unless a completed notice of cancellation form, the language of which is set forth in that subsection, is attached to the contract or receipt.

The question here is whether the Act may be construed as allowing a seller to obtain equitable relief notwithstanding a violation of its provisions. The words of the Act do not specifically preclude equitable relief if a seller violates any provision of the Act, nor do the legislature's declarations of the Act's purpose support such a blanket prohibition. When the Arizona legislature originally passed the Act in 1970, it declared its purpose was "to regulate, not prohibit, home solicitations sales by [*inter alia*] granting the buyer a statutory period during which time the contract may be canceled." Similarly, in amending the Act in 1973 the legislature declared its purpose was "to make void any attempt to waive buyer cancellation rights in home solicitation sales." Those express legislative purposes underlying the Act would not be furthered or achieved by automatically depriving the seller of equitable recourse and relief for material and labor it has furnished to a buyer under the circumstances of this case.

G & B's contract was dated, signed by and furnished to defendants. In language almost identical to that required by §44-5004(B), the contract provided immediately above defendants' signatures that they "may cancel this transaction at any time prior to midnight of the third business day after the date of this transaction." It is undisputed that defendants were aware of that provision and never sought to cancel the transaction. Although the contract did not fully comply with the requirements of §44-5004, it fulfilled the basic legislative purpose of "[g]ranting the buyer a [three business day] period during which time the contract may be canceled." There was no evidence that defendants would have acted differently had the contract fully complied with §44-5004; nor was there evidence that defendants were harmed by the noncomplying contract.

One commentator has suggested that Arizona's Act may have been modeled on Connecticut's Home Solicitation Sales Act. If so, we generally would consider the Connecticut courts' construction of their Act, at least prior to adoption of the Arizona Act in 1970, as persuasive but not binding authority. In a 4-3 decision, the Connecticut Supreme Court held that a contractor whose agreement admittedly failed to comply with and was unenforceable under that state's Home Improvement Contractors Act could not recover in quasi-contract by demonstrating unjust enrichment of the homeowner for whom the contractor had performed work. Barrett Builders v. Miller, 215 Conn. 316, 576 A.2d 455 (1990). The dissent rejected "an interpretation [of the Act] so fraught with the danger of exploitation by the unscrupulous," and noted that neither the statutory language nor its policy mandated that conclusion, which effectively "result[ed] in forfeitures enriching the homeowners regardless of the merits of the disputes or the value of the work performed." That would be the result here. As noted, defendants knew of and never exercised their right to cancel the contract within three business days of the transaction. G & B commenced and completed its work only after that time frame had elapsed.

The trial court found that "Defendants never complained to [G & B] about the siding or the installation until after the complaint was filed." On appeal, defendants do not challenge the quality of G & B's work, its timeliness, or the reasonable value of its material and labor.

Defendants admittedly received the benefit of G & B's services at a price customarily charged for such jobs, yet paid nothing and incurred no debt for those services. Moreover, the trial court specifically found that G & B made no fraudulent misrepresentations, a finding not challenged on appeal, and there was no evidence that G & B intentionally or knowingly violated the Act. Under the circumstances, assuming *arguendo* the Act applied and precluded G & B from recovering on its contract, it was "entitled to recovery on *quantum meruit* for the reasonable value of the improvements [defendants have] received." Beley v. Ventura County Mun. Court, 100 Cal. App. 3d 5, 8, 160 Cal. Rptr. 508, 509 (1979).

In sum, we are persuaded by and therefore adopt the position of the dissent in *Barrett Builders*. That position is consistent with other authorities, including the Restatement (Second) of Contracts, §197 (1981) ("Except as stated in §§198 and 199, a party has no claim in restitution for performance that he has rendered under or in return for a promise that is unenforceable on grounds of public policy *unless denial of restitution would cause disproportionate forfeiture*"). It also comports with restitution principles recognized and applied in analogous Arizona cases. See, *e.g.*, Evans v. Mason, 82 Ariz. 40, 45, 308 P.2d 245, 248 (1957) (where an oral contract is within the statute of frauds and no action can be maintained thereon for that reason, "one who has rendered services pursuant thereto is not remediless for he can sue on a quantum meruit, a promise to pay the reasonable value thereof being implied"); Ruck Corp. v. Woudenberg, 125 Ariz. 519, 522, 611 P.2d 106, 109 (Ct. App. 1980) ("If a person performs work, renders services, or expends money under an agreement which is unenforceable, but not illegal, he may recover in quantum meruit for the value of the services and expenses reasonably incurred in good faith").

We also agree with the reasoning of the California court of appeals in *Beley*, a case upon which the trial court relied, that "there was nothing illegal or immoral about the contract itself or the nature of the services and materials to be furnished under it." Unlike the "heir finder" agreement at issue in Landi v. Arkules, 172 Ariz. 126, 835 P.2d 458 (Ct. App. 1992), G & B's contract for the sale and installation of vinyl siding did not involve performance of any "unlawful act" and was neither "void as against public policy" nor inherently "illegal."

Affirmed.

Unenforceable for "informality"

1. When the defendant has received a valuable performance under a contract that is unenforceable by reason of the Statute of Frauds, courts will often avoid a forfeiture by invoking a rule to the effect that—in certain cases at

least—"performance takes the case out of the statute." In Towsley v. Moore, 30 Ohio St. 184 (1876), Olive Towsley "then being a minor about eleven years old, with the advice and consent of her mother, agreed to work for defendant in his household and kitchen, until she arrived at the age of 18; for which defendant was to board, clothe, and furnish her with schooling, and at the expiration of her period of service, pay her what such service was reasonably worth." Olive performed her end of the bargain, and defendant Moore refused to pay. Reviewing numerous cases in which a defendant's receipt of performance—in money, property, or services—had been held to "take the case out of the Statute," the Ohio court explained them in these terms:

> When courts say that performance takes a case out of the statute, or that where the contract has been fully completed on both sides, or where it has been completed on one side and payment alone remains, the statute has no application, it is only an artificial method of stating a very simple proposition. That is this: When one has received money, goods, or benefits from another, justice and equity demand that he should pay therefor, and the law will, if necessary, imply a promise to that effect. And although such benefits may have been rendered under a void contract, or one that can not be enforced, it cannot be allowed that a defendant can retain his advantage without compensation. This would be unconscionable. In the case before us plaintiff agreed to labor for defendant for board and clothing, and such sum as her services were reasonably worth. If this contract cannot be enforced by reason of the statute, the law can imply a promise precisely like it. The defendant has received the benefit of the services, whatever they were, and it would be a reproach to the law if he were permitted to retain these benefits without just payment.

Id. at 194. Why didn't this reasoning help the plaintiffs in *Boone v. Coe?*

2. Should it make a difference *which* statute makes the parties' contract unenforceable? In other words, should a court show the same deference toward the Statute of Frauds and toward a modern regulatory statute such as the one involved in *Pelletier v. Johnson?*

---

(2) Illegal contract

His Excellency Abdulaziz Bin Ibrahim Al–Ibrahim v. Edde
897 F. Supp. 620 (D.D.C. 1995)

PAUL L. FRIEDMAN, District Judge.

George Edde has filed a counterclaim alleging that his former employer, Sheikh Abdulaziz Bin Ibrahim Al–Ibrahim, breached an oral contract to reimburse Mr. Edde for tax liability Edde incurred when he fraudulently claimed some of the Sheikh's gambling winnings as his own and paid federal income taxes on those winnings. In addition to this breach of contract claim, Mr. Edde seeks restitution of the amount of money he paid to the IRS, $400,000, plus interest.

According to Mr. Edde's description of the events leading up to this contentious dispute, a promise of employment by Sheikh Al–Ibrahim lured him away from his home in California during the mid 1980's. Mr. Edde found himself occupied as the Sheikh's constant companion. He alleges that the Sheikh, a frequent high stakes gambler, required Mr. Edde to accompany him on numerous visits to casinos in the United States and "insisted that Mr. Edde . . . claim credit for [Sheikh Al–Ibrahim's gambling] winnings." Mr. Edde admits that he signed for the Sheikh's winnings on documents that were submitted to the Internal Revenue Service. Mr. Edde asserts that he "clearly understood that his signing for the Sheikh's gambling winnings was a condition of his employment and that if he refused to do so, he would be discharged."

In 1991 Mr. Edde's circumstances deteriorated. Sheikh Al–Ibrahim's demands left Mr. Edde at the point of exhaustion, he began to have marital difficulties, and the IRS began to contact him about taxes due on the gambling winnings he had signed for. Mr. Edde gave notice of his resignation to Sheikh Al–Ibrahim because "he could no longer continue to work for him at such a pace," and left the Sheikh's employ in late 1991. After leaving the Sheikh, Mr. Edde began negotiations with the IRS regarding the unpaid taxes on the gambling winnings. In August 1992, Mr. Edde reached an agreement with the IRS by which he would pay past obligations, interest and penalties on the gambling winnings he had claimed as his own. Mr. Edde asserts that as a result of representations made by the Sheikh both during and after his employment, he understood that the Sheikh would reimburse him for his tax obligations. Mr. Edde never informed the IRS that the gambling winnings actually were won by and retained by Sheikh Al–Ibrahim.

Mr. Edde seeks reimbursement for the taxes he paid and compensation for breach of contract, fraud and intentional infliction of emotional distress. He maintains that "[t]o the extent Mr. Edde may have participated in an illegal act, he was not equally in the wrong with the Sheikh. Mr. Edde's payment of the Sheikh's tax obligations was solely for the benefit of the Sheikh." Sheikh Al–Ibrahim has moved to dismiss, arguing, essentially, that Mr. Edde is a dishonorable character who should not be permitted to use the federal courts to enforce an illegal contract.

A.   *Breach of contract claim*

Generally, a contract to perform an illegal act, such as the alleged contract between Mr. Edde and Sheikh Al–Ibrahim, is void and unenforceable. The purpose of this rule is to prevent wrongdoers from using or abusing the legitimate judicial process to resolve disputes over their illegal undertakings. Whether an action is brought in equity or at law, "neither party to an illegal contract will be aided by the court, whether to enforce it or to set it aside. If the contract is illegal, affirmative relief against it will not be granted at law or in equity." United States v. Farrell, 606 F.2d 1341, 1348–49 (D.C. Cir. 1979) (quoting St. Louis R.R. v. Terre Haute R.R., 145 U.S. 393, 407 (1892)). The rule denying recovery is "based on public policy rather than a desire to benefit or punish either party." United States v. Farrell, 606 F.2d at 1349; see Crylon Steel Co. v. Globus, 185 F. Supp. 757, 760 (S.D.N.Y.1960) ("Where a transaction is a fraud upon the public and is contrary to public policy, courts will leave the parties where it finds them.")

The courts of California and Nevada have recognized two exceptions to this otherwise accepted rule that fraud or illegality renders contracts unenforceable. A party who performed under an illegal contract may recover from a breaching party only if: (1) permitting relief to the non-breaching party would promote enforcement of the underlying law that led to the invalidity of the contract, or (2) denying relief would result in a harsh forfeiture when weighed against the seriousness of the illegality or the relative culpability of the parties. Applying these principles, the Court must consider the nature and the degree of the illegality, the public policy or policies to be served by enforcing or by refusing to enforce the contract, and the relative culpability of the parties.

While not denying that his conduct was illegal, Mr. Edde argues that his conduct was not terribly serious compared with that of Sheikh Al–Ibrahim. Under a comparative culpability analysis, he contends that because the Sheikh avoided his tax obligation entirely while Mr. Edde paid the IRS, the Sheikh is the real culprit in the case. Indeed, at oral argument, counsel for Mr. Edde repeatedly argued that what Mr. Edde did was to make a "lawful payment" to the IRS. He therefore maintains that the Sheikh is the more culpable and that public policy would be served by holding the Sheikh liable in contract.

Mr. Edde's characterization of this aspect of his conduct as lawful must be rejected. A United States citizen, Mr. Edde made false statements to the Internal Revenue Service in an effort to frustrate the lawful and timely collection of taxes. The fact that Mr. Edde ultimately paid the IRS does not excuse his behavior. According to the facts alleged in his own counterclaim, he broke the law. To enforce the contract between Mr. Edde and Sheikh Al–Ibrahim would be to excuse Mr. Edde's conduct, to enforce a contract that had as its purpose the commission of illegal acts, and to permit the judicial process to be used in violation of public policy. Mr. Edde's breach of contract claim is dismissed.

B.   Restitution

Mr. Edde contends that even if he is not entitled to damages for breach of contract, he should be permitted to maintain an action for restitution to ensure that the Sheikh is not unjustly enriched for his unlawful acts. He argues that he and the Sheikh were not equally culpable or *in pari delicto* (of equal fault). He asserts that he was induced, if not coerced, to take part in the illegal conduct by the influence of Sheikh Al–Ibrahim's superior economic and bargaining position. Mr. Edde maintains that he is entitled to restitution because the Sheikh masterminded the tax avoidance scheme and was the only one who profited from it.

There is no mechanical rule by which to determine whether one party to an illegal contract is *in pari delicto* with another party to the contract. In considering the question on a motion to dismiss, the Court must accept the allegations made by the pleader. The Court therefore accepts Mr. Edde's assertion that the Sheikh had a strong influence over him that enabled the Sheikh to make unusually burdensome demands, that the Sheikh expressed in angry terms his insistence that Mr. Edde sign for his gambling winnings, that Mr. Edde believed that signing for the winnings was a condition of his continued employment (although there is no allegation that the Sheikh threatened to fire him if he did not), and that Sheikh Al–Ibrahim was able to induce Mr. Edde's illegal conduct because of his superior economic position in the relationship.

If the remedy of restitution originates from the Court's equitable powers, then the Court is guided by the principle that "he who comes to equity must come with clean hands." The doors of a court of equity are traditionally closed to one who acted inequitably, in bad faith or illegally in relation to the matter as to which he seeks relief; "however improper may have been the behavior of the defendant," the court will not be "the abettor of inequity."

If restitution is an action brought at law, as most courts and commentators maintain, then the Court is guided by similar principles to those that bar Mr. Edde's breach of contract claim. In a case involving a void, unenforceable contract, restitution is available only in exceptional circumstances. The cases cited by Mr. Edde do not provide support for the proposition that the exception should be invoked in this case. In Karpinski v. Collins, [252 Cal. App. 2d 711, 60 Cal. Rptr. 846 (1967)], the Court concluded that the parties were not *in pari delicto* because the small dairyman who had been forced to pay a bribe in order to keep his milk contract had virtually no economic alternative but to pay the bribe. While Mr. Edde maintains that his participation in the illegal contract was a condition of his job, his counterclaim is very carefully drafted. He does not allege that he was ever threatened with loss of employment and does not set forth any facts, only conclusory statements, from which the Court could infer that he was truly under economic duress or that he lacked an economic alternative to working for Sheikh Al–Ibrahim. Mr. Edde's claim for restitution is dismissed.

For these reasons, plaintiff's motion to dismiss defendant's counterclaim is granted.

More illegal contracts

1. [Note], *The Highwayman's Case*, 9 L.Q. Rev. 198 (1897), describes an equity proceeding of 1725 in which a highway robber sued his partner for an accounting. The plaintiff alleged that he was "skilled in dealing with several

sorts of commodities"; that the partners had "proceeded jointly in said dealings with good success on Hounslow Heath, where they dealt with a gentleman for a gold watch"; that in other locations they had obtained "divers watches, rings, swords, canes, hats, cloaks, horses, bridles, saddles, and other things . . . at a very cheap rate," resulting in profits "to the amount of £2000 and upwards"; finally, that "the defendant would not come to a fair account with the plaintiff touching and concerning the said partnership." The case was dismissed for "scandal and impertinence"; plaintiff and defendant were both hanged; their lawyers were arrested and fined £50 each for contempt of court.

2. In Chapman v. Haley, 117 Ky. 1004, 80 S.W. 190 (1904), the facts were stated as follows:

> Chapman, who lived in Laurel county, came to the home of Haley, in Madison county, and there proposed to him that if he would meet him in Cincinnati, Ohio, he would sell to him $3,000 of "good" money for the sum of $300. This proposition was accepted by Haley, who, not having the $300, took two of his neighbors into his golden venture, each of whom contributed $62.50. In pursuance of this arrangement, Haley met Chapman in Cincinnati, in a small room, at night, and there turned over to him the sum of $300, relying upon the word of the latter to return in 15 or 20 minutes with the promised $3,000 of good money in exchange for his $300. To his great surprise, Chapman failed to return, and Haley neither saw nor heard of him again until just prior to the institution of this action.
>
> The following excerpts from his evidence, as shown by the bill of exceptions, will fully illustrate what he knew of the moral quality of the transaction: "He [Chapman] told me he would give me $3,000 for $300, and showed me the kind of money. He showed me new bills, one 2 and a 20, and I think a 5 and a 10, and he had plenty of it, apparently. The money I was to get was to be just like those he showed me. Silver certificates, and not counterfeit. Q. Was there any agreed time as to when he was to return with your $3,000? A. He told me to sit down here on the walls of the waterworks, and he would step right across the street here, and would get it and be back in twenty minutes, and he never returned." In answer to a question regarding the character of the money, Haley stated that "he [Chapman] told me it was good money, and said there was only one trouble about this money, and that was, when deposited in bank, two numbers running of the same date might be detected in that way. He said that was the only trouble. Q. What did you understand there was wrong with that money, that bankers might detect? A. Just only what he said about the numbers. I did not doubt the money at all. Q. Did you really believe that you were going to get $3,000 good and lawful money for $300? A. Yes, sir."

Obviously Haley was not very bright. But if he was telling the truth about his understanding of the transaction, should he be allowed to recover $300 from Chapman?

3. In Keller v. Central Bank of Nigeria, 277 F.3d 811 (6th Cir. 2002), the facts were stated as follows:

> In the fall of 1994, plaintiff Keller, a sales representative for a Michigan-based manufacturer of prefabricated mobile hospital and medical centers, was contacted by an individual identifying himself as Prince Arthur Ossai, who said that he was royalty and a government official in Nigeria. Ossai suggested that plaintiff grant him the exclusive distribution rights for plaintiff's hospital and emergency care facilities in Nigeria. This deal would be funded, said Ossai, with $25,000,000 on deposit at the Central Bank of Nigeria as the result of a previous government contract that had been overfunded. Ossai and plaintiff entered into an agreement, and Ossai, stating that he was acting as an agent for the Nigerian government, placed an order for five of plaintiff's mobile medical units. The following payment arrangements were agreed upon: (1) Keller would give Ossai exclusive distribution rights to sell in Nigeria mobile hospital and medical equipment supplied by Keller; (2) Ossai would then sell to Nigeria $4.1 million worth of Keller's mobile hospital and medical equipment for a purchase price of $6.63 million; (3) Nigeria would pay to Keller the $6.63 million for the equipment, plus a $7.65 million "licensing fee"; (4) Ossai would receive from the government a $9.945 million commission; and (5) the $1.275 million remaining from the $25.5 million would be used for attorney's fees, wire charges, and so on. Ossai explained that, to make the deal work, the entire $25.5 million would have to be transferred into an escrow account set up by Keller himself, and disbursements made from there.
>
> The funds, however, were not transferred to plaintiff's account, and defendants Paul Ogwuma, Alhaji M.R. Rasheed, and Alhaji M.A. Sadiq, professing to act for the CBN, told plaintiff that he had to pay certain fees, wire charges, and assessments before the funds would be transferred. Plaintiff eventually paid a total of $28,950 in fees and charges. He also agreed to go to London to pick up the funds. No representative of the CBN showed up in London.

Does a criminal conspiracy to defraud others fall within the rule of *The Highwayman's Case* if the "highwayman" plaintiff is himself one of the fraud victims? Decisions go both ways. The intricate facts of these complex swindles make the cases too long for casebook purposes, but they are highly recommended as recreational reading. See, *e.g.*, Adler v. Federal Republic of Nigeria, 219 F.3d 869 (9th Cir. 2000) (another scheme to extract funds from Nigerian bank accounts); In re Himber, 296 B.R. 217 (Bankr. C.D. Cal. 2002) (scheme to launder $15 million in blackened U.S. currency, stored in metal canisters in Budapest, using expensive secret chemicals); Stewart v. Wright, 147 F. 321 (8th Cir. 1906) (confidence scheme involving wagers on fraudulent footraces, organized by the notorious "Buckfoot Gang" of Webb City, Missouri).

4. Illegal contracts are unenforceable, but they are often performed, at least in part. Is a party who performs an illegal contract entitled to restitution from

the recipient of performance? The question has given rise to a vast amount of law, of which the present examples merely scratch the surface. That law has been made more difficult because of a pervasive tendency to decide the cases on the basis of mottoes rather than reasons.

The first of these mottoes asserts simply that when the parties have made an illegal contract, "the law will leave them where it finds them"—neither enforcing the contract nor entertaining a claim of restitution to the extent the contract has been performed. As a starting proposition this appears to describe the result in a case like *Al-Ibrahim* or *The Highwayman's Case*, but some simple counter-examples show that there is more to it than that. The court in *Al-Ibrahim* mentions some of the countervailing considerations that are summarized by R3RUE §32, *infra*.

Instead of directly addressing the factors that might lead to the grant or denial of restitution in particular cases of illegal contracts, courts traditionally have tried to explain their results by reference to a second motto. According to a maxim introduced or popularized by Lord Mansfield, *in pari delicto, potior est conditio defendentis*. In other words, "if the parties are equally at fault *(in pari delicto)*, the defendant is in the stronger position." But a defendant who seeks to avoid liability in restitution on the basis of this maxim invites the inevitable reply from the plaintiff that "we may have both been engaged in an illegal transaction, but we were not *in pari delicto*, because you were more to blame than I." Actually, a judgment about the parties' relative culpability is rarely the best explanation of the outcome. The Restatement suggests that the cases depend more realistically on (i) the consequences of allowing restitution for the policy underlying the illegality, (ii) the consequences of denying restitution for the policy against unjust enrichment, and (iii) the possibility that a litigant may be "equitably disqualified" from asserting an otherwise valid claim in restitution.

Restatement Third, Restitution and Unjust Enrichment

§32. ILLEGALITY.

A person who renders performance under an agreement that is illegal or otherwise unenforceable for reasons of public policy may obtain restitution from the recipient in accordance with the following rules:

(1) Restitution will be allowed, whether or not necessary to prevent unjust enrichment, if restitution is required by the policy of the underlying prohibition.

(2) Restitution will also be allowed, as necessary to prevent unjust enrichment, if the allowance of restitution will not defeat or frustrate the policy of the underlying prohibition. There is no unjust enrichment if the claimant receives the counterperformance specified by the parties' unenforceable agreement.

(3) Restitution will be denied, notwithstanding the enrichment of the defendant at the claimant's expense, if a claim under subsection (2) is foreclosed by the claimant's inequitable conduct (§63).

Farnsworth, *Restitution* 79-80 (2014):

Sometimes the law is hostile in some way to the agreement the parties tried to make (or maybe hostile to one of the parties); something in what at least one of the parties tried to do offended a public policy. That same hostility may make a court hesitate before ordering restitution if one of the parties performed and got nothing back.

In *National Recovery Systems v. Ornstein*, 541 F. Supp. 1131 (E.D. Pa. 1982), for example, Ornstein borrowed thousands of dollars from a pair of casinos, lost the money, and did not repay it. The plaintiff sought to collect Ornstein's debts. The court held that while Ornstein's gambling was itself legal, loans made to finance gambling by the debtor are not enforceable. But shouldn't Ornstein at least be obliged to give back the money, since otherwise he would be unjustly enriched? No, because making him give back the money is too close to enforcing the loan agreement. In other words, allowing restitution would undermine the policy that caused the parties' contract to be unenforceable in the first place.

A similar analysis applies to *Womack v. Maner*, 227 Ark. 786, 301 S.W.2d 438 (1957). Womack paid a bribe to a judge, and then—perhaps after the judge defaulted on his performance—sued for the return of the money. Their contract was illegal, of course, so the judge had no need to fear that he would have to pay expectation damages. But nor could the plaintiff even get back his money. This time it is not because restitution would circumvent the prohibition (it wouldn't). It is because the plaintiff's conduct is so bad that the law is not interested in helping him—a case of "equitable disqualification" for relief, where the claimant is said to have unclean hands and so is barred from seeking a remedy. This is the usual result when a claimant has made a contract in pursuit of some criminal design. Note that the defense of equitable disqualification is not limited to claims seeking equitable relief. It is potentially available to fend off a restitution claim of any kind when the plaintiff committed misconduct in the transaction that gave rise to the suit. Its most common application is to cases where the plaintiff wants restitution of benefits received by the defendant under an illegal contract.

Lewy v. Crawford
5 Tex. Civ. App. 293, 23 S.W. 1041 (1893)

FLY, J.

The facts, in brief, are that Peck and Crawford, on the day of the state and national election, 1892, made a wager with each other on the pending election for governor, each one putting into the hands of Lewy as stakeholder the sum of $170. Crawford bet that J. S. Hogg would be elected governor by 10, 000 majority—whether over George Clark or the field is left in doubt. A few days after the election, Crawford notified stakeholder Lewy not to pay his $170 over to Peck, but to give it back to him. Lewy declined to do this, and had never paid the money over to any one, but still had it. The terms of the bet, or who was winner or loser, can cut no figure in the decision of this case. The whole transaction was clearly against public policy, and in open violation of one of the penal statutes of Texas. In every state and government wherever the right of suffrage has been retained by the people the deleterious and degrading effect of any species of gambling upon the result of a popular election has been recognized and unqualifiedly condemned. More especially is this true in a government like ours, where the stability and efficacy of the government rests upon the purity of the ballot box [the court continues in this vein at some length].

A gaming contract being illegal and void, courts have invariably refused to interfere between the parties to the wager, who, being *in pari delicto*, cannot invoke the aid of the courts in carrying out their contracts. The question, however, presented to this court is not whether it will enforce or affirm a gambling contract, but whether it will permit one of the parties to disaffirm it. We have investigated a large number of American cases, and in nearly all of them the rule is laid down that, as long as the money is in the hands of a stakeholder, either party has a right to demand his part of the money, and, if refused, can maintain an action at law, whether demand is made on the stakeholder before or after the happening of the contingency upon which the wager is suspended. This is the English rule, and is fortified by age, and hallowed by precedent.

One of the earliest cases to which we have had access, and one which has been very widely and favorably cited, is the case of Vischer v. Yates, 11 Johns. 28 (N.Y. Sup. Ct. 1814). The opinion in this case was rendered by Chief Justice Kent, the great commentator on American law, and in a fine review of English decisions he lays down the broad rule, since followed by most courts, that courts must frown down in every legitimate manner any unholy tampering with or corruption of the ballot; that bets on election are illegal and void, and that courts will lend their aid in disaffirming such contracts, and will hold the stakeholder responsible, when notice is given by a party to a wager that he desires to withdraw his money. This learned judge struck the keynote that has in most American courts given tone to decisions on the subject:

> The stakeholder ought not to be permitted to hold the money in defiance of both parties. There would be no equity in such a defense, and, if the plaintiff cannot recover back the deposit in this case, the winner cannot recover it; for that would be compelling the execution of an illegal contract as if it were legal, and would at once prostrate the law that declares such contracts illegal. The English rule is the true rule on this subject. On the disaffirmance of the illegal and void contract, and before it has been carried into effect, and while the money remains in the hands of the stakeholder, each party ought to be allowed to withdraw his own deposit.

The court will then be dealing equitably with the case. It will be answering the policy, and putting a stop to the contract before it is perfected. The courts have gone quite far enough when they have refused to help either party, as against the other, in respect to these illegal contracts.

It is true that this decision was overruled by the "court for the correction of errors," the decision being rendered by a divided court, but no court of any respectability, except perhaps that of California, has ever followed in the noisome wake of the decision of Senator Sanford, the mouthpiece of the New York court.

Senator Sanford makes his decision turn on the question of the happening of the contingency concerning which the wager is laid. We quote from his opinion as follows:

> Before the event has happened, and while it is uncertain who will be the winner or the loser, neither is much injured, and perhaps not at all, by declaring the contract void. If it is necessary for the public good that the contract should not proceed further, the decision is made without any sacrifice of justice between the parties. Not so if the hazard has ceased, and the wager has been lost or won, according to contract. If the losing party may vacate his contract, after the event has happened and is known, he is allowed to practice fraud upon the adverse party. To allow the loser to retract his contract because he is the loser would give sanction to the grossest perfidy and injustice. If this party wins, he profits by the contract, and takes the fruit of it; if he loses, he abjures the contract, and exonerates himself from its obligation. If he wins, he holds the wager by the laws of honor; if he loses, he refuses payment, or reclaims the wager, if paid, by the laws of the land. According to the result, he avails himself either of the laws of honor or of the laws of the land. While the event is uncertain and unknown, he stands upon the laws of honor. When it has happened, and is against him, he retires to the laws of the land. While he contracts upon the basis of hazard, he incurs no risk. When he promises, he deceives; and while he pledges his faith, he betrays. It is only the loser who repents. However bitter and sincere his repentance may be, it is not that he has offended against public policy, but that he has lost his money. To prove the sincerity of his repentance, and as an atonement of his sin against public policy, he proposes to cheat his adversary, and take back his own money after it has been lost.

We are unable to see the cogency of this rule. It is not the business of courts to determine at what point in the proceeding a man must repent, for repentance has nothing to do with the solution of the question. Doubtless repentance after losing a bet is like unto that which follows a drunken debauch, short–lived, and the offspring of a disordered liver or depleted pocket; but the senator never apprehended the great truth put by Judge Kent that it was not a question of sorrow and repentance, but one of disaffirming and destroying a contract made in violation of law and morals. Neither does his rule work harm to any one, but it leaves the parties exactly where they were when the violation of the law was initiated, and no one in law or morals has been defrauded of anything.

We hold that the wager made, between Crawford and Peck was illegal, and *ab initio* null and void, and the stakeholder occupies the same position towards them that he would have done had they voluntarily left their money in his hands without any stipulations; and, being a bailee, he is responsible to each of the depositors for the amount of his deposit. We are not assisting in executing an illegal contract; we ignore it; we treat it as though it did not, and could not exist. Crawford does not rely on the illegal contract to establish his right to the money, but he says that appellant Lewy has his money on deposit, and he wants it. It is the policy of courts, as hereinbefore indicated, to pursue that course that will discountenance gambling on elections, and have a tendency to check it; and when it is known that the loser can, at any time before the money is paid over, reclaim it from the stakeholder, it will have a discouraging effect on those who have the desire to stake their money on the result of popular elections. We are of the opinion that there was no error in the judgment of the lower court, and it is affirmed.

Crocodile tears

1. The theme of "repentance" stems from the notion that the law of restitution, like the law in various other contexts, may recognize a doctrine of *locus poenitentiae,* or "opportunity of repentance." This is the idea that one who embarks on a course of conduct may think better of it, withdraw, and be treated as if he had never begun—so long as he renounces the transaction before some decisive step has been taken.

2. Courts generally recognized a *locus poenitentiae* allowing recovery of a wager from a *stakeholder* before the race had been run or the election decided. Cases like *Lewy v. Crawford* asked whether the loser could reclaim his bet from a stakeholder after the outcome was known, but before the money had been paid over to the winner. The California decision that "followed in the noisome wake of Senator Sanford" likewise involved a claim against a stakeholder. Johnston made bets with several people that Horatio Seymour would defeat Ulysses Grant in the 1868 presidential election. The parties to these wagers deposited their stakes with Russell. Three weeks after the election, Johnston wrote Russell as follows:

> SACRAMENTO CITY, November 23, 1868.
>
> Mr. P. H. Russell: I notify you that if you pay any of the money held by you as stakeholder in the bets made by me with Freeman, Miller, and

Howard, you will do so at your own peril, as I repudiate said bets, and refuse to pay any of them.

W. F. Johnston.

Russell paid nevertheless, and Johnston sued him. The court held that his repentance had come too late:

> If the parties to an illegal wager repent and desire to withdraw before the wager has been decided, let them be encouraged to do so by allowing them to recover their stakes from each other, or from the stakeholder, if one has been employed. In times of political excitement persons may be provoked to make wagers which they may regret in their cooler moments. No obstacle should be thrown in the way of their repentance, and if they retract before the bet has been decided, their money ought to be returned to them. But persons who allow their stakes to remain until after the bet has been decided, and the result has become generally known, are entitled to no such consideration. Their tears, if any, are not repentant tears, but such as crocodiles shed over the victims they are about to devour. To allow them to recover is not to reward repentance—not to promote the public good; for as to that, the mischief has already been done, but to reward hypocrisy and promote the private interests of such as are found willing to violate not only the law of the land, but the law of honor also. After the money has been lost and won, and the result generally known, neither party ought to be heard in a Court of justice.

Johnston v. Russell, 37 Cal. 670, 676 (1869).

3. Before the advent of state-sponsored lotteries and casinos, a combination of common law and statute in nearly every jurisdiction made bets or wagers illegal and unenforceable. (Outside the exceptions carved out for state-approved gambling, they probably still are.) It follows that a winner has no legal claim against a loser who refuses to pay. If a loser pays a winner, then changes his mind and asks for his money back, the result at common law was equally clear: no restitution. This much presumably follows from *The Highwayman's Case*—but public policy may be more complicated.

Statutes in many jurisdictions altered the common-law rule by creating a cause of action permitting the recovery of gambling losses from *winners* (as well as from stakeholders). Former N.Y. Penal Law §994 was to this effect:

> Any person who shall pay, deliver or deposit any money, property or thing in action, upon the event of any wager or bet prohibited, may sue for and recover the same of the winner or person to whom the same shall be paid or delivered, and of the stakeholder or other person in whose hands shall be deposited any such wager, bet or stake, or any part thereof, whether the same shall have been paid over by such stakeholder or not.

In Watts v. Malatesta, 262 N.Y. 80, 186 N.E. 210 (1933), the facts were summarized as follows:

> The plaintiff and the defendant are two gamblers, the defendant being a bookmaker at the race tracks, and the plaintiff placing his bets on the races with the defendant through himself and his betting agent. These transactions covered the period between April 27, 1928, and May 28, 1929, during which time the plaintiff won nearly $250,000, and had lost about $150,000. His gains over losses were about $100,000. All the money he won was paid to him. He now brings this action under §994 of the Penal Law to recover his losses but makes no offer to repay his winnings—these he wants to keep.
>
> In his complaint he alleges that between the dates stated he paid to John B. Malatesta $37,773 as his wagers upon horse races at the Belmont track, the Jamaica race track and the Empire City race track; that having lost, he demanded back his money which the defendant failed to pay.
>
> The defendant in his answer admits that between the dates mentioned he and the plaintiff entered into a series of wagers upon horse races but denies that the plaintiff's losses have not been repaid. He further alleges, as a counterclaim, the fact that he paid the plaintiff $95,938, his winnings at the track over and above the losses, and demands judgment for its return.

The courts were sharply divided over allowing the bookmaker's counterclaim—though they agreed that the proper construction of the statute was the one that would best achieve the legislative purpose, namely, to discourage gambling. Which one was that?

---

(3) Supervening circumstances

Cutter v. Powell
6 Term Rep. 320, 101 Eng. Rep. 573 (K.B. 1795)

To assumpsit for work and labour done by the intestate, the defendant pleaded the general issue. And at the trial at Lancaster the jury found a verdict for the plaintiff for 31*l*. 10*s*. subject to the opinion of this Court on the following case.

The defendant being at Jamaica subscribed and delivered to T. Cutter the intestate a note, whereof the following is a copy: "Ten days after the ship 'Governor Parry,' myself master, arrives at Liverpool, I promise to pay to Mr. T. Cutter the sum of thirty guineas, provided he proceeds, continues and does his duty as second mate in the said ship from hence to the port of Liverpool. Kingston, July 31st, 1793." The ship "Governor Parry" sailed from Kingston on the 2d of August, 1793, and arrived in the port of Liverpool on the 9th of

October following. T. Cutter went on board the ship on the 31st of July, 1793, and sailed in her on the 2d day of August, and proceeded, continued and did his duty as second mate in her from Kingston until his death, which happened on the 20th of September following, and before the ship's arrival in the port of Liverpool. The usual wages of a second mate of a ship on such a voyage, when shipped by the month out and home is four pounds per month; but when seamen are shipped by the run from Jamaica to England, a gross sum is usually given. The usual length of a voyage from Jamaica to Liverpool is about eight weeks.

Arguments for the plaintiff. The plaintiff is entitled to recover a proportionable part of the wages on a *quantum meruit* for work and labour done by the intestate during that part of the voyage that he lived and served the defendant; as in the ordinary case of a contract of hiring for a year, if the servant dies during the year, his representatives are entitled to a proportionable part of his wages.

Arguments on behalf of the defendant. Nothing can be more clearly established than that where there is an express contract between the parties, they cannot resort to an implied one. It is only because the parties have not expressed what their agreement was that the law implies what they would have agreed to do had they entered into a precise treaty; but when once they have expressed what their agreement was, the law will not imply any agreement at all.

LORD KENYON Ch. J.—I should be extremely sorry that in the decision of this case we should determine against what had been the received opinion in the mercantile world on contracts of this kind, because it is of great importance that the laws by which the contracts of so numerous and so useful a body of men as the sailors are supposed to be guided should not be overturned. Whether these kind of notes are much in use among the seamen, we are not sufficiently informed; and the instances now stated to us from Liverpool are too recent to form any thing like usage. But it seems to me at present that the decision of this case may proceed on the particular words of this contract and the precise facts here stated, without touching marine contracts in general. That where the parties have come to an express contract none can be implied has prevailed so long as to be reduced to an axiom in the law. Here the defendant expressly promised to pay the intestate thirty guineas, provided he proceeded, continued and did his duty as second mate in the ship from Jamaica to Liverpool; and the accompanying circumstances disclosed in the case are that the common rate of wages is four pounds per month, when the party is paid in proportion to the time he serves: and that this voyage is generally performed in two months. Therefore if there had been no contract between these parties, all that the intestate could have recovered on a *quantum meruit* for the voyage would have been eight pounds; whereas here the defendant contracted to pay thirty guineas provided the mate continued to do his duty as mate during the whole voyage, in which case the latter would have received nearly four times as much as if he were paid for the number of months he served. He stipulated to receive the larger sum if the whole duty were performed, and nothing unless the whole of that duty were performed: it was a kind of insurance. On this particular contract my opinion is formed at present; at the same time I must say that if we were assured that these notes are in universal use, and that the commercial world have received and acted upon them in a different sense, I should give up my own opinion.

[Judgment reversed. The plaintiff, Cutter's executor, recovers nothing.]

_____

On or off the contract?

1. The famous case of *Cutter v. Powell* introduces what is probably the most fundamental problem in this subdivision of "restitution and contract." The plaintiff has rendered a valuable performance pursuant to contract, but the anticipated course of performance has gone off the rails somehow, and the contract does not explicitly cover the situation in which the parties find themselves. Does the contract still supply an answer—at least to the extent of excluding or limiting certain possibilities? To the extent it does so, we have remedies and defenses "on the contract." If not, the parties are closer to dealing with each other as if there had never been a contract between them. In that event, the performing party will seek to recover "off the contract"—in other words, in restitution—for the value of his performance.

This is why the scope of restitution in cases of contractual "frustration" is intimately connected to questions of contract interpretation. Has the risk of such-and-such contingency (such as T. Cutter's death en route) already been allocated between the parties, and if so, how? Note that in the cases worth arguing about, any relevant allocation will usually be *implicit,* somewhere between the lines of what the parties actually said. More flexible contract interpretation—a willingness to find more implied terms—means less "frustration," more remedies "on the contract," and less restitution.

2. Lord Kenyon's statement "[t]hat where the parties have come to an express contract none can be implied" is both true and potentially misleading. (The concluding observation by the New York court in *Simkin v. Blank* is a good example of how the idea is misunderstood.) What he calls an "express contract" includes what we would call the *implied terms* of the parties' agreement: for example, an "implied condition" that the death of a performing party excuses performance and allows a ratable recovery. (He says he is open to the contention that "the received opinion in the mercantile world" or the maritime usage at Liverpool would support such a reading of the agreement between Cutter and Powell: the problem was a lack of sufficient evidence to that effect.) The true proposition is that where the parties have dealt with some question in their contract (express or implied), there is no room for a contract "implied in law"—in other words, a claim in restitution—that would vary their agreement. So understood, Lord Kenyon's statement is fully in accord with the usual modern understanding. See R3RUE §2(2) ("A valid contract defines the obligations of the parties as to matters within its scope, displacing to that extent

any inquiry into unjust enrichment"). By contrast, the existence of an express contract does *not* preclude either the existence of implied contract terms or a claim based on unjust enrichment as to matters the parties have not explicitly addressed.

3. How plausible is it that Cutter and Powell made a bargain that was "a kind of insurance" (actually more like a wager), with the effect that if Cutter performed faithfully for only seven weeks of an eight-week voyage he was to receive nothing for his work? Of course they might have done so, in which case there is no problem of unjust enrichment. But isn't the apparent injustice of the result a reason to assume they did not? Recall Jacob & Youngs, Inc. v. Kent, 230 N. Y. 239, 29 N.E. 889 (1921). The contract specified "wrought iron pipe of Reading manufacture." By an innocent mistake, the builder used some pipe manufactured in Cohoes—pipe that was otherwise identical to pipe manufactured in Reading. The contract also said that the builder would not be paid the final installment of the price unless the architect certified that all specifications had been met; because of the Cohoes pipe, the architect refused to do so. The first problem in this famous case, much as in *Cutter v. Powell*, was whether the contract imposed the condition on which the owner relied in refusing to pay. Had the parties really *intended* this harsh result—that the builder should forfeit the unpaid price of the work for an insignificant failure to follow specifications?

> From the conclusion that promises may not be treated as dependent to the extent of their uttermost minutiæ without a sacrifice of justice, the progress is a short one to the conclusion that they may not be so treated without a perversion of intention. Intention not otherwise revealed may be presumed to hold in contemplation the reasonable and probable. If something else is in view, it must not be left to implication. There will be no assumption of a purpose to visit venial faults with oppressive retribution.

Id. at 242, 29 N.E. at 891 (Cardozo, J.).

4. In another famous Cardozo opinion, Matter of Buccini v. Paterno Constr. Co., 253 N.Y. 256, 170 N.E. 910 (1930), the facts were stated as follows:

> Alberto Buccini made a contract with the Paterno Construction Company to decorate the ballroom, banquet hall and swimming pool in a dwelling described as "Paterno's Castle" on Riverside Drive in the city of New York. The character of the decorations was such as to call for the exercise of artistic skill, and there is a provision that all the decorative figured work shall be done by Buccini personally and that only the plain work may be delegated to mechanics.
>
> Buccini died while the work was in progress. The contract being personal, the effect of his death was to terminate the duty of going forward with performance, but to leave the owner liable for benefits received.

Buccini's widow sued Paterno in restitution; the dispute was about the proper measure of the defendant's enrichment. Cardozo emphasized the continuing relevance of the parties' agreement to this question—even an agreement that had been frustrated, terminated, and discharged:

> Into every contract of personal service the law reads "the implied condition" that sickness or death shall be an excuse for non-performance. The parties may say by their contract what compensation shall be made in the event of that excuse. The award will then conform to the expression of their will. They may leave the subject open, to be governed by the law itself. The award will then conform to the principles of liability in *quasi*-contract and to the considerations of equity and justice by which that liability is governed. In either event the controversy is one that has its origin in the contract and in the performance of the work thereunder, just as much as if the work had been completed under a contract silent as to price, and the controversy had relation to the reasonable value.
>
> Death of the contractor has not nullified the contract in the sense of emancipating the claimant (Mrs. Buccini) from the restraint of its conditions. They limit her at every turn. She cannot stir a step without reference to the contract, nor profit by a dollar without adherence to its covenants. The interrupted work may have been better than any called for by the plans. Even so, there can be no recovery if the contractor willfully and without excuse has substituted something else (Jacob & Youngs, Inc., v. Kent, 230 N. Y. 239). The value proportionately distributed may be greater than the contract price. Even so, the price, and not the value, will be the maximum beyond which the judgment may not go (Clark v. Gilbert, 26 N. Y. 279, 283). "The recovery in such a case cannot exceed the contract price, or the rate of it for the part of the service performed" (*Clark v. Gilbert*, supra). The question to be determined is not the value of the work considered by itself and unrelated to the contract. The question to be determined is the benefit to the owner in advancement of the ends to be promoted by the contract.

Id. at 258-259, 170 N.E. at 911. Assume that the contract price for Buccini's work was $10,000, and that he completed exactly half the job. What recovery in restitution in the following hypothetical cases? (1) Mrs. Buccini can show that the fair market value of the work done is $6,000. (2) Defendant Paterno Construction can show that it will cost $6,000 to have the work completed.

5. In Parker v. Arthur Murray, Inc., 10 Ill. App. 3d 1000, 295 N.E.2d 487 (1973), the facts were stated as follows:

> In November, 1959 plaintiff went to the Arthur Murray Studio in Oak Park to redeem a certificate entitling him to three free dancing lessons. At that time he was a 37 year-old college-educated bachelor who lived alone in a one-room attic apartment in Berwyn, Illinois. During the free lessons

the instructor told plaintiff he had "exceptional potential to be a fine and accomplished dancer" and generally encouraged further participation. Plaintiff thereupon signed a contract for 75 hours of lessons at a cost of $1,000. At the bottom of the contract were the bold-type words, "NON-CANCELLABLE NEGOTIABLE CONTRACT." This initial encounter set the pattern for the future relationship between the parties. Plaintiff attended lessons regularly. He was praised and encouraged regularly by the instructors, despite his lack of progress. Contract extensions and new contracts for additional instructional hours were executed. Each written extension contained the bold-type words, "NON-CANCELLABLE CONTRACT," and each written contract contained the bold-type words, "NON-CANCELLABLE NEGOTIABLE CONTRACT." Some of the agreements also contained the bold-type statement, "I UNDERSTAND THAT NO REFUNDS WILL BE MADE UNDER THE TERMS OF THIS CONTRACT."

On September 24, 1961 plaintiff was severely injured in an automobile collision, rendering him incapable of continuing his dancing lessons. At that time he had contracted for a total of 2,734 hours of lessons, for which he had paid $24,812.80. Despite written demand defendants refused to return any of the money, and this suit in equity ensued.

As might possibly have been predicted, the court found a way to order a refund for the prepaid lessons that had not yet been given. But what is the best rationale for reaching that result?

Angus v. Scully
176 Mass. 357, 57 N.E. 674 (1900)

HAMMOND, J.

The contract was that the plaintiffs should move a large building belonging to the defendants from a lot on Third street to a lot on First street, and also change the location of two other buildings, of which one was on the First street lot, and one on the Third Street lot; and the defendant was to pay them $840. In accordance with the agreement, the plaintiffs began the work. "They first moved the house on the Third street lot, and then began to move the large building from the Third street lot across certain open lots towards the lot on First street. When said last-named building had been moved about half the distance to said lot on First street it was entirely consumed by fire at some time during the night, and thereupon, with the assent of the defendant, no further work was done in moving either of the other buildings." In this action the plaintiffs seek to recover the fair value of the services rendered by them in the work done down to the time of the fire. The court refused to rule as requested by the defendant, that the plaintiffs could not recover, and submitted the case to the jury upon instructions which would authorize them to find for the plaintiffs if they were satisfied that the fire was not attributable to any negligence of the plaintiffs.

We see no error in the rulings under which the case thus went to the jury. Clearly, one of the implied conditions of the contract was that the building should continue to exist. Upon the destruction of the building, the work could not be completed according to the contract. Authorities differ as to the rights of the parties in such a case, but so far as respects this commonwealth the rule is well settled. As stated by Knowlton, J., in Butterfield v. Byron, 153 Mass. 517, 523, 27 N.E. 669:

> The principle seems to be that when, under an implied condition of the contract, the parties are to be excused from performance if a certain event happens, and by reason of the happening of the event it becomes impossible to do that which was contemplated by the contract, there is an implied assumpsit for what has properly been done by either of them; the law dealing with it as done at the request of the other, and creating a liability to pay for its value, to be determined by the price stipulated in the contract, or in some other way if the contract price cannot be made applicable.

Stated more narrowly, and with particular reference to the circumstances of this case, the rule may be said to be that where one is to make repairs or do any other work on the house of another under a special contract, and his contract becomes impossible of performance on account of the destruction of the house without any fault on his part, then he may recover for what he has done. This case comes clearly within this rule. Exceptions overruled.

Half of nothing?

1. The contract in *Angus v. Scully* would have called for full payment on completion of the job, but completion became impossible. Now the plaintiff ends up with half the price for moving the house half the distance. What is basis of such a recovery? The reference to "implied assumpsit" (quoted here from *Butterfield v. Byron*) is inherently ambiguous: it might mean either an implied term of the parties' agreement or a liability based on unjust enrichment. How plausible is either approach on facts like these?

An implied agreement to pay *pro rata* for the portion of the work performed might make sense in some long-term employment cases, but does it make sense here? Many people conclude that the rationale has to be restitution rather than contract, but it is difficult to see enrichment in circumstances where there appear only to be losses. A contemporary New York court tried to meet this objection, using the hypothetical of a painter who "agrees to paint a certain house and the house is destroyed before the painting is finished":

Why should not the painter be paid for his part performance? It was no fault of his that full performance was impossible. But why should the owner pay? Because every stroke of the painter's brush converted something of the painter's labor and material into the property of the owner, and thus the fire destroyed the owner's property and not the painter's.

Hayes v. Gross, 9 App. Div. 12, 13, 40 N.Y.S. 1098, 1099 (1896). In the words of one commentator:

> Some authorities argue that the property owner is enriched by each stroke of the hammer or the paint brush; but others refuse to accept this somewhat Pickwickian conclusion. At all events the measure of restitution to the plaintiff exceeds the amount of increase in the assets of the defendant, since the increment of value due to half-painting a house, for instance, seems scarcely equal to the value of the labor and materials used in half-painting it. [At any event] recovery is limited to the benefits received by the owner; he would not be liable for materials which the painter had bought for this purpose but had not yet used on the house.

Patterson, *The Scope of Restitution and Unjust Enrichment*, 1 Mo. L. Rev. 223, 230 (1936).

2. Given the difficulty of finding a persuasive enrichment rationale, are the courts that award restitution for benefits conferred in these cases merely looking for a way to distribute casualty losses?

---

(4) Plaintiff in breach

Vines v. Orchard Hills, Inc.
181 Conn. 501, 435 A.2d 1022 (1980)

PETERS, Associate Justice.

The facts underlying this litigation are straightforward and undisputed. When the purchasers contracted to buy their condominium in July 1973, they paid $7,880, a sum which the contract of sale designated as liquidated damages.[1] The purchasers decided not to take title to the condominium because Euel D. Vines was transferred by his employer to New Jersey; the Vines so informed the seller by a letter dated January 4, 1974. There has never been any claim that the seller has failed, in any respect, to conform to his obligations under the contract, nor does the complaint allege that the purchasers are legally excused from their performance under the contract. In short, it is the

---

1. Paragraph 9 of the contract of sale provided: "DEFAULT: In the event Purchaser fails to perform any of the obligations herein imposed on the Purchaser, the Seller performing all obligations herein imposed on the Seller, the Seller shall retain all sums of money paid under this Contract, as liquidated damages, and all rights and liabilities of the parties hereto shall be at an end."

purchasers and not the seller whose breach precipitated the present cause of action.

In the proceedings below, the purchasers established that the value of the condominium that they had agreed to buy for $78,800 in 1973 had, by the time of the trial in 1979, a fair market value of $160,000. The trial court relied on this figure to conclude that, because the seller had gained what it characterized as a windfall of approximately $80,000, the purchasers were entitled to recover their down payment of $7,880. Neither the purchasers nor the seller proffered any evidence at the trial to show the market value of the condominium at the time of the purchasers' breach of their contract or the damages sustained by the seller as a result of that breach.

The ultimate issue on this appeal is the enforceability of a liquidated damages clause as a defense to a claim of restitution by purchasers in default on a land sale contract. Although the parties, both in the trial court and here, have focused on the liquidated damages clause *per se*, we must first consider when, if ever, purchasers who are themselves in breach of a valid contract of sale may affirmatively invoke the assistance of judicial process to recover back moneys paid to, and withheld by, their seller.

I

The right of a contracting party, despite his default, to seek restitution for benefits conferred and allegedly unjustly retained has been much disputed in the legal literature and in the case law. Although earlier cases often refused to permit a party to bring an action that could be said to be based on his own breach, many of the more recent cases support restitution in order to prevent unjust enrichment and to avoid forfeiture.

A variety of considerations, some practical and some theoretical, underlie this shift in attitude toward the plaintiff in breach. As Professor Corbin pointed out in his seminal article, "The Right of a Defaulting Vendee to the Restitution of Instalments Paid," 40 Yale L.J. 1013 (1931), the anomalous result of denying any remedy to the plaintiff in breach is to punish more severely the person who has partially performed, often in good faith, than the person who has entirely disregarded his contractual obligations from the outset. Only partial performance triggers a claim for restitution, and partial performance will not, in the ordinary course of events, have been more injurious to the innocent party than total nonperformance. Recognition of a claim in restitution is, furthermore, consistent with the economic functions that the law of contracts is designed to serve. The principal purpose of remedies for the breach of contract is to provide compensation for loss, and therefore a party injured by breach of contract is entitled to retain nothing in excess of that sum which compensates him for the loss of his bargain. Indeed, there are those who argue that repudiation of contractual obligations is socially desirable, and should be encouraged, whenever gain to the party in breach exceeds loss to the party injured by breach.

To assign such primacy to inferences drawn from economic models requires great confidence that the person injured by breach will encounter no substantial difficulties in establishing the losses for which he is entitled to be compensated. It is not necessary to push the principle of compensatory damages that far, or to disregard entirely the desirability of maintaining some incentives for the performance of promises. A claim in restitution, although legal in form, is equitable in nature, and permits a trial court to balance the equities, to take into account a variety of competing principles to determine whether the defendant has been unjustly enriched. "Even though we adhere to the rule that only compensatory damages are to be awarded, there are other important questions of policy to be considered. One is whether aid is to be given to one who breaches his contract, particularly when the breach is deliberate and without moral justification. Another is whether restitution can be administered without leaving the innocent party with uncompensated damages." 1 Palmer, Restitution §5.1, p. 574 (1978).

Recognition that there are circumstances under which a defaulting purchaser may be entitled to restitution for benefits conferred upon the innocent seller of land is consistent with parallel developments elsewhere in the law of contracts. Judicial resistance to enforcement of forfeitures has of course long been commonplace, particularly with regard to contract clauses purporting to liquidate damages. Despite the deference afforded by nineteenth-century courts to freedom of contract in other areas, clauses that might impose forfeitures were invariably carefully scrutinized and frequently denounced as penal. The law of conditional sales contracts came to recognize that avoidance of forfeiture was more important than retention of title, so that conditional sales, like chattel mortgages, were enforced in such a way as to preserve the debtor's equity. In a similar vein, in real property transactions courts have long protected a debtor's equity from forfeiture by allowing the debtor to show by parol evidence that a deed although absolute on its face was actually intended to be a mortgage.

We have never directly decided whether a purchaser of real estate may, despite his breach, recover payments made to his seller. But [consistent with related developments elsewhere] we conclude that a purchaser whose breach is not willful has a restitutionary claim to recover moneys paid that unjustly enrich his seller. In this case, no one has alleged that the purchasers' breach, arising out of a transfer to a more distant place of employment, should be deemed to have been willful. The trial court was therefore not in error in initially overruling the seller's demurrer and entertaining the purchasers' cause of action.

II

The purchaser's right to recover in restitution requires the purchaser to establish that the seller has been unjustly enriched. The purchaser must show more than that the contract has come to an end and that the seller retains moneys paid pursuant to the contract. To prove unjust enrichment, in the ordinary case, the purchaser, because he is the party in breach, must prove that the damages suffered by his seller are less than the moneys received from the purchaser. It may not be easy for the purchaser to prove the extent of the seller's damages, it may even be strategically advantageous for the seller to come forward with relevant evidence of the losses he has incurred and may expect to incur on account of the buyer's breach. Nonetheless, only if the breaching party satisfies his burden of proof that the innocent party has sustained a net gain may a claim for unjust enrichment be sustained. Dobbs, Remedies §12.14 (1973); 1 Palmer, Restitution §5.4 (1978); [R3RUE §36, Comment c].

In the case before us, the parties themselves stipulated in the contract of sale that the purchasers' down payment of 10 percent of the purchase price represents the damages that would be likely to flow from the purchasers' breach. The question then becomes whether the purchasers have demonstrated the seller's unjust enrichment in the face of the liquidated damages clause to which they agreed.

This is not a suitable occasion for detailed review of the checkered history of liquidated damages clauses. Despite the judicial resistance that such clauses have encountered in the past, this court has recognized the principle that there are circumstances that justify private agreements to supplant judicially determined remedies for breach of contract. This court has however refused to enforce an otherwise valid liquidated damages clause upon a finding that no damages whatsoever ensued from the particular breach of contract that actually occurred.

Most of the litigation concerning liquidated damages clauses arises in the context of an affirmative action by the party injured by breach to enforce the clause in order to recover the amount therein stipulated. In such cases, the burden of persuasion about the enforceability of the clause naturally rests with its proponent. In the case before us, by contrast, where the plaintiffs are themselves in default, the plaintiffs bear the burden of showing that the clause is invalid and unenforceable. It is not unreasonable in these circumstances to presume that a liquidated damages clause that is appropriately limited in amount bears a reasonable relationship to the damages that the seller has actually suffered. The seller's damages, as Professor Palmer points out, include not only his expectation damages suffered through loss of his bargain, and his incidental damages such as broker's commissions, but also less quantifiable costs arising out of retention of real property beyond the time of the originally contemplated sale. 1 Palmer, Restitution §§5.4, 5.8 (1978). A liquidated damages clause allowing the seller to retain 10 percent of the contract price as earnest money is presumptively a reasonable allocation of the risks associated with default.

The presumption of validity that attaches to a clause liquidating the seller's damages at 10 percent of the contract price in the event of the purchaser's unexcused nonperformance is, like most other presumptions, rebuttable. The purchaser, despite his default, is free to prove that the contract, or any part thereof, was the product of fraud or mistake or unconscionability. In the alternative, the purchaser is free to offer evidence that his breach in fact caused the seller no damages or damages substantially less than the amount stipulated as liquidated damages.

The trial court concluded that the plaintiff purchasers had successfully invoked this principle by presenting evidence of increase in the value of the real property between the date of the contract of sale and the date of the trial. That conclusion was in error. The relevant time at which to measure the seller's damages is the time of breach. Benefits to the seller that are attributable to a rising market subsequent to breach rightfully accrue to the seller. Beckley v. Munson, 22 Conn. 299, 313 (1853); Baffa v. Johnson, 35 Cal. 2d 36, 39-40, 216 P.2d 13 (1950). There was no evidence before the court to demonstrate that the seller was not injured at the time of the purchasers' breach by their failure then to consummate the contract. Neither the seller's status as a developer of a condominium project nor the absence of willfulness on the part of the purchasers furnishes a justification for disregarding the liquidated damages clause, although these factors may play some role in the ultimate determination of whether the seller was in fact unjustly enriched by the down payment he retained.

Because the availability of, and the limits on, restitutionary claims by a plaintiff in default have not previously been clearly spelled out in our cases, it is appropriate to afford to the purchasers herein another opportunity to proffer evidence to substantiate their claim. What showing the purchasers must make cannot be spelled out with specificity in view of the sparsity of the present record. The purchasers may be able to demonstrate that the condominium could, at the time of their breach, have been resold at a price sufficiently higher than their contract price to obviate any loss of profits and to compensate the seller for any incidental and consequential damages. Alternatively, the purchasers may be able to present evidence of unconscionability or of excuse, to avoid the applicability of the liquidated damages clause altogether. The plaintiffs' burden of proof is not an easy one to sustain, but they are entitled to their day in court.

There is error, the judgment is set aside, and the case is remanded for further proceedings in conformity with this opinion.

Restitution or forfeiture

1. Suppose a party performs extensively under a contract but then breaches it—and now wants to be paid for performance as far as it went. A party can't sue to enforce the contract he has breached. So a "plaintiff-in-breach" case is necessarily "off the contract"—yet the defendant's enrichment, if any, is still measured by reference to his contractual expectation. If a plaintiff's unpaid performance prior to breach was worth $100, but the breach caused contract damages of $50, the defendant's net enrichment will not exceed $50. But the contract measures enrichment for the benefit of the plaintiff as well. Suppose that Euel D. Vines accepts the court's invitation "to offer evidence that his breach in fact caused the seller no damages"—by showing that, at the time of the breach, the market price of the condo exceeded the contract price by more than the expense of resale. Now the defaulting plaintiff relies on the terms of the contract he has breached

to show that Orchard Hills has been enriched, by comparison to its contractual expectation, by the full value of the plaintiff's performance.

2. In modern cases, the issue of restitution in favor of the party in default under a contract of sale is most often presented as it was in *Vines v. Orchard Hills*. The contract specifies that some or all of a prepaid sum shall be retained as liquidated damages in the event of the buyer's default, so a question of unjust enrichment tends to dissolve into a question of liquidated damages. (In contracts for the sale of goods, UCC §2-718 sets off the defaulting buyer's restitution claim against the seller's liquidated damages—or against statutory liquidated damages, if the contract does not provide any.) Straight restitution claims—without the liquidated damages aspect—will still arise when the plaintiff confers benefits in the form of services (rather than money), then abandons the job or otherwise defaults before the contract price becomes due.

3. The role of unjust enrichment analysis in "judicial resistance to enforcement of forfeitures" has become harder to visualize—and the conflict between restitution and contract on this point has been greatly diminished—because old-style, no-holds-barred forfeiture clauses have simply vanished from U.S. contract law. A brief look at how they used to operate—and not so long ago, in our more red-blooded jurisdictions—gives a better sense of what was at stake.

Quinlan v. St. John, 28 Wyo. 91, 201 P. 149 (1921), illustrates a simple version of the traditional "contract for deed" as a method of real estate finance. The agreement read as follows:

Lander, Wyo., Dec. 20, 1911.

To Ben Sheldon: This envelope contains a deed from Edward T. St. John to Beatrice Bright, which you are requested to hold in escrow upon and under the following conditions, viz: The said Beatrice Bright is to pay to you the sum of $75 on the 9th day of each and every month until the full sum of $3,900.00 shall be paid, said payment of $75 to commence on the 9th day of January, 1912. When the full sum of $3,900 is paid, you are authorized to deliver said deed to the said Beatrice Bright. In the default of the payment to you of 75.00 each month at the time and in the manner hereinbefore provided, then and in that event you are authorized to deliver said deed to the said Edward T. St. John.

In witness whereof we have hereunto subscribed our names.

Edward T. St. John.
Beatrice Bright.

Thereafter, "plaintiff met the payments regularly and on time until the sum of $2,250 was paid, and during said time she placed valuable improvements on the land to the value of approximately $900." But at this point, under circumstances that were disputed,

plaintiff was unable to meet the installment due July 9, 1914, in the amount of $75 on the exact day it became due. [Plaintiff] further says that she pleaded with defendant for an extension of a few days' time in which to meet said installment, but that defendant refused to extend the time, and recalled said deed from escrow, and on July 25, 1914, sold the property in question to another person, "also taking possession of and appropriating to his own use the said improvements so placed on said property by the plaintiff."

Plaintiff sued for "the $2,250 paid on the contract, with interest from the dates of the several payments, and for $900, the value of the improvements, with interest from July 25, 1914." Her claim for restitution under both these headings was dismissed.

This kind of contractual forfeiture is now considered so objectionable that a contract for deed in these terms will probably be given effect only as a mortgage. The result is to limit the seller to the benefit of his bargain, granting restitution to the buyer (in effect) for anything paid beyond the amount required to compensate the seller. Assuming that a $75 late payment actually permits Edward St. John to terminate the contract and resell the property, how does Beatrice Bright calculate her recovery in restitution?

4. The facts of Ruxley Electronics & Construction Ltd. v. Forsyth, [1996] 1 App. Cas. 344 (H.L. 1995), were summarized for the House of Lords by Lord Jauncey of Tullichettle:

> My Lords, the respondent entered into a contract with the appellants for the construction by them of a swimming pool at his house in Kent. The contract provided for the pool having a maximum depth of 7 feet 6 inches but, as built, its maximum depth was only 6 feet. The respondent sought to recover as damages for breach of contract the cost of demolition of the existing pool and construction of a new one of the required depth. The trial judge made the following findings which are relevant to this appeal: (1) the pool as constructed was perfectly safe to dive into; (2) there was no evidence that the shortfall in depth had decreased the value of the pool; (3) the only practicable method of achieving a pool of the required depth would be to demolish the existing pool and reconstruct a new one at a cost of £21,560; (4) he was not satisfied that the respondent intended to build a new pool at such a cost; (5) in addition such cost would be wholly disproportionate to the disadvantage of having a pool of a depth of only 6 feet as opposed to 7 feet 6 inches and it would therefore be unreasonable to carry out the works; and (6) that the respondent was entitled to damages for loss of amenity in the sum of £2,500.

In real life, *Ruxley* involved the builder's claim for the unpaid balance of the contract price, set against the owner's counterclaim for breach of contract. The focus of the discussion was accordingly on the measure of damages for the builder's breach: what we would call "diminution of value" vs. "cost of cure." We can improve the facts by supposing that Builder has completed the 6-foot pool before Owner has paid any of the price. Owner refuses to pay; when Builder sues Owner, his claim is necessarily in restitution. What result if Builder's breach was the result of an innocent mistake? What result if Builder was trying to save money on excavation and calculated that Owner would never notice the difference?

Restatement Third, Restitution and Unjust Enrichment

§36. RESTITUTION TO A PARTY IN DEFAULT.

(1) A performing party whose material breach prevents a recovery on the contract has a claim in restitution against the recipient of performance, as necessary to prevent unjust enrichment.

(2) Enrichment from receipt of an incomplete or defective contractual performance is measured by comparison to the recipient's position had the contract been fully performed. The claimant has the burden of establishing the fact and amount of any net benefit conferred.

(3) A claim under this section may be displaced by a valid agreement of the parties establishing their rights and remedies in the event of default.

(4) If the claimant's default involves fraud or other inequitable conduct, restitution may on that account be denied (§63).

Farnsworth, *Restitution* 90-91 (2014):

Since the defendant asked for whatever he got, it usually will be clear that he valued it and should pay something for it. But here again the law is protective of his interests. After all, once the plaintiff has breached, by making either an incomplete performance or a defective one, the defendant continues to have the right to a complete performance at the contract price. He thus can hire a replacement to finish the job. The defaulting plaintiff gets paid for his partial performance out of whatever money is left over after the replacement has been paid—and there may be nothing left over. Indeed, the defaulting plaintiff will have to pay the costs of completing the job to the extent those costs exceed the contract price. To put the point another way, the contract price is a ceiling on what the defendant can be made to pay out in all directions, both to the breaching plaintiff and to whoever is completing the contract instead, and the breaching plaintiff gets paid last.

And if the plaintiff's breach is tainted by fraud he can recover nothing in restitution at all. In *Dodge v. Kimball*, 203 Mass. 364, 89 N.E. 542 (1909), Kimball hired Dodge to construct a building for $96,500. The contract called for a particular type of mortar to be used in the plastering and said that "this mixture must be strictly adhered to without any deviation whatever." Dodge intentionally departed from those specifications and used a somewhat less expensive mortar. The cheaper mortar caused the building to be worth $800 less than it would have been if the contract had been obeyed. The cost of removing and redoing the plaster would have been $7,000. Kimball had made progress payments to Dodge but had yet to pay him $9,215 of the contract price. So what did Kimball owe Dodge? The court's answer had the charm of simplicity: Kimball owed nothing. It is a case of equitable disqualification; the law of restitution will not recognize a claim by a plaintiff who has committed a fraud of this kind.

This is a striking result to modern ears because it imposes a potentially massive forfeiture on the breacher. It seems to imply that if the defendant had not yet paid anything for the plaintiff's construction work, he would end up paying nothing for it at all, ever, because the plaintiff cannot sue for breach of contract (since he is the breacher) and his hands would be too unclean to permit him to sue in restitution. That penalty for the plaintiff's fraud bears no relation to the actual damages suffered by the other side. The harsh result is tolerated to punish the contractor for trying to slip one past the homeowner. But courts nowadays do not often tolerate forfeitures of quite such an extreme kind, and it is not clear that they would do so here. The new *Restatement* takes the same hard-line position as *Dodge v. Kimball*, but the cases it relies on—the only good cases out there—are old. And the possible forfeiture on facts of this kind is generally limited as a practical matter by progress payments the plaintiff made while the house was under construction. Even in the old cases (including *Dodge*), the usual result of the fraud is that the buyer just withholds the last payment for the work, not *all* payment (nor does he sue to get back the payments already made). These patterns keep too much pressure from being put on the rule.

C. ALTERNATIVE REMEDIES FOR BREACH OF AN ENFORCEABLE CONTRACT

(1) Rescission and restitution for breach

Mobil Oil Exploration & Producing Southeast, Inc. v. United States
530 U.S. 604 (2000)

Justice BREYER delivered the opinion of the Court.

Two oil companies, petitioners here, seek restitution of $156 million they paid the Government in return for lease contracts giving them rights to explore for and develop oil off the North Carolina coast. The rights were not absolute, but were conditioned on the companies' obtaining a set of further governmental permissions. The companies claim that the Government repudiated the contracts when it denied them certain elements of the permission-seeking opportunities that the contracts had promised. We agree that the Government broke its promise; it repudiated the contracts; and it must give the companies their money back.

A description at the outset of the few basic contract law principles applicable to this action will help the reader understand the significance of the complex factual circumstances that follow. "When the United States enters into contract relations, its rights and duties therein are governed generally by the law applicable to contracts between private individuals." United States v. Winstar Corp., 518 U.S. 839, 895 (1996). As set forth in the Restatement of Contracts, when one party to a contract repudiates that contract, the other party "is entitled to restitution for any benefit that he has conferred on" the repudiating party "by way of part performance or reliance." Restatement (Second) of Contracts §373 (1979).

As applied to this action, these principles amount to the following: If the Government said it would break, or did break, an important contractual promise, thereby "substantially impair[ing] the value of the contract[s]" to the companies, then (unless the companies waived their rights to restitution) the Government must give the companies their money back. And it must do so whether the contracts would, or would not, ultimately have proved financially beneficial to the companies. The Restatement illustrates this point as follows:

> A contracts to sell a tract of land to B for $100,000. After B has made a part payment of $20,000, A wrongfully refuses to transfer title. B can recover the $20,000 in restitution. The result is the same even if the market price of the land is only $70,000, so that performance would have been disadvantageous to B.

Id., §373, Comment *a*, Illustration 1.

In 1981, in return for up-front "bonus" payments to the United States of about $156 million (plus annual rental payments), the companies received 10-year renewable lease contracts with the United States. In these contracts, the United States promised the companies, among other things, that they could explore for oil off the North Carolina coast and develop any oil that they found (subject to further royalty payments), provided that the companies received exploration and development permissions in accordance with various statutes and regulations to which the lease contracts were made "subject."

The statutes and regulations, the terms of which in effect were incorporated into the contracts, made clear that obtaining the necessary permissions might not be an easy matter. In particular, the Outer Continental Shelf Lands Act (OCSLA) and the Coastal Zone Management Act of 1972 (CZMA) specify that leaseholding companies wishing to explore and drill must successfully complete the following four procedures. . . .

[The Court recounts in detail the statutory and regulatory maze that the lessees would have had to penetrate, at both federal and state levels, before they could ever have extracted oil under their leases—assuming they found any. In the event, the process of obtaining federal approval of their "Exploration Plan" was cut short in 1990 when Congress passed the Outer Banks Protection Act (OBPA). The OBPA substantially changed prior law concerning oil exploration off the North Carolina coast—the law under which plaintiffs' leases had been issued—making it impossible for federal officials to approve the Exploration Plan in the manner contemplated by the parties.]

In October 1992, petitioners joined a breach-of-contract lawsuit brought in the Court of Federal Claims. On motions for summary judgment, the court found that the United States had broken its contractual promise to follow OCSLA's provisions, in particular the provision requiring Interior to approve an Exploration Plan that satisfied OCSLA's requirements within 30 days of its submission to Interior. The United States thereby repudiated the contracts. And that repudiation entitled the companies to restitution of the up-front cash "bonus" payments they had made. Conoco Inc. v. United States, 35 Fed. Cl. 309 (1996).

A panel of the Court of Appeals for the Federal Circuit reversed, one judge dissenting. The panel held that the Government's refusal to consider the companies' final Exploration Plan was not the "operative cause" of any failure to carry out the contracts' terms because [North Carolina's] objection to the companies' plans would have prevented the companies from exploring regardless. 177 F.3d 1331 (1999).

[The complexity of the licenses at issue and their shifting statutory background, combined with the theoretical problems of deciding when an act of Congress constitutes a breach or repudiation of a pre-existing contractual obligation of the United States, account for the difficulty of *Mobil Oil Exploration* and the lion's share of the opinion. Concluding its analysis of these matters, the Court held that "in communicating to the companies its intent to follow OBPA, the United States was communicating its intent to violate the contracts."]

The Government argues that repudiation could not have hurt the companies. Since the companies could not have met the CZMA consistency requirements, they could not have explored (or ultimately drilled) for oil in any event. Hence, OBPA caused them no damage. As the Government puts it, the companies have already received "such damages as were actually caused by the [Exploration Plan approval] delay," namely, none. This argument, however, misses the basic legal point. The oil companies do not seek damages for breach of contract. They seek restitution of their initial payments. Because the Government repudiated the lease contracts, the law entitles the companies to that restitution whether the contracts would, or would not, ultimately have produced a financial gain or led them to obtain a definite right to explore. If a lottery operator fails to deliver a purchased ticket, the purchaser can get his money back—whether or not he eventually would have won the lottery. And if one party to a contract, whether oil company or ordinary citizen, advances the other party money, principles of restitution normally require the latter, upon repudiation, to refund that money. Restatement §373.

Contract law expresses no view about the wisdom of OBPA. We have examined only that statute's consistency with the promises that the earlier contracts contained. We find that the oil companies gave the United States $156 million in return for a contractual promise to follow the terms of pre-existing statutes and regulations. The new statute prevented the Government from keeping that promise. The breach "substantially impair[ed] the value of the contract[s]." *Id.*, §243. And therefore the Government must give the companies their money back.

For these reasons, the judgment of the Federal Circuit is reversed. We remand the cases for further proceedings consistent with this opinion. *It is so ordered.*

––––––––––––––

Rescission as a remedy for breach of contract

1. Before the Supreme Court decided *Mobil Oil Exploration*, the leading case on rescission as a means of escape from an unfavorable bargain was Bush v. Canfield, 2 Conn. 485 (1818). *Bush v. Canfield* involved a forward contract for 2,000 barrels of flour at $7 a barrel. Buyer paid $5,000 in advance. Scllcr failed to deliver, although the market price of flour at the time and place fixed for delivery was only $5.50 a barrel. Buyer sued to recover his $5,000. Seller argued that Buyer's damages were only $2,000. What result in this famous case? According to U.C.C. §2-711, a buyer confronted with nondelivery or repudiation may recover damages (by the standard expectation measures) "in addition to recovering so much of the price as has been paid."

2. Was the buyer in *Bush v. Canfield* injured or benefited by the seller's breach? If the seller is liable for the flour or its value, is he unjustly enriched if he benefits from the change in market price—or is that risk allocation the essence of the contract? If there is neither injury to the plaintiff nor unjust enrichment of the defendant, what is the point of restitution in such a case?

3. The paradoxical facts of *Bush v. Canfield* (and to a lesser extent *Mobil Oil Exploration*) make them memorable instances of the remedy for breach called "rescission and restitution," but the cases are untypical in the extreme. According to the Restatement:

> Such outcomes are rare, because a prepaid seller will almost never forfeit a profit that might be earned, at the seller's option, by performing the contract or simply by releasing the buyer. The striking results . . . are the fortuitous consequence of the law's adherence to a simple rule rather than a complex one. The simple rule is that a plaintiff who seeks only the return of a prepaid price will not (for reasons of both fairness and economy) be put to the burden of proving damages from the defendant's breach.

R3RUE §37, Comment *a*.

4. The availability of restitution instead of damages as a remedy for breach is subject to some important limits. How does each of them relate to the justification of "rescission and restitution" as an alternative to contract enforcement?

(a) While damages are available for any breach of contract, rescission for breach is an option only when the breach is the kind that courts call "material," "essential," or "substantial." In Smith v. Continental Bank, 130 Ariz. 320, 636 P.2d 98 (1981), the Smiths paid $33,000 for a previously occupied house that the Bank had acquired in foreclosure. After they moved in, the Smiths complained about defective conditions; when the Bank did not respond to their satisfaction, they sued to rescind the contract. Finding that the defects in the house could be repaired for $2,235, the court ruled that the Bank's breach of warranty was not "substantial" enough to justify rescission of a $33,000 purchase. Why not give the Smiths their preferred remedy of a money-back guarantee?

(b) As an initial proposition, rescission for breach requires a two-way restitution in which each party returns whatever has been obtained from the other, so that both are restored to the *status quo ante*. Cases in which the plaintiff has paid money in advance and received nothing in exchange are perfect candidates for rescission, as are cases in which any values exchanged are easily returned in both directions—e.g., Blackacre for Whiteacre, a horse for a cow. Where performance consists of nonreturnable property or services, rescission is only available to the extent a court is prepared to deviate from the *status quo ante* ideal. Depending on circumstances, a court may disregard certain nonreturnable benefits or defects in the values being restored; or it may permit the substitution of a money allowance to compensate for an imperfect restitution. Such methods encounter a limit at some point where the egg cannot be unscrambled, and the plaintiff is left to a remedy in damages; but the variety of circumstances is so great that the availability of "rescission and restitution" is in important respects a matter of judicial discretion. These matters are discussed at length in R3RUE §54 ("Rescission and restitution"), with its accompanying Comments and Illustrations.

(c) Restitution instead of damages is not available against a defendant whose default in performance is exclusively the nonpayment of money. See R3RUE §37(2); Restatement Second, Contracts §373(2). In practical terms, a prepaying buyer can have restitution (of the price) from a defaulting seller; but a credit seller cannot have restitution (of the goods) from a buyer who fails to pay. The result would be the same in the inverse case to *Bush v. Canfield*—supposing, for example, that the seller had sold flour on credit at $5.50 a barrel, and that the market price on the date of the buyer's default had increased to $7. (If the buyer is insolvent, obviously the seller would like to get the flour back whatever the current market price; but he cannot.) What explains this asymmetry of treatment between buyers and sellers?

5. In Bollenback v. Continental Casualty Co., 243 Or. 498, 414 P.2d 802 (1966), Bollenback held a policy of health and accident insurance issued by Continental in 1954. Premiums due every six months had been paid without interruption. In September 1963, Bollenback was hospitalized for six days with a back injury. He subsequently filed a claim for $107.33—the first and only claim he had made under the policy. Continental ignored the claim and failed to respond to subsequent correspondence. Pressed for a reply, Continental eventually informed Bollenback that his policy had lapsed in

1959 for nonpayment of premiums. (This assertion, demonstrably false, was the result of a clerical error on the part of Continental.) After the failure of repeated efforts to clarify the matter, Bollenback filed suit "stating that he had elected to rescind the contract because of its repudiation by defendant and requesting judgment against defendant for all premiums previously paid under the policy in the sum of $2,166.50."

An initial question was whether an insurer's repudiation *by mistake* could be sufficient to justify rescission:

> Defendant cites a number of cases holding that a breach of contract based upon a mistake of fact was not such an unequivocal repudiation of the contract as to merit rescission by the other party. Mobley v. New York Life Ins. Co., 295 U.S. 632 (1934); New York Life Ins. Co. v. Viglas, 297 U.S. 672 (1935); Daley v. People's Bldg., Loan & Sav. Ass'n, 178 Mass. 13, 59 N.E. 452 (1901). In both *Mobley* and *Viglas* there was a dispute as to whether the insured was completely incapacitated from work which was a condition precedent to the insurer's obligation to pay. The position of the insurers was not that they would not be bound in any event, but only that they would not pay unless the insured was completely incapacitated. "Petitioner did not disclaim the intention or the duty to shape its conduct in accordance with the provisions of the contract. Far from repudiating those provisions, it applied to their authority and endeavored to apply them." 297 U.S. at 676 (Cardozo, J.).
>
> In *Daley* the defendant mistakenly sent a notice of forfeiture of plaintiff's stock in defendant because of the claimed nonpayment of dues. Plaintiff elected to treat the notice as a repudiation. Speaking for the court, Judge Holmes said, "It would be straining the facts and the law to say that this imported a refusal, before any demand, to pay any sum under the policy even if the defendant's mistake should be pointed out, and that therefore it was a repudiation." (178 Mass. at 18.)

The Oregon court distinguished these cases, reasoning that Continental's obdurate persistence in denying coverage—despite Bollenback's repeated efforts to enlighten it—made it responsible for a "willful" failure to pay. "If defendant wants to indulge in the luxury of omnipotence, it must be responsible when it commits error. The plaintiff is entitled to rescind because of defendant's material breach of the contract."

The more characteristic issue concerned the restitutionary obligation of the policyholder seeking rescission:

> The theory of relief on an action for restitution is placing both parties *in statu quo ante*. Because insurance protection cannot be returned to defendant, the theory of recovery necessarily means the return to plaintiff of all premiums less the value of any benefits the plaintiff has actually received under the contract. Defendant contends plaintiff received the value of the protection for the ten year period which, upon loss, could

have been asserted by plaintiff at any time despite defendant's subsequent disavowal of the contract.

Defendant's assertion upon repudiating the contract was that the policy had lapsed in 1959. There is no reason to believe that after that date defendant would have been any more willing to honor claims by plaintiff than it was in 1964 when it refused payment. By its own assertion that the policy lapsed in 1959 defendant demonstrated its unwillingness to meet contractual obligations since that time. Plaintiff therefore could not have been receiving the protection for which his premiums were being paid.

Plaintiff is not entitled to recover for those premiums paid prior to the year 1959 because it appears from the record that he received the protection these payments afforded. It would be inequitable for him to recover them. Defendant having wrongfully terminated plaintiff's policy in 1959, plaintiff is entitled to recover all premiums paid subsequent to January 1, 1959.

Id. at 518-520, 414 P.2d at 812. Did the court correctly measure the benefit received by Bollenback in exchange for his insurance premiums? (Continental's immediate response to the lawsuit had been to pay the amount of $107.33 into court.)

6. Courts of an earlier day saw a significant "election of remedies" in the plaintiff's choice either to affirm the contract (by seeking damages for breach) or to disaffirm the contract (by seeking rescission). Logically one might have damages or rescission, but not both. The more modern approach asks whether restitution and damages are duplicative or inconsistent remedies in the context of a particular dispute. So long as the effect of the *cumulative* remedies is to restore the plaintiff to the *status quo ante*—as is normally the function of what are called "incidental" or "reliance" damages—there is unlikely to be any inconsistency.

Thus in McCrae v. Lonsby, 130 F. 17 (6th Cir. 1904), defendant-buyers were sued on their promissory note for $3,300. By way of defense, they pleaded that their note had been given for the purchase price of

the parts of the dismantled steamboat called the Byron Trerice, consisting of the hull, the boiler, the engine, and machinery; that at the time of the purchase all except the hull had been removed and was stored on land; that the hull was lying submerged in Lake Erie, near Leamington, Ontario, where she had suffered the loss of her upper parts by fire and was sunk.

The purchase had been made in reliance on seller's representations as to the condition of the hull; but when the buyers attempted to raise it, at a cost of $500, the found that the seller's representations had been false and that the hull was worthless. The court ruled that the buyers were entitled to rescind the contract, to recover their promissory note, and to damages of $500 besides:

The rescission of the contract by the defendants did not prevent their recovery for the damages they were brought to suffer by relying on the false representations which induced it. Not having got what they bought, they were not obliged to go on and keep and pay for a thing they had not bought and did not want. Nor would the refunding the price paid— that is to say, the recovery of the note—restore to them the expense they had incurred by reason of the plaintiff's fraud, a consequence which the plaintiff must have known the defendants would suffer.

Id. at 20-21. The court in *McCrae* found that the seller's representations had been fraudulent, but the result would be the same under the Uniform Commercial Code in a case of rescission (alias "revocation of acceptance") for an equivalent but nonfraudulent breach of warranty. See U.C.C. §2-608, O.C. 1 ("the buyer is no longer required to elect between revocation of acceptance and recovery of damages for breach. Both are now available to him").

Farnsworth, *Restitution* 95-96 (2014):

The requirement [of rescission] that it be possible to return both parties to their precontractual positions is not absolute. The rigors of it can be adjusted according to other facts in the case. If a seller commits a major breach, the buyer can generally get his money back without fussing about whether the seller is now out a little money for his initial efforts. So suppose I lease a house from you for a year; then move out after the first week because I discover it is overrun with rats and is uninhabitable. I can rescind the lease and get back whatever I have paid you. There need not be any deduction for my one week spent there. Likewise if you pay for schooling and receive just a little of it before the defendant breaches. The breach is large enough, or sufficiently material in nature, to allow rescission even with a loose end or two.

The examples just mentioned all involved breaching defendants who were allowed to be shortchanged a bit by rescission. But the law demands greater exactitude when approaching the problem from the other side and fashioning relief for the innocent plaintiff who was the victim of the breach. The defendant may have to not only return what he has received but also pay incidental damages to bring the plaintiff all the way back to where he was before the contract was signed. Thus in another swimming-pool case, *Bause v. Anthony Pools, Inc.*, the plaintiff hired the defendant to build a pool, and the defendant did a terrible job; the pool contained cracks that leaked 150 gallons per day. The court awarded the plaintiff the entire amount he had paid the defendant plus the cost of removing the pool and refilling the hole where it had been. The result amounted not to damages but to rescission. The plaintiff got his money back and returned the pool at the builder's expense.

The builder's obligation to remove the bad pool illustrates a point noted earlier: rescission for breach of a valid contract is not based—not very precisely, anyway—on the need to correct the defendant's unjust enrichment. If it were, the defendant would not be obliged to pay incidental damages to bring the plaintiff all the way back to his original position. Payments of that kind can be driven only by the wish to compensate, and have nothing to do with the defendant's enrichment. We find this discrepancy because here we are not dealing now with the law of unjust enrichment per se. We are dealing with the law of contracts, which occasionally awards remedies that it refers to as rescission and restitution and that proceed upon a similar and overlapping logic, but not an identical one.

---

(2) Performance-based damages

Boomer v. Muir
24 P.2d 570 (Cal. Dist. Ct. App. 1933)

DOOLING, Justice pro tem.

R.C. Storrie & Co., a copartnership composed of Robert B. Muir and Robert C. Storrie, had a general contract with the Feather River Power Company to build a hydroelectric project in the high mountains on certain tributaries of the north fork of the Feather river. The project was one of great magnitude, and under their contract Storrie & Co. were to receive a flat price of $7,691,889. The project involved, as one item, the construction of a storage dam in Buck's Valley to impound the waters of Buck's creek.

On May 28, 1926, Storrie & Co. entered into a subcontract with H.H. Boomer for the construction by him of the Buck's creek dam, the work to be done in accordance with the plans and specifications of the Feather River Power Company and to the satisfaction of that company's engineer. Under this subcontract Storrie & Co. were to deliver at the dam site to Boomer all cement, gravel, sand, steel and other metal work which was to be a permanent part of the dam. Boomer was to furnish all other materials and labor and equipment.

It was further agreed that work was to commence immediately and be completed on or before December 1, 1927. Boomer was to be paid for his work according to an agreed schedule of unit prices for quantities which were to be estimated by the engineers of the Feather River Power Company, such estimates to be made monthly for work completed during the previous month. On the basis of such estimates Storrie & Co. were to pay Boomer monthly 90 percent of the estimate, the remaining 10 percent to be paid upon the completion of the contract.

When Boomer commenced performance of his subcontract, almost immediately friction developed between Boomer and Storrie & Co., and such friction and disputes continued as long as Boomer remained on the job. A discussion of the nature and character of these disputes will be deferred to a later portion of this opinion [and radically abridged here]. Suffice it to say here that, when Boomer shut down for the winter at the end of 1926, a much smaller portion of the work had been done by him than the parties had anticipated at the inception of their contract. In a mutual effort to speed up the work in 1927, Boomer and Storrie & Co. entered into a supplemental agreement on March 4, 1927, whereby the original contract between them was considerably modified. By this supplemental agreement it was provided that Boomer should open up the work not later than April 1, 1927, and that commencing with May 1927, Boomer should place not less than 40,000 cubic yards of material each month until the completion of the dam. Storrie & Co. agreed to pay Boomer all of the 10 percent estimates previously retained under their original contract with Boomer. The unit prices for loose rock fill were materially increased; it being recited that such increase should be construed as covering any cost Boomer had theretofore or might thereafter incur for stripping quarries, transportation of rock, and developing new quarries. Storrie & Co. waived their right to retain 10 percent of the monthly estimates, but after May 1, 1927, if during any month 40,000 cubic yards of loose rock should not be placed in the dam, the 10 percent for such month was to be retained by Storrie & Co. until completion.

Boomer proceeded with the work on the dam in 1927, and the disputes between Boomer and Storrie & Co. continued much as before, culminating with Boomer's leaving the job uncompleted in December 1927.

[Suits and countersuits involving all parties and their sureties] were ultimately combined for trial and tried before a jury in San Francisco. Boomer's actions contained inconsistent counts; one of them being upon a *quantum meruit* for the reasonable value of the work done less the payments received. This count proceeded upon the theory of rescission of the contract on the ground that performance had been prevented by Storrie & Co.'s failure to deliver materials as required by the contract. During the course of the trial, upon motion of Storrie & Co. and Storrie's sureties, the court compelled Boomer to elect the theory upon which he should proceed. Boomer elected to proceed upon the theory of rescission for prevention of performance. The jury brought in a verdict against Storrie & Co., and Storrie's sureties for $257,965.06.

We have said that the disputes between Boomer and Storrie & Co. were practically continuous throughout the time Boomer was on the job. These disputes fell into four principal classes: (1) Disputes concerning compressed air; (2) disputes concerning the cut-off trench; (3) disputes concerning material deliveries by Storrie & Co.; and (4) disputes concerning roads and quarries. . . .

While he was on the job, Boomer repeatedly complained to Storrie & Co. about delays in furnishing materials and for several months before December 1927, he informed them that if the materials were not supplied as needed, he would quit the job and hold Storrie & Co. responsible. There is testimony which would support a finding that Storrie & Co. did not furnish materials as rapidly as Boomer needed them, and that this slowed up Boomer's progress and increased his cost. On December 3, 1927, Boomer finished pouring the third slab on the inner face of the dam. At that time all that remained to be done was to pour the fourth slab and complete the superstructure of the dam. It was Boomer's testimony that at that time there were not sufficient materials on hand to complete or proceed further with the work; that he waited until December 15, 1927, and, no further materials having been supplied to him, he moved off the job and never returned.

It is well settled in California that a contractor who is prevented from performing his contract by the failure of the other party to furnish materials has a choice of three remedies: He may treat the contract as rescinded and recover upon a *quantum meruit* so far as he has performed; he may keep the contract alive, offering complete performance, and sue for damages for delay and expense incurred; or he may treat the repudiation as putting an end to the contract for purposes of performance and sue for the profits he would have realized. McConnell v. Corona City Water Co., 149 Cal. 60, 85 P. 929. Storrie & Co. and Storrie's sureties admit this rule, but claim that the evidence will not support a finding that Boomer was prevented from performance by Storrie & Co.'s failure to furnish materials. They argue that Boomer did not intend to go any further than the pouring of the third tier, and that Storrie & Co. knew this. However, the jury was not bound to find that Boomer ever agreed to a modification of the contract so as to provide only for the completion of the third slab in 1927. In his wire of November 27 he explicitly stated: "I am prepared to complete my contract on time." He was entitled under the law to quit the job at that time for failure to supply materials . . . [T]he jury must have found that Boomer intended to proceed if materials were furnished. We are satisfied that under the evidence this was a question of fact for the determination of the jury, and that their implied finding on this point is not without substantial support in the evidence.

It is further urged that, "assuming that prevention of performance was shown, the contractor may not, where the contract has been fully liquidated up to a given stage, reopen the part of the contract which has been fully executed on both sides and seek to have his past work revalued." In this connection it is pointed out that, at the time Boomer left the job in December 1927, the monthly estimates provided for in the contract had been made up to November 25, 1927, and Boomer had been paid in full for all work covered by these estimates, with the exception of the retained percentage of 10 percent, for three months after May 1927, in which months Boomer had not placed 40,000 cubic yards of material in the dam as provided in the supplemental agreement. It is conceded that the general rule, and the one followed in California, is that, where a contract has been rescinded for prevention of performance, the plaintiff may recover the reasonable value of what he has done or supplied under the contract, even though such recovery may exceed the contract price. It is insisted, however, that this general rule does not apply in cases where specific payment is provided in the contract for specific portions of the work, and such portions have been fully performed and payment for which has been fully ascertained and liquidated prior to the breach by the adverse party. In support of this contention are cited Rodemer v. Gonder, 9 Gill (Md.) 288; Doolittle v. McCullough, 12 Ohio St. 360; Wellston Coal Co. v. Franklin Paper Co., 57 Ohio St. 182, 48 N.E. 888; City of Philadelphia v. Tripple, 230 Pa. 481, 79 A. 703. . . . [But] we are not impressed by the rule announced in these cases. It being settled as the general rule that upon prevention of performance the injured plaintiff may treat the contract as rescinded and recover upon a *quantum meruit* without regard to the contract price, why should he be limited to the contract price in case payments for portions of the entire contract have been made or liquidated? Those payments were received in full only on condition that the entire contract be performed. But, if the contract is rescinded, the prices fixed by the contract are also rescinded. As aptly said by the Pennsylvania Supreme Court in *City of Philadelphia v. Tripple*: "Where the defendant undertakes to limit the plaintiff's recovery by treating the contract price as a limitation upon such recovery, he is asserting a right under the very contract which he himself has discharged."

To hold that payments under the contract may limit recovery where the contract is afterwards rescinded through the defendant's fault seems to us to involve a confusion of thought. A rescinded contract ceases to exist for all purposes. How then can it be looked to for one purpose, the purpose of fixing the amount of recovery? We conclude that the defendant, by his own wrong having put an end to the contract, cannot insist on its terms to limit the recovery, even though part payments have been made for part performance, because the payments are received as satisfaction only on condition that the entire contract be performed according to its terms; but that, the contract having been rescinded through defendant's fault, he should place the plaintiff as nearly as possible *in statu quo* by paying the reasonable value of plaintiff's performance.

Storrie & Co. and Storrie's sureties say that to permit such recovery in this case is to allow Boomer to recover over $250,000, when if he had completed the contract, he would have received no more than $20,000. The answer to this is found in the language of *City of Philadelphia v. Tripple*:

> Let it be assumed that, in an extreme case, a builder has actually expended in the course of his work a sum in excess of the contract price and has not yet completed performance. If, under such circumstances, the builder finishes his work, the owner, upon paying the contract price, will receive the benefit of a large expenditure actually made, in return for the payment of a smaller sum of money.
>
> Let it further be supposed, however, that the owner, who finds himself in this position of advantage, voluntarily puts an end to his contract rights in the premises. The situation which then presents itself is one in which the builder has in good faith expended money in the course of work done for the benefit of the owner, and has, in the absence of contract, an equitable claim to be reimbursed. The owner, on the other hand, has deprived himself of the legal right which would have sufficed

to defeat the equity. He accordingly stands defenseless in the presence of the builder's claim.

Even if it were true, then, that Boomer would only have received an additional $20,000 for the completion of his contract, we are of the opinion that that does not prevent him from recovering the reasonable value of his services upon its rescission for Storrie & Co.'s breach. But Boomer points out that he had large claims for damages against Storrie & Co. for continued delays and increased expense of operation due to their misconduct. Upon the rescission of the contract, it ceased to exist for all purposes, including the purpose of relying upon its terms for the purpose of recovering damages for any breach. If Boomer had valid claims for damages arising under the contract by reason of the fact that his cost of operation had been wrongfully increased, it would seem inequitable to limit him to the recovery of the contract price upon a rescission for Storrie & Co.'s failure of performance.

The jury might well have found that Boomer's cost of operation had been substantially increased by Storrie & Co.'s continuing breaches. . . . On the whole case, without further discussing the evidence, we are satisfied that the money judgment finds ample support and should be affirmed.

Kehoe v. Rutherford
56 N.J.L. 23, 27 A. 912 (1893)

DIXON, J.

On October 15, 1888, the plaintiff and defendant entered into a written contract, under seal, by which the plaintiff became bound to grade, work, shape, level, smooth, and roll Montross avenue, in the borough of Rutherford, to its entire width, according to the established grade, commencing at Washington avenue, and ending at Pierpont avenue, and the defendant became bound to pay him therefor 65 cents per lineal or running foot. Soon afterwards, the plaintiff began the work, and continued until it was discovered that some of the land to be graded under the contract was private property. Then, being forbidden by the owners to enter upon this property, the plaintiff stopped the work, by direction of the borough authorities, and concluded to abandon it. In the mean time, he had been paid $1,850 of the contract price. On this state of facts, he brought suit against the defendant, relying, in one count of his declaration, upon the breach of the special contract, and, in another, on a *quantum meruit* for the work done. At the trial in the Bergen circuit the plaintiff's evidence tended to prove that the length of the whole work required by the contract was 4,220 feet, which, at the contract rate—65 cents per lineal foot—made the aggregate price $2,743; that about 3,500 feet in length had been substantially graded, but still needed trimming up and finishing; that in doing this work he had excavated about 8,000 cubic yards of earth, and had put in about 1,300 cubic yards of filling; that, to complete the job, about 14,000 cubic yards of filling were still necessary, besides the trimming up and finishing of the entire length of the street. His evidence further indicated that the fair cost of the work done was:

8,000 cubic yards of excavation, at 35 cents	$2800
900 cubic yards of filling, at 21 cts.	189
400 cubic yards of filling, at 41 cts.	164
Making a total of	$3153

—and that the fair cost of the work remaining to be done, in completely performing the contract, was:

14,000 cubic yards of filling, at 12 cents	$1680
4,220 feet of finishing, at 5 cents	211
Making a total of	$1891

—thus showing the fair cost of the whole work required by the contract to be $5,044. These calculations are, in every instance, based upon the testimony most favorable to the plaintiff; allowing him the highest estimates for what he had done, and reckoning the residue at the lowest. If his own estimates, or those of any single witness, were taken throughout, the result would be more to his disadvantage.

Upon the evidence thus presented, the plaintiff was nonsuited, and a rule allowed that the defendant show cause why a new trial should not be awarded. The nonsuit was ordered upon the theory that the plaintiff could recover, for the work done, only such a proportion of the contract price as the fair cost of that work bore to the fair cost of the whole work required, and, in respect of the work not done, only such profit, if any, as he might have made by doing it for the unpaid balance of the contract price. Under this theory, his recovery for the work done was to be limited to such a proportion of $2,743 as 3,153 bears to 5,044, viz. $1,715; and as to the work not done, since it would cost him $1,891 to do it, while the unpaid balance of the price was only $893, no profit could be earned by doing it. Hence, it was considered that he had been overpaid to the extent of the difference between $1,850 and $1,715. But the contention of the plaintiff was and is that, as he was prevented from completing the contract without fault on his part, he is entitled to the reasonable value of the work done, without reference to the contract price; and if this be the correct rule, undoubtedly the case should have gone to the jury. But, at the very threshold, we are confronted with this possible result of the application of the rule contended for: That the plaintiff might recover $3,153 for doing about three-fifths of the work, while, if he had done it all, he could have recovered only $2,743. The absurdity of the result condemns the application of such a rule.

Circumstances may exist in which, for work done under a special contract, the plaintiff will recover its fair value. Thus, if the contract be within the prohibition of the statute of frauds, (McElroy v. Ludlum, 32 N. J. Eq. 828;) or if, the work being only partly done, that which is done, or that which is left undone, cannot be measured, so as to ascertain its price at the rate specified in the contract, (Derby v. Johnson, 21 Vt. 17,) or, in the absence of evidence to the contrary, it may be assumed that the rate specified is a reasonable one, (U. S. v. Behan, 110 U. S. 338.) But, generally, when it can be determined what, according to the contract, the plaintiff would receive for that which he has done, and what profit he would have realized by doing that which, without fault, he has been prevented from doing, then these sums become the legal, as they are the just, measure of his damages. He is to lose nothing, but, on the other hand, he is to gain nothing, by the breach of the contract, except as the abrogation of a losing bargain may save him from additional loss. This is the rule applied in the case of Masterton v. Mayor, etc., of Brooklyn, 7 Hill, 61, where the plaintiff was to receive $271,600 for 88,819 feet of marble, and after he had delivered 14,779 feet the defendant stopped him. He was awarded the contract price for the 14,779 feet, and the profit which he would have made by delivering the balance. The same principle was declared by this court in Boyd v. Meighan, 48 N. J. Law, 404, 4 Atl. Rep. 778, and accords with the fundamental doctrines laid down by Mr. Sedgwick, (1 Sedg. Dam. [200] 432:) First, that the plaintiff must show himself to have sustained damage, or, in other words, that actual compensation will only be given for actual loss; and, second, that the contract itself furnishes the measure of damages. Sometimes it has been held that if the contract binds the defendant to pay otherwise than in money, and he refuses, then the plaintiff may recover the cash value of what he has done or delivered. Ankeny v. Clark, 148 U. S. 345. But in New Jersey the rule is that he shall recover the cash value of what he was to receive, (Hinchman v. Rutan, 31 N. J. Law, 496,) thus maintaining the standard fixed by the contract.

The refusal of the defendant to pay, after all the work is done, is no less a breach of the contract than is his refusal to permit the plaintiff to do all that the bargain entitled him to do; but neither breach does or ought to put the parties in the position they would have occupied if no contract had been made. In both cases, what is done was done under the contract, and should be paid for accordingly. If, on partial performance, the plaintiff confines himself to the common counts, he excludes by his pleading any claim for what he has not performed, but he does not thereby enhance his deserts for what he has performed; and therefore, in order to obtain complete justice on breach of a profitable bargain, he must resort to a special count. Our conclusion is that, as the plaintiff had been paid up to the full measure of the contract for the work done, and could have made no profit by its further prosecution, the nonsuit was substantially right. The rule to show cause is discharged.

Losing contracts

1. The problem of "losing contracts" is easily stated: does restitution for part performance allow the plaintiff to escape from an unfavorable bargain or not? But the messy real-life facts of a case like *Boomer* add an important dimension to the problem:

(a) Even supposing the Feather River contract had been priced more favorably—making it a job on which Boomer would earn a normal profit—the constant friction between Boomer and Storrie suggests a transaction destined to break down at some point. After the performing party either walks off the job or is fired, each party sues the other for breach. Presented with ample evidence of justified grievances on both sides, a jury has the nearly impossible task of deciding which party committed the first "material breach." Normally, the threat of an unpredictable liability in damages should encourage cooperation and compromise. How are the incentives to cooperation affected, on either side, if the terms of the contract oblige one party to perform at a loss?

(b) In the concluding passages of its opinion (mostly omitted here), the court refers to Boomer's "large claims for damages against Storrie & Co. for continued delays and increased expense of operation due to their misconduct." Damages of this kind may be real but difficult to prove; a judgment ostensibly in *quantum meruit* for the reasonable value of the work done might be an indirect means of awarding these damages to the injured contractor. "A suspicion that the plaintiff has a losing contract *because* the defendant is in breach goes a long way toward justifying a recovery without an expectancy ceiling." 3 Dobbs, Law of Remedies §12.7(5) (1993). In support of this hypothesis, a careful examination of landmark losing-contract cases such as *Boomer v. Muir* and *Philadelphia v. Tripple* concludes that "well over half the cases that award restitution of costs above contract price can be explained in the same way." Gergen, *Restitution as a Bridge Over Troubled Contractual Waters*, 71 Fordham L. Rev. 709, 711-13 (2002).

2. The court says that Boomer proceeded "on a theory of rescission of the contract," but references to "rescission" in this context are potentially misleading. "Rescission and restitution," as we saw in the preceding section, unwinds contractual performance by requiring—within limits—that each party restore to the other whatever benefits it has received by way of performance. That kind of restoration is obviously impossible in cases like *Boomer* and *Kehoe*, where the performance on one side consists of nonreturnable labor and materials. These cases involve a different mode of "restitution for breach": one in which the plaintiff recovers a money substitute for his nonreturnable performance, rather than the performance itself.

When the word "rescission" was used to describe such a claim, the idea was that a material breach in the course of performance was "tantamount" to an offer to rescind by the breaching party. This gave the injured party a choice of remedies: either to enforce his contract rights, usually by an action for damages, or to treat the contract as "rescinded" or *nullified*. (This is what the *Boomer* court means when it says, "A rescinded contract ceases to exist for all purposes.") If that conclusion could be taken seriously, the obligations of the parties would be the same as if there had never been a valid contract between them—as if Boomer's work on the Buck's Creek Dam had been obtained by Storrie's fraud, or if Boomer had built the dam by mistake. In such circumstances, of course, restitution would give Boomer at least the reasonable value of the work he had done.

3. Judicial authority on the *Boomer/Kehoe* debate has long been sharply divided, though reported decisions are distinctly rare. The question continues to attract sustained academic attention, with a perceptible tendency in recent decades favoring *Kehoe*. The proposition that a plaintiff should receive more money for a partial than for a completed performance has always been hard to explain, and commentators accustomed to think of contracts as risk-allocation devices are probably predisposed to see contract terms as the measure of benefit and injury on either side. As late as 1981, *Boomer* still retained the (lukewarm) endorsement of Restatement Second, Contracts §373, Comment *d*, but R3RUE is emphatically to the contrary:

> [A rule] allowing damages measured by the value of performance unlimited by the contract price permits the injured party to reallocate or revalue risks that it is the function of contract to price and to assign. Such an outcome is contrary to fundamental objectives of contract law and inconsistent with the other remedies for breach of contract, all of which take the parties' agreement as the benchmark by which the plaintiff's remedies are measured.
>
> The argument to the contrary [frequently] asserts that the defendant is unjustly enriched if he retains the benefit of a contract (goods or services on below-market terms) that he has failed to perform on his side. But the benefit to the defendant in such a case is the result of the contract, not of the breach. [The consequence of breach] is not to benefit the defendant at the plaintiff's expense, but to benefit the plaintiff at the defendant's expense, by releasing the plaintiff from the expense of a further performance at a loss. In summary, the fact that the defendant has committed a material breach does not mean that the contract is to be disregarded, allowing the plaintiff to seek restitution as if there had never been a contract between the parties. Such precisely is the legal response where the contract was never valid to begin with, as in a case of rescission for fraud. It is not and has never been the remedy for breach of a valid and enforceable contract.

R3RUE §38, Comment *d*. Numerous additional authorities on the "losing contract" problem are described in the accompanying Reporter's Note.

Glendale Federal Bank v. United States

239 F.3d 1374 (Fed. Cir. 2001)

PLAGER, Senior Circuit Judge.

The Federal Savings and Loan Insurance Corporation was established by Congress to insure the deposits of savings and loan institutions (also known as "S & Ls" or "thrifts"), and the Federal Home Loan Bank Board was established to safeguard the soundness of those institutions. Pursuant to this regulatory scheme, thrifts that desired to provide depositors with the insurance guaranteed under the program were required to maintain a certain level of capital.

Interest rates soared during the late 1970s and early 1980s, causing the savings and loan industry serious economic problems. At that time, thrifts' liabilities were principally short-term deposits, while their assets were primarily long-term fixed-rate mortgages. When interest rates soared, the value of the long-term fixed-rate assets plummeted, and the thrifts had to pay higher rates on their liabilities. As a result, many thrifts experienced difficulty remaining solvent and many became insolvent.

The Government's insurance fund lacked sufficient funds to liquidate even a small percentage of the thrifts that became insolvent. Consequently, the FSLIC and the FHLBB began to consider proposals for outside investors and thrifts to acquire other thrifts through mergers to prevent an exhaustion of the insurance fund.

Mergers were attractive to solvent thrifts because they enabled the thrifts to acquire previously prohibited interstate branches, to acquire high-quality assets that suffered only from the current interest rate squeeze, and to transform an insolvent thrift's net liabilities into an intangible asset called "supervisory goodwill." The accounting device was important to the acquiring thrift because the FHLBB allowed thrifts to include supervisory goodwill in the calculation of its regulatory capital requirements. Further, regulators in some instances would permit the goodwill to be amortized over a period of forty years.

In 1981, the Government and Glendale, an S & L institution primarily doing business in California, entered into negotiations concerning Glendale's possible acquisition of First Federal Savings and Loan Association of Broward County, Florida. The FHLBB found that Broward's financial condition was deteriorating and projected that Broward's regulatory capital would fall to zero by June 1982. Although Glendale was also losing money, the federal regulators determined that Glendale was nevertheless a financially strong institution, had no material management problems, and had the strength to absorb Broward and remain viable for some years.

In November 1981, the FHLBB approved Glendale's acquisition of Broward in a voluntary merger, and the Government and Glendale entered into a contract memorializing the arrangement. At the time of the merger, the market value of the liabilities of Broward exceeded the market value of its assets by $734 million. Pursuant to its contract with the Government, Glendale was permitted to book Broward's resulting market value deficit or net excess liabilities (negative net worth) as supervisory goodwill, an asset for purposes of meeting regulatory capital requirements. This supervisory goodwill was to be amortized over forty years, or until 2021.

Not long after the merger, interest rates declined, and the asset squeeze experienced by the industry eased. For a variety of reasons, some in the Government began to doubt the wisdom of the contracts that had been made with the salvaging S & Ls. In August of 1989, Congress enacted the Financial Institutions Recovery, Reform and Enforcement Act. FIRREA, among other things, greatly restricted the use of goodwill and other intangible assets in the calculation of regulatory capital.

Beyond that, FIRREA and its implementing regulations repudiated the Government's obligation to recognize Glendale's goodwill as an asset for purposes of regulatory capital over the contract's forty-year amortization period by requiring Glendale to deduct goodwill in determining its regulatory capital on a greatly accelerated schedule.

Glendale brought this action claiming the enactment of FIRREA breached an agreement by the Government to give Glendale favorable regulatory treatment in connection with its merger with Broward. The courts that reviewed the matter held that FIRREA's enactment rendered the Government liable to Glendale for breach of contract; the matter was remanded to the trial court for a trial on damages. [United States v. Winstar Corp., 518 U.S. 839 (1996).]

The primary issue in this case is damages, how much and why. A review of basic principles of contract damages will illuminate the issues and their resolution. . . .

One way the law makes the non-breaching party whole is to give him the benefits he expected to receive had the breach not occurred. See Restatement (Second) of Contracts §344(a) (1981). The benefits that were expected from the contract, "expectancy damages," are often equated with lost profits, although they can include other damage elements as well. See Restatement (Second) of Contracts §347. The problems of proof attendant on the burden placed on the non-breaching party of establishing lost profits—on establishing what might have been—are well recognized. Even with a generous standard of proof applied in such cases, the proof problems can in some situations prove to be insurmountable.

In the case at hand, Glendale sought expectancy damages; the trial court concluded that on the facts of the case Glendale was not entitled to expectancy damages. This conclusion appears to rest upon problems of proof. In this appeal, Glendale does not challenge that ruling by the trial court.

When proof of expectancy damages fails, the law provides a fall-back position for the injured party—he can sue for restitution. The idea behind restitution is to restore—that is, to restore the non-breaching party to the position he would have been in had there never been a contract to breach. See Acme Process Equip. Co. v. United States, 347 F.2d 509, 528 (Ct. Cl. 1965); In re First Penn Corp., 793 F.2d 270, 272 (10th Cir. 1986) ("The object of restitution is to return the parties to the position that existed before the transaction occurred"); John D. Calamari & Joseph M. Perillo, The Law of Contracts,

§15.4 (4th ed. 1998) ("The basic aim of restitution is to place the plaintiff in the same economic position as the plaintiff enjoyed prior to contracting"); *cf.* Restatement (Second) of Contracts §384, cmt. *a* ("A party who seeks restitution of a benefit that he has conferred on the other party is expected to return what he has received from the other party. The objective is to return the parties, as nearly as practicable, to the situation in which they found themselves before they made the contract"). In other words, the objective is to restore the parties to the status quo ante. This is typically not as good as lost profits, from the viewpoint of the non-breacher, but a lot better than nothing.

Restitution is sometimes described in terms of taking from the breaching party any benefits he received from the contract and returning them to the non-breaching party. That requires determining what benefit from the contract the breaching party has received, and restoring that to the nonbreaching party. This approach makes good sense when viewed, for example, from the perspective of a typical contract for the sale of goods. B contracts to buy 1,000 widgets from S, for $10 a widget. B gives S $1,000 down, the balance of $9,000 to be paid on delivery. S defaults on the contract; B sues for restitution. B gets his $1,000 back. The amount that S is wrongfully benefited by the contract is taken from S, and restored to B.

In the case before us, the trial court, faced with a situation in which expectancy damages were ruled out but with a legitimate claim by the plaintiff for a remedy for the Government's breach, fashioned a restitutionary remedy based on the assumed risk that Glendale undertook when it acquired Broward. This was done by taking the value of Broward's obligations or debts at the time the contract was made, and subtracting from it Broward's then-assets. The resulting figure, a negative $798,291,000, was deemed to be the amount that the Government benefited from the contract, and to which Glendale was entitled as restitutionary damages.

The Government's response is that the real figure should be zero. The Government never received a $798,291,000 benefit from the contract because the Government would not have liquidated Broward in the absence of a merger with Glendale, and the Government would have been responsible for Glendale and Broward if interest rates had not fallen and both institutions failed.

We conclude that both approaches are flawed. . . . The action taken by the purchasing S & L in acquiring the failing thrift did not result in the Government saving the dollar value of the net obligations of the thrift. It is not at all clear that but for Glendale's purchase of Broward the Government would have been called upon to make up that deficit then and there. Glendale was only one of a number of potential acquirers of Broward. Alternatively, rather than approve a merger, the Government had open to it the option of hiring new and better management to run Broward and make a go of it, just as Glendale itself did. In a very real sense, what the Government received in exchange for its promise was time—time to deal with other failing S & Ls, time to see what the market would do before having to commit substantial resources to the problem. Though the value of time was more than zero, there is no proof of what in fact it was worth.

It is important to remember that, even after Glendale's merger with Broward, the Government was not free of potential liability for the failing thrift. Had interest rates not come down, and Broward, and perhaps Glendale as well, failed, the Government's contingent liability would have matured, and the FSLIC would have had to step in at that time and assume the very losses that Glendale now claims were benefits the Government received.

Fortunately for both the industry and the Government, the facts of the case are that interest rates did come down, market forces allowed the thrift industry to escape impending doom, and neither Glendale nor the Government was called upon to pay the potential losses the fear of which was the motivation for the scenario in the first place.

This case, then, presents an illustration of the problem in granting restitution based on an assumption that the non-breaching party is entitled to the supposed gains received by the breaching party, when those gains are both speculative and indeterminate. We do not see how the restitution award granted by the trial court, measured in terms of a liability that never came to pass, and based on a speculative assessment of what might have been, can be upheld; accordingly we vacate the trial court's damage award on this theory.

This does not mean that Glendale is without a remedy. Glendale recognized the problems in the restitution award, and cross-appealed, arguing that, should the court reject that award, Glendale nevertheless would be entitled to damages on a reliance theory.

The underlying principle in reliance damages is that a party who relies on another party's promise made binding through contract is entitled to damages for any losses actually sustained as a result of the breach of that promise. See Restatement (Second) of Contracts §344(b) ("[Judicial remedies serve to protect the promisee's] reliance interest, which is his interest in being reimbursed for loss caused by reliance on the contract by being put in as good a position as he would have been in had the contract not been made"); 3 Dan B. Dobbs, Law of Remedies §12.3(1) (2d ed. 1993) ("The reliance recovery is a reimbursement for losses the plaintiff suffers in reliance on the defendant's contractual promise"). As a general proposition, these damages are available for injuries resulting from activities that occurred either before or after the breach.

In a case like the one before us, for all the reasons we have explained, we conclude that, for purposes of measuring the losses sustained by Glendale as a result of the Government's breach, reliance damages provide a firmer and more rational basis than the alternative theories argued by the parties. We recognize the appeal in the restitution approach, but we find that keying an award to a liability that was at most a paper calculation, and which ignores the reality of subsequent events as they impacted the parties, and particularly the plaintiff, is not justifiable. Reliance damages will permit a more finely tuned calculation of the actual losses sustained by plaintiff as a result of the Government's breach.

Accordingly, we vacate the trial court's award of damages, and remand the matter to the court for a determination of total reliance damages to which plaintiff may be entitled. Because the matter is being returned to the trial court for further proceedings, we do not now undertake a piecemeal review of the specific items of reliance damages already awarded; that review will await the final award review when and if it is appealed.

Restitution and reliance

1. Reading between the lines in *Glendale Federal*, we can see traces of a significant uncertainty about the meaning of "restitution" in a contractual context. Uncertainty was aggravated by an unacknowledged shift in definitions between the first and second Restatements of Contract. The original Restatement of Contracts (1932) was published before the original Restatement of Restitution (1937) adopted the word "restitution" to mean "liability based on unjust enrichment." For the first Restatement of Contracts, "restitution" in a contract setting meant either "rescission and restitution" (as in *Mobil Oil Exploration*) or else what we now tend to call "reliance damages." Either form of relief achieves "restitution" in the sense of *restoration*, by restoring the plaintiff to his pre-contract position. *Glendale Federal* draws on this first-Restatement definition when it concludes that the objective of restitution as a remedy for breach is "to restore the parties to the *status quo ante*." Unjust enrichment has no necessary relation to such a remedy.

By contrast, Restatement Second, Contracts (1981) attempted at several points to accommodate the idea of "restitution" as a contract remedy to the word's new meaning—preventing the unjust enrichment of the breaching party. Pointing to these passages from the Restatement Second, the S & L plaintiffs in the *Winstar Cases* told the courts, in effect: "Since we can't prove our expectation damages, the remedy of restitution allows us to recover the benefits we conferred on the Government." This was the reasoning behind Glendale's claim for $798,291,000. After enough of these cases had been litigated, a consensus emerged within the Federal Circuit that "benefits conferred on the Government" by the acquiring S & Ls were not recoverable as a remedy for breach, if only because they were impossible to measure.

2. The analysis in *Glendale Federal* stops just short of a helpful final step. If "restitution" and "reliance damages" are both "fall-back" remedies for breach of contract—in that both seek to restore the injured party to the *status quo ante* as a second-best alternative to expectation damages—then the only difference between them is how they calculate the damages needed to put the plaintiff back where he started. One measures the value of the plaintiff's uncompensated performance; the other measures its cost. Subsequent decisions in the *Winstar* line of cases made these parallels explicit:

> There are two alternative measures of relief in restitution. The first is the value of the benefits received by the defendant due to the plaintiff's

performance. The second is the cost of the plaintiff's performance, which includes both the [cost] of the benefits provided to the defendant and the plaintiff's other costs incurred as a result of its performance under the contract. *See Acme Process Equip. Co. v. United States*, 347 F.2d 509, 530 (1965) ("As the best means of restoring the *status quo ante*, cost of performance is often used").

Landmark Land Co. v. FDIC, 256 F.3d 1365, 1372 (Fed. Cir. 2001).

> When restitution damages are based on recovery of the expenditures of the non-breaching party in performance of the contract, the award can be viewed as a form of reliance damages, wherein the non-breaching party is restored to its pre-contract position by returning as damages the costs incurred in reliance on the contract. . . . The principle of restitution damages is to return the costs incurred in performing the contract, costs sometimes conveniently measured by the benefits conferred on the breaching party . . . .

LaSalle Talman Bank v. United States, 317 F.3d 1363, 1376 (Fed. Cir. 2003).

3. The "losing contract" question—the issue of expectancy as a limit on restitution/reliance—did not arise in the *Winstar Cases*, where the acquiring thrifts' expectations or lost profits were acknowledged to be unknowable. On the "reliance" side, the question has long had a definitive answer. See Restatement Second, Contracts §349. As expressed by the leading opinion on the topic:

> The decisions leave much to be desired. . . . Much the fullest discussion of the whole subject is Professor Fuller's in the Yale Law Journal. [Fuller & Perdue, *The Reliance Interest in Contract Damages*, 46 Yale L.J. 52, 373 (1936-1937).] The situation at bar was among those . . . for which he favors the rule we are adopting. It is one instance of his "very simple formula: We will not in a suit for reimbursement of losses incurred in reliance on a contract knowingly put the plaintiff in a better position than he would have occupied, had the contract been fully performed."

L. Albert & Son v. Armstrong Rubber Co., 178 F.2d 182 (2d Cir. 1949) (L. Hand, J.).

"Reliance damages" for breach of contract cannot exceed the plaintiff's expectation from performance because the recovery will be reduced, dollar for dollar, to the extent the defendant can prove the plaintiff would have lost money had the contract been performed. This limitation makes "reliance damages" functionally identical to *quantum meruit* for any court that adopts the position of *Kehoe* (rather than *Boomer*) in the "losing contract" cases. Seen in conjunction, the two sorts of recovery are then variants of a single rule—one that permits the plaintiff to elect a monetary form of "restitution" as an alternative to expectation damages, but subject to provable expectation as a limit. This is how the remedies are presented in R3RUE §38, set forth *infra*.

4. In Wellston Coal Co. v. Franklin Paper Co., 57 Ohio St. 182, 48 N.E. 888 (1897), the parties contracted in August for a year's supply of coal at a fixed rate of $1 per ton. The market price of coal varies with the season. Buyer took delivery through the winter months, then repudiated the contract in May. Supposing that Buyer's fluctuating "requirements" make Seller's expectancy unknowable, what is the remedy for breach? According to R3RUE §38(2)(b), Seller can recover "the market value of the plaintiff's uncompensated performance, not exceeding the price of such performance as determined by reference to the parties' agreement." Does the contract in *Wellston Coal* fix a price for the coal that was delivered over the winter?

5. One of the Restatement's illustrations of performance-based damages is based on the classic western movie "Red River," with John Wayne and Montgomery Clift (directed by Howard Hawks, 1948):

> Boss hires Wrangler as one of 25 hands engaged to drive a herd of longhorns from Texas to Kansas. Wages are $5 per day, to be paid in gold if and when the cattle reach the railhead at Wichita; but no wages are earned if the herd is lost. After 60 days on the trail, Wrangler is wrongfully discharged for an alleged breach of discipline. One week later, the entire herd is lost in a stampede that Wrangler could have done nothing to prevent.

R3RUE §38, Illustration 16. What is Wrangler's recovery?

Restatement Third, Restitution and Unjust Enrichment

§38. PERFORMANCE-BASED DAMAGES.

(1) As an alternative to damages based on the expectation interest (Restatement Second, Contracts §347), a plaintiff who is entitled to a remedy for material breach or repudiation may recover damages measured by the cost or value of the plaintiff's performance.

(2) Performance-based damages are measured by

(a) uncompensated expenditures made in reasonable reliance on the contract, including expenditures made in preparation for performance or in performance, less any loss the defendant can prove with reasonable certainty the plaintiff would have suffered had the contract been performed (Restatement Second, Contracts §349); or

(b) the market value of the plaintiff's uncompensated contractual performance, not exceeding the price of such performance as determined by reference to the parties' agreement.

a. General principles and scope. The remedy described in the present section is one of the two principal devices sometimes referred to as "restitution for breach of contract," the other being rescission (§37). It is distinguished from ordinary contract damages, measured by the plaintiff's expectation interest, because it permits a plaintiff who cannot prove expectation to recover damages calculated on an alternative basis.

Damages of this kind have traditionally been associated with the idea of "restitution" because they tend to "restore": they restore the plaintiff to the precontractual position, or they restore to the plaintiff either the cost or the value of the plaintiff's uncompensated performance. Cost of performance is the measure more frequently employed: the plaintiff recovers damages measured by unreimbursed expenditure in reliance on the contract, subject to provable expectation as a cap. Less often, the basis of the performance-based damage calculation is the value of the plaintiff's uncompensated performance, not exceeding the price of such performance at the contract rate. Damages measured by expenditure are commonly called "reliance damages." Damages measured by the value of performance go by various names, including both "restitution" and "reliance" as well as "*quantum meruit.*" Conceptual and terminological confusion has obscured the fact that the measures of cost and value are—for the most part—parallel versions of a single alternative damage remedy.

Either approach to damages under this section yields a second-best, "fall-back" alternative to damages measured by expectancy. A plaintiff who can prove expectation damages will seek to recover them, because they yield the benefit of a favorable bargain and the highest recovery. . . . The usual application of the rule of §38, therefore, is either to a case in which the plaintiff's contractual expectation cannot be established at all, or to a case in which—although the plaintiff's expectancy cannot be known with certainty—it can be shown to lie somewhere within an upper limit. In either case, an alternative damage calculation by the rule of §38 protects the plaintiff's expectancy so far as the evidence permits, based on a rebuttable presumption that the plaintiff was neither performing at a loss nor selling at less than market value. More specifically, the presumption is that the plaintiff's earnings from performance would have been at least sufficient to defray the plaintiff's reliance expenditures; alternatively, that the plaintiff's unknown expectancy would have been at least equal to the market value of the plaintiff's performance. Either presumption may be rebutted by the defendant, on proof that the plaintiff's contractual expectancy was something less than the damages sought by this alternative measure.

Farnsworth, *Restitution* 96-99 (2014):

Rescission calls for the return of whatever has passed between the parties—a refund of money paid or a handing back of things traded. So-called restitution when a contract has been breached can also take a different form: a demand by the plaintiff that the defendant pay over the value of the work the plaintiff has done (along with consequential and incidental damages). It is a bit misleading—though common—to call damages awarded on this theory in a contract case a form of "restitution," because courts awarding them make no real effort to figure out how much the defendant valued what he received from the plaintiff. Instead they basically just award the plaintiff the value of the performance he made, using its market value so long as that isn't any greater than the rate shown in the contract. When a plaintiff finds this remedy attractive, it is usually because expectation damages—that is, what he would have been due if the contract had been fully performed—are hard to prove. A plaintiff in that position has the option of seeking to recover the cost of the performance (reliance damages) or the value of it (performance-based damages). Those amounts will often be similar, but not always. Sometimes it is easier to show the market value of what the plaintiff did than to show what it cost the plaintiff to do it. And sometimes the plaintiff would like to recover the value of the performance (the "quantum meruit" measure) because it is greater than the contract rate.

To start with the old and simple facts of *Brown v. St. Paul, Minneapolis & Manitoba R. Co.*, 36 Minn. 236, 31 N.W. 941 (1886), the plaintiff performed lawyerly services for a railroad in return for the promise of a lifetime pass to ride its trains. The railroad repudiated the contract. The plaintiff sued for breach, and the railroad's liability was clear—but what should be the remedy? Assume, as the court did, that expectation damages would be hard to figure because lifetime passes are rarely given to anyone and there is no market for them. Rescission is no help here because the plaintiff gave the railroad nothing that it can return. So the plaintiff was permitted to recover in quantum meruit—that is, in restitution—a cash amount that reflected the reasonable market value of his services. Since the plaintiff's expectation damages are hard to prove, he demands payment at a market rate for whatever he actually did.

So far none of this is controversial. But a difficulty can arise when we *do* know what the plaintiff's expectation damages would be and his claim for restitutionary damages is greater. [Professor Farnsworth here quotes the *Red River* hypothetical, given in the last preceding note.] The example is good because it puts the issue starkly. Wrangler did a lot of work, and (let us suppose) his sixty days of labor had some market value that could be determined easily enough. We might use that market value as a benchmark for restitutionary damages if his expectation damages were difficult to settle—if, for example, Boss had called off the entire project because he lost interest in the cattle drive. In that case, Wrangler would have been deprived of a chance that the cattle might make it to Wichita, and the value of that chance would be hard to calculate, so restitution (here simply the market value of the services rendered) becomes a natural measure of recovery. But that isn't what happened in the illustration. The herd was lost in a stampede. So we *do* know what Wrangler's expectation damages would have been: nothing. That is the amount he would have collected if he had not been wrongfully discharged and the contract had been fully performed. Why should he collect more than all the other wranglers just because he was wrongfully fired? He shouldn't. He should collect nothing, just like the rest of them.

This result is partly a matter of holding Wrangler to the method of valuing his services that he agreed to in the contract. But there is a point of policy as well. Suppose Wrangler realized that the cattle drive was not going well and that his prospects for collecting the gold were getting worse by the day. If a breach by Boss would entitle Wrangler to compensation on a daily basis regardless of the fate of the cattle, then it would be in Wrangler's interest to see such a breach occur. In fact, it would be in the interest of all the wranglers to see Boss breach, since then they all would get paid something. So the wranglers would have an incentive to provoke a breach if they could find some way to do it without seeming too blameworthy. This is not the sort of incentive the law wants to create. It would raise the cost of the enterprise.

Kehoe v. Rutherford might look distant from the wrangler's case, but the logic is the same. The fact that the defendant breached does not mean that we now set the contract aside and start reasoning from scratch about how to value the benefits the plaintiff provided. The contract itself laid down a rate for the work, and that rate sets the terms of the plaintiff's entitlement whether the contract is performed or breached. And, again, the contract rate also is the right measure as a matter of policy. Otherwise the plaintiff in *Kehoe* would have an incentive, perhaps late in the performance period, to induce a breach on the defendant's part so that the plaintiff can collect the higher rate of market-measured restitutionary damages rather than the lower rate called for by the contract that the plaintiff no doubt regrets.

D. PROFITABLE BREACH OF CONTRACT

Y.J.D. Restaurant Supply Co. v. Dib
98 Misc. 2d 462, 413 N.Y.S.2d 835 (Sup. Ct. 1979).

LOUIS GROSSMAN, J.

In this nonjury case, the evidence is clear and overwhelming that the defendant breached an agreement with the plaintiff in that defendant willfully and deliberately violated a covenant not to compete with the plaintiff within a five-block radius for a period of three years. At the conclusion of the trial, this court directed an interim order making a temporary injunction, heretofore issued at Special Term by Justice Beatrice Shainswit, permanent in nature.

The facts adduced at the trial showed that prior to the trial the defendant sold the competing business, which he had unlawfully opened, for a price of

$250,000. It was further testified to that the defendant had various expenses and costs which he incurred in the opening and running of said competing business in the amount of $214,500. Therefore, the defendant admitted that he had realized a profit to himself of $35,500 from the sale of said competing business.

In addition to the permanent injunction, the plaintiff seeks to recover monetary damages incurred as a result of the breach of the aforesaid agreement, namely the portion thereof not to compete with the plaintiff. In the instant case, albeit labeled as one in equity, the court feels justified in awarding monetary damages as well as a permanent injunction to the plaintiff against the defendant. The authority for doing so was best expressed in Birnbaum v. Rollerama, Inc. (232 NYS2d 188, 191): "Equity will mold its decrees to suit the needs of the particular case."

The plaintiff attempted to introduce evidence concerning the loss of profits in the store which he had purchased from the defendant. However, the plaintiff failed to adequately sustain or meet his burden of proof in order to establish any loss of profits. The plaintiff failed to produce his business records, and his evidence regarding loss of profits failed to impress the court. There were too many elements of uncertainty in what little proof was adduced to prove any loss of profits by the plaintiff. It was shown that too many competitive and economic factors were involved herein to prove any correct or even fair estimate of the amount of damages sustained as a result of loss of profits by the plaintiff.

On the other hand, the court finds that the plaintiff herein is entitled to recover the full profit made by the defendant on the sale of his competing business, which he opened unlawfully. It is a well-established doctrine that equity will not aid any scheme or project which might lead to undeserved profit. It is stated in N.Y. JUR. (vol 20, Equity, §95) as follows: "The doctrine that a person cannot be advantaged by his own wrong is applicable only to willful wrongs as distinguished from carelessness." In our instant case, the breach of the defendant in opening the competing business in the forbidden area within the prohibited time limit was indeed a willful act on his part. It must therefore be held that the defendant herein should not profit from his own misconduct.

In the old case of Riggs v. Palmer (115 NY 506, 511-512) the Court of Appeals recognized that nobody shall be permitted to profit by his own wrong: "No one shall be permitted to profit by his own fraud, or to take advantage of his own wrong, or to found any claim upon his own inequity, or to acquire property by his own crime. These maxims are dictated by public policy, have their foundation in universal law administered in all civilized countries, and have nowhere been superseded by statutes." The same principle was enunciated by Mr. Justice Black, writing for the United States Supreme Court in Glus v Brooklyn Eastern Term. (359 U.S. 231, 232-233): "To decide the case we need look no further than the maxim that no man may take advantage of his own wrong. Deeply rooted in our jurisprudence this principle has been applied in many diverse classes of cases by both law and equity courts."

In our instant situation, the defendant, on the sale of his original store to the plaintiff, must be presumed to have obtained part of the purchase price thereof for goodwill and for his covenant not to compete in a certain area within a certain period of time. By wrongfully breaching the covenant, the defendant cannot sustain any gain by such willful misconduct on his part. He was, in effect, selling his goodwill twice—once to the plaintiff and then to the purchaser of the competing store. Since the competing store will remain in business and continue to compete against the plaintiff, the profit made on the sale of the competing store by the defendant should properly be awarded to the plaintiff.

Accordingly, in addition to the permanent injunction heretofore granted to the plaintiff against the defendant, the plaintiff is awarded a monetary judgment against the defendant in the sum of $35,500 with interest from June 9, 1978, together with the costs and disbursements of this action.

Attorney-General v. Blake
[1998] Ch. 439 (Ct. App. 1997)

LORD WOOLF M.R. handed down the following judgment of the court.

The facts are well known and can be summarised very shortly. The defendant was a former member of the Secret Intelligence Service who in 1944 signed an undertaking not to divulge any official information gained as a result of his employment. Between 1951 and his arrest in 1960 the defendant became an agent for the Soviet Union and betrayed this country by disclosing secret information of considerable value. On 3 May 1961 the defendant pleaded guilty to five counts of unlawfully communicating information, contrary to section 1(1)(c) of the Official Secrets Act 1911. He was sentenced to 42 years' imprisonment, but in 1966 he escaped from prison and eventually arrived in Moscow, where he now lives.

The action arises out of the autobiography of the defendant which is entitled *No Other Choice*. It was published by Jonathan Cape Ltd. on 17 September 1990. In addition to other matters, in his autobiography he describes his activities on behalf of the K.G.B. and his trial and imprisonment and subsequent escape. As Sir Richard Scott V.-C. found at trial:

> The book may fairly be described as his apologia for the course his life has taken. Substantial parts of the contents relate to the defendant's activities as a member of the S.I.S. and are based on information acquired by him while an S.I.S. officer.

The Government did not have any knowledge of the book until its publication was first announced in the press. The defendant had not sought, nor has he received, any licence or permission from the Crown for the publication of the book and the manuscript was not submitted for prior approval. A sum of £90,000 remains payable by the publishers. Their contract with him provided for royalties of £50,000 payable on signing the contract, £50,000 on delivery of the final manuscript and £50,000 on publication of the book.

It is obvious that, if the defendant had not been a notorious spy who had also dramatically escaped from prison, royalties of this order would never have been paid to him for his autobiography.

The Attorney-General has never sought to restrain publication of the book. Instead he seeks to extract from the defendant any financial benefit he may obtain from the publication of the book. He also now contends that he is entitled to an injunction to restrain the defendant from receiving any financial proceeds derived from the book which have not yet been paid, or any benefit which represents those proceeds. The sums already paid to the defendant are realistically regarded as irrecoverable.

A.   *Breach of fiduciary duty*

In order to found the claim, the Attorney-General contends that, in submitting the book for publication, the defendant acted not only in breach of contract, which would entitle the Crown to claim relief by way of injunction and damages, but also in breach of this fiduciary duty, thereby making available equitable remedies. The characterisation of the defendant's wrongdoing as a breach of fiduciary duty is remedy-led, despite Sopinka J.'s salutary warning in Norberg v. Wynrib, (1992) 92 D.L.R. (4th) 449, 481: "Fiduciary duties should not be superimposed on those common law duties simply to improve the nature or extent of the remedy."

[The court concludes that Blake did *not* breach a fiduciary duty by publication of his memoir both (i) after his employment had terminated and (ii) after the information it contained had ceased to be confidential.]

B.   *Breach of contract*

By submitting the manuscript for publication, without having first obtained clearance, the defendant committed a clear breach of the express undertaking which he signed when he joined the public service. This was a breach of contract which prima facie entitled the Crown to an injunction and damages. The Crown has not sought an injunction to prevent publication, and now cannot establish any loss. It is not, therefore, entitled to other than nominal damages.

In the course of the initial hearing we invited submissions on a second issue which had not previously been considered. The second issue is whether, in the particular circumstances of the present case, the Crown might have a private law claim to restitutionary damages for breach of contract. After giving further consideration to the matter, the Attorney-General decided that the Crown did not desire to advance such a claim.

Since the subject is of some importance, we will express our own views on the subject, even though they are obiter and, being without benefit of argument, necessarily tentative.

The general rule is that damages for breach of contract are compensatory not restitutionary, that is to say, they are measured by the loss to the plaintiff and not by the gain to the defendant. It is unnecessary to cite authority for this proposition, since it is beyond dispute. Its elevation into a fundamental principle which admits of no exceptions, however, has been disputed, attributed to inertia and has attracted widespread (though not universal) academic criticism: see, for example, Daniel Friedmann, "Restitution of Benefits Obtained Through the Appropriation of Property or the Commission of a Wrong," (1980) 80 Col. L. R. 504, 513 et seq.; Gareth Jones, "The Recovery of Benefits Gained from a Breach of Contract," (1983) 99 L.Q.R. 443; Peter Birks, "Profits of Breach of Contract," (1993) 109 L.Q.R. 518; per contra I. M. Jackman, "Restitution for Wrongs," [1989] C.L.J. 302 , 318-321; Andrew Burrows, "No Restitutionary Damages for Breach of Contract: *Surrey County Council v. Bredero Homes*," [1993] L.M.C.L.Q. 453. Even its proponents recognise that some flexibility is desirable, Jackman (for example) suggesting that the moral calibre of the defendant's conduct might justify an award of restitutionary damages for a cynical breach of contract.

Judicial opinion is also divided. The exclusively compensatory basis of damages for breach of contract does not lack judicial critics, and there are signs that the traditional view that the rule admits of no exceptions may not long survive.

If the court is unable to award restitutionary damages for breach of contract, then the law of contract is seriously defective. It means that in many situations the plaintiff is deprived of any effective remedy for breach of contract, because of a failure to attach a value to the plaintiff's legitimate interest in having the contract duly performed. In our opinion, the time has come to accept Professor Jones's view, expressed as long ago as 1983 [99 L.Q.R. 443, 452], that the law is now sufficiently mature to recognise a restitutionary claim for profits made from a breach of contract in appropriate circumstances. The difficult question is not whether restitutionary damages should ever be available for breach of contract, but in what circumstances they should be made available.

We do not think that the basis on which damages are awarded should depend on the defendant's moral culpability alone. The fact that his breach of contract is deliberate and cynical is not by itself a good ground for departing from the normal basis on which damages are awarded. It is not only that the line cannot easily be drawn in practice; it is rather that the defendant's motives will normally be irrelevant. To adapt an observation of Lord Keith of Kinkel made in a different context in Attorney-General v. Guardian Newspapers Ltd. (No. 2) [1990] 1 A.C. 109, 261, a natural desire to deprive a deliberate wrongdoer of profit is not a valid ground for departing from the normal measure of damages for breach of contract.

The mere fact that the defendant's breach of his contract with the plaintiff has enabled him to enter into a more profitable contract with someone else should also not be sufficient: Teacher v. Calder [1899] A.C. 451 is sound law. Nor should it suffice that, by entering into the later and more profitable contract, the defendant has put it out of his power to perform his contract with the plaintiff: the distinction between the two cases is not one of substance. But we think that there are at least two situations in which justice requires the award of restitutionary damages where compensatory damages would be inadequate.

The first may be described as the case of skimped performance. This is where the defendant fails to provide the full extent of the services which he has contracted to provide and for which he has charged the plaintiff. Professor Jones cites the Louisiana case of City of New Orleans v. Firemen's

Charitable Association (1891) 9 So. 486 as an example. The defendant contracted with the plaintiff to provide a firefighting service and was paid the full contract price. After the expiry of the contract the plaintiff discovered that the defendant had not provided the stipulated number of firemen or horses or the promised length of hosepipe. The defendant had saved itself substantial expense by the breach, but had not failed to put out any fires in consequence. The court ruled that the plaintiff had not proved that it had suffered any loss and was unable to recover more than nominal damages. Justice surely demands an award of substantial damages in such a case, and the amount of expenditure which the defendant has saved by the breach provides an appropriate measure of damages. This could be achieved by presuming that the plaintiff has suffered a loss of an amount corresponding to the amount by which he has been overcharged for the service actually provided; and the presumption could be justified by invoking the notion of the "consumer surplus." But it would surely be preferable, as well as simpler and more open, to award restitutionary damages.

The second case is where the defendant has obtained his profit by doing the very thing which he contracted not to do. In his article "Restitutionary Damages for Breach of Contract: *Snepp* and the Fusion of Law and Equity," [1987] L.M.C.L.Q. 421, 434, Professor Birks observed: "If you promise not to pursue a particular profit-making activity and then do pursue it, nothing is more apt than that you should make restitution of your profits."

This covers the present case exactly. The defendant's breach of contract in submitting the book for publication did not merely provide him with an opportunity for profit; nor did his contract with the publishers merely put it out of his power to perform his contractual obligations to the Crown. The connection between the breach and the profit is far more direct. He promised not to disclose official information and he did so for profit. He earned the profits by doing the very thing which he had promised not to do.

The two cases have this in common: that in both the profits in question are occasioned directly by the breach, which does not merely provide the defendant with the opportunity to make them; and in both compensatory damages are an inadequate remedy if regard is paid to the objects which the plaintiff sought to achieve by the contract.

Only time will tell whether these distinctions are tenable. They may not hold. But it appears to us that the general rule that damages for breach of contract are compensatory can safely be maintained without denying the availability of restitutionary damages in exceptional cases.

C.   *Conclusion*

In Snepp v. United States, 444 U.S. 507, a majority of the United States Supreme Court awarded restitutionary damages for breach of contract in circumstances closely resembling those of the present case. They did so by invoking the concept of the remedial constructive trust impressed on the proceeds of publication without prior clearance. We find the conclusion more attractive than the route by which it was reached. We would prefer to award restitutionary damages directly for breach of contract, rather than distort the equitable concepts of fiduciary duty or constructive trust in order to accommodate them.

In the absence of a claim for substantial damages for breach of contract, however, we dismiss the Crown's private law claims.

"*Opportunistic breach*"

1. *Snepp v. United States*, cited in *A-G v. Blake*, involved similar facts and legal theories:

> Based on his experiences as a CIA agent, Frank Snepp published a book about certain CIA activities in South Vietnam. Snepp published the account without submitting it to the Agency for prepublication review. As an express condition of his employment with the CIA in 1968, however, Snepp had executed an agreement promising that he would "not publish any information or material relating to the Agency, its activities or intelligence activities generally, either during or after the term of [his] employment, without specific prior approval by the Agency."

444 U.S. 507, 507-08 (1980). Unauthorized publication had caused the Government "irreparable harm," the trial court found, though it was agreed that "the actual damages attributable to a publication such as Snepp's generally are unquantifiable. Nominal damages are a hollow alternative, certain to deter no one. Proof of the tortious conduct necessary to sustain an award of punitive damages might force the Government to disclose some of the very confidences that Snepp promised to protect." The Government sought to strip Snepp of the profits of publication by subjecting his royalties to a constructive trust. Its theory against Snepp, like that of the British Crown against Blake, was that its agent had breached not just a contractual but also a fiduciary duty. If this were the case it would make the argument for restitution relatively easy: profits earned through breach of fiduciary duty make the paradigm case for disgorgement of wrongful gain. The *Snepp* majority accepted the Government's claim about fiduciary duty. *A-G v. Blake* makes the more instructive decision of this pair, because the English Court of Appeal was prepared to impose a disgorgement liability based on breach of contract alone.

2. What is the most important reason for restitution in a case like *Y.J.D. Restaurant Supply Co. v. Dib*? How much of it is just "a natural desire to deprive a deliberate wrongdoer of profit"? Compare the famous case of the New Orleans Firefighters, discussed in *A-G v. Blake*. Isn't this a perfect example of "No harm, no foul"? If justice demands that the City be awarded the

amount of the firemen's saved expenditure—and notice that the Louisiana court did not think it did—what is being achieved?

3. Recall from Contracts class the case of Peevyhouse v. Garland Coal & Mining Co., 382 P.2d 109 (Okla. 1962). Garland agreed to strip-mine the Peevyhouse homestead, paying a royalty per ton of coal extracted. They also agreed to restore the surface of the land when mining operations were completed—because the Peevyhouses refused to allow strip-mining unless restoration was part of the deal. Garland took the coal and paid the royalty, but walked away from the job without restoring the land. The Oklahoma Supreme Court declined to award damages for breach of contract: comparing the negligible "diminution of value" of the farm with Garland's substantial "cost to complete," an award of more than nominal damages would be "economic waste." Shouldn't the Peevyhouses have been asking for restitution rather than damages? What would they have to prove to be able to argue—by analogy to *Y.J.D. v. Dib*—that the promised work of restoration was something they had already paid for? What if the court suspects that they will just take the money and move to Florida, rather than restore the land?

4. As Lord Woolf observes, "The difficult question is not whether restitutionary damages should ever be available for breach of contract, but in what circumstances they should be made available." The Restatement's answer is that restitution is available for profitable and "opportunistic" breach, a term that is glossed in the following comment:

> The common rationale of every instance in which restitution allows a recovery of profits from wrongdoing, in the contractual context or any other, is the reinforcement of an entitlement that would be inadequately protected if liability for interference were limited to provable damages. Cases in which restitution reaches the profits from a breach of contract are those in which the promisee's contractual position is vulnerable to abuse. Vulnerability in this context stems from the difficulty that the promisee may face in recovering, as compensatory damages, a full equivalent of the performance for which the promisee has bargained. A promisor who was permitted to exploit the shortcomings of the promisee's damage remedy could accept the price of the promised performance, then deliver something less than what was promised. Such an outcome results in unjust enrichment as between the parties. The mere possibility of such an outcome undermines the stability of any contractual exchange in which one party's performance may be neither easily compelled nor easily valued.
>
> A promisor who recognizes this possibility and attempts to profit by it commits what is here called an "opportunistic breach." The label suggests the reasons why a breach of this character is condemned, but there is no requirement under this section that the claimant prove the motivation of the breaching party.

R3RUE §39, Comment *b*.

5. Is the Restatement conception of "opportunistic breach" (quoted in the preceding note) unnecessarily cumbersome? How about this instead: "Restitution of breach-created profits is available in cases where—if the timing were different—the court would grant equitable relief, either enjoining breach or ordering performance"? By traditional equity rules, a remedy by injunction or specific performance was available only where a plaintiff had no adequate remedy at law by an action for damages. The Restatement's observation about allowing an opportunistic promisor "to exploit the shortcomings of the promisee's damage remedy" looks like an elaboration of equity's simple rule of thumb.

6. On April 26, 1909, Farmer Johnson sold 2,000 bushels of No. 2 merchantable wheat to Acme Mills at $1.03 per bushel, "to be delivered from thresher 1909." On July 13, 1909, Johnson "of his own wrong and without right or legal authority or the consent of appellant" sold the same quantity of wheat to Liberty Mills at the price of $1.16 per bushel. Johnson failed to deliver wheat under his contract with Acme, and Acme sued for damages in the amount of $240. Johnson "admitted the execution and breach of the contract, but denied that Acme was damaged. He further pleaded that he threshed his wheat after the 25th of July, that this was the time fixed for delivery, and wheat was then worth only about 97-1/2 cents per bushel." Acme Mills & Elevator Co. v. Johnson, 141 Ky. 718, 133 S.W. 784 (1911).

As a reasonably sophisticated grain dealer, Acme must have realized that it would not be injured by Johnson's failure to deliver fungible wheat at a contract price exceeding market. What was the point of the litigation? What sort of facts could Acme have pleaded to give it a viable claim in restitution?

7. An inadvertent breach is not "opportunistic," but it might justify restitution nevertheless. The Restatement offers this hypothetical, suggested by Jacob & Youngs, Inc. v. Kent, 230 N.Y. 239, 244, 129 N.E. 889, 891 (1921):

> Builder and Owner agree on the construction of a house at a price of $2 million. The specifications call for foundations to be made of Vermont granite, and the work has been bid and priced on that basis. By mistake and inadvertence, Builder constructs the foundations of granite quarried in New Hampshire. This fact comes to light when construction has been completed. The difference in the appraised value of Owner's property as a result of the nonconformity is nil. The cost to cure the default would far exceed the total price of the house. Because New Hampshire granite is less expensive than comparable stone from Vermont, Builder has saved $15,000 as a result of his negligent breach of contract.

R3RUE §39, Illustration 13. What result? (Is this "damages"?)

———————————

Chapter 7

Restitution for Wrongs

Farnsworth, *Restitution* 61-63 (2014):

Every case of liability in this chapter will feature a defendant who violated the rights of a plaintiff and thus committed a wrong in the eyes of some source of law. That source may be a criminal statute. It may be the common law — usually the law of torts. Or the defendant's conduct may be viewed as wrongful in equity; in that case we might now speak of it as recognized as wrongful by the law of restitution itself. These different sources of condemnation make this branch of restitution law conceptually messy in two ways. First, it means that a plaintiff often has a choice between bringing a restitution claim or a claim based on some other body of law. Compare a case where I *mistakenly* send money to you: the legal analysis usually can have nothing to do with tort law, with contract law, with statutes, or with anything else except the common law of restitution. Now suppose instead that I enter your land, cut down your trees, and take them away to make furniture. I committed a trespass and an act of conversion — two torts. You can sue in tort to collect your damages or in restitution to collect my gains. In olden days a plaintiff who chose restitution for whatever reason was said to "waive the tort," but this expression is misleading and best avoided. The plaintiff really isn't "waiving" anything. He is just choosing a legal theory — though it is true that he must pick one or the other and cannot have both tort damages and a recovery in restitution. So how does a plaintiff decide which to try?

The answers are matters of strategy. Of course restitution may be preferable, first, because it leads to a larger recovery. This may be the case if the defendant has gained more from the wrong than the plaintiff lost, or if the thing taken has since grown in value, or if the defendant's gains are easier to prove than the plaintiff's losses. Or the plaintiff may prefer restitution because the remedies it offers will allow him to recover property directly without competing against other creditors of the defendant. Or a plaintiff may prefer restitution because the limitations period for such a claim usually is longer than for a tort and sometimes may be set flexibly by the doctrine of laches.

There is a second way that this branch of restitution can be complicated by other sources of law bearing on it. Sometimes restitution will borrow a conclusion of wrongfulness from one of those other bodies of law; in other words, it will regard the defendant as unjustly enriched because he obtained his gains in a way that is said to be wrongful by tort law, or criminal law, or a statute. (In the latter case the statute has to be examined carefully to see whether it allows restitution by its terms, and if not, whether it leaves room for a common-law restitution claim in the event of a violation.) As noted a moment ago, however, there also are a few areas where the law of restitution itself identifies the wrong—and is quicker to recognize the wrong than the law of tort or any other branch of law would be. These sometimes are matters that historically would have been considered wrongful as a matter of equity. A breach of the duty of loyalty owed by a fiduciary is an example. That sort of wrong is always a good basis for a restitution claim. Many such cases would provide a good basis for a tort claim, too, but the restitution law on point borrows nothing from the law of torts, and restitution more easily captures cases in which the fiduciary made wrongful gains but the plaintiff suffered no injury. Historically the correction of such misconduct was secured by a device that is one of the predecessors to the modern law of restitution: a bill in equity that sought an accounting from the defendant or some other specific relief. The practical result is that restitution law tends to be more hospitable than the law of torts to claims that involve breaches of trust. The same could be said about the sensitivity of tort and restitution law to some types of deceit.

A. TRESPASS AND CONVERSION

Edwards v. Lee's Administrator
265 Ky. 418, 96 S.W.2d 1028 (1936)

STITES, Justice.

This is an appeal from a judgment of the Edmonson circuit court sitting in equity. Appellants argue but two points in this court: (1) That the court below applied an improper measure of damages; and (2) even if the measure of damages was correct, the amount was erroneously computed. Due to the unique nature of the case, a somewhat detailed statement of the facts is necessary.

About twenty years ago L. P. Edwards discovered a cave under land belonging to him and his wife, Sally Edwards. The entrance to the cave is on the Edwards land. Edwards named it the "Great Onyx Cave," no doubt because of the rock crystal formations within it which are known as onyx. This cave is located in the cavernous area of Kentucky, and is only about three miles distant from the world-famous Mammoth Cave. Its proximity to Mammoth Cave, which for many years has had an international reputation as an underground wonder, as well as its beautiful formations, led Edwards to embark upon a program of advertising and exploitation for the purpose of bringing visitors to his cave. Circulars were printed and distributed, signs were erected along the roads, persons were employed and stationed along the highways to solicit the patronage of passing travelers, and thus the fame of the Great Onyx Cave spread from year to year, until eventually, and before the beginning of the present litigation, it was a well-known and well-patronized cave. Edwards built a hotel near the mouth of the cave to care for travelers. He improved and widened the footpaths and avenues in the cave, and ultimately secured a stream of tourists who paid entrance fees sufficient not only to cover the cost of operation, but also to yield a substantial revenue in addition thereto. The authorities in charge of the development of the Mammoth Cave area as a national park undertook to secure the Great Onyx Cave through condemnation proceedings, and in that suit the value of the cave was fixed by a jury at $396,000.

In April, 1928, F. P. Lee, an adjoining landowner, filed this suit against Edwards and the heirs of Sally Edwards, claiming that a portion of the cave was under his land, and praying for damages, for an accounting of the profits which resulted from the operation of the cave, and for an injunction prohibiting Edwards and his associates from further trespassing upon or exhibiting any part of the cave under Lee's land. At the inception of this litigation, Lee undertook to procure a survey of the cave in order that it might be determined what portion of it was on his land. The chancellor ordered that a survey be made, and Edwards prosecuted an appeal from that order to this court. The appeal was dismissed because it was not from a final judgment. Edwards v. Lee, 230 Ky. 375, 19 S.W.(2d) 992. Thereupon Edwards sought a writ of prohibition in this court against the circuit judge to prevent the carrying out of the order of survey. The writ was denied. Edwards v. Sims, 232 Ky. 791, 24 S.W.(2d) 619, 620.

In this last case the maxim, "*Cujus est solum, ejus est usque ad cœlum et ad inferos*" (to whomsoever the soil belongs, he owns also to the sky and to the depths) was considered and applied, and an analogy drawn between trespassing through mining beneath another's land and passing under it through a cave. A tremendous amount of proof was taken on each side concerning the title of Lee to the land claimed by him; how much, if any, of the cave is under the land of Lee; the length of the exhibited portion of the cave and the amount thereof under the land of Lee; the net earnings of the cave for the years involved; the location of the principal points of interest in the cave and whether they were under the lands of Edwards or of Lee; and whether or not Edwards and his associates had knowledge of the fact that they were trespassing on Lee's property. An appeal was taken to this court from a judgment fixing the boundaries between the lands of Edwards and Lee, and that judgment was affirmed. An injunction was granted prohibiting Edwards and his associates from further trespassing on the lands of Lee. On final hearing the chancellor stated separately his findings of law and of fact in the following language:

> The Court finds as a matter of law the plaintiff is entitled to recover of defendants the proportionate part of the net proceeds defendants received from exhibiting Great Onyx Cave from the years 1923 to 1930, inclusive, as the footage of said cave under Lee's land bears to the entire footage of the cave exhibited to the public for fees during the years 1923 to 1930, inclusive, with 6% interest on plaintiff's proportionate part of said fund for each year from the first day of the following year as set out in the memorandum opinion.
>
> 1. The Court finds as a matter of fact the true boundary line between the Lee and Edwards land is as set out in a former judgment of this Court in this case which was affirmed in Edwards v. Lee, 250 Ky. 166, 61 S.W.(2d) 1049.
>
> 2. The Court finds as a matter of fact there was 6,449.88 feet of said cave exhibited to the public during 1923 to 1930, inclusive, and that 2,048.60 feet of said footage was under Lee's lands making plaintiff entitled to 2048.60 / 6449.88 or 1/3 of the proceeds.
>
> 3. The Court finds as a matter of fact the proof failed to show the proceeds received for the years 1923 and 1924 and there can be no recovery for those years. That the net proceeds for 1925 amounted to $3,090.31 and plaintiff's one-third thereof is $1,030.10, with 6% interest from January 1st, 1926, and that the net proceeds for the other years were:
>
> | | |
> |------|------------|
> | 1926 | $ 4,039.56 |
> | 1927 | 7,288.57 |
> | 1928 | 14,632.99 |
> | 1929 | 24,551.96 |
> | 1930 | 23,340.51 |
>
> and the plaintiffs are entitled to one-third of the net proceeds for each of said years, with 6% interest thereon from January 1st of each succeeding year.

Appellants, in their attack here on the measure of damages and its application to the facts adduced, urge: (1) That the appellees had simply a hole in the ground, about 360 feet below the surface, which they could not use and which they could not even enter except by going through the mouth of the cave on Edwards' property; (2) the cave was of no practical use to appellees without an entrance, and there was no one except the appellants on whom they might confer a right of beneficial use; (3) Lee's portion of the cave had no rental value; (4) appellees were not ousted of the physical occupation or use of the property because they did not and could not occupy it; (5) the property has not in any way been injured by the use to which it has been put by appellants, and since this is fundamentally an action for damages arising from trespass, the recovery must be limited to the damages suffered by appellees (in other words, nominal damages) and cannot properly be measured by the benefits accruing to the trespasser from his wrongful use of the property; (6) as a result of the injunction, appellees have their cave in exactly the condition it has always been, handicapped by no greater degree of uselessness than it was before appellants trespassed upon it.

Appellees, on the other hand, argue that this was admittedly a case of willful trespass; that it is not analogous to a situation where a trespasser simply walks across the land of another, for here the trespasser actually used the property of Lee to make a profit for himself; that even if nothing tangible was taken or disturbed in the various trips through Lee's portion of the cave, nevertheless there was a taking of esthetic enjoyment which, under ordinary circumstances, would justify a recovery of the reasonable rental value for the use of the cave; that there being no basis for arriving at reasonable rental values, the chancellor took the only course open to him under the circumstances and properly assessed the damages on the basis of the profits realized from the use of Lee's portion of the cave. Appellees have taken a cross-appeal, however, on the theory that, since the trespass was willful, their damages should be measured by the gross profits realized from the operation of the cave rather than from its net profits.

As the foregoing statement of the facts and the contentions of the parties will demonstrate, the case is *sui generis*, and counsel have been unable to give us much assistance in the way of previous decisions of this or other courts. We are left to fundamental principles and analogies.

We may begin our consideration of the proper measure of damages to be applied with the postulate that appellees held legal title to a definite segment of the cave and that they were possessed, therefore, of a right which it is the policy of the law to protect. We may assume that the appellants were guilty of repeated trespasses upon the property of appellees. The proof likewise clearly indicates that the trespasses were willful, and not innocent.

Appellees brought this suit in equity, and seek an accounting of the profits realized from the operation of the cave, as well as an injunction against future trespass. In substance, therefore, their action is *ex contractu* and not, as appellants contend, simply an action for damages arising from a tort. Ordinarily, the measure of recovery in assumpsit for the taking and selling of personal property is the value received by the wrongdoer. On the other hand, where the action is based upon a trespass to land, the recovery has almost invariably been measured by the reasonable rental value of the property. . . . [But] it is apparent that rental value has been adopted, either consciously or unconsciously, as a convenient yardstick by which to measure the proportion of profit derived by the trespasser directly from the use of the land itself. In other words, rental value ordinarily indicates the amount of profit realized directly from the land as land, aside from all collateral contracts. Clearly, the unjust enrichment of the wrongdoer is the gist of the right to bring an action *ex contractu*. Rental value is merely the most convenient and logical means for ascertaining what proportion of the benefits received may be attributed to the use of the real estate.

In the current proposed final draft of the Restatement of Restitution and Unjust Enrichment (March 4, 1936), Part I, §136, it is stated:

> A person who tortiously uses a trade name, trade secret, profit a prendre, or other similar interest of another, is under a duty of restitution for the value of the benefit thereby received.

The analogy between the right to protection which the law gives a trade-name or trade secret and the right of the appellees here to protection of their legal rights in the cave seems to us to be very close. In all of the mineral and timber cases, there is an actual physical loss suffered by the plaintiff, as well as a benefit received by the defendant. In other words, there is both a plus and a minus quantity. In the trade-name and similar cases, as in the case at bar, there may be no tangible loss other than the violation of a right. The law, in seeking an adequate remedy for the wrong, has been forced to adopt profits received, rather than damages sustained, as a basis of recovery. In commenting on the section of the Restatement quoted above, the reporter says:

> Persons who tortiously use trade names, trade secrets, water rights, and other similar interests of others, are ordinarily liable in an action of tort for the harm which they have done. In some cases, however, no harm is done and in these cases if the sole remedy were by an action of tort the wrongdoer would be allowed to profit at little or no expense. In cases where the damage is more extensive, proof as to its extent may be so difficult that justice can be accomplished only by requiring payment of the amount of profits. Where definite damage is caused and is susceptible of proof, the injured person, as in other tort cases, can elect between an action for damages and an action for the value of that which was improperly received. The usual method of seeking restitution is by a bill in equity, with a request for an accounting for any profits which have been received, but the existence of a right to bring such a bill does not necessarily prevent an action at law for the value of the use.

We are led inevitably to the conclusion that the measure of recovery in this case must be the benefits, or net profits, received by the appellants from the use of the property of the appellees. The philosophy of all these decisions is that a wrongdoer shall not be permitted to make a profit from his own wrong. Our conclusion that a proper measure of recovery is net profits, of course, disposes of the cross-appeal. Appellees are not entitled to recover gross profits. They are limited to the benefits accruing to the appellants.

This brings us to a consideration of appellants' second contention, namely, that even if the measure of recovery was correct, the amount was erroneously computed. It is argued that the appellants ceased to exhibit the portion of the cave on appellees' land after electric lights were put into that part of the cave on the appellants' property. The proof on this question was conflicting. Various witnesses testified concerning the particular points of interest that were exhibited, and many of these were shown to have been on appellees' land. Likewise, it was established that tourists entering the cave, even after it had been electrified to the limits of appellants' property, carried lanterns, which, presumably, would only be of use if they were going into its unlighted portions, and advertisements of the cave published after the electrification continued to feature points of interest on the appellees' land. Under the circumstances, therefore, we cannot say that the chancellor did not correctly conclude that the entire cave was exhibited even after the portion of it on appellants' land had been equipped with electric lights.

In determining the profits which might fairly be said to arise directly from the use of appellees' segment of the cave, the chancellor considered not only the footage exhibited, but the relative value of the particular points of interest featured in advertising the cave, and their possible appeal in drawing visitors. Of thirty-one scenes or objects in the cave advertised by appellants, twelve were shown to be on appellees' property. Several witnesses say that the underground Lucikovah river, which is under the appellees' land for almost its entire exhibited length, is one of the most attractive features of the cave, if not its leading attraction. Other similar attractions are shown to be located on appellees' property. The chancellor excluded profits received by the appellants from the operation of their hotel, and we think the conclusion that one-third of the net profits received alone from the exhibition of the cave is a fair determination of the direct benefits accruing to the appellants from the use of the appellees' property.

Profitable trespass

1. The Great Onyx Cave was "admittedly a case of wrongful trespass." What if the underground trespass had been inadvertent? Trespass (like conversion) is a strict-liability tort, so a defendant may be subject to liability for conduct that is not only unintentional but entirely free from negligence or other fault. Both types of defendant—the "conscious wrongdoer," as well as the person who is liable without fault—are liable in restitution for any benefits obtained by their tortious conduct or other wrongdoing, but there is often a distinction in the way those benefits are measured. As a first approximation: even an innocent tortfeasor (like an unwitting trespasser) is liable for the measurable value of what he has taken—the use of the owner's property—and this is so even if the injury to the property is nil. But the unjust enrichment of a conscious wrongdoer is fixed by a "disgorgement" measure, designed to strip the defendant of wrongful gains and to eliminate the possibility that such conduct might be profitable. Profitable

exploitation of a cave lends itself to this sort of calculation, but placing a cash value on the intentional interference with legal rights is often more difficult.

2. In Don v. Trojan Construction Co., 178 Cal. App. 2d 135, 2 Cal. Rptr. 626 (1960), the essential facts were as follows:

> On February 21, 1957, plaintiffs, husband and wife, bought a commer-cially zoned lot in the city of Campbell. They intended to build a super-market on the lot, and placed a sign on it announcing their intention to do so, but conditions on the stock market, in which they had holdings, were not favorable to them at the time, so they postponed construction of the market. They did not intend to rent the lot to anyone, and Mr. Don testified that he would not have accepted a proposal to rent, although he might have allowed a brief use of the lot without charge had he been asked for it.
>
> On or about June 1, 1957, Trojan Construction Company was build-ing a subdivision near the Don lot. Streets had to be built, and there was dirt to be taken away and stored somewhere. [Trojan had at one time owned the lot in question. Trojan sold it to Ad-Mor, and Ad-Mor sold it to the Dons. Trojan said it had asked Ad-Mor's permission to store dirt on the lot, and that Ad-Mor—which no longer owned it—had agreed.]
>
> During June and July, 1957, dirt was being put on the land and taken off. In August 1957, Trojan decided it did not need any of the dirt, and advertised that free dirt was available. The public began to remove the dirt. It was stipulated that in March, 1958, there was still "substantial dirt on it," but by the end of March, 1958, there was no dirt on the property.
>
> On November 26, 1957, plaintiffs filed the action, alleging that defen-dant Trojan placed large quantities of dirt on plaintiffs' land, without their permission. They alleged the rental value of the land to be $750 per month, and they prayed damages in the amount of $750 per month until all the dirt should have been removed.
>
> The trial court found that the value of the lot [once the dirt had been removed] was neither greater nor less by reason of the use of the land by defendants; that the average rental value during the period when the land was used by defendants was $550 per month, and the total $5,500. However, the court found that plaintiffs would not have made any use of the land during that time, nor did they intend to rent it out for any pur-pose, and would not have rented it had an offer been made. The court found that the only damages "are nominal damages sustained by reason of the technical invasion of their possessory rights in the land." The court awarded damages against defendants in the total amount of $200, and no costs to plaintiffs.

Plaintiffs thought the damage award was insufficient. How would you decide the case on appeal?

3. In Beck v. Northern Natural Gas Co., 170 F.3d 1018 (10th Cir. 1999), the facts were stated as follows:

> This case involves the vertical migration of natural gas between two subsurface geological reservoirs, or formations, located in the Cunningham Field, once one of the most prolific production areas of oil and gas in Kansas. Such formations, once depleted of native natural gas, can be injected with natural gas for storage to enable pipeline companies to ensure supply of natural gas during times of peak demand. In 1977, Northern was authorized by the Kansas Corporation Commission (KCC) and the Federal Power Commission to store gas in the Viola formation underlying 23,000 acres of the landowners' property. Under leases subsequently negotiated with the landowners, Northern obtained storage rights to this formation, and began injecting gas in August of 1978.
>
> Sometime after Northern began storing gas, some of the gas vertically migrated from the Viola to the Simpson formation, a smaller formation directly beneath the Viola. In September of 1993, a well was drilled and completed in the Simpson formation, and composition and pressure data indicated that the gas produced was storage gas from the Viola formation. In response, Northern thoroughly evaluated the Simpson formation and determined that geological faults had allowed gas to migrate from the Viola into the Simpson formation. Northern then sought certification of the Simpson formation before the KCC. After a public hearing, the KCC determined that the formation was suitable for gas storage, and that such storage was in the public interest. Northern subsequently obtained lease agreements from approximately two-thirds of the affected landowners, and exercised its eminent domain rights against the remaining landowners, including the plaintiffs.

The disaffected Simpson landowners brought suit against Northern, alleging trespass and unjust enrichment for the time the gas was migrating, up to the date on which they were compelled to lease their storage rights. Northern's pipeline and storage business was highly profitable throughout the period in question, and the landowners had evidence supposedly showing what portion of Northern's overall profits for this period was attributable to the unlicensed use of the Simpson formation. What (if anything) are the landowners entitled to recover?

4. From 1974 to 1976, the MGM Grand Hotel in Las Vegas presented 1,700 performances of an elaborate musical revue entitled "Hallelujah Hollywood." Four of the 10 acts in the show were "tributes" to famous MGM movies — one of them "Kismet," made in 1955. Plaintiffs held copyrights to the original *Kismet* musical (produced in 1953), and they alleged that "Hallelujah Hollywood" infringed those rights. MGM was found liable for infringement, though the trial court initially found that plaintiffs had not shown any damages. On an initial appeal, it was held that plaintiffs were entitled to (i) an apportionment of the profits from the performances of "Hallelujah Hollywood," and

moreover (ii) a share of "indirect profits" from the "nontheatrical" operations of the MGM Grand Hotel, including its casino. Frank Music Corp. v. Metro-Goldwyn-Mayer, Inc., 772 F.2d 505 (9th Cir. 1985). Should MGM have been liable for a share of hotel and casino profits? Why were hotel profits awarded in Las Vegas but not at the Great Onyx Cave?

Olwell v. Nye & Nissen Co.
26 Wash. 2d 282, 173 P.2d 652 (1946)

MALLERY, J.

On May 6, 1940, plaintiff, E. L. Olwell, sold and transferred to the defendant corporation his one-half interest in Puget Sound Egg Packers, a Washington corporation having its principal place of business in Tacoma. By the terms of the agreement, the plaintiff was to retain full ownership in an "Eggsact" egg-washing machine, formerly used by Puget Sound Egg Packers. The defendant promised to make it available for delivery to the plaintiff on or before June 15, 1940.

It appears that the plaintiff arranged for and had the machine stored in a space adjacent to the premises occupied by the defendant but not covered by its lease. Due to the scarcity of labor immediately after the outbreak of the war, defendant's treasurer, without the knowledge or consent of the plaintiff, ordered the egg washer taken out of storage. The machine was put into operation by defendant on May 31, 1941, and thereafter, for a period of three years, was used approximately one day a week in the regular course of the defendant's business.

Plaintiff first discovered this use in January or February of 1945, when he happened to be at the plant on business and heard the machine operating. Thereupon, plaintiff offered to sell the machine to defendant for six hundred dollars or half of its original cost in 1929. A counteroffer of fifty dollars was refused, and, approximately one month later, this action was commenced to recover the reasonable value of defendant's use of the machine, and praying for twenty-five dollars per month from the commencement of the unauthorized use until the time of trial. A second cause of action was alleged, but was not pressed and hence is not here involved. The court entered judgment for plaintiff in the amount of ten dollars per week for the period of 156 weeks covered by the statute of limitations, or $1,560, and gave the plaintiff his costs.

Defendant has appealed to this court, assigning error upon the judgment, upon the trial of the cause on the theory of unjust enrichment, upon the amount of damages, and upon the court's refusal to make a finding as to the value of the machine, and in refusing to consider such value in measuring damages.

The theory of the respondent was that the tort of conversion could be "waived" and suit brought in quasi-contract, upon a contract implied in law, to recover, as restitution, the profits which inured to appellant as a result of its wrongful use of the machine. With this the trial court agreed and, in its findings of facts, found that the use of the machine

> resulted in a benefit to the users, in that said use saves the users approximately $1.43 per hour of use as against the expense which would be incurred were eggs to be washed by hand; that said machine was used by Puget Sound Egg Packers and defendant, on an average of one day per week from May of 1941, until February of 1945 at an average saving of $10.00 per each day of use.

In substance, the argument presented by the assignments of error is that the principle of unjust enrichment, or quasi-contract, is not of universal application but is imposed only in exceptional cases because of special facts and circumstances and in favor of particular persons; that respondent had an adequate remedy in an action at law for replevin or claim and delivery; that any damages awarded to the plaintiff should be based upon the use or rental value of the machine and should bear some reasonable relation to its market value. Appellant therefore contends that the amount of the judgment is excessive.

It is uniformly held that in cases where the defendant tortfeasor has benefited by his wrong, the plaintiff may elect to "waive the tort" and bring an action in assumpsit for restitution. Such an action arises out of a duty imposed by law devolving upon the defendant to repay an unjust and unmerited enrichment. Woodward, The Law of Quasi-Contracts 439, §272(2); Keener on Quasi-Contracts 160. See, also, Professor Corbin's articles, "Waiver of Tort and Suit in Assumpsit," 19 Yale Law Journal 221, and "Quasi-Contractual Obligations," 21 Yale Law Journal 533.

It is clear that the saving in labor cost which appellant derived from its use of respondent's machine constituted a benefit.

According to the Restatement of Restitution §1 (Comment *b*):

> A person confers a benefit upon another if he gives to the other possession of or some other interest in money, land, chattels, or choses in action, performs services beneficial to or at the request of the other, satisfies a debt or a duty of the other, or in any way adds to the other's security or advantage. *He confers a benefit not only where he adds to the property of another, but also where he saves the other from expense or loss.* The word "benefit," therefore, denotes any form of advantage. (Italics ours.)

It is also necessary to show that, while appellant benefited from its use of the egg-washing machine, respondent thereby incurred a loss. It is argued by appellant that, since the machine was put into storage by respondent, who had no present use for it, and for a period of almost three years did not know that appellant was operating it, and since it was not injured by its operation and the appellant never adversely claimed any title to it, nor contested respondent's right of repossession upon the latter's discovery of the wrongful operation, that

7. Restitution for Wrongs

the respondent was not damaged, because he is as well off as if the machine had not been used by appellant.

The very essence of the nature of property is the right to its exclusive use. Without it, no beneficial right remains. However plausible, the appellant cannot be heard to say that its wrongful invasion of the respondent's property right to exclusive use is not a loss compensable in law. To hold otherwise would be subversive of all property rights, since its use was admittedly wrongful and without claim of right. The theory of unjust enrichment is applicable in such a case.

We agree with appellant that respondent could have elected a "common garden variety of action," as he calls it, for the recovery of damages. It is also true that, except where provided for by statute, punitive damages are not allowed, the basic measure for the recovery of damages in this state being compensation. If, then, respondent had been limited to redress in tort for damages, as appellant contends, the court below would be in error in refusing to make a finding as to the value of the machine. In such case, the award of damages must bear a reasonable relation to the value of the property. Hoff v. Lester, 25 Wash. 2d 86, 168 P.2d 409 (1946).

But respondent here had an election. He chose rather to waive his right of action in tort and to sue in assumpsit on the implied contract. Having so elected, he is entitled to the measure of restoration which accompanies the remedy.

> Actions for restitution have for their primary purpose taking from the defendant and restoring to the plaintiff something to which the plaintiff is entitled, or if this is not done, causing the defendant to pay the plaintiff an amount which will restore the plaintiff to the position in which he was before the defendant received the benefit. If the value of what was received and what was lost were always equal, there would be no substantial problem as to the amount of recovery, since actions of restitution are not punitive. In fact, however, the plaintiff frequently has lost more than the defendant has gained, and sometimes the defendant has gained more than the plaintiff has lost.
>
> In such cases the measure of restitution is determined with reference to the tortiousness of the defendant's conduct or the negligence or other fault of one or both of the parties in creating the situation giving rise to the right to restitution. If the defendant was tortious in his acquisition of the benefit he is required to pay for what the other has lost although that is more than the recipient benefited. *If he was consciously tortious in acquiring the benefit, he is also deprived of any profit derived from his subsequent dealing with it.* If he was no more at fault than the claimant, he is not required to pay for losses in excess of benefit received by him and he is permitted to retain gains which result from his dealing with the property. (Italics ours.) Restatement of Restitution 595-96.

Respondent may recover the profit derived by the appellant from the use of the machine.

Respondent has prayed "on his first cause of action for the sum of twenty-five dollars per month from the time defendant first commenced to use said machine subsequent to May 1940 (1941) until present time." In computing judgment, the court below computed recovery on the basis of ten dollars per week. This makes the judgment excessive, since it cannot exceed the amount prayed for. We therefore direct the trial court to reduce the judgment, based upon the prayer of the complaint, to twenty-five dollars per month for thirty-six months, or nine hundred dollars.

Conversion

1. "If A, being a liveryman, keeps his horse standing idle in the stable, and B, against his wish or without his knowledge, rides or drives it out, it is no answer to A for B to say: 'Against what loss do you want to be restored? I restore the horse. There is no loss. The horse is none the worse; it is the better for the exercise.'" Watson, Laidlaw & Co. v. Pott, Cassels & Williamson, [1914] Sess. Cas. (H.L.) 18, 31 (Scot.) (Lord Shaw of Dunfermline).

2. The facts of Langton v. Waite, (1868) L.R. 6 Eq. 165 (Ch.), are paraphrased by the Restatement as follows:

> Borrower pledges to Lender 1,000 shares of Grand Trunk Railway, currently worth about $100,000, as collateral for a loan. The term of the loan is 90 days with no right of prepayment. Absent an event of default, Lender has no right under the contract or applicable law to make any disposition of the collateral. Thirty days later, Lender sells Borrower's shares in a rising market for $220,000. When Borrower repays the loan at maturity, the market has fallen: Lender reacquires 1,000 shares of Grand Trunk for $170,000 and delivers them to Borrower.

R3RUE §41, Illustration 18. Lender's sale of Borrower's shares constitutes conversion, but has Borrower been injured in any way? Is Borrower entitled to restitution—and if so, of what?

3. In Corey v. Struve, 170 Cal. 170, 149 P. 48 (1915), the parties' contentions were as follows:

> The complaint contained allegations that plaintiff leased to defendants certain land in Monterey County for a term of years; that while defendants were in possession of the said land plaintiff was the owner of certain beet-tops which had been cut from beets grown upon said property under said lease; that defendants, without right, converted said beet-tops to their

own use, sold said personal property, and received therefor the sum of $3,271.27, which was the value thereof at the time of conversion.

Defendants admitted plaintiff's ownership of the beet-tops, but alleged that such ownership was limited and special, for the sole purpose of having the beet-tops remain upon the ground where they had been grown and cut, defendants being entitled to the possession of said beet-tops for the purpose of plowing them under as a fertilizer. They further alleged that with plaintiff's permission they had sold the beet-tops to be fed to cattle on the premises and averred that the fertilizing effect of feeding the beet-tops upon the ground where they had been grown and cut was greater than that produced by plowing under, and they denied that plaintiff had been injured by their conduct, but asserted that he had been greatly benefited thereby.

We can assume that defendants did not, in fact, have plaintiff's permission to sell the beet-tops, but that defendants' theory about their "fertilizing effect" was substantially correct. Has plaintiff been injured? Is he entitled to any recovery?

4. In Schlosser v. Welk, 193 Ill. App. 3d 448, 550 N.E.2d 241 (1990), the case on appeal was stated as follows:

The defendant, Rhonda Welk, appeals from a $549 judgment entered in favor of the plaintiff, Marianne Schlosser, d/b/a Select-A-Video. The record shows that the defendant was an employee of Select-A-Video until her termination on October 5, 1987. As a general policy, employees were allowed to take video tapes home for their personal use without checking the tapes out or paying a rental fee. On the day the defendant was terminated, she had placed eight video tapes in her car. At the end of the work day, the defendant was told that she was being terminated. The defendant took the tapes home and during a conversation with her husband placed them in a storage closet. She testified that a number of weeks later she discovered the tapes while cleaning. She also testified that the tapes were never viewed by her or her family while they were in her possession. She returned the video tapes to the plaintiff's store on December 10, 1987.

At the conclusion of the bench trial, the court found that an implied contract existed between the parties. The court then ruled that the plaintiff was entitled to $549, which was the amount the defendant would have owed if she had rented the tapes for the two months she kept them.

What result on appeal? Does it matter that the defendant never watched the movies?

B. FRAUD AND MISREPRESENTATION

Ward v. Taggart
51 Cal. 2d 736, 336 P.2d 534 (1959)

Traynor, J.

At plaintiff William R. Ward's request in February 1955, LeRoy Thomsen, a real estate broker, undertook to look for properties that might be of interest to Ward for purchase. During a conversation about unrelated matters, defendant Marshall W. Taggart, a real estate broker, told Thomsen that as exclusive agent for Sunset Oil Company he had several acres of land in Los Angeles County for sale. Thomsen said that he had a client who might be interested in acquiring this property. When Thomsen mentioned to Taggart that another broker named Dawson had a "For Sale" sign on the property, Taggart replied that Sunset had taken the listing away from Dawson. With Ward's authorization Thomsen submitted an offer on his behalf to Taggart of $4,000 an acre. Taggart promised to take the offer to Sunset.

Taggart later told Thomsen that Sunset had refused the offer and would not take less for the property than $5,000 an acre, one-half in cash. Thomsen conveyed this information to Ward, who directed Thomsen to make an offer on those terms. Thomsen did so in writing. At Taggart's direction, Thomsen inserted in the offer a provision for payment by Sunset of a 10 percent commission, which Taggart and Thomsen agreed to divide equally. On the following day Thomsen informed Ward of the provision for the commission and Ward agreed to it. Subsequently, Taggart told Thomsen that Sunset had accepted Ward's offer and presented to him proposed escrow instructions naming Taggart's business associate, defendant H. M. Jordan, as seller acting for Taggart. Taggart stated that his designation as principal would enable him to "clear up the Dawson exclusive listing" as well as certain blanket mortgages on the property. Thomsen told Ward of this arrangement when he submitted the escrow instructions to him. When Ward asked why Jordan was to be the payee of the notes and the beneficiary of the trust deeds, Thomsen replied that Taggart had said the arrangement was prompted by certain tax and other problems of the Sunset Oil Company and that the trust deeds would be turned over to Sunset after the escrow. Plaintiffs paid $360,246 for the 72.0492 acres conveyed to them.

Plaintiffs did not learn until after they had purchased the property that Taggart had never been given a listing by Sunset and that he had never presented to Sunset and never intended to present plaintiffs' offers of $4,000 and $5,000 per acre. Instead, he presented his own offer of $4,000 per acre, which Sunset accepted. He falsely represented to plaintiffs that the least Sunset would take for the property was $5,000 per acre, because he intended to purchase the property from Sunset himself and resell it to plaintiffs at a profit of $1,000 per acre. All the reasons he gave for the unusual handling of the sale were fabrications. He never disclosed Ward's offer to Sunset until after the escrow papers were signed. All of the money he used to pay Sunset the purchase price came from the Ward escrow.

Plaintiffs brought an action in tort charging fraud on the part of Taggart and Jordan. The case was tried without a jury, and the court entered judgment against both defendants for $72,049.20 compensatory damages, and against Taggart for $36,000 exemplary damages. The judgment also enjoined defendants from transferring notes and trust deeds received from plaintiffs and ordered them to discharge these and thereby reduce the amount of the judgment. Defendants appeal.

Defendants contend that the judgment must be reversed on the ground that, there can be no recovery in a tort action for fraud without proof of the actual or "out-of-pocket" losses sustained by the plaintiff and that in the present case there was no evidence that the property was worth less than plaintiffs paid for it. Defendants invoke §3343 of the Civil Code, which provides that one "defrauded in the purchase, sale or exchange of property is entitled to recover the difference between the actual value of that with which the defrauded person parted and the actual value of that which he received." Although, as defendants admit, the evidence is clearly sufficient to support the finding of fraud, the only evidence submitted on the issue of damages was that the property was worth at least $5,000 per acre, the price plaintiffs paid for it. Since there was no proof that plaintiffs suffered "out-of-pocket" loss, there can be no recovery in tort for fraud. (Bagdasarian v. Gragnon, 31 Cal. 2d 744, 762-763, 192 P.2d 935 (1948).)

Plaintiffs contend, however, that their recovery is not limited to actual damages, on the ground that §3343 does not apply to a tort action to recover secret profits [citing several California cases]. These cases all involved situations in which the defendant was the agent of the defrauded person or in which a confidential or fiduciary relationship existed between the parties. They rest on the theory that "the principal's right to recover does not depend upon any deceit of the agent, but is based upon the duties incident to the agency relationship and upon the fact that all profits resulting from that relationship belong to the principal." In the present case, however, there is no evidence of an agency or other fiduciary relationship between plaintiffs and defendant Taggart or defendant Jordan. Plaintiffs dealt at arms length with Taggart through their agent Thomsen. At no time did Taggart purport to act for plaintiffs. There is no evidence of any prior dealings between the parties or any acquaintanceship or special relationship that would create a fiduciary duty of defendants to plaintiffs. In the absence of a fiduciary relationship, recovery in a tort action for fraud is limited to the actual damages suffered by the plaintiff.

Even though Taggart was not plaintiff's agent, the public policy of this state does not permit one to "take advantage of his own wrong" (Civ. Code §3517), and the law provides a quasi-contractual remedy to prevent one from being unjustly enriched at the expense of another. Section 2224 of the Civil Code provides that one "who gains a thing by fraud . . . or other wrongful act, is, unless he has some other and better right thereto, an involuntary trustee of the thing gained, for the benefit of the person who would otherwise have had it." As a real estate broker, Taggart had the duty to be honest and truthful in his dealings. The evidence is clearly sufficient to support a finding that

Taggart violated this duty. Through fraudulent misrepresentations he received money that plaintiffs would otherwise have had. Thus, Taggart is an involuntary trustee for the benefit of plaintiffs on the secret profit of $1,000 per acre that he made from his dealings with them.

Although the facts pleaded and proved by plaintiffs do not sustain the judgment on the theory of tort, they are sufficient to uphold recovery under the quasi-contractual theory of unjust enrichment since that theory does not contemplate any factual situation different from that established by the evidence in the trial court. Defendants were given ample opportunity to present their version of the transaction involved, and the issue of whether or not their actions constituted fraud was decided adversely to them by the trial court.

Accordingly, the judgment for $72,049.20, representing the $1,000 per acre secret profit, against defendant Taggart must be affirmed. The judgment against defendant Jordan, however, must be reversed. Although she permitted her name to be used in the dual escrows, she did not share in the illicit profit that Taggart obtained. One cannot be held to be a constructive trustee of something he has not acquired.

Taggart contends that if recovery is based on the theory of unjust enrichment, the judgment for exemplary damages must be reversed. The argument runs that under this theory the law implies a promise to return the money wrongfully obtained, that the plaintiff waives the tort and sues in assumpsit on an implied contract, and that since such an action is "contractual" in nature, it does not admit of the exemplary damages allowed under §3294 of the Civil Code. That section authorizes exemplary damages "in an action for the breach of an obligation not arising from contract, where the defendant has been guilty of oppression, fraud, or malice." The word "contract" is used in this section in its ordinary sense to mean an agreement between the parties, not an obligation imposed by law despite the absence of any such agreement. Taggart's obligation does not arise from any agreement between him and plaintiffs. It arises from his fraud and violation of statutory duties. His fraud is not waived, for it is the very foundation of the implied-in-law promise to disgorge. (See Corbin, *Waiver of Tort and Suit In Assumpsit*, 19 Yale L.J. 221, 243-246.) The promise is purely fictitious and unintentional, originally implied to circumvent rigid common law pleading. It was invoked not to deny a remedy, but to create one "for the purpose of bringing about justice without reference to the intention of the parties." 1 Williston, Contracts (rev. ed.) p.9; see Desny v. Wilder, 46 Cal. 2d 715, 735 (1956). Since Taggart's obligation for his fraud does not arise from contract but is imposed by law, the judgment for exemplary damages clearly falls within §3294.

Courts award exemplary damages to discourage oppression, fraud, or malice by punishing the wrongdoer. Such damages are appropriate in cases like the present one, where restitution would have little or no deterrent effect, for wrongdoers would run no risk of liability to their victims beyond that of returning what they wrongfully obtained. The record herein discloses no abuse of discretion in the award of exemplary damages.

Taggart finally contends that he is entitled to a deduction of the cost to him of the transaction except those items incurred to accomplish his fraud. He seeks to reduce the compensatory damages by $25,563.10, representing the commission of $15,012.30 paid to Thomsen; the $5,900 commission paid to Harvey Nelson, former land manager of Sunset Oil Company; the $616 cost of the two escrows, one of which channeled title from Sunset to Jordan and the other from Jordan to plaintiffs; and the $4,034.80 paid to Dawson, who had an exclusive agency on the property, to cancel his contract. The $5,900 paid to Nelson and the cost of the Jordan escrow were expenses incurred to accomplish the fraud; they would not have been necessary to a legitimate transaction. It is clear that these expenses must be disallowed. Since it is entirely speculative whether the commissions paid to Thomsen and Dawson and the cost of the second escrow would have been paid by plaintiffs or Sunset had the transaction been a legitimate one, it would be inequitable to permit Taggart to deduct any of these expenses from plaintiffs' recovery.

The judgment against Taggart is affirmed. The judgment against Jordan is reversed.

Gains from misrepresentation

1. When a claimant has been induced to enter into a disadvantageous transaction by fraudulent misstatements, the first-choice remedy is normally rescission—as in *Earl v. Saks & Co.* or *Porreco v. Porreco*. Sometimes the claimant would prefer to keep the transaction in place with compensation for the defendant's wrong. Tort and contract theories may or may not yield a claim for damages. If Seller sells goods to Buyer for $10,000, falsely representing that they are worth that much when in fact they are worth only $5,000, Buyer can probably keep the goods and recover $5,000 damages—either in tort (for deceit) or for breach of warranty. But damage claims become elusive as the seller's misrepresentation shifts. A traditional rule, evoked in *Ward v. Taggart*, limited damages for fraud to the difference in value (if any) between what the fraud victim gave up and received in exchange. Restitution adds considerable flexibility, because it regards profits gained by fraudulent misrepresentation as unjust enrichment at the expense of the person defrauded—without reference to any difference in value of the assets exchanged.

2. A material (though nonfraudulent) misrepresentation will likewise support a claim based on unjust enrichment. In Murkofsky v. Jerry, 152 Misc. 2d 141, 584 N.Y.S.2d 707 (Sup. Ct. 1992), the facts were stated as follows:

> Plaintiff rendered psychiatric services to decedent from 1981 through 1986, comprising 148 office visits on an out-patient basis. During this five-year period of treatment, plaintiff accepted Medicare assignments, limited to $250 annually or a total compensation of $1,250. Plaintiff testified

that he accepted no assignments and submitted no bills to Medicare or decedent in excess of this maximum annual allowance, relying upon decedent's representation that she was impoverished.

Decedent died intestate in December 1986, leaving an estate of approximately $100,000. Following rejection of plaintiff's written claim of $9,850, which plaintiff had presented in August 1988 (148 visits x $75 per visit less $1,250 received), plaintiff commenced the instant action. After trial, the court below awarded $312.50 to plaintiff, who now appeals.

Held: reversed, and new trial ordered. "Significantly, restitution may be had for services obtained by an 'innocent but material misstatement' as well as a consciously false statement."

By the standard rule in contract law, a misrepresentation will justify rescission if the misrepresentation is *either* fraudulent or material, materiality being defined in terms of inducing assent. R3RUE §13 (and cases like *Murkofsky v. Jerry*) carry over the contract rule to define claims for restitution.

3. Can the defendant be unjustly enriched if the fraudulent misrepresentation is made by someone else? The Restatement offers an illustration inspired by Scrushy v. Tucker, 955 So. 2d 988 (Ala. 2006):

> Corporation pays $45 million in bonuses to its President, based on its reported net income during a five-year period. It is subsequently revealed that Corporation's net income for the period was artificially inflated, in consequence of an accounting fraud perpetrated by certain officers and directors. (Corporation was actually operating at a loss.) Corporation sues President to recover $45 million plus interest.

Corporation does not claim that President participated in the fraud, or that President was aware the earnings were overstated. What result? See R3RUE §13, Illustration 13.

Janigan v. Taylor
344 F.2d 781 (1st Cir. 1965)

ALDRICH, Chief Judge.

This is a personal action brought by plaintiffs as a class in the district court for the district of Massachusetts in which they allege violations by the defendant of Rule 10b-5 of the Securities and Exchange Commission promulgated pursuant to section 10 of the Securities Exchange Act of 1934, hereinafter the Act. The cause of action arises by implication of the Act. The basic facts are simple. The plaintiffs are former stockholders, some of whom were also the controlling directors, of Boston Electro Steel Casting, Inc. (BESCO). For convenience they will be called stockholders, directors, or, collectively, plaintiffs. The defendant was the president, general manager and a director of BESCO.

In early 1956, following a directors' meeting on December 27, 1955, defendant purchased plaintiffs' stock (virtually all of the outstanding stock of the company) for approximately $40,000. In December 1957 he sold it for $700,000. Suit was brought in October 1958. Plaintiffs' action rests upon a statement by the defendant admittedly made at the December 27 meeting in response to a question by one of the directors. Asked whether he "knew of any material change in the affairs of the company or in the past months which could cause us to have any different opinion about the company," his answer was, "There was none, it was about the same." For convenience we will call this the representation. Trial was had without jury. The district court found the representation consciously and materially false and, to the degree hereinafter set forth, that plaintiffs relied on it, and awarded as damages defendant's net profits. Defendant appeals.

[The court discusses at length whether the action was timely; whether the defendant's representation was false; whether it was fraudulent; and whether it was relied upon by the plaintiffs. Each of these points was debatable, but the judgment of the district court is ultimately affirmed in all these respects.]

We turn to the remedy. With respect to damages we draw a distinction between cases where, by fraud, one is caused to buy something that one would not have bought or would not have bought at that price, and where, by fraud one is induced to convey property to the fraudulent party. In the former case the damages are to be reckoned solely by "the difference between the real value of the property at the date of its sale to the plaintiffs and the price paid for it, with interest from that date, and, in addition, such outlays as were legitimately attributable to the defendant's conduct, but not damages covering 'the expected fruits of an unrealized speculation.'" Sigafus v. Porter, 1900, 179 U.S. 116, 125. On the other hand, if the property is not bought from, but sold to the fraudulent party, future accretions not foreseeable at the time of the transfer even on the true facts, and hence speculative, are subject to another factor, viz., that they accrued to the fraudulent party. It may, as in the case at bar, be entirely speculative whether, had plaintiffs not sold, the series of fortunate occurrences would have happened in the same way, and to their same profit. However, there can be no speculation but that the defendant actually made the profit and, once it is found that he acquired the property by fraud, that the profit was the proximate consequence of the fraud, whether foreseeable or not. It is more appropriate to give the defrauded party the benefit even of windfalls than to let the fraudulent party keep them. See Marcus v. Otis, 2 Cir., 1948, 168 F.2d 649, 660, 169 F.2d 148. We may accept defendant's position that there was no fiduciary relationship and that he was dealing at arm's length. Nonetheless, it is simple equity that a wrongdoer should disgorge his fraudulent enrichment. Falk v. Hoffman, 1922, 233 N.Y. 199, 135 N.E. 243 (per Cardozo, J.); 4 Scott, Trusts §§507, 508, 508.1 (2d ed. 1956); Restatement, Restitution §§151, 202, Comments *b, c* (1937); [R3RUE §13].

There are, of course, limits to this principle. If an artist acquired paints by fraud and used them in producing a valuable portrait we would not suggest that the defrauded party would be entitled to the portrait, or to the proceeds of its sale. However, those limits are not reached in the case at bar. In answers to interrogatories defendant stated that following the acquisition he did nothing different, and worked no harder than he had before. In his pretrial memorandum he stated that the company's "turnaround" was due to price rises, increased efficiency, and an improvement in the business cycle particularly affecting BESCO's customers. Since defendant received his salary for his personal efforts, which would have been his regular duty, no extraordinary gains in the company's affairs attributable to himself fall within the principle suggested by our artist hypothetical.

Securities fraud "disgorgement"

1. The term "disgorgement" has become a familiar label for a particular form of restitution: a judicial order that requires a wrongdoing defendant to surrender wrongful gains, even (in fact, particularly) when those gains exceed any quantifiable injury from the defendant's misconduct. The term came into current use in securities cases, though a liability to surrender unjust gains has nothing in particular to do with securities violations. Rather it is the central focus of a major branch of the law of restitution and the theme of many of the cases in this chapter, epitomized by the rule that "a person is not permitted to profit by his own wrong." (R3RUE §3.)

2. The source of restitution/disgorgement as a remedy for securities fraud depends in part on the difference between private and public remedies. When *Janigan v. Taylor* held that a fraud victim's restitution claim was necessarily part of the victim's (implied) private right of action for fraud under Rule 10b-5, the court found its authority in the same principles of unjust enrichment that explain recovery in a case like *Ward v. Taggart*. When SEC lawsuits under the 1934 Act began to seek disgorgement of the profits from securities fraud—there being nothing in the statute to authorize such a remedy—the federal courts held that their own "inherent" and "historic" equity powers included a power to fashion appropriate remedies, and that disgorgement in securities cases was obviously an appropriate remedy:

> Clearly the provision requiring the disgorging of proceeds received in connection with the [securities violation] was a proper exercise of the district court's equity powers. The effective enforcement of the federal securities laws requires that the SEC be able to make violations unprofitable. The deterrent effect of an SEC enforcement action would be greatly undermined if securities law violators were not required to disgorge illicit profits. As Judge Waterman said in SEC v. Texas Gulf Sulphur Co., 446 F.2d at 1308: "It would severely defeat the purposes of the Act if a violator of Rule 10b-5 were allowed to retain the profits from his violation."

SEC v. Manor Nursing Centers, Inc., 458 F.2d 1082, 1104 (2d Cir. 1972). The availability of restitution has since been extended to administrative—that is, nonjudicial—enforcement proceedings, where there is naturally no "inherent equity power" on the part of the agency to shape necessary remedies. By an amendment to the 1934 Act (adopted in 2000), Congress authorized the SEC and other agencies to "enter an order requiring accounting and disgorgement" in addition to imposing penalties for violations. 15 U.S.C. §78u-2(e).

3. According to *Janigan v. Taylor*, "If an artist acquired paints by fraud and used them in producing a valuable portrait we would not suggest that the defrauded party would be entitled to the portrait, or to the proceeds of its sale." Why not? What *would* be the appropriate remedy for the defrauded party?

4. Most equitable remedies in restitution (such as constructive trust) confer rights in identifiable ("traceable") assets: specific property that was previously misappropriated, or the "product" or proceeds thereof. By contrast, the "disgorgement" of ill-gotten gains—in cases as different as *Olwell v. Nye & Nissen Co.*, *Ward v. Taggart*, and *Janigan v. Taylor*—requires no identification or tracing of specific misappropriated property. If the starting principle is that "a person is not permitted to profit by his own wrong," the case for restitution requires a showing of *causation*—that defendant has been enriched in consequence of his wrongdoing, and in what amount—but not the identification of any particular property in the hands of the defendant.

5. The question of causation becomes prominent in measuring the profits of securities fraud. In SEC v. MacDonald, 699 F.2d 47 (1st Cir. 1983), the Commission sought to compel the disgorgement of gains from insider trading realized by one MacDonald, chairman of a company called RIT. The facts were simple. At a meeting of the RIT board on December 15, 1975, MacDonald learned of material, nonpublic information favorable to the near-term prospects of the company. On December 16, MacDonald's wife purchased 100 shares of RIT at 4¼. On December 23, MacDonald himself purchased an additional 9,500 shares at 4⅝. RIT announced its good news in a press release issued December 24. "The price of RIT stock then jumped from 4⅝ to 5½ in two days of trading—a rise of 19%—and closed the year at 5¾. Defendant held on to the stock until 1977 when it was sold at an average price of over $10 per share." The issue on appeal was not the possibility of a disgorgement remedy, but the measure of unjust enrichment:

> The district court ordered defendant to disgorge, for restitution to defrauded shareholders, the sum of $53,012 representing the profits he realized upon reselling the 9,600 shares of stock in early 1977 at roughly $10 per share. The court noted that since the essence of defendant's inside information was made public on December 24, 1975, "any changes in the market after a fairly reasonable period of time after the 24th of December were because of other developments." But it felt that it would be "inequitable to permit the defendant to retain the benefits of a bargain that was clearly illegal, and that he should be required to disgorge the entire profits." Defendant complains.

would measure assessments by purely fortuitous circumstances. If two fraudulent insiders bought at the same time and price, but, well after public disclosure, sold at different times and prices, their assessments would be measured by their selling dates, choices they made entirely independent of the fraud. To call the additional profits made by the insider who held until the price went higher "ill-gotten gains," or "unjust enrichment," is merely to give a dog a bad name and hang him.

Rejecting this outcome, the appellate court looked for a measure of unjust enrichment that would yield "consistent" results in a number of situations:

We put four hypotheticals, predicated on the assumption that an insider fraudulently bought shares at $4.00, and that, throughout the entire month after the undisclosed information became public, the stock sold at $5.00:

(1) Insider sold forthwith for $5.00.
(2) Stock declined thereafter and insider sold at $3.00.
(3) Stock rose a year later to $10.00, but then declined, and insider ultimately sold at $3.00.
(4) When the stock rose to $10.00, insider sold at $10.00.

What is the implied solution to each of the court's hypotheticals?

C. INFRINGEMENT AND THE LIKE

Sheldon v. Metro-Goldwyn Pictures Corp.
309 U.S. 390 (1940)

Mr. Chief Justice HUGHES delivered the opinion of the Court.

The questions presented are whether, in computing an award of profits against an infringer of a copyright, there may be an apportionment so as to give to the owner of the copyright only that part of the profits found to be attributable to the use of the copyrighted material as distinguished from what the infringer himself has supplied, and, if so, whether the evidence affords a proper basis for the apportionment decreed in this case.

Petitioners' complaint charged infringement of their play "Dishonored Lady" by respondents' motion picture "Letty Lynton," and sought an injunction and an accounting of profits. The Circuit Court of Appeals, reversing the District Court, found and enjoined the infringement and directed an accounting. 2 Cir., 81 F.2d 49. Thereupon the District Court confirmed with slight modifications the report of a special master which awarded to petitioners all the net profits made by respondents from their exhibitions of the motion picture, amounting to $587,604.37. D.C., 26 F. Supp. 134, 136. The Circuit Court of Appeals reversed, holding that there should be an apportionment and fixing petitioners' share of the net profits at one-fifth. 2 Cir., 106 F.2d 45, 51. In view of the importance of the question, which appears to be one of first impression in the application of the copyright law, we granted certiorari.

Petitioners' play "Dishonored Lady" was based upon the trial in Scotland, in 1857, of Madeleine Smith for the murder of her lover—a *cause célèbre* included in the series of "Notable British Trials" which was published in 1927. The play was copyrighted as an unpublished work in 1930, and was produced here and abroad. Respondents took the title of their motion picture "Letty Lynton" from a novel of that name written by an English author, Mrs. Belloc Lowndes, and published in 1930. That novel was also based upon the story of Madeleine Smith, and the motion picture rights [to the novel] were bought by respondents. There had been negotiations for the motion picture rights in petitioners' play [as well], and the price had been fixed at $30,000, but these negotiations fell through.

As the Court of Appeals found, respondents in producing the motion picture in question worked over old material: "the general skeleton was already in the public demesne. A wanton girl kills her lover to free herself for a better match; she is brought to trial for the murder and escapes." (106 F.2d 50.) But not content with the mere use of that basic plot, respondents resorted to petitioners' copyrighted play. They were not innocent offenders. From comparison and analysis, the Court of Appeals concluded that they had "deliberately lifted the play"; their "borrowing was a deliberate plagiarism." It is from that standpoint that we approach the questions now raised.

Respondents contend that the material taken by infringement contributed in but a small measure to the production and success of the motion picture. They say that they themselves contributed the main factors in producing the large net profits; that is, the popular actors, the scenery, and the expert producers and directors. Both courts below have sustained this contention.

The District Court (26 F. Supp. 141) thought it "punitive and unjust" to award all the net profits to petitioners. The court said that, if that were done, petitioners would receive the profits that the "motion picture stars" had made for the picture "by their dramatic talent and the drawing power of their reputations." "The directors who supervised the production of the picture and the experts who filmed it also contributed in piling up these tremendous net profits." The court thought an allowance to petitioners of 25 percent of these profits "could be justly fixed as a limit beyond which complainants would be receiving profits in no way attributable to the use of their play in the production of the picture." But, though holding these views, the District Court awarded all the net profits to petitioners, feeling bound by the decision of the Court of Appeals in Dam v. Kirk La Shelle Co., 2 Cir., 175 F. 902, 903, a decision which the Court of Appeals has now overruled.

The Court of Appeals was satisfied that but a small part of the net profits was attributable to the infringement, and, fully recognizing the difficulty in finding a satisfactory standard, the court decided that there should be an apportionment and that it could fairly be made. The court was resolved "to avoid the one certainly unjust course of giving the plaintiffs everything, because the defendants cannot with certainty compute their own share." The court would not deny "the one fact that stands undoubted," and, making the best estimate it could, it fixed petitioners' share at one-fifth of the net profits, considering that to be a figure "which will favor the plaintiffs in every reasonable chance of error."

Petitioners insist fundamentally that there can be no apportionment of profits in a suit for a copyright infringement; that it is forbidden both by the statute and the decisions of this Court. We find this basic argument to be untenable.

The Copyright Act in Section 25(b) provides that an infringer shall be liable —

> (b) To pay to the copyright proprietor such damages as the copyright proprietor may have suffered due to the infringement, as well as all the profits which the infringer shall have made from such infringement . . . or in lieu of actual damages and profits such damages as to the court shall appear to be just . . . .

We agree with petitioners that the "in lieu" clause is not applicable here, as the profits have been proved and the only question is as to their apportionment.

Petitioners stress the provision for recovery of "all" the profits, but this is plainly qualified by the words "which the infringer shall have made from such infringement." This provision in purpose is cognate to that for the recovery of "such damages as the copyright proprietor may have suffered due to the infringement." The purpose is thus to provide just compensation for the wrong, not to impose a penalty by giving to the copyright proprietor profits which are not attributable to the infringement.

Prior to the Copyright Act of 1909 there had been no statutory provision for the recovery of profits, but that recovery had been allowed in equity both in copyright and patent cases as appropriate equitable relief incident to a decree for an injunction. Stevens v. Gladding, 17 How. 447, 455. That relief had been given in accordance with the principles governing equity jurisdiction, not to inflict punishment but to prevent an unjust enrichment by allowing injured complainants to claim "that which, *ex aequo et bono*, is theirs, and nothing beyond this." Livingston v. Woodworth, 15 How. 546, 560. Statutory provision for the recovery of profits in patent cases was enacted in 1870. The principle which was applied both prior to this statute and later was thus stated in the leading case of Tilghman v. Proctor, 125 U.S. 136, 146:

> The infringer is liable for actual, not for possible, gains. The profits, therefore, which he must account for, are not those which he might

reasonably have made, but those which he did make, by the use of the plaintiff's invention; or, in other words, the fruits of the advantage which he derived from the use of that invention over what he would have had in using other means then open to the public and adequate to enable him to obtain an equally beneficial result. If there was no such advantage in his use of the plaintiff's invention, there can be no decree for profits, and the plaintiff's only remedy is by an action at law for damages.

Petitioners invoke the cases of Callaghan v. Myers, 128 U.S. 617, and Belford, Clarke & Co. v. Scribner, 144 U.S. 488. In the *Callaghan* case, the copyright of a reporter of judicial decisions was sustained with respect to the portions of the books of which he was the author, although he had no exclusive right in the judicial opinions. On an accounting for the profits made by an infringer, the Court allowed the deduction from the selling price of the actual and legitimate manufacturing cost. With reference to the published matter to which the copyright did not extend, the Court found it impossible to separate the profits on that from the profits on the other. And in view of that impossibility, the defendant, being responsible for the blending of the lawful with the unlawful, had to abide the consequences, as in the case of one who has wrongfully produced a confusion of goods. A similar impossibility was encountered in Belford, Clarke & Co. v. Scribner, *supra*, a case of a copyright of a book containing recipes for the household. The infringing books were largely compilations of these recipes, "the matter and language" being "the same as the complainant's in every substantial sense," but so distributed through the defendants' books that it was "almost impossible to separate the one from the other." The Court ruled that when the copyrighted portions are so intermingled with the rest of the piratical work "that they cannot well be distinguished from it," the entire profits realized by the defendants will be given to the plaintiff.

We agree with the court below that these cases do not decide that no apportionment of profits can be had where it is clear that all the profits are not due to the use of the copyrighted material, and the evidence is sufficient to provide a fair basis of division so as to give to the copyright proprietor all the profits that can be deemed to have resulted from the use of what belonged to him. Both the Copyright Act and our decisions leave the matter to the appropriate exercise of the equity jurisdiction upon an accounting to determine the profits "which the infringer shall have made from such infringement."

The principle as to apportionment of profits was clearly stated in the case of Dowagiac Mfg. Company v. Minnesota Moline Plow Co., 235 U.S. 641, 646 (1915)—a case which received great consideration. The Court there said:

> We think the evidence, although showing that the invention was meritorious and materially contributed to the value of the infringing drills as marketable machines, made it clear that their value was not entirely attributable to the invention, but was due in a substantial degree to the unpatented parts or features.

In so far as the profits from the infringing sales were attributable to the patented improvements they belonged to the plaintiff, and in so far as they were due to other parts or features they belonged to the defendants. But as the drills were sold in completed and operative form, the profits resulting from the several parts were necessarily commingled. It was essential, therefore, that they be separated or apportioned between what was covered by the patent and what was not covered by it; for, as was said in Westinghouse Electric & Mfg. Co. v. Wagner Electric & Mfg. Co., 225 U.S. 604, 615 (1912): "In such case, if plaintiff's patent only created a part of the profits, he is only entitled to recover that part of the net gains."

Petitioners stress the point that respondents have been found guilty of deliberate plagiarism, but we perceive no ground for saying that in awarding profits to the copyright proprietor as a means of compensation, the court may make an award of profits which have been shown not to be due to the infringement. That would be not to do equity but to inflict an unauthorized penalty. To call the infringer a trustee *ex maleficio* merely indicates "a mode of approach and an imperfect analogy by which the wrongdoer will be made to hand over the proceeds of his wrong." Larson Company v. Wm. Wrigley, Jr., Co., 277 U.S. 97, 99, 100 (1928) (Holmes, J.). He is in the position of one who has confused his own gains with those which belong to another. Where there is a commingling of gains, he must abide the consequences, unless he can make a separation of the profits so as to assure to the injured party all that justly belongs to him. When such an apportionment has been fairly made, the copyright proprietor receives all the profits which have been gained through the use of the infringing material, and that is all that the statute authorizes and equity sanctions.

Both courts below have held in this case that but a small part of the profits were due to the infringement, and, accepting that fact and the principle that an apportionment may be had if the evidence justifies it, we pass to the consideration of the basis of the actual apportionment which has been allowed.

The controlling fact in the determination of the apportionment was that the profits had been derived, not from the mere performance of a copyrighted play, but from the exhibition of a motion picture which had its distinctive profit-making features, apart from the use of any infringing material, by reason of the expert and creative operations involved in its production and direction. In that aspect the case has a certain resemblance to that of a patent infringement, where the infringer has created profits by the addition of non-infringing and valuable improvements. And, in this instance, it plainly appeared that what respondents had contributed accounted for by far the larger part of their gains.

Respondents had stressed the fact that, although the negotiations had not ripened into a purchase, the price which had been set for the motion picture rights in "Dishonored Lady" had been but $30,000. And respondents' witnesses cited numerous instances where the value, according to sales, of motion picture rights had been put at relatively small sums. But the court below rejected as a criterion the price put upon the motion picture rights, as a bargain had not been concluded and the inferences were too doubtful. The court also ruled that respondents could not count the effect of "their standing and reputation in the industry." The court permitted respondents to be credited "only with such factors as they bought and paid for: the actors, the scenery, the producers, the directors and the general overhead."

The testimony showed quite clearly that in the creation of profits from the exhibition of a motion picture, the talent and popularity of the "motion picture stars" generally constitutes the main drawing power of the picture, and that this is especially true where the title of the picture is not identified with any well-known play or novel. Here, it appeared that the picture did not bear the title of the copyrighted play and that it was not presented or advertised as having any connection whatever with the play. It was also shown that the picture had been "sold," that is, licensed to almost all the exhibitors as identified simply with the name of a popular motion picture actress before even the title "Letty Lynton" was used. In addition to the drawing power of the "motion picture stars," other factors in creating the profits were found in the artistic conceptions and in the expert supervision and direction of the various processes which made possible the composite result with its attractiveness to the public.

Upon these various considerations, with elaboration of detail, respondents' expert witnesses gave their views as to the extent to which the use of the copyrighted material had contributed to the profits in question. The underlying facts as to the factors in successful production and exhibition of motion pictures were abundantly proved, but, as the court below recognized, the ultimate estimates of the expert witnesses were only the expression "of their very decided opinions." These witnesses were in complete agreement that the portion of the profits attributable to the use of the copyrighted play in the circumstances here disclosed was very small. Their estimates given in percentages of receipts ran from five to twelve percent; the estimate apparently most favored was ten percent as the limit. One finally expressed the view that the play contributed nothing. There was no rebuttal. But the court below was not willing to accept the experts' testimony "at its face value." The court felt that is must make an award "which by no possibility shall be too small." Desiring to give petitioners the benefit of every doubt, the court allowed for the contribution of the play twenty percent of the net profits.

What we said in the *Dowagiac* case is equally true here—that what is required is not mathematical exactness but only a reasonable approximation. Equity is concerned with making a fair apportionment so that neither party will have what justly belongs to the other.

The judgment of the Circuit Court of Appeals is affirmed.

———————————

Attributable to the underlying wrong

1. As indicated in *Sheldon*, courts allowed the recovery of infringers' profits in patent and copyright cases before the remedy was spelled out in the

statutes—"not to inflict punishment but to prevent an unjust enrichment." Compare the judicial response by which "disgorgement" was added to the available remedies for securities violations, as illustrated by the preceding materials.

2. Even with a perfect apportionment, remember that the plaintiff is asking for a share of the defendant's profits (rather than damages) only because a share of profits is larger than the value of what the defendant misappropriated. The film rights to the play "Dishonored Lady" were presumably not worth more than $30,000—the price Sheldon had been asking. (MGM had bought the film rights to "Gone With the Wind" for $50,000.) Yet the 20 percent of MGM's net profits awarded to Sheldon amounted to $117,520. Is it fair to put MGM to work for Sheldon in this way? Consider these observations in a more recent copyright case:

> It is true that if the infringer makes greater profits than the copyright owner lost, because the infringer is a more efficient producer than the owner or sells in a different market, the owner is allowed to capture the additional profit even though it does not represent a loss to him. It may seem wrong to penalize the infringer for his superior efficiency and give the owner a windfall. But it discourages infringement. By preventing infringers from obtaining any net profit it makes any would-be infringer negotiate directly with the owner of a copyright that he wants to use, rather than bypass the market by stealing the copyright and forcing the owner to seek compensation from the courts for his loss. Since the infringer's gain might exceed the owner's loss, especially as loss is measured by a court, limiting damages to that loss would not effectively deter this kind of forced exchange. This analysis also implies that some of the "windfall" may actually be profit that the owner would have obtained from licensing his copyright to the infringer had the infringer sought a license.

Taylor v. Meirick, 712 F.2d 1112, 1120 (7th Cir. 1983) (Posner, J.).

3. Since 1946, the statutory remedies for patent infringement no longer impose liability for profits in most cases—probably because the problems of attribution (as required by *Dowagiac*) came to be regarded as too difficult and time-consuming. Federal statutes continue to provide for recovery of profits from infringement of design patents, copyrights, and trademarks. The problem of attribution and accounting imposed by *Sheldon* is a necessary part of any such case, even if—as Judge Learned Hand had already warned—"Strictly and literally, it is true that the problem is insoluble." Sheldon v. Metro-Goldwyn Pictures Corp., 106 F.2d 45, 48 (2d Cir. 1939). Is there any reason why federal statutes should allow the recovery of infringers' profits for copyrights and trademarks but not patents? See Caprice L. Roberts, *The Case for Restitution and Unjust Enrichment Remedies in Patent Law*, 14 Lewis & Clark L. Rev. 653 (2010).

4. The attribution and accounting issues brought to the forefront in *Sheldon* are not limited to cases of infringement. R3RUE §51 manages to describe the overall objective of disgorgement remedies in fairly simple terms:

(4) [T]he unjust enrichment of a conscious wrongdoer, or of a default-ing fiduciary without regard to notice or fault, is the net profit attribut-able to the underlying wrong. The object of restitution in such cases is to eliminate profit from wrongdoing while avoiding, so far as possible, the imposition of a penalty. Restitution remedies that pursue this object are often called "disgorgement" or "accounting."

But in the very next subsection, it leaves the door wide open to accounting controversies and a pervasive judicial discretion:

(5) In determining net profit the court may apply such tests of causa-tion and remoteness, may make such apportionments, may recognize such credits or deductions, and may assign such evidentiary burdens, as reason and fairness dictate, consistent with the object of restitution as specified in subsection (4).

Applying this test, how would you decide the following questions of apportionment?

(a) Hollywood studios used to own a lot of movie theaters. Are plaintiffs entitled to a share of the profits on ticket sales for "Letty Lynton" in theaters owned by MGM's corporate affiliates? What about profits from their conces-sion stands while "Letty Lynton" was showing? What about ticket and popcorn sales in theaters that are independently owned?

(b) In calculating MGM's net profits from "Letty Lynton," the special mas-ter credited the defendants "only with such factors as they bought and paid for: the actors, the scenery, the producers, the directors and the general overhead." Does "general overhead" include expenses that MGM would have incurred with or without "Letty Lynton"—for example, salaries for janitors or studio executives? Assuming we have a figure for MGM's general overhead for 1932, what proportion should be charged against revenues from "Letty Lynton"?

(c) MGM paid corporate income tax of 30 percent in 1932. Should MGM be allowed to deduct from its liability to Sheldon the tax previously paid by MGM on Sheldon's 20 percent share of the profits?

Farnsworth, *Restitution* 117-118 (2014):

The most pervasive challenge in cases involving intellectual property is sep-aration of what the defendant gained by infringing the plaintiff's rights from what the defendant would have gained legitimately without the infringement. In some cases this may involve complex problems of accounting. Thus in one famous case, *Sheldon v. Metro-Goldwyn Pictures Corp.*, the defendants were found liable for deliberate infringement of the plaintiff's copyrighted play. Determining the amount of net profit earned by the infringing movie—one of dozens released by the studio that year—was a challenging task by itself, involving the allocation of overhead expenses between one production and another. Assume this number has been found; that still is not the end of the task, because the plaintiff must show what proportion of those net profits were attributable to the plaintiff's play, as opposed to all the other elements that made the film profitable: the stars, the advertising, and so on. Such calculations may be impossible to make with any certainty and so will often be decided as a result of presumptions about the burden of proof. These tend to resolve doubts against the wrongdoer, and so may force him, in effect, to pay more than he really gained. (This was almost certainly the case in *Sheldon*.) But such results accord with the longstanding legal principle that a defendant should not benefit from uncertainties that result from his own misconduct.

O'Brien v. Pabst Sales Co.
124 F.2d 167 (5th Cir. 1941)

HUTCHESON, Circuit Judge.

Plaintiff, in physique as in prowess as a hurler, a modern David, is a famous football player. Defendant, in bulk, if not in brass and vulnerability, a modern Goliath, is a distributor of Pabst beer. Plaintiff, among other honors received during the year 1938, was picked by Grantland Rice on his Collier's All American Football Team. Defendant, as a part of its advertising publicity for 1939, following its custom of getting out football schedule calendars, placed an order with the Inland Lithographing Company, to prepare for and furnish to it, 35,000 Pabst 1939 football calendars.

At the top of the calendar, as thus printed and circulated, were the words "Pabst Blue Ribbon." Directly underneath were the words "Football Calendar, 1939"; to the left of these words was a photograph of O'Brien in football uniform characteristically poised for the throw; to the right of them was a glass having on it the words "Pabst Breweries, Blue Ribbon Export Beer"; and to the right of the glass still, a bottle of beer, having on it "Pabst Blue Ribbon Beer." Directly below these was the intercollegiate football schedule for 1939, and in the center of the calendar were pictures, including that of O'Brien, of Grantland Rice's All American Football Team for 1938. Near the bottom was the schedule of the national football league and on the very bottom margin, were the words "Pabst Famous Blue Ribbon Beer." Claiming that this use of his photograph as part of defendant's advertising was an invasion of his right of privacy and that he had been damaged thereby, plaintiff brought this suit.

The defenses were three. The first was that if the mere use of one's picture in truthful and respectable advertising would be an actionable invasion of privacy in the case of a private person, the use here was not, as to plaintiff, such an invasion, for as a result of his activities and prowess in football, his chosen field, and their nationwide and deliberate publicizing with his consent and in his interest, he was no longer, as to them, a private but a public person, and as to their additional publication he had no right of privacy. The second defense was that plaintiff, in his own interest and that of Texas Christian University, had posed for and had authorized the publicity department of T.C.U. to distribute his picture and biographical data to newspapers, magazines, sports journals and the public generally, and that the particular picture whose use is complained of had been in due course obtained from and payment for it had been made to the T.C.U. publicity department. Third, no injury to appellant's person, property or reputation had been or could be shown, and there was therefore no basis for a recovery.

The testimony fully supported these defenses. It showed that plaintiff, then 23 years old, had been playing football for 14 years, four years of that time with Texas Christian University, and two with the Philadelphia Eagles, a professional football team. During that period he had received many and distinguished trophies and honors as an outstanding player of the game. He had in fact been the recipient of practically every worthwhile football trophy and recognition, being picked by Grantland Rice on his Collier's All American Football Team, and by Liberty on their All Players All American Team, and many other so-called All American Football Teams. Plaintiff testified that he had not given permission to use his picture, indeed had not known of the calendar until some time after its publication and circulation; that he was a member of the Allied Youth of America, the main theme of which was the doing away with alcohol among young people; that he had had opportunities to sell his endorsement for beer and alcoholic beverages and had refused it; and that he was greatly embarrassed and humiliated when he saw the calendar and realized that his face and name was associated with publicity for the sale of beer. But he did not, nor did anyone for him, testify to a single fact which would show that he had suffered pecuniary damage in any amount. In addition, on cross-examination he testified: that he had repeatedly posed for photographs for use in publicizing himself and the T.C.U. football team; that Mr. Ridings, director of publicity and news service of T.C.U., without obtaining particular, but with his general, approval and consent, had furnished numberless photographs to various people, periodicals and magazines; and that the pictures of those composing Grantland Rice's All American Football Team which appeared on the calendar, including his own picture, were first publicized in Collier's magazine, a magazine of widest circulation.

On defendants' part, it was shown that following the instructions given by the defendant, the calendar company had written to the T.C.U. Director of Publicity for, and obtained from him, the photograph for use in the calendar, paying him $1 therefor, and that the photograph had been used in the belief that the necessary consent to do so had been obtained. The proof that plaintiff had posed for many football pictures for the publicity department of T.C.U. for the purpose of having them widely circulated over the United States was overwhelming and uncontradicted. Mr. Riding, director of publicity, testified that Davey O'Brien was perhaps the most publicized football player of the year 1938-39; that it was the function of his office to permit and increase the publicity of football players; that his office had furnished some 800 photographs of plaintiff to sports editors, magazines, etc.; that if anybody made a request for a picture of O'Brien he would ordinarily grant the request without asking what they were going to do with it; that the picture in the upper left hand corner of the calendar is a very popular picture of O'Brien and perhaps his most famous pose, and that the publicity department had general authority to furnish plaintiff's pictures for publicity purposes but had never knowingly furnished any for use in commercial advertising except with O'Brien's consent and approval.

The District Judge agreed with defendant that no case had been made out. He was of the opinion: that considered from the standpoint merely of an invasion of plaintiff's right of privacy, no case was made out, because plaintiff was an outstanding national football figure and had completely publicized his name and his pictures. He was of the opinion too, that considered from the point of view that the calendar damaged him because it falsely, though only impliedly, represented that plaintiff was a user of or was commending the use of, Pabst beer, no case was made out because nothing in the calendar or football schedule could be reasonably so construed; every fact in it was truthfully stated and there was no representation or suggestion of any kind that O'Brien or any of the other football celebrities whose pictures it showed were beer drinkers or were recommending its drinking to others; the business of making and selling beer is a legitimate and eminently respectable business and people of all walks and views in life, without injury to or reflection upon themselves, drink it, and that any association of O'Brien's picture with a glass of beer could not possibly disgrace or reflect upon or cause him damage. He directed a verdict for defendant.

Assuming then, what is by no means clear, that an action for right of privacy would lie in Texas at the suit of a private person, we think it clear that the action fails; because plaintiff is not such a person and the publicity he got was only that which he had been constantly seeking and receiving; and because the use of the photograph was by permission, and there were no statements or representations made in connection with it, which were or could be either false, erroneous or damaging to plaintiff. Nothing in the majority opinion purports to deal with or express an opinion on the matter dealt with in the dissenting opinion, the right of a person to recover on *quantum meruit*, for the use of his name for advertising purposes. That was not the case pleaded and attempted to be brought. The case was not for the value of plaintiff's name in advertising a product but for damages by way of injury to him in using his name in advertising beer. Throughout the pleadings, the record and the brief, plaintiff has uniformly taken the position that he is not suing for the reasonable value of his endorsement of beer, on the contrary, the whole burden of his pleading and brief is the repeated asseveration, that he would not and did not endorse beer, and the complaint is that he was damaged by the invasion of his privacy in so using his picture as to create the impression that he was endorsing beer.

The judgment was right. It is affirmed.

HOLMES, Circuit Judge (dissenting).

The right of privacy is distinct from the right to use one's name or picture for purposes of commercial advertisement. The latter is a property right that belongs to every one; it may have much or little, or only a nominal, value; but it is a personal right, which may not be violated with impunity.

The great property rights created by the demands of modern methods of advertising are of comparatively recent origin, and may not have been in existence in January 1840, but the common law of Texas is subject to growth and adaptation in the land of its adoption, as well as it was in the country of its origin. The capacity of the common law of Texas "to draw inspiration from every fountain of justice" has not been diminished by time, though a century has passed since its adoption by the legislature of that state.

No one can doubt that commercial advertisers customarily pay for the right to use the name and likeness of a person who has become famous. The evidence in this case shows that appellant refused an offer by a New York beer company of $400 for an endorsement of its beer, and the appellee apparently recognized that it was necessary to obtain the consent of the various football players, because it required that releases be obtained from them. This admittedly was not done. The fact that appellant made this stipulation with the publishers of the calendars may save it from the infliction of punitive damages, but cannot relieve it from the payment of actual damages measured by the value of the unauthorized use of appellant's picture.

The decision of the majority leaves the appellant without remedy for any non-libelous use made of his picture by advertisers of beer, wine, whiskey, patent medicines, or other non-contraband goods, wares, and merchandise. It also places every other famous stage, screen, and athletic star in the same situation. If one is popular and permits publicity to be given to one's talent and accomplishment in any art or sport, commercial advertisers may seize upon such popularity to increase their sales of any lawful article without compensation of any kind for such commercial use of one's name and fame. This is contrary to usage and custom among advertisers in the marts of trade. They are undoubtedly in the habit of buying the right to use one's name or picture to create demand and good will for their merchandise. It is the peculiar excellence of the common law that, by general usage, it is shaped and moulded into new and useful forms

Appellant's pleadings allege facts that entitle him to recover for either a violation of his right of property or right of privacy, and because the court does not think he is entitled to recover for the latter does not relieve us of the duty of deciding whether or not any right of property was violated.

It appears from the complaint that the appellee committed a tort in misappropriating a valuable property right of appellant. Even if forms of action were not abolished, the appellant might seek damages for the tort or waive the tort and sue upon an implied promise to pay the reasonable value of the right appropriated. Appellant has not sought the wrong relief. He was not required to plead the law (ordinarily it is improper to do so); he was only required to state the ultimate facts upon which he relied for relief. If a litigant pleads the wrong law, it is the court's duty nevertheless to apply the correct law to the facts of the case. This was true even before the new rules, and it is doubly true since their adoption.

———————————

Restitution and right of publicity

1. Plainly, the dissenting judge in *O'Brien v. Pabst* better appreciated the significance of this new property right. But the majority opinion demonstrates the way in which the evolving "right of publicity" could hardly be protected without a theory of liability for unjust enrichment. At least some of the time, the owners of patents, copyrights, and trademarks can show damages from infringement in the form of lost sales. By contrast, a heavily-promoted celebrity like Davey O'Brien of T.C.U. could hardly complain about an invasion of privacy; whether he could show injury to reputation from appearing on a beer calendar was evidently in the eye of the beholder. Unjust enrichment is the theory by which O'Brien's rights are vindicated, precisely because it requires no showing of quantifiable harm. It is like trespass to an underground cave, or temporary conversion of an egg-washing machine.

2. Assume that the "right of publicity" is now protected as property, and that T.C.U. had no authority to license its use in the case of Davey O'Brien. Isn't it possible that Pabst's correspondence with the T.C.U. Director of Publicity made Pabst—at worst—an innocent rather than an intentional tortfeasor? What is the measure of Pabst's liability in that case?

———————————

D.   FIDUCIARY OR CONFIDENTIAL RELATION

Keech v. Sandford
Sel. Cas. T. King 61, 25 Eng. Rep. 223 (Ch. 1726)

Lease of a market devised to a trustee for the benefit of an infant; lessor, before expiration of the lease, refuses to renew to the infant; trustee takes it himself, shall be obliged to convey to the infant, and account for the profits.

THE LORD CHANCELLOR (Baron King): I must consider this as a trust for the infant; for I very well see, if a trustee, on the refusal to renew, might have a lease to himself, few trust estates would be renewed to *cestui que use*; though I do not say there is a fraud in this case, yet he should rather have let it run out, than to have had the lease to himself. This may seem hard, that the trustee is the only person of all mankind who might not have the lease: but it is very proper that rule should be strictly pursued, and not in the least relaxed: for it is very obvious what would be the consequence of letting trustees have the lease, on refusal to renew to *cestui que use*. So decreed, that the lease should be assigned to the infant, and that the trustee should be indemnified from any covenants comprised in the lease, and an account of the profits made since the renewal.

Hamberg v. Barsky
355 Pa. 462, 50 A.2d 345 (1947)

STERN, J.

Plaintiff, a registered optometrist, had been occupying for seven years the premises No. 14 South 52nd Street, Philadelphia; his current lease was for a term of one year beginning July 1, 1944. Defendants operate a retail business for the sale of ladies' dresses at several shops in Philadelphia, among them a store at No. 6 South 52nd Street. Being threatened with the loss of their tenancy of the latter premises they thought it would be desirable to obtain a lease of No. 16, which was next door to the premises occupied by plaintiff. Defendant George Barsky, who had been on friendly terms for many years with plaintiff and at one time his employer, met him in the latter part of August, 1944, and told him that he knew the owner of the properties Nos. 14 and 16 very well, and that he, Barsky, was interested in obtaining a lease of No. 16. He told plaintiff to "leave everything" to him; that he would see the owner and "rent both places, and by renting both we will get a better price and we will split the cost," and that, when he made that arrangement, plaintiff could occupy No. 14 and defendants No. 16. Plaintiff replied: "I was going myself [to the owner], but all right." In September, again in October, and again in November, plaintiff telephoned to Barsky inquiring about the progress of the negotiations and was each time assured that the latter was "working on it" and that plaintiff should not "worry about it" but should "leave it" to him. On November 28, 1944 plaintiff received a notice from the agent for the owner notifying him that his lease had been terminated; he reported this to Barsky who assured him that "that doesn't mean anything. I am working on it. Everything is all right." In January Barsky finally confessed to plaintiff that in the course of his negotiations with the owner he had found that he could not rent No. 16 because it was occupied by a soldier whom the owner did not wish to dispossess and accordingly he had leased for himself and his partners the place at No. 14. He followed this announcement with the brazen statement: "Well, Doc, that is good business. If we are sharp enough to outsmart you that is too bad for you."

Barsky denied practically all of these facts, but the chancellor, sustained by the court en banc, accepted the version given by plaintiff and his witnesses. Barsky admits that already on November 14, 1944 he had obtained from the owner a lease of the premises No. 14 South 52nd Street which he took in the name of defendant Thelma Barsky, his wife, the term being for five years and seven months commencing July 1, 1945.

Defendants, on this appeal, pointing out that all the dealings between Barsky and plaintiff consisted of oral conversations, claim that plaintiff is disentitled to relief because of the Statute of Frauds. But it is elementary that these statutes do not apply to constructive trusts or to trusts *ex maleficio.* Indeed, the act expressly provides that "where any conveyance shall be made of any lands or tenements by which a trust or confidence shall or may arise or result by implication or construction of law . . . then and in every such case such trust or confidence shall be of the like force and effect as if this act had not been passed."

Defendants challenge the court's finding that there existed a confidential relationship between Barsky and plaintiff, who, they say, were not in any position toward one another of trustee and *cestui que trust,* guardian and ward, attorney and client, or agent and principal, and were not even *intimate* friends. This contention reveals a misapprehension on their part as to what constitutes, in the eyes of equity, a confidential relationship. It is not limited, as defendants apparently believe, to one which arises from circumstances or relations preceding the occurrence which gives rise to the controversy but may spring from the dealings and conversations between the parties in connection with the very transaction itself. It exists between two persons whenever "one has gained the confidence of the other and purports to act or advise with the other's interest in mind." Restatement, Restitution §166, comment *d*; [R3RUE §43, Comment *f*].

> Confidential relation is not confined to any specific association of the parties; it is one wherein a party is bound to act for the benefit of another, and can take no advantage to himself. It appears when the circumstances make it certain the parties do not deal on equal terms, but, on the one side there is an overmastering influence, or, on the other, weakness, dependence or trust, justifiably reposed; in both an unfair advantage is possible. . . . No precise language can define the limits of the relation or fetter the power of the court to control these conditions. . . . In some cases the confidential relation is a conclusion of law, in others it is a question of fact to be established by the evidence. (citations omitted)

A clearer case of confidential relationship than that revealed in the present record could hardly be imagined. . . .

The present is not the first case in which the courts of this State have been called upon to denounce the betrayal of a confidential relationship similar to that which existed here and to apply the remedy which equity affords. There is a host of authorities all of which announce and enforce the principle that if one be induced to confide in the promise of another that he will acquire property for him or for both of them, and is thereby led to do what otherwise he would have forborne or to forbear what he contemplated to do in order to acquire such property, and the promisor acquires the property in his own name, the attempted denial of the confidence is such a fraud as will operate to convert the promisor into a trustee *ex maleficio*. "A trust will spring from the fraud practiced where one employed to negotiate for another takes advantage of the opportunity to obtain a conveyance to himself." No one can acquire rights in property antagonistic to the person whose interest he has committed himself to protect, nor hold any benefit acquired by fraud or breach of duty; this is one of the fundamental principles of equity jurisprudence.

Decree affirmed; costs to be paid by defendants.

Meinhard v. Salmon
249 N.Y. 458, 164 N.E. 545 (1928)

CARDOZO, Ch. J.

On April 10, 1902, Louisa M. Gerry leased to the defendant Walter J. Salmon the premises known as the Hotel Bristol at the northwest corner of Forty-second street and Fifth avenue in the city of New York. The lease was for a term of twenty years, commencing May 1, 1902, and ending April 30, 1922. The lessee undertook to change the hotel building for use as shops and offices at a cost of $200,000. Alterations and additions were to be accretions to the land.

Salmon, while in course of treaty with the lessor as to the execution of the lease, was in course of treaty with Meinhard, the plaintiff, for the necessary funds. The result was a joint venture with terms embodied in a writing. Meinhard was to pay to Salmon half of the moneys requisite to reconstruct, alter, manage and operate the property. Salmon was to pay to Meinhard 40 percent of the net profits for the first five years of the lease and 50 percent for the years thereafter. If there were losses, each party was to bear them equally. Salmon, however, was to have sole power to "manage, lease, underlet and operate" the building.

The two were coadventurers, subject to fiduciary duties akin to those of partners (King v. Barnes, 109 N. Y. 267). As to this we are all agreed. The heavier weight of duty rested, however, upon Salmon. He was a coadventurer with Meinhard, but he was manager as well. During the early years of the enterprise, the building, reconstructed, was operated at a loss. If the relation had then ended, Meinhard as well as Salmon would have carried a heavy burden. Later the profits became large with the result that for each of the investors there came a rich return. For each, the venture had its phases of fair weather and of foul. The two were in it jointly, for better or for worse.

When the lease was near its end, Elbridge T. Gerry had become the owner of the reversion. He owned much other property in the neighborhood, one lot adjoining the Bristol Building on Fifth avenue and four lots on Forty-second street. He had a plan to lease the entire tract for a long term to some one who would destroy the buildings then existing, and put up another in their place. In the latter part of 1921, he submitted such a project to several capitalists and dealers. He was unable to carry it through with any of them. Then, in January, 1922, with less than four months of the lease to run, he approached the defendant Salmon. The result was a new lease to the Midpoint Realty Company, which is owned and controlled by Salmon, a lease covering the whole tract, and involving a huge outlay. The term is to be twenty years, but successive covenants for renewal will extend it to a maximum of eighty years at the will of either party. The existing buildings may remain unchanged for seven years. They are then to be torn down, and a new building to cost $3,000,000 is to be placed upon the site. The rental, which under the Bristol lease was only $55,000, is to be from $350,000 to $475,000 for the properties so combined. Salmon personally guaranteed the performance by the lessee of the covenants of the new lease until such time as the new building had been completed and fully paid for.

The lease between Gerry and the Midpoint Realty Company was signed and delivered on January 25, 1922. Salmon had not told Meinhard anything about it. Whatever his motive may have been, he had kept the negotiations to himself. Meinhard was not informed even of the bare existence of a project. The first that he knew of it was in February when the lease was an accomplished fact. He then made demand on the defendants that the lease be held in trust as an asset of the venture, making offer upon the trial to share the personal obligations incidental to the guaranty. The demand was followed by refusal, and later by this suit. A referee gave judgment for the plaintiff, limiting the plaintiff's interest in the lease, however, to 25 percent. The limitation was on the theory that the plaintiff's equity was to be restricted to one-half of so much of the value of the lease as was contributed or represented by the occupation of the Bristol site. Upon cross-appeals to the Appellate Division, the judgment was modified so as to enlarge the equitable interest to one-half of the whole lease. With this enlargement of plaintiff's interest, there went, of course, a corresponding enlargement of his attendant obligations. The case is now here on an appeal by the defendants.

Joint adventurers, like copartners, owe to one another, while the enterprise continues, the duty of the finest loyalty. Many forms of conduct permissible in a workaday world for those acting at arm's length, are forbidden to those bound by fiduciary ties. A trustee is held to something stricter than the morals of the market place. Not honesty alone, but the punctilio of an honor the most sensitive, is then the standard of behavior. As to this there has developed a tradition that is unbending and inveterate. Uncompromising rigidity has been the attitude of courts of equity when petitioned to undermine the rule of undi-vided loyalty by the "disintegrating erosion" of particular exceptions (Wendt v. Fischer, 243 N. Y. 439, 444). Only thus has the level of conduct for fiduciaries been kept at a level higher than that trodden by the crowd. It will not con-sciously be lowered by any judgment of this court.

The owner of the reversion, Mr. Gerry, had vainly striven to find a tenant who would favor his ambitious scheme of demolition and construction. Baffled in the search, he turned to the defendant Salmon in possession of the Bristol, the keystone of the project. He figured to himself beyond a doubt that the man in possession would prove a likely customer. To the eye of an observer, Salmon held the lease as owner in his own right, for himself and no one else. In fact he held it as a fiduciary, for himself and another, sharers in a common venture. If this fact had been proclaimed, if the lease by its terms had run in favor of a partnership, Mr. Gerry, we may fairly assume, would have laid before the partners, and not merely before one of them, his plan of reconstruction. The pre-emptive privilege, or, better, the pre-emptive opportunity, that was thus an incident of the enterprise, Salmon appropriated to himself in secrecy and silence. He might have warned Meinhard that the plan had been submitted, and that either would be free to compete for the award. If he had done this, we do not need to say whether he would have been under a duty, if successful in the competition, to hold the lease so acquired for the benefit of a venture then about to end, and thus prolong by indirection its responsibilities and duties. The trouble about his conduct is that he excluded his coadventurer from any chance to compete, from any chance to enjoy the opportunity for benefit that had come to him alone by virtue of his agency. This chance, if nothing more, he was under a duty to concede. The price of its denial is an extension of the trust at the option and for the benefit of the one whom he excluded.

No answer is it to say that the chance would have been of little value even if seasonably offered. Such a calculus of probabilities is beyond the science of the chancery. Salmon, the real estate operator, might have been preferred to Meinhard, the woolen merchant. On the other hand, Meinhard might have offered better terms, or reinforced his offer by alliance with the wealth of oth-ers. Perhaps he might even have persuaded the lessor to renew the Bristol lease alone, postponing for a time, in return for higher rentals, the improvement of adjoining lots. We know that even under the lease as made the time for the enlargement of the building was delayed for seven years. All these opportuni-ties were cut away from him through another's intervention. He knew that Salmon was the manager. As the time drew near for the expiration of the lease, he would naturally assume from silence, if from nothing else, that the lessor was willing to extend it for a term of years, or at least to let it stand as a lease from year to year. Not impossibly the lessor would have done so, whatever his protestations of unwillingness, if Salmon had not given assent to a proj-ect more attractive. At all events, notice of termination, even if not necessary, might seem, not unreasonably, to be something to be looked for, if the busi-ness was over and another tenant was to enter. In the absence of such notice, the matter of an extension was one that would naturally be attended to by the manager of the enterprise, and not neglected altogether. At least, there was nothing in the situation to give warning to anyone that while the lease was still in being, there had come to the manager an offer of extension which he had locked within his breast to be utilized by himself alone. The very fact that Salmon was in control with exclusive powers of direction charged him the more obviously with the duty of disclosure, since only through disclosure could opportunity be equalized. If he might cut off renewal by a purchase for his own benefit when four months were to pass before the lease would have an end, he might do so with equal right while there remained as many years. He might steal a march on his comrade under cover of the darkness, and then hold the captured ground. Loyalty and comradeship are not so easily abjured.

Little profit will come from a dissection of the precedents. None precisely similar is cited in the briefs of counsel. What is similar in many, or so it seems to us, is the animating principle. Equity refuses to confine within the bounds of classified transactions its precept of a loyalty that is undivided and unselfish. Certain at least it is that a "man obtaining his *locus standi*, and his opportunity for making such arrangements, by the position he occupies as a partner, is bound by his obligation to his co-partners in such dealings not to separate his interest from theirs, but, if he acquires any benefit, to communicate it to them" (Cassels v. Stewart, 6 App. Cas. 64, 73). Certain it is also that there may be no abuse of special opportunities growing out of a special trust as manager or agent (Matter of Biss, 1903, 2 Ch. 40; Clegg v. Edmondson, 8 D. M. & G. 787, 807 [44 Eng. Rep. 593 (Ch. 1857)]). If conflicting inferences are possible as to abuse or opportunity, the trier of the facts must make the choice between them. There can be no revision in this court unless the choice is clearly wrong. It is no answer for the fiduciary to say "that he was not bound to risk his money as he did, or to go into the enterprise at all" (Beatty v. Guggenheim Exploration Co., 225 N. Y. 380, 385 [1919]). "He might have kept out of it altogether, but if he went in, he could not withhold from his employer the benefit of the bargain." (*Id.*). A constructive trust is then the remedial device through which preference of self is made subordinate to loyalty to others. (*Id.*). Many and varied are its phases and occasions (Selwyn & Co. v. Waller, 212 N. Y. 507, 512 [1914]; Robinson v. Jewett, 116 N. Y. 40 [1889]; *cf.* Tournier v. Nat. Prov. & Union Bank, 1924, 1 K. B. 461).

We have no thought to hold that Salmon was guilty of a conscious purpose to defraud. Very likely he assumed in all good faith that with the approaching end of the venture he might ignore his coadventurer and take the extension for himself. He had given to the enterprise time and labor as well as money. He had made it a success. Meinhard, who had given money, but neither time nor labor, had already been richly paid. There might seem to be something grasping in his insistence upon more. Such recriminations are not unusual when coadventurers fall out. They are not without their force if conduct is to be judged by the common standards of competitors. That is not to say that they have pertinency here. Salmon had put himself in a position in which thought of self was to be renounced, however hard the abnegation. He was much more than a coadventurer. He was a managing coadventurer. For him and for those like him, the rule of undivided loyalty is relentless and supreme. A different question would be here if there were lacking any nexus of relation between the business conducted by the manager and the opportunity brought to him as an incident of management (Dean v. MacDowell, 8 Ch. D. 345, 354 [1878]; Aas v. Benham, 1891, 2 Ch. 244, 258; Latta v. Kilbourn, 150 U. S. 524 [1893]). For this problem, as for most, there are distinctions of degree. If Salmon had received from Gerry a proposition to lease a building at a location far removed, he might have held for himself the privilege thus acquired, or so we shall assume. Here the subject-matter of the new lease was an extension and enlargement of the subject-matter of the old one. A managing coadventurer appropriating the benefit of such a lease without warning to his partner might fairly expect to be reproached with conduct that was underhand, or lacking, to say the least, in reasonable candor, if the partner were to surprise him in the act of signing the new instrument. Conduct subject to that reproach does not receive from equity a healing benediction.

WILLIAM ANDREWS, J. (dissenting).

A tenant's expectancy of the renewal of a lease is a thing, tenuous, yet often having a real value. It represents the probability that a landlord will prefer to relet his premises to one already in possession rather than to strangers. Less tangible than "good will," it is never included in the tenant's assets, yet equity will not permit one standing in a relation of trust and confidence toward the tenant unfairly to take the benefit to himself. At times the principle is rigidly enforced. Given the relation between the parties, a certain result follows. No question as to good faith, or injury, or as to other circumstances is material. Such is the rule as between trustee and cestui (Keech v. Sanford, Select Cas. in Ch. 61); as between executor and estate (Matter of Brown, 18 Ch. Div. 61; as between guardian and ward (Milner v. Harewood, 18 Ves. 259, 274).

At other times some inquiry is allowed as to the facts involved. Fair dealing and a scrupulous regard for honesty is required. But nothing more. It may be stated generally that a partner may not for his own benefit secretly take a renewal of a firm lease to himself. Mitchell v. Reed, 61 N. Y. 123 (1874). Where the trustee, or the partner or the tenant in common, takes no new lease but buys the reversion in good faith, a somewhat different question arises. Here is no direct appropriation of the expectancy of renewal. Here is no offshoot of the original lease. We so held in Anderson v. Lemon, 8 N. Y. 236 (1853), and although Judge Dwight casts some doubt on the rule in *Mitchell v. Reed*, it seems to have the support of authority. The issue, then, is whether actual fraud, dishonesty, or unfairness is present in the transaction. If so, the purchaser may well be held as a trustee.

With this view of the law I am of the opinion that the issue here is simple. Was the transaction, in view of all the circumstances surrounding it, unfair and inequitable? I reach this conclusion for two reasons. There was no general partnership, merely a joint venture for a limited object, to end at a fixed time. The new lease, covering additional property, containing many new and unusual terms and conditions, with a possible duration of 80 years, was more nearly the purchase of the reversion than the ordinary renewal with which the authorities are concerned.

The findings of the referee are to the effect that before 1902, Mrs. Louisa M. Gerry was the owner of a plot on the corner of Fifth avenue and Forty-Second street, New York, containing 9,312 square feet. On it had been built the old Bristol Hotel. Walter J. Salmon was in the real estate business, renting, managing and operating buildings. On April 10th of that year Mrs. Gerry leased the property to him for a term extending from May 1, 1902, to April 30, 1922. The property was to be used for offices and business, and the design was that the lessee should so remodel the hotel at his own expense as to fit it for such purposes, all alteration and additions, however, at once to become the property of the lessor. The lease might not be assigned without written consent.

Morton H. Meinhard was a woolen merchant. At some period during the negotiations between Mr. Salmon and Mrs. Gerry, so far as the findings show without the latter's knowledge, he became interested in the transaction. Before the lease was executed he advanced $5,000 toward the cost of the proposed alterations. Finally, on May 19th he and Salmon entered into a written agreement. "During the period of twenty years from the 1st day of May, 1902," the parties agree to share equally in the expense needed "to reconstruct, alter, manage and operate the Bristol Hotel property" and in all payments required by the lease, and in all losses incurred. During the same term net profits are to be divided. Mr. Salmon has sole power to "'manage, lease, underlet and operate" the premises.

The referee finds that this arrangement did not create a partnership between Mr. Salmon and Mr. Meinhard. In this he is clearly right. He is equally right in holding that while no general partnership existed, the two men had entered into a joint adventure, and that while the legal title to the lease was in Mr. Salmon, Mr. Meinhard had some sort of an equitable interest therein. Mr. Salmon was to manage the property for their joint benefit. He was bound to use good faith. He could not willfully destroy the lease, the object of the adventure, to the detriment of Mr. Meinhard.

Mr. Salmon went into possession and control of the property. The alterations were made. At first came losses. Then large profits which were duly distributed. At all times Mr. Salmon has acted as manager.

Some time before 1922 Mr. Elbridge T. Gerry became the owner of the reversion. He was already the owner of an adjoining lot on Fifth avenue and of four lots adjoining on Forty-Second Street, in all 11,587 square feet, covered by five separate buildings. Obviously, all this property together was more valuable than the sum of the value of the separate parcels. Some plan to develop the property as a whole seems to have occurred to Mr. Gerry. He arranged that all leases on his five lots should expire on the same day as the Bristol Hotel lease. Then in 1921 he negotiated with various persons and corporations seeking to obtain a desirable tenant who would put up a building to cover the entire tract, for this was the policy he had adopted. These negotiations lasted for some months. They failed. About January 1, 1922, Mr. Gerry's agent approached Mr. Salmon and began to negotiate with him for the lease of the entire tract. Upon this he insisted, as he did upon the erection of a new and expensive building covering the whole. He would not consent to the renewal of the Bristol lease on any terms. This effort resulted in a lease to the Midpoint Realty Company, a corporation entirely owned and controlled by Mr. Salmon. For our purposes the paper may be treated as if the agreement was made with Mr. Salmon himself.

In many respects, besides the increase in the land demised, the new lease differs from the old. Instead of an annual rent of $55,000 it is now from $350,000 to $475,000. Instead of a fixed term of twenty years it may now be, at the lessee's option, eighty. Instead of alterations in an existing structure costing about $200,000 a new building is contemplated costing $3,000,000. Of this sum $1,500,000 is to be advanced by the lessor to the lessee, "but not to its successors or assigns," and is to be repaid in installments. Again no assignment or sale of the lease may be made without the consent of the lessor.

This lease is valuable. In making it Mr. Gerry acted in good faith without any collusion with Mr. Salmon and with no purpose to deprive Mr. Meinhard of any equities he might have. But as to the negotiations leading to it or as to the execution of the lease itself Mr. Meinhard knew nothing. Mr. Salmon acted for himself to acquire the lease for his own benefit.

Under these circumstances the referee has found, and the Appellate Division agrees with him, that Mr. Meinhard is entitled to an interest in the second lease, he having promptly elected to assume his share of the liabilities imposed thereby. This conclusion is based upon the proposition that under the original contract between the two men "the enterprise was a joint venture, the relation between the parties was fiduciary and governed by principles applicable to partnerships," therefore, as the new lease is a graft upon the old, Mr. Salmon might not acquire its benefits for himself alone.

Were this a general partnership between Mr. Salmon and Mr. Meinhard I should have little doubt as to the correctness of this result, assuming the new lease to be an offshoot of the old. We have here a different situation governed by less drastic principles. I assume that where parties engage in a joint enterprise each owes to the other the duty of the utmost good faith in all that relates to their common venture. Within its scope they stand in a fiduciary relationship. I assume *prima facie* that even as between joint adventurers one may not secretly obtain a renewal of the lease of property actually used in the joint adventure where the possibility of renewal is expressly or impliedly involved in the enterprise.

What then was the scope of the adventure into which the two men entered? It is to be remembered that before their contract was signed Mr. Salmon had obtained the lease of the Bristol property. Having the lease Mr. Salmon assigns no interest in it to Mr. Meinhard. He is to manage the property. It is for him to decide what alterations shall be made and to fix the rents. But for twenty years from May 1, 1902, Salmon is to make all advances from his own funds and Meinhard is to pay him personally on demand one-half of all expenses incurred and all losses sustained "during the full term of said lease," and during the same period Salmon is to pay him a part of the net profits. There was no joint capital provided.

It seems to me that the venture so inaugurated had in view a limited object and was to end at a limited time. There was no intent to expand it into a far greater undertaking lasting for many years. The design was to exploit a particular lease. Doubtless in it Mr. Meinhard had an equitable interest, but in it alone. This interest terminated when the joint adventure terminated. There was no intent that for the benefit of both any advantage should be taken of the chance of renewal—that the adventure should be continued beyond that date. Mr. Salmon has done all he promised to do in return for Mr. Meinhard's undertaking when he distributed profits up to May 1, 1922. Suppose this lease, non-assignable without the consent of the lessor, had contained a renewal option. Could Mr. Meinhard have exercised it? Could he have insisted that Mr. Salmon do so? Had Mr. Salmon done so, could he insist that the agreement to share losses still existed or could Mr. Meinhard have claimed that the joint adventure was still to continue for twenty or eighty years? I do not think so. The adventure by its express terms ended on May 1, 1922. The contract by its language and by its whole import excluded the idea that the tenant's expectancy was to subsist for the benefit of the plaintiff. On that date whatever there was left of value in the lease reverted to Mr. Salmon, as it would had the lease been for thirty years instead of twenty. Any equity which Mr. Meinhard possessed was in the particular lease itself, not in any possibility of renewal. There was nothing unfair in Mr. Salmon's conduct.

So far I have treated the new lease as if it were a renewal of the old. As already indicated, I do not take that view. Such a renewal could not be obtained. Any expectancy that it might be had vanished. What Mr. Salmon obtained was not a graft springing from the Bristol lease, but something distinct and different—as distinct as if for a building across Fifth avenue. I think also that in the absence of some fraudulent or unfair act the secret purchase of the reversion even by one partner is rightful. Substantially this is such a purchase. Because of the mere label of a transaction we do not place it on one side of the line or the other. Here is involved the possession of a large and most valuable unit of property for eighty years, the destruction of all existing structures and the erection of a new and expensive building covering the whole. No fraud, no deceit, no calculated secrecy is found. Simply that the arrangement was made without the knowledge of Mr. Meinhard. I think this not enough.

The judgment of the courts below should be reversed and a new trial ordered, with costs in all courts to abide the event.

Punctilio

1. The expiring lease in *Meinhard v. Salmon* was to the old Hotel Bristol, at Fifth Avenue and 42nd Street. The owner of the property—holder of the reversion under the headlease to Salmon—was Elbridge T. Gerry, wealthy New York lawyer, landowner, and social reformer. (His grandfather was a signer of the Declaration of Independence and the inventor of the Gerrymander).

This photograph of the Hotel Bristol was taken about 1898, but the upper stories of the building would have looked the same in 1922. (Salmon's 1902 lease required him to convert the ground floor to retail space.) The hotel occupied the NW corner of the intersection; the New York Public Library (built in 1911) occupied the SW corner across the street. By 1922, Gerry had acquired additional property adjoining the hotel on both sides: one lot on Fifth Avenue to the north, and four lots on 42nd Street to the west. Following the 1922 lease to Salmon, Midpoint Realty (Salmon's company) redeveloped the combined tract to construct 500 Fifth Avenue. Built in 1929-1931, 59 stories high, it is an art deco masterpiece and a designated New York City landmark.

According to the NYC Landmarks Preservation Commission (in 2000):

> When it opened in March 1931, 500 Fifth Avenue was the crowning
> achievement of real estate developer Walter J. Salmon, who was respon-
> sible for rebuilding the north side of West 42nd Street between Fifth and
> Sixth Avenues in the first decades of the 20th century. Shreve, Lamb &
> Harmon [which designed the building] was one of the leading architec-
> tural firms in the country specializing in skyscraper design.

As Cardozo reminds us, Meinhard's victory in litigation left him liable for 50
percent of the lessee's obligations under the new headlease—construction of

a $3 million building beginning in 1929, and annual rent of $350,000 for the combined tract. Meinhard died in 1931, the year the building was completed. When his estate was settled two years later, a glut of new buildings (including the Empire State Building, designed by the same architects) amid the depressed market for mid-Manhattan office space meant that Meinhard's 50 percent interest in 500 Fifth represented a *liability* of $845,000 (and a corresponding benefit to Salmon). Apparently the Meinhard estate eventually sold out to Salmon—at what price we don't know—so the appreciation in Manhattan real estate for the rest of the 20th century (the new lease could be renewed until 2002) went to Salmon after all. See Robert B. Thompson, "The Story of *Meinhard v. Salmon*," in *Corporate Law Stories* 105-33 (Ramseyer ed. 2009).

2. What should Salmon have done—consistent with "the punctilio of an honor the most sensitive"—on receiving Gerry's proposal in 1922?

3. Is Cardozo correct to see the opportunity for a new and expanded real estate deal as one that belonged to the Meinhard/Salmon joint venture? He appears to view the question of Salmon's duty of loyalty as all or nothing. Andrews gives a more nuanced answer, weighing two intersecting variables: first the nature of relationship between Meinhard and Salmon, then the nature of the opportunity presented. Compare the following relationships:

a) *Keech v. Sandford*, in which the defendant was a trustee and the Infant held 100 percent of the beneficial interest.

b) A hypothetical variant in which "Meinhard & Salmon" is a general partnership doing business in real estate investment and management. Both Meinhard and Salmon are engaged in running the Hotel Bristol for the benefit of the partners, and actively involved in other real estate ventures besides.

c) A hypothetical variant in which Meinhard died in 1912. For the last 10 years, Salmon has been managing the Hotel Bristol, making quarterly payments to Meinhard's widow.

Now compare the following opportunities:

d) Gerry offers to renew the Hotel Bristol lease for 20 years on existing terms.

e) Gerry offers a new lease of different property, across the street from the Hotel Bristol.

f) Gerry offers to sell his interest in the Hotel Bristol tract (*i.e.*, the reversion of the fee simple absolute).

4. Cardozo's opinion in *Meinhard v. Salmon* cites his own famous opinion in Beatty v. Guggenheim, 225 N.Y. 380, 122 N.E. 378 (1919), an "opportunity" case in which the equities were more clear-cut:

> The plaintiff was sent to the Yukon to investigate mining claims which were the subject of an option. He found certain other claims which were not included in the option, but which he believed to be essential to the

successful operation of those that were included. In conjunction with Perry, he purchased rights in the new claims. The two were partners in the venture. Later his employer, appreciating the importance of the claims, determined to buy them for itself. We think it had the right to say to the agent that he must renounce the profits of the transaction and transfer the claims at cost. A different situation would be presented if the claims had no relation to those which the plaintiff was under a duty to investigate. But they had an intimate relation. One could not profitably be operated without the other. Let us suppose that the plaintiff, instead of buying the claims as a partner with Perry, had bought them alone. No one, we think, would say that he could have retained them against his employer, and held out for an extravagant price, as, of course, he could have done if the purchase was not affected by a trust. It is not an answer to say that he was not bound to risk his money as he did, or to go into the enterprise at all. He might have kept out of it altogether, but if he went in, he could not withhold from his employer the benefit of the bargain.

A constructive trust is the formula through which the conscience of equity finds expression. When property has been acquired in such circumstances that the holder of the legal title may not in good conscience retain the beneficial interest, equity converts him into a trustee. We think it would be against good conscience for the plaintiff to retain these profits unless his employer has consented. The tie was close between the employer's business and the forbidden venture. Of course it is true that if Perry had made the purchase alone, without the aid of plaintiff, the employer might be no better off. That is true whenever an agent goes into some competing venture. His associates might have succeeded in diverting equal profits without him. The disability is personal to him. Others may divert profits from the business of the principal. He may not. If he does, he must account for them.

We conclude, therefore, that the plaintiff was chargeable as a trustee if the employer so elected. But the Appellate Division has found upon sufficient evidence that the employer consented to the investment. . . .

The remark about constructive trust being "the formula through which the conscience of equity finds expression" is probably the most frequently cited definition of the remedy. What does it mean? What does Cardozo mean when he says that the disloyal agent "must renounce the profits of the transaction and transfer the claims at cost"?

5. A modern case of "corporate opportunity," Thorpe v. CERBCO, 676 A.2d 436 (Del. 1996), is summarized by the Restatement as follows:

Controlling Shareholders who are also directors of Corporation are approached by Buyer interested in purchasing corporate Subsidiary. Shareholders instead engage in negotiations with Buyer regarding a sale of their interest in Corporation. Buyer pays Shareholders $75,000 for a purchase option, but the sale is never consummated. In a derivative suit brought on behalf of Corporation, the court finds that the potential sale of Subsidiary represented a corporate opportunity under local law, and that Shareholders breached their duty of loyalty by failing to present this opportunity to the Corporation. Shareholders object that Corporation has suffered no injury, because Shareholders would have exercised their power to veto any transaction between Corporation and Buyer.

R3RUE §43, Illustration 15. Does your intuition—based on the preceding cases—tell you how this dispute will be resolved?

Lum v. Clark
56 Minn. 278, 57 N.W. 662 (1894)

Action by Leon E. Lum against D. H. Clark and others for the cancellation of a note executed by plaintiff in Clark's favor. There was judgment for plaintiff, and, from an order denying defendants' motion for a new trial, defendant L. B. McEwen appeals. Affirmed.

MITCHELL, J.

It is only necessary to consider one of numerous questions argued by counsel. The defendant McEwen was the superintendent and general manager of the business of the Northern Mill Company. That company had a sawmill on Gull River eight miles from Brainerd, and also a logging railroad extending from Kilpatrick Lake, 25 miles from Brainerd, some distance out into the woods. The mill company had under consideration a plan for remodeling its mill, and extending its logging road to Gull River, where the mill was situated. At this juncture of affairs, in consideration of McEwen's agreement to use his influence and authority as superintendent and manager of the mill company to secure the removal of its mill and the extension of its road to Brainerd, the plaintiff executed the obligation in suit, by which he promised to pay to defendant Clark $5,000 nine months after date, on condition that within that time the mill company extended its logging railroad to Brainerd, and built within the limits of that city a sawmill of a specified capacity. This note was given for the benefit of McEwen, but was made payable to Clark, in order to conceal McEwen's connection with the matter.

That this contract was illegal and void on grounds of public policy will not admit of a moment's doubt. Loyalty to his trust is the first duty which an agent owes to his principal. Reliance upon an agent's integrity, fidelity, and capacity is the moving consideration in the creation of all agencies; and the law condemns, as repugnant to public policy, everything which tends to destroy that reliance. The agent cannot put himself in such relations that his own personal interests become antagonistic to those of his principal. He will not be allowed to serve two masters without the intelligent consent of both. Actual injury is not the principle the law proceeds on, in holding such transactions void. Fidelity in the agent is what is aimed at, and, as a means of securing it, the law will not permit him to place himself in a position in which he may be tempted by his own private interests to disregard those of his principal.

In the matter of determining the policy of removing the mill and extending the road, McEwen, in the discharge of his duties, whether merely that of making recommendations, or of exercising authority to act, owed to his principal the exercise of his best judgment and ability, uninfluenced by any antagonistic personal interests of his own. His attempt to secure $5,000 to himself was calculated to bias his mind in favor of the policy upon which the payment of the money was conditioned, regardless of the interests of the mill company. It is not material that no actual injury to the company resulted, or that the policy recommended may have been for its best interest. Courts will not inquire into these matters. It is enough to know that the agent in fact placed himself in such relations that he might be tempted by his own interests to disregard those of his principal. The transaction was nothing more or less than the acceptance by the agent of a bribe to perform his duties in the manner desired by the person who gave the bribe. Such a contract is void. This doctrine rests on such plain principles of law, as well as common business honesty, that the citation of authorities is unnecessary. The fact that the validity of such a transaction is attempted to be sustained in courts of justice does not speak well for the state of the public conscience on the subject of loyalty to trusts in business affairs.

This was an action by the maker of the instrument to have it surrendered up and canceled. In view of the relation which he bears to the transaction, there may be some doubt whether courts should give him affirmative relief. But defendants do not raise the point, and we only advert to it in order that this case may not be considered an authority on the question. Order affirmed.

Fidelity in the agent

1. Suppose that the $5,000 bribe in *Lum v. Clark* had been paid in advance, in cash, rather than merely promised in the form of a note. What result if the Northern Mill Co. sues McEwen in restitution to get the money? What result if Lum sues McEwen in restitution to get the money back? Leaving the facts as they are, what if the court denies "affirmative relief" in this lawsuit, then Lum's note is dishonored, whereupon Clark sues Lum to enforce the note?

2. Liability for insider trading is usually explained, not as a species of securities fraud (though that was the idea in *SEC v. Macdonald*), but in terms of a breach of the insider's fiduciary duty to the corporation. Here as well it may be difficult to find quantifiable injury:

> It is true that the complaint before us does not contain any allegation
> of damages to the corporation but this has never been considered to be
> an essential requirement for a cause of action founded on a breach of

fiduciary duty. This is because the function of such an action, unlike an ordinary tort or contract case, is not merely to *compensate* the plaintiff for wrongs committed by the defendant but, as this court declared many years ago (Dutton v. Willner, 52 N. Y. 312, 319), "to *prevent* them, by removing from agents and trustees all inducement to attempt dealing for their own benefit in matters which they have undertaken for others, or to which their agency or trust relates." (Emphasis supplied.)

Diamond v. Oreamuno, 24 N.Y.2d 494, 498 (1969). This suggests that insider trading by a corporate officer resembles the taking of a bribe by an agent. What if the person who profits by trading on inside information has no power to influence the actions of the corporation?

3. Reading v. Attorney-General, (1951) A.C. 507 (H.L.), was conveniently summarized in a New Jersey decision involving official corruption:

> Reading, a sergeant in the British Army Medical Corps stationed in Egypt, received about £20,000 from a group of smugglers for riding in uniform on various trucks which they were using in their smuggling activities into Cairo, the idea being that the truck would not be stopped by the Egyptian police if a British soldier in uniform was riding upon it. The English government seized the money, and after serving a term in prison Reading brought a petition to recover the money. It is important to the decision of the case at bar to note that the money in question in the *Reading* case never belonged to the government, nor was it in any way out-of-pocket in the transaction. Nevertheless, the House of Lords held that the government was entitled to the money on the ground that Reading obtained it illegally as a result of the misuse of his position as a soldier in the English Army.

Jersey City v. Hague, 18 N.J. 584, 594, 115 A.2d 8, 14 (1955) (Vanderbilt, C.J.). Was Sergeant Reading a fiduciary? Did that matter to the result?

E.   OTHER TORTS

Marmo v. Tyson Fresh Meats, Inc.
457 F.3d 748 (8th Cir. 2006)

MAGNUSON, District Judge.

Carol Marmo appeals from the final judgment entered on a jury verdict awarding her $17,500.00 on a nuisance claim against Tyson Fresh Meats, Inc., f/k/a IBP, Inc. ("IBP"). We affirm.

The complaint alleged three theories of recovery: nuisance, negligence, and strict liability. In each claim, Marmo asserted that she had been damaged by hydrogen sulfide gas emitted from the wastewater treatment lagoons at IBP's beef processing plant. Marmo later attempted to amend the complaint to add an unjust enrichment claim based on a pollution easement theory. Specifically, Marmo claimed that IBP inequitably saved $70 million by not installing appropriate pollution control equipment. The district court rejected the proposed amendment as futile, concluding that the unjust enrichment claim based on the facts presented was a novel cause of action that the Nebraska courts had not recognized.

[Marmo's tort claims based on allegations of physical injury were rejected by the district court. On the facts of the case there could be no "strict liability" under Nebraska law, because the defendant's wastewater treatment was not an "ultrahazardous activity." Claims based on negligence were barred by the statute of limitations: Marmo was aware of "her alleged difficulties with hydrogen sulfide," and its source in the defendant's activities, more than four years before her action was commenced in September 2000.] Marmo's nuisance claim for the four-year period preceding September 2000 was submitted to the jury, which returned a verdict of $17,500.00 for Marmo.

Marmo sought leave to amend her complaint to add an unjust enrichment claim based on the theory that IBP unjustly profited from its failure to install adequate pollution control equipment. The district court denied leave, reasoning that the attempt was futile because Nebraska law did not recognize an unjust enrichment claim based on the theory advanced by Marmo.

An unjust enrichment claim embodies the equitable doctrine that one will not be allowed to profit or enrich oneself unjustly at the expense of another. Hoffman v. Reinke Mfg. Co., 227 Neb. 66, 416 N.W.2d 216, 219 (1987). When the inequitable and unconscionable retention of a benefit occurs, Nebraska law requires the recipient to pay for the reasonable value of the benefit received. Bush v. Kramer, 185 Neb. 1, 173 N.W.2d 367, 369 (1969). "Unjust enrichment requires restitution, which measures the remedy by the gain obtained by the defendant, and seeks disgorgement of that gain." Trieweiler v. Sears, 268 Neb. 952, 689 N.W.2d 807, 834 (2004). Thus, a defendant will be liable for the unjust benefit it receives—and not the harm sustained by the plaintiff.

Marmo admits that neither the Nebraska Supreme Court nor the Nebraska Legislature has recognized an unjust enrichment claim based on a pollution easement theory, but nonetheless argues that Nebraska case law supports her claim. Nebraska courts have recognized an unjust enrichment claim to allow a purchaser who made valuable improvements to a property to recover the reasonable value of the improvement. See McIntosh v. Borchers, 201 Neb. 35, 266 N.W.2d 200, 203 (1978). They have also recognized an unjust enrichment claim to require payment for land use when an individual disavowed an obligation to pay for the use. *Bush*, 173 N.W.2d at 369.

However, no Nebraska state court has recognized a negative unjust enrichment claim based on the pollution easement theory, which seeks disgorgement of profits unjustly saved by a polluter.[1] Rather, Nebraska courts focus on how the pollution injures the plaintiff, and that claim is properly brought under the law of nuisance. See Bargmann v. Soll Oil Co., 253 Neb. 1018, 574 N.W.2d 478, 486 (1998); Karpisek v. Cather & Sons Constr., Inc., 174 Neb. 234, 117 N.W.2d 322, 326-27 (1962). There is no indication that the Nebraska Supreme Court would recognize an unjust enrichment claim on the facts of this case. Thus, the proposed amendment would have been futile, and the district court did not err in denying Marmo leave to amend the complaint.

MORRIS ARNOLD, Circuit Judge, dissenting.

I respectfully disagree with the court's conclusion that the courts of the State of Nebraska would not recognize a claim for unjust enrichment in the circumstances of this case. The law of restitution, as the court seems to recognize, is well established in Nebraska. Generally speaking, restitution is available whenever a person acquires a benefit that in justice he or she ought not to retain. Ahrens v. Dye, 208 Neb. 129, 133, 302 N.W.2d 682, 684-85 (1981). The generality of this principle may account for the court's reluctance here to entertain this suit, but in truth the principle is not unbounded and there are well-defined and well-developed categories into which claims for restitution fit. One of those is when a person wrongfully uses the property of another for profit. See Restatement (Third) of Restitution and Unjust Enrichment §40. Nebraska law specifically recognizes, moreover, that in a proper case a person who is unjustly enriched must disgorge the profits produced by the wrongful act that he or she committed. See Trieweiler v. Sears, 268 Neb. 952, 979, 689 N.W.2d 807, 834 (2004).

These are the principles, well established in Nebraska law, that the plaintiff seeks to have applied to her case. She claims that the defendant has wrongfully used her property and that allowing it to keep the gains that it realized from its tort would unjustly enrich it. There is nothing particularly exotic or radical about this claim. It is true that no Nebraska court has recognized a claim that is the exact duplicate of the one raised here, but the present claim is constructed from the basic building blocks of the law of restitution, which is very much a part of Nebraska law. Our job is simply to apply the law that we believe the Supreme Court of Nebraska would apply in the circumstances. For the reasons given, I have no doubt that that court would recognize this claim.

The court notes, correctly, that the plaintiff cites no Nebraska case directly on point. But it is also true that the defendant does not point to any Nebraska case that rejects a claim like the plaintiff's. In fact, though the court acknowledges numerous cases from other jurisdictions that provide restitutionary relief

---

1. The theory is not entirely novel, as other jurisdictions have recognized it. See Branch v. Mobil Oil Corp., 778 F. Supp. 35, 35-36 (W.D. Okla.1991); N.C. Corff P'ship, Ltd. v. OXY USA, Inc., 929 P.2d 288, 295 (Okla. Ct. App. 1996); Evans v. City of Johnstown, 96 Misc. 2d 755, 410 N.Y.S.2d 199, 205-07 (Sup. Ct. 1978); see also generally Allan Kanner, *Unjust Enrichment in Environmental Litigation*, 20 J. Envtl. L. & Litig. 111 (2005). Indeed, since we heard oral argument in this case, another district court from the District of Nebraska ruled that Nebraska law supports such a claim. Schwan v. CNH Am. LLC, 2006 WL 1215395 (D. Neb. May 4, 2006). Notably, however, the district court in *Schwan* relied heavily on Oklahoma law—not Nebraska law. *Id.* Nebraska courts have not interpreted unjust enrichment claims so broadly as to include the pollution easement theory.

in the present circumstances, it is highly suggestive that the court does not advert to a single instance in which a court turned away a similar claim. The reason for the lack of such authority, I believe, is that the plaintiff's case presents essentially a mine-run, routine restitutionary claim that calls for a relatively straightforward application of familiar legal principles. Another federal district court in Nebraska has correctly recognized this. See Schwan v. CNH Am. LLC, 2006 WL 1215395 (D. Neb. May 4, 2006).

The court also points out that Nebraska courts provide an action of nuisance for damages in the present circumstances; but it is unclear exactly why the court thinks that the nuisance remedy would be exclusive. It is certainly not true, as the defendant repeatedly suggests in its brief, that restitution is an equitable remedy and therefore is available only when an action at law is not. Restitution is not an equitable remedy: It is part of the substantive law of obligations, like the law of tort and contract, and the Nebraska courts have recognized that it is in ordinary courts of law that restitutionary actions lie. See Collection Bureau of Grand Island, Inc. v. Fry, 9 Neb. App. 277, 282-84, 610 N.W.2d 442, 446-48 (2000). Nor is there any other principled reason why the mere existence of a nuisance remedy for damages should oust the plaintiff from her restitutionary remedy. Restitution is simply there at the plaintiff's option: She may waive the tort and sue for unjust enrichment. As Judge Posner has said, "Restitution is available in any intentional-tort case in which the tortfeasor has made a profit that exceeds the victim's damages (if the damages exceed the profit, the plaintiff will prefer to seek damages instead)." Williams Electronics Games, Inc. v. Garrity, 366 F.3d 569, 576 (7th Cir. 2004).

Though the availability of the restitutionary claim is plain enough, it is not altogether clear what remedy the Nebraska courts would provide in the present case. If an injunction would not have been issued under Nebraska law to enjoin the defendant's emissions, it is likely that disgorgement of the profits realized from them would not be available as a remedy in this case. Instead, a Nebraska court might well enter a judgment in an amount equal to the reasonable cost of a license to trespass or commit a nuisance — the market price, in other words, of a so-called pollution easement. See Restatement (Third) of Restitution and Unjust Enrichment §40, Illus. 15; *cf.* Daniel Friedmann, *Restitution of Benefits Obtained Through the Appropriation of Property or the Commission of a Wrong*, 80 Colum. L. Rev. 504, 531-32 (1980). This is a matter that the district court ought to explore on a more fully developed record.

For the reasons given, I would reverse the district court's summary judgment on the plaintiff's unjust enrichment claim and remand for further proceedings.

Wrongful interference, wrongful economy

1. The Restatement puts *Marmo v. Tyson* within a residual or catchall rule of restitution for profitable wrongdoing:

§44. Interference with Other Protected Interests.

(1) A person who obtains a benefit by conscious interference with a claimant's legally protected interests (or in consequence of such interference by another) is liable in restitution as necessary to prevent unjust enrichment, unless competing legal objectives make such liability inappropriate.

Most of the "conscious interference" falling under this heading consists of actionable wrongs not elsewhere classified—most prominently, the "interference torts" protecting a party's business arrangements and expectations against illegitimate disruption. A plaintiff who can show wrongful interference with contractual relations or unfair competition, for example, will sue for restitution rather than damages whenever the defendant's profits are greater (or easier to prove).

2. Saved expenditure is easily identifiable as a benefit for restitution purposes. Should there be liability in restitution for savings realized by engaging in low-cost tortious conduct rather than more careful and costly alternatives? In most tort cases the possibility would not be worth pursuing:

> The most common kind of tort is the negligent infliction of a personal injury—one car hits another, or a sponge is left inside a patient on the operating table. In these cases the plaintiff has obvious damages, and the defendant has no gains; or if the defendant does have gains, they consist of the tiny savings from skipping a precaution that would have spared the plaintiff some grief. Whether those sorts of gains can be the subject of a restitution claim might be of some theoretical interest, but in practice that question does not come up. The reason is that the defendant's savings will invariably be smaller than the damages suffered by the plaintiff. If the savings were *larger*, the plaintiff's negligence claim would be at risk of failing because the accident was not worth preventing—the implication of Learned Hand's formula for measuring reasonable care. That is why no victims of conventional negligently inflicted personal injuries chose to bring restitution claims against their injurers. They are better off recovering their damages.

Farnsworth, *Restitution* 63 (2014). Suppose the plaintiff in *Marmo* can prove what she alleges: that the defendant made a conscious decision to manage its wastewater treatment in a way that would constitute a nuisance, because the least expensive non-tortious (and environmentally friendly) alternative would have cost it an additional $70 million. Should she and her neighbors be entitled to restitution in the amount of $70 million, or would such proof undermine the basis ("unreasonable interference") of the nuisance tort?

3. According to Judge Arnold, "If an injunction would not have been issued under Nebraska law to enjoin the defendant's emissions, it is likely that disgorgement of the profits realized from them would not be available as a remedy in this case." Why not?

4. The tort of wrongful interference with actual or prospective contractual relations is interesting from the restitution point of view, because such interference can be profitable even when it is not harmful. The Restatement presents this simplified version of Federal Sugar Refining Co. v. United States Sugar Equalization Board, 268 F. 575 (S.D.N.Y. 1920):

> Seller contracts with Buyer to deliver one million pounds of sugar at 25¢ per pound. By acts that are tortious under local law, Competitor induces Buyer to repudiate its contract with Seller and to purchase the same quantity from Competitor at 30¢ per pound. The market price of sugar at the time and place of delivery specified in Seller's contract with Buyer is 27¢ per pound. Competitor realizes a profit of $30,000 from its transaction with Buyer. Seller has a cause of action for breach but no claim for contract damages against Buyer; Seller has a cause of action for wrongful interference but no claim for tort damages against Competitor.

R3RUE §44, Illustration 4. What if Seller sues Competitor in restitution?

F. DIVERSION OF PROPERTY RIGHTS AT DEATH

Neiman v. Hurff
11 N.J. 55, 93 A.2d 345 (1952)

VANDERBILT, C.J.

On July 31, 1950 the defendant killed his wife and thereafter pleaded *non vult* to an indictment for second degree murder for which he is now confined in prison. During her lifetime the decedent and the defendant owned a residence in Collingswood, New Jersey, as tenants by the entirety. In her will the decedent named as her sole beneficiary the Damon Runyon Memorial Fund for Cancer Research, Inc.

The plaintiff Alberta A. Neiman as executrix of the decedent sought the direction of the court in regard to the rights of the Cancer Fund and of the defendant respectively . . . . The Cancer Fund sought an adjudication that the real property held by the entirety be held in trust for it by the defendant and that he be ordered to convey such property to the Fund. The defendant contended that the title to the realty vested in him on his wife's death.

The trial court ruled, 14 N.J. Super. 479, 82 A.2d 471, that the decedent having met her death at the hands of the defendant, the title to the realty was vested in him as trustee for himself individually and for the Cancer Fund; that its value at the time of her death was $14,000; that the value of the Cancer Fund's interest was $11,597.98 (this sum representing the difference between $14,000 and "the commuted value as of the date of decedent's death of the net income of one-half of said property for the number of years of defendant's expectancy of life as determined according to the mortality tables used by this

Court"); that $11,597.98 was imposed as a lien on the real property in favor of the Cancer Fund; that the defendant pay the Cancer Fund $11,597.98 within 45 days of service of the judgment or that the Cancer Fund have execution issue. From this judgment the defendant appealed to the Appellate Division of the Superior Court, and we have certified the case on our own motion.

The question here presented is whether or not a murderer can acquire by right of survivorship and keep property the title to which he had held jointly with his victim. This question has never been before a court of last resort in this State, although it has been considered at length in the former Court of Chancery, Sorbello v. Mangino, 108 N.J. Eq. 292, 155 A. 6 (1931); Sherman v. Weber, 113 N.J. Eq. 451, 167 A. 517 (1933); and Whitney v. Lott, 134 N.J. Eq. 586, 36 A.2d 888 (1944). Some states have held that the legal title passes to the murderer despite his crime and that he may retain it, see Wenker v. Landon, 161 Or. 265, 88 P.2d 971 (1939); Beddingfield v. Estill & Newman, 118 Tenn. 39, 100 S.W. 108 (1907), each involving real property held by the entirety. Some other states have held that the legal title will not pass to the murderer at all, see Van Alstyne v. Tuffy, 103 Misc. 455, 169 N.Y.S. 173 (Sup. Ct. 1918), likewise involving real property held by the entirety. A third group of states has held that legal title passes to the murderer but that equity will treat him as a constructive trustee because of his unconscionable acquisition of the property and compel him to convey it to those to whom it has been devised or bequeathed by the will of his victim, or in the absence of a will to the heirs or next of kin of the decedent exclusive of the murderer. See, in addition to the three New Jersey cases hereinbefore mentioned, In re King's Estate, 261 Wis. 266, 52 N.W.2d 885 (1952); Colton v. Wade, 80 A.2d 923 (Del. Ch. 1951); Grose v. Holland, 357 Mo. 874, 211 S.W.2d 464 (1948); all involving property held by the entirety.

To permit the murderer to retain title to the property acquired by his crime as permitted in some states is abhorrent to even the most rudimentary sense of justice. It violates the policy of the common law that no one shall be allowed to profit by his own wrong, *"Nullus commodum capere potest de injuria sua propria."* This doctrine, as Vice Chancellor Jayne pointed out in Whitney v. Lott, *supra*, 134 N.J. Eq. at 589, "so essential to the observance of morality and justice, has been universally recognized in the laws of civilized communities for centuries and is as old as equity. Its sentiment is ageless. Domat, pt. 2, bk. 1; Code Nap. 272; Mackelday's Roman Law, 530; Coke's Littleton 148-B; Broom's Legal Maxims, 9th Ed. 197." On the other hand, to divest the surviving murderer of all legal title violates or does violence to the doctrine of vested rights and would conflict with N.J.S. 2A:152-2: "No conviction or judgment for any offense against this state, shall make or work corruption of blood, disinherison of heirs, loss of dower, or forfeiture of estate."

But to follow the principle enunciated in the cases in our former Court of Chancery does not interfere with vested legal rights, yet by applying the equitable doctrine of a constructive trust force is given to the sound principle of equity that a murderer or other wrongdoer shall not enrich himself by his inequity at the expense of an innocent person. To quote from "Can a Murderer Acquire Title by His Crime and Keep It?" in Ames, *Lectures on Legal History* (1913), 310, at 321:

> The results reached in these cases must commend themselves to every-
> one's sense of justice. But all will admit that these results could not be
> accomplished by common-law principles alone. The common law would
> make the criminal remainderman in the one case, and the criminal joint
> tenant in the other case, the absolute owner of the land. Equity alone, by
> acting *in personam*, can compel the criminal to surrender what, in spite
> of his crime, the common law has suffered him to acquire.

This doctrine is so consistent with the equitable principles that have obtained here for centuries that we have no hesitancy in applying it, and we find no merit at all in the defendant's argument that the decision below works a corruption of blood or a forfeiture of estate. It would be a strange system of jurisprudence that would be able to grant relief against many kinds of accidents, mistake and fraud, by compelling a defendant to act as constructive trustee with respect to property vouchasfed him by the common law, and yet be unable similarly to touch the legal rights of a defendant who sought to profit by a heinous crime.

A more difficult question is involved in determining how much, if any, of the realty shall be held in constructive trust by the defendant for the benefit of the Cancer Fund. In the ordinary course of events the estate by the entirety in the real property would vest in the survivor absolutely, but it is now impossible here to determine whether husband or wife would have survived in the ordinary course of events and thus which would have become the sole owner of the property in question. Inasmuch as the husband by his wrongful act has prevented the determination in the natural course of events of whether he or his wife would survive, it is not inequitable to presume that the decedent would have survived the wrongdoer. In this situation there is no justification for determining survivorship according to the mathematical life expectancies of the decedent and her murderer. The wrongdoer, having prevented the natural ascertainment of the answer to the question of survivorship, should not be permitted to avail himself of mortality tables which may have no applicability as between him and the decedent in respect to their respective individual possibilities of survivorship. Equity therefore conclusively presumes for the purpose of working out justice that the decedent would have survived the wrongdoer. In no other way can complete justice be done and the criminal prevented from profiting through his crime, Vesey v. Vesey, 54 N.W.2d 385 (Minn. 1952).

This view inevitably leads us to the conclusion that the Cancer Fund is entitled in equity to an absolute one-half interest and a remainder interest in the other half, subject only to the value of the life estate of the defendant in such half. Thus the defendant will hold the realty in trust for the Cancer Fund subject to a lien thereon for the commuted value at the time of the decedent's death of the net income of one-half of the real property for the number of years of his expectancy of life as determined according to the mortality tables used in our courts, *i.e.*, $2,402.02.

Murdering heirs, remaindermen, insurance beneficiaries

1. The answer to Dean Ames's question—"Can a Murderer Acquire Title by His Crime and Keep It?"—seems obvious today, but only because this is one area of law in which the triumph of equity has been nearly universal. According to strictly legal rules, a murderer could inherit from a victim, or take as legatee under a will, or as beneficiary under an insurance policy; likewise a remainderman could speed the possession of his future interest by doing away with the life tenant. These unattractive consequences appeared to be dictated by the statutes of descent and distribution, by the Wills Act, by a literal-minded reading of the insurance contract, or simply by the law of estates. Equity saw the results as intolerable and intervened to prevent them. Whether title to property was reassigned by means of "constructive trust" or some other device was a manner of speaking and a detail. One way or another, the murderer would not be permitted to profit.

In one small corner of this landscape a question remains. What happens when one joint tenant (or tenant by the entireties) murders the other? The purely legal answer is that the murderer takes the whole property by the right of survivorship, and courts have so held. Others have held that the murderer forfeits any entitlement, with the result that the entire property goes to the estate of the victim. Both solutions are now considered unsatisfactory, given wide acceptance of the starting proposition—likewise derived from equity—that (ideally) the wrongdoer should neither gain by his crime nor forfeit any interest already vested. Punishment is the province of criminal law, not the law of property.

Accordingly, the choice today generally lies between two middle-ground approaches. The more conscientiously equitable solution is the one applied and explained in *Neiman v. Hurff*. The property—usually a family house—goes to the estate of the victim, except that the murderer retains what he already was sure of: in effect, a life interest in an undivided one half. If the next step (as is likely) is a partition by sale, the murderer can be awarded the commuted value of the life interest, with the balance of the proceeds paid to the estate of the victim. The principal alternative is to hold that the murder effects a severance of the joint tenancy—with the result that the murderer and the estate of the victim hold the property as 50/50 tenants in common. On a subsequent partition, the murderer takes half the value of the fee simple absolute.

The equitable approach seen in *Neiman v. Hurff* was recommended by the original Restatement of Restitution §188 (1937) and carried forward by R3RUE §45. The principal current authority for the severance approach is the Uniform Probate Code and the numerous state statutes that incorporate it to some extent. See UPC §2-803 (1990). Some courts have attempted to justify the severance idea by reasoning that the murderer was free to sever the joint tenancy at any time before the crime—so that treating the murder as a severance gives the murderer no more than the rights he had already. Is this persuasive? The UPC's adherence to severance is probably explained by different considerations: in particular, a consistent policy favoring an equal division of assets wherever possible, without examining the individual claimants' fault or desert.

2. When we consider who are the real parties in interest in a particular case, there will be circumstances in which "severance" appears to yield the more equitable outcome. R3RUE offers two stylized illustrations, based on real cases, to draw this contrast:

> 14. H and W hold the family home as tenants by the entireties and some investments in securities as joint tenants. H murders W, is convicted of the crime, and is imprisoned for life. In the ensuing litigation about the disposition of the co-owned property, H proposes that the murder of one spouse by the other should be deemed to sever their cotenancy, thereby allowing him to retain a one-half interest as a tenant in common with W's estate. In the contest between H and W's estate, the equities do not favor H. On the facts supposed, no reason appears why the court should distribute the property as if H had made lawful dispositions he did not make—by taking title as tenant in common in the first place, by obtaining a legal dissolution of his marriage to W, or by obtaining W's agreement to change the registered ownership of the securities. H's interest in the property is accordingly limited to his preexisting life interest in one-half, or its commuted value.

> 15. Same facts as Illustration 14, except that H commits suicide after killing W. Both H and W had children of previous marriages, and the beneficiaries of their respective estates are not the same. Unlike the case presented by Illustration 14, in which the equitable contest is between the murderer and the estate of the victim, here the contest is between two overlapping groups of innocent parties whose equities are equal. Under these circumstances, the reason of the slayer rule—which seeks to prevent the killer from acquiring property by homicide—has no application to the persons whose interests are directly in issue. (If the rule of this section were applied to limit H's successors to H's preexisting life interest in the co-owned property, the result would be an arbitrary distribution favoring W's estate over H's estate.) To reach a result that is equitable on the facts of the case, the court may decree a severance of the co-ownership between H and W, with the result that the estate of each spouse succeeds to a one-half interest in the co-owned property.

R3RUE §45, Comment *h*. Illustration 15 is based on cases such as Johansen v. Pelton, 8 Cal. App. 3d 625, 87 Cal. Rptr. 784 (1970).

3. In Estate of Foleno v. Estate of Foleno, 772 N.E.2d 490 (Ind. Ct. App. 2002), the facts were stated as follows:

> On the morning of July 15, 2000, Billy Foleno found his wife of thirty-five years, Charlotte Foleno, and her companion, Barry Crowle, at a Holiday

Inn hotel room in Fremont, Indiana. Armed with a .45 caliber automatic pistol, Billy shot Charlotte at least three times as she ran from the hotel room into the hallway. Following her into the hallway, Billy shot Charlotte in the head. He then returned to the room and shot Crowle, who survived the attack. Believing that he had killed both Charlotte and Crowle, Billy ended his own life. The parties agree that Charlotte died before Billy.

Billy owned a life insurance policy carrying a death benefit of $40,000, designating Charlotte as the primary beneficiary. In the event there was "no designated beneficiary living at the death of the insured," the insurance company would "pay the benefits to the persons surviving the Insured who are listed in the order they appear:"

1. first the Insured's spouse;
2. next the Insured's children;
3. next the Insured's parents;
4. next the Insured's brothers and sisters.

Under the terms of the policy, Billy was the insured. Both Charlotte and Billy died intestate with no children. Billy was survived by his three brothers, Rick, Keith, and Barry Foleno.

Indiana's "slayer statute" prohibits a murderer from gain by the death of the victim—but it has nothing to say about the problem at hand. The administrator of Charlotte's estate sued Rick, Keith, and Barry, arguing that the proceeds of Billy's life insurance should be distributed as if Billy had predeceased Charlotte. What is the reasoning of such a claim? How should the lawsuit be decided?

Pope v. Garrett
147 Tex. 18, 211 S.W.2d 559 (1948)

SMEDLEY, Justice.

This suit is by Claytonia Garrett against James Pope and others, the heirs of Carrie Simons, a negro woman, to impress a trust upon property that passed to the heirs on the death of Carrie Simons intestate, after she, during her last illness, had been forcibly prevented by two of the heirs from executing a will devising the property to Claytonia Garrett.

Following trial before a jury the district court rendered judgment awarding to the plaintiff, Claytonia Garrett, the beneficial title to the whole of the property. The Court of Civil Appeals affirmed the trial court's judgment in part and reversed and rendered it in part, holding that a trust should not be impressed upon the interests of those of the heirs who had not participated in the wrongful act. 204 S.W.2d 867.

The jury made the following findings: That Carrie Simons, some days before her death, requested Thomas Green to prepare a will for her leaving all of her property to Claytonia Garrett; that the will so prepared by Green was read by him to Carrie Simons; that after having heard the instrument read to her, Carrie Simons, in the presence of Reverend Preacher, Jewel Benson and others, declared it to be her last will; that Carrie Simons prepared to sign her name to the will but the defendants, Evelyn Jones and Lillie Clay Smith, by physical force or by creating a disturbance, prevented her from carrying out her intention to execute the will; that Carrie Simons was of sound mind at the time and was not in an unconscious condition; and that shortly after this incident she suffered a severe hemorrhage, lapsed into a semicomatose condition and remained in that condition continuously until her death, which was on November 3, 1944. There is no proof that any of the heirs of Carrie Simons other those above named were present or were in any way connected with the violence that prevented the execution of the will.

We find no difficulty in approving the conclusion reached both by the trial court and by the Court of Civil Appeals as to the interests of the heirs who were guilty of the wrongful acts: that when they acquired, by the inheritance, the legal title to interests in the property, they became constructive trustees for Claytonia Garrett. According to the facts found by the jury, title undoubtedly would have passed to her under Carrie Simons' will but for the acts of violence. The case is a typical one for the intervention of equity to prevent a wrongdoer, who by his fraudulent or otherwise wrongful act has acquired title to property, from retaining and enjoying the beneficial interest therein, by impressing a constructive trust on the property in favor of the one who is truly and equitably entitled to the same. It has been said that "The specific instances in which equity impresses a constructive trust are numberless,—as numberless as the modes by which property may be obtained through bad faith and unconscientious acts." Pomeroy's Equity Jurisprudence, 5th Ed., Vol. 4, §1045.

The argument is often made that the imposition of the constructive trust in a case like this contravenes or circumvents the statute of descent and distribution, the statute of wills, the statute of frauds, or particularly a statute which prohibits the creation of a trust unless it is declared by an instrument in writing. It is generally held, however, that the constructive trust is not within such statutes or is an exception to them. It is the creature of equity. It does not arise out of the parol agreement of the parties. It is imposed irrespective of and even contrary to the intention of the parties. Resort is had to it in order that a statute enacted for the purpose of preventing fraud may not be used as an instrument for perpetrating or protecting a fraud.

In this case Claytonia Garrett does not acquire title through the will. The trust does not owe its validity to the will. The statute of descent and distribution is untouched. The legal title passed to the heirs of Carrie Simons when she died intestate, but equity deals with the holder of the legal title for the wrong done in preventing the execution of the will and impresses a trust on the property in favor of the one who is in good conscience entitled to it.

The second question is more difficult. Shall the trust in favor of Claytonia Garret extend to the interests of the heirs who had no part in the wrongful acts? From the viewpoint of those heirs, it seems that they should be permitted to retain and enjoy the interests that vested in them as heirs, no will having been executed, and they not being responsible for the failure of Carrie Simons to execute it. On the other hand, from the viewpoint of Claytonia Garrett, it appears that a court of equity should extend the trust to all of the interests in the property in order that complete relief may be afforded her and that none of the heirs may profit as the result of the wrongful acts.

The policy against unjust enrichment argues in favor of the judgment rendered herein by the district court rather than that of the Court of Civil Appeals. But for the wrongful acts the innocent defendants would not have inherited interests in the property. Dean Roscoe Pound speaks of the constructive trust as a remedial institution and says that it is sometimes used "to develop a new field of equitable interposition, as in what we have come to think the typical case of constructive trust, namely, specific restitution of a received benefit in order to prevent unjust enrichment." 33 Harvard Law Review, pp.420, 421. Further and in the same trend, it has been said that equity is never wanting in power to do complete justice. Hill v. Stampfli, 290 S.W. 522, 524 (Tex. Comm'n of App. 1927).

We realize that a constructive trust does not arise on every moral wrong and that it cannot correct every injustice. It must be used with caution, especially where as here proof of the wrongful act rests in parol, in order that it may not defeat the purposes of the statute of wills, the statute of descent and distribution, or the statute of frauds.

In view of the authorities and equitable principles which have been cited and discussed, it is our opinion that the judgment of the district court should be affirmed in order that complete justice may be done.

Non-homicidal interference

1. The facts of Brazil v. Silva, 181 Cal. 490, 185 P. 174 (1919), were stated as follows:

> Frank V. Silva died in May 1910. Four years before he had made a will, leaving all his property to the defendant whom he described as his wife. The will was admitted to probate in April 1912. Thereafter the plaintiffs commenced a contest to revoke its probate and the contest was decided against them. In April 1915, a decree of distribution was made distributing the estate to the defendant. The present action [to impose a constructive trust on the property so distributed] was commenced November 20, 1915.
>
> It is averred that the defendant was not in fact the wife of Silva and that the plaintiffs are his sole heirs at law, that Silva when he made

his will delivered it to the defendant, that thereafter he demanded it back from her for the purpose of destroying it and thereby revoking it, that she thereupon in the presence of Silva and at his request destroyed by burning an envelope which she falsely stated to him to contain his will but which in fact did not, that this false statement was made by the defendant for the purpose of preserving the will without the knowledge of Silva so that she might take advantage of its terms in case of his death, and, finally, that Silva from that time on believed that the will had been destroyed and that he had no will and died in that belief.

Given that Frank Silva's will has already been contested and found valid in probate, what can the law of restitution do about this situation?

2. A probate court, in the traditional view, had no power either to enforce a will that had not been made (the problem in *Pope v. Garrett*), or to refuse enforcement of a will that had been validly made and not revoked (the problem in *Brazil v. Silva*). Restitution was employed to fill these gaps. Courts could disclaim any interference with legal and statutory dispositions—in particular, the requirements of the Wills Act—because of the way constructive trust was understood to operate. As the court in *Pope v. Garrett* was careful to insist, property passed to the defendants in these cases according to the strict rules of probate. But if it came into the hands of the wrong recipient—judged by equitable principles—that person could be ordered (by a proceeding outside probate) to convey it to the person with the better equitable claim.

3. The facts of In re Estate of Mollard, 98 So. 2d 814 (Fla. Dist. Ct. App. 1957), were stated as follows:

The appellee, a licensed practicing nurse, hereinafter referred to as the petitioner, was employed on February 22, 1950 by Mary Mitchell Mollard who on April 24, 1953 executed a will bequeathing $5,000 to petitioner on condition that she was still in the employ of testator at the time of her death. The residuary legatee was John Thorne Mollard, testator's husband, who was familiar with the will and the subject legacy long prior to testator's death on September 2, 1954, following which he qualified as executor thereof.

Petitioner continued actively in performance of the duties of her employment until August 13, 1954—approximately 20 days prior to decedent's death and over a year after the will was executed—when testator's husband summarily required her to leave the premises where she carried on her duties. Upon his refusal, as executor of the will, to recognize the legacy, she petitioned the County Judge's Court to determine her right thereto, and the answer of the respondent executor sought to justify his action on the ground that petitioner was not in the employ of testator at the time of her death.

Did Mr. Mollard do anything wrong when he discharged the nurse, whose employment was presumably "at will"?

Farnsworth, *Restitution* 73-74 (2014):

So far we have been occupied with cases where one person uses or takes the property of another in some way. But property can end up in the wrong hands through less direct means. In *Riggs v. Palmer*, 115 N.Y. 506, 22 N.E. 188 (1889), Elmer Palmer was the largest beneficiary named in the will of his grandfather, Francis Palmer. Worried that the grandfather might change his mind, Elmer poisoned him. It might seem obvious that a party in Elmer's position cannot be allowed to have the money that the decedent's will leaves to him. The bad incentive it would create is plain enough, though letting Elmer collect would seem intolerable even if his motive hadn't been to obtain the money (e.g., if he hadn't known about the will when he poisoned Francis). But just *how* a party like Elmer Palmer is to be denied the inheritance has caused occasional puzzlement. The slayer is criminally liable for the murder, obviously, but the consequences of that liability are set by statute, and the statute may just call for a prison sentence and say nothing about money. Meanwhile other parts of the statute law, not to mention the decedent's will, may indicate that the slayer is entitled to the money and contain no qualifications or exceptions to cover the problem of the murdering heir.

The court in *Riggs* held that since the legislature would not have wanted the murderer to gain from his crime, the statutes should be construed to forbid that result. *Riggs* has played a part in debates about whether and when courts have to step beyond the authoritative legal materials bearing on a case to reach a just result in it. But when viewed as a restitution case, the correct handling of *Riggs* is not so remarkable: declare that the grandson has been unjustly enriched and that he holds the money in constructive trust for the proper beneficiaries. Or use the same principles to prevent the murderer from ever acquiring legal title to the assets in the first place. On this view the difficulties associated with *Riggs* merely illustrate the limits of law as distinct from equity.

The particular doctrine of restitution that prevents the murdering heir from profiting is sometimes called the "slayer rule." Identifying and proving the unjust enrichment in such a case tends to be simple so long as the defendant's criminal liability is clear enough. If he has been convicted of murder, the findings in the criminal case probably will be regarded as conclusive in the civil suit under the doctrine of collateral estoppel. But who gets the money if the slayer doesn't? The answer usually will be the other beneficiaries in the decedent's will, or the other payees of his insurance policy, or any alternative or contingent beneficiaries named in the will or policy—in other words, those whom the decedent thought should receive his property if the slayer were unable to receive it or, where none of these sources of guidance are helpful, whoever would succeed to legal ownership in the slayer's absence (perhaps some distant kin of the decedent). If there are no heirs in view, the state can take title to the decedent's property by escheat.

The approach just described, rather than the approach of *Riggs v. Palmer*, has been the most common judicial handling of the murdering heir, at least until the jurisdiction adopts a statute that directs a similar outcome without need for help from judges. Most states do now have statutes of that kind, but they do not always cover all the variations that can arise on this fact pattern. When they don't, traditional principles of restitution continue to fill the gaps. For example, the statutes are likely to speak of inheritance by the slayer without addressing the problem of insurance benefits payable to him. Restitution reaches all such cases, because they all involve unjust enrichment.

Chapter 8

Remedies

A. RESTITUTION IN MONEY: THE MEASURE OF ENRICHMENT

(1) Innocent recipients

Vickery v. Ritchie
202 Mass. 247, 88 N.E. 835 (1909)

KNOWLTON, C.J.

This is an action to recover a balance of $10,467.16, alleged to be due the plaintiff as a contractor, for the construction of a Turkish bath house upon land of the defendant on Carver Street in Boston. The parties signed duplicate contracts in writing, covering the work. At the time when the plaintiff signed both copies of the contract, the defendant's signature was attached, and the contract price therein named was $33,721. When the defendant signed them the contract price stated in each was $23,200. Until the building was completed, the plaintiff held a contract under which he was to receive the larger sum, while the defendant held a contract for the same work, under which he was to pay only the smaller sum. This resulted from the fraud of the architect who drew the contracts, and did all the business and made all the payments for the defendant. The contracts were on typewritten sheets, and it is supposed that the architect accomplished the fraud by changing the sheets on which the price was written, before the signing by the plaintiff, and before the delivery to the defendant. The parties did not discover the discrepancy between the two writings until after the building was substantially completed. Each of them acted honestly and in good faith, trusting the statements of the architect. The architect was indicted, but he left the Commonwealth and escaped punishment.

The auditor found that the market value of the labor and materials furnished by the plaintiff, not including the customary charge for the supervision of the work, was $33,499.30, and that their total cost to the plaintiff was $32,950.96. He found that the land and building have cost the defendant much more than their market value. The findings indicate that it was bad judgment on the part of the defendant to build such a structure upon the lot, and that the increase in the market value of the real estate, by reason of that which the plaintiff put upon it, is only $22,000. The failure of the parties to discover the difference between their copies of the contract was caused by the frequently repeated fraudulent representations of the architect to each of them.

The plaintiff and defendant were mistaken in supposing that they had made a binding contract for the construction of this building. Their minds never met in any agreement about the price. The labor and materials were furnished at the defendant's request and for the defendant's benefit. From this alone the law would imply a contract on the part of the defendant to pay for them. The fact that the parties supposed the price was fixed by a contract, when in fact there was no contract, does not prevent this implication, but leaves it as a natural result of their relations. Both parties understood and agreed that the work should be paid for, and both parties thought that they had agreed upon the price. Their mutual mistake in this particular left them with no express contract by which their rights and liabilities could be determined. The law implies an obligation to pay for what has been done and furnished under such circumstances, and the defendant, upon whose property the work was done, has no right to say that it is not to be paid for. The doctrine is not applicable to work upon real estate alone. The rule would be the same if the work and materials were used in the repair of a carriage, or of any other article of personal property, under a supposed contract with the owner, if, through a mutual mistake as to the supposed agreement upon the price, the contract became unenforceable.

If the law implies an agreement to pay, how much is to be paid? There is but one answer. The fair value of that which was furnished. No other rule can be applied. Under certain conditions the price fixed by the contract might control in such cases. In this case there was no price fixed. The right of recovery depends upon the plaintiff's having furnished property or labor, under circumstances which entitle him to be paid for it, not upon the ultimate benefit to the property of the owner at whose request it was furnished.

It follows that the plaintiff is entitled to recover the fair value of his labor and materials.

Unrequested benefits; splitting losses

1. The facts of Campbell v. Tennessee Valley Authority, 421 F.2d 293 (5th Cir. 1969), can be gleaned from the following paragraphs of the majority and dissenting opinions:

Campbell entered into an oral agreement with Earl Daniel, Director of the TVA Technical Library, to reproduce 13 sets of technical trade journals on 16 mm. microfilm at a price of $90 per roll. Mr. Daniel had no authority to make such a purchase for TVA and entered into the agreement with Campbell without the knowledge of his superiors. Campbell photographed, developed and processed 336 rolls of 16 mm. film containing the journals in question, placed the film in cartridges and delivered them to the TVA Technical Library at Muscle Shoals. Under the terms of the oral agreement, the charge for this work was to have been $30,240. The cartridges were placed on the shelves of the library and were available to its patrons for approximately two months. [There is evidence in the record that in this two-month period, three of the cartridges were each used once.]

The microfilm cartridges were then returned to Campbell by registered mail along with a letter from Daniel stating that there was no contract for their reproduction, that he had no authority to enter into such a contract, and that the price of the film was excessive. Campbell refused to accept the film and it was returned to the library, where it has since been stored. TVA has refused to pay for the film. The journals reproduced by Campbell were destroyed upon instruction by Daniel.

Robert Holladay, Manager of the Microfilm Office at Xerox University Microfilm, "the largest supplier of microfilm outside of the federal government," testified that his company would have duplicated Campbell's work for $10,000 and in addition would have returned the original journals to TVA, whereas Campbell, at Daniel's direction, destroyed them.

Shirley Nichols, who seems to have succeeded Earl Daniel as TVA's librarian, testified at trial about the value of the microfilm:

> Q. How about the ability to get to either one of the materials, say the materials on microfilm as opposed to going through the hard cover? Which is faster?
> A. Going to the hard cover is much more satisfactory.
> Q. It is faster and more satisfactory for the person in pure research?
> A. Yes.
> Q. As a librarian, do you personally prefer microfilm or hard copy?
> A. Hard copy.

Campbell had no claim on the express contract (why not?), so like the builder in the Turkish bathhouse case he sued in *quantum meruit*. The Court of Appeals affirmed a trial court judgment of $30,240. What kind of *quantum meruit* was that? What was the value of Campbell's work to the TVA?

2. Restitution measures unjust enrichment differently depending on whether the defendant is an "innocent recipient" or a "conscious wrongdoer." Both *Vickery v. Ritchie* and *Campbell v. TVA* show us "innocent recipients,"

where the question of unjust enrichment is not "what were these benefits worth?" but rather "what were they worth to the defendant?"

At this point it makes a difference whether the benefits in question were *requested*. A claimant who has conferred a benefit that an innocent defendant did not ask for might recover much less than its market value—and might not recover at all. This was the problem in *Michigan Central* (misdelivered coal) and *Continental Forest Products* (plywood delivered by wrong supplier). By contrast, liability for something the defendant has requested from the claimant is ordinarily not less than its market value.

Vickery v. Ritchie and *Campbell v. TVA* are both cases in which it might appear at first blush that the defendant asked for what he received. On closer examination, we see that both transactions were involuntary in critical respects. (Do you see why?) They are also cases that most observers (as well as the Restatement) think were wrongly decided. (For another example of the same problem, recall *Upton-on-Severn RDC v. Powell*—the case of the "wrong fire department" in Chapter 2.) Is the problem in all three cases the persistent confusion between different meanings of "implied contract"?

3. The liability of an innocent recipient for unrequested, nonmoney benefits is sometimes described as "cost or benefit, whichever is less." Cases of mistaken improvements offer some of the clearest examples. Almost invariably, the value added to defendant's property by a mistaken improvement is less than the cost of the claimant's labor and materials. (Why should this be?) Occasionally—at least in theory—a mistaken improvement might add value exceeding its cost. But the measure of enrichment in either case is the cost to the claimant or the increased value of the property, *whichever is less*. Courts say things like, "the owner cannot be said to have been unjustly enriched in excess of the improver's cost." Madrid v. Spears, 250 F.2d 51 (10th Cir. 1957). Why not?

4. Students who read *Vickery v. Ritchie* before they have internalized an orthodox analysis in terms of unjust enrichment often want to split the loss between Vickery and Ritchie. Do you see why neither contract nor restitution will yield that result? (Nor will tort, unless we make one of the parties responsible for the conduct of the architect, which does not appear to have been the case.) Can you define a legal principle that would make it possible to split losses in a case like this?

5. A famous English case of successive frauds, Ingram v. Little, [1961] 1 Q.B. 31 (Ct. App. 1960), can be summarized as follows:

> Three ladies in Bournemouth placed an advertisement in the local paper offering to sell their used motorcar: "1957 Dauphine, 3800 miles, sky blue, £725 o.n.o." A rogue calling himself Hutchinson came to look at the car. He talked at length about himself, offered £700, agreed on £717, and persuaded the ladies to take a check. He informed them that he was a reputable person named P.G.M. Hutchinson, of Stanstead House,

Stanstead Road, Caterham, and when the sellers found just such a person listed in the telephone directory they were convinced their visitor was telling the truth. Three days later, "Hutchinson" (now calling himself "Hardy") sold the car to Little, a used-car dealer in Blackpool, who gave him £605 in trade against the price of a Ford Consul. Little was acting in good faith. The check for £717 was returned unpaid. Sellers sued Little for conversion.

Kull, *Ponzi, Property, and Luck*, 100 Iowa L. Rev. 291, 320-21 (2014). Following existing legal principles the result is necessarily all or nothing, one way or the other: either Little is protected as a bona fide purchaser against the sellers' restitution claim (in which case they take the entire loss), or he is not (in which case he does). A dissenting opinion in *Ingram* rejected this alternative:

> The true spirit of the common law is to override theoretical distinctions when they stand in the way of doing practical justice. For the doing of justice, the relevant question in this sort of case is not whether the contract was void or voidable, but which of two innocent parties shall suffer for the fraud of a third. The plain answer is that the loss should be divided between them in such proportion as is just in all the circumstances. If it be pure misfortune, the loss should be borne equally; if the fault or imprudence of either party has caused or contributed to the loss, it should be borne by that party in the whole or in the greater part.

[1961] 1 Q.B. at 73-74 (Devlin, L.J.).

Fabian v. Wasatch Orchard Co.
41 Utah 404, 125 P. 860 (1912)

STRAUP, J.

The case was tried to the court, without a jury. The court found: That the defendant had invested a considerable sum of money in growing asparagus for canning purposes, and that the asparagus plants had reached a stage where they would be producing in considerable quantities. That the defendant was heavily in debt and in straightened financial circumstances. That it had a large quantity of such product on hand, but had no market or outlet for it. That it desired to convert the products into cash, regardless of the profit from the sales thereof, and to create a market therefor in Eastern cities, especially in Kansas City, St. Louis, Cincinnati, Chicago, Pittsburgh, Boston, New York, and Philadelphia, and to advertise and introduce its products in such markets. That thereupon the plaintiff, a merchant broker at Salt Lake City, at the solicitation and request of the general manager of the defendant, and for and on its behalf, visited such cities and there advertised the defendant's products, and devoted time and services in introducing them and in creating a market for them, and solicited and obtained orders amounting, at the prices fixed for the products, to the aggregate sum of between $30,000 and $35,000. That the defendant accepted the benefit of such services, and, to the extent of its capacity, filled such orders to the amount of at least $16,000, and that the reasonable value of plaintiff's services was $2,300.

The court further found that, in consideration of the services to be rendered, the defendant's general manager orally agreed to give plaintiff for three years the exclusive right to sell the defendant's products in Utah and Southern Idaho, and to give him 2½ percent commission of all sales made in such territory during such time, either by himself or others.

[By the end of the year, Wasatch was out of the canning business. Because his oral contract of employment was unenforceable under the Statute of Frauds, Fabian sued in restitution for the value of his services selling Wasatch asparagus. Fabian recovered $2,300, and Wasatch appeals.]

In its brief it states the proposition for consideration to be: "There is but one question in this case, and that is: Was the defendant enriched in any manner by the part performance of the oral contract, which was within the statute of frauds, and what was the value of that enrichment? In other words, what was the value of the benefits received by the defendant from the part performance of the oral contract by the plaintiff?"

The defendant urges that the court erred in permitting the plaintiff to prove the reasonable value of the services, and in giving the plaintiff a judgment for the sum of $2,300, the found reasonable value thereof, and further assails the judgment for the reason, as contended by it, that the products sold by it in the Eastern markets on the orders solicited and procured by the plaintiff were sold for less than cost of manufacturing them, and were therefore sold, not to the defendant's profit or gain, but to its loss; and hence the defendant received no "benefit" from the services rendered by the plaintiff and accepted and received by it.

It is not contended that the services rendered by the plaintiff, or the orders obtained by him, were not rendered or obtained in accordance with the contract. No such claim is made. The claim made is that the defendant did not profit, "was not enriched," by the transaction. The defendant's contention leads to this: If A should orally employ B for a period of three years to do the labor in the manufacture of 100,000 brick (assuming such a contract to be within the statute of frauds), and if B, on the faith of and in accordance with the contract, should, within the first nine months, make and produce 20,000, which were received and accepted by A, and A should then repudiate the contract and refuse to longer engage B's services, B could not recover the reasonable value of the services on a *quantum meruit*, but to entitle him to recover it would be essential for him to show that the market value of the brick so made by him and received by A was more than the cost of manufacture; otherwise A received no "benefit" from B's services. Or, if A should orally employ B to work on his farm for a term of three years and agree to give him 10 acres of land at the end of that period, and if B, on the faith of the contract, should work nine months on the farm for A in tilling the soil, sowing grain, and reaping crops, and A should then repudiate the contract and refuse to longer engage B's services, again B could not recover the reasonable value of his services; and if it were made to appear that because of drought or a falling market, or other causes not due to his negligence or willfulness, the market price of the products was less than the cost of productions, then A received no benefit from B's services, and the latter could not recover from the former.

We think the well-established rule is that, where one who, not in default, on the faith of and in accordance with a contract unenforceable because within the statute of frauds, but not *malum prohibitum* nor *malum in se*, has, in pursuance of the contract, rendered services for the adversary party, who, with knowledge or acquiescence, accepted them and received the benefit of them and repudiated the contract, he may recover on a *quantum meruit* the reasonable value thereof—not the profit or gain resulting to the adversary party by reason of the transaction, nor the loss suffered or sustained by the other, but compensation for the reasonable value of the services rendered by the one and accepted and received by the other.

Requested benefits

1. The Statute of Frauds is central to the issue in *Fabian v. Wasatch*, because it meant that recovery could only be in restitution—not on the contract. But compare the position if Fabian had managed to obtain a written contract on the same terms. How does he establish his entitlement to contract damages from future commissions in Utah and southern Idaho? As we saw in Chapter 6, there is a version of "restitution for breach" that uses the value of benefits conferred as an alternative measure of damages.

2. According to the scheme of the Restatement, the fact that makes Wasatch liable for the market value of Fabian's services—here $2,300—is that his services were *requested*. What would be the measure of recovery in restitution on the following variations of the facts? (In each case, Fabian achieves the same sales results described in the opinion.)

(a) Instead of promising a future sales agency in Utah and southern Idaho, the general manager promises Fabian $300 a week for selling asparagus. Fabian worked 10 weeks before his position was terminated.

(b) The sales trip to Eastern markets was Fabian's own idea. He made no agreement ahead of time, but he felt sure Wasatch would pay for his valuable services.

(c) The person who sent Fabian on the asparagus tour (and who promised him the future exclusive territory) was a former salesman for Wasatch, impersonating the general manager. This salesman had recently been fired, and he thought the episode would make a good joke on the general manager.

See R3RUE §2(3) (reproduced at the beginning of Chapter 5); R3RUE §§49-50 (reproduced immediately below).

3. Does the price term of an unenforceable contract fix the value of performance for purposes of restitution? The Restatement proposes that it depends on the reason for unenforceability. A contract induced by fraud might be of no weight in measuring values conferred on the defrauded party. At the other extreme, a contract that is unenforceable only because of the failure to satisfy some formal requirement (like the Statute of Frauds) might still constitute the best evidence of the parties' independent valuation of a requested performance. Thus in *Pelletier v. Johnson* (Chapter 6), an unenforceable contract for installation of vinyl siding was still used to measure the benefit conferred on the homeowner when the contractor did the work.

In Gregory v. Lee, 64 Conn. 407, 30 A. 53 (1894), a Yale undergraduate—an "infant" under Connecticut law at the time—rented a room for 40 weeks (September to June) at $10 per week, then moved out in February. Landlady sued Student to collect the rent from February to June. This claim failed: because Student lacked legal capacity, he could not make a contract that Landlady could enforce. There was no problem about the rent for September to February, because Student paid regularly so long as he occupied the room. What if Student was six weeks behind in the rent on the day he moved out, and the going rate for a room in New Haven was $9 per week?

Restatement Third, Restitution and Unjust Enrichment

§49. RESTITUTION IN MONEY; MEASURES OF ENRICHMENT

(1) A claimant entitled to restitution may obtain a judgment for money in the amount of the defendant's unjust enrichment.

(2) Enrichment from a money payment is measured by the amount of the payment or the resulting increase in the defendant's net assets, whichever is less.

(3) Enrichment from the receipt of nonreturnable benefits may be measured by

(a) the value of the benefit in advancing the purposes of the defendant,

(b) the cost to the claimant of conferring the benefit,

(c) the market value of the benefit, or

(d) a price the defendant has expressed a willingness to pay, if the defendant's assent may be treated as valid on the question of price.

(4) When restitution is intended to strip the defendant of a wrongful gain, the standard of liability is not the value of the benefit conferred but the amount of the profit wrongfully obtained.

---

§50. INNOCENT RECIPIENT

(1) An "innocent recipient" is one who commits no misconduct in the transaction concerned and who bears no responsibility for the unjust enrichment in question.

(2) If nonreturnable benefits would be susceptible of different valuations by the standards identified in §49(3), the liability of an innocent recipient is determined as follows:

(a) Unjust enrichment from unrequested benefits is measured by the standard that yields the smallest liability in restitution.

(b) Unjust enrichment from requested benefits is measured by their reasonable value to the recipient. Reasonable value is normally the lesser of market value and a price the recipient has expressed a willingness to pay.

(3) The liability in restitution of an innocent recipient of unrequested benefits may not leave the recipient worse off (apart from the costs of litigation) than if the transaction giving rise to the liability had not occurred.

(4) The liability in restitution of an innocent recipient of unrequested benefits may not exceed the cost to the claimant of conferring the benefits in question.

---

(2) Enrichment by misconduct

De Camp v. Bullard
159 N.Y. 450, 54 N.E. 26 (1899)

VANN, J.

In 1894 the plaintiff owned a large quantity of land on John Brown's tract in the Adirondack wilderness, through which the north branch of the Moose river runs, as it winds and turns, for between twenty and thirty miles. John A. Dix and Edward Thomson, Jr., having purchased the softwood trees standing on lands farther in the forest than those of the plaintiff, were preparing to float logs down the north branch to their mill some thirty miles below. On the 26th of June, 1896, the plaintiff recovered a judgment against Dix and Thomson perpetually restraining them from entering upon his lands and from interfering in any manner with that part of the north branch flowing over them for the purpose of floating, driving or transporting logs thereon, and from increasing or diminishing the natural flow of water in the stream over said lands by the use of dams or artificial means.

[A year later, the permanent injunction against trespass was "suspended" for a period of six weeks, on condition that the defendants give a formal undertaking to indemnify the plaintiff "against any and all loss or damage whatsoever sustained by the plaintiff" as a result of the trespass that was now being permitted to take place.] The object of this order was to enable Dix and Thomson to float to their mill a large quantity of logs which they had cut under the advice of counsel, and in the belief that they had the right to use the river for that purpose. An undertaking was given accordingly, signed by the defendants as sureties.

The question presented for decision is whether the words "any and all damages and loss whatsoever," as used in said undertaking, include the tollage, or the reasonable value of the use of the river for the purpose of floating logs, as claimed by the plaintiff, or simply the damage done to the banks of the river and the property of the plaintiff adjacent thereto, as claimed by the defendants. The question is presented by an exception to evidence given in behalf of the plaintiff as to the value of the tollage and by an exception to a denial of the defendants' motion to direct a verdict of six cents in favor of the plaintiff, who furnished no evidence tending to show actual injury to his property or that he had any use for the stream at the time, or that he had lost an opportunity to rent it to others during the period in question.

It appeared, however, that after the undertaking was filed, and during the period of suspension, Dix and Thomson floated over that part of the north branch which flows through plaintiff's land 2,000,000 feet of logs for a distance of sixteen miles. Witnesses for the plaintiff testified that this privilege was worth two cents a mile per thousand feet, while witnesses for the defendant stated that the tollage was worth nothing upon a stream in the situation and condition of the north branch at the time. No question was raised as to the validity of the undertaking, or as to any point except the measure of damages. The jury was instructed to give the plaintiff fair compensation for the use of the river to float the 2,000,000 feet of logs upon, and the defendant took no exception to the charge. A verdict was rendered in favor of the plaintiff for $500, and the judgment entered thereon having been affirmed by the Appellate Division, the defendants come here.

The defendants insist that the measure of damages is not what the privilege of trespassing was worth to the trespassers, but what the plaintiff actually lost through interference with his business, loss of rent and the like. As there was no proof of actual loss of this character, they further insist that the plaintiff is entitled to nominal damages only. This position would place a premium on trespassing, because it makes the position of the trespasser more favorable than that of one lawfully contracting. If a man's house is vacant with no prospect of a tenant and no intention on his part of occupying it himself, and a trespasser occupies it, he must pay as damages for the trespass the value of the use and occupation, for this would be the duty of a tenant contracting upon a *quantum meruit* for the use, by consent, of that which the trespasser uses without consent.

In cases of involuntary trespass the damages are restricted as much as possible, but when the trespass is deliberate, intentional and continuous, they include, at least, the value of the use of the premises for the period that the owner is kept out of possession. "If," says Mr. Sutherland, "the defendant derives a benefit from the tortious use of the plaintiff's premises, the plaintiff will be entitled to damages measured by the benefit to the defendant. Where the trespass suspends or impairs the enjoyment of the premises, compensation may be given on the basis of rental value in the absence of any ground for special damages or in addition to such special damages." (Sutherland on Damages, vol. 3, pp. 366-7.)

We think that the promise, under all the circumstances, embraced more than mere indemnity against the unimportant consequences of a bare infringement of a legal right, and that it included damages in the nature of compensation for the value of the use of the river for floating logs. Such would be the measure of damages in an action against Dix and Thomson, and we regard the stipulation of the sureties as co-extensive with the obligation of their principals. The language used, and the facts surrounding the parties when it was used, show that substantial and complete indemnity was intended, and this of necessity includes the tollage or the income which the river ought to bring when used to float logs. Whatever the plaintiff might have received from a prudent use or renting of the property, had he not been deprived of its possession, the defendants, by signing the undertaking, placed themselves under obligation to pay.

The judgment should be affirmed, with costs.

Taking without asking

1. The dispute in *De Camp v. Bullard* was somewhat convoluted, but once the situation comes into focus it makes a useful paradigm. The lower court issued an injunction against trespass, then later changed its mind. (Probably the reasoning was "balance of hardships.") But the fact that there was no injunction did not mean that the unauthorized use of the Moose River was not a trespass. After all that litigation, the trespass could hardly be inadvertent. And yet the log owners were not willful wrongdoers either—having obtained, in a sense, the court's permission to trespass.

2. Trespass is a strict-liability tort, in the sense that the loggers would have been tortfeasors even if they had been innocently mistaken about permission to use the river. In Restatement terms, the use of the river was a benefit obtained by "misconduct of the defendant, culpable or otherwise" and therefore measured by the rules of R3RUE §51 (see the following extracts). One of these rules is that if benefits obtained by misconduct have a market

value—"identified, where appropriate, with the reasonable cost of a license"—that valuation of what the defendant has wrongfully obtained is the minimum liability in unjust enrichment. *De Camp v. Bullard* gives us a perfect example of this kind of valuation (in the customary "tollage" for log-floating), and the court gives a perfect explanation of why such liability is necessarily imposed.

3. With its verdict of $500, the jury seems to have assessed tollage toward the high end of the range suggested by the witnesses, though not at the very top ($640). What recovery would we anticipate if the loggers had been innocently mistaken about the course of the Moose River, making their trespass on plaintiff's property entirely inadvertent? What if they had floated their logs in defiance of the original injunction?

4. As a "conscious wrongdoer," an intentional trespasser is liable for "the net profit attributable to the underlying wrong." R3RUE §51(4). But as we saw in the context of copyright infringement in Chapter 7, the question of how much profit is "attributable to the underlying wrong" can be difficult to resolve.

In America Online, Inc. v. National Health Care Discount, Inc., 174 F. Supp. 2d 890 (N.D. Iowa 2001), professional emailers working for NHCD had been advertising its "discount optical and dental service plans" using "unsolicited bulk email" ("UBE" or "spam"). In violation of federal statutes (and of local tort law on trespass to chattels), NHCD's agents sent 135 million items of UBE to customers of AOL. Damages to AOL—measured by the incremental cost of handling these unwanted messages—were calculated at 78¢ per thousand, or $105,300. AOL argued that liability should be measured instead by what it would have charged NHCD for 135 million "impressions" achieved through paid advertising at an average rate of $8.56 per thousand, or $1,155,600.

> The court agrees AOL's damages should not be limited to the amount NHCD's wrongful conduct cost AOL. Such a result would permit NHCD, and others in a similar position, to appropriate the use of AOL's equipment at cost, without compensating AOL for any profit. On the other hand, the court sees significant differences between the value of a banner advertisement and the value of UBE. Banner advertisements are much larger on a computer screen than incoming e-mail messages. Banners usually are in color, with eye-catching graphics. They often have moving text. They can be linked directly to an advertiser's website, taking the viewer to the site with a single click of the mouse. While AOL stresses the similarities between UBE and banner advertisements, and argues that UBE, in several respects, is actually more valuable than a banner advertisement, the court is not convinced. AOL's own witnesses stressed the almost universal hostility of AOL members to UBE, while the same hostility apparently does not exist as to banner advertisements.
>
> Considering all of the circumstances, the court finds a rate of $2.50 per thousand pieces of UBE is appropriate. Using this rate, the court finds AOL's actual damages are $337,500. This is an appropriate amount both to charge NHCD and to compensate AOL for the NHCD's e-mailers'

use of AOL's computer system. It also is approximately the same amount NHCD paid to its e-mailers for the leads produced from UBE sent to AOL members, which supports the court's conclusion that it is a fair and reasonable amount.

Id. at 900-901. Has the court overlooked another possible measure—possibly more appropriate—of NHCD's liability to AOL?

————————————

Restatement Third, Restitution and Unjust Enrichment

§51. ENRICHMENT BY MISCONDUCT; DISGORGEMENT; ACCOUNTING

(1) As used in this section, the term "misconduct" designates an actionable interference by the defendant with the claimant's legally protected interests . . . .

(2) The value for restitution purposes of benefits obtained by the misconduct of the defendant, culpable or otherwise, is not less than their market value. Market value may be identified, where appropriate, with the reasonable cost of a license.

(3) A "conscious wrongdoer" is a defendant who is enriched by misconduct and who acts

(a) with knowledge of the underlying wrong to the claimant, or

(b) despite a known risk that the conduct in question violates the rights of the claimant.

(4) Unless the rule of subsection (2) imposes a greater liability, the unjust enrichment of a conscious wrongdoer, or of a defaulting fiduciary without regard to notice or fault, is the net profit attributable to the underlying wrong. The object of restitution in such cases is to eliminate profit from wrongdoing while avoiding, so far as possible, the imposition of a penalty. Restitution remedies that pursue this object are often called "disgorgement" or "accounting."

————————————

Farnsworth, *Restitution* 69-70 (2014):

What if a deliberate wrong produces no damages or consequential gains? In *Jacque v. Steenburg Homes*, 209 Wis. 2d 605, 563 N.W.2d 154 (1997), the defendant sought to deliver a mobile home to a neighbor of the plaintiffs. The easiest way was to convey it across the plaintiffs' land. The alternate route was covered with seven feet of snow and contained a turn that would have required expensive equipment to navigate. The plaintiffs refused to permit the defendant to come onto their property. The defendant did it anyway. The plaintiffs sued for trespass, and the defendant replied that the plaintiffs could show no actual damages. The court agreed that the plaintiffs' damages were nominal but awarded them $100,000 in punitive damages anyway. The court noted with apparent disapproval that the defendant had considered the affair a laughing matter. The *Restatement* suggests, plausibly, that the case might as easily been dealt with as a matter of restitution. How to measure the defendant's gains? Not just by awarding the market value of a license to cross the plaintiffs' property, for that would put the defendant on the same footing as someone who did the right thing by bargaining for permission (and also on the same footing as someone who committed the mistake innocently). A more suitably aggressive measure would account for what the defendant would have had to spend if the plaintiffs' property had not been available: the cost of plowing through the snow and using pricey equipment to get around the bend in the road.

This general approach to valuation—making the defendant pay the cost avoided by invading the plaintiff's rights—is an especially attractive measure in a case like *Jacque* where the plaintiffs had specifically denied permission to the defendant to take or use the property in question. It also can serve as a fallback measure in cases where consequential damages exist but can't be calculated with confidence. It might seem more direct to treat such a case as a matter of tort law and award punitive damages, especially since the punitive award is more likely to not only make the defendant's conduct valueless to him but to ensure that it has a negative expected value. Restitution, however, has the advantage of being less arbitrary (in *Jacque* there was no particular basis for the $100,000 the court authorized; it was a round number). And awards of punitive damages are, partly on account of that sort of arbitrariness, subject to constitutional challenges that are not likely to be an issue in a restitution case.

E.E. Bolles Wooden Ware Co. v. United States
106 U.S. 432 (1882)

Miller, J.

This was an action in the nature of trover, brought by the United States for the value of 242 cords of ash timber, or wood suitable for manufacturing purposes, cut and removed from that part of the public lands known as the reservation of the Oneida tribe of Indians, in the state of Wisconsin. This timber was knowingly and wrongfully taken from the land by Indians, and carried by them some distance to the town of Depere, and there sold to the defendant, which was not chargeable with any intentional wrong or misconduct or bad faith in the purchase. The timber on the ground, after it was felled, was worth 25 cents per cord, or $60.71 for the whole, and, at the town of Depere, where defendant bought and received it, $3.50 per cord, or $850 for the whole quantity. The question on which the judges divided was whether the liability of the defendant should be measured by the first or the last of these valuations. It was the opinion of the circuit judge that the latter was the proper rule of damages, and judgment was rendered against the defendant for that sum.

We cannot follow counsel for the plaintiff in error through the examination of all the cases, both in England and this country, which his commendable research has enabled him to place upon the brief. In the English courts the decisions have in the main grown out of coal taken from the mine, and in such cases the principle seems to be established in those courts that when suit is brought for the value of the coal so taken, and it has been the result of an honest mistake as to the true ownership of the mine, and the taking was not a willful trespass, the rule of damages is the value of the coal as it was in the mine before it was disturbed, and not its value when dug out and delivered at the mouth of the mine.

The doctrine of the English courts on this subject is probably as well stated by Lord HATHERLY in the House of Lords, in the case of Livingston v. Rawyards Coal Co. (1880) L.R. 5 App. Cas. 33, as anywhere else. He said:

> There is no doubt that if a man furtively, and in bad faith, robs his neighbor of his property, and because it is underground is probably for some little time not detected, the court of equity in this country will struggle, or I would rather say, will assert its authority, to punish the fraud by fixing the person with the value of the whole of the property which he has so furtively taken, and making him no allowance in respect of what he has so done, as would have been justly made to him if the parties had been working by agreement. [But] when once we arrive at the fact that an inadvertence has been the cause of the misfortune, then the simple course is to make every just allowance for outlay on the part of the person who has so acquired the property, and to give back to the owner, so far as is possible under the circumstances of the case, the full value of that which cannot be restored to him in specie.

There seems to us to be no doubt that in the case of a willful trespass the rule as stated above is the law of damages both in England and in this country. On the other hand, the weight of authority in this country as well as in England favors the doctrine that where the trespass is the result of inadvertence or mistake, and the wrong was not intentional, the value of the property when first taken must govern, or if the conversion sued for was after value had been added to it by the work of the defendant, he should be credited with this addition.

While these principles are sufficient to enable us to fix a measure of damages in both classes of torts where the original trespasser is defendant, there remains a third class where a purchaser from him is sued, as in this case, for the conversion of the property to his own use. In such case, if the first taker of the property were guilty of no willful wrong, the rule can in no case be more stringent against the defendant who purchased of him than against his vendor. But the case before us is one where, by reason of the willful wrong of the party who committed the trespass, he was liable, under the rule we have supposed to be established, for the value of the timber at Depere the moment before he sold it, and the question to be decided is whether the defendant who purchased it then with no notice that the property belonged to the United States, and with no intention to do wrong, must respond by the same rule of damages as his vendor should if he had been sued.

It seems to us that he must. The timber at all stages of the conversion was the property of plaintiff. Its purchase by defendant did not divest the title nor the right of possession. The recovery of any sum whatever is based upon that proposition. This right, at the moment preceding the purchase by defendant at Depere, was perfect, with no right in any one to set up a claim for work and labor bestowed on it by the wrongdoer. If the case were one which concerned additional value placed upon the property by the work or labor of the defendant after he had purchased, the same rule might be applied as in case of the inadvertent trespasser. But here he has added nothing to its value. He acquired possession of property of the United States at Depere, which, at that place, and in its then condition, is worth $850, and he wants to satisfy the claim of the government by the payment of $60. He founds his right to do this, not on the ground that anything *he* has added to the property has increased its value by the amount of the difference between these two sums, but on the proposition that in purchasing the property, he purchased of the wrongdoer a right to deduct what the labor of the latter had added to its value. If, as in the case of an unintentional trespasser, such right existed, of course defendant would have bought it and stood in his shoes; but, as in the present case, of an intentional trespasser, who had no such right to sell, the defendant could purchase none.

Such is the distinction taken in the Roman law as stated in the Inst. Just. lib. 2, tit. 1, §34. After speaking of a painting by one man on the tablet of another, and holding it to be absurd that the work of an Apelles or Parrhasius should go without compensation to the owner of a worthless tablet, if the painter had possession fairly, he says, as translated by Dr. Cooper: "But if he, *or any other,* shall have taken away the tablet feloniously, it is evident the owner may prosecute by action of theft."

To establish any other principle in such a case as this would be very disastrous to the interest of the public in the immense forest lands of the government. It has long been a matter of complaint that the depredations upon these lands are rapidly destroying the finest forests in the world. Unlike the individual owner, who, by fencing and vigilant attention, can protect his valuable trees, the government has no adequate defense against this great evil. Its liberality in allowing trees to be cut on its land for mining, agricultural, and other specified uses, has been used to screen the lawless depredator who destroys and sells for profit. To hold that when the government finds its own property in hands but one remove from these willful trespassers, and asserts its right to such property by the slow processes of the law, the holder can set up a claim for the value which has been added to the property by the guilty party in the act of cutting down the trees and removing the timber, is to given encouragement and reward to the wrong-doer, by providing a safe market for what he has stolen and compensation for the labor he has been compelled to do to make his theft effectual and profitable.

We concur with the circuit judge in this case, and the judgment of the circuit court is affirmed.

Innocent converters vs. thieves

1. In U.S. law, the pervasive contrast between the liabilities of unintentional and willful tortfeasors was most sharply drawn in numerous cases about the conversion of timber. Conditions in the forest meant that there would be many cases of both intentional and unintentional trespass and conversion. Furthermore, the work involved in conversion—cutting the timber and then hauling it to the lumberyard—normally accounted for the lion's share of the value of the goods by the time they were discovered: timber that was worth $60 on the stump might be worth $850 at the yard. Defendant was a tortfeasor either way (being both a trespasser and a converter), whether he intended to steal plaintiff's timber or merely lost his way in the woods. For the resulting liability, however, it made all the difference.

The rules stated in the influential *Wooden Ware* decision might be summarized as follows: (1) The owner can retake his converted timber *in specie* wherever he can find it, so long as the property is still identifiable. (2) Supposing that the trespasser has sold the timber, and the owner sues the trespasser for damages, (a) an innocent trespasser is liable only for "stumpage value" ($60 in *Wooden Ware*), but (b) a willful trespasser is liable for the full value at the point of sale ($850). (3) If the owner sues the lumberyard—an innocent purchaser of stolen property—the lumberyard's liability for conversion depends on the state of mind of the trespasser from whom the lumberyard has purchased: either $60 or $850 as the case may be.

Viewed strictly as a matter of tort damages, these rules are paradoxical. How could the injury to the landowner depend on the state of mind of the tortfeasor? Even more curious, how could the liability of an innocent purchaser depend on the state of mind of his seller? The paradox is resolved if we see how these rules about tort damages incorporate ideas about *restitution*, ideas that are closer to the surface in *Wooden Ware* than they would be in later cases. By cutting down the trees and hauling the logs to the yard, the trespasser has dramatically improved the owner's property—taking something worth $60 and making it into something worth $850. Damages for conversion are measured by the value of the property "at the time and place of conversion," which the owner is free to identify as the time and place of a subsequent sale by the converter. But an *innocent* trespasser was allowed an implicit restitutionary counterclaim for the value added to the owner's property ($790) by what was, in effect, his mistaken improvement of the timber. A willful trespasser—a timber thief—would not be allowed to force an owner to pay for an improvement he had not requested.

Justice Miller explains why the same distinction carries over to the liability of the innocent purchaser. The purchaser acquires what the seller has to sell. When it purchases from an innocent converter, the lumberyard acquires an inchoate restitution claim to be set off against its liability in damages, but a timber thief has no such claim to convey. Fixing the purchaser's liability in conversion at $60 rather than $850 would allow the purchaser to charge the owner for the value of the thief's logging activity—while indemnifying the purchaser, to that extent, against the risk of buying stolen logs.

2. What is the connection between converted logs in northern Wisconsin and the fantasies of the Roman jurists about a valuable painting on someone else's tablet? (In *Janigan v. Taylor*, a decision about securities fraud in Chapter 7, the court mentioned a case in which "an artist acquired paints by fraud and used them in producing a valuable portrait.") The painting hypotheticals would ordinarily be deployed to illustrate the doctrine of *accession*, whereby a person who expends substantial effort on the transformation of someone else's chattel may become the owner of the more valuable product. (The line between conversion and accession is a matter of degree. If a trespasser cuts down someone else's tree he is a converter of the log. If he mills the log into staves which he uses to make barrels, he may become the owner of the barrels.) In the usual understanding, an innocent converter can acquire ownership of the improved chattel by accession, but a conscious wrongdoer cannot. (A converter who becomes an owner by accession must still compensate the original owner for the value of what was taken.) The Restatement offers the following paradigm:

> Distiller converts corn worth $50 and makes it into whiskey worth $500. Owner of the corn discovers what has happened and demands the whiskey. If Distiller is a thief, Owner is entitled to recover the whiskey as the product of the corn, without [compensating Distiller] for other costs of production. If Distiller is an innocent converter, Distiller owns the product of the corn by the doctrine of accession. In the latter case, Owner's entitlement by the rule of this section is limited to $50, secured by an equitable lien on the whiskey.

R3RUE §40, Illustration 14, based on Silsbury & Calkins v. McCoon & Sherman, 3 N.Y. 379 (1850) (corn thief makes whiskey), and Wetherbee v. Green, 22 Mich. 311 (1871) (innocent converter of timber makes hoops).

B. ASSET-BASED RESTITUTION: FOLLOWING PROPERTY INTO ITS PRODUCT

(1) Constructive trust

Kent v. Klein
352 Mich. 652, 91 N.W.2d 11 (1958)

SMITH, Justice.

This is a family case, an effort to impose a constructive trust on one of the daughters. It involves a piece of land, the ownership of which is disputed. The mother of the children here involved was Mrs. Barbara Klein. She owned real estate in Oakland county. She had 6 children, but she was going to split her property only 5 ways. The reason for this was that the 6th child, a daughter living in California, had been helped in other ways.

Actually, however, there were only 4 grantees to her real property. The son who would normally have been the 5th grantee, John, was not well. He had undergone treatment, at times, in various mental institutions. His mother felt it would be unwise to vest title in him. Consequently, acting upon the advice of another son, Harold, and a son-in-law, she put the title to certain acreage intended for John (according to the proofs and the findings of the trial chancellor) in the name of his sister, Edith Klein, defendant here. On the same date she conveyed to Edith other acreage, in fact intended for her, and concerning which no question is raised. Thus on the same date the mother conveyed to her daughter, Edith, by 2 separate deeds, 2 separate parcels of real estate, one admittedly intended for her, the other allegedly for her at-times incompetent brother, John. Edith was selected as titleholder, it was testified, because she had no creditors.

Edith's deed was delivered to her. The one allegedly intended for John was not. Although the latter deed was recorded, it was kept in Harold's possession. Edith was not present when the arrangement was worked out and the proofs do not disclose whether or not she knew anything about it right away. She did not take the stand. She did know about it, however, at the time of John's death, because she was told of it by Harold, who later asked her to convey the land to John's widow. She refused. Plaintiffs (John's widow and only son) brought this bill in chancery to impress a constructive trust upon the property and "to obtain specific performance of said trust." The trial chancellor found that it was the intention on the part of the mother to have the property held for the benefit of the brother and "for that purpose only," that a valid trust had been established, and "that the deed was given for the benefit of the incompetent son." Conveyance was accordingly decreed to plaintiffs. Defendant appeals.

The appellant sets up the statute of frauds[1] as preventing the imposition of an express trust and asserts that the record does not support the imposition of a constructive trust. It is said that there is no evidence of a confidential or fiduciary relationship, and that mere family ties are not enough, citing Funk v. Engel, 235 Mich. 195, 209 N.W. 160, and similar cases. It is possible that defendant's self-interest has distorted her objectivity. She holds this land not merely because John was her brother but because, in addition, he was her incompetent brother. She holds this land because her mother implicitly trusted her honor, her integrity, and her familial solicitude. A bond the mother demanded not, nor writing, nor, indeed, a promise. Foolish it may have been for her to have trusted so blindly, but it lies ill in the mouth of the honored child to assert selfish advantage therefrom. The sister's cupidity in seeking a

---

1. "No estate or interest in lands, other than leases for a term not exceeding 1 year, nor any trust or power over or concerning lands, or in any manner relating thereto, shall hereafter be created, granted, assigned, surrendered or declared, unless by act or operation of law, or by a deed or conveyance in writing, subscribed by the party creating, granting, assigning, surrendering or declaring the same, or by some person thereunto by him lawfully authorized by writing." C.L.1948, § 566.106 (Stat. Ann. § 26.906).

double portion at the expense of her incompetent brother gains nothing in either justification or luster by ranging it alongside a mother's possibly foolish trust or, indeed, blind gullibility. Trust and confidence there was, in abundant measure. What was clear to the trial chancellor (that the land was intended for John) is equally clear to us and, as far as the sister is concerned, chancery will not permit one to enrich himself at the expense of another by closing his eyes to what is clear to the rest of mankind. Equity, to paraphrase, regards that as seen which ought to be seen, and, having so seen, as done that which ought to be done.

But what of the statute of frauds? Defendant urges again and again that she made no promise whatever to hold in trust, that nothing was said about a trust, and, as a clincher, that even if she had so orally promised the promise would have been unenforceable under the statute of frauds. Her conclusion is that she keeps the land.

What is overlooked in all of this is the fact that the constructive trust is not a trust at all, any more than a quasi-contract is a contract. See Scott on the Law of Trusts, §462.1. Both are remedial devices. The constructive trust, as it was put by Mr. Justice Cardozo, "is the formula through which the conscience of equity finds expression. When property has been acquired in such circumstances that the holder of the legal title may not in good conscience retain the beneficial interest, equity converts him into a trustee." Beatty v. Guggenheim Exploration Co., 225 N.Y. 380, 386, 122 N.E. 378, 380. It arises by operation of law. (*Cf.* "unless by act or operation of law" in C.L.1948, §566.106 quoted in footnote, *supra.*) That defendant made no promise to hold in trust is utterly irrelevant. The constructive trust is as contemptuous of promises not made as of promises broken. The fact that a thief fleeing with his loot promises nothing avails him nothing. He remains a constructive trustee. Lightfoot v. Davis, 198 N.Y. 261, 91 N.E. 582. Fraud in the inception we do not require, nor deceit, nor chicanery in any of its varied guises, for it is not necessary that property be wrongfully acquired. It is enough that it be unconscionably withheld. McCreary v. Shields, 333 Mich. 290, 52 N.W.2d 853; Rudenberg v. Clark, D.C., 72 F. Supp. 381. Nor is it necessary, to move the chancellor's conscience, that plaintiffs have suffered a loss, although in most cases there is both a loss to the plaintiffs and a like gain to the defendant. United States v. Carter, 217 U.S. 286; Olwell v. Nye & Nissen Co., 26 Wash. 2d 282, 173 P.2d 652; Carey v. Safe Deposit & Trust Co., 168 Md. 501, 178 A. 242.

It is enough, to compel the surrender, that one feed and grow fat on that which in good conscience belongs to another, that he enjoy a windfall resulting in his unjust enrichment, that he reap a profit in a situation where honor itself furnishes rich reward, where profit, the mainspring of the market place, is both foreign and inimical to the trust reposed. These principles have been firmly established in this jurisdiction for many years and we do not propose to depart therefrom.

Finally, appellant argues, even if she be found to be holding the land as constructive trustee, she should be ordered to convey it back to the estate of the mother, rather than to plaintiffs. Conveyance to them, we are told, "would be taking the constructive trust doctrine too far toward enforcement of an oral agreement concerning land." This journey, if, indeed, it be such, does not appall us. When the remedial device of the constructive trust is employed, chancery orders whatever conveyance will remedy the wrong suffered, whether back to transferor, or to some intended third person. Here, as the trial chancellor held, the land was intended for John. It shall to his heirs, the plaintiffs, be conveyed.

Affirmed. Costs to appellees.

DETHMERS, C. J., and EDWARDS, KELLY, CARR, BLACK, VOELKER and KAVANAGH, JJ., concur.

Newton v. Porter
69 N.Y. 133 (1877)

CHARLES ANDREWS, J.

This is an equitable action brought to establish the right of the plaintiff to certain securities, the proceeds of stolen bonds, and to compel the defendants to account therefor.

In March, 1869, the plaintiff was the owner of $13,000 of government bonds, and of a railroad bond for $1,000, negotiable by delivery, which, on the 12th of March, 1869, were stolen from her, and soon afterwards $11,500 of the bonds were sold by the thief and his confederates, and the proceeds divided between them. William Warner loaned a part of his share in separate loans and took the promissory notes of the borrower therefor. George Warner invested $2,000 of his share in the purchase of a bond and mortgage, which was assigned to his wife Cordelia without consideration.

In January, 1870, William Warner, George Warner, Cornelia Warner and one Lusk were arrested upon the charge of stealing the bonds, or as accessories to the larceny, and were severally indicted in the county of Cortland. The Warners employed the defendants, who are attorneys, to defend them in the criminal proceedings, and in any civil suits which might be instituted against them in respect to the bonds, and to secure them for their services and expenses, and for any liabilities they might incur in their behalf, William Warner transferred to the defendants Miner and Warren promissory notes taken on loans made by him out of the proceeds of the stolen bonds, amounting to $2,250 or thereabouts, and Cordelia Warner, for the same purpose, assigned to the defendant Porter the bond and mortgage above mentioned.

The learned judge at Special Term found that the defendants had notice at the time they received the transfer of the securities, that they were the avails and proceeds of the stolen bonds, and directed judgment against them for the value of the securities, it appearing on the trial that they had collected or disposed of them and received the proceeds.

The doctrine upon which the judgment in this case proceeded, viz.: that the owner of negotiable securities stolen and afterwards sold by the thief may pursue the proceeds of the sale in the hands of the felonious taker or his assignee with notice, through whatever changes the proceeds may have gone, so long as the proceeds or the substitute therefor can be distinguished and identified, and have the proceeds or the property in which they were invested subjected, by the aid of a court of equity, to a lien and trust in his favor for the purposes of recompense and restitution, is founded upon the plainest principles of justice and morality, and is consistent with the rule in analogous cases acted upon in courts of law and equity. It is a general principle of the law of personal property that the title of the owner cannot be divested without his consent. The purchaser from a thief, however honest and *bona fide* the purchase may have been, cannot hold the stolen chattel against the true proprietor, but the latter may follow and reclaim it wherever or in whosoever hands it may be found. The right of pursuit and reclamation only ceases when its identity is lost and further pursuit is hopeless; but the law still protects the interest of the true owner by giving him an action as for the conversion of the chattel against anyone who has interfered with his dominion over it, although such interference may have been innocent in intention and under a claim of right, and in reliance upon the title of the felonious taker. The extent to which the common law goes to protect the title of the true owner has a striking illustration in those cases in which it is held that where a willful trespasser converts a chattel into a different species, as for example, timber into shingles, wood into coal, or corn into whiskey, the product in its improved and changed condition belongs to the owner of the original material. (Silsbury v. McCoon, 3 N. Y., 380, and cases cited.) The rule that a thief cannot convey a good title to stolen property has an exception in case of money or negotiable securities transferable by delivery, which have been put into circulation and have come to the hands of *bona fide* holders. The right of the owner to pursue and reclaim the money and securities there ends, and the holder is protected in his title. The plaintiff was in this position. The bonds, with the exception stated, had, as the evidence tends to show, been sold to *bona fide* purchasers, and she was precluded from following and reclaiming them.

[Thus] the plaintiff, by the sale of the bonds to *bona fide* purchasers, lost her title to the securities. She could not further follow them. She could maintain an action as for a conversion of the property against the felons. But this remedy in this case would be fruitless, as they are wholly insolvent. Unless she can elect to regard the securities in which the bonds were invested as a substitute, *pro tanto*, for the bonds, she has no effectual remedy. The thieves certainly have no claim to the securities in which the proceeds of the bonds were invested as against the plaintiff. They, without her consent, have disposed of her property, and put it beyond her reach. If the avails remained in their hands, in money, the direct proceeds of the sale, can it be doubted that she could reach it? And this equitable right to follow the proceeds would continue and attach to any securities or property in which the proceeds were invested, so long as they could be traced and identified, and the rights of *bona fide* purchasers had not intervened.

In Taylor v. Plumer, 3 M. & Sel. 562, [105 Eng. Rep. 721 (K.B. 1815)], an agent, intrusted with a draft for money to buy exchequer bills for his principal, received the money and misapplied it by purchasing American stocks and bullion, intending to abscond and go to America, and absconded, but was arrested before he quitted England, and surrendered the securities and bullion to his principal, who sold them and received the proceeds. It was held that the principal was entitled to withhold the proceeds from the assignee in bankruptcy of the agent, who became bankrupt on the day he received and misapplied the money. Lord ELLENBOROUGH, in pronouncing the opinion in that case, said: "It makes no difference, in reason or law, into what other form different from the original the change may have been made, for the product or substitute for the original thing, still follows the nature of the thing itself so long as it can be ascertained to be such, and the right only ceases when the means of ascertainment fail."

In courts of equity the doctrine is well settled and is uniformly applied that when a person, standing in a fiduciary relation, misapplies or converts a trust fund into another species of property, the beneficiary will be entitled to the property thus acquired. The doctrine is illustrated and applied most frequently in cases of trusts, where trust moneys have been, by the fraud or violation of duty of the trustee, diverted from the purposes of the trust and converted into other property. In such case a court of equity will follow the trust fund into the property into which it has been converted, and appropriate it for the indemnity of the beneficiary. It is immaterial in what way the change has been made, whether money has been laid out in land, or land has been turned into money, or how the legal title to the converted property may be placed. Equity only stops the pursuit when the means of ascertainment fail, or the rights of *bona fide* purchasers for value, without notice of the trust, have intervened. The relief will be moulded and adapted to the circumstances of the case, so as to protect the interests and rights of the true owner.

It is insisted by the counsel for the defendants that the doctrine which subjects property acquired by the fraudulent misuse of trust moneys by a trustee to the influence of the trust, and converts it into trust property and the wrongdoer into a trustee at the election of the beneficiary, has no application to a case where money or property acquired by felony has been converted into other property. There is, it is said, in such cases, no trust relation between the owner of the stolen property and the thief, and the law will not imply one for the purpose of subjecting the avails of the stolen property to the claim of the owner. It would seem to be an anomaly in the law, if the owner who has been deprived of his property by a larceny should be less favorably situated in a court of equity, in respect to his remedy to recover it, or the property into which it had been converted, than one who, by an abuse of trust, has been injured by the wrongful act of a trustee to whom the possession of trust property has been confided. The law in such a case will raise a trust *in invitum* out of the transaction, for the very purpose of subjecting the substituted property to the purposes of indemnity and recompense. "One of the most common cases," remarks Judge Story, "in which a court of equity acts upon the ground of implied trusts *in invitum*, is when a party receives money which he cannot conscientiously withhold from another party." (Story, Equity Jurisprudence §1255.) And he states it to be a general principle that "whenever the property of a party has been wrongfully misapplied, or a trust fund has been wrongfully converted into another species of property, if its identity can be traced, it will be held in its new form liable to the rights of the original owner, or the *cestui que trust*" (§1258).

We are of opinion that the absence of the conventional relation of trustee and *cestui que trust* between the plaintiff and the Warners, is no obstacle to giving the plaintiff the benefit of the notes and mortgage, or the proceeds in part of the stolen bonds.

It is, however, strenuously insisted that the defendants had no notice when they received the securities that they were the avails or proceeds of the bonds. That if they had notice they would stand in the position of their assignors, and that the property in their hands would be affected by the same equities as if no transfer had been made, is not denied. The learned judge, at Special Term, found, as has been stated, that the defendants had notice of the larceny of the bonds, and the use made of the money arising from their sale, at the time they received the notes and mortgage.

The testimony was conflicting. The circumstances under which the defendants took the transfer of the securities were certainly unusual, and the facts then known by the defendants were calculated to create a strong presumption that the notes and mortgage came from investments of the stolen property. It was for the trial court to weigh the testimony, and, in the light of all the facts developed on the trial, to determine the question of notice. It would be a useless labor to collate the testimony on this subject, and we content ourselves with stating our conclusion, that the finding was warranted by the evidence.

The judgment should be affirmed.

What is a constructive trust?

1. *Kent v. Klein* illustrates the equitable inspiration of the constructive trust idea. In order to avoid an injustice, a defendant who is not subject to any formal trust obligation—and against whom the injured party might have no legal (as opposed to equitable) claim at all—is treated in equity "as if she were a trustee" of contested property. The analogy to trust goes no further than this: that the "constructive" (or "as if") trustee holds legal title to property whose real owner, from an equitable standpoint, is someone else. The only "trust duty" of the constructive trustee is to hand over the property to the person with the superior equitable claim. So while the form of the decree is usually "Defendant holds X in constructive trust for plaintiff," or words to that effect, the Michigan court—in its indignation—skips the polite formula and simply orders that "the land shall to the plaintiffs be conveyed."

2. Cases of specific restitution are often complicated by two additional factors. The claimant's original property may have been exchanged for something

else—and the process of substitution may have been repeated one or more times—with the result that the claimant seeks to recover property different from what he originally lost. A second consequence of these exchanges is frequently that the constructive trust claim is asserted against someone other than the person by whom the claimant was originally dispossessed. These critical themes of equitable (asset-based) remedies in restitution are distinctly visible in *Newton v. Porter*, but they are easier to see once the ideas have become familiar. Consider the following synopsis:

(a) Suppose a dishonest trustee holds Blackacre subject to trust. In breach of trust, he exchanges Blackacre for Whiteacre, sells Whiteacre for cash, uses the cash to buy shares of stock, then exchanges the stock for bonds. Now the facts come to light. Equity developed rules that permitted a trust beneficiary to "follow" the original trust property through successive changes of form into its ultimate product—here, the bonds—and then to claim the bonds as trust property. Obviously the bonds were not subject to an express trust by the usual rules—the trustee was trying to steal this property for himself, not hold it for the beneficiary—but equity treated them *as if they were*. The bonds were said to be subject to a "constructive trust," using the word "constructive" in its professional connotation of "deemed" or "let's pretend."

(b) *Newton v. Porter* marks a watershed in American law, because it denied that these property-following and "constructive trust" devices were limited to cases in which the parties had previously occupied a trust relationship. The defendants argue that it is absurd to find a trust relationship arising from a theft. The court responds, in effect, "What is it about 'constructive' that you don't understand?" Ever since, the accepted American view has been that a constructive trust is "not a real trust, only a remedy," or more accurately, that constructive trust is "only a manner of speaking." When a court orders that "A holds X in constructive trust for B," it is ordering that A hand X over to B—no more and no less.

(c) Of course a thief acquires no title at all, while "constructive trust" implies that a constructive trustee (like an express trustee) has legal title to the property in question. If A steals B's cow, A has nothing: B's remedy is trover or replevin, not constructive trust. But if A gives the stolen cow to C in exchange for a horse, A acquires what C had: legal title to the horse. At this point B has a choice of remedies, and one of them is to claim the horse from A as the product of his stolen cow. (This will obviously be B's preferred remedy if C has disappeared with the stolen cow.) The court grants this remedy by an order that A holds the horse in constructive trust for B. In *Newton v. Porter*, the stolen bonds were in bearer form, which meant the purchasers from the thieves acquired good title to the bonds if they took them without notice (as the court tells us they did). This is why plaintiff is not suing those purchasers. Instead her claim is to recover the ultimate product (or proceeds) of her stolen property—namely, the proceeds of the securities the defendants acquired from the thieves, which the thieves (in turn) had bought with the sale proceeds of the original stolen bonds.

(d) In a constructive trust case, someone has acquired legal title subject to the claimant's equitable interest—sometimes this is called "voidable title"— and between these immediate parties, the claimant will prevail. In *Newton v. Porter*, the plaintiff would have been entitled to restitution from the thieves— including constructive trust over substitute assets, if need be—but the proceeds of the stolen bonds had already been transferred to third parties, in this case the thieves' lawyers. Someone who has voidable title can convey good title to a bona fide purchaser, at which point the claimant's interest in the property is extinguished. This is why *Newton v. Porter* considers whether the defendants (the lawyers) had notice of the fact that the securities in question "were the avails and proceeds of the stolen bonds."

3. The name "constructive trust" causes more confusion today than it did at the time of *Newton v. Porter* (or even *Kent v. Klein*) because the origins of the term have become progressively less familiar. The following excerpt is one attempt at demystification:

> Given that a "constructive trust" was not really a trust—a proposition that was U.S. legal orthodoxy after the 1870s—the expression could only be employed in a figurative sense. It is accordingly as metaphor that the most influential U.S. statements have to be understood:
>
>> If one party obtains the legal title to property, not only by fraud, or by violation of confidence or of fiduciary relations, but in any other unconscientious manner, so that he cannot equitably retain the property which really belongs to another, equity carries out its theory of a double ownership, equitable and legal, by impressing a constructive trust upon the property in favor of the one who is in good conscience entitled to it, and who is considered in equity as the beneficial owner. (1 Pomeroy, Equity Jurisprudence §155, at 137-138 (1881).)
>>
>> A constructive trust is the formula through which the conscience of equity finds expression. When property has been acquired in such circumstances that the holder of the legal title may not in good conscience retain the beneficial interest, equity converts him into a trustee. (Beatty v. Guggenheim Exploration Co., 225 N.Y. 380, 386 (1919) (Cardozo, J.).)
>
> To say that equity "impresses a constructive trust," or that it "converts the holder of legal title into a trustee," was convenient shorthand for what equity actually did in these cases. Elsewhere an analogous remedy already had a convenient name. If defrauded A was entitled to recover X from B by a simple "rescission and restitution," B was unlikely to be called a "constructive trustee" of the property—not because it was illogical, but because it was unnecessary. If A by mistake had conveyed to B more land than the parties intended, A had an "equity of reformation," and there

was no need to convert B into a trustee of the additional parcel—though courts might have done so and occasionally did. If A's money had been used by mistake to discharge a lien on B's Blackacre, giving A a remedy that already had a name (subrogation), there was no need to impress an equitable lien on Blackacre, or to say that "equity converts A into a mortgagee." But these alternative expressions would have meant the same thing.

In cases like these, in other words, the conscience of equity already had a formula. "Constructive trust" was the formula for cases in which the vindication of A's equitable interest lacked any such convenient label. To describe the remedy without the metaphor, we would have to say that equity "carried out its theory of a double ownership" by recognizing and enforcing—not by creating—A's equitable interest in X, and that it did this by ordering B (or C) to restore X to A, on such conditions as the court might direct. It was much simpler to say that B or C would be treated (in this one critical respect) as if he were a trustee.

Kull, *The Metaphorical Constructive Trust*, 18 Trusts & Trustees 945, 950 (2012).

Farnsworth, *Restitution* 122-123 (2014):

"Constructive trust" is an obscure name for a fairly simple idea. The court declares that property to which the defendant has legal title belongs in equity to the plaintiff, and orders that he be given possession of it. To express the idea in the simplest way, the judge looks at property held by the defendant, gestures toward the plaintiff, and says, in effect, "It is his; give it to him." The second instruction ("give it to him") is easy to understand. But the first part of the constructive trust—"it is his"—adds something important. It makes clear that the plaintiff has a better claim to the property than the defendant who has some sort of title to it.

The constructive trust can reach further than replevin does. It is the standard device for recovering proceeds from property that was stolen and then sold; for equity allows a dispossessed owner to show what has been done with his property and to claim, as a substitute, the *product* of his original asset. This is the simplest version of a remedial mechanism often called "tracing." So suppose you steal my money and buy a car with it. I cannot take the car from you by means of replevin, because it is not mine and never was. You bought it and have title to it. But the constructive trust allows the court to make me the owner of the car anyway by saying that I have a better equitable right to it than you do, since you bought it with money that was mine. The same would be true if, instead of stealing my money and buying a car, you stole my car and sold it for money. My ownership of the car is turned, by operation of the constructive trust, into ownership of the money you received for it. (To be technical about this, my legal title to the car produces an equitable claim to the money.) How far this process can go—how many transactions and transformations the property can endure and still be seized by the plaintiff—is the subject of more detailed rules about tracing that we will consider soon.

Church of Jesus Christ of Latter-Day Saints v. Jolley
24 Utah 2d 187, 467 P.2d 984 (1970)

CROCKETT, Chief Justice.

This appeal challenges a judgment and decree of the district court which impressed against the defendant Vickie C. Jolley a constructive trust upon two new automobiles, a 1968 Pontiac Firebird and a 1968 Chevrolet Corvette, which had been given her by one LaMar Kay, who had purchased the cars with money embezzled from the plaintiff church. On appeal defendant makes two contentions: 1) that a constructive trust can be imposed only on a fiduciary or confidant and not upon a third person with respect to whom no such relationship exists; and 2) that even if such a constructive trust could be imposed it should extend only to the amount of funds which were identified as being embezzled from the plaintiff and traced into that property.

The said LaMar Kay was an accountant employed by the plaintiff church. During 1967 and 1968, by the use of fictitious firm names and pretended payment of claims, he was engaged in a scheme of embezzling funds. In April of 1968 he drew from a fictitious account in the name of "Barker and Clayton" in the Murray State Bank [to which embezzled Church funds had been deposited] a check in the amount of $4,305.57 made payable to Peck and Shaw, automobile dealers, with which he paid $4,224.62 for the Pontiac Firebird in question.

In August 1968, he drew another check on the same account in the amount of $3,000 with which he purchased a cashier's check payable to Capital Chevrolet; this check was then presented to the latter company as part payment for the 1968 Chevrolet Corvette which had a total purchase price of $5,008.87. The balance on this car was paid by $50 cash on August 26, 1968, and $1,958.87 on August 30, 1968. The latter two cash payments admittedly were not traced directly through the "Barker and Clayton" account of embezzled funds into the Corvette automobile. But the evidence does show that a few days before he made those cash payments on that automobile, LaMar Kay had drawn $2,700 in cash from that account.

Upon completion of the purchases as above stated, the titles to both of these automobiles were transferred to the defendant Vickie C. Jolley; and there is no evidence nor contention made that she gave any legal consideration for them. Inasmuch as she is not a bona fide purchaser for value, her defenses in raising the question as to her lack of knowledge of the source of the funds which purchase the automobiles, and her averment that a constructive trust can only be impressed upon the wrongdoing fiduciary or confidant are of no avail to her. Where one has stolen or embezzled the money or property of another, he obtains no title whatsoever. A constructive trust may be impressed upon it in his hands; and equity may continue the trust effective against any subsequent transferee, unless transferred to a bona fide purchaser and under circumstances where equity would require a different result. The evidence in this case justified the court in its conclusion that the defendant had no better title to these automobiles than LaMar Kay had, and that they were held in constructive trust for the benefit of the plaintiff.

As to the defendant's second contention: that the plaintiff is not entitled to recover an equitable portion of the Corvette represented by the $1,958.87 and $50 cash payments which were not traced directly to the embezzled funds, this is to be said: Such direct tracing of funds is not an indispensable requisite to the conclusion arrived at. In the nature of the function of determining facts it is essential that the court or jury have the prerogative of finding not only facts based upon direct evidence, but also those which may be established from the reasonable inferences that may be deduced therefrom. The circumstances here shown concerning the associations of the defendant with LaMar Kay, including the facts that she went with him on the occasion of the purchase of the automobile, and that a few days previous to making the payments in question he had withdrawn $2,700 from the embezzled funds account, provide a reasonable basis for the trial court to believe that it was paid for entirely by money embezzled from plaintiff.

Affirmed. Costs to plaintiff (respondent).

HENRIOD, Justice (dissenting).

Without expressing any opinion as to the rest of the main opinion and its conclusion, I dissent from that portion which includes $50 and $1,958.87 cash, in any amount upon which a purported trust could be impressed. The main opinion's own language reflects the weakness of the decision with respect to those amounts, which is compounded by the obvious conjecture indulged by "guessing" that such amounts must have been a part of a much greater withdrawal.

Provencher v. Berman
699 F.2d 568 (1st Cir. 1983)

BREYER, Circuit Judge.

This court first considered this case three years ago. See Berman v. Provencher, 614 F.2d 823 (1st Cir. 1980). In an opinion that criticized the bankruptcy court's decision, the state of the record, and the parties' briefs, we wrote that the bankrupt Provenchers had improperly failed to disclose to the trustee Berman one of their important assets—namely, an equitable interest in a corporation called Ramblewood Associates, Inc. Ramblewood apparently served as a Provencher alter ego. The Provenchers had deposited in a Ramblewood bank account money that rightfully belonged to the bankruptcy estate and had used that money to help buy land and build a house for themselves. The trustee, not the Provenchers, was entitled to that money.

In our earlier opinion, we rejected the trustee's claim to the entire property. We noted that in buying the land and building the house, estate funds had been commingled with the Provenchers' own funds; we held that the trustee was therefore entitled to some but not all of the real property. We stated that the trustee could either assert a lien against the house for the amount of the estate money invested in it or "to the extent that [the trustee] can follow the [estate] funds into the real estate . . . he may claim the proportionate share of the real estate attributable thereto." *Provencher I*, 614 F.2d at 825.

On remand, despite these explicit holdings, the parties again became embroiled in complex arguments. For one thing, the parties strongly contested whether each of the many items of value (*e.g.*, checks, cash, labor provided in kind) that went into the creation of the house properly belonged to the estate or were earned by (or given to) the Provenchers after the filing of the bankruptcy petition. The bankruptcy judge eventually decided that 47.9 percent of the property investment (not attributable to the mortgages on the property) had been contributed by the trustee. For another thing, the trustee asked the bankruptcy judge to convey his interest (*i.e.*, 47.9 percent) to him directly in the form of an undivided interest in the property. Instead, the bankruptcy judge valued the house at $70,000 and gave the trustee a *money judgment* equal to approximately 47.9 percent of this amount less the face value of the outstanding mortgage. In doing so, the bankruptcy court appears in effect to have partitioned the property and to have used only the Provenchers' testimony to determine its value. (The trustee presented no appraisal evidence.)

The district court affirmed the judgment of the bankruptcy court, and both parties appeal from that judgment. Many of the points raised are better suited for decision by an accountant than a judge. Nonetheless, to expedite this litigation, we shall decide as many of the issues as possible.

We deal first with the most important point of law: the trustee says that he was entitled to an undivided interest in the real property rather than a money judgment reflecting the value of the property. The trustee is correct. This court in *Provencher I* explicitly stated that the trustee, if he chose, could "claim the proportionate share of the real estate." We did not say he could claim only a proportionate share of the "value" of the real estate. We followed the analysis of Professor Scott, which we explicitly cited. See 5 A. Scott, The Law of Trusts (3d ed. 1967). We described the trustee's rights as Professor Scott and the Restatement describe the rights of an innocent party against a "conscious wrongdoer" who uses commingled funds to buy property, see Restatement of Restitution §202 (1937); 5 A. Scott, *supra*, at §508. In such a situation, the innocent party can choose either to enforce a lien on the property for the value of the estate's funds or to enforce a constructive trust on the property.

Further, Professor Scott explains precisely how courts treat property held subject to a constructive trust. The holders of the property, here the Provenchers, have "an equitable duty *to convey it*" to the beneficiary, here the trustee. 5 A. Scott, *supra*, at §462 (emphasis added); see Loring v. Baker, 329 Mass. 63, 66-67, 106 N.E.2d 434 (1952); Restatement of Restitution §160; 1 G. Palmer, The Law of Restitution §1.3 (1978). The trustee as beneficiary is entitled to an *undivided share of the property* equivalent to the proportion which his funds bore to the total amount (other than mortgage loans) used by the Provenchers to buy the house. The trustee would be entitled to the entire property only if the Provenchers had used solely estate funds (or estate funds plus borrowed funds) to buy the property—not the case here. Where, as in this case, the holder used commingled funds to buy the property subject to a mortgage, according to the authorities we cited the beneficiary of the constructive trust (here the trustee in bankruptcy) may take title to a proportionate share of the entire property, subject to the mortgage.

On remand, however, the bankruptcy court not only determined the parties' relative interests in the property, it went on to award a money judgment to the trustee against his will. In doing so the court acted contrary to the authority just cited. And, if it was doing so by virtue of some inherent power to partition real property among owners of undivided interests, we believe it erred. For one thing, the parties had not formally petitioned for a partition of the property. For another thing, this case arose under the Bankruptcy Act of 1898 which, unlike the present Bankruptcy Code of 1978, contains no provision for partition or a partition-like remedy. *Cf.* Bankruptcy Code §363. Furthermore, we see no reason to make new law by allowing partition in this case. Massachusetts has a perfectly adequate procedure for partition. See Mass. Gen. Laws Ann. ch. 241, §§1-37. Indeed, that procedure will protect the parties' rights far more completely than the procedure the bankruptcy court followed here. We hold that the bankruptcy court should require the Provenchers to provide the trustee with an undivided interest in the property. If such an arrangement proves impractical, the parties are free to seek partition in the state courts.

We next turn to several adjustments that must be made because of our holding that the trustee is entitled to an undivided 47.9 percent interest in the property. First, the trustee is, as to this share, effectively the Provenchers' landlord. Thus, unless the bankruptcy court finds on remand that the trustee waived the argument, the Provenchers must pay the trustee a reasonable rent. This rent will equal the fair rental value of the property during the years in question multiplied by .479. Second, the trustee must pay the Provenchers 47.9 percent of the property taxes they have paid during the years in question. The trustee must also pay a fair share of the mortgage payments (principal plus interest) that the Provenchers have made. To determine the fair share, the bankruptcy court will have to determine first what proportion of the borrowed money was used for the property (for the trustee need not contribute to the repayment of funds that the Provenchers did not invest in the property). If, for example, the Provenchers had borrowed $25,000 and used $20,000 for the property, the court should divide four-fifths of each mortgage payment between the Provenchers and the trustee. In such a case, the trustee would pay 47.9 percent of four-fifths of each mortgage payment. We leave it to the bankruptcy court to work out the details in its discretion.

Vacated and remanded.

No identification—no lien

1. The "tracing requirement" is usually mentioned in judicial opinions as something that (almost) everybody knows: "It is hornbook law that before a constructive trust may be imposed, a claimant to a wrongdoer's property must trace his own property into a product in the hands of the wrongdoer." United States v. Benitez, 779 F.2d 135, 140 (2d Cir. 1985). A step above hornbook law are some still-quotable statements from older cases:

> Clearly a thief having sold stolen goods may be treated as a trustee of the proceeds and also of any property into which they have been transformed, so long as either may be identified. Under such circumstances broader relief may be obtained in equity than at law. Where necessary, an accounting may be had. A lien may be declared. A surrender of the trust property may be decreed. (Newton v. Porter, 69 N. Y. 133; American S. R. Co. v. Fancher, 145 N. Y. 552; Hammond v. Pennock, 61 N. Y. 145; Jaffe v. Weld, 220 N. Y. 443.) The added reason that the defendant is insolvent is not essential. Such was not found to be the fact either in *Newton v. Porter* or in *Jaffe v. Weld*.
>
> Where, however, the specific proceeds, in their original or in their transformed shape may not be traced, then no lien may be obtained. (Matter of Cavin, 105 N. Y. 256; Matter of Hicks, 170 N. Y. 195.) No identification—no lien. The complaint will not be dismissed, however, if ultimately it is determined that such proceeds are not found in possession of the defendant. . . . If equity has properly obtained jurisdiction it may retain it so as to afford proper relief—personal judgment in such a case against the wrongdoer.

Fur & Wool Trading Co. v. Fox, Inc., 245 N.Y. 215, 218, 156 N.E. 670, 671 (1927) (William Andrews, J.).

2. In *Provencher v. Berman,* the heavy lifting on the tracing issue is done offstage, "better suited for decision by an accountant." Someone has determined that X percent of the funds invested in Ramblewood (47.9 percent in this case) were the property of the bankruptcy estate. Whatever X turns out to be, how does the trustee decide whether he prefers (i) an equitable lien on Ramblewood, or (ii) a constructive trust on X percent of Ramblewood? What if the trustee is in doubt? If the property is going to be sold either way, a claimant can seek equitable lien or constructive trust in the alternative—making the final election once values have been determined.

3. Tracing requirements are satisfied when the claimant's assets (or their product) can be identified in the hands of the defendant, without regard to the form they take. Land, a car, shares of stock, money in the bank, or a reduction in the amount of a debt will all do nicely. But the asset-based remedies are only available to reach the *identifiable* assets of the defendant into which the claimant's property can be traced. It is not sufficient, in other words, for a

claimant to prove that "yesterday defendant took $100 from me, so his assets today must be greater by $100 than they would have been otherwise," even if claimant's demonstration is logically airtight. The idea is most easily presented in the form of a hypothetical case:

> Suppose that Vendor and Purchaser agree on the sale of Blackacre for $500. Small-town Bank is acting as Vendor's agent: Vendor executes a deed which Bank is instructed to deliver to Purchaser on receipt of the price. Purchaser arrives one morning at 9 A.M., hands Bank teller a $500 bill (something seldom seen in this town), and takes the deed. Bank closes that day at 3 P.M. — never to reopen, because it is insolvent. Assets coming into the hands of Bank's receiver include all the cash on hand at the end of the day, but no $500 bill.
>
> Bank's relation to its depositors is that of debtor and creditor, but its relation to Vendor is fiduciary under local law. Bank cannot use trust funds to pay its own creditors — the depositors. Has Vendor traced "his" $500 into the receiver's hands? (In other words, can Vendor demand his $500 from Receiver, or must Vendor stand in line with the depositors?) Teller's account for the last day's business is in perfect balance, so there is no doubt that Bank's cash on hand is $500 more than if Purchaser's payment had not been made.

(Suggested by Francis v. Evans, 69 Wis. 115, 33 N.W. 93 (1887).) Older decisions that held this form of tracing to be sufficient — the ones that would give Vendor an equitable lien for $500 on these facts — created a doctrine known as "swollen assets." In the modern U.S. law of restitution, the idea of "swollen assets" is uniformly rejected. (For a contemporary example, see R3RUE §58, Illustration 19.) If Purchaser's $500 bill were still in the cash drawer, Bank's receiver — if playing by orthodox rules — would hand it over to Vendor. If not, Vendor can get in line with the others. But if tracing is denied, aren't Bank's debts to its depositors being paid with trust assets?

What is the reasoning that explains the rejection of "swollen assets"? The underlying question is to determine the extent, if any, to which trust assets are being used to repay Bank's unsecured creditors. In rare circumstances, a case like the $500 hypothetical seems to present a "closed loop," in which a particular payment to an account must still be present in the closing balance, because there appears to have been no opportunity for any offsetting disbursement. Usually there will have been some lapse of time between receipt of the funds and the point at which a claimant tries to trace into a closing balance. Payment by the claimant may have influenced the debtor to make other expenditures or just do things differently — which normally makes it impossible to conclude with certainty that the claimant's money is "still there." The law sidesteps these complications with an arbitrary rule of thumb: "No identification, no lien."

4. Every so often — when a wrongdoer has invested the claimant's money in life insurance or lottery tickets — the most obvious advantage of asset-based

restitution may be that it captures for the claimant a resulting consequential gain. Usually, however, the claimant seeks restitution from property in order to obtain priority over the general creditors of the wrongdoer. The question of priority is the most controversial aspect of restitution in modern law, and it is examined in more detail in Chapter 10. In a nutshell, however, the proposition is this: asset-based restitution makes the claimant an owner or lienor of property in the hands of the defendant, whereas a personal judgment for money (measured by the defendant's unjust enrichment) makes him only a creditor. As a creditor of the defendant, the restitution claimant has to fight over the defendant's assets with all of the defendant's other creditors. As an owner or lienor, he gets paid off the top.

Because this underlying contest between restitution claimants and general creditors is the principal issue being regulated by the asset-based remedies in restitution, it stands to reason that the explanation of the tracing requirement might be found in the same place. The Restatement puts the matter as follows:

> Frequently, the most important result of the claimant's ability to trace is the consequence for the claimant's position vis-à-vis the recipient's general creditors.
>
> The restitution claimant bases a right to recovery on the avoidance of a transaction that is invalid for reasons such as fraud or mistake; the general creditor has made a valid extension of credit. The equitable theory of divided interests in property permits the restitution claimant to assert the rights of a dispossessed owner as opposed to the rights of a creditor. Yet the fact that the competing claims are easily distinguished in this respect would not suffice to establish, as a matter of first impression, the degree of priority (if any) that should be accorded the owner's claim over the creditor's. At one extreme, a claim arising from an invalid transfer might be given absolute priority over the claims of general creditors. (The now-discredited form of tracing known as the doctrine of "swollen assets" produced something close to this result.) At the other extreme, the claim of an owner dispossessed by fraud or theft might be ranked *pari passu* with the rights of general creditors.
>
> Modern law effects a compromise between these two extremes through the mediating principle of unjust enrichment. The equitable owner (the restitution claimant) recovers in priority to general creditors, but only to the extent that the creditors would otherwise be unjustly enriched at the owner's expense. Logically, the condition of unjust enrichment in these circumstances would not be difficult to state: the creditors of the recipient/debtor are unjustly enriched to the extent that the assets available for distribution have been increased as a result of the invalid (and usually wrongful) transaction between the restitution claimant and the recipient. But this logical test is too difficult to meet with direct evidence. In particular, the possibility that the transaction with the claimant might have influenced subsequent transactions by the debtor—for example, by encouraging wasteful expenditures that would not otherwise have been made—makes it impossible to calculate with certainty, outside the realm

of hypothetical examples, the assets that would be available for distribution if the transaction with the claimant had never taken place.

The law of restitution meets this difficulty by substituting a rough proxy test—the "tracing rules"—for the direct inquiry into but-for causation. Assets available for distribution to creditors are presumed to have been increased (thereby creating a potential for unjust enrichment) to the extent, and only to the extent, that the claimant's property or its traceable product may be identified in the assets available for distribution. In any three-party restitution contest (between the claimant and the creditors or other successors of the recipient), the principal function of the tracing rules is to give effect to the compromise just described.

R3RUE §58, Comment *b*.

---

(2) Equitable lien

Gladowski v. Felczak
346 Pa. 660, 31 A.2d 718 (1943)

HORACE STERN, Justice.

This case involves the application of the doctrines of "unjust enrichment" and "restitution"—modern terms of legal nomenclature which have come largely to supplant the former designation of "quasi contracts."

The earlier events in the controversy out of which the present action arises are recited in the opinion of the Court in Polish Falcons of America v. American Citizens Club for Poles of Natrona, 338 Pa. 218, 13 A.2d 27. Polish Falcons, Nest No. 290 of Natrona, an unincorporated, subordinate lodge of Polish Falcons of America, was the owner of a valuable clubhouse in Natrona. The greater part of the building was occupied by the American Citizens Club, the Nest and the Club having largely a common membership. On August 13, 1936, the Nest conveyed the property to the Club through the agency of trustees appointed for that purpose. In August 1937, Polish Falcons of America, together with one or more of the members of the Nest (which had meanwhile undergone a reorganization), brought a bill in equity to have the deed cancelled, the principal ground urged for the granting of this relief being that the constitution of the parent body provided that its consent was a prerequisite to the transfer or sale of the property of a subordinate lodge, and such consent had not been given to this conveyance. The court decreed that the deed was illegal and void, and made an order for reconveyance of the property. Accordingly the Club deeded the building back to the Nest on June 3, 1940.

At the time of the conveyance to the Club in August 1936, the building had been seriously damaged, indeed almost demolished, by the great flood of March 17, 1936, and the Nest was wholly without funds for its repair. Moreover, there was a judgment lien against it of $3,000 held by the First National Bank of Natrona, and the taxes were in arrears. After the Club obtained title it borrowed $6,000 from plaintiffs, Joseph and Sophia Gladowski, and on November 30, 1936, executed to them its bond in that amount secured by a mortgage on the property. It used this money partly to pay the bank the sum of $3,044.50 in satisfaction of its judgment, and partly, together with funds of its own, to pay the sum of $3,475 to a contractor whom it had engaged to make the repairs necessary to restore the building. During the four years it held color of title it paid to plaintiffs $2,000 in reduction of their mortgage.

Plaintiffs filed the present bill in equity to have the mortgage declared a lien upon the property. The court below entered such a decree to the extent of $4,000, being the balance due on the mortgage, together with interest thereon from March 1, 1940.

As the deed from the Nest to the Club was judicially determined to be illegal and void the mortgage executed by the Club is necessarily also invalid. But, although the mortgage itself is invalid because of the invalidity of the title of the Club which executed it, plaintiffs are not beyond the pale of equitable relief.

The crucial fact is that the mortgage money was used wholly for the benefit of the property which has now been restored to the ownership and possession of the Nest. As already stated, when the latter conveyed the property to the Club the building, due to the ravages of the flood, was totally unfit for occupancy, and it was saddled with a judgment lien which the Nest had no means to satisfy. If the Nest were to be allowed, without any equitable obligation on its part, to hold the property freed of that judgment and with its clubhouse restored by the repairs made upon it, and plaintiffs were to be denied the right to recover the money loaned by them in good faith and used, in the manner indicated, for the ultimate benefit of the Nest, every proper conception of morals and fair dealing would be violated. It is not as if the mortgage money had been devoted to the erection on the premises of some structure or improvements which the Nest, as owner, neither required nor desired.

In the Restatement of the Law of Restitution, §43(c), it is said: "Where a person lends money to another who contracts to use the money for the discharge of a lien upon property which the other represents as belonging to him and where the money so lent is used for the discharge of such lien, the lender is entitled to have the lien reinstated for his benefit if, unknown to him, the property was not owned by the other" [cf. R3RUE §8]. And in §162 it is stated: "Where property of one person is used in discharging an obligation owed by another or a lien upon the property of another, under such circumstances that the other would be unjustly enriched by the retention of the benefit thus conferred, the former is entitled to be subrogated to the position of the obligee or lienholder" [cf. R3RUE §57]. That the law in most jurisdictions is in accord with these statements is shown by the long list of authorities in support of them.

Their application to the present situation would assure to plaintiffs the right of subrogation to the judgment lien of the bank, and equitable considerations require that plaintiffs should also be given the protection of a lien in order to be able to recoup the portion of the money advanced by them which was used for restoring the building, the total relief being limited, of course, to the sum of $4,000 and the interest remaining due on the mortgage. It is immaterial whether such relief be afforded in part through the application of the doctrine of subrogation or wholly by means of an equitable lien impressed upon the premises. In the Restatement of Restitution, §161, it is said: "Where property of one person can by a proceeding in equity be reached by another as security for a claim on the ground that otherwise the former would be unjustly enriched, an equitable lien arises" [*cf.* R3RUE §56]. The object to be attained is the prevention of the unjust enrichment of defendants and the securing for plaintiffs of that to which they are justly and in good conscience entitled.

In the original proceedings between the Nest and the Club, the former claimed rent for the period of the Club's occupancy, and against this claim the Club set off the payments it had made in satisfaction of the lien of the bank and for the repairs to the building. The court in those proceedings held that the two claims balanced one another, and allowed no money judgment to either party. The Nest contends, therefore, that it has already paid for the items which were liquidated out of the mortgage money. But plaintiffs have not been reimbursed, nor are they concerned with any accounting has between the Nest and the Club. Moreover, the Nest failed to call the court's attention to the fact that the Club had not actually made all the payments out of its own funds but most of them out of moneys obtained on a mortgage loan, and had merely substituted a new lien, in a larger amount, for the one previously existing on the property of the Nest.

The decree of the court that plaintiffs' mortgage constitutes a lien upon the premises is modified to read: "It is ordered, adjudged and decreed that an equitable lien be and hereby is impressed, as of November 30, 1936, upon the property of Polish Falcons, Nest No. 290 of Natrona, in Harrison Township, Allegheny County, Pennsylvania, referred to and described in the second paragraph of plaintiffs' bill, in favor of plaintiffs, Joseph Gladowski and Sophia Gladowski, in the amount of $4,000 and interest on that sum from March 1, 1940." As thus modified, the decree is affirmed. Costs to be paid by defendants.

Cox v. Waudby
433 N.W.2d 716 (Iowa 1988)

CARTER, Justice.

Defendants, Clell Waudby and Helen Waudby, appeal from a district court order establishing that their jointly owned homestead property is subject to levy and sale as a result of tracing proceeds of a fraudulent transaction carried out by defendant Clell Waudby. We affirm the judgment of the district court.

I.   *Facts and Proceedings Below.*

On December 8, 1986, the trial court entered a final judgment and decree in favor of plaintiffs and against Clell Waudby in the underlying fraud action.

Although defendant Helen Waudby was also a party to the action, there were no findings of fraud on her part and no relief was granted directly against her.

The judgment in the underlying fraud action was based on transactions occurring between 1970 and 1974 in which defendant Clell Waudby obtained title to 420 acres of land owned by plaintiffs through fraudulent representations. While title was held in their name, defendants granted the Federal Land Bank a mortgage against the land to secure a loan. The court determined that Helen Waudby was unaware of her husband's fraudulent activities in obtaining the farm from plaintiffs and was not liable for any of the damages suffered. The court found Clell Waudby personally liable for compensatory damages for fraudulent misrepresentation and a breach of confidential relationship and also imposed punitive damages.

The court, in its judgment and decree, returned ownership of this land to the plaintiffs, subject, however, to the Federal Land Bank mortgage which defendants had placed on the farm. The compensatory damages granted the plaintiffs included the sum of $61,084.71, representing the proceeds from the Federal Land Bank mortgage distributed to the Waudbys for their personal use. The defendants did not appeal from the district court's 1986 judgment and decree.

The present appeal is brought by defendants from the district court's October 29, 1987, order overruling their motion to quash plaintiffs' attempt to execute a levy against their homestead property. In denying the motion to quash, the district court determined that the defendants had used $33,331.32 of the Federal Land Bank mortgage proceeds to retire a purchase money mortgage against the defendants' homestead property. The court held that the property was subject to execution and sale for the sum of $33,331.32 as a result of tracing proceeds of the fraudulent transaction. The defendants do not contest that proceeds from the Federal Land Bank mortgage were invested in their present homestead. In seeking to quash the levy, defendants rely on its homestead character and on the joint tenancy interest of Helen Waudby, an innocent party. Defendants assert that either or both of these circumstances preclude levy and sale of their homestead.

II. *Tracing Trust Proceeds into Homestead Property.*

The first issue we address is whether the district court erred in holding that the homestead nature of the defendants' property does not prevent plaintiffs from tracing the proceeds of a constructive trust or equitable lien into the property. Defendants assert Iowa Code §561.21 (1985) identifies the only exceptions to the homestead exemption and that principles of statutory interpretation require we find the express exceptions are exclusive.

It is true that homestead property is ordinarily immune from the attachment of nonpurchase money judgment liens. Iowa Code §624.23(2). However, it is clear that plaintiffs' interest in the property is greater than that of an ordinary judgment lien. As a general proposition, a party in whose favor a constructive trust has been established may trace the property to where it is held and may reach whatever has been obtained through the use of it, including profits or income generated through its use. Where the trust funds have been invested in property, the beneficiary may have an equitable lien thereon established up to the amount of the trust funds invested.

This court has already indicated that the homestead nature of property does not shield it from the right of a constructive trustee to trace proceeds of the trust property. In In re Munsell's Guardianship, 239 Iowa 307, 31 N.W.2d 360 (1948), we held that, where funds from a ward's bank account were wrongfully used to make a mortgage payment on the guardian's home, a constructive trust would attach to the homestead for payment of the wrongfully diverted funds. In McGaffee v. McGaffee, 244 Iowa 879, 58 N.W.2d 357 (1953), we held that an equitable lien could be impressed against the defendants' homestead property to the extent that funds originating from a fraudulently acquired business were used to pay a mortgage and other charges against the homestead.

The listing of specific exceptions to the homestead exemption in the statute does not change the analysis. Although exemption statutes are to be liberally construed in favor of the debtor, our construction must not extend the debtor privileges not intended by the legislature. We conclude the legislature never contemplated or intended that a homestead interest could be created or maintained with wrongfully appropriated property. Where wrongfully obtained funds are used to purchase property, the property does not belong to the purchasers, and therefore, to the extent of the illegal funds used, they never acquire a homestead interest. The same principle applies where the funds are used to retire debt against the homestead.

IV.   *Tracing Trust Proceeds into Joint Tenancy Property.*

Defendants contend that Helen Waudby's joint tenancy interest in the property prevents judicial sale of the premises, referring to the general rule that property held in joint tenancy is not subject to execution and sale for the debt of one joint owner.

The ability of beneficiaries to trace the proceeds of trust property may be cut off by the superior rights of innocent third parties. State v. Hawkeye Oil Co., 253 Iowa 148, 158, 110 N.W.2d 641, 647 (1961); Bogle v. Goldsworthy, 202 Iowa 764, 771, 211 N.W. 257, 260 (1926). Equity will not impress a constructive trust upon property that has passed into the hands of a good faith purchaser for value who takes the property without notice of the trust. Harris v. Warner, 199 Iowa 1000, 1003-04, 203 N.W. 279, 281 (1925); Restatement of Restitution §172 (1937) [*cf.* R3RUE §66]. However,

> Where property is held by one person upon a constructive trust for another, and the former transfers the property to a third person who is not a bona fide purchaser, the interest of the beneficiary is not cut off, and

the defrauded person can maintain a suit in equity for specific restitution against the third person.

Restatement of Restitution §168 [*cf.* R3RUE §58].

The spouse of a person who acquires property with stolen or misappropriated funds does not occupy the position of a bona fide purchaser, and the spouse's interest cannot cut off the interests of beneficiaries unless he or she gives consideration for his or her acquisition of title to the property. A constructive trust is imposed not because of the intention of the parties but because the person holding title to the property would profit by a wrong *or* would be unjustly enriched if he or she were permitted to keep the property. Restatement of Restitution §160, comment *b* (1936). As a person who acquired title to the property without paying value, Helen Waudby is not a bona fide purchaser but a gratuitous transferee. A constructive trust or equitable lien can be imposed on the product of wrongfully obtained property in the hands of a gratuitous transferee. Restatement of Restitution §161, comment *d*, § 168 (1937).

We find the district court correctly determined that plaintiffs are entitled to a constructive trust and an equitable lien on defendants' homestead property to the extent of the $33,331.32 invested in that property which was obtained by borrowing against the plaintiffs' farm. The district court was also correct in authorizing levy and sale of the property to enforce that obligation. We affirm the order of the district court.

Equitable lien and exempt property

1. The Coxes recover their 420 acres—"subject, however, to the Federal Land Bank mortgage which defendants had placed on the farm." Why did the Bank's mortgage survive the return of the land from the Waudbys to the Coxes, when the Gladowskis' mortgage from the Club was treated as a nullity? If and when the Coxes collect their judgments against the Waudbys, they will have the funds needed to retire this unwanted mortgage on the farm.

2. The most frequent comparison of equitable lien to constructive trust arises when a defendant (frequently an embezzler) uses money of the plaintiff to make improvements on property the defendant already owns. Notice how using someone else's funds to pay down a mortgage (the case in both *Gladowski* and *Cox*) produces a similar situation. Either way, the claimant's property is commingled with that of the defendant, though no distinct part of the whole can be identified as the product of the money.

3. Although the court refers (rather confusingly) to a judgment for "compensatory damages," the simpler way to explain *Cox v. Waudby* is that the $61,084.71 lent by the Bank on the security of the Coxes' 420 acres was the partial *product* of the Coxes' land. Of this amount, the Coxes were able to *trace* $33,331.32 into a different kind of "improvement" of the Waudbys' homestead property: instead of using the money to build a new barn, the Waudbys

used it to pay off a preexisting mortgage loan. Either way, the textbook remedy for the Coxes in this situation is equitable lien. They get a judge-made lien (effectively, here, a first-priority mortgage) securing their claim to $33,331.32. An equitable lien is enforced in the same way as a consensual one: either the defendants pay to discharge it, or else plaintiffs foreclose, compel the sale of the property, and take their $33,331.32 out of the proceeds. If Clell Waudby had used the same $33,331.32 to buy some other Blackacre outright—instead of using it to retire a mortgage—the Coxes could identify Blackacre as the product of their money and claim ownership via constructive trust.

4. "Homestead" laws in every jurisdiction make certain categories of property, within specified limits, exempt from the claims of creditors. (The fact that some jurisdictions are so much more generous than others explains why people with significant debts and significant assets tend to establish residence in a few well-known states.) But debt is one thing; misappropriation is something else. No jurisdiction will permit a person to acquire property by fraud or theft, then put it beyond the reach of its owner by using it to purchase exempt assets. This is why the court in *Cox v. Waudby* says that the "homestead nature" of property does not shield it against the remedies of constructive trust or equitable lien. The rule is universal, though rarely (if ever) mentioned in the homestead statutes themselves.

————————————

Farnsworth, *Restitution* 127-128 (2014):

The logic of an equitable lien much resembles the logic of a constructive trust. Again the court recognizes the plaintiff's rights in property to which the defendant has title. But whereas the constructive trust causes the property to be transferred to the plaintiff, the equitable lien does not. It just gives the plaintiff a security interest in the property. Usually this means the right to force a sale and collect what is owed out of the proceeds.

When an equitable lien makes more sense than a constructive trust, it is typically because the plaintiff has only a limited claim to the defendant's property. Suppose, for example, that the defendant improved his own property by spending some of the plaintiff's money on it. Since the plaintiff's assets contributed just some fraction of the property's total value, it would be overkill to transfer all of the property in question to the plaintiff by means of a constructive trust. But since the plaintiff can follow his stolen money into the defendant's property, he surely should have some rights in it. An equitable lien reflects this mixed state of affairs. If the defendant pays what he owes to the plaintiff, the lien is discharged and the property is no longer encumbered. The defendant has exercised his "right of redemption." Otherwise the plaintiff can foreclose the lien; that is, he can insist on a judicial sale of the property and satisfy his claim out of whatever money it brings in. The defendant keeps whatever amount may be left over afterward. (The court has discretion to relax these rules if the defendant was not a conscious wrongdoer, as by saying the plaintiff gets his money *if* the property is sold—but not ordering the sale.)

————————————

(3) Subrogation

Equity Savings & Loan Association v. Chicago Title Insurance Co.
190 N.J. Super. 340, 463 A.2d 398 (App. Div. 1983)

BRODY, J.A.D.

Harvey Goldberg misused his position as an attorney in arranging the placement of two mortgages on the same property. He falsely represented to each mortgagee that its mortgage was a first lien. Their priorities are at issue in this foreclosure suit.

Goldberg's machinations began while the property was encumbered by a $12,000 first mortgage to Philip Raben and a $40,000 second mortgage to Valley Savings and Loan Association. In order to obtain a $48,000 mortgage loan from Equity Savings and Loan Association, Goldberg secured a subordination of the Raben mortgage but falsely certified to Equity that he had cancelled the Valley mortgage. In fact, he did not pay the Valley mortgage which by virtue of the subordination became the first mortgage on the property. About a year later Goldberg obtained a $54,000 mortgage loan from Spencer Savings and Loan Association for his corporation Trunc Enterprises, Inc. which by then had acquired title to the property. Goldberg disclosed to Spencer only the Valley mortgage and satisfied it out of the proceeds of the Spencer loan. He concealed the Equity and Raben mortgages. When the truth came out, Chicago Title Insurance Co. paid Spencer under its policy, took an assignment of the Spencer mortgage and purchased the Raben mortgage. This left the record priorities as follows: Equity, Chicago (Raben) and Chicago (Spencer). The present dispute is between Equity and Chicago. Relying on the state of the record and finding the equities equally balanced, the trial judge concluded that Equity was first. We reverse.

Since part of the proceeds of the Spencer loan was used to satisfy the Valley mortgage, Chicago, Spencer's assignee, stands in the shoes of Valley as though the Valley mortgage had been assigned to Spencer instead of cancelled. A refinancing lender whose security turns out to be defective is subrogated by equitable assignment "to the position of the lender whose lien is discharged by the proceeds of the later loan, there being no prejudice to or justified reliance by a party in adverse interest." Kaplan v. Walker, 164 N.J. Super. 130, 138, 395 A.2d 897 (App. Div. 1978).

The trial judge declined to apply the doctrine of subrogation by equitable assignment because, as he viewed it, there is no equitable reason to give Spencer an advantage over Equity since each was identically defrauded by Goldberg into believing its junior mortgage was first. We disagree. The difference between the two is that while there is no evidence of what Goldberg did with Equity's money, he used part of Spencer's money to cancel Valley's mortgage, thereby gratuitously enhancing Equity's security. Since Spencer's money was obtained by fraud (the concealment of the Equity and Raben mortgages), Equity's windfall may be viewed as a product of the money stolen from Spencer. When stolen property or its product can be traced, it must be returned to its true owner. *Cf.* Restatement, Restitution, §215 at 866 (1937);

Baisch v. Publishers' Typographic Serv., Inc., 70 N.J. Super. 340, 175 A.2d 485 (Ch. Div. 1961) (owner of unidentifiable portion of commingled property in hands of receiver not entitled to priority over general creditors). Here the return of Spencer's money is accomplished through application of the doctrine of subrogation by equitable assignment.

The mortgage priorities are therefore as follows: (1) Chicago in the amount it paid to satisfy the Valley mortgage, (2) the Equity mortgage, and (3) the Chicago mortgages.

Reversed and remanded for further proceedings consistent with this opinion.

Tracing into discharge of a lien

1. Notice the way each of the cases in this section turns on a finding, more or less explicit, that the claimant's property (or its product) has come into the defendant's hands. This kind of identification or "tracing" is the universal and critical requirement of the asset-based remedies in restitution. A claimant who cannot show what happened to his property may still have a valid claim in restitution, but it will not be enforceable by the remedies of constructive trust, equitable lien, or subrogation. That leaves the claimant with judgment for money against the defendant, in the amount of the defendant's unjust enrichment.

2. How the claimant has managed to satisfy the tracing requirement is more obvious in some cases than others. In *Equity Savings*, the "product" of Spencer's money was the payment of the Valley mortgage and the consequent promotion of Equity's mortgage. In other words, Equity's unjust enrichment can be identified in the enhanced value of its security interest. Since Valley cannot be required to give back the money, subrogation does the next best thing by allowing Spencer to enforce the secured obligation (with its priority) that Spencer's money was used to discharge. (Recall that subrogation is sometimes called "equitable assignment.") This gives Spencer what was "bought" with Spencer's money, and it restores Equity to the position it occupied before the fraud on Spencer.

Farnsworth, *Restitution* 130-131 (2014):

Suppose a defendant acquires the plaintiff's money by fraud or mistake and uses it to pay off a creditor. The plaintiff has a good claim against the defendant for return of the money, but that just makes the plaintiff yet another creditor who may be competing with many others. The interesting question is whether the plaintiff can somehow get a specific claim to any of the defendant's property. A constructive trust or equitable lien will not work here, because the plaintiff's money has not been exchanged for property that the defendant can seize or seek to have sold. But another route may be possible. The plaintiff can step into the shoes of the creditor who was paid with his money. If that creditor had a security interest—a lien by contract—in the defendant's property, then the plaintiff now has that same lien with the same priority. If the defendant defaults, the plaintiff can foreclose the lien, force a judicial sale of the property, and get his money ahead of other creditors (though the defendant has the same defenses against the plaintiff that he would have had against the creditor in whose shoes the plaintiff now stands). Putting the plaintiff into the creditor's position this way is called "subrogation," an old word for "substitution." It resembles the other devices just reviewed because again the plaintiff can gain rights in specific property held by the defendant. He just gets those rights less directly. He inherits them, so to speak, from the party who was paid with his money.

From the defendant's point of view, the effect of the subrogation is that he never paid his creditor after all. To be precise, he paid him with money that belonged to someone else, so now the someone else simply takes the old creditor's place. Notice that if the creditor who was paid off by the defendant was unsecured—in other words, if he had no lien on any of the defendant's property and the defendant merely owed him money—then the plaintiff still *could* step into his shoes, but there would be no point. It would just give the plaintiff a money claim against the defendant, which is what the plaintiff already has anyway when he wins his restitution suit. It is only worth bothering with subrogation as a remedy when it gives the plaintiff something more: not rights against the defendant, but rights in the defendant's property (and perhaps priority over other claimants).

---

(4) More problems of following or tracing

Brodie v. Barnes
56 Cal. App. 2d 315, 132 P.2d 595 (1942)

PETERS, P. J.

W. B. Barnes died May 15, 1939. For many years prior to his death Barnes had been employed by Brodie Bros., Inc., a corporation [since dissolved, to which plaintiff Brodie is the successor]. After his death it was discovered that from 1934 to the time of his death Barnes had embezzled substantial sums from his employer. A claim for [the total amount embezzled] was filed by plaintiff in the estate proceedings and was rejected, and this action was then instituted. Among other things, the plaintiff alleged that certain of the misappropriated funds had been used to purchase a piece of real property at 1976 Waltonia Drive, Montrose, California, and some of such funds had been used to pay premiums on a $2,000 life insurance policy issued by defendant John Hancock Mutual Life Insurance Company, in which policy Evadna Barnes was named beneficiary. Plaintiff prayed for a judgment against the estate in the amount of the embezzled funds, for a determination that Mrs. Barnes held the real property in trust for plaintiff, and for a determination that the proceeds of the insurance policy should be ordered paid to him.

The trial court, at the request of the parties, appointed a referee, with instructions to investigate and report back to the court the extent and disposition of all misappropriated funds. The referee found that the total amount of the peculations by Barnes for the period 1934 to 1939 was $5,815.03. The trial court ruled that the statute of limitations barred the collection of any sums misappropriated prior to May 29, 1936, thus applying the three-year statute of limitations, the complaint having been filed May 29, 1939. The correctness of this ruling must be assumed on this appeal, plaintiff not having appealed. The trial court also found that the amount embezzled prior to May 29, 1936, was $2,450, which amount he held should be deducted from the total sum misappropriated. Judgment was given plaintiff for $3,365.03. The trial court also imposed a trust on the proceeds of the life insurance policy and on the real property, and decreed that the total of the proceeds of the life policy should be paid to plaintiff, that the realty should be sold to satisfy the judgment, plaintiff to get no more than $3,365.03 in any event, and the excess turned over to Evadna Barnes, and gave judgment against the estate of Barnes for any deficiency.

The appellants contend that there was not a sufficient tracing of the misappropriated funds to justify the imposition of a constructive trust on the real property and insurance policy. So far as this contention is predicated upon the alleged insufficiency of the evidence to support the findings of the referee and trial court, it is without merit. So far as the real property located on Waltonia Drive is concerned, there is no merit to the contention that the findings do not support the conclusion that the misappropriated money was used to purchase this property. The referee found that this property was purchased in 1936 for a total purchase price of $3,150, of which $1,234 was paid in cash; that installments were paid from the Bank of America account in which salary and additional sums (obviously part of the misappropriated funds), were deposited; that at the death of Mr. Barnes there was on deposit with the Bank of Commerce $2,721 (which account contained the balance of the misappropriated funds); that Mrs. Barnes, the day following Mr. Barnes' death, withdrew this entire account, and, after paying $500 for funeral expenses, deposited the balance in her account; that within a week of Mr. Barnes' death, Mrs. Barnes withdrew $1,528 from this account and paid the balance due on the real property. The referee found in detail the various financial transactions of Barnes, and it is the reasonable inference from those findings that the money used to purchase the real property was all taken from the accounts in which the misappropriated funds were deposited. The trial court found in accordance with this inference. It found that the original deposit and the balance due on the mortgage were paid from the funds misappropriated from plaintiff, and that "as to the fact that it was the money and property of plaintiff that was used by said W. B. Barnes . . . in paying the purchase money on said real estate, defendant Evadna L. Barnes at all times had and now has full knowledge." This was a sufficient tracing of the funds to authorize the court in imposing the trust. It will be noted that the trial court did not give plaintiff the real property as it might well have done. It limited plaintiff's rights to a lien, ordered the property sold, and provided that the recovery by plaintiff should be limited to the amount embezzled.

As to the insurance policy, a different situation exists. Both the referee and the trial court found that the policy was issued for $2,000 on the life of W. B. Barnes by the John Hancock Mutual Life Insurance Company on December 1, 1931, and that the premiums after April 9, 1934, were paid by Barnes with money stolen from plaintiff. Obviously, the premiums from December 1, 1931, to April 9, 1934, must have been paid with Barnes' own funds. Moreover, appellant's plea of the statute of limitations was sustained as to all funds taken prior to May 29, 1936. Whether that determination was correct or not is immaterial, plaintiff not having appealed from the judgment is bound thereby. As a result, plaintiff has no legal right to any portion of the policy, the premiums for which were paid prior to May 29, 1936. There is no finding as to the total amount of the premiums that were paid into the policy, nor is there any finding as to the total amount of the premiums that were paid with misappropriated funds. Nevertheless, the trial court by its judgment ordered the insurance company to pay the total amount of the insurance policy over to plaintiff on the theory there was a constructive trust of the entire policy. This was error. Although there seems to be no case directly in point in this state, there is a line of authorities in other states to the effect that where a person has embezzled funds and used them for the payment of premiums for insurance on his life, a trust is created in favor of the person from whom they were embezzled, and that such person is entitled to such proportion of the total insurance as the amount of premiums which have been paid from the embezzled funds bears to the total amount of the premiums paid. There is some authority that the defrauded person is limited to recovering the amount of premiums paid with the misappropriated funds, but the better reasoned cases permit a *pro tanto* recovery.

That portion of the judgment providing that plaintiff should be paid the entire insurance policy is reversed with instructions to the trial court to ascertain the amount of the total premiums on the policy and the amount of such premiums paid since May 29, 1936, and to grant plaintiff a *pro tanto* interest in the policy; the balance of the judgment is affirmed.

Limits to profitable recovery

1. Following property into its product will sometimes give the claimant the benefit of an intervening appreciation in value. Dramatic windfalls—as where a thief uses a victim's funds to buy winning lottery tickets—are easy to imagine but nearly impossible to find in reported cases. The real-life examples of stolen

funds invested at exceptionally high returns involve the use of someone else's money to pay life-insurance premiums. The extent to which the eventual death benefit should be regarded as the product of the funds used to pay the premiums has been vigorously debated. *Brodie v. Barnes* adopts the consensus position in favor of a pro rata division, but this is by no means the only logical possibility. What if the embezzler has purchased term life insurance, using his own funds to pay annual premiums in prior years but his victim's funds for the year in which he dies?

2. One of the reasons for the recurrent controversy over life insurance proceeds is that the facts of such cases are potentially awkward. On a strict tracing approach, the bank that employs a dishonest cashier might recover many times its loss if the cashier has bought insurance with bank funds—while the cashier's widow and orphan children are left penniless. Considering the problem more broadly, many observers think it unfair that rules of tracing (or following property into its product) should give some claimants restitution exceeding their losses, if other creditors of the wrongdoer remain unpaid.

According to the usual logic by which one asset is regarded as the product of another, the employer in *Brodie v. Barnes* was entitled to the house on Waltonia Drive (all of it) and possibly to all of the life insurance proceeds. The trial court limited the employer's claim against the house to the amount of its loss within the period of limitations; the appellate court ordered that the insurance proceeds be shared as well. The reasoning is not made explicit, but it can only reflect judicial concern for the support of the widow. Notice that Evadna's character was not spotless either.

3. In the view of the Restatement, the results in cases like *Brodie v. Barnes* reflect a more general principle: that the claimant's right to a *profitable* recovery in restitution—that is, to recover more than he lost—will be subordinated to the claims of the unpaid creditors and dependents of the wrongdoer.

> Given the starting premise that conscious wrongdoing ought not to be profitable, the law permits the victim to recover more than the loss so that the wrongdoer may be stripped of the gain. But the justification of the remedy disappears if a supracompensatory award to the restitution claimant would come at the expense of a third party who is innocent of the underlying wrong: typically, an unpaid creditor or a surviving dependent of the wrongdoing recipient.
>
> The assumption that restitution to the claimant is made at the expense of a wrongdoer underlies every justification for the possibility of a recovery exceeding the claimant's loss. But if the wrongdoer is insolvent—so that the wrongdoer's assets are inadequate to satisfy both a liability to the claimant in restitution and the claims of general creditors—this critical assumption no longer holds. If circumstances are such that restitution to the claimant reduces the assets available to the recipient's creditors, a case that begins as a contest between victim and wrongdoer is transformed into a competition for limited assets between innocent claimants.

Rules permitting a recovery in restitution in excess of the claimant's loss are accordingly limited, by their own rationale, to cases in which restitution to the claimant is made at the expense of the wrongdoer. The initial result of this limitation is that the portion of an entitlement to restitution that exceeds the claimant's loss is subordinated to the claims of creditors of the recipient/debtor.

The limitation of the claimant's recovery required by this section is often accomplished simply by substituting one remedy for another. A claimant who would be entitled to a constructive trust vis-à-vis the wrongdoer may be restricted to an equitable lien, when the effective contest is with the wrongdoer's general creditors.

R3RUE §61, Comments *a* & *b*.

Simonds v. Simonds
45 N.Y.2d 233, 380 N.E.2d 189 (1978)

Chief Judge Breitel.

Plaintiff Mary Simonds, decedent's first wife, seeks to impress a constructive trust on proceeds of insurance policies on decedent's life. The proceeds had been paid to the named beneficiaries, defendants Reva Simonds, decedent's second wife, and their daughter Gayle. Plaintiff, however, asserts as superior an equitable interest arising out of a provision in her separation agreement with decedent. Special Term granted partial summary judgment to plaintiff and impressed a constructive trust to the extent of $7,000 plus interest against proceeds of a policy naming the second wife as beneficiary, and the Appellate Division affirmed. Defendant Reva Simonds, the second wife, appeals.

On March 9, 1960, decedent Frederick Simonds and his wife of 14 years, plaintiff Mary Simonds, entered into a separation agreement which, on March 31, 1960, was incorporated into an Illinois divorce decree granted to plaintiff on grounds of desertion. The agreement provided, somewhat inartfully:

> The husband agrees that he will keep all of the policies of Insurance now in full force and effect on his life. Said policies now being in the sum of $21,000.00 and the Husband further agrees that the Wife shall be the beneficiary of said policies in an amount not less than $7,000.00 and the Husband further agrees that he shall pay any and all premiums necessary to maintain such policies of Insurance and if for any reason any of them now existing the policies shall be cancelled or be caused to lapse. He shall procure additional insurance in an amount equal to the face value of the policies having been cancelled or caused to lapse.

Thus, the husband was to maintain, somehow, at least $7,000 of life insurance for the benefit of his first wife as a named beneficiary.

On May 26, 1960, less than two months after the divorce, decedent husband married defendant Reva Simonds. Defendant Gayle Simonds was born to the couple shortly thereafter.

Sometime after the separation agreement was signed, the then existing insurance policies were apparently canceled or permitted to lapse. It does not appear from the record why, how, or when this happened, but the policies were not extant at the time of decedent husband's death on August 1, 1971. In the interim, however, decedent has acquired three other life insurance policies, totaling over $55,000, none of which named plaintiff as a beneficiary. At his death, decedent had one policy in the amount of $16,138.83 originally issued in 1962 by Metropolitan Life Insurance Company, a second policy for $34,000 issued in 1967 through decedent's employer by Travelers Insurance Company, and a third policy for $5,566 issued in 1962 by the Equitable Life Assurance Society of Iowa. The first two policies named Reva Simonds, defendant's second wife, as beneficiary, and the third policy named their daughter. Hence, at the time of decedent's death he had continuously violated the separation agreement by maintaining no life insurance naming the first wife as a beneficiary.

There is no question that decedent breached his obligation to maintain life insurance with his first wife as beneficiary. Consequently, the first wife would of course be entitled to maintain an action for breach against the estate. The estate's insolvency, however, would make such an action fruitless. Thus, the controversy revolves around plaintiff's right, in equity, to recover $7,000 of the insurance proceeds.

Born out of the extreme rigidity of the early common law, equity in its origins drew heavily on Roman law, where equitable notions had long been accepted (see 1 Pomeroy, Equity Jurisprudence [5th ed], §§2-29). "Its great underlying principles, which are the constant sources, the never-failing roots, of its particular rules, are unquestionably principles of right, justice, and morality, so far as the same can become the elements of a positive human jurisprudence" (*id.*, §67, at p 90). Law without principle is not law; law without justice is of limited value. Since adherence to principles of "law" does not invariably produce justice, equity is necessary (Aristotle, Nichomachean Ethics, Book V, ch. 9, pp.1019-1020 [McKeon, ed Oxford: Clarendon Press, 1941]). Equity arose to soften the impact of legal formalisms; to evolve formalisms narrowing the broad scope of equity is to defeat its essential purpose.

Whatever the legal rights between insurer and insured, the separation agreement vested in the first wife an equitable interest in the insurance policies then in force. An agreement for sufficient consideration, including a separation agreement, to maintain a claimant as a beneficiary of a life insurance policy vests in the claimant an equitable interest in the policies designated. This interest is superior to that of a named beneficiary who has given no consideration, notwithstanding policy provisions permitting the insured to change the designated beneficiary freely.

This is not to say that an insurance company may not rely on the insured's designation of a beneficiary. None of this opinion bears on the rights or responsibilities of the insurer in law or in equity.

Obviously, the policies now at issue are not the same polices in existence at the time of the separation agreement. But it has been held that mere substitution of policies, or even substitution of insurance companies, does not defeat the equitable interest of one who has given sufficient consideration for a promise to be maintained as beneficiary under an insurance policy (see Locomotive Engrs. Mut. Life & Acc. Ins. Assn. v Locke, 251 App. Div. 146, 149 (1937); see also Dixon v Dixon, 184 So. 2d 478, 481 (Fla. Dist. Ct. App. 1966)). The persistence of the promisee's equitable interest is all the more evident where the agreement expressly provides for a change in policies, and in effect provides further that the promisee's right shall attach to the new policies.

For a certainty, the first wife's equitable interest would be easier to trace if the new policies were *quid pro quo* replacements for the original policies. The record does not reveal whether this was so. But inability to trace plaintiff's equitable rights precisely should not require that they not be recognized, much as in the instance of damages difficult to prove. The separation agreement provides nexus between plaintiff's rights and the later acquired policies. The later policies were expressly contemplated by the parties, and it was agreed that plaintiff would have an interest in them. No reason in equity appears for denying plaintiff that interest, so long as no one who has given value for the policies or otherwise suffered a detriment is involved. The second wife's innocence does not offset the wrong by the now deceased husband.

The conclusion is an application of the general rule that equity regards as done that which should have been done (2 Pomeroy, Equity Jurisprudence [5th ed], §364). Thus, if an insured, upon lapse or cancellation of insurance, followed by replacement with new insurance, has a contractual obligation to designate a particular person as beneficiary, equity will consider the obligee as a beneficiary.

In this case, then, the first wife's interest in the original policies extended as well to the later acquired policies. The husband, upon lapse or cancellation of the earlier policies, had by virtue of the separation agreement an obligation to name her as beneficiary on the later policies, an obligation enforceable in equity despite the husband's failure to comply with the terms of the separation agreement. Due to the husband's failure to do what he should have done, the first wife acquired not only a right at law to sue his estate for breach of contract, a right now worthless, but also an equitable right in the policies, a right which, upon the husband's death, attached to the proceeds.

And, since the first wife was entitled to $7,000 of the insurance proceeds at the time of the husband's death, she is no less entitled because the proceeds have already been converted by being paid, erroneously, to the named beneficiaries. Her remedy is imposition of a constructive trust.

In the words of Judge Cardozo, "A constructive trust is the formula through which the conscience of equity finds expression. When property has been acquired in such circumstances that the holder of the legal title may not in good conscience retain the beneficial interest, equity converts him into a trustee" (Beatty v Guggenheim Exploration Co., 225 N.Y. 380, 386). Thus, a constructive trust is an equitable remedy. It is perhaps more different from an express trust than it is similar (5 Scott, Trusts [3d ed], §461). As put so well by

Scott and restated at the Appellate Division, "He is not compelled to convey the property because he is a constructive trustee; it is because he can be compelled to convey it that he is a constructive trustee" (*id.*, §462).

More precise definitions of a constructive trust have been termed inadequate because of the failure to recognize the broad scope of constructive trust doctrine (*id.*). As another leading scholar has said of constructive trusts, "[t]he Court does not restrict itself by describing all the specific forms of inequitable holding which will move it to grant relief, but rather reserves freedom to apply this remedy to whatever knavery human ingenuity can invent"(Bogert, Trusts and Trustees [2d ed. Rev., 1978], §471). For a single example [of its flexible application], one who wrongfully prevents a testator from executing a new will eliminating him as beneficiary will be held as a constructive trustee even in the absence of a confidential or fiduciary relation, a promise by the "trustee," and a transfer in reliance by the testator (see, e.g., Latham v Father Divine, 299 N.Y. 22, 26-27). As then Judge Desmond said in response to the argument that a breach of a promise to the testator was necessary for imposition of a constructive trust, "A constructive trust will be erected whenever necessary to satisfy the demands of justice. . . . [I]ts applicability is limited only by the inventiveness of men who find new ways to enrich themselves unjustly by grasping what should not belong to them."

It is agreed that the purpose of the constructive trust is prevention of unjust enrichment. Unjust enrichment, however, does not require the performance of any wrongful act by the one enriched. Innocent parties may frequently be unjustly enriched. What is required, generally, is that a party hold property "under such circumstances that in equity and good conscience he ought not to retain it" (Miller v Schloss, 218 N.Y. 400, 407). A bona fide purchaser of property upon which a constructive trust would otherwise be imposed takes free of the constructive trust, but a gratuitous donee, however innocent, does not.

The unjust enrichment in this case is manifest. At a time when decedent was, certainly, anxious to remarry, he entered into a separation agreement with his wife of 14 years. As part of the agreement, he promised to maintain $7,000 in life insurance with the first wife as beneficiary. Later he broke his promise, and died with insurance policies naming only the second wife and daughter as beneficiaries. They have collected the proceeds, amounting to more than $55,000, while the first wife has collected nothing. Had the husband kept his promise, the beneficiaries would have collected $7,000 less in proceeds. To that extent, the beneficiaries have been unjustly enriched, and the proceeds should be subjected to a constructive trust.

The issues in this case should not generate significant controversy. The action is in equity, and the equities are clear. True, some courts have decided the issues differently (Rindels v Prudential Life Ins. Co. of Amer., 83 NM 181 (1971); Lock v Lock, 8 Ariz App 138, 143 (1968); see, also, Larson v. Larson, 226 Ga 209, 211 (1970)). Those cases, however, rely heavily on formalisms and too little on basic equitable principles, long established in Anglo-American law and in this State and especially relevant when family transactions are involved. "A court of equity in decreeing a constructive trust is bound by no unyielding formula. The equity of the transaction must shape the measure of relief" (Beatty v Guggenheim Exploration Co., 225 NY 380, 389 [Cardozo, J.]).

Accordingly, the order of the Appellate Division should be affirmed, with costs.

Wife 1 v. Wife 2

1. In a recurrent scenario, former Husband promises to maintain or obtain life insurance in favor of Wife 1 (or their children). He fails to do so, then dies leaving other life insurance proceeds to Wife 2. Husband's Estate is liable for his breach of contract but has no assets. Wife 1 looks for a theory to support a restitution claim against Wife 2. As the court recognizes in *Simonds*, the problem is to explain how the insurance proceeds paid to Wife 2 (or some part of them) constitute property to which Wife 1 has a prior equitable claim. This is easier in some cases than in others:

(a) Husband changes the beneficiary designation on an existing policy from Wife 1 to Wife 2.

(b) Husband leaves his current job, where his employee life insurance named Wife 1 as beneficiary. At his new job he is issued a new policy in favor of Wife 2.

(c) Husband allows an existing policy in favor of Wife 1 to lapse. Years later he buys a new policy (different terms, different company) for the benefit of Wife 2.

(d) Husband promises to insure his life for the benefit of Wife 1 but never does so. After his remarriage, he insures his life for the benefit of Wife 2.

Courts have usually handled the simpler cases with a "tracing" analysis. If Wife 1 can show that benefits paid to Wife 2 were a substitute for benefits promised to Wife 1—easy enough with a substitution of beneficiaries or exchange of policies—it is not difficult to apply a standard analysis in constructive trust. Where there is no substitution of one policy for another, finding a solution requires a more flexible conception of equitable rights, one that permits an equitable owner to trace property despite a break in continuity. Courts that refuse to do this might grant restitution to Wife 1 in cases (a) and (b) and refuse it in cases (c) and (d). But *Simonds* is correct in holding that a person can have an equitable interest in property that has not yet been acquired.

2. The Restatement offers the following comparison:

> Some courts attempt to explain these outcomes [in cases of subsequently-acquired policies] by invoking a relaxed version of "tracing." See Rogers v.

Rogers, 63 N.Y.2d 582, 473 N.E.2d 226 (1984) (asserting a "need to relax the tracing requirement in exceptional circumstances" in concluding that an unrelated second policy might be regarded as a replacement for a previous policy that had been allowed to lapse). But the reference to tracing rules (which are naturally impossible to satisfy in these cases) makes the problem of the subsequently-acquired policy more difficult than it need be. As held in [*Simonds v. Simonds*], a court may recognize a promisee's equitable interest in property subsequently acquired by the promisor, without insisting that such property be the traceable product of an asset previously held. Such an interest may be enforced against a third party (in these cases, the second wife) who does not take the new asset as a bona fide purchaser.

The real-property doctrine of estoppel by deed offers a helpful analogy. Here A gives B a deed to Blackacre, but B takes nothing because (at the time of the conveyance) A has no interest in the property. When A subsequently acquires Blackacre, A is estopped to deny B's title; B becomes the equitable owner of Blackacre from the moment of A's acquisition. B's title is likewise good against A's successor, C, so long as C is not a bona fide purchaser. See, e.g., Dalessio v. Baggia, 57 Mass. App. Ct. 468, 783 N.E.2d 890 (2003) (affirming the doctrine of estoppel by deed while holding that a bona fide purchaser from the common grantor can take free of the interest of the estoppel grantee). Real property law is helpful in the present context, because it demonstrates that a claimant may indeed assert a "springing" equitable interest (so to speak) in subsequently acquired property of the defendant that is *not* the product of anything in which the claimant previously had an interest.

R3RUE §48 (Reporter's Note to Comment g). Estoppel by deed is usually explained as one application of "the general rule that equity regards as done that which should have been done," to which Chief Judge Breitel refers in *Simonds*.

People v. $35,315.00 United States Currency
64 N.E.3d 754 (Ill. Ct. App. 2016)

Justice POPE delivered the judgment of the court, with opinion:

The State appeals the trial court's judgment the proceeds of a winning lottery ticket were not forfeitable under the Illinois Drug Asset Forfeiture Procedure Act (Forfeiture Act) (725 ILCS 150/1 to 14 (West 2014)). We reverse.

I. Background

On November 18, 2014, Macon County police officers executed a search warrant at the residence of Terrance Norwood. Claimant, Tykisha Lofton, lived with Norwood. Police recovered cannabis, cocaine, a digital scale, packaging material, a loaded SKS assault rifle, ammunition, and approximately $200 cash.

During an interview with police, Norwood admitted he sold drugs. Norwood stated he was unemployed and had no source of income other than drug sales. Norwood explained he was going to stop selling drugs because he had recently purchased a scratch-off lottery ticket at the Price Rite in Decatur and won $50,000.

[A few days later, Norwood was charged with a series of drug-related crimes.] On January 14, 2015, the State filed a complaint for forfeiture, seeking the proceeds of the winning lottery ticket, *i.e.*, $35,315. (The parties appear to agree that figure represents the lump sum value of the $50,000 prize.) The State alleged those funds were subject to forfeiture as proceeds traceable to Norwood's illegal drug sales.

[At a bench trial of the forfeiture complaint, the court first heard from Macon County sheriff's deputy Brian Hickey.] During an interview with Hickey, Norwood stated he had been unemployed for several months and admitted he was selling cocaine and cannabis. Norwood stated he was selling drugs to pay the bills until he got "that little bit of money." When Hickey asked Norwood what he meant by "that little bit of money," Norwood explained he had won $50,000 on a $3 scratch-off lottery ticket. The ticket had been turned in to the lottery office in Springfield, and Norwood was waiting to get paid. Hickey testified Norwood told him he purchased the ticket in the beginning of November and he let Lofton scratch it off.

[After Lofton's motion for a directed verdict was denied, her trial testimony was significantly different.] Lofton testified she and Norwood had been living together "for years." Lofton lived at the residence with her three children (ages five, six, and eight). Lofton maintained Norwood did not give her the money to purchase the ticket. Lofton testified she was unemployed both at the time of the hearing and at the time the lottery ticket was purchased. Although she last babysat in September, Lofton claimed to have received payment for those services in October 2014. Lofton explained she purchased the first ticket, which yielded a free ticket, with money she received from babysitting. According to Lofton, the free ticket was the winning ticket.

At the conclusion of the hearing, the trial court found in favor of Lofton. With regard to who purchased the ticket, the trial court found the following:

> This Court believes that Mr. Norwood purchased the lottery ticket. This Court believes that he purchased the ticket more likely than not with drug money. [Norwood] indicated at that time that drug money was his only source of income. He used the [drug] money to pay his bills and to help support his family. And by the way, he was going to change because he had won this ticket and so on and so forth. Before Mr. Norwood and [Lofton] understood the consequences, this is what Mr. Norwood told the authorities and what [Lofton] told the authorities. This Court does find that Detective Hickey's testimony on this point is credible and [Lofton's] testimony on the point is not credible.

However, the trial court denied the State's complaint on the basis that although the ticket was purchased with drug money, it was not forfeitable under the Forfeiture Act. Specifically, the court found the following:

> This Court does not believe that forfeiting the proceeds that were purchased from a lottery ticket was what the Forfeiture Act was intended to do. The proceeds in this particular case were the windfall of purchasing one $3 lottery ticket. They were not derivative from the sales of drugs except, perhaps, for the $3. They did not stem from the sale of drugs.
>
> I did carefully review the [*Betancourt*] case, which, of course, says just the opposite in terms of what I am stating. I do not agree with the reasoning in that particular case. I am not bound by the decision of a federal [court] out of the state of Texas. And just to comment briefly, I think, at some point in time the—the argument that everything stems from something has to stop.
>
> What if, for instance, they had taken the proceeds and invested [them] in some type of successful dry cleaning business or some such thing, and they're making $100,000 a year from the dry cleaning business, are those proceeds then forfeitable?
>
> What if, for instance, some cannabis dealer had earned $10,000 selling cannabis, and he decided he was going to put himself through medical school or something with that money, earned a medical degree and was out successfully working? Is that money then forfeitable? At some point the—the connection has to stop.

The trial court concluded forfeiture was not appropriate under the circumstances presented by this case. This appeal followed.

II. *Analysis*

The Illinois General Assembly passed the Forfeiture Act to establish uniform procedures for the civil forfeiture of property "attributable to" certain drug-related violations of, *inter alia*, the Illinois Controlled Substances Act and the Cannabis Control Act. People v. $280,020 United States Currency, 372 Ill. App. 3d 785, 791, 866 N.E.2d 1232, 1239 (1st Dist. 2007). Both of those acts provide, in relevant part, *all proceeds traceable* to an exchange for a substance in violation of the acts are subject to forfeiture. 720 ILCS 570/505(a)(5) (West 2014); 720 ILCS 550/12(a)(5) (West 2014).

In United States v. Betancourt, 422 F.3d 240, 242 (5th Cir. 2005), a case with very similar facts to the instant matter, the defendant appealed the district court's order for forfeiture of a $5 million lottery prize because the winning ticket was purchased with the proceeds of his drug trafficking. In affirming the district court's decision, the Fifth Circuit Court of Appeals found the proceeds of drug selling used to win the Texas lottery made the lottery winnings subject to forfeiture. *Betancourt*, 422 F.3d at 252. The court

reasoned, "All proceeds obtained from unlawful conduct and property traceable to those proceeds are subject to criminal forfeiture." *Betancourt*, 422
F.3d at 250; see also United States v. Four Million, Two Hundred Fifty–
Five Thousand, 762 F.2d 895, 905 (11th Cir.1985) (rejecting the argument
forfeited money did not constitute the proceeds of narcotics transactions
where the money had been exchanged for goods because the forfeiture
statute does not limit forfeiture to property found in the hands of a drug
dealer but applies to all proceeds traceable to drug dealing). According to
Betancourt, the fact "[the defendant] used his drug proceeds to generate a
very large return by winning the Texas lottery is of no import in the forfeiture
analysis." *Betancourt*, 422 F.3d at 251.

In this case, the trial court found Norwood purchased a scratch-off lottery
ticket with proceeds derived from his drug dealing. While Lofton testified
she made the purchase and did not know Norwood sold drugs, the court
found her testimony was not credible. According to Lofton, the initial ticket
yielded a free ticket, which ended up being the winning ticket. Because of
the direct link between the lottery winnings and the funds used to purchase
the original ticket, the winnings can reasonably be considered "proceeds
traceable" to Norwood's illegal drug sales. As such, those proceeds are forfeitable under the Forfeiture Act. The trial court's conclusion to the contrary
was error.

For the reasons stated, we reverse the trial court's judgment.

Everything stems from something

1. The world is still waiting for a case of common-law restitution in which a
defendant uses misappropriated funds to purchase a winning lottery ticket. But
drug dealers occasionally win the lottery, and the courts interpret the criminal
forfeiture statutes to incorporate the standard logic of following and tracing.

2. In *United States v. Betancourt*, the 5th Circuit decision mentioned in the
course of the Illinois opinion, the winning ticket had been purchased by the
drug dealer's neighbor:

> In the forfeiture phase of trial, the government intended to show that
> Betancourt's interest in the winning Texas lottery ticket was purchased
> with proceeds from the sale of cocaine. Guadalupe Rosales, Betancourt's
> neighbor, would regularly pick the numbers for lottery tickets with the
> understanding that while Betancourt contributed ten dollars and Rosales
> only five dollars, the two men would split any winnings from the Texas
> lottery equally. Every time that Betancourt paid Rosales for his share of
> the lottery tickets, Betancourt would reach into the black bag he always
> carried to retrieve the money; this was the same bag into which he was
> regularly seen placing his drug proceeds.

422 F.3d 240, 244. Is the evidence of the black bag sufficient by itself to establish the source of the funds used to pay Rosales? (See *Knatchbull v. Hallett*, the next principal case.) Assuming that it is, how much of the $5,481,462.91 prize should the government be allowed to take?

3. In the words of the Illinois trial court, "at some point in time the—the argument that everything stems from something has to stop." Where does it stop? How would you answer the court's two hypotheticals?

4. Do the forfeiture statutes allow the government to seize life insurance proceeds? In United States v. $465,789.31 Seized From Term Life Insurance, 150 F. Supp. 3d 175 (D. Conn. 2015), a deceased Ponzi-scheme operator and cancer victim had paid insurance premiums from a bank account "funded principally" with money obtained from fraud victims. The United States claimed the insurance proceeds via civil forfeiture (18 U.S.C. §981(a)(1)(C))—seeking the money, so far as appears, for the government's own "use and benefit" and not as a means of redress for the fraud victims. The widow moved to dismiss on the ground that the premium payments had not been adequately traced. The court ruled that the action might proceed, to allow the government to show "by a preponderance of evidence that the insurance proceeds are traceable to wire fraud."

As we have seen in connection with *Brodie v. Barnes*, a court adjudicating a private restitution claim would not award a life-insurance windfall to an embezzlement victim at the expense of the embezzler's widow and children. R3RUE §61(b). Do the policies behind civil forfeiture justify putting the government into competition with the wrongdoer's surviving dependents? Does it matter if the survivors are left destitute?

5. In Ruffin v. Ruffin, 2000 WL 198078 (Va. Ct. App.), the facts were stated as follows:

> Calvin Cornell Ruffin, Sr. and Andreania (Pace) Ruffin appeal the final decree of divorce entered by the circuit court. In his appeal, husband contends that the trial court erred in awarding wife $1,000 in monthly spousal support. In her appeal, wife contends that the trial court erred by failing to find that husband held his lottery winnings in a constructive trust for the benefit of wife and the parties' two children.
>
> The parties married in 1989, had two children, and separated in November 1995. The wife filed a bill of complaint for divorce on August 19, 1996. The trial court entered a *pendente lite* order on [September 19], 1996, directing husband to pay $120 a week in child support and $80 a week in spousal support, beginning September 20, 1996. Husband did not make any support payments until January 1997. On September 28, 1996, husband won $4.9 million in a lottery, with a gross payout for twenty years exceeding $243,000 per annum. After husband claimed his winnings in January 1997, wife filed a motion to increase support. By order entered March 30, 1998, the trial court ordered husband to pay $2,446 in monthly child support.
>
> Wife contends that the trial court erred by failing to find that husband's lottery winnings were subject to a constructive trust for her benefit

and that of the parties' children. Wife argues that husband used his last available funds to purchase the lottery tickets instead of paying his court-ordered child and spousal support.

Wife contends that the $2 husband used to purchase the winning lottery ticket on September 28, 1996 were already owed to her and their children pursuant to the *pendente lite* order of the trial court at the September 19, 1996 hearing. She argues that a constructive trust arose as of September 20, 1996, the date when his first support payments were due. However, no fund existed on that date upon which to impose a constructive trust, as husband did not win the lottery until eight days later. It is true that husband's first and second weekly payments were outstanding on the day husband purchased the winning lottery ticket. However, as acknowledged by wife, husband had limited funds on September 20 due in part to the fact he recently had purchased a car. Although husband's car payments were undoubtedly a greater drain on his ability to pay support than the $2 he used to purchase the lottery tickets, wife argued that the money husband used to purchase the tickets was traceable solely to funds obligated for support.

What is the best answer to Mrs. Ruffin's constructive trust claim? The court concluded, "We cannot say that husband's good fortune so reeked of injustice as to require the imposition of a constructive trust on his lottery winnings" — but is that the test?

C. COMMINGLED FUND

In Re Hallett's Estate (Knatchbull v. Hallett)
L.R. 13 Ch. D. 696 (Ct. App. 1880)

JESSEL, M.R.:
The question we have to consider depends on very few facts. A Mr. *Hallett*, a solicitor, was a trustee of some bonds. Without authority and improperly he sold them, and on the 14th of November, 1877, by his direction the proceeds of these bonds were paid to his credit at Messrs. *Twinings' Bank*, and there mixed with moneys belonging to himself, to the credit of the same banking account, and he also drew out by ordinary cheque moneys from the banking account, which he used for his own purposes. He died in February 1878, and at his death the account stood in this way: that there was more money to the credit of the account than the sum of trust money paid into it; but if you applied every payment made after November 1877, to the first items on the credit side in order of date, a large portion of the trust money would have been paid out. The question really is, whether or not, under these circumstances, the beneficiaries — that is, the persons entitled to the trust moneys, who are the present Appellants — are or are not entitled to say that the moneys subsequently drawn out — that is, drawn

out by Mr. *Hallett* subsequently to November 1877—and applied for his own use, are to be treated as appropriated to the repayment of his own moneys, or whether the Respondents, the executors, are right in their contention that they are to be treated as appropriated in the way I have mentioned, so as to diminish the amount now applicable to the repayment of the trust funds.

Now, first upon principle, nothing can be better settled, either in our own law, or, I suppose, the law of all civilised countries, than this, that where a man does an act which may be rightfully performed, he cannot say that that act was intentionally and in fact done wrongly. Wherever it can be done rightfully, he is not allowed to say, against the person entitled to the property or the right, that he has done it wrongfully. That is the universal law.

When we come to apply that principle to the case of a trustee who has blended trust moneys with his own, it seems to me perfectly plain that he cannot be heard to say that he took away the trust money when he had a right to take away his own money. The simplest case put is the mingling of trust moneys in a bag with money of the trustee's own. Suppose he has a hundred sovereigns in a bag, and he adds to them another hundred sovereigns of his own, so that they are commingled in such a way that they cannot be distinguished, and the next day he draws out for his own purposes £100, is it tolerable for anybody to allege that what he drew out was the first £100, the trust money, and that he misappropriated it, and left his own £100 in the bag? It is obvious he must have taken away that which he had a right to take away, his own £100. What difference does it make if, instead of being in a bag, he deposits it with his banker, and then pays in other money of his own, and draws out some money for his own purposes? Could he say that he had actually drawn out anything but his own money? His money was there, and he had a right to draw it out, and why should the natural act of simply drawing out the money be attributed to anything except to his ownership of money which was at his bankers.

Notes on commingled funds

1. When lawyers speak specifically of "tracing rules" or "tracing fictions," they are usually referring to the special presumptions that make it possible to trace property through a "commingled fund." The usual commingled fund, as in *Hallett's Estate*, consists of money of the claimant that has been wrongfully combined with money of the defendant in a single bank account. (The same rules would apply if claimant's wheat were combined with defendant's wheat in a single grain elevator.) It is not the initial act of commingling that causes the problem. If the defendant misappropriates $6,000 from the claimant and deposits it in an account where he already has $4,000 of his own, it is easy to conclude that the parties now own the $10,000 pro rata. A subsequent investment of the whole fund is likewise easy to deal with. If the defendant withdraws the $10,000 and uses it to buy shares of stock, we can say that the parties own the shares in the same proportion, and that the claimant's money can be traced into a 60 percent ownership of the investment.

2. The commingled fund problem appears in the more typical case involving multiple deposits and withdrawals. Suppose that the defendant in the previous example has $3,000 in the bank. He deposits claimant's $6,000 into the same account. Then he deposits a further $1,000 of his own funds. This produces a commingled fund of $10,000. Half of the money is then withdrawn and dissipated—meaning that the defendant spends it without acquiring any identifiable asset in exchange. Now the facts come to light, and the expenditures stop. Who owns the $5,000 that remains? There is no answer to this question that does not depend on a presumption. The principal candidates have been:

(a) Claimant owns $4,000 and defendant owns $1,000, because debits to an account are charged against credits in the order they are made. This means that the $5,000 withdrawal was charged first to the $3,000 that was already in the account, then to the subsequent deposit of claimant's $6000. This is the "first in, first out" accounting rule of Clayton's Case, 1 Mer. 572, 35 Eng. Rep. 781 (Ch. 1816).

(b) Claimant owns $3,000 and defendant owns $2,000, because they own the $5,000 in the same proportion (60/40) that they owned the whole $10,000 fund. This is the rule of strict proportionality that was proposed, unsuccessfully, by Austin W. Scott in the first Restatement of Restitution §211 (1937).

(c) Claimant owns $5,000 and defendant owns nothing, because defendant is presumed to have acted lawfully (so far as possible)—and thus to have withdrawn his own money first. This is the rule announced in *Hallett's Estate*, better known as "The Rule of Jessel's Bag."

Despite the efforts of Scott in the original Restatement, the consistent answer in U.S. law has been "Jessel's Bag"—expanded as explained in the following notes.

3. Suppose that the sequence of events is reversed: defendant withdraws $5,000 and uses the money to make a valuable investment, then dissipates the rest. Now the parties will be contesting the ownership of the investment property. What result under each of the foregoing rules? Both the problem and the solution were described by Judge Learned Hand in Primeau v. Granfield, 184 F. 480, 484 (C.C.S.D.N.Y. 1911):

> The language about presumed intent in *Knatchbull v. Hallett*, which Sir George Jessel laid down with his customary vigor, was merely a way of giving an explanation by a fiction of the right of the beneficiary to elect to regard his right as a lien. That it is a fiction appears clearly enough in this case, where Granfield could have had no intention about the investments as he meant to use all the money for himself anyway. To say that in such a case he will be "presumed" to intend to take his own money out first is merely a disingenuous way, common enough, to avoid laying down a rule upon the matter.

This fiction in Re Oatway, (1903) 2 Ch. Div. 356, would have brought the usual injustice which fictions do bring, when pressed logically to their conclusion. Logically, the trustee's widow, in that case, was quite right in claiming the first withdrawal, although the trustee had invested it profitably, and had subsequently wasted all of the fund which had remained in the bank. That was, of course, too much for the sense of justice of the court, which awarded to the wronged beneficiary the investment, intimating that the rule in *Knatchbull v. Hallett* applied only where the withdrawals were actually spent and disappeared. If to that rule be added the qualification that if the first withdrawals be invested in losing ventures, then the beneficiary is to have a lien, if he likes, till he uses up that whole investment, and then may elect to fall back for the balance upon the original mixed account from which the withdrawal was made, there is no objection, but it is a very clumsy way of saying that he may elect to accept the investment if he likes, or to reject it. The last is the only rule which will preserve to the beneficiary the option which he has when the investment is made wholly with his money.

Combining these first two rules—*Jessel's Bag* and *In re Oatway*—yields a composite rule that is even simpler. Between an innocent claimant and a wrongdoing defendant, withdrawals from a commingled fund will be attributed or "marshaled" in whatever way is most advantageous for the claimant:

> The usual formula is to say that, where a fund is composed partly of the defrauded claimant's money and partly of the fiduciary's own money, the fiduciary is presumed to intend to draw out the money he can legally use rather than that of the claimant. Central National Bank v. Insurance Co., 104 U. S. 54; Cunningham v. Brown, 265 U. S. 1, 12; Knatchbull v. Hallett, 13 Ch. D. 696. But, when courts speak of "presumed intent," they mean that a rule of law is announced which takes no account at all of the actor's real intent. Equity marshals the withdrawals against the fiduciary's own funds so long as it can because that result is deemed fairer.

In re Kountze Bros., 79 F.2d 98, 101-02 (2d Cir. 1935) (Swan, J.).

4. One further presumption—a highly significant one—completes the rules for tracing through a commingled fund. Change the sequence of events in the preceding hypothetical once more, so that the account stands as follows:

	Account balance
1. Starting balance	-0-
2. Deposit $3,000 of defendant's funds	$3,000.
3. Deposit $6,000 of claimant's funds	$9,000.
4. Unauthorized withdrawal of $5,000 (dissipated)	$4,000.
5. Deposit $1,000 of defendant's funds	$5,000.

At this point the facts come to light, and the account is frozen. Who owns the $5,000 closing balance? The answer depends on whether the defendant's *subsequent* deposit of $1,000—following the unauthorized withdrawal—is treated as restoring the funds of the claimant that were previously misappropriated. Applying a *Knatchbull*-like rule that the defendant is presumed to act lawfully, it might be presumed that a subsequent deposit of the defendant's own funds is intended to restore what was stolen from the claimant. But the actual rule is to the contrary. Absent clear evidence that the wrongdoer has acted with the intention of restoring what he previously took from the claimant—evidence that will very rarely be available—the law follows the opposite presumption: that subsequent deposits of the defendant's own money do *not* increase the claimant's interest in the commingled fund, as it stood following the most recent withdrawal. The result in the example just given is that the claimant is entitled to only $4,000 of the $5,000 closing balance.

This final presumption leads directly to the best-known and most frequently applied of the tracing rules: the rule of "Lowest Intermediate Balance." Because subsequent additions of the defendant's money do not restore funds previously misappropriated—absent positive evidence that they were so intended—the claimant's share of the commingled fund can never exceed the low balance of the account reached between T1 (the time at which claimant's money was added) and T2 (the time at which the claimant's share of the account is being calculated). Of course, the claimant's share of the account can be increased by a further deposit of the claimant's funds. Note that the rule of LIB limits both (1) the claimant's share of the closing balance, and (2) the claimant's share of any beneficial interim withdrawals—those used by the defendant (as in *Oatway*) to acquire assets of which the claimant would now like to be the owner.

An account of any complexity will involve multiple deposits and withdrawals, and only some of the withdrawals will traceable into assets whose value has been preserved. Taken together, the tracing rules split the difference (very roughly) between the restitution claimant and the real parties in interest on the other side—typically the defendant's general creditors. The claimant can marshal the withdrawals in whatever way yields the most favorable result, with the benefit of hindsight; but this reconstruction of whose money went where is always subject to the rule of Lowest Intermediate Balance.

5. What is the claimant's remedy in each of the following scenarios? We can assume in every case that the wrongdoer's assets are insufficient to pay his general creditors.

(a) Grower delivers 500 turkeys to Processor, who commingles them with 500 turkeys of his own. Of the resulting mass of turkeys, Processor sells 500 to Buyer A and 500 to Buyer B. The proceeds from the sale to A are dissipated, but the proceeds from the sale to B are still due and payable when Processor files for bankruptcy. The court holds that Grower's delivery to Processor was a bailment, not a sale, and that Processor's sale of Grower's turkeys constituted conversion.

(b) On Monday, Lawyer deposits $1,000 of Client's funds in a personal bank account that already contains $1,000 of Lawyer's funds. On Tuesday, Lawyer withdraws $1,500 from this account and loses the money in a card game. On Wednesday, Lawyer deposits $2,500 of legitimate income in the same account, producing a balance of $3,000. On Thursday, Lawyer withdraws $2,000 and uses the money to purchase shares of XYZ Corp. Client discovers the facts on Friday, when the balance in the bank account is still $1,000 and the XYZ shares are worth $2,100.

(c) Same facts as (b), except that on Friday the XYZ shares have declined in value to $1,900.

(d) On July 1, Lawyer misappropriates $50,000 of Client's funds and deposits the money in a personal account in which there is a preexisting balance of $200,000. Between July 1 and December 31, Lawyer makes numerous withdrawals from the commingled account and numerous deposits of his own funds. On September 1, when the account contained $275,000, Lawyer withdrew $100,000 and used the money to purchase a certificate of deposit; but no one can determine what was done with any of the other withdrawals. Between July 1 and September 1, the daily balance of Lawyer's account fluctuated between a high of $400,000 (on July 18) and a low of $20,000 (on August 10). Between September 1 and December 31, the daily balance of Lawyer's account was as high as $500,000 at one point in October, but on two dates in November the account was overdrawn. On December 31, before the misappropriation is discovered, Lawyer files for bankruptcy. The closing balance of Lawyer's account is $350,000, and these funds (along with Lawyer's other assets) are now in the hands of the bankruptcy trustee.

In re JD Services, Inc.
284 B.R. 292 (Bankr. D. Utah 2002)

GLEN E. CLARK, Chief Judge.

This matter came before the Court on April 9, 2002, on the "Motion for Summary Judgment Regarding Recovery of Funds Received as a Result of Bank Encoding Error" filed by Bank of America, N.A.

Undisputed Facts

1. On August 24, 2000, the Debtor filed its voluntary petition commencing this case under Chapter 11 of the Bankruptcy Code.

2. On August 28, 2000, Lone Star Pre-paid Inc., a subsidiary of the Debtor, deposited a check in the amount of $7,250.00 into account number

0016–3224–5892 at Bank of America in Texas. Bank of America (the "Bank") gave immediate credit for the check.

3. At the time of accepting the deposit, the check and deposit were improperly encoded by the Bank for $725,000.00 rather than $7,250.00.

4. On August 28, 2000, the Debtor opened an account, account number 222–00087–06 (the "Account") at First Security Bank of Utah, N.A.

5. On August 30, 2000, Debra W. Ricks, an owner of the Debtor, initiated a wire transfer from Lone Star account number 0016–3224–5892 to the Account at First Security in the amount of $800,000.00.

6. Of the $800,000.00 sent by wire transfer from Lone Star to the Account at First Security, $717,750.00 (the "Disputed Funds") did not belong to Lone Star, but was erroneously transferred to the Debtor account at First Security as a result of the above-described encoding error.

7. Each day beginning August 28, 2000, the Debtor deposited funds into the Account, some in the form of cash deposits, some in the form of wire transfers, some in the form of official checks, money orders or checks written on other First Security accounts (and similar items), and some in the form of local checks as defined in 12 C.F.R. §229.2(r) (2001), and some in the form of non-local checks as defined in 12 C.F.R. §229.2(v) (2001).

8. Prior to September 1, 2000, deposits to the Account by the Debtor in the form of cash deposits and in the form of wire transfers, official checks, money orders or checks written on other First Security accounts (and similar items) were immediately available for withdrawal by the Debtor.

9. First Security was not immediately informed that the Debtor was in bankruptcy when the Debtor opened the Account, and First Security did not impose any extraordinary holds for local and non-local checks deposited into the Account when the account was opened.

10. On or about September 1, 2000, as a result of several checks being returned to First Security unpaid as a result of insufficient funds or stop payment orders on checks previously deposited into the Account, First Security imposed a longer hold on the Account for local and non-local checks deposited into the account.

11. For local checks deposited by the Debtor to the Account, First Security only made the funds available for withdrawal by the Debtor seven business days after deposit.

12. For non-local checks deposited by the Debtor, First Security only made the funds available for withdrawal by the Debtor eleven business days after deposit.

13. Stephen Austin Hansen ("Hansen"), the First Security branch manager in charge of the Account, believed that the holds of seven and eleven business days placed on the Account were the longest holds allowed under the federal banking regulations.

14. On September 5, 2000, Bank of America notified the Debtor that it had erroneously credited the Lone Star account for $725,000.00 on a deposit of $7,250.00 and that the Debtor received $717,750.00 that did not belong to the Debtor as part of the August 30, 2000, wire transfer.

15. Bank of America demanded return of the Disputed Funds received in error by the Debtor by letter dated September 6, 2000.

16. On or before September 8, 2000, First Security put an administrative freeze on the Account that required Hansen to designate which checks or other items were being paid from the Account, and allowed him to review any deposits to the Account.

17. On September 13, 2000, the Debtor and First Security agreed to placing a hold on the Account in the amount of $717,750.00.

18. Between August 24, 2000, the petition date, and September 13, 2000, the Debtor, as a Chapter 11 debtor-in-possession, operated as a going concern collecting funds and paying its postpetition creditors in the ordinary course of business with approximately $6,500,000.00 passing through the Account.

19. There is no allegation that payments to creditors between August 24, 2000, and September 13, 2000, were made outside the Debtor's ordinary course of business or for less than equivalent value.

20. The parties stipulated to information contained in a report prepared by or at the direction of Hansen reflecting the activity with regard to the Account covering the period from August 28, 2000, to September 26, 2000 (the "Report").

21. The last entry in the fifth column for any particular day reflects the available balance at the close of business for the day.

22. Given the information contained in the Report, the Debtor's account balance can be analyzed from two different approaches. One approach is to analyze the amounts on deposit as the "Collected Balance," which is the total funds on deposit in the Bank regardless of whether or not the funds are available for withdrawal or use by the Debtor. The other approach is to analyze the amounts on deposit as the "Available Balance," which is the total funds available to the Debtor for withdrawal at any given time. The available balance approach takes into account only local deposits that have been on deposit for at least seven business days and non-local checks that have been on deposit for at least eleven business days.

23. If the Account balance is analyzed using the Collected Balance approach, the lowest intermediate balance for the time period between August 30, 2000, and September 13, 2000, would be no less than $717,750.00 at the end of any given day.

24. If the Account balance is analyzed using the Available Balance approach, the lowest intermediate balance for the time period between August 30, 2000,

and September 13, 2000, would be no less than $394,460.47 at the end of any given day.

25. Page 4 of the Report shows that on September 6, 2000, the Account balance using the Available Balance approach may have dropped to as low as $162,524.28. However, the Trustee and First Security agree that the Report does not necessarily reflect the order that individual items were received by First Security or processed during the day. It is undisputed that at the end of the day on September 6, 2000, the Available Balance was $394,460.47.

Discussion

UNJUST ENRICHMENT

This dispute involves a transfer that resulted in $725,000.00 being credited to Debtor's bank account instead of $7,250.00 because of a bank encoding error. It is undisputed that the encoding error and transfer of the Disputed Funds took place postpetition, and that prior to the transfer, the Debtor held no claim or interest in the Disputed Funds. The Bank argues that the Disputed Funds remain property of the Bank, that the Trustee's interest[2] in the Disputed Funds is nothing more than a mere possessory interest, and that to permit the Debtor to retain the Disputed Funds would unjustly enrich the estate. The Trustee argues that the estate's interest is more than a possessory interest and that the encoding error and transfer of Disputed Funds should place the Bank on the same footing as any other postpetition administrative creditor. In the alternative, the Trustee argues that if the Disputed Funds are held by the estate in constructive trust, the Bank's claim to recovery of the Disputed Funds should be limited to those funds that can be traced using the lowest intermediate balance rule.

In a bankruptcy setting, state law controls the determination of whether or not the bankruptcy estate has an interest in the property in controversy. Amdura National Distribution Co. v. Amdura Corp., Inc., 75 F.3d 1447 (10th Cir. 1996). Under Utah law, unjust enrichment occurs whenever a person has and retains money that in justice and equity belongs to another. In order for a claim based on unjust enrichment to be successful, there must be (1) a benefit conferred on one person by another; (2) an appreciation or knowledge by the conferee of the benefit; and (3) the acceptance or retention by the conferee of the benefit under such circumstances as to make it inequitable for the conferee to retain the benefit without payment of its value. Berrett v. Stevens, 690 P.2d 553, 557 (Utah 1984). The Bank has met each of these elements and the Court finds that on August 30, 2000, the Debtor was unjustly enriched in the amount of $717,750.00.

---

2. Although it is the Trustee and not the Debtor that now represents the estate, the Trustee takes subject to all valid claims, liens, and equities which might have been asserted against the Debtor and can take no greater rights than the Debtor itself had. Sender v. Simon, 84 F.3d 1299 (10th Cir. 1996). "Congress intended the trustee to stand in the shoes of the debtor and take no greater rights than the debtor himself had." In re Hedged–Investments Associates, Inc. v. Buchanan, 84 F.3d 1281, 1285 (10th Cir. 1996).

CONSTRUCTIVE TRUST

Unjust enrichment will support a constructive trust. A constructive trust is an equitable doctrine used for the purpose of working out justice where there is no intention of the parties to create a trust and no express, implied, written or verbal declaration of the trust. Parks v. Zions First Nat'l Bank, 673 P.2d 590 (Utah 1983); In re McGavin, 189 F.3d 1215 (10th Cir. 1999) (Utah law bases constructive trust on the principle of unjust enrichment). Here, the undisputed facts clearly and convincingly support the imposition of a constructive trust on the Disputed Funds in favor of the Bank. In re Hal Taylor, 133 F.3d 1336 (10th Cir. 1998) (circumstances requiring imposition of a constructive trust must be found to exist by clear and convincing evidence). Had the Disputed Funds never been commingled and it were possible to readily distinguish the Disputed Funds from other assets of the estate, the Bank would be entitled to the immediate return of the entire $717,750.00. In re M & L Business Mach. Co., Inc., 59 F.3d 1078 (10th Cir. 1995) (assets held by a debtor that were never property of the estate are properly returned to their rightful owner so long as the assets are readily distinguishable from assets to which general creditors have a claim). Unfortunately for the Bank, the Disputed Funds were commingled with other funds to which general creditors have a claim.

TRACING OF FUNDS

After receiving the Disputed Funds, the Debtor continued to conduct its business as a Chapter 11 debtor-in-possession, depositing funds from its business into the Account and disbursing funds to its postpetition creditors in the ordinary course of business. If funds held in constructive trust have been commingled, the beneficiary of the constructive trust must trace the funds using the lowest intermediate balance rule. In re Foster, 275 F.3d 924, 927 (10th Cir. 2001).

11 U.S.C §541(d) provides that property [in which the debtor holds, as of the commencement of a case, only legal title and not an equitable interest,] such as constructive trust funds, does not become property of the bankruptcy estate. The Court finds that the Disputed Funds never became property of this bankruptcy estate. Although the Disputed Funds never became property of the estate, tracing of the Disputed Funds is required in this case to verify that the Disputed Funds were not disbursed by the Debtor in the ordinary course of business to good faith purchasers for value. Once funds of a constructive trust are paid in good faith[3] to a purchaser for value who had no notice of the trust, then neither the debtor nor the trust beneficiary have any claim to the disbursed funds. See Research–Planning, Inc. v. Segal (In re First Capital Mortgage Loan Corporation), 917 F.2d 424 (10th Cir. 1990); Peterson v. Peterson, 112 Utah 554, 190 P.2d 135 (1948). By tracing the constructive trust funds, the Court can determine if, and to what extent, the Disputed Funds

---

3. There is no allegation that the Debtor failed to act in good faith.

were disbursed to good faith purchasers who had no notice of the origin of the funds. Funds that were so transferred are lost from the trust res, the remaining funds constitute the trust res to which the Bank has a claim.

A constructive trust, like any other trust, must have a trust res at all times. A trust is created in property and exists only so long as there is an identified and ascertainable interest in property to be the trust res. Begier v. I.R.S., 496 U.S. 53 (1990). In circumstances where a constructive trust is declared postpetition, the beneficiary of the constructive trust must trace the funds to identify the trust res in the same manner as if there were no bankruptcy. "Property interests are created and defined by state law. Unless some federal interest requires a different result, there is no reason why such interests should be analyzed differently simply because an interested party is involved in a bankruptcy proceeding." Butner v. United States, 440 U.S. 48 (1979). Bankruptcy Courts are directed to apply "reasonable assumptions" to govern the tracing of trust funds. *Begier*, 496 U.S. at 67. To impose the same tracing requirements as are required under state law is reasonable and will cause no greater hardship on the bank than it would experience outside a bankruptcy setting. Furthermore, a tracing requirement is reasonable when weighed against bankruptcy policy which demands equality of distribution among creditors of equal rank. If the Bank successfully traces its funds, return of the trust res to the Bank will not violate bankruptcy policy because the Bank will be receiving its own money and not property of the estate. If the Bank cannot trace the funds, the Bank becomes a creditor to the extent of its loss, see Cunningham v. Brown, 265 U.S. 1 (1924), and must be treated on an equal basis with other postpetition creditors who advanced funds, goods and services postpetition. While this may seem harsh, "[i]t is the nature of bankruptcies to result in hardship even as they seek to fairly allocate scarce assets under the law in order to reflect policies accepted by Congress." *Amdura*, 75 F.3d 1447, fn.2.

For the above reasons, the Bank must trace its funds held in constructive trust utilizing the lowest intermediate balance rule.

COLLECTED BALANCE VS AVAILABLE BALANCE

Under the lowest intermediate balance rule, any funds removed from a commingled account are presumed to be the Debtor's funds to the extent the funds [in the account] exceed the beneficiary's equitable interest. If the Trustee deposits other funds into the commingled account, it is generally held that the Trustee is not replenishing trust funds. New deposits are not subject to the equitable claim of the trust beneficiary, and subsequent withdrawals are presumed to draw first upon the new funds. Applying the rule, a constructive trust beneficiary may retrieve the lowest balance recorded after the funds were commingled. *Foster*, 275 F.3d at 927. In this case, the Court is provided with two approaches by which it may trace the constructive trust funds placed in the Account: Collected Balance and Available Balance. The Collected Balance approach focuses only on the dates of deposit and withdrawal of funds and ignores the hold imposed upon new deposits to the Account. The Available

Balance approach takes into account the hold imposed by First Security on new deposits to the Account. The additional information utilized by the Available Balance approach adds precision to the tracing process and minimizes the commingling of constructive trust funds with new deposits.

Of the two approaches, the Available Balance approach most accurately traces the actual funds that were placed into the Account and will be used by this Court for purposes of computing the lowest intermediate balance of funds held in constructive trust. Use of the Available Balance approach to compute the lowest intermediate balance of the constructive trust funds entitles the Bank the return of constructive trust funds totaling $394,460.47.

INTEREST

The Bank, in its motion for summary judgment, seeks entitlement to the interest actually earned on the funds held in constructive trust. Because the funds held in constructive trust have always belonged to the Bank, it is entitled to the interest actually earned by the $394,460.53 in constructive trust funds held from August 28, 2000, until paid.

ADMINISTRATIVE CLAIM

It is uncontested that the Bank is entitled to a postpetition administrative priority claim for the unpaid balance of the Disputed Funds. Accordingly, the Bank is entitled to a postpetition administrative priority claim in the amount of $323,289.53, which represents the difference between the $717,750.00 originally transferred by mistake and the amount successfully traced using the lowest intermediate balance method. Because the $323,289.53 is unsecured, it is not entitled to the accrual of interest. United Sav. Ass'n v. Timbers of Inwood Forest, 484 U.S. 365 (1988). Therefore, it is hereby

ORDERED that the Bank is entitled to immediate payment of $394,460.47, plus interest actually earned, from funds held by the Trustee in constructive trust in behalf of the Bank; and it is further ORDERED that the Bank is entitled to a postpetition administrative priority claim in the amount of $323,289.53 without accrual of interest.

Commingled funds of multiple victims

1. Ruddle v. Moore, 411 F.2d 718 (D.C. Cir. 1969), illustrates the next phase of the commingled-fund problem. Now the conflict is no longer victim v. malefactor but victim v. victim:

> The question on this appeal is what rule governs the distribution of funds recovered from a confidence man who swindled different victims

at different times and then commingled the lucre. The District Court was unable to trace the recovered funds to the deposit of any one victim or to conclude that any victim's deposit had been wholly dissipated prior to the recovery. Accordingly, following equitable principles, it distributed the funds among the victims pro rata according to their respective losses.

In other words, some of the funds obtained by the swindler had been recovered and were available for distribution, but it was impossible to tell whose they were. One of the victims, however, could prove that she had been the *last* to be swindled. Was that a basis for awarding her restitution ahead of the earlier victims? The District Court held that it was not, and distributed the available funds *pro rata*.

Mrs. Ruddle appealed, arguing that by the rule in Clayton's Case, 1 Mer. 572 (Ch. 1816), the last victim is entitled to be repaid first. *Clayton's Case* adopted the simple accounting rule of first in, first out (or FIFO). Because the funds of earlier victims are presumed to be paid out first, the last victim has first claim on anything that remains. *Clayton's Case* is familiar from its application in a variety of commercial contexts: if we need to know which bank deposits have been withdrawn and which are still in an account, *Clayton's Case* gives us the answer. But does it makes sense if we are tracing trust funds wrongly commingled in a trustee's personal account? In *Knatchbull v. Hallett*, the rule of *Clayton's Case* had to be rejected to clear the way for the rule of Jessel's Bag. What if our problem is to trace the commingled funds of multiple fraud victims?

That question was still officially unanswered in the D.C. Circuit in 1969, but leading authorities had long dismissed the relevance of *Clayton's Case* to this kind of tracing issue. According to the court in *Ruddle*:

> the rule makes sense as a statement of the presumed intent of parties to an agreement (e.g., between bank and depositor), when a court must decide which funds among those paid in from time to time must be deemed to have been paid out. But it has nothing to be said for it as a principle governing conflicting claims to restitution by equally wronged parties. See Scott, *The Right To Follow Money Wrongfully Mingled with Other Money*, 27 Harv. L. Rev. 125, 130 n15 (1913).

411 F.2d at 719. The court went on to quote an influential statement by Judge Learned Hand:

> The rule in Clayton's Case is to allocate the payments upon an account. Some rule had to be adopted, and though any presumption of intent was a fiction, priority in time was the most natural basis of allocation. It has no relevancy whatever to a case like this. Here two people are jointly interested in a fund held for them by a common trustee. There is no reason in law or justice why his depredations upon the fund should not be borne equally between them. To throw all the loss upon one, through the

mere chance of his being earlier in time, is irrational and arbitrary, and is equally a fiction as the rule in Clayton's Case. When the law adopts a fiction, it is, or at least it should be, for some purpose of justice. To adopt it here is to apportion a common misfortune through a test which has no relation whatever to the justice of the case.

Id. (quoting In re Walter J. Schmidt & Co., 298 F. 314, 316 (S.D.N.Y. 1923)).

2. So far, so good—but there are more layers of complexity to come. When Judge Hand says "There is no reason in law or justice why [the trustee's] depredations upon the fund should not be borne equally between them," he is assuming that the contributions of the two victims are impossible to trace. But what if we have more information about the sequence of the victims' contributions and the swindler's withdrawals? Hand's opinion continues as follows:

> It does not follow, however, that the claimants should divide the fund in the proportions of their original deposits. An illustration will perhaps be clearest. Suppose three claimants, A, B, and C, for $5,000 each, whose money was deposited at intervals of a month, January, February, and March. Suppose that the fund had been reduced on some day in January to $3,000. A has lost $2,000, which he cannot throw on B. Hence, when B's money is deposited on February 1st, A and B will share $8,000 in the proportion of 3 to 5. Suppose that during February the account gets as low as $4,000. A and B cannot throw this loss on C, and when C's money is deposited they will share the $9,000 in the proportion of 3, 5, and 10. But any subsequent depletion below $9,000 they must bear in that proportion, just as A and B bore theirs in February. At least, to me it would be a parody of justice if, out of a remainder, for example, of $7,000, C should get $5,000, B $2,000, and A get nothing at all. Such a result, I submit with the utmost respect, can only come from a mechanical adherence to a rule which has no intelligible relation to the situation.

In re Walter J. Schmidt & Co., 298 F. at 316. Hand's famous hypothetical actually contemplates three possible ways to divide "a remainder of $7,000" between A, B, and C. What are the three possibilities? Which solutions do A, B, and C advocate? Which one do you consider most equitable?

3. A final exercise in this vein combines Hand's idea about the sequence of victim contributions with the *Oatway* possibility that withdrawals might be traceably invested by the wrongdoer, not simply dissipated. Consider this composite hypothetical:

> Acting in breach of his fiduciary obligations, Attorney deposits $10,000 of Client A's trust funds into Attorney's personal account at Chase Bank, where there is a preexisting balance of $10,000, making a total of $20,000. (The preexisting balance consists of Attorney's legitimate earnings.) Subsequent transactions take place in this order:

> 1) Attorney withdraws $15,000 from the Chase account, which he dissipates in Las Vegas.
> 2) Attorney deposits another $10,000 of legitimate earnings to the Chase account, creating a balance of $15,000.
> 3) Attorney withdraws $3,000 from the Chase account, which he uses to buy shares of ABC Corp., leaving a balance of $12,000.
> 4) Attorney deposits $8,000 of Client B's trust funds to the Chase account, creating a balance of $20,000.
> 5) Attorney withdraws $15,000 from the Chase account, which he uses to buy shares of XYZ Corp.

Attorney dies at this point. His estate contains property of various kinds, but his indebtedness far exceeds his assets, and his wife and children have been left penniless. The final balance in the Chase account is $5,000. The executor takes possession of the Chase account, sells the ABC shares for $9,000, and sells the XYZ shares for $7,500.

Clients A and B seek restitution from Attorney's estate. Applying orthodox tracing rules, who is entitled to what at each step of the way?

In working out this problem, bear in mind (i) the *Oatway* rule that permits a claimant either to trace into an investment or not, depending on how it turns out; (ii) the claimant's usual choice between constructive trust and equitable lien (mentioned in such cases as *Provencher v. Berman* and *Primeau v. Granfield*); and (iii) the rule of R3RUE §61 (discernible in *Brodie v. Barnes*) to the effect that restitution will not yield a net profit to a victim at the expense of surviving dependents or unpaid creditors of the wrongdoer.

Cunningham v. Brown
265 U.S. 1 (1924)

Mr. Chief Justice TAFT delivered the opinion of the Court.

These were six suits in equity brought by the trustees in bankruptcy of Charles Ponzi to recover of the defendants sums paid them by the bankrupt within four months prior to the filing of the petition in bankruptcy on the ground that they were unlawful preferences. The actions were tried together in the District Court, and were argued together in the Circuit Court of Appeals, and all the bills were dismissed in both courts.

The litigation grows out of the remarkable criminal financial career of Charles Ponzi. In December 1919, with a capital of $150, he began the business of borrowing money on his promissory notes. He did not profess to receive money for investment for account of the lender. He borrowed the money on his credit only. He spread the false tale that on his own account he was engaged in buying international postal coupons in foreign countries and selling them in other countries at 100 percent profit, and that this was made possible by the

excessive differences in the rates of exchange following the war. He was willing, he said, to give others the opportunity to share with him this profit. By a
written promise in 90 days to pay them $150 for every $100 loaned, he induced
thousands to lend him. He stimulated their avidity by paying his 90-day notes
in full at the end of 45 days, and by circulating the notice that he would pay
any unmatured note presented in less than 45 days at 100 percent of the loan.
Within eight months he took in $9,582,000, for which he issued his notes for
$14,374,000. He paid his agents a commission of 10 percent. With the 50
percent promised to lenders, every loan paid in full with the profit would cost
him 60 percent. He was always insolvent, and became daily more so, the more
his business succeeded. He made no investments of any kind, so that all the
money he had at any time was solely the result of loans by his dupes.

The defendants made payments to Ponzi as follows:

Benjamin Brown, July 20th	$ 600
Benjamin Brown, July 24th	600
H. W. Crockford, July 24th	1,000
Patrick W. Horan, July 24th	1,600
Frank W. Murphy, July 22d	600
Thomas Powers, July 24th	500
H. P. Holbrook, July 22d	1,000

By July 1st, Ponzi was taking in about $1,000,000 a week. Because of an
investigation by public authority, Ponzi ceased selling notes on July 26th, but
offered and continued to pay all unmatured notes for the amount originally
paid in, and all matured notes which had run 45 days, in full. The report
of the investigation caused a run on Ponzi's Boston office by investors seeking payment, and this developed into a wild scramble when, August 2nd, a
Boston newspaper, most widely circulated, declared Ponzi to be hopelessly
insolvent, with a full description of the situation, written by one of his recent
employees. To meet this emergency, Ponzi concentrated all his available
money from other banks in Boston and New England in the Hanover Trust
Company, a banking concern in Boston, which had been his chief deposi-
tory. There was no evidence of any general attempt by holders of unmatured
notes to secure payment prior to the run which set in after the investigation
July 26th.

The money of the defendants was paid by them between July 20th and July
24th and was deposited in the Hanover Trust Company. At the opening of business July 19th, the balance of Ponzi's deposit accounts at the Hanover Trust
Company was $334,000. At the close of business July 24th it was $871,000.
This sum was exhausted by withdrawals of July 26th of $572,000, of July 27th
of $228,000, and of July 28th of $905,000, or a total of more than $1,765,000.
In spite of this, the account continued to show a credit balance, because new
deposits from other banks were made by Ponzi. It was finally ended by an overdraft on August 9th of $331,000. The petition in bankruptcy was then filed.
The total withdrawals from July 19th to August 10th were $6,692,000. The

claims which have been filed against the bankrupt estate are for the money lent, and not for the 150 percent promised.

Both courts held that the defendants had rescinded their contracts of loan for fraud and that they were entitled to a return of their money; that other dupes of Ponzi who filed claims in bankruptcy must be held not to have rescinded, but to have remained creditors, so that what the latter had paid in was the property of Ponzi; that the presumption was that a wrongdoing trustee first withdrew his own money from a fund mingled with that of his cestuis que trustent, and therefore that the respective deposits of the defendants were still in the bank and available for return to them in rescission; and that payments to them of these amounts were not preferences, but merely the return of their own money.

We do not agree with the courts below. The outstanding facts are not really in dispute. It is only in the interpretation of those facts that our difference of view arises.

In the first place, we do not agree that the action of the defendants constituted a rescission for fraud and a restoration of the money lent on that ground. As early as April, his secretary testifies that Ponzi adopted the practice of permitting any who did not wish to leave his money for 45 days to receive it back in full without interest, and this was announced from time to time. Two of the defendants expressly testified to this. It was reiterated in the public press in July and by the investigating public authorities. There is no evidence that these defendants were consciously rescinding a contract for fraud. Certainly Ponzi was not returning their money on any admission of fraud. The lenders merely took advantage of his agreement to pay his unmatured notes at par of the actual loan. Such notes were paid under his agreement exactly as his notes which were matured were paid at par and 50 percent. The real transaction between him and those who were seeking him is shown by the fact that there were 500 to whom he gave checks in compliance with his promise, and who were defeated merely because there were no more funds.

The District Court found that, when these defendants were paid on and after August 2d, they had reason to believe that Ponzi was insolvent. The statute (section 60b of the Bankruptcy Act) requires that, in order that a preference should be avoided, its beneficiary must have reasonable cause to believe that the payment to him will effect a preference; that is, that the effect of the payment will be to enable him to obtain a greater percentage of his debt than others of the creditors of the insolvent of the same class. The requirement is fully satisfied by the evidence in this case, no matter where the burden of proof. On the morning of August 2nd, when news of Ponzi's insolvency was broadly announced, there was a scramble and a race. The neighborhood of the Hanover Bank was crowded with people trying to get their money, and for eight days they struggled. Why? Because they feared that they would be left only with claims against an insolvent debtor. In other words, they were seeking a preference by their diligence. Thus they came into the teeth of the Bankruptcy Act, and their preferences in payment are avoided by it.

But, even if we assume that the payment of these unmatured notes was not according to the contract with Ponzi, and that what the defendants here did was a rescission for fraud, we do not find them in any better case. They had one of two remedies to make them whole. They could have followed the money wherever they could trace it and have asserted possession of it on the ground that there was a resulting [constructive] trust in their favor, or they could have established a lien for what was due them in any particular fund of which he had made it a part. These things they could do without violating any statutory rule against preference in bankruptcy, because they then would have been endeavoring to get their own money, and not money in the estate of the bankrupt. But to succeed they must trace the money, and therein they have failed. It is clear that all the money deposited by these defendants was withdrawn from deposit some days before they applied for and received payment of their unmatured notes. It is true that by the payment into the account of money coming from other banks and directly from other dupes the bank account as such was prevented from being exhausted; but it is impossible to trace into the Hanover deposit of Ponzi after August 1st, from which defendants' checks were paid, the money which they paid him into that account before July 26th. There was, therefore, no money coming from them upon which a constructive trust, or an equitable lien could be fastened. Schuyler v. Littlefield, 232 U. S. 707; In re Mulligan (D. C.), 116 Fed. 715; In re Matthews' Sons, 238 Fed. 785; In re Stenning, [1895] 2 Ch. 433. In such a case, the defrauded lender becomes merely a creditor to the extent of his loss and a payment to him by the bankrupt within the prescribed period of four months is a preference. Clarke v. Rogers, 228 U. S. 534; In re Door, 196 Fed. 292; In re Kearney (D. C.), 167 Fed. 995.

Lord Chancellor Eldon, in Clayton's Case, [1816] Ch. 1 Merivale, 572, held that, in a fund in which were mingled the moneys of several defrauded claimants insufficient to satisfy them all, the first withdrawals were to be charged against the first deposits, and the claimants were entitled to be paid in the inverse order in which their moneys went into the account. Ponzi's withdrawals from his account with the Hanover Trust Company on July 26, 27, and 28 were made before defendants had indicated any purpose to rescind. Ponzi then had a defeasible title to the money he had received from them, and could legally withdraw it. By the end of July 28th he had done so, and had exhausted all that was traceable to their deposits. The rule in Clayton's Case has no application.

The courts below relied on the rule established by the English Court of Appeals in Knatchbull v. Hallett, L. R. 13 Ch. D. 696, in which it was decided by Sir George Jessel, Master of the Rolls, and one of his colleagues, that, where a fund was composed partly of a defrauded claimant's money and partly of that of the wrongdoer, it would be presumed that in the fluctuations of the fund it was the wrongdoer's purpose to draw out the money he could legally and honestly use rather than that of the claimant, and that the claimant might identify what remained as his res, and assert his right to it by way of an equitable lien on the whole fund, or a proper pro rata share of it. National Bank v. Insurance Co., 104 U. S. 54, 68; Hewitt v. Hayes, 205 Mass. 356, 91 N. E. 332. To make the rule applicable here, we must infer that in the deposit and withdrawal of more than $3,000,000 between the deposits of the defendants prior to July 28th, and the payment of their checks after August 2nd, Ponzi kept the money of defendants on deposit intact and paid out only his subsequent deposits. Considering the fact that all this money was the result of fraud upon all his dupes, it would be running the fiction of *Knatchbull v. Hallett* into the ground to apply it here. The rule is useful to work out equity between a wrongdoer and a victim; but, when the fund with which the wrongdoer is dealing is wholly made up of the fruits of the frauds perpetrated against a myriad of victims, the case is different. To say that, as between equally innocent victims, the wrongdoer, having defeasible title to the whole fund, must be presumed to have distinguished in advance between the money of those who were about to rescind and those who were not, would be carrying the fiction to a fantastic conclusion.

After August 2nd the victims of Ponzi were not to be divided into two classes, those who rescinded for fraud and those who were relying on his contract to pay them. They were all of one class, actuated by the same purpose to save themselves from the effect of Ponzi's insolvency. Whether they sought to rescind, or sought to get their money as by the terms of the contract, they were, in their inability to identify their payments, creditors, and nothing more. It is a case the circumstances of which call strongly for the principle that equality is equity, and this is the spirit of the bankrupt law. Those who were successful in the race of diligence violated not only its spirit, but its letter, and secured an unlawful preference. The decrees are reversed.

Ponzi and after

1. The defendants in *Cunningham* won the "race of diligence" among Ponzi's victims. They pushed their way through the panicky crowds during the first week of August and succeeded in withdrawing their funds before Ponzi's accounts were exhausted. Ponzi's bankruptcy trustees sued to recover these payments as voidable *preferences*. (Bankruptcy Code §547(b) would give the trustees the same remedy, with a "preference period" of 90 days in place of the former four months.) The defendants offered a different characterization of their withdrawals, one that will not fit the definition of a "preference." What was the defendants' reasoning? Before you dismiss it as fanciful, observe that the defendants' analysis was accepted by both the district court and the court of appeals before the case reached the Supreme Court.

2. Assuming for the sake of argument that the defendants had in fact acted to rescind their investments:

> They could have followed the money wherever they could trace it and have asserted possession of it on the ground that there was a resulting [Chief Justice Taft means "constructive"] trust in their favor, or they

could have established a lien for what was due them in any particular fund of which he had made it a part. These things they could do without violating any statutory rule against preference in bankruptcy, because they then would have been endeavoring to get their own money, and not money in the estate of the bankrupt. But to succeed they must trace the money, and therein they have failed.

What was the tracing theory or presumption on which defendants relied in *Cunningham*? Why did the Supreme Court reject it?

3. What about all the money that Ponzi had paid out to investors *before* the "wild scramble" that started on August 2? It sounds as though the bulk of the payouts to investors were made during the four months preceding his bankruptcy filing. Weren't all these payments equally preferential? (See the Court's reference to Bankruptcy Act §60b — a provision that was dropped from the current Bankruptcy Code.)

4. Leaving bankruptcy out of it, is it equitable that earlier "victims" walked away with 150 percent of their original investments, when later victims recovered pennies on the dollar (if that)? "[Ponzi] made no investments of any kind, so that all the money he had at any time was solely the result of loans by his dupes." This means every dollar paid out to early investors came from the money obtained by fraud from later investors. Could later investors (as a class) state a valid claim in restitution against earlier investors who were repaid with later investors' money? Should they recover the whole payout of 150 percent? Just the 50 percent "profit"? Nothing?

5. Questions like these were posed dramatically in the collapse of the fraudulent investment scheme promoted by Bernard Madoff — previously seen from another angle in *Simkin v. Blank* (Chapter 6). Unfortunately, the resulting litigation did relatively little to illuminate them:

> In the aftermath of the greatest Ponzi scheme in history, involving thousands of victims and billions of dollars in losses, lawyers and judges have begun the task of "sorting out decades of fraud." The complex sorting process involves claims against multiple parties on a variety of legal theories, but the central feature of the Madoff controversy is readily apparent from newspaper accounts. As in any Ponzi scheme, purported investment returns were paid with money obtained from subsequent fraud victims. More fortunate investors — the "net winners" — withdrew more money from the scheme than they put in, while others — the "net losers" — withdrew less than they invested or nothing at all. A natural question is whether in these circumstances net winners are liable to net losers; if so, why, and to what extent.
>
> An extensive body of law deals with precisely these questions, but that law is described in places where many modern lawyers and judges will not

think to look. Rights and remedies between fraud victims are addressed by the common law of restitution and unjust enrichment, including (significantly) the equitable rights and remedies that make up much of this part of the law. Because the claims of net losers against net winners turn on textbook restitution issues, the Madoff liquidation is also the greatest restitution case in history, measured by the amounts at stake. A wave of Madoff litigation has begun to flow through the courts. But to judge by the published opinions in the cases so far, it appears that no one involved in these lawsuits—on either side of the bench—has thought to ask how the central issues would be analyzed and decided as a matter of common law. The significance of the law of restitution has been almost entirely overlooked.

The Madoff liquidation is taking place in a quasi-bankruptcy setting, and the courts' disregard of the underlying restitution questions is part of an increasingly familiar pattern. Bankruptcy law determines how property rights and claims of various parties are adjusted and reconciled, but it does not say what those rights are in the first place. Property interests, whether legal or equitable, are part of the state-law background on which the bankruptcy statutes impose a procedural overlay. Restitution claims of the kind asserted in bankruptcy typically involve equitable property interests: a category of property rights and associated remedies that began to recede from professional awareness when American law schools stopped teaching equity. The problem is that when lawyers no longer perceive the common-law background, they try to find statutory answers to questions the statutes do not address. The attempt necessarily distorts both the meaning of the statute and the rules of the background law that are being ignored.

Kull, *Common-Law Restitution and the Madoff Liquidation*, 92 B.U. L. Rev. 939 (2012).

United States v. Durham
86 F.3d 70 (5th Cir. 1996)

REYNALDO G. GARZA, Circuit Judge:

Background

Intervenor/Plaintiff-Appellant, Claremont Properties, Inc. ("Claremont"), challenges the district court's method of distributing assets seized by the United States from Defendants-Appellees, Jannetta E. Durham, et al. The Defendants perpetrated a "scheme to defraud consumers through an advance fee loan financing business." They created various front corporations purportedly operating a legitimate loan brokerage business in order to obtain money from consumers by falsely representing their ability to obtain financing for large projects, or to directly finance those projects.

These grifters were successful in their venture until apprehended by the FBI. A total of $806,750 was defrauded from thirteen entities or individuals. Upon Defendants' arrest, roughly $83,495.52 of the money was left. The Defendants were indicted for wire fraud, money laundering, and conducting financial transactions with money derived from unlawful activity. Upon motion from the United States, the district court permanently enjoined the Defendants from further fraudulent action and froze their assets. The next order of business was to divide the seized $83,495.52 among the thirteen claimants.

The charlatans used multiple accounts and company names to implement their scheme. However, by the end, they had only one account (Cypress, Ltd.) with assets (the $83,495.42) at one bank, Pavilion National. It is uncontested by court or party that all but $8,803.99 of the money in the Pavilion accounts could be traced to seven claimants, one of which was Claremont Properties. Only four of these seven filed claims. The Defendants had deposited and withdrawn almost all the money defrauded from the other claimants. A few days after Claremont funds were deposited, the Defendants were arrested.

Over Claremont's objection, the district court elected in the interest of equity, to distribute the $83,000 pro rata rather than giving the bulk of it to Claremont and the other three victims whose funds had been traced. The court added the total claims, $806,750, and allocated the $83,000 by percentage against the total claim. Claremont's total claim was $161,750—20% of the total claims. Therefore it would receive only $16,740,83. Uncontroverted evidence from the FBI showed that, if tracing were applied, Claremont was due $70,970.13 of the $83,000.

The district court rejected Claremont's bid that the court trace the funds. The court justified its decision to distribute pro rata stating,

> In determining a plan for distribution, the Court must act to determine the most equitable result. In the instant action, all claimants stand equal in terms of being victimized by the defendant defrauders. The ability to trace the seized funds to Claremont and Northernaire is the result of the merely fortuitous fact that the defrauders spent the money of the other victims first. Allowing Claremont and Northernaire to recover from the funds seized to the exclusion of the other victims under the tracing principle would be to elevate the position of those two victims on the basis of the actions of the defrauders. The Court sees no justification in equity for this result. (Order Overruling Objections of Claremont, p.3.)

The district court granted Claremont's motion to intervene in the government's action for injunctive relief, allowing Claremont to make this timely appeal. For the reasons stated herein, we affirm.

Discussion

The Court is offered this question to decide: did the district court abuse its discretion in distributing the assets pro rata? Typically, when a party can trace its assets, that party is entitled to seek a constructive trust or equitable lien on its portion of those funds that remain. Restatement (First) of Restitution §211(1) (1937); Cunningham v. Brown, 265 U.S. 1, 11 (1924) (discussing the infamous Ponzi scheme). A constructive trust may be created regardless of the intentions of the parties "where equity and justice demand." Rosenberg v. Collins, 624 F.2d 659, 663 (5th Cir. 1980). When tracing is impossible, a claimant has merely a personal claim against the wrongdoer and the funds are distributed ratably. *Cunningham*, 265 U.S. at 11; Restatement (First) of Restitution §213 cmt. c., illus. 3-6 (1937).

No one can dispute that tracing would have been permissible under the circumstances of this case. *Cunningham*, 265 U.S. at 11. Claremont identified its funds and had a right *to seek* imposition of a constructive trust on the traced funds. The government in fact suggested that Claremont receive the traced funds. However, the court, in exercising its discretionary authority in equity, was not obliged to apply tracing. See S.E.C. v. Elliott, 953 F.2d 1560 (11th Cir. 1993) (district court's decision to disallow tracing was well within broad equitable powers); United States v. Vanguard Inv. Co., 6 F.3d 222, 227 (4th Cir. 1993) ("a district court in its discretionary supervision of an equitable receivership may deny remedies like rescission and restitution where the equities of the situation suggest such a denial would be appropriate"). As noted above, the court imposes a constructive trust only "*where equity and justice demand.*" *Rosenberg*, 624 F.2d at 663.

The lower court in this case chose not to impose a constructive trust in Claremont's favor because it seemed inequitable to allow Claremont to benefit merely because the defendants spent the other victims' funds first. Claremont would obtain a preferred claim over funds if the court were to impose the constructive trust. To the district court, all the fraud victims were in equal positions and should be treated as such. We cannot say that the district court's assessment of the facts and the resulting order were an abuse of discretion.

Sitting in equity, the district court is a "court of conscience." Wilson v. Wall, 73 U.S. (6 Wall.) 83, 90 (1867). Acting on that conscience, the lower court in the instant case rationally considered the positions of the victims and held that following the tracing principle would be inequitable. Claremont's frustration with the lower court's ruling is understandable, but the court was not required to impose a constructive trust in Claremont's favor. Because the court used its discretion in a logical way to divide the money, the court committed no error requiring our intervention. For us to hold otherwise would be to chain the hands of the court in Equity to do what is right under the circumstances. We will not rob the lower court of the discretion essential to its function. The restitution order is AFFIRMED.

Following property or comparative fault?

1. In United States v. Central National Bank of Cleveland, 429 F.2d 5 (8th Cir. 1970), a man named Edward Owen Watkins was arrested in Montana for bank robbery. When they arrested Watkins, FBI agents found $4,350.71 in currency either on his person or in his house. The United States initiated an interpleader action to determine ownership of the money: the defendants/claimants were ten banks that Watkins had robbed, as well as Watkins and his wife. The ten banks had lost various sums, amounting in the aggregate to $128,342.26. Of the $4,350.71 recovered by the FBI, the district court "found that $300 of the sum on deposit was 'bait money,' marked and traceable to the Minneapolis Federal Savings & Loan Association," but it was impossible to tell where the remaining $4,050.71 had come from. How do you suppose the 8th Circuit decided this question in 1970? Would the *Durham* court have agreed in 1996? What had happened in the meantime?

2. *United States v. Durham* is not the strongest example of a judicial refusal to let an owner retake identifiable property, because the identification in *Durham* (by the FBI) might have involved a tracing of funds through a commingled bank account. The extreme case is represented by SEC v. Elliott, 953 F.2d 1560 (11th Cir. 1992):

> Elliott talked investors into "loaning" him their securities. He convinced the investors that he could get them a return on their money far greater than they were currently earning in dividends from their securities. In exchange for the securities, Elliott gave them a promissory note, equal to the market value of the securities, promising to make monthly interest payments. The investors delivered the securities to Elliott with executed powers of attorney attached. Elliott could satisfy his obligation to pay either by returning the securities or by making a cash payment. The district court found, and we agree, that what in fact transpired was that the investors unwittingly transferred legal title in the securities to Elliott.
>
> The appellants argue that they are entitled to rescission of the agreements and restitution of the securities because the agreements were induced by fraud. Elliott had sold many of the securities given to him, but he also kept many of them. These investor/appellants are attempting to recover the securities that Elliott retained with their names on them. Legally, these investors occupy the same position as the other investors whose securities were sold. All investors were defrauded. All investors were cleverly persuaded to part with their securities. The district court held:
>
>> To allow any individual to elevate his position over that of other investors similarly "victimized" by asserting claims for restitution and/or reclamation of specific assets based upon equitable theories of relief

such as fraud, misrepresentation, theft, etc., would create inequitable results, in that certain investors would recoup 100% of their investment while others would receive substantially less. . . . [I]n the context of this receivership the remedy of restitution to various investors seeking to trace and reclaim specific assets as originating with them is disallowed as an inappropriate equitable remedy.

The Supreme Court has recognized that, in equity, certain tracing rules should be suspended. Cunningham v. Brown, 265 U.S. 1 (1924). In *Cunningham*, creditors argued that they were rescinding their contracts with Ponzi because of fraud. They attempted to use a tracing presumption to remove their money from a fund before other defrauded creditors could reach it. However, the Supreme Court recognized that the money in the account belonged to other victims, not Ponzi, and that the use of this presumption would harm other victims. Moreover, since these creditors occupied the same legal position as other creditors, equity would not permit them a preference; for "equality is equity."

Does the situation in *Elliott* involve any "tracing" or the use of any "presumption"? Does *Cunningham* support the denial of a "preference" to claimants who can point to registered securities with their names on them?

3. If the entire subject of equitable remedies in restitution can be reduced to a single cardinal rule, that rule—paraphrasing slightly from *Newton v. Porter*— is that the owner of misappropriated property "may follow and reclaim it wherever or in whosoever hands it may be found," and that this "right of pursuit and reclamation only fails when the identity of the property is lost and further pursuit is hopeless" (or, we might add, when the property comes into the hands of a bona fide purchaser). So long as property law is the accepted starting point, it cannot be inequitable for a more fortunate fraud victim "to benefit merely because the defendants spent the other victims' funds first." Such an outcome is merely one illustration of a well-known fact of life: that casualty or mischance inevitably falls on A while leaving some more or less proximate neighbor B unaffected.

The courts in *Durham* and *Elliott* see the equities differently because they take a different starting point. Their idea is more familiar from tort law than from property and restitution: namely, that losses should be divided in proportion to fault. If "all claimants stand equal in terms of being victimized by the defendant defrauders," then losses from fraud should be ratably allocated. The proposition advanced in these cases was novel, but not entirely so. Recall that the trial court in *Equity Savings*—in the judgment reversed by the Appellate Division—had denied subrogation in that case, seeing "no equitable reason to give Spencer an advantage over Equity since each was identically defrauded by Goldberg into believing its junior mortgage was first."

Restatement Third, Restitution and Unjust Enrichment

§59. Tracing into or through a commingled fund

(2) If property of the claimant has been commingled by a recipient who is a conscious wrongdoer or a defaulting fiduciary (§51) or equally at fault in dealing with the claimant's property (§52):

(a) Withdrawals that yield a traceable product and withdrawals that are dissipated are marshaled so far as possible in favor of the claimant.

(b) Subsequent contributions by the recipient do not restore property previously misappropriated from the claimant, unless the recipient affirmatively intends such application.

(c) After one or more withdrawals from a commingled fund, the portion of the remainder that may be identified as the traceable product of the claimant's property may not exceed the fund's lowest intermediate balance.

(4) If a fund contains the property of multiple restitution claimants (such as the victims of successive fraud by the recipient):

(a) Each claimant's interest in the fund and any product thereof is determined by the proportion that such claimant's contributions bear to the balance of the fund upon each contribution and withdrawal, but only if the accounting necessary to this calculation can be established without using the presumptions or marshaling rules of §59(2).

(b) If the evidence does not permit the court to distinguish the interests of multiple restitution claimants by reference to actual transactions, such claimants recover ratably from the fund and any product thereof in proportion to their respective losses.

g. *Multiple claimants: ratable recovery.* The rule of *Cunningham v. Brown* establishes that the presumptions or "fictions" of §59(2)—properly employed to divide a commingled fund and its products between a claimant and a wrongdoer—will not be mechanically applied to answer an altogether different question: namely, the proportions of a commingled fund and its products to which competing restitution claimants are entitled. By contrast, *Cunningham v. Brown* does not hold, and §59(4) does not provide, that ordinary tracing principles are irrelevant to a contest between competing restitution claimants; that the sequence of otherwise identical transactions is irrelevant to the outcome; or that the resolution of competing restitution claims (or claims of fraud victims) is necessarily by hotchpot or ratable distribution. The law of unjust enrichment does not impose a rule of contribution or loss-sharing between the victims of common or related injuries, and individual outcomes will frequently depend on the circumstances that determine whether a particular claimant's assets (or their traceable product) may be identified in the property available for distribution.

Thus it is a familiar consequence that a fraud victim whose funds are applied directly to acquire a traceable product may obtain ownership of the product via constructive trust, while a victim whose funds are dissipated has only an unsecured claim against the wrongdoer. Similarly, the victim whose funds are used to discharge a prior mortgage indebtedness will be subrogated both to the lien and to its priority, while the victim whose funds are used to discharge an unsecured obligation is in the same position as the victim whose funds have been lost.

Farnsworth, *Restitution* 140-141 (2014):

[*United States v. Durham*] is like a case where a bank robber has stolen money from many banks, but when caught is found to just have bills that are still wrapped and labeled as coming from First National. First National takes those bills back directly, and the robber's other victims are out of luck. But in *Durham* the court "elected in the interest of equity, to distribute the $83,000 pro rata rather than giving the bulk of it to [the] victims whose funds had been traced." The court reasoned that giving the money back to the two claimants who could trace it would "elevate the position of those two victims on the basis of the actions of the defrauders."

The third *Restatement* is critical of *Durham* and other recent cases like it, concluding that they are the result of "error and inattention"—and in particular a misunderstanding by the judges about the extent of their discretion under traditional principles of equity. The basis of the criticism is that these cases depart from long-standing case law without clear justification and without evident recognition that the old rules even exist. But the new cases might nevertheless make sense as a matter of policy. The old rules allow the perpetrator of a fraud to favor some of his victims over others by keeping the funds of the favored ones separate and traceable. Then if the scheme collapses, the favored claimants take all their money back and the unfavored ones, whose money was spent, collect less or nothing. It might seem unlikely that a typical defrauder would have preferences of that kind about his victims or enough legal knowledge to give effect to such preferences in the way just described. But the authors of some well-known Ponzi schemes have conned their friends and family members as well as strangers, and in some cases, they have shown sophistication in structuring their transactions. It is understandable that courts want to avoid rules that would reward such efforts.

Granted, one could object that this logic proves too much. It might imply that if the schemer almost fleeced his grandmother but stopped short at the last minute, she should share in the losses suffered by those he did fleece. After all, why should the defendant get to decide who suffers and who does not? But the old tracing rules don't just allow the defrauder to play favorites. In cases that involve Ponzi schemes, they also might encourage his friends to play along in the hope that they will have a better chance of getting all their money back if the scheme collapses. If it can be proven that those friends were collaborators, then they will be held liable regardless of the tracing rules. But the modern departures from those rules help to discourage the kind of silent and hopeful collaboration with a Ponzi schemer that is hard to prove.

Chapter 9

Defenses

A. CHANGE OF POSITION

Painewebber, Inc. v. Levy
293 N.J. Super. 325, 680 A.2d 798 (1995)

Russell, P.J.S.C.

On April 6, 1987, defendant Carl Levy purchased 20,000 shares of Juice International, Inc. stock at three cents per share from plaintiff PaineWebber. Between January 1994 and April 1994, Levy sold 7,500 shares of the stock, receiving proceeds totaling $25,635.07. However, on April 19, 1993, there had been a 1 for 100 reverse split of the stock. Thus, although prior to the reverse split Levy had owned 20,000 shares, he only owned 200 shares when he began selling it in January 1994. It is uncontroverted that between January 1994 and April 1994, Levy was the beneficiary of a mistaken overpayment by plaintiff PaineWebber of $24,835.07. Levy was notified of the mistake on April 21, 1994, by which time he claims to have spent the entire amount of the overpayment. Levy has explained that $500 was used to pay a past debt to his veterinarian. He spent $10,000 to $12,000 on his daughter's college tuition and expenses, including $2,500 for a new computer. The balance was spent on Levy's own living expenses. For purposes of this motion, it is uncontested that Levy would not have purchased the computer, but for the overpayment.

PaineWebber now seeks summary judgment for $22,335.07, the amount of the overpayment, less the cost of the computer. Levy cross-moves for summary judgment as to the full amount of the overpayment.

It is considered unjust enrichment to permit the recipient of money paid under mistake of fact to keep it, unless the circumstances are such that it would be inequitable to require its return. One who has paid money under a mistake of fact may have restitution from the payee, notwithstanding that the mistake

461

was unilateral and a consequence of the payor's negligence, unless such restitution will prejudice the payee. Great American Ins. Co. v. Yellen, 58 N.J. Super. 240, 156 A.2d 36 (App. Div. 1959).

In order to defeat an action for restitution due to prejudice, the payee's change in circumstances must be detrimental to the payee, material and irrevocable and such that the payee cannot be placed in the status quo. Jonklaas v. Silverman, 117 R.I. 691, 370 A.2d 1277 (1977); Westamerica Securities, Inc. v. Cornelius, 214 Kan. 301, 520 P.2d 1262 (1974). For example, the payee is not required to make restitution if, by reason of the mistaken payment, he has assumed liabilities and obligations that he would not otherwise have assumed. See Lake Gogebic Lumber Co. v. Burns, 331 Mich. 315, 320, 49 N.W.2d 310, 313 (1951); Restatement of Restitution, §142, comment *b* (1937); [R3RUE §65].

Prejudice to the payee does not occur when the payee has used the money to cover ordinary living expenses or to pay preexisting debt. See United States v. Reagan, 651 F. Supp. 387, 389 (D. Mass.1987) (neither incapacity alone nor the mere fact that the taxpayer spent the erroneously paid tax refund to repay previous debts was sufficient to prevent United States' action for restitution); Ohio Co. v. Rosemeier, 32 Ohio App. 2d 116, 288 N.E.2d 326, 329 (1972) (purchase of new car with insurer's overpayment held not sufficient change of position barring restitution). This is the equitable result, since the payee would have assumed such liabilities and obligations regardless of the overpayment. Therefore, the payee cannot be said to have detrimentally changed his position in reliance on the overpayment.

This court disagrees with the proposition that a payee demonstrates sufficient prejudice to defeat restitution simply by not retaining the value originally represented by the overpayment. See Home Ins. Co. v. Honaker, 480 A.2d 652, 655 (Del. Super. 1984) (restitution not required when, but for a $20,000 tort settlement, payee lacked sufficient funds to repay a $14,907 overpayment by the insurer). This view of prejudice would lead to unjust enrichment. Where a payee uses the overpayment to pay a past debt, no detrimental reliance occurs and restitution returns the parties to the status quo. The payee is placed in no worse a position, because he simply pays the amount of his prior obligation as restitution to the mistaken payor instead of the creditor (who has already been paid). Similarly, the payee expects to pay his ordinary living expenses. Requiring restitution of monies expended on ordinary living expenses prevents the payee from realizing a windfall and moves the parties closer to the position reasonably expected by each before the overpayment.

The payee is prejudiced when he incurs new debts or extraordinary living expenses in good faith reliance upon his right to the overpayment. The payee must prove that but for the mistaken overpayment he would not have incurred these costs or liabilities. See Lincoln National Life Ins. Co. v. Rittman, 790 S.W.2d 791, 793-94 (Tex. Ct. App. 1990) (restitution not required where insured would have discontinued his daughter's medical treatment absent the mistaken overpayment of the insurance company). In such circumstances the payee has detrimentally relied upon the mistaken overpayment, and equity will not require restitution. The payee cannot be placed in the status quo, where the overpayment induces him to incur new debt he would not have otherwise assumed.

It is unclear whether Levy would have paid for his daughter's college tuition and expenses absent the overpayment. He had paid for her tuition during prior semesters, but in September 1993, both Levy and his wife were discharged from Chapter 7 bankruptcy. If Levy would have paid for his daughter's college expenses (approximately $12,000) without the benefit of the overpayment, then restitution of that amount is appropriate.

How to change position

1. Besides the question of what expenditures count as a change of position, the facts of *PaineWebber v. Levy* raise a question of *notice*. The two ideas are interconnected, because it is only "a recipient without notice" who is entitled to a defense based on change of position (R3RUE §65). What is the likelihood that Carl Levy—just discharged from bankruptcy—believed in 1994 that his investment in Juice International, Inc. was worth more than 100 times what he had paid for it seven years earlier?

2. In Wachovia Bank of S.C. v. Thomasko, 339 S.C. 592, 529 S.E.2d 554 (2000), the facts were stated as follows:

> On March 10, 1997, Martha B. Thomasko presented 183,000 Mexican pesos and 78,000 Spanish pesetas to the Wachovia branch in Spartanburg and requested United States currency in exchange. The teller mistakenly calculated the value of the foreign currency as $21,741.10. The teller issued Thomasko a cashier's check in the amount of $21,503.44.
>
> Two days later, Wachovia determined the currency presented by Thomasko was actually worth $527.46, instead of $21,741.10. The error arose from the teller's miscalculation of the pesos' value. In January 1993, the Mexican government devalued the peso by a factor of 1,000. The Mexican government issued "nuevo pesos" that equaled 1,000 old pesos. The government circulated the new pesos and the old pesos jointly. Due to the devaluation, Thomasko's old pesos were actually worth only 183 new pesos. On March 10, 1997, the exchange rate for new pesos was 8.6179 cents per peso.
>
> Immediately upon discovering its error, Wachovia contacted Thomasko seeking recovery of the overpayment. Wachovia informed Thomasko of the error and sought a return of the $21,216.64 overpayment. Thomasko, however, refused to repay Wachovia. After several subsequent attempts to collect the overpayment failed, Wachovia filed an action for unjust enrichment on May 5, 1997.
>
> In her answer, Thomasko maintained she should not be required to return the excess funds because she had already spent the money to pay

previously incurred medical bills. She also alleged she was financially incapable of returning the overpayment. Thomasko further alleged she relied upon Wachovia's representations as to the value of the foreign currency and Wachovia was negligent in ascertaining its true value.

What result?

3. What about an innocent recipient of mistaken payments over an extended period—for example, an extra $50 per month in pension income—who has simply used the money for ordinary household expenses and has no realistic prospect of being able to repay? Where restitution would appear inequitable, we may expect that it will not be ordered, even if there has been no textbook "change of position."

On the topic of "overpayments and underpayments," the Social Security Act provides as follows:

> In any case in which more than the correct amount of payment has been made, there shall be no adjustment of payments to, or recovery by the United States from, any person who is without fault if such adjustment or recovery would defeat the purpose of this subchapter or would be against equity and good conscience.

42 U.S.C. §404(b)(1).

4. Consider Bank of New York v. Thomas W. Simmons & Co., 117 Misc. 103, 190 N.Y.S. 602 (App. Term 1921), which is paraphrased by the Restatement as follows:

> Customer directs Bank to collect certain drafts from the drawees in Rio de Janeiro; to pay $50,000 of the proceeds to its Brazilian Creditor; and to remit the balance to Customer in New York. Bank follows these instructions but neglects to deduct the payment made to Creditor from its eventual remittance to Customer, who is accordingly overpaid in the amount of $50,000. Creditor arrives in New York, calls on Customer, and requests payment of the debt. Ascertaining from Bank's erroneous bookkeeping that Creditor has apparently not been paid, Customer pays the $50,000 a second time. Creditor returns to Brazil.

R3RUE §65, Illustration 19. Bank sues Customer for restitution of the overpayment. What result between these parties? What resolution is possible, if Brazilian Creditor is worth pursuing?

5. From the final examination in Contracts (second year) at Harvard Law School, June 1888 (Assistant Professor Keener):

> By a mutual mistake A made an overpayment of $100 to B. Shortly after receiving it, B without fault on his part was robbed of the amount. What are A's rights?

How would you answer?

6. A case of mistaken payment normally involves some negligence on the part of the payor. But what if the payor's mistake is predominantly the result of negligence on the part of the payee? There is naturally no problem so long as the money is sitting around waiting to be repaid, but questions of fault arise when the payor seeks restitution and the payee defends on the ground of change of position. The Restatement gives this example:

> Seller agrees to send Buyer three shipments of goods at a price of $10,000 each. After receiving a large quantity of goods, Buyer concludes that the shipments are complete and pays Seller $30,000, without examining the goods received. A year later, the parties discover that one of the shipments was consigned by Seller to a nonexistent address. Carrier held the misdirected shipment for six months, then sold the goods to satisfy its lien for storage charges. Carrier's actions were proper under the circumstances, and Carrier is under no liability to anyone. Buyer sues Seller in restitution to recover the $10,000 paid for goods it never received. Seller defends on the ground that—as a result of Buyer's negligent delay in reporting the missing shipment—Seller has lost its recourse against Carrier. The court concludes that both parties were negligent, but that "the origin and real cause of the loss" was not Buyer's delay in discovering the mistaken payment but Seller's negligence in misdirecting the shipment. Seller is not entitled to the defense of change of position.

R3RUE §65, Illustration 26. (This point about loss allocation is further addressed in the following extracts.)

Restatement Third, Restitution and Unjust Enrichment

§52. RESPONSIBILITY FOR ENRICHMENT

(3) If the defendant rather than the claimant is primarily responsible for the defendant's unjust enrichment, the defendant may not assert the defense of change of position (§65). When responsibility is based on negligence, the defense of change of position is unavailable if the defendant's negligence in the transaction concerned exceeds that of the claimant.

---

§65. CHANGE OF POSITION

If receipt of a benefit has led a recipient without notice to change position in such manner that an obligation to make restitution of the original benefit would be inequitable to the recipient, the recipient's liability in restitution is to that extent reduced.

h. Restitution and loss allocation. Restitution is primarily concerned with benefits, not losses, and it is a familiar proposition that a liability to restore unjust enrichment is independent of fault. Yet many of the transactions for which a claimant is entitled to restitution involve losses as well as benefits. In the simplest restitution scenario, involving recovery from an innocent recipient, the most basic element of loss—the amount by which the cost to the claimant of conferring the benefit exceeds its value in the recipient's hands—is implicitly allocated to the claimant. This is not because the claimant is necessarily at fault, but as a result of the rule that a liability in unjust enrichment may not be disadvantageous to an innocent recipient (§50(3)). By contrast, if the recipient is more to blame than the claimant for the transaction resulting in unjust enrichment—and for any loss sustained as a result—the limitations of §50 no longer hold, and the loss will be reassigned (predictably) on the basis of fault. (The foregoing remarks do not apply to cases of restitution from wrongdoers, where liability is measured on a fundamentally different basis. See §51.)

Change-of-position cases pose essentially the same problem, with the loss being incurred at a different stage of the transaction. The liability of an innocent recipient must be net of any loss sustained as a result of the transaction for which the claimant seeks restitution, if liability is to be justified in terms of unjust enrichment. Yet if the recipient rather than the claimant is principally to blame for the sequence of events—as when, in some of the foregoing Illustrations, misstatement or negligence on the part of the recipient causes the claimant's mistaken payment, leading in turn to the recipient's loss by change of position—then the loss in question is once again assigned on the basis of fault. In short, the basic defense of change of position reallocates a loss from the recipient to the claimant, in obedience to the rule of §50(3); while the qualifications of §52(3) reallocate again (from the claimant back to the recipient) on the basis of the recipient's greater fault.

Farnsworth, *Restitution* 142-143, 145 (2014):

Claims for restitution of mistaken payments are heavily influenced by two principles. The first is that the recipient is strictly liable for the payment's return, even if he had no responsibility for it and even if the claimant was negligent. The second principle mitigates the harshness of the first: liability in restitution cannot make an innocent recipient worse off than he was before the transfer occurred. The change-of-position defense is really just an application of this second principle. If Levy made decisions on account of the overpayment that cannot be taken back, then making him repay the money to PaineWebber would leave him poorer than he was before the mistake. He would be stuck with the decisions that the overpayment caused him to make but without the money needed to bear the consequences of them; in this case he will have a computer that he can't afford.

It helps to think about how the rules change when there is a loss to allocate between the parties. Holding Levy (or any recipient of a mistaken payment) liable without fault is fine if it requires nothing more than returning money. He is not then being asked to bear a loss—except for the bother, likely minor, of giving back what he shouldn't have received. A case that involves a change of position is different because now there *is* a loss that somebody will have to bear. The defendant bought something that we now realize he shouldn't have bought—a bit of waste that will have to be allocated to one side or the other. The law allocates the waste to the party who was in the best position to prevent the misfortune—here, the claimant—in the name of fairness and perhaps for the sake of deterring the carelessness that leads to these fiascos.

A change of position can take other forms as well. The defendant invests the mistakenly received money and then the investment goes down. This is a change of position. Making him pay back the entire amount he received would leave him worse off than before it arrived. The result is the same in the simpler case where a thief steals the money from the mistaken recipient of it or where the property is demolished by accident. If the defendant obtained the money by fraud, he would bear the risk of any such losses; since he obtained it by mistake, the losses are assigned to the plaintiff. Or suppose the claimant thinks he is liable in tort for some loss the defendant has suffered (but actually he isn't liable for it). He therefore sends money to the defendant, and by the time this is discovered to be a mistake, the statute of limitations has expired on any claims the defendant would have had against the parties who really are liable. The defendant's failure to go after those parties while there still was enough time is a change of position—assuming it was a reasonable choice, assuming he *would* have gone after them if the claimant had not mistakenly paid him, and assuming, finally, that the payment from the claimant was the claimant's idea.

B. BONA FIDE PURCHASE

Restatement Third, Restitution and Unjust Enrichment

§66. BONA FIDE PURCHASER

A purchaser for value and without notice acquires the legal interest that the grantor holds and purports to convey, free of equitable interests that a restitution claimant might have asserted against the property in the hands of the grantor.

Bona fide purchase: a crib sheet

I. BFP BASICS

The equitable doctrine of bona fide purchase is a fundamental rule of property and commercial law that functions *inter alia* as a defense to restitution. There are circumstances in which the rights and liabilities it regulates would not be described in terms of unjust enrichment. On the other hand, every restitution claim asserting an interest in identifiable property is potentially limited by the doctrine of good-faith purchase if the interests of third parties have intervened. If so, the step-by-step inquiry proceeds as follows:

(1) Is the third party's interest that of a *purchaser*? "Purchase" in this context means "taking by sale, lease, discount, negotiation, mortgage, pledge, lien, security interest, issue or reissue, gift, or any other *voluntary transaction creating an interest in property*" (to borrow the definition of UCC §1-209(29)). By contrast, a *successor in interest*—someone who merely steps into the predecessor's shoes by operation of law—is not a purchaser. Trustees and receivers are not purchasers. Donees are purchasers, but heirs are not. Consensual lien creditors are purchasers, but judicial lienors are not.

(2) Has the purchaser given *value* for the rights acquired? People who put their hands in their pockets to pay for something give what is called "present value," and they are protected. Donees are purchasers, but they are not protected because they don't give value. The difficult questions about value turn on finer distinctions:

- By the traditional rule, a promise of performance constitutes value only insofar as the promise has been performed. (This is the quickest way to distinguish value from contract law's "consideration.") Someone who buys property for $100 and has only paid $50 might have a defense to restitution as to the half-interest he has paid for, yet be liable in restitution as to the rest.

- A more complex limitation relates to the status of "antecedent debt." B owes C $10,000—perhaps the debt is overdue—and C eventually agrees to take Blackacre in satisfaction. After the deed has been delivered, it transpires that B acquired the land by defrauding A. When A sues C in restitution, the question is whether C gave value. In the earliest and most purely equitable version of the doctrine, the answer would be no. If C is liable to restore Blackacre to A, C is left exactly where he started—with no Blackacre and with a valid claim against B for $10,000. In the equitable viewpoint, if there was no prejudice to C, there was no "intervening equity" giving C an affirmative defense against A.

- Commercial law—where the central concern is the finality of money payments and the validity of security interests—eventually developed a different rule: that a person gives value for rights if (among other possibilities) he takes them in payment of a preexisting debt or as security therefor. See UCC §1-204 (defining "value"). Because a purchase of real property (as in the A-B-C hypothetical) is not governed by the UCC, the status of antecedent debt as value would still be governed by the old common-law precedents, with the answer uncertain in many jurisdictions.

(3) Did the purchaser take with *notice*? An "innocent purchaser"—a purchaser entitled to the defense—is one who takes without notice of the facts underlying the equitable claim the defense will cut off. Notice is often established by inference—*e.g.*, what knowledge should be imputed where direct evidence is lacking—and the test can be more or less stringent. A defendant whose conduct amounts to "willful blindness" will usually be found to have notice of what he would have preferred not to know; but so too, in some circumstances, will the defendant whose knowledge of certain facts should have "put him on inquiry" as to certain others. See R3RUE §69 ("Notice"); UCC §1-202 ("Notice; Knowledge"). If C pays B $50 for goods obviously worth $500, and A sues C in restitution (alleging that B acquired the goods from A by fraud), C is a purchaser for value—the "value" requirement is satisfied by anything more than nominal value—but C might be found to have purchased with notice, given the evident inadequacy of price.

(4) Bona fide purchase is Latin for "good-faith purchase." Many people conclude, understandably, that a potential bfp must satisfy an independent, fourth requirement of *good-faith conduct* in the transaction concerned. This is an error—fostered in no small part by recent amendments to the UCC, but an error nonetheless. In context, "bona fide purchaser," "good-faith purchaser," and sometimes "innocent purchaser for value" are merely familiar names for the defendant who qualifies for protection as a "purchaser for value without notice." See R3RUE §66, Comment *d*.

II. DO WE HAVE TO TALK ABOUT "LEGAL" AND "EQUITABLE"?

R3RUE §66 states the rule of bona fide purchase in terms of the traditional distinction between legal and equitable ownership of property. If A's transfer of X to B is influenced by fraud or mistake, one way to describe the situation is to say that B acquires legal title to X subject to A's equitable interest. (A's "equitable interest" is a valid claim in restitution against B to undo or correct the defective transfer—which is why B's interest can also be described as a "voidable title.") Now X moves from B to C. If C acquires B's rights as a successor in interest, C takes what B had—a legal title that is "voidable" because it is subject to A's equitable interest (or restitution claim). But if C qualifies as a "bona fide purchaser," C takes free of A's equitable interest, with the result that A's claim to recover X is cut off. The consequence—that C can acquire better rights in X than B had to give—makes a striking illustration of the alchemy of equity.

For anyone impatient with this terminology, it is entirely possible to describe the same property relations without referring to "law" and "equity." Consider the following propositions:

(1) Some asset X moves from A to B by a transaction that is ineffective to create definitive rights in B. X might be Blackacre, a cow, or money in some form.

(2) The deficiencies of the transaction may be such that B acquires no rights at all, as when B steals X or A conveys it at gunpoint. In the associated vocabulary, any purported transaction is "void," B has "no title," and A has a legal claim to recover X under one label or another.

(3) Alternatively, a transfer from A to B may convey imperfect rights of ownership. Standard examples are cases in which the transfer is induced by A's mistake or B's fraud. B's rights are imperfect in the practical sense that, so long as A finds X in B's hands, A can get it back from B. Lawyers sometimes say that B has something called "voidable title."

(4) So long as the dispute remains a two-party contest between A and B, it is irrelevant whether B has imperfect rights or no rights at all. In either case, A is entitled to specific restitution of X if that is his preferred remedy and still possible.

(5) The distinction becomes relevant when there has been a subsequent transaction in which third-party C acquires rights in X in competition with A. If B acquired no rights from A, then C gets no rights from B, because "the thief gets no title and gives none." But if B acquired imperfect ownership rights from A (as in proposition (3) above), resolution of the commercially significant case (A v. C) depends on the nature of transaction between B and C.

(6) If C takes X merely as B's successor, or as a gift from B, or with notice of A's rights, C acquires B's rights and no more, so A defeats C. If C takes X as a bona fide purchaser from B (a category that includes B's secured creditors), C acquires good title, so C defeats A.

(7) Because C acquires by transfer at least what B had (call it "voidable title"), C—although not protected himself—can still convey a good title to bona fide purchaser D, and so on. This is why so many cases say that the dispossessed owner can follow his property "through any number of transfers and changes of form, until it comes into the hands of an innocent purchaser for value."

III. WHY IS THE DEFINITION OF "VALUE" THE HARD PART OF THE DOCTRINE?

The relevance of the "value" question to deciding whether a given purchaser is protected becomes easier to understand when the giving of value is seen as a formalized proxy for change of position. The Restatement quotes the following excerpt from La Fon v. Grimes, 86 F.2d 809, 812-13 (5th Cir. 1936):

The principle upon which the doctrine of innocent purchaser for value rests, like equitable principles in general, is not a hard and fast rule of narrow application, but one to be liberally and equitably applied. Under it relief is denied to a purchaser without notice who has not paid value, on the ground that his equity arises, not out of his mere lack of notice, but out of injury to him, through an innocent change of position to his prejudice. It is therefore denied where the matter of the payment remains executory between purchaser and seller, and there is no irrevocable change of position. It is granted where either the buyer has paid the purchase price or has entered with third persons into a binding obligation with regard to it, whether the obligation arises out of the execution or the assumption of negotiable promissory notes, or other form of undertaking which the buyer is able to perform, and from which he cannot in law withdraw.

R3RUE §66 (Reporter's Note to Illustration 17). In other words, "the defense of purchase for value may be nothing more than an instance of change of position grown doctrinaire." Cohen, *Change of Position in Quasi-Contracts*, 45 Harv. L. Rev. 1333, 1342 (1932).

IV. IN WHAT SENSE IS THE DOCTRINE PURELY DEFENSIVE?

Purchase for value without notice does not yield a total immunity to restitution claims, because (like other equitable defenses) it is "a shield and not a sword." It confirms in the protected purchaser a legal title free of competing "equities," but it will not validate a conveyance that was not made. This is why R3RUE §66 says that the bfp acquires "the legal interest that the grantor *holds and purports to convey*." These words comprise two independent qualifications.

(a) The first means that the bfp does not acquire a legal title that the grantor did not have to give:

- A owns Blackacre. A sells to B, delivering a deed which (by a mistake in description) purports to convey both Blackacre and Whiteacre, the property of C. B is by every test a bfp, but B acquires no interest in Whiteacre by A's conveyance.

(b) The second qualification is that while the bfp acquires a protected title to whatever he was supposed to get (if his grantor had it to give), his status as an innocent purchaser for value does not give him anything more. Consider the following real-life scenario:

In 1945 defendant [Jensen] and her late husband acquired approximately 15 acres of land. In 1958 they conveyed all of that land, except the parcel that comprised their home, yard and garden, to Ray and Georgia Jones with the mutual understanding and intent that the boundary line of the property to be conveyed was the existing fence and that it would divide their respective properties. However, as was determined 22 years later, the metes and bounds description in the deed of conveyance prepared by a third party did not follow the fence line but included a plot of approximately .78 acres to the north of the fence, which includes much of defendant's yard and garden spot. This acreage is the subject matter of this dispute.

A few years after the conveyance to the Joneses, they conveyed the property to N.E. Anglin, who in turn conveyed to D.A. Dove. All deeds used the same metes and bounds description as was contained in the original conveyance from defendant to the Joneses. However, it was stipulated that all of the parties understood and intended the fenceline to be the boundary between the two properties. In 1973 Dove conveyed the property to the plaintiffs [Hottingers], utilizing the original metes and bounds description. Plaintiffs treated the fenceline as the boundary until 1980. In 1980 plaintiffs had the property surveyed. The survey revealed that the deed description put the boundary some 90 feet north of the fence and within a few feet of defendant's house. Plaintiffs thereupon asserted ownership of the property as described by the deed, tore down the existing fence and erected a fence at the claimed boundary. Defendant objected, whereupon plaintiffs brought suit to quiet title in plaintiffs to the disputed property. Defendant counterclaimed asking reformation of the deed to conform to the previously understood boundary.

Hottinger v. Jensen, 684 P.2d 1271, 1272-73 (Utah 1984). The Hottingers were unquestionably bfps. Does this give them a defense against Jensen's "equity of reformation"? How would we have to change the facts to make the defense relevant?

BFP REVIEW

Test your knowledge of the basics of the doctrine with the following hypotheticals based on *Church of Jesus Christ of Latter-Day Saints v. Jolley* from Chapter 8. In that case, as you may recall, LaMar Kay bought two cars with funds he embezzled from the Church. He gave both cars to his girlfriend, Vickie Jolley. The Church found the cars and sued Vickie to get them back.

1) In the actual case, Vickie did not know that LaMar was an embezzler. Why was she not protected as a bona fide purchaser?

2) Before she learns the facts—and before the Church finds her—Vickie Jolley sells the Corvette to a used-car dealer, Beehive Motors. LaMar Kay had paid $5,000 for this car, but Beehive pays Vickie only $2,500. Now the Church finds the car and sues Beehive. Is Beehive protected as a bfp?

3) What if Beehive paid Vickie only $500? What if a former Beehive employee is willing to testify that "the manager thought she didn't know what the car was worth, so we could take advantage of her"?

4) Assume again that Beehive paid Vickie $2,500. The Church finds the Corvette on the Beehive lot and threatens a lawsuit to get it back. The

story of LaMar Kay and his cars gets into the newspapers. Collector reads about the dispute and sees an opportunity to get a late-model Corvette at a reasonable price. Beehive is glad to get this problem off its hands, and sells the car to Collector for $3,000. Is Collector protected as a bfp?

5) LaMar bought the car with stolen money. What if LaMar had stolen the car instead of the money?

Finally, consider a fraudulent purchase of real property, as in *Cox v. Waudby* in Chapter 8:

6) Instead of mortgaging the Coxes' farm to the bank, Waudby (the fraudulent buyer) sells it to a neighbor, Farmer Jones. The price is $300,000, payable $50,000 in cash with the balance in monthly instalments. By the time the Coxes discover Waudby's fraud, Farmer Jones has paid $100,000 toward the price while making improvements that add $25,000 to the value of the farm. How will this situation be resolved?

———————

C. CREDITOR/PAYEES

Wilson v. Newman
463 Mich. 435, 617 N.W.2d 318 (2000)

PER CURIAM.

This appeal arises out of a postjudgment garnishment proceeding. The plaintiffs obtained a judgment against defendant Newman, which they sought to enforce through a writ of garnishment directed to garnishee First Allmerica Financial Life Insurance Company. The garnishee paid the judgment in the mistaken belief that it was indebted to the defendant. The circuit court denied its request for relief from the garnishment order, and the Court of Appeals denied leave to appeal.

We conclude that the case on which the lower courts relied, Shield Benefit Administrators, Inc. v. Univ. of Michigan Bd. of Regents, 225 Mich. 467, 571 N.W.2d 556 (1997), improperly rejected prior Michigan precedent in adopting Restatement of Restitution §14 (1937). We adhere to prior Michigan law, which permits recovery of mistaken payments absent detrimental reliance by the payee. We therefore reverse the judgments of the Court of Appeals and the circuit court and remand the case to the circuit court for further proceedings.

I

Defendant Newman borrowed money from the plaintiffs. When he failed to repay the debt, plaintiffs brought this action to recover the remaining loan

balance, together with interest and attorney fees. Ultimately, Newman agreed
that he owed the debt, and a consent judgment was entered in plaintiffs' favor.
The plaintiffs obtained issuance of a writ of garnishment directed to garnishee
First Allmerica Financial Life Insurance Company, seeking any funds owed
by First Allmerica to Newman.

In preparing the response to the writ of garnishment, First Allmerica's staff
discovered several insurance policies owned by a Robert L. Newman and
disclosed indebtedness to defendant Newman as a result. When no objections to the disclosure were received, it sent a check to the plaintiffs in care
of their attorney dated September 1, 1998, in the amount of $43,021.58. The
funds were withdrawn from two life insurance policies owned by its insured.
Shortly thereafter, the garnishee discovered that the policies were not those of
defendant Newman, but rather of a Colorado resident with a different social
security number. First Allmerica contacted plaintiffs' counsel on September
18 to advise of the error and requested return of the funds in a letter dated
September 23, 1998. Plaintiffs refused to return the funds, and on November
3, 1998, the garnishee filed a motion for relief from the garnishment order.

The circuit court denied relief, relying on *Shield Benefit, supra.* It opined
that the garnishee, the party making the mistake, should bear the loss. The
court noted that there was no claim that the plaintiffs made any misrepresentations or knew of the mistake. The garnishee filed a delayed application for
leave to appeal with the Court of Appeals. The application was denied with an
order citing *Shield Benefit.*

II

Shield Benefit involved a claim that health insurance benefits were mistakenly paid. The case was submitted on stipulated facts, which the Court of
Appeals summarized as follows:

> The husband of Claudette Hodge was an employee of plaintiff Oven-
> Fresh Bakeries, Inc., through which he and his dependents were insured
> under a group health plan. Plaintiff Shield Benefit Administrators, Inc.
> is a third-party administrator that administers Oven-Fresh's health plan.
> Hodge was insured under the Oven-Fresh health plan and received treat-
> ment at the University of Michigan Medical Center. The medical care
> was delivered during the first five months of 1994 and cost $4,260. Before
> each provision of service to Hodge, the Medical Center obtained preau-
> thorization from a Shield agent. The Medical Center obtained an assign-
> ment from Hodge and directly billed Shield for the services rendered to
> Hodge. Shield submitted full payment to the Medical Center for Hodge's
> treatments.
>
> After making the payment to the Medical Center, Shield discovered
> that benefits had been paid in excess of Hodge's maximum plan ben-
> efit for the applicable period. Accordingly, in November 1994, Shield

notified the Medical Center that Shield should not have paid for Hodge's services, and Shield requested that the payment be refunded. The Medical Center refused to return the $4,260 paid by Shield for the services rendered to Hodge. Shield then filed this action. [225 Mich. App. at 468-469, 571 N.W.2d 556.]

The *Shield Benefit* majority recognized that there was a well-settled rule that payment made under a mistake of fact can be recovered even if the mistake could have been avoided by the payor. Couper v. Metropolitan Life Ins. Co., 250 Mich. 540, 544, 230 N.W. 929 (1930); Madden v. Employers Ins. of Wausau, 168 Mich. App. 33, 40, 424 N.W.2d 21 (1988). The Court noted, however, that neither case involved a third-party creditor, such as the hospital in that case. The Court was thus faced with the question whether to apply the traditional rule in the third-party case or whether to adopt the position expressed in Restatement, Restitution §14(1), which creates an exception to the general mistake-of-fact rule when a third-party creditor is involved:

> A creditor of another or one having a lien on another's property who has received from a third person any benefit in discharge of the debt or lien, is under no duty to make restitution therefor, although the discharge was given by mistake of the transferor as to his interests or duties, if the transferee made no misrepresentation and did not have notice of the transferor's mistake.

Relying on a number of cases that have adopted the Restatement principle in the context of payments by insurers to medical care providers, particularly Federated Mut. Ins. Co. v. Good Samaritan Hosp., 191 Neb. 212, 214 N.W.2d 493 (1974), the *Shield Benefit* Court adopted the Restatement position and held that the insurer could not recover the erroneous payments.

Judge Young, dissenting in *Shield Benefit*, saw no reason to abandon the well-settled rule that a voluntary payment made under a mistake of material fact may be recovered. Montgomery Ward & Co. v. Williams, 330 Mich. 275, 47 N.W.2d 607 (1951). He noted also the recognition of an exception—the recipient may retain the mistaken payment when the recipient has changed position in detrimental reliance on it. Leute v. Bird, 277 Mich. 27, 31, 268 N.W. 799 (1936). Noting the hospital's request to adopt §14(1) of the Restatement, Judge Young said:

> I am unconvinced that the Michigan rule is inadequate, as contended, to cover sufficiently and equitably the circumstances of this case. As a rule of equity, it seems reasonable to require the return of a mistaken payment, particularly when the payee can demonstrate no change of position or detrimental reliance as a consequence of receiving the mistaken payment. Such has been Michigan's rule for more than one hundred years, and it is well understood. [225 Mich. App. at 474, 571 N.W.2d 556.]

Judge Young went on to question the appropriateness of changing the long-standing rule regarding restitution of payments made by mistake, noting the lack of information about the effect of such a policy change.

III

We agree with the dissent in *Shield Benefit* that it was inappropriate for the Court of Appeals to have adopted the principle of §14 of the Restatement of Restitution in that case. The longstanding Michigan authority on the subject is sound, and provides all the necessary exceptions to protect payees where it is appropriate to do so. We summarized those principles in General Motors Corp. v. Enterprise Heat & Power Co., 350 Mich. 176, 86 N.W.2d 257 (1957):

> The general rule relative to the right to recover money paid through a mistake of fact is well stated in Smith v. Rubel, 140 Or. 422, 426, 427 (13 P.2d 1078, 87 A.L.R. 644) [1932], where it was said: "As a general rule, a payment made under a mistake of fact which induces the belief that the other party is entitled to receive the payment when, in fact, the sum is neither legally nor morally due to him, may be recovered, provided the payment has not caused such a change in the position of the payee that it would be unjust to require the refund."

Michigan has generally followed this rule. In Walker v. Conant, 65 Mich. 194, 197, 198 [31 N.W. 786 (1887)], we said:

> The rule is general that money paid under a mistake of material facts may be recovered back, although there was negligence on the part of the person making the payment; but this rule is subject to the qualification that the payment cannot be recalled when the situation of the party receiving the money has been changed in consequence of the payment, and it would be inequitable to allow a recovery.

In Pingree v. Mutual Gas Co., 107 Mich. 156, 159, 160 [65 N.W. 6 (1895)], we said: "Payments made by reason of a mistake or ignorance of a material fact are regarded as involuntarily made. Ignorance of a fact may be equivalent to a mistake of fact." In State Savings Bank of Ann Arbor v. Buhl, 129 Mich. 193, 197 [88 N.W. 471 (1901), we said:

> While it may be difficult to find a case on all fours with this, it may be said the courts almost unanimously now hold that, although the mistake of facts is caused by the negligence of one party, that party is not precluded thereby from availing himself of the mistake if the other party can be relieved of any prejudice caused thereby.

The plaintiffs have contended that they in fact were prejudiced by the defendant's mistaken payment, for example, forgoing other collection efforts that may not now be available. Such claims are available under the Michigan cases cited earlier. If the plaintiffs can demonstrate a change of position or detrimental reliance as a consequence of having received the mistaken payment, they may be entitled to retain all or part of the funds mistakenly paid by Allmerica. However, given the disposition of the case by the lower courts, the record has not been developed on this issue and cannot be decided by this Court.[1]

The traditional Michigan rule permitting restitution of mistaken payments, with appropriate exceptions, produces a just result in the instant case. It is undisputed that the property held by garnishee Allmerica Financial was not that of defendant Newman, but rather of another person with the same name, making this a case of payment by mistake within the general rule. As many Michigan cases have said, the fact that the mistake is the result of negligence by the payor is not dispositive.

Courts often say that when one of two innocent parties must suffer a loss, it should be borne by the one whose conduct made the loss possible. E.g., Langschwager v. Pinney, 351 Mich. 473, 88 N.W.2d 276 (1958). However, such analysis does not apply in this case. Under the result reached by the lower courts, Allmerica Financial will unquestionably suffer a loss. It will have paid more than $43,000 to the plaintiffs, and will also continue to owe that amount to its Colorado policyholder, whom it mistakenly believed to be defendant Newman. By contrast, absent some showing of specific prejudice, as discussed further below, the plaintiffs will not suffer loss as a result of restitution. The plaintiffs had a judgment against defendant Newman, which they were entitled to collect by whatever means the law permits. After restitution of the mistaken payment by Allmerica, they would be left in exactly the same position, possessed of the same judgment, which they may proceed to attempt to collect.

Accordingly, we reverse the decision of the lower court that precluded recovery of the mistaken payment on the basis of §14 of the Restatement of Restitution. We remand the case to the Oakland Circuit Court for further proceedings to determine whether, on the facts of this case, restitution of the mistaken payment is appropriate.

Change of position, antecedent debt, and "discharge for value"

1. The opinion in *Wilson v. Newman* makes it apparent that there are competing theories about a creditor/payee's liability for restitution of a mistaken payment, but it does not explain very well what the alternatives are. The choice

---

1. Indeed, even under the established Michigan law, denial of reimbursement in *Shield Benefit* may well have been appropriate. In that case, before providing service to the patient, the defendant medical center obtained preauthorization from a Shield Benefit agent. Thus, the medical center was arguably relying on the expected payments from Shield Benefit in rendering services to the insured.

lies between competing equitable and commercial responses to the problem, where what was once a crucial distinction is only visible in a historical perspective. The equitable idea was (and is) that while the creditor/payee must be protected against prejudice resulting from the claimant's mistake, he should not be allowed to profit at the claimant's expense—being left better off than if the mistaken payment had not been made. The contrasting commercial idea emphasizes the special need for finality in payment transactions.

Nineteenth-century bankers and brokers—dealers in negotiable instruments and other commercial paper—wanted to reinforce their legal status as protected purchasers and secured lenders. As we have seen, the tricky part of bfp doctrine has always been the definition of "value," and the argument about value is mostly about the status of "antecedent debt." From the equity viewpoint, where the idea of value is assimilated to detrimental change of position, it is hard to see how a creditor gives value if he merely takes money or other property in satisfaction of (or as security for) a preexisting debt. If such a creditor has to give back the money—supposing it was paid by mistake, as in *Wilson v. Newman*—he is left back where he started and no worse off. From the banker's viewpoint, this equity thinking was dangerously subversive. Probably the majority of the banker's day-to-day dealings in commercial paper involve antecedent debt in one form or another. Commercial paper, likely maturing in 30, 60 or 90 days, is constantly being renewed and replaced. Every day the banker is taking new notes to refinance old notes that are coming due. Even more important, the banker's status as a secured lender—then as now—is only valid if he gives value for the collateral. If his outstanding loans have longer maturities than the paper he holds as collateral, the bulk of the assets he holds for this purpose have been acquired as security for antecedent debt. Unless the banker gives value for this replacement collateral, he is merely an unsecured creditor in the event of the borrower's bankruptcy.

Bankers and their lawyers had a simple solution to any doubts on this score. Whatever "value" might mean in other contexts, taking negotiable instruments in satisfaction of antecedent debt, or as security for antecedent debt, had to qualify as a purchase "for value." Not everyone was convinced that this step was necessary. The debate about the status of antecedent debt as value produced an epic struggle between jurisdictions, in which the heavyweight championship matched Coddington v. Bay, 20 Johns. 637 (N.Y. 1822), against Swift v. Tyson, 41 U.S. (16 Pet.) 1 (1842). The original object of the "federal common law" announced by Justice Joseph Story in *Swift v. Tyson* was to ensure that antecedent debt would count as "value" in the federal courts, no questions asked. The New York courts continued to reject that proposition, at least in the unqualified form favored by Story, for most of the 19th century.

Story's position ultimately prevailed, and law is written by the victors—in this case at UCC §1-204, which provides that "a person gives value for rights if the person acquires them [*inter alia*] as security for, or in total or partial satisfaction of, a preexisting claim." ("Value" for transactions in negotiable instruments is separately defined at UCC §3-303.) The expansive UCC definitions of value settle the bfp question for any transaction within the scope of the Code. For example, a creditor who takes goods in satisfaction of an outstanding debt is protected as a bfp—with the result that the creditor prevails over the former owner of the goods, when it transpires that the goods delivered in payment by the debtor were obtained from the former owner by fraud. UCC §2-403(1). By contrast, if the transaction that gives rise to a restitution claim is *not* regulated by the UCC—such as a conveyance of real property, or the mistaken payment in *Wilson v. Newman*—the question is whether the common law of the jurisdiction, after carving out the UCC transactions, follows the equitable or the commercial rule regarding antecedent debt.

Section 14(1) of the 1937 Restatement, quoted by the court in *Wilson v. Newman*, proposed that the commercial rule be applied across the board in restitution cases—by stating that a creditor who takes property without notice in discharge of a debt or lien is "under no duty to make restitution therefor." As explained in their published notes, the Reporters of the original Restatement thought that the question was one that could be decided either way:

> The question is one of legal mechanics, or the operation of rules which determine who, as between equally innocent persons, is entitled to the subject matter. . . .
>
> It becomes clear, therefore, that as a new matter and from the standpoint of justice the result reached in any particular case might equally well be opposite to the result now reached under the rules. In other words, the rules as to bona fide purchase are not, as are the rules normally applicable to questions involving restitution, based upon the balance of justice between the parties, but merely upon technicalities.

W.A. Seavey & A.W. Scott, Notes on Certain Important Sections of Restatement of Restitution 7-8 (1937). What was the "balance of justice between the parties" in *Wilson v. Newman*—or don't we care?

2. The most prominent modern decision adopting the rule of "discharge for value" in mistaken-payment cases is Banque Worms v. BankAmerica Int'l, 77 N.Y.2d 362, 570 N.E.2d 189 (1991). Consider the following synopsis from Kull, *Defenses to Restitution: The Bona Fide Creditor,* 81 B.U.L. Rev. 919, 919-22 (2001):

> Spedley Securities, a broker in Australia, had a payment due on its loan from Banque Worms in New York. Spedley also owed money to another bank in New York, National Westminster Bank USA (Natwest). Spedley asked its local bank to send $2 million to Banque Worms by electronic funds transfer. Before anyone was paid, Spedley changed its mind: Spedley told its bank to cancel the first transfer and send the money to Natwest instead. Somebody down the line failed to get the message, and Security Pacific, an intermediary in the funds-transfer chain, made both payments by mistake. Discovering what had happened within a matter of

hours, Security Pacific asked Banque Worms for its money back. Banque Worms refused. According to Banque Worms, the fact that it had received the money without notice of any mistake, in satisfaction of a valid debt owed by a third party (Spedley), gave it an affirmative defense to what would otherwise be a valid restitution claim. The question was whether these circumstances made out a good defense under New York law. The New York Court of Appeals held that they did.

Banque Worms v. BankAmerica International makes a dramatic illustration of the rule in question, because if a defense to restitution is available on these facts the result is unmistakably harsh. Consider first that Security Pacific would have had an unanswerable claim in restitution to recover the same $2 million if it had been sent by mistake to almost anyone else in the world: specifically, to any payee who was neither a creditor of Spedley nor indebted to his own bank. Consider next that Banque Worms would have been entitled to an affirmative defense in any U.S. court if it could have demonstrated that it had suffered a detrimental change of position in reliance on the payment. (Release of security for Spedley's loan would be a good example of change of position.) In this case, by contrast, it appears that at the time it received notice of the mistake, Banque Worms had done nothing at all. At most it had made an entry on a ledger, one that might be reversed by another entry.

Consider finally that Spedley has become insolvent. Thus while the loser of the contest between Security Pacific and Banque Worms has an iron-clad claim for $2 million against Spedley (Banque Worms on the loan contract; Security Pacific on a restitution theory), the result of allowing the affirmative defense is that a $2 million loan loss is shifted from Banque Worms to Security Pacific as the result of a clerical error. If the issue between the parties is a matter of unjust enrichment, then something is wrong with this picture.

The question presented in *Banque Worms* is in fact a very old one. A traditional formulation might run as follows: In order to establish an affirmative defense to an action for restitution of a mistaken payment, must the recipient establish a good-faith change of position—this will concededly suffice—or is it enough to have taken the money in good faith in payment of a valid obligation? There are many New York cases bearing on precisely this controversy, offering significant authority on both sides of the issue. Without attempting to reconcile or even to understand this split in its own decisions, the Court of Appeals in *Banque Worms* suggested that the old quarrel was probably irrelevant in the new era of electronic payments. The fact that payments are being made faster and in greater volume enhances—the court implied, without quite saying why—the payee's interest in finality. Moreover, the bank that makes a mistaken payment is clearly in a better position to avoid the mistake by taking better care. Putting the loss on the payor bank—that is, allowing an affirmative defense to the payee—should decrease the incidence of payment mistakes in the long run.

There is less to this analysis than meets the eye. The first argument, about electronic versus paper payments, is sheer makeweight. It is not apparent why the speed and volume of electronic payments give the electronic payee any greater interest in the security of receipt than payees in cash or paper have always had. Insofar as there is a relation between the speed of the payment system and the availability of restitution for mistake, the most plausible inference—in this as in other contexts—is still that liberal restitution favors prompt payment.

The second error in the reasoning of the Court of Appeals is more interesting, because it is relatively common in this context. The problem between the immediate parties (Security Pacific and Banque Worms) was a mistaken payment. Obviously the payor, not the payee, is in the better position to avoid such mistakes in the future. Assigning the loss to Security Pacific on the facts of this case was "particularly appropriate," the court felt, in view of the payor's deplorable carelessness: "The undisputed facts demonstrate that Security Pacific executed Spedley's initial order directing payment to Banque Worms notwithstanding having already received a cancellation of that order." This is the reflexive, rudimentary reasoning of modern tort law, by which a party identified as a superior risk-bearer is chosen to bear some associated loss. But the court in *Banque Worms* has mixed up the different risks and losses in the case. Apart from the administrative expense of straightening things out—a cost that is negligible if the matter is not litigated—Security Pacific's payment mistake has not in fact caused any loss to the parties. The only real loss anywhere on the horizon—and the only reason the parties are in court—is the loss of $2 million caused by Spedley's default. The only significant consequence of Security Pacific's mistake is that this loss on the Spedley loan has been fortuitously shifted from Banque Worms (which voluntarily assumed the associated credit risk and was paid for doing so) to Security Pacific (which had nothing to do with the loan transaction from which the loss resulted). The result in *Banque Worms* cannot be justified by reference to superior risk bearing, because the risk in question does not correlate to the loss being assigned.

Commercial law has a legitimate interest in payment finality, but must it override any concern for "the balance of justice between the parties"? Is there any way to insulate "ordinary course" transactions without foreclosing restitution in a case like *Wilson v. Newman* or *Banque Worms*?

3. As seen in the last chapter, restitution adopts extremely protective rules for measuring the benefit conferred on an innocent recipient—to ensure that a defendant's liability in restitution not leave the defendant worse off than if the transaction had never occurred. On the reverse of the same coin is the equitable view of affirmative defenses. A defendant should not be allowed to profit from a plaintiff's mistake, being left better off—at the plaintiff's expense—than if the transaction had never occurred. This equitable view readily recognizes change of position as a defense to an action based on mistaken payment, to the

extent that a liability in restitution would leave the defendant worse off than if the mistake had not been made. But in cases like *Wilson v. Newman* and *Banque Worms*, we see defendants who have not changed position—who by returning the mistaken payment would be restored to the position they would occupy had there been no mistake. Are the defendants in these cases simply fighting to hold onto a windfall gain at someone else's expense?

Today's answer may be that such questions are no longer relevant—that the equitable inquiry has been displaced, in cases about money payments, by the commercial rule that treats antecedent debt as value, "no questions asked." But it is worth remembering that the rule about antecedent debt was no part of the law of restitution at the outset. A hard-headed commercial judge like Lord Mansfield was fully prepared to find that a creditor/payee who could not show a prejudicial change of position was not entitled to a defense. In Buller v. Harrison, 2 Cowp. 565, 98 Eng. Rep. 1243 (K.B. 1777), the plaintiff insurer had promptly paid a claim in the amount of £2,100, "thinking the loss was fair." Payment was made to the defendant in London, as agent of the insureds who were "resident at New York." Discovering shortly thereafter that in fact "it was a foul loss," the insurer sued the agent to recover the money. The agent's defense was that the insureds, at the time of the payment, had been indebted to him in the amount of £3,000, and that he had credited the insurer's £2,100 against this antecedent debt. Lord Mansfield rejected the agent's defense in memorable terms:

> [S]hall a man, though innocent, gain by a mistake, or be in a better situation than if the mistake had not happened? Certainly not. In this case, there was no new credit, no acceptance of new bills, no fresh goods bought or money advanced. In short, no alteration in the situation which the defendant and his principals stood in towards each other on the 20th of April. What then is the case? The defendant has trusted Ludlow and Co. and given them credit. He trafficks to the country where they live, and has agents there who know how to get the money back. The plaintiff is a stranger to them and never heard of their names. Is it conscientious then, that the defendant should keep money which he has got by their misrepresentation, and should say, though there is no alteration in my account with my principal, *this is a hit, I have got the money and I will keep it?*

Id. at 568, 98 Eng. Rep. at 1245 (emphasis added).

Contingent obligations

1. Even if antecedent debt counts as value, "no questions asked"—in particular, no questions about the cash value of the obligation—what about an obligation that is contingent in some respect? In Mohamed v. Kerr, 91 F.3d 1124 (8th Cir. 1996), the issue on appeal was summarized as follows:

After summary judgment was granted in favor of his client, appellee's counsel transferred judgment proceeds received from the court to his client, except for a portion which he retained for himself, at least in part, as payment of his contingent legal fee. The summary judgment was subsequently reversed on appeal. Appellants seek to compel the attorney to return that portion of the judgment which he retained. Their motion was denied. We reverse.

The court agreed that an "innocent payee" of the judgment proceeds from the client—including, for example, a supermarket where the client bought groceries, or a lawyer who was charging an hourly rate—would *not* be required to make restitution if the judgment in favor of the client were reversed on appeal. What is the reasoning by which courts apply a different rule to lawyers who charge a contingent fee?

2. If you like *Mohamed v. Kerr*, consider In re Deepwater Horizon, 845 F.3d 634 (5th Cir. 2017). A commercial fisherman named Burrle claimed losses from the BP oil spill: he received $50,000 from the court-supervised settlement program. Burrle's claim was later determined to be fraudulent. By the time the program administrators sought restitution, Burrle had used $20,000 of his settlement to repay a creditor: not a supermarket or a contingent-fee attorney, but a litigation-finance entity called "Woodbridge Baric Pre-Settlement Funding, LLC." The terms of the "pre-settlement funding" provided that the "advance" made by Woodbridge Baric to Burrle need not be repaid if Burrle's claim against BP was not successful. Perceiving an analogy to cases like *Mohamed v. Kerr*, the special master handling the settlement argued that Woodbridge Baric was like a contingent-fee attorney: not a bona fide creditor, but more like an assignee *pro tanto* of the settlement proceeds. The district court agreed with this analysis and ordered restitution. The Fifth Circuit reversed:

> Woodbridge Baric's right to Burrle's repayment of the principal amount of its loan did not depend solely on the success of Burrle's claims: Woodbridge Baric's contracts with Burrle expressly required Burrle to indemnify and hold Woodbridge Baric harmless for the loss of the principal amount of the loan if his representations to Woodbridge Baric regarding his claims were not accurate and complete in all respects. Although Woodbridge Baric assumed some of the risks associated with non-recovery in its contracts with Burrle, it specifically disclaimed the risk that Burrle had asserted fraudulent claims and withheld that information from it. Accordingly, Woodbridge Baric was entitled to Burrle's full repayment of the principal under their contracts. In other words, because Burrle's payment to Woodbridge Baric discharged an unconditional, bona fide obligation, Woodbridge Baric is not liable in restitution to the settlement program.

Id. at 639. Why not order restitution and let Woodbridge Baric pursue Burrle on his "unconditional, bona fide obligation"?

Farnsworth, *Restitution* 150 (2014):

Note that creditors—that is, people paid money—get more protection than purchasers of real estate or goods. A creditor who receives *money* in good faith keeps it even if it was stolen. The best explanation for that rule lies in the importance of treating money payments as final for the sake of reducing uncertainty in their recipients. Someone who receives money generally will find it harder than the recipient of a car, a painting, and so on, to research whether the money came into the payor's hands unlawfully. And perhaps it is true that money received tends to be combined quickly with other money and then spent, invested, and so forth, so that the burden of trying to show an actual change of position in every case would be costly and usually not necessary. A danger in thinking about rationales of this kind, though, is that they can be beguiling enough to make the rule sound inevitable. It isn't. Until fairly recently New York's courts required a showing of an actual change of position before allowing the recipient of a mistaken payment to keep it. This did not cause the wheels of commerce to come to the halt that the rationale for the usual rule might suggest.

Gaffner v. American Finance Co.
120 Wash. 76, 206 P. 916 (1922)

BRIDGES, J.

This was an action for money had and received. The facts as found by the trial court (and which are clearly supported by the evidence) are as follows: One Hughes stole an automobile in California and drove it to Seattle. Some time thereafter he sought to obtain a loan on it from the finance company. It did not know Hughes, and did not know anything about the title to the machine. After making such investigation as it could, it concluded that Hughes owned the machine, and made him a loan thereon in the sum of $465.22. It took from him a chattel mortgage covering the machine, as security for the money loaned, which mortgage was duly recorded in the office of the auditor of King county. Thereafter Hughes entered into negotiations with the appellant for the sale of the automobile. Appellant was informed by Hughes that the finance company held a mortgage on it. The price was agreed upon. Hughes and the appellant went to the office of the finance company for the purpose of closing the deal. While there, the appellant paid the finance company the balance due it, secured a release of the mortgage and a surrender of the note which had been given by Hughes, and paid the balance of the purchase price directly to Hughes. Some days thereafter the police of Seattle found the machine on the street, and took it, and ultimately it was returned to the person from whom it had been stolen. The plaintiff brought this action to recover the amount he had paid to the finance company. There was a judgment for the defendants. The plaintiff has appealed.

The general principle of law upon which the appellant seeks reversal is that where one pays money to another through mistake he is entitled to recover it.

The cases which may be considered directly in point are few and not altogether harmonious. . . .

In the case of Walker v. Conant, 69 Mich. 321, 37 N. W. 292 (1888), the facts were as follows: Henry Van Riper was the owner of certain real estate, and Edgar Van Riper was his son. The son, pretending to represent the father, obtained a loan of $1,000 from Maria S. Conant. Young Van Riper forged his father's name to a note and mortgage, and appropriated the money received. Later the son, still pretending to represent his father, obtained from E.C. Walker a loan of $3,000. To get this money he again forged the name of his father to the note and mortgage. One thousand of the $3,000 loaned by Mr. Walker was paid to Mrs. Conant to secure a release of her mortgage. The son appropriated all of these amounts, and the father was ignorant of all the transactions. After the frauds were discovered, Walker, the second mortgagee, sought to recover from Mrs. Conant, the first mortgagee, the $1,000 thus paid to her. Held, that the plaintiff could not recover.

In the case of Merchants' Ins. Co. v. Abbott et al., 131 Mass. 397 (1881), the facts were: Abbott had a policy of insurance on some property which was destroyed by fire. At the same time he owed certain amounts to Denny, Rice & Co., and assigned to them all moneys which he claimed he was entitled to receive on account of his insurance. The insurance company, being aware of the assignment, paid the insurance money directly to Denny, Rice & Co. Later it developed that Abbott had been criminally connected with the fire, and had defrauded the insurance company, which then brought suit against Abbott and the Denny-Rice Company, wherein it sought judgment against Abbott for the full amount of the insurance money, and against Denny, Rice & Co. for the amount paid to it, on the ground that the money was paid through mistake of fact, and that the company had no right to retain it. It was held that judgment could be recovered against Abbott for the full amount, but denied any recovery against Denny, Rice & Co.

The general rule is that an action for money had and received can be maintained whenever one has received money from another by mistake, and which the receiver ought not, in equity and good conscience, to retain. We are of the opinion, however, that the facts of this case do not come within that rule. The respondent had made a bona fide loan to Hughes, not upon a forged note, but upon that given by the borrower himself. Hughes actually became indebted to the respondent. It is true the mortgage given to secure the indebtedness was upon a stolen machine, and was consequently fraudulently made and probably invalid, but the mortgage was a mere incident of the loan. Though the mortgage was invalid and worthless, the debt it secured was actual and enforceable. The appellant tried to purchase Hughes' automobile, but wished it to be clear of the apparent incumbrance. The money which was paid to the respondent was to discharge a bona fide indebtedness; consequently, it cannot be said that there was no consideration for the payment, or that the respondent cannot, in good conscience, keep the money. The situation is different than in those cases where both the note and mortgage were tainted with fraud. Here there was no mistake as to the indebtedness which was paid.

If we look at this case from a purely equitable viewpoint, the result to which we must come will not be different than that above announced. Appellant made the payment to the respondent in the belief that he was paying a bona fide, valid, indebtedness due from Hughes, and in so supposing there was no mistake. As to the mortgage; if the [appellant] was innocent, so was the [respondent]. The equities in favor of the respondent are not less great than those running with the appellant. We think the judgment of the trial court was right, and it is affirmed.

Victim v. victim; taxes; racehorses

1. Successive-fraud cases of the kind described in *Gaffner* make a dramatic illustration of the fundamental issue about the creditor/payee's defense to restitution. Is it enough to have received payment in satisfaction of a debt—real or supposed—or must the payee show a genuinely prejudicial change of position? To put it differently, what should be the result when the "value" given in exchange for the money is demonstrably worthless? In *Walker v. Conant*, one of the famous cases epitomized in *Gaffner*, a dissenting opinion attacked the defense on just these points:

> Mrs. Conant, by releasing her mortgage, did not release her debt against Edgar Van Riper. Her claim still remains as good as it ever was against him. Mr. Walker never received anything from her, or any one else, for the money he let her have. The mortgage she discharged was the only thing she parted with for it, and that was worthless and void. Under such circumstances, to permit Mrs. Conant to withhold the money she received from Mr. Walker would not only be inequitable and unjust, but would be allowing her to reap the fruits of the crime committed by young Van Riper. . . . It is said by my Brother MORSE, in regard to Mrs. Conant's giving up her note and mortgage: "Her situation is changed, and without her fault, beyond all possible return or restoration." If by this it is meant she has given up for destruction a forged note and mortgage which she received for a loan of money made, it is true; but if by it is meant that her legal or equitable rights are changed, in the event she is obliged to return the money she received of Mr. Walker, I confess my inability to discover such change.

69 Mich. at 330-31, 37 N.W. at 296 (Sherwood, C.J.). The same Morse and Sherwood, JJ., had been the authors one year earlier of the competing opinions in Sherwood v. Walker, 66 Mich. 568, 33 N.W. 919 (1887). This was the famous case of mutual mistake (noted in Chapter 6) regarding the fertility of Rose 2d of Aberlone, a purebred Aberdeen-Angus cow.

2. If the defenses of "bona fide purchase" and "bona fide payee" are set side by side—the way they are presented in R3RUE §§66-67—they are clearly two versions of the same idea, but with two important distinctions. The first, already discussed, relates to the question of "value." If receipt of payment in satisfaction of antecedent debt is "value" by definition, then every repaid creditor has a defense to restitution so long as he takes the money without notice. The second is the fact that a protected purchaser of money—an innocent creditor/payee—acquires good title even when the property in question (the money) has been stolen from someone else. This is a consequence of what is often called the "money rule," famously explained by Lord Mansfield in Miller v. Race, 1 Burr. 452, 97 Eng. Rep. 398 (K.B. 1758):

> It is a pity that reporters sometimes catch at quaint expressions that may happen to be dropped at the Bar or Bench; and mistake their meaning. It has been quaintly said, "that the reason why money cannot be followed is, because it has no ear-mark:" but this is not true. The true reason is, upon account of the currency of it: it cannot be recovered after it has passed in currency. So, in case of money stolen, the true owner cannot recover it, after it has been paid away fairly and honestly upon a valuable and bonã fide consideration: but before money has passed in currency, an action may be brought for the money itself.

3. The fact that money *usually* has no ear-mark means that restitution claims for stolen money are rare, but they do happen. In Transamerica Ins. Co. v. Long, 318 F. Supp. 156 (W.D. Pa. 1970), the court found

> that on April 22, 1964, William Hanzl, acting in conspiracy with others, robbed the Punxsutawney National Bank of the sum of $18,500 for which crime he was later apprehended and convicted.
>
> On April 24, 1964, two days after the robbery, Hanzl paid in excess of $4,500 to Revenue Officer Francis Klaus in satisfaction of his federal income tax liability for the years 1960 and 1962.
>
> Hanzl was arrested on April 29, 1964. Shortly after his arrest on that date he stated to agents of the Federal Bureau of investigation "that he had been given $2,000 as proceeds of the robbery and that he had paid this money to the Internal Revenue Service."
>
> Thereafter, "agent Klaus was told that Mr. Hanzl might have robbed a bank to pay tax obligations," and that "Mr. Hanzl might have been involved in a robbery of the Dayton Branch of the Punxsutawney National Bank on April 22, 1964, and that this robbery might have made possible his April payments to the Internal Revenue Service."

What factual issue remains to be litigated? According to the court, "It seems clear that an obligation to pay income taxes constitutes a valid preexisting debt, and the transfer of currency in payment of that debt is for value."

4. In granting an affirmative defense to a creditor/payee, at what point is the payee protected? In ordinary bfp cases, the purchase transaction must be completed before the purchaser acquires notice. For example, the deed to Blackacre must be delivered (and paid for) before the purchaser learns that his grantor's title was affected by fraud or mistake. But what is the relevant time at which to test the issue of notice to the payee in a payment transaction? Consider the pertinent facts of In re Calumet Farm, Inc., 398 F.3d 555 (6th Cir. 2005):

> This case arises out of a botched electronic wire transfer from Calumet Farm, Inc. to Peter M. Brant and White Birch Farm, Inc. (collectively, White Birch). On Friday, March 8, 1991, Calumet initiated the wire transfer of $77,301.58 by a payment order to its bank, First National Bank & Trust Company. This amount was calculated by Calumet as a payment of interest on its outstanding debt of over $1 million due to White Birch. When Calumet received written confirmation of the wire transfer from First National on the following Monday, March 11, 1991, it learned that $770,301.58, rather than $77,301.58, had mistakenly been transferred. White Birch refused to return the additional $693,000, and Calumet subsequently declared bankruptcy. First National is now seeking restitution from White Birch for the excess payment. Both the bankruptcy court and district court ruled in favor of White Birch.
>
> White Birch is a thoroughbred horse farm in Connecticut owned by Peter Brant. In 1986, Calumet purchased a one-half interest in the thoroughbred stallion Mogambo from White Birch and executed a $6,500,000 promissory note ("the Mogambo note") evidencing the obligation. On October 31, 1990, Calumet defaulted in making its annual principal payment of [$1,300,000] on the debt. Brant and J.T. Lundy, president of Calumet, reached an agreement whereby Calumet would make the payment on or before March 15, 1991. Calumet also defaulted in making several intervening interest payments and, as of March 7, 1991, owed White Birch approximately $103,057.50 in interest and penalties.
>
> On March 8, 1991, Lundy instructed Calumet's bookkeeper, Angela Holleran, to pay the interest due to White Birch as of January 31, 1991, amounting to $77,301.58. Holleran thereupon called First National to arrange payment by wire transfer, and also called White Birch to inform it that a wire transfer payment was forthcoming; however, the substance of these conversations is disputed as to the amount that White Birch was to receive. The wire transfer, referenced as "MOGAMBO INT," was made to White Birch's account at Citibank in New York on March 8, 1991.
>
> On March 11, 1991, Holleran received written confirmation of the wire transfer from First National and realized that $770,301.58, rather than $77,301.58, had been transferred. Holleran notified First National of the mistake and First National contacted Citibank to request reversal of the wire transfer. Because the money already had been credited to White Birch's account, Citibank refused to reverse the wire transfer.
>
> The undisputed record shows that White Birch did not credit the funds to Calumet's account until the afternoon of March 11, 1991. [Yet]

there is no dispute that Holleran notified White Birch of the error on the morning of March 11, 1991.

Furthermore, White Birch's behavior establishes that it was aware of the error as soon as it was informed of the wire transfer by its own bank. When White Birch discovered on the morning of March 11, 1991 that Citibank had credited its account for $770,301.58, it immediately transferred the additional $693,000 to Brant's personal account at Citibank, ostensibly so that "everything could be sorted out." It did not apply that amount to reduce Calumet's debt on the Mogambo note until later that day. If White Birch did not know or at least suspect that it had erroneously received the additional funds, it would have had no reason to segregate them into its owner's personal account. The fact that it segregated the precise amount of the overage, moreover, is strong evidence that White Birch knew exactly how much it was supposed to receive from Calumet. Even the wire transfer itself, after all, was referenced as "MOGAMBO *INT.*"

The strongest arguments in favor of "finality of payment"—and thus, for the broadened affirmative defense of a creditor/payee without notice—are usually framed in terms of stability and reliability. In other words, "I have to be able to spend the money people send me, without having to prove a change of position every time." If that is the rationale of the defense, at what point should be issue of notice be tested? When payment is received by Citibank for the account of White Birch? When White Birch is advised that $770,301.58 is in its Citibank account? What if notice to White Birch that a payment has been received makes it simultaneously obvious that a mistake has been made?

D. EQUITABLE DISQUALIFICATION (UNCLEAN HANDS)

Norton v. Haggett
117 Vt. 130, 85 A.2d 571 (1952)

BLACKMER, J.

The plaintiff, K. E. Norton, seeks equitable relief because he paid and discharged a note and the mortgage securing it. The bill alleges that the payment was made under a mutual mistake, and that the defendants, Roy M. and Hazel C. Haggett and the Northfield Savings Bank, are guilty of fraud and conspiracy. The case was heard by the chancellor, facts found, and a decree entered dismissing the bill; it is here on the plaintiff's exceptions.

So far as it is necessary to state them, the chancellor found these facts. The bank held a note and mortgage given to it by the Haggetts. On November 30, 1948, the plaintiff went to the bank for the purpose of securing possession of this note and mortgage. He told the clerk on duty that he wanted to "take up" the Haggett note and mortgage. Whereupon the clerk asked the plaintiff if he wanted to pay off the note, and the plaintiff replied "yes." The amount due was computed, and the plaintiff gave the bank his check for that amount. The clerk made the proper entries to cover the transaction; he stamped the note "Paid" with a large stamp with red ink, and prepared a discharge for the signature of the bank's president. As the president executed the discharge he said to the plaintiff, "You junk men must be making plenty of money in order to be paying someone else's mortgage"; the plaintiff made no reply. The cancelled note and discharged mortgage was handed to the plaintiff, the clerk telling him to be sure to have the mortgage discharge recorded. The plaintiff made no examination of either the note or the mortgage when he received them from the clerk. The plaintiff was well acquainted with notes and mortgages; he understood the process of executing and discharging mortgages, and the meaning of a stamp "paid" on a note. Both the clerk and the president understood that the plaintiff desired to pay the debt. On the same day the plaintiff wrote Roy M. Haggett that he had purchased the note and mortgage. This was the first dealing about the note and mortgage between the plaintiff and the Haggetts. Roy M. Haggett was much disturbed, because the plaintiff had had recent arguments with him on two occasions, and was apparently desirous of harming him. On December 1, Roy M. Haggett communicated with the bank, which told him the note had been paid, not sold. The bank furnished the Haggetts a second discharge of the mortgage, which discharge was recorded. The plaintiff interfered in the business relation between the bank and the Haggetts without any occasion, reason or inducement on the part of the Haggetts. As between the plaintiff and the Haggetts there has never been any indebtedness based on the note and mortgage; the debt due and evidenced by the note and mortgage has been paid and discharged.

[As between the plaintiff and the bank] we are dealing with a unilateral mistake, not a mutual mistake as claimed in the bill. It is quite safe to infer from the findings that the plaintiff intended to purchase the note and mortgage, and not to pay the note and discharge the mortgage. But the bank did not share in the plaintiff's mistake. It understood and acted in accordance with the plaintiff's expressed wish, which was to pay. The bank cannot be charged with a mistake simply because it did not know that the plaintiff entertained an unexpressed intent which was the opposite of his mistakenly expressed desire.

Insofar as the plaintiff's mistake is involved, the bank can be removed immediately from the picture. A person who confers a benefit upon another, manifesting that he does so as an offer of a bargain which the other accepts, is not entitled to restitution because of a mistake which the other does not share and the existence of which the other does not suspect. Restatement, Restitution, §12. The equitable principle by which a person is entitled to restitution for what he has transferred to another by mistake is modified by the principle that a person is entitled to the benefit of a bargain made by him without fraud or duress. Ordinarily, therefore, a person entering into a transaction in which another gives or promises consideration is not entitled to the return of what he gives merely because he is mistaken as to the nature of what he gives or receives, or as to other facts which cause him to enter into the transaction. A contracting party who is unaware of and does not share the mistake made by the transferor is entitled to retain that which he has received if what he gives is sufficient consideration for a simple contract. Idem. Comment pp.47, 48.

The situation as to the Haggetts stands differently. They were not a party to the bargain; they have not changed their position; they parted with no consideration; they will gain an unearned benefit if the plaintiff is refused relief. However, whether a mistake is to be corrected depends always upon the circumstances of the case. (1) The plaintiff has no one and nothing to blame except his own negligence and inattention. (2) He was an intermeddler, and officiousness is not to be encouraged. (3) His good faith was apparently questionable. (4) He had no motive of self-interest; he was not protecting any interest which he had or thought he had; nor was he discharging any duty which he owed or thought he owed. (5) He was not related to, nor even friendly with the Haggetts, nor was he protecting any interest of theirs. (6) To give the plaintiff restitution from the Haggetts would be to substitute him for the bank as creditor of the Haggetts without the consent of either the bank or the Haggetts. No protection is deserved by one who intermeddles by paying another's debt either without reason or to secure rights against the debtor without the consent of the creditor. Restatement, Restitution, Comment on §43, p.173. These latter considerations weigh more than the former, and dictate that the loss remain where it has fallen.

The plaintiff also briefs eight exceptions to the refusal of the chancellor to find as requested on the subjects of fraud and conspiracy. The facts sought to be found may be summarized thus. After the bank learned that the plaintiff claimed to have bought the note and mortgage, its president immediately and personally presented the plaintiff's check for payment at the drawee bank. The plaintiff seasonably on advice from his lawyer returned to the bank and informed the president that he had bought the mortgage, and that the clerk had made a mistake. He offered to rescind the transaction, but the bank refused, the president informing the plaintiff that "in my opinion he had already made Mr. Haggett a Christmas present." The second discharge was immediately recorded. All the above, read with the facts found, fail to show fraud and conspiracy. The acts requested to be found as facts were within both the legal and equitable competence of the defendants, as has been demonstrated.

No error has been made to appear.

Producers Lumber & Supply Co. v. Olney Building Co.
333 S.W.2d 619 (Tex. Civ. App. 1960)

MURRAY, Chief Justice.

This suit was instituted by Producers Lumber & Supply against Olney Building Company, seeking to recover damages resulting from the conduct of

H. P. Orts, president of defendant, when he caused his construction superintendent and a large crew of men to go upon Lot 8, Block 9, New City Block 12459, Northeast Park, owned by plaintiff, and demolish a dwelling constructed thereon by Olney Building Company.

The trial was to a jury and, based partly upon the verdict of the jury, the trial court rendered judgment in favor of plaintiff against defendant in the sum of $600. Producers Lumber & Supply has prosecuted this appeal, contending that the judgment should have been in the sum of $5,900.

The issues submitted to the jury and the answers thereto are as follows:

> Question No. 1: Do you find from a preponderance of the evidence that H. P. Orts, as president of Olney Building Company, acted in good faith in erecting the building on the plaintiff's lot? Answer Yes or No.
>
> We, the jury, answer: Yes.
>
> Question No. 2: What do you find from a preponderance of the evidence would be the reasonable and necessary cost of restoring the lot in question to substantially the same condition that it was in immediately before the construction was commenced thereon? Answer by stating the cost.
>
> We, the jury, answer: $600.00.
>
> Question No. 3: Do you find from a preponderance of the evidence that H. P. Orts, as president of Olney Building Company, acted maliciously in removing the building from the lot in question? Answer Yes or No.
>
> We, the jury, answer: Yes.
>
> Question No. 4: What sum of money, if any, do you find from a preponderance of the evidence is the plaintiff, Producers Supply & Lumber Company, entitled to receive as exemplary damages, if any, as that term is defined hereinbelow? Answer by stating the amount, if any.
>
> We, the jury, answer: $300.00.

The parties stipulated that the dwelling on Lot 8 had a value of $5,000, and that the dwelling had enhanced the value of Lot 8 by $5,000.

It might be well here to make a rather complete statement of the evidence in the case. H. P. Orts owned several corporations and was the head and general manager of them all, including Olney Building Company. Prior to November 1, 1956, Elliott Construction Co. was the owner of Lot 8, Block 9, Now City Block 12459, involved herein. On that date H. P. Orts executed a warranty deed, which was properly recorded, from Elliott to Producers Lumber & Supply, conveying Lot 8 for a consideration of $1,428. The lot was purchased by Producers with the intention that later its general manager, George R. Montgomery, and his wife would build a home for themselves thereon. Montgomery and wife had the lot graded and planted some trees and grass on it. On or about February 27, 1958, Orts and Elliott decided to construct nine dwellings, one on Lot 8 and eight on other nearby lots. Orts called A. L. Burden, secretary-treasurer of Olney, and asked him whether Lot 8 had been sold. Burden, after consulting a map on the wall, assured Orts it had not been sold. Orts inspected Lot 8 and noticed the trees planted there, he thought it was nice of someone to plant trees on this lot. Shortly thereafter the construction of the nine houses was begun. On April 1, 1958, Olney ordered Stewart Title Company to issue a Title Binder covering all nine lots to Frost National Bank in connection with interim financing. On April 14, 1958, Orts learned from the Title Company that Lot 8 had been sold to Producers. Orts then notified Mr. Montgomery of the circumstances, and this was the first notice to appellant that construction had been commenced on its lot. The dwelling on Lot 8 had been almost completed when the discovery was made. The house had been constructed without the knowledge or consent of Producers and against its wishes, and contrary to the plans that Montgomery and wife had for their own home. Orts began negotiations with Montgomery, trying to reach an amicable settlement of the matter. Orts told Montgomery that he, Montgomery, had him at his mercy. Various offers and counter-offers were made, but no settlement had been reached, when suddenly on April 22, 1958, Orts broke off negotiations and sent his construction superintendent with a large crew of men and heavy equipment to Lot 8, and demolished the dwelling constructed thereon, leaving nothing but a heap of crude building material and debris. With reference to the destruction of this dwelling, Orts testified as follows:

> Q. Now, you did, on or about April 22, 1958, remove those improvements, did you not? A. That is correct, sir.
> Q. Did you notify Mr. Montgomery or anyone from Producers Lumber and Supply Company that you were going to remove them? A. No, sir.
> Q. How many men do you remember employing on the job of removal? A. Does this have to be exact, or will an approximation do?
> Q. Well, if you know, tell me exactly; otherwise, it has to be approximately. A. I will say—I am going to say ten.
> Q. Approximately ten? A. Yes.
> Q. Isn't it a fact that you started the removal of these improvements about 2:00 o'clock in the afternoon? A. That is correct, sir.
> Q. Isn't it a fact that by 6:00 o'clock in the afternoon, by the use of a bulldozer and a dozen or more men, you had completely removed everything but the slab? A. That's right.
> Q. Isn't it a fact that you made no effort to salvage anything on the removal? A. No, sir.
> Q. You say that is not true? A. No, sir.
> Q. What did you salvage? A. All of the interior partitions, the exterior partitions, the siding, not the siding but the exterior sheeting, the roof sheeting, electrical and plumbing.

Q. Well, now, actually what happened was that several of your men went out and tore the roof off, isn't that right? A. That's right.

Q. And then you, for lack of a better word I will say unjointed, the corners and then you hooked on with a dozer and dragged the partitions and framing and roof trusses across the street, is that right? A. Partially, that is correct.

Q. You say that is not true? A. Not all of it.

Q. What is not true? A. The side walls were taken down piece by piece.

Q. The side walls were taken down piece by piece? A. Yes, sir.

Q. You said that you salvaged the electrical? A. Yes.

Q. Now, who did you employ to remove the slab? A. My superintendent.

Q. How did Crea Brothers get on the job? A. I hired their equipment.

Q. What equipment did you hire from Crea Brothers? A. A D–12 tractor, and I believe that slab was so good they couldn't get it up with a D–12 and finally they had to get a crane with a drop hammer, and I told my superintendent if Crea Brothers didn't have the—well, frankly, I don't know where I got the crane with the drop hammer.

Q. Isn't it a fact that they also used a couple of air hammers? A. Oh, yes.

Q. Air hammers, and they had to use torches to cut the steel? A. That is correct.

With reference to the destruction of the dwelling Orts further testified as follows:

Q. So the night you tore that house down, $2,768.00 went down the drain; is that right? A. Yes, sir. My money.

Q. Yes, sir. $2,768.00 went up just like that (slapping hands together)? A. That is right.

Q. As if you had set a match to it, didn't it? A. That is right.

It cost more than $1,300 to put the concrete foundation in, and, of course, it was worthless after the crane and drop hammer, cutting torches, etc., had been used upon it. This and other evidence clearly supports the finding of the jury that H. P. Orts, as president of Olney, acted maliciously in removing the building from Lot 8.

The law at one time was quite clear that where a person erects a building upon the land of another without his knowledge and consent the building became a fixture and belonged to the owner of the land and the builder was without remedy. This rule was regarded as harsh, but was thought necessary to make people careful with reference to their examination of the title to the land upon which they place buildings and other permanent improvements. It is only where a person places permanent improvements upon land belonging to another in a good faith belief that he is the owner of the land, that he has any remedy at all. Where he has built such improvements in good faith, he has a somewhat limited right to go into court, and upon proof of such good faith ask the court to grant him equitable relief. Under such circumstances, a court of equity may grant relief in several ways. If the building can be removed without great injury to the building or to the land, the court may permit the improver to move the building. Where the building cannot well be removed the court or jury can find the market value of the land before and after the making of the improvement, and allow the improver to recover for the amount of this enhanced value, if any. The landowner will first be permitted to pay the enhanced value and keep the land, but if he is unable or unwilling to do so, then the improver may be permitted to pay the value of the land before the improvements were placed thereon, and thus become the owner of the land and the improvements. Rzeppa v. Seymour, 230 Mich. 439, 203 N.W. 62 (1925). If the landowner is unable to pay for the improvements and the improver is unable to pay for the land, then the court may order the land and the improvements sold to the highest bidder and the money divided between the owner and the improver as their respective interests appear. Or the court may give the improver judgment for the amount the lot has been enhanced in value, together with a lien against the lot to secure the payment of the judgment.

Under no circumstances is an improver authorized to go upon the land of another, without his knowledge and consent, and demolish the improvements that he has through mistake placed thereon, and if he does so he commits waste and can be required to pay the landowner for such waste.

When Orts went upon Lot 8 without the knowledge or consent of appellant and demolished the dwelling he had placed thereon, he committed waste and must pay appellant for the value of the dwelling he destroyed, which as stipulated by the parties is the sum of $5,000. And Orts will not be heard to claim, in equity, reimbursement for the amount he had enhanced the value of the lot by the erection of the dwelling thereon. He resorted to self-help and took the law into his own hands, and before a court of equity could determine the rights of the parties he went upon Lot 8, which at the time he well knew belonged to Producers, and demolished the dwelling stipulated to be worth $5,000, thereby causing great destruction of property. He cannot now come into court, with unclean hands, and seek the equitable remedy of reimbursement for the amount he had enhanced the value of Lot 8 by the erection of the dwelling thereon.

The judgment of the trial court will be amended so as to permit appellant, Producers Lumber & Supply Company, to recover the sum of $5,000, the stipulated value of the dwelling demolished by Orts, and $300, found by the jury as exemplary damages, in addition to the sum of $600 awarded by the trial court, thus making the total amount of the judgment the sum of $5,900, and as thus amended the judgment will be affirmed. The cost of this appeal is adjudged against Olney.

BARROW, Justice (dissenting).

I do not concur in the opinion of the majority. My objection is that it allows the appellant to recover the sum of $5,000, the value of the house built by Olney on Producers' lot.

There is no doubt that appellant is entitled to recover such damages as it suffered to its lot, which is all that it had at the inception of this transaction. Producers is also entitled to recover exemplary damages under the jury finding that the house was torn down and removed maliciously, but I cannot agree that it is entitled to recover compensatory damages for the removal of the house.

The majority opinion holds that Olney is not entitled to reimbursement for the amount its improvements enhanced the value of Producers' land because it resorted to "self-help," and took the law into its own hands, and demolished the building, causing great destruction of property, and by reason thereof Olney does not come into equity with clean hands, and therefore cannot seek equitable relief. I cannot agree with such reasoning.

It appears from the record that immediately upon discovery of the mistake, Olney contacted Producers and sought to adjust the difficulty. It first offered to buy the lot, and Producers asked $3,600 or $3,700 for the lot, although it cost $1,428. Producers' manager and witness Montgomery testified the lot was worth $1,700 or $1,800. Olney then offered to trade any lot in the subdivision for Producers' lot. Producers declined on the ground that none of the lots would fit the plan of house that had been planned for its manager's home, although it was admitted that several of the lots offered were more valuable than Producers' lot. In that connection, it appears that the manager's home was not built on the lot in question, but was built on Walzen Road. Olney offered to sell the house to Producers either in its incomplete condition, or to complete it according to F.H.A. specifications at its cost. Producers declined and finally made a counter offer that it would give $7,000 for the house as so completed. The evidence shows that when completed the house would cost Olney $10,400. Montgomery testified that the completed house with the lot would be of the value of $12,000 to $12,900. When Producers made the offer of $7,000 for the completed house, it notified Olney that it was its final offer, although, at the time Montgomery was instructed to make the offer, Producers' president told Montgomery that he would give $8,000 for the house. This was not communicated to Olney, they said: "Let's offer him $7,000." Producers never at any time offered to pay the amount of the stipulated enhancements of its lot. Thus the record shows that Producers, having Olney "at its mercy" attempted to drive an unconscionable bargain. It was at this point that Olney proceeded to tear down the house and remove it. In that connection, I have found no authority which makes any distinction between moving the improvements intact or tearing it down and removing it, so long as the land is not damaged.

Keeping in mind that Producers seeks to recover as damages the value of a house that it did not build and has not one dollar invested in, and that it seeks to recover such damages against Olney, which at its own expense built the house in question, I cannot in good conscience agree to such an inequitable decision. Producers has sustained no injury so far as the house is concerned.

Chief Justice Bickett, formerly of this Court, in Bush v. Gaffney, 84 S.W.2d 759, 764 (Tex. Civ. App. 1935), said:

> It would ill comport with the principles of equity for the court to visit upon the defendants a sort of punishment to the pecuniary profit of the complainant and consequent loss of the defendants. A court of equity is a court of conscience, but not a forum of vengeance. It will make restitution, but not reprisals. It will fill full the measure of compensation, but will not overflow it with vindictive damages.

There is no sound reason to exact of appellee additional punitive damages in the sum of $5,000 and make the donation to appellant, as chastisement for appellee's alleged uncleanliness of hands, after full restitution has been made in awarding to appellant all damages which the jury found it suffered, as well as the exemplary damages found by the jury. Equity looks on that done which ought to be done.

As said by the Supreme Court in French v. Grenet, 57 Tex. 273, 279 (1881), in a situation similar to that involved here:

> In such case, the question is not whether a mistake of law shall vest title, but whether the penalty for that mistake, however innocently made and however diligently guarded against, shall be the forfeiture for a claim for improvements which enhanced the value of that property. To so decide would palpably violate that maxim, founded in the highest natural equity, that no one should be made richer to the damage and wrong of another.

I respectfully dissent.

———————

Unclean hands?

1. Accepting K.E. Norton's version of events, what is the best case you can make for Norton in his suit against the Haggetts? Against the Northfield Savings Bank? Has the court achieved full poetic justice here, or is there some lingering inequity?

2. What result in *Producers Lumber v. Olney* if H.P. Orts had been a mild-mannered law professor instead of a quick-tempered building contractor? Which of these adversaries—Orts or Montgomery—displayed the finer regard for principles of "equity and good conscience"?

———————

E. LIMITATION OF ACTIONS

Federal Deposit Insurance Corp. v. Bank One, Waukesha
881 F.2d 390 (7th Cir. 1989)

EASTERBROOK, Circuit Judge.

Robert Nanz carried on an elaborate check kite. The First National Bank of Waukesha was one of its victims, as well as the recipient of some of the proceeds of Nanz's fraud. (The First National Bank of Waukesha has been absorbed into Bank One, Waukesha; we call it "the Bank" for brevity.) Nanz funneled money from the American City Bank & Trust Co. of Milwaukee (ACB) to his account at the Bank. ACB failed, and the Federal Deposit Insurance Corporation, as ACB's receiver, sold to itself in its corporate capacity some of ACB's assets, including the right to pursue the Bank as the recipient of the proceeds. After some pretrial maneuvering, including a decision by this court refusing to direct the district judge to hold a jury trial, First National Bank of Waukesha v. Warren, 796 F.2d 999 (7th Cir. 1986), the case went to judgment—before a jury, the district judge having changed his mind after reading our opinion. The jury brought back a verdict of $2.174 million (including prejudgment interest) in the FDIC's favor.

Nanz was a prominent real estate developer with close ties to the Bank. The Bank foolishly allowed Nanz to write checks against uncollected funds; it even certified Nanz's checks despite the absence of good funds. During 1973, Nanz Realty had gross receipts of $7.4 million but deposited some $70 million into its account at the Bank, a sure sign of monkey business. Check kiting landed him in jail and his banks in red ink. United States v. Nanz, 471 F. Supp. 968 (E.D. Wis. 1979). The jury was entitled to find that in late 1973 the kite had approached its inevitable collapse. To postpone the evil day, Nanz had two friends—one of them Scott K. Lowry, a prominent figure in Waukesha and the Chairman of the Board of the Bank—borrow $250,000 apiece from ACB, which furnished funds on the strength of Lowry's financial statements, which were as bogus as Nanz's checks. The proceeds ended up in Nanz's account at the Bank, enabling it to pay some outstanding instruments, including one for $428,000 that it had certified. When in June 1974 the kite finally collapsed, ACB was out the $500,000 (plus interest), as the borrowers never repaid.

FDIC's theory is that the Bank was unjustly enriched as of January 1974 by $500,000. The Bank replies that it could not have been unjustly enriched because in a check kite the money flows out faster than it comes in. Although the $500,000 enabled it to cover the $428,000 check and other instruments, Nanz just wrote more paper, and the Bank never showed a positive (collected) balance in the account or controlled how Nanz used the money. When the kite came down, the Bank still was some $250,000 in the hole. The jury adopted the FDIC's position, finding in special verdicts that the loans conferred a benefit on the Bank, that retention of the benefit would be inequitable, and that the damages are $2.174 million.

Buried in the Bank's scattershot appellate brief (seven questions, with sub-parts) lies one difficult issue: whether the FDIC filed this suit on time. ACB made the loans in January 1974. The kite collapsed in June 1974. The Comptroller of the Currency closed ACB in October 1975. On August 30, 1976, the FDIC objected to the discharge of Nanz in bankruptcy, contending that Nanz and Lowry jointly had injured ACB by procuring the loans, and in December 1976 the FDIC similarly objected to the discharge of Herbert Cleveland, the other borrower—so by 1976 the FDIC was on the scent. Because the FDIC did not file this suit until February 1980, the Bank says it is too late under 28 U.S.C. §2415(b), which gives the United States only three years to begin litigation "founded upon a tort." This litigation is "founded," the Bank believes, on the fraud Nanz, Lowry, and Cleveland committed against ACB.

FDIC emphasizes in turn that the claim does not depend on *the Bank's* tort but sounds instead in "quasi-contract" or "unjust enrichment." The Bank got a benefit from the fraud of Nanz and Lowry; it would be unjust for the Bank to retain this benefit; hence there is an implied obligation to repay. If the basis of the claim is contractual, the FDIC may use 28 U.S.C. §2415(a):

> [E]very action for money damages brought by the United States or an officer or agency thereof which is founded upon any contract express or implied in law or fact, shall be barred unless the complaint is filed within six years after the right of action accrues.

Unjust enrichment claims are conceived as contracts implied in law. Even if the Bank is vicariously liable for Lowry's torts, the FDIC asserts that it may waive that remedy and pursue the quasi-contract claim, with its longer statute of limitations. Because even diligent investigation would not have informed ACB about the delicts more than six years before February 1980, the FDIC concludes that its suit is timely.

The district judge did not choose between §2415(a) and §2415(b) but concluded, unbidden by either party, that the suit is timely under Wisconsin law. The Bank contends on appeal, and the FDIC agrees, that federal law applies because this suit was filed by an "agency" of the United States. The district court's approach is untenable, and we must decide whether styling the claim "unjust enrichment" extends the period of limitations to six years.

We have considerable sympathy with the Bank's position. "Quasi-contract" allows the victim to follow the proceeds of the fraud, collecting them from the pocket in which they land, but does not change the gravamen of the wrong— here, fraud. No tort, no unjust enrichment. Because the FDIC could not have sued Nanz or Lowry more than three years after learning of their misdeeds, and because recovering "unjust enrichment" is simply a way to recoup the loss caused by the tort, it seems strange to think that a different caption on the pleadings, a demand against a person farther removed from the wrong, means a longer period of limitations. Unjust enrichment is a remedy in search of a wrong; as a remedy its period of limitations might logically be assimilated to that for the wrong.

Statutes of limitation frequently draw the same distinction as §2415 between tort and contract, providing a longer period for contracts. It is an historical accident that "unjust enrichment" is treated as part of contract. Long ago, when the forms of action ruled, English courts shoehorned restitution into the writ of *assumpsit*, indulging the (useful) fiction that the beneficiary had "agreed" to repay what it did not deserve to receive. English courts allowed victims to recover that which "natural justice" dictated the beneficiaries should not keep, Moses v. Macferlan, [1760] 97 Eng. Rep. 676 (Mansfield, L.J.), and American courts took over the concept as part of contract law, Prosser & Keeton on Torts §94 (5th ed. 1984). Still, the form of action from which unjust enrichment descended has no logical relation to the period of limitations.

Legislatures rarely give reasons for longer periods of limitations in contract cases (Congress, in particular, did not when enacting §2415), but it is not hard to see what the reasons might be. Contracts, ordinarily written, provide evidence that is apt to be more enduring than that in the run of tort cases; moreover, because most persons monitor the performance of their contracting partners, a breach will come to light quickly, and the parties can preserve evidence. Litigation six years later thus is apt to be more accurate than deferred litigation in tort cases. Legislatures also might believe that those who do not do what they voluntarily undertook should stand ready to make amends for longer periods than those who may be sued by strangers. Each of these grounds implies that unjust enrichment belongs with tort rather than with contract.

On first principles, then, the period of limitations for unjust enrichment actions should track that of the wrong. Two district judges have reached this conclusion for purposes of §2415(b). Blusal Meats, Inc. v. United States, 638 F. Supp. 824 (S.D.N.Y. 1986); United States v. Vicon Construction Co., 575 F. Supp. 1578 (S.D.N.Y. 1983). Unfortunately, however, first principles are the only support for this conclusion. For hundreds of years, courts in England and the United States have been doing things otherwise, and this conclusion is too well established to be overthrown. History has its claims:

> [I]f we consider the law of contract, we find it full of history. The distinctions between debt, covenant, and assumpsit are merely historical. The classification of certain obligations to pay money, imposed by law irrespective of any bargain as quasi contracts, is merely historical. The doctrine of consideration is merely historical.

Oliver Wendell Holmes, *The Path of the Law*, 10 Harv. L. Rev. 457 (1897), reprinted in Collected Legal Papers 192 (1920). History becomes the foundation of statutes such as §2415(b). When Congress uses words such as "any contract express or implied in law or fact," it uses a phrase with an established (maybe even understood) meaning, and to toss it away on the ground that it is "mere" history, and at war with instrumental considerations, is to revise the statute in the bargain.

No one doubts—though many regret—that the common law allowed the victim of a tort to elect the quasi-contract claim with its longer period of limitations. Voices have been raised in opposition, most prominently that of Arthur Linton Corbin, who thought the privilege to use the longer period of limitations a bit of historical fluff that could be blown away. *Waiver of Tort and Suit in Assumpsit*, 19 Yale L.J. 221, 234–38 (1910). Corbin and others huffed and puffed, but the detritus stayed just where it was. New York, the only important jurisdiction that had followed Corbin's view, reversed course in 1953. Dentists' Supply Co. v. Cornelius, 281 App. Div. 306, 119 N.Y.S.2d 570, affirmed without opinion, 306 N.Y. 624, 116 N.E.2d 238 (1953). So when Congress enacted §2415 in 1966, providing that suits "founded upon any contract express *or implied in law* or fact" could be brought within six years, such a provision had a definite meaning in common law jurisdictions. The statute was designed to put the United States as plaintiff on the same footing as private litigants. Because private litigants have been able to use the period of limitations for contracts ever since "unjust enrichment" landed in the "contract" cubbyhole in the seventeenth century, our contrary assessment does not justify a different result.

The two courts of appeals that have examined the question before us reached the conclusion that the United States may choose the six-year period in unjust enrichment cases. See United States v. P/B STCO 213, 756 F.2d 364, 374–76 (5th Cir. 1985); United States v. Neidorf, 522 F.2d 916 (9th Cir. 1975). *Blusal* and *Vicon*, the only cases going the other way under §2415, displayed no awareness of the history of this problem—or of the appellate decisions on the subject, for that matter. The FDIC unequivocally chose quasi-contract as the basis of its claim, jettisoning any hope for punitive damages. Its choice must be respected. So although we hold that federal law supplies the period of limitations, we agree with the district court's conclusion that the suit is timely.

Unjust enrichment is impossible without enrichment, and the Bank denies that it was enriched. True, it paid the certified check with the loaned funds, but Nanz kept on washing money through the account. Perhaps the Bank could have stopped payment, had the loan not been made, despite its "acceptance" of the instrument in advance by the act of certification, so long as the check had not passed to a holder in due course. See Farmers & Merchants State Bank v. Western Bank, 841 F.2d 1433 (9th Cir. 1987). Maybe the Bank could have dishonored other checks. In the end the Bank lost $250,000, and it asks us to conclude that as a matter of law it got no benefit.

Whether the Bank received a benefit is a factual question, which the jury resolved adversely to it. As happens too frequently in commercial litigation, the parties spent all of their energy on the merits and devoted little more than fulmination to damages. Here the FDIC simply pointed to the $500,000 and claimed it as the benefit. The Bank pointed to Nanz's control of the account and protested that there could have been no benefit. Forced to choose one of these two simplistic positions, the jury was entitled to select the FDIC's. In retrospect there were other options. Because the loans kept the kite aloft, one logical measure of the Bank's gain is the difference between its loss had things been wrapped up in January 1974 and its actual loss of $250,000 when the kite came apart in June. At oral argument we asked the parties what the record shows about the Bank's exposure had the kite come down on the date the $500,000 was deposited, and the Bank done the same kinds of things it did in June (such as not paying any item it had not irrevocably accepted). According to counsel, the record does not reveal this sum, because no one thought it important, although it does show that the negative balance when the $500,000 arrived in January was about $1.3 million. Perhaps, then, the Bank gained more than $500,000 by keeping Nanz in business; perhaps it gained less. Appellate courts do not reconstruct the case the parties should have litigated; they decide whether there was error in the case *as* litigated. The record in the case that was put before the jury supports its verdict.

"Waiver of tort"

1. The choice between alternative causes of action in tort and restitution can be highly significant for limitations purposes, and the problem is by no means restricted to the federal statute discussed in *FDIC v. Bank One.*

The explanation takes us back to the beginning of the story, when the emergence of the "common counts" in 18th-century pleading gave rise in some circumstances to an overlap between available causes of action. To take a simple example: Suppose that A steals B's horse (stipulated value $100), then sells it to C for $125. C disappears, taking the horse with him. But when B finds A, B has a choice of legal theories. An action in tort for conversion will yield $100 damages. But an action on one of the "common counts"—probably "money had and received"—gives B a claim to restitution of $125. Recovery was on the theory of a fictitious promise: "A stole my horse, then sold it, and promised to pay me the sale proceeds." The plaintiff's election of the quasi-contractual cause of action was called "waiver of tort and suit in assumpsit."

While the primary reason to choose restitution over tort damages is obviously the possibility of a greater recovery, a further advantage may be the expanded time for the plaintiff to bring suit. In most states, B's action in tort for conversion would be subject to a relatively short limitations period—typically two or three years. By contrast, B's action in restitution to recover the value of the horse will be governed by a longer period, often the one applicable to implied contracts—typically five or six years. This makes "waiver of tort" a way to expand the limitations period, even where the amount of recovery in tort and restitution would be the same. Does it make sense that a cause of action seeking what may be the same monetary relief, based on the same facts, should be either viable or time-barred depending on how it is pleaded?

> The fact that a statute of limitations includes no explicit provision for restitution claims presents a significant problem when plausible choices among the available classifications are subject to different limitations periods. The dilemma is most commonly associated with the election

made by a claimant who pursues an action in restitution for wrongs, a choice traditionally known as "waiver of tort." Liability in restitution in these circumstances is an alternative to liability for damages in tort, and the claimant will choose restitution when the wrongdoer's profits exceed the claimant's damages (or are easier to establish).

Commentators have long disagreed about the proper characterization of the claimant's election, which might be seen either as a choice between two overlapping theories of liability or as a choice of remedies for what is fundamentally a liability in tort. Here, in the one place where the distinction makes a practical difference, courts have adhered to the view that a claim in restitution asserts a separate cause of action, not subject (unless by coincidence) to the statute of limitations for tort claims. As a result, there are circumstances in which a dilatory tort plaintiff may avoid the relatively short period of limitations applicable to tort actions by choosing to designate the action as one in restitution. (The limitations period governing the restitution claim—typically characterized for limitations purposes as an action on an implied or unwritten contract—will almost certainly be longer.)

R3RUE §70, Comment *e*.

2. Judge Easterbrook says, "No tort, no enrichment," but it is not as simple as that. (He also says that "Unjust enrichment is a remedy in search of a wrong.") If the FDIC were suing Nanz and Lowry instead of the bank, it might be reasonable to say "there should not be two limitations periods for the same tort liability, depending on how the action is labeled." But the FDIC is not suing Nanz and Lowry in this case. Does the FDIC allege that FNB Waukesha committed a tort? Suppose we eliminate all fraud from the story: ACB made a mistake and transferred $500,000 to FNB Waukesha when that money was intended for someone else. Which of the limitations periods from 28 U.S.C. §2415 governs the FDIC's action to recover the mistaken payment?

Further notes on limitations and laches

1. Applying statutes of limitations to restitution cases can be a matter of some difficulty. There is often a threshold issue in deciding how to categorize a given restitution claim for limitations purposes. Because no U.S. jurisdiction has ever enacted a statute that limits "claims based on unjust enrichment," analysis normally depends on analogy and interpolation. Frequently an answer is found by treating restitution as a species of *implied contract*—part of the legacy of restitution's origins in the fictitious promises of the "common counts." Statutes of limitations in many jurisdictions include a category for "contracts not in writing," and garden-variety restitution claims for mistaken payments or unrequested services are often brought within a jurisdiction's

"miscellaneous contracts" rubric. Because the question depends on the local statute, however, the answers reached in different kinds of restitution cases differ widely from one jurisdiction to another. Some statutes specify a limitations period for claims based on fraud or mistake, or claims to recover real or personal property, or claims "not elsewhere classified"—all of which might be held to apply to restitution claims in particular cases.

2. Claims founded on unjust enrichment may be wholly or partly equitable in origin, and many remedies in restitution are obviously (or at least arguably) equitable as well. Statutes in a few jurisdictions include a specific reference to claims for equitable relief. But a nearly universal problem, which may or may not have a clear answer under local law, concerns the status of the equitable defense of laches vis-à-vis the statute of limitations.

The doctrine of laches, in a nutshell, is that a plaintiff whose unreasonable delay in bringing suit is prejudicial to the defendant may on that account be precluded from suit. Given equity's sensitivity to opportunism and unfair advantage-taking, the strongest examples of laches are those in which the delay in bringing suit is not only prejudicial to the defendant but calculated, speculative, or strategic on the part of the plaintiff. Certain restitution plaintiffs—such as parties who lie low and wait to see how prices develop, before deciding whether to ratify or rescind a voidable transaction—offer textbook examples of the conduct that laches is designed to frustrate.

The merger of law and equity has left it uncertain, in many jurisdictions, to what extent laches is still available as a separate defense—independent of the statute of limitations—to claims seeking equitable relief. Elsewhere it may be contended that in a merged court system the doctrine of laches should restrict legal and equitable claims without distinction—like the (formerly) equitable doctrine of unconscionability. Delay in asserting restitution claims is likely to test the possibilities of laches, either because the relief sought is unmistakably equitable (such as constructive trust) or because the remedy resists classification one way or the other (such as disgorgement of profits outside the context of express trusts). It is easy to find judicial statements to the effect that restitution in general is an equitable doctrine, but the student who has got this far will know that is not so.

3. Applying a statute of limitations requires the court to decide when a particular cause of action has *accrued*, subject to qualification in some cases by the equitable idea of "tolling." Restitution claims often originate in transactions that occur in a surprising or unexpected manner, and for this reason—perhaps—it can be more difficult to pin down the time when they "accrue" than with the usual claims for tort or breach of contract. If you owe me $100 a month and stop paying—and I fail to notice—my claim for your breach will be held to accrue month by month, and I will not be able to recover amounts that became due and payable more than the specified period before my action is commenced. By contrast, if you owe me $100 a month and (as a result of some computer malfunction) you begin paying me $200 a month—and I again fail to notice—is it equally clear that your claim for restitution should be held to

accrue month by month, with the result that you can only recover the over-payments that were made within the limitations period? Clear or not, such is the usual rule—as seen when the plaintiff in *Brookside Memorials* (Chapter 4) sought to recover its overpaid sewer taxes.

By contrast, there are cases of continuing, incremental enrichment in which a court may hold that the plaintiff's cause of action only accrues when the relationship between the parties is at an end. The issue is discussed at some length in the cohabitation case of *Maglica v. Maglica* (Chapter 5). Claire's claim in *quantum meruit* for the value of her services was subject to a two-year limitations period. She worked for Anthony for 22 years before bringing suit. Anthony argued that she could recover only for the last two years of employment; Claire naturally took the position that the limitations period only began to run upon termination. The court agreed with Claire, but it treated the question as a difficult one, which necessarily involved "parsing the exact nature of the circumstances in a particular case, since fine gradations can lead to wildly divergent results."

4. The last two aspects of the limitations problem (laches and accrual), and the potential relation between them, were illustrated by Petrella v. Metro-Goldwyn-Mayer, Inc., 134 S. Ct. 1962 (2014). The suit was for restitution: specifically, disgorgement of profits from copyright infringement, very much along the lines of *Sheldon v. MGM* (Chapter 7). In this case, however, the alleged infringement consisted in the production and distribution of a movie, *Raging Bull*, that had been released by MGM in 1980 and shown continually ever since. Not later than 1991, the plaintiff had become sole owner of the copyright in a screenplay which the film allegedly infringed; she filed suit for infringement in 2009. Copyright infringement is subject to a three-year statute of limitations, so the plaintiff sought a share of MGM's profits from *Raging Bull* since 2006. She had not sued earlier because "the film hadn't made money." Meanwhile MGM "had made a large investment in *Raging Bull*, believing it had complete ownership and control of the film."

MGM argued that these facts established laches on the part of the plaintiff, barring her suit without reference to its merits. Both the District Court and the Court of Appeals agreed. *Petrella*, 695 F.3d 946 (2012). The Supreme Court reversed. In the opinion of the majority, the inclusion in the Copyright Act of an explicit three-year limitation for infringement actions precluded any shortening of the "three-year window" during which—on this view—Congress had decreed that Petrella could recover a share of MGM's profits from infringement.

There was strong dissent in *Petrella*, and many readers will find it more persuasive on the question the Court was debating: namely, the applicability of the doctrine of laches to the viability of copyright claims. But neither the majority nor the dissenters in *Petrella* chose to question the rule of *accrual* that gave rise to the problem: a "separate-accrual rule" for copyright claims, according to which "when a defendant commits successive violations, the statute of limitations runs separately from each violation." Such a rule makes better sense in some cases than others. If a newspaper infringes my copyright by an unauthorized publication, then repeats its offense five years later, it is easy to conclude that I can bring suit within three years of the second publication, arguing that "each act of infringement is a distinct harm giving rise to an independent claim for relief." But it seems myopic to apply the same rule where the alleged infringement consists in the production and exhibition of a movie, resulting in countless "acts of infringement"—*e.g.*, in movie theaters, on television, over the internet—every day thereafter for the foreseeable future. The result of "separate accrual" in such a case is that the plaintiff's cause of action *never* accrues for limitations purposes until the plaintiff decides that it should—then selects the date of accrual, three years after the fact, by the filing of a complaint. That is not how statutes of limitation are supposed to work. Still, if this is really the proper interpretation of "separate accrual" for a case like *Petrella*, the need for a supplemental laches principle would appear all the more obvious.

F. "PAYABLE IN POINT OF HONOR AND HONESTY"

Moses v. Macferlan
2 Burr. 1005, 1010, 1012, 97 Eng. Rep. 676, 679, 680-81 (K.B. 1760)

MANSFIELD, L.J.

[The action "for money had and received"] is equally beneficial to the defendant. It is the most favourable way in which he can be sued: he can be liable no further than the money he has received; and against that, may go into every equitable defence, upon the general issue; he may claim every equitable allowance; he may prove a release without pleading it; in short, he may defend himself by every thing which shews that the plaintiff, ex aequo & bono, is not intitled to the whole of his demand, or to any part of it.

This kind of equitable action, to recover back money, which ought not in justice to be kept, is very beneficial, and therefore much encouraged. It lies only for money which, ex aequo et bono, the defendant ought to refund: it does not lie for money paid by the plaintiff, which is claimed of him as payable in point of honor and honesty, although it could not have been recovered from him by any course of law; as in payment of a debt barred by the Statute of Limitations, or contracted during his infancy, or to the extent of principal and legal interest upon an usurious contract, or, for money fairly lost at play: because in all these cases, the defendant may retain it with a safe conscience, though by positive law he was barred from recovering. But it lies for money paid by mistake; or upon a consideration which happens to fail; or for money got through imposition, (express, or implied;) or extortion; or oppression; or an undue advantage taken of the plaintiff's situation, contrary to laws made for the protection of persons under those circumstances.

In one word, the gist of this kind of action is, that the defendant, upon the circumstances of the case, is obliged by the ties of natural justice and equity to refund the money.

"Absence of enrichment" as an affirmative defense?

1. The complicated procedural history of Atlantic Coast Line R. Co. v. State of Florida, 295 U.S. 301 (1935), can be summarized as follows. Freight rates for the shipment of logs within Florida were alleged to be *too low*, resulting in "unjust discrimination" against interstate log shipments. The Interstate Commerce Commission conducted proceedings and ordered that the Florida rates be increased. Log shippers objected, and the Supreme Court eventually upheld their complaint: the order was vacated, because the Commission had not made the factual findings required by law. Florida rates went back down. The ICC reopened the matter and eventually reinstated its previous order—this time including the required findings. Log shippers sued railroads to recover the increased freight charges they had paid during the period in which the ICC's original (illegal) order had been in effect. Restitution was denied in an opinion by Justice Cardozo:

> A cause of action for restitution is a type of the broader cause of action for money had and received, a remedy which is equitable in origin and function. Moses v. Macferlan, 2 Burr. 1005; Bize v. Dickason, 1 Term Rep. 285 (K.B. 1786) (Mansfield, C.J.); Farmer v. Arundel, 2 Wm. Bl. 824; Kingston Bank v. Eltinge, 66 N.Y. 625. The claimant, to prevail, must show that the money was received in such circumstances that the possessor will give offense to equity and good conscience if permitted to retain it. The question no longer is whether the law would put him in possession of the money if the transaction were a new one. The question is whether the law will take it out of his possession after he has been able to collect it.

> By the time the present claim for restitution had been heard by the master and passed upon by the reviewing court, the Commission had cured the defects in the form of its earlier decision. During the years affected by the claim there existed in very truth the unjust discrimination against interstate commerce that the earlier decision had attempted to correct. If the processes of the law had been instantaneous or adequate, the attempt at correction would not have missed the mark. It was foiled through imperfections of form, through slips of procedure, as the sequel of events has shown them to be. Unjust discrimination against interstate commerce, "forbidden" by the statute, and there "declared to be unlawful," does not lose its unjust quality because the evil is without a remedy

until the Commission shall have spoken. . . . The blunders being now corrected, the verities of the transaction are revealed as they were from the beginning. We think the better view is that in the light of its present knowledge the court will stay its hand and leave the parties where it finds them.

The federal court by its inaction . . . does not undertake to say that the rates collected by the carrier were lawful in the sense that a suit would lie to recover them if credit had been given to the shipper and a balance were now unpaid. All that the federal court does is to announce that it will stand aloof. It discovers through the evidence submitted to the Commission and renewed in the present record that what was charged would have been lawful as well as fair if there had been no blunders of procedure, no administrative delays. Learning those things, it says no more than this, that, irrespective of legal rights and remedies, it will not intervene affirmatively, in the exercise of its equitable and discretionary powers, to change the status quo. This is not usurpation. It is not action of any kind. It is mere inaction and passivity in line with the historic attitude of courts of equity for centuries.

295 U.S. at 309-312, 314-315. What kind of restitution claim is shipper asserting against railroad, and why does it not succeed? How troubling is the paradox here? Cardozo acknowledges that the disputed rates would *not* be enforceable—even now—"if credit had been given to the shipper and a balance were now unpaid." The decision in *Atlantic Coast Line* was by a closely divided Court. Cardozo had the votes of Justices Butler, McReynolds, Sutherland, and Van Devanter. A dissenting opinion by Justice Roberts was supported by Chief Justice Hughes and Justices Brandeis and Stone.

2. The Restatement includes this illustration based on Buel v. Boughton, 2 Denio 91 (N.Y. Sup. Ct. 1846):

> A agrees to settle a debt by giving B a promissory note for $5,000, payable in two years with interest. By a clerical error, the note delivered by A to B omits any reference to interest. The note is thereafter negotiated by B to C, and by C to D, all parties acting in the mistaken belief that the note calls for payment of interest. At maturity, A pays D $5,000 plus accrued interest of $600. When he examines the canceled instrument, A discovers that interest was not due by its terms; whereupon A sues D to recover $600 as money paid by mistake.

R3RUE §62, Illustration 3. What result?

3. A bank is under no obligation to pay a forged check. If it recognizes the forgery it will naturally refuse to pay, and the holder of the worthless check has no rights against the bank. But if the bank pays by mistake, and the payee took the forged check for value and without notice, the bank has no claim in restitution against the payee. (The common-law rule comes from another of Lord

Mansfield's famous decisions—Price v. Neal, 3 Burr. 1354, 97 Eng. Rep. 871 (K.B. 1762)—now codified at U.C.C. §3-418. This was one of the extraneous points raised by the defendant in *Bank of Naperville v. Catalano* in Chapter 2.) Because the bank cannot charge the account on which the forged check purported to be drawn, the effect of the rule is to shift a loss from fraud from the innocent and mistaken holder to the innocent and mistaken bank.

A forged check for $50,000, purportedly drawn on an account at a New York bank, was made payable to a resident of Mexico. The innocent payee presented the check for payment in New York, and it was paid by mistake. When the bank learned the facts (doubtless from its customer), it advised the Mexican payee that his $50,000 check was a forgery. Under Mexican law—or so he believed—the payee would have been obliged to reimburse the bank. Acting under a mistake about his legal obligations, the honest payee sent the $50,000 back to the New York bank. The bank was delighted to get the money back. But when the payee learned from his New York lawyers that he had been under no obligation to repay the money, he asked them to sue the bank in restitution. How should they advise him? See Zechariah Chafee, Jr., Reissued Notes on Bills and Notes 122-123 (1943).

———————————————

Chapter 10

Priority

A. CLAIMANT V. CREDITOR IN INSOLVENCY

In re Berry
147 F. 208 (2d Cir. 1906)

COXE, Circuit Judge.

Raborg & Manice, during all the time in question, were brokers on the New York Stock Exchange and Berry & Co., the bankrupts, were also brokers on the Consolidated Stock Exchange, in the same city, and had an active speculative account with Raborg & Manice.

On November 11, 1904, by virtue of a sale of stock made by Raborg & Manice for Berry & Co., the latter received a credit of $2,675 on the books of the former and on the same day the money was paid over to Berry & Co. On November 14, 1904, through a mistake of the bookkeeper of Raborg & Manice, the said amount of $2,675 was again credited to Berry & Co., but the mistake was not discovered until after their failure, on November 26, 1904, when they made a general assignment for the benefit of their creditors. On the day previous, November 25th, between 2 and 3 o'clock in the afternoon, in response to a demand for "some money" by Berry & Co., Raborg & Manice, after consulting the books and learning from the bookkeeper that there was a balance of about $2,500 due, drew two checks for $1,000 and $500, respectively, and sent them by messenger to Berry & Co., who deposited them about 3 o'clock to their credit in the Hanover National Bank. On November 28, 1904, a petition in bankruptcy was filed against Berry & Co. by their creditors.

There is no dispute as to the fact that through a mistake in bookkeeping, growing out of the failure of Berry & Co. to deliver certificates on their stock sale which were a good delivery on the Stock Exchange, a credit of $2,675 was given them to which they were not entitled. Relying on this credit, the payment of $1,500 was made. The fact was that at the time the balance was the other way, Berry & Co. owing Raborg & Manice the sum of $139. Had the true situation been known the additional payment would not have been made. Stripped of all complications and entanglements we have this naked fact that Raborg & Manice by mistake paid Berry & Co. $1,500, which they did not owe and which Berry & Co. could not have retained without losing the respect of every honorable business man.

It is conceded on all hands that had not insolvency and bankruptcy intervened, Raborg & Manice could have recovered the money on an implied assumpsit in the event that Berry & Co. declined to return it after knowledge of the facts—a highly improbable contingency. Of course such an action would lie. On no possible theory could the retention of the money by Berry & Co. be justified; it was paid to them and received by them under mistake, both parties believing that Raborg & Manice owed the amount.

If $1,500 had been placed in a package by Raborg & Manice and delivered to a messenger with instructions to deposit it in their bank, and the messenger, by mistake, had delivered it to Berry & Co., it will hardly be pretended that the latter would acquire any title to the money, and yet the actual transaction in legal effect gave them no better right.

It is urged that to compel restitution now will work injustice to the general creditors of the bankrupts, but this contention loses sight of the fact that the money in dispute never belonged to the bankrupts, and their creditors, upon broad principles of equity, have no more right to it than if the transaction of November 25th had never taken place. If the trustees succeed on this appeal the creditors will receive $1,500, the equitable title to which was never in the bankrupts. There can be no doubt of the fact that the payment to Berry & Co. was a mistake and that by reason of this mistake the trustees have in their possession $1,500 which, otherwise, they would not have. The proposition that Raborg & Manice, who have done no wrong, shall be deprived of their property and that it shall be divided among creditors to whom it does not fairly belong, is not one that appeals to the conscience of a court of equity.

The rule invoked by the District Court is well stated by Judge Story:

> The receiving of money which consistently with conscience cannot be retained is in equity sufficient to raise a trust in favor of the party for whom or on whose account it was received. This is the governing principle in all such cases. And, therefore, whenever any interest arises, the true question is not whether money has been received by a party of which he could not have compelled the payment, but whether he can now, with a safe conscience, *ex aequo et bono* retain it. Illustrations of this doctrine are familiar in cases of money paid by accident, or mistake, or fraud. . . . . Still, however, there are many cases of this sort where it is indispensable to resort to courts of equity for adequate relief, and especially where the transactions are complicated, and a discovery from the defendant is requisite. Story Eq. Jurisp., vol. 2, Secs. 1255-1256.

See, also, Nat. Bank v. Ins. Co., 104 U.S. 54; Am. Sugar Ref. Co. v. Fancher, 145 N.Y. 552, 40 N.E. 206.

When the money was paid under a plain mistake of fact, equity impressed upon it a constructive trust which followed it through the bank and into the hands of the trustees.

The account of Berry & Co. was never overdrawn during the day of November 25th; there was as much as $5,000 to their credit during that day and at no time did the withdrawals reduce the balance below $1,500. It is true that large sums were checked out after the deposit of the $1,500, but the law presumes that the amounts withdrawn were not those impressed with the trust. In other words, so long as $1,500 remained in the bank the presumption is that it was the trust fund.

It is unnecessary to enter further into details of the bank's transactions subsequent to the failure; it is enough to say that as the final result of the bank's liquidation of the account $6,310.41 was delivered to the trustees in bankruptcy. But for the mistake of Raborg & Manice this sum would have been $4,810.31, which is all the bankrupts' creditors are entitled to. The $1,500 should be paid by the trustees to Raborg & Manice, its lawful owners.

The language of Judge Jenkins in Standard Oil Co. v. Hawkins, 74 F. 395 (7th Cir. 1896), is applicable to the present situation. At page 402 he says:

> Here the receiver is an officer of the law, having the assets *in custodia legis*. He has no interest in the fund, save to see that it shall be distributed among those entitled to it according to the highest principles of honesty and of equity. The assets of the bank received by him are, with respect to the question in hand, to be treated as an entirety. Those assets have been swelled by the property of the appellant wrongfully obtained by the bank, and which went into the possession of the receiver. That in the payment of dividends he has disbursed the actual money so received can make no difference, so long as assets remain out of which restitution can be made. The creditors have received that to which they were not entitled, and that which belonged to the appellant. If restitution be made out of the assets still remaining, the creditors will receive no less than that to which they were originally entitled, and the appellant will only receive that which was its due. To compass such a result is the highest equity, since otherwise the appellant will be deprived of its own, and the general creditors will receive that to which they have no right.

The order of the District Court is affirmed with costs.

Every honorable businessman?

1. "Stripped of all complications and entanglements," according to Judge Coxe, "we have this naked fact that Raborg & Manice by mistake paid Berry

& Co. $1,500, which they did not owe and which Berry & Co. could not have retained without losing the respect of every honorable business man." If Berry & Co. were still in business—honorable or not—would they even attempt to retain the money? According to Judge Jenkins, "the bankruptcy trustee has no interest in the fund, save to see that it shall be distributed among those entitled to it according to the highest principles of honesty and of equity." Is that what the trustee is doing here?

2. The court says that the case is the same as if Raborg's messenger had delivered by mistake a package containing $1,500 in identifiable currency. If that is true as a matter of law, why is it true? Would the "look and feel" of Raborg's restitution claim be different in the case of misdelivered cash, and (if so) should that make a difference in the result?

Owner v. tax collector

In James v. United States, 366 U.S. 213 (1961), the Supreme Court overruled earlier decisions to hold that embezzled funds would thereafter constitute taxable income to the embezzler in the year of embezzlement. Prior authority was to the contrary, and the Court held that its new ruling should have only prospective effect. This meant that Eugene C. James, a corrupt union official, had been wrongly convicted of evading tax on $738,000 in stolen funds—but future embezzlers would not escape tax liability.

Reaching this conclusion required the Court to circumvent a threshold paradox. IRC §61(a) defines "gross income" to mean "all income from whatever source derived." But the embezzler acquires no right whatever to the embezzled funds: they remain legally and equitably the property of the victim. In what sense do they constitute "income"? Loan proceeds are not "income" to the borrower. Conceding for the sake of argument, however, that "income" can be whatever Congress and the courts say it is, the interesting result of taxing the proceeds of embezzlement—or the proceeds of some other theft, extortion, or fraud—is the way it sets up a priority contest between the taxing authority and the owner of the misappropriated funds.

The facts of one representative case—Atlas, Inc. v. United States, 459 F. Supp. 1000 (D.N.D. 1978)—were stated as follows:

> On or about October 9, 1972, Mrs. Arlene Dohn, a bookkeeper for Atlas, Inc., began embezzling funds from Atlas. She continued to embezzle funds until her activities were discovered in October of 1975. During the period October 9, 1972 to October 10, 1975, Mrs. Dohn embezzled a total of $390,723.48 from Atlas. The funds were obtained by altering checks drawn on Atlas and depositing them in the personal checking account of Mrs. Dohn in the Dakota Northwestern Bank, Bismarck, North Dakota.

When Mrs. Dohn's activities were discovered, a lawsuit was started against her by Atlas in the Burleigh County District Court. Atlas prayed for judgment against Mrs. Dohn in the total of the embezzlement and further requested that a constructive trust be imposed on certain properties she had purchased through the use of embezzled funds. Among the properties Atlas sought to have a constructive trust imposed upon was the personal residence of Arlene Dohn. In conjunction with the action against Mrs. Dohn, a *lis pendens* was filed on October 12, 1975.

The house Mrs. Dohn lived in at the time of her employment by Atlas was purchased by her in December of 1967 for $19,700. She paid $2,400 down and financed the balance with the First Federal Savings and Loan Association, Bismarck, North Dakota. Mrs. Dohn made payments of $160 per month on the home and on September 27, 1972, the payment date immediately preceding her first embezzlement of funds, the balance due and owing on her house was $15,882.67. During the period she was embezzling funds from Atlas, Mrs. Dohn continued to make her monthly payments of $160 per month. On October 8, 1975, Mrs. Dohn paid to First Federal a personal check in the amount of $13,931.93. Of this amount, $13,849.35 went to pay off the principal due on the house at the time.

Based on a standard tracing analysis, the court concluded that monthly loan payments prior to this date were made from Mrs. Dohn's legitimate funds. By contrast, this final principal payment, as well as some improvements "including an expenditure of $5,465.51 for a cement patio and fence," had been made with embezzled funds.

On December 1, 1976, the Internal Revenue Service filed with the Burleigh County Register of Deeds a Notice of Federal Tax Lien under the Internal Revenue Laws. The amount of the lien was $220,757.49 and the tax liability arose because the funds that Mrs. Dohn embezzled from Atlas, Inc. were not declared by her as income.

On February 22, 1977, the District Court of Burleigh County entered judgment for Atlas and against Arlene Dohn for the sum of $289,546.70, and for a constructive trust on, among other properties, the home which is the subject matter of this lawsuit.

In this subsequent lawsuit, Atlas and the U.S. Treasury were asserting competing claims to Mrs. Dohn's house. Both sides seem to have assumed that the question involved a simple race to the Burleigh County courthouse. The government's Notice of Federal Tax Lien was filed after Atlas's notice of *lis pendens*, but before the entry of judgment in favor of Atlas against Mrs. Dohn. Which party's lien had priority?

The court held that a notice of *lis pendens* is not a judgment lien—so the tax lien came first—but that the lawyers had missed the forest for the trees. The real answer to the priority contest is in the federal tax lien statute, reading it more carefully:

If any person liable to pay any tax neglects or refuses to pay the same after demand, the amount (including any interest, additional amount, addition to tax, or assessable penalty, together with any costs that may accrue in addition thereto) shall be a lien in favor of the United States upon all property and rights to property, whether real or personal, *belonging to such person.* 26 U.S.C. §6321 (emphasis added).

1. Assuming that North Dakota law adheres to standard principles of restitution and unjust enrichment—and the court in *Atlas v. United States* said that it did—what is the proper resolution of the contest between Atlas and the U.S. Treasury?

2. Isn't there something extraordinary about this claim on the part of the Government? Embezzler is liable for income tax on embezzled funds. But Embezzler's principal asset has been acquired with the same embezzled funds that produced her tax liability. (This must have been evident by the time the tax was assessed.) Now the U.S. Treasury argues that its tax lien gives it a better claim to the asset than that of the embezzlement victim whose funds were demonstrably used to purchase the asset. What's wrong with this picture?

3. If Arlene Dohn had carefully segregated the proceeds of her embezzlement in a separate account at Dakota Northwestern Bank, and the embezzled funds were still sitting there untouched, would the Treasury be arguing that its tax lien on that bank account was superior to Atlas's claim to get its money back? If not, why not?

Osin v. Johnson
243 F.2d 653 (D.C. Cir. 1957)

BURGER, C.J.

Appellant, a woman of more than average business experience, agreed to sell a parcel of improved real estate to appellee Johnson and subsequently executed and delivered a deed, taking back a note for the full purchase price of $30,000. There was no down payment. Johnson represented to appellant that he would prepare, execute and record a trust on the property to secure his purchase money note.

After delivery of the deed to him, Johnson recorded the deed but did not prepare and record the trust instrument as he had promised appellant he would do. For this breach of faith and fraud Johnson was thereafter indicted, tried and convicted, and testimony in the criminal case forms part of the record in this case.

Without disclosing appellant's prior unrecorded lien against his title, Johnson borrowed $11,000 from appellee Perpetual Building Association, executing deeds of trust against the property. Later Johnson borrowed an additional $3,300 on second deeds of trust from appellee Glorius. Thereafter, creditors of Johnson obtained judgments which became liens on the real estate under D.C. Code §15-103 (1951 ed.).[1] When foreclosure proceedings were commenced under the trust deeds executed by Johnson, appellant brought this suit for equitable relief, joining the trust holders, with the judgment creditors of Johnson subsequently intervening.

The trial court properly heard the case without a jury since this suit was plainly addressed to the equity jurisdiction of the court. The trial judge found that appellant conveyed title to Johnson knowingly and in reliance on Johnson's assurances that he would record all the documents including the deed of trust which secured the purchase money note. Upon this finding the court concluded that appellee trust holders and judgment creditors had acquired interests in the property superior to that of appellant's unrecorded claim.

Appellant contends she did not knowingly execute and deliver the deed, and that Johnson fraudulently procured her signature on an instrument represented to be a sales contract. However, appellant's pre-litigation actions and letters expressly refute this contention and provide ample basis for the trial court's finding contrary to her testimony. Nor do we find merit in appellant's other allegations of error on the part of the trial court.

I

The trial court apparently did not consider whether Johnson's fraudulent conduct might give rise to the imposition of a constructive trust on the real estate in appellant's favor, although appellant's prayer for equitable relief, while not specifically requesting this remedy, was sufficiently broad to enable a court of equity to impress a trust upon the property.

A constructive trust is a purely equitable device which can be applied with great flexibility. It arises by operation of law from the occurrence of an unconscionable act for which no traditional relief is available. A constructive trust can be imposed wherever one unfairly holds title or a property interest and where the holder would be unjustly enriched if permitted to retain such interest. Specifically, the acquisition of property through the fraudulent misrepresentation of a material fact has been held sufficient grounds to fasten a constructive trust on the property. Howard v. Howe, 7 Cir., 1932, 61 F.2d 577. Since the District Court in the instant case found that appellant was induced to convey her title to the real estate by a fraudulent promise of Johnson that he would execute

---

1. "Every final judgment at common law . . . for the payment of money from the date when the same shall be rendered, every judgment of the municipal court when docketed in the clerk's office of the District Court . . . shall be a lien on all the freehold . . . estates, legal and equitable, of the defendants bound by such judgment . . . in any lands, tenements, or hereditaments in the District."

Appellant's Brief urges us to take judicial notice of certain facts of record in the cases of Umbricht v. Johnson, No. M-7187-55, Municipal Court of District of Columbia, and Hakim v. Johnson, No. 771-55, United States District Court for the District of Columbia, to wit: Umbricht sold Johnson an Oldsmobile car taking Johnson's note for $1,875, against which Johnson later paid $400. Hakim sold a Cadillac car to Johnson taking the latter's note for $4,500 upon which he later defaulted.

It would appear from the nature of these transactions that neither judgment creditor dealt with Johnson in reliance on the state of the record title as to the realty.

518
10. Priority

and record a deed of trust, the court could have properly considered whether, under all the circumstances, a constructive trust should have been imposed. It thus becomes necessary to consider whether the existence of a constructive trust would give appellant a superior claim to the interests of the trust holders and Johnson's judgment creditors, should it be found that a constructive trust exists.

II

We turn first to the holders of the first and second deeds of trust. Whatever the nature of appellant's interest, the District Court was correct in holding the fraud in the relationship between appellant and Johnson did not give appellant a claim superior to that of the trust holders who occupy the position of bona fide purchasers. Colorado Coal & Iron Co. v. United States, 1887, 123 U.S. 307, 314; Davison v. Morgan, 1931, 60 App. D.C. 161, 50 F.2d 311.

The record demonstrates, and the lower court so found, that the holders of the trust deeds were innocent purchasers for value without notice of appellant's prior equity, and thus they clearly fall within the purview of the recording act, D.C. Code, §45-501 (1951 ed.), protecting bona fide purchasers against unrecorded conveyances.[2] The logical and rational basis for preferring the bona fide purchaser over the grantor of the record title holder is that as between two innocent parties, *i.e.*, appellant and the bona fide lenders such as Perpetual and other trust holders, appellant must yield to those who in good faith relied on the state of the record which her negligence allowed to exist. It would manifestly defeat the whole point of recording statutes to permit Mrs. Osin to assert her admitted equities at the expense of those who relied in good faith on a state of the record title which her acts created.

Even in the absence of recording acts or, as discussed under point III *infra*, if the recording statute is inapplicable, a bona fide purchaser's rights have always been held superior to prior equitable interests. A purchaser for value, without notice of the facts which lead to the creation of a constructive trust, will cut off the trust beneficiary's rights. Restatement, Restitution, §172 (1937); 4 Scott, Trusts §468 (2d ed. 1956). Therefore, the holders of the deeds of trust would prevail over appellant even if a constructive trust were to be imposed on the property.

III

The same rationale does not have equal validity when applied to judgment creditors of the fraudulent grantee. A judgment creditor possessing a statutory

---

2. "Any deed conveying real property in the District, or interest therein, executed and acknowledged and certified as provided . . . and delivered to the person in whose favor the same is executed, shall be held to take effect from the date of the delivery thereof, except that as to creditors and subsequent bona fide purchasers and mortgagees without notice of said deed, and others interested in said property, it shall only take effect from the time of its delivery to the recorder of deeds for record." D.C. Code, §45-601 (1951 ed.) provides that deeds of trust are to be recorded and to take effect as against "bona fide purchasers and mortgagees and creditors" in the same manner as absolute deeds under §45-501.

lien on property does not occupy a position equivalent to that of a purchaser for value and thus "if the land of the debtor is subject to equities, the judgment creditor's lien is subject to such equities." 3 Scott, Trusts §308.1 (2d ed. 1956). See also Restatement, Restitution §173, comment *j* (1937); [R3RUE §60]. As a matter of simple ordinary fairness, which is the essence of equity, there is every reason why a defrauded grantor of title should command a higher priority than creditors of the fraudulent grantee, since such creditors usually do not rely on the record title in their extension of credit. The equitable considerations dictating the priority of an equitable right over subsequently acquired judgment liens was aptly summarized by this court many years ago:

> Unless precluded by the terms of some statute expressly intended to change it, the rule has always prevailed that the equity under a trust or a contract *in rem* is superior to that under a judgment lien. The claimant under the contract *in rem* has an equity to the specific thing which binds the conscience of his grantor; whilst the judgment creditor, who has advanced nothing on the faith of the specific thing, is entitled only to that which his debtor really has, at the time, or could honestly convey or encumber; his beneficial interest and nothing more. Hume v. Riggs, 1898, 12 App. D.C. 355, 367.

The appellee judgment creditors, however, point to the recording acts as altering the equitable rule and giving them a preference over appellant's unrecorded interest. This jurisdiction, like approximately half of the states, has adopted a recording statute which specifically lists "creditors" among those classes given precedence to prior interests not recorded. Despite early intimations to the contrary, it is now well settled that the statutory reference to "creditors" includes a good faith judgment creditor holding a statutory lien obtained under D.C. Code, §15-103. Thus, as to instruments required to be recorded and capable of being recorded, the recording act elevates a judgment creditor to the same legal plane as a bona fide purchaser for value.

But since the preference accorded a judgment lien depends upon the statute, it extends only to such interests as the statute requires to be recorded. It has long been acknowledged that recording acts similar to that enacted in the District of Columbia do not apply to interests incapable of record. Where an equitable interest is not created by a written instrument or conveyance but rather arises by operation of law, such an interest "is not within the statute and is not subject to the lien of a judgment (creditor)." 2 Freeman, Judgments 2043 (5th ed. 1925). Other jurisdictions have recognized that a constructive trust, by its nature not susceptible of record, is not within the reach of recording acts and thus retains priority over judgment liens. In re Rosenberg, D.C.S.D. Tex. 1925, 4 F.2d 581; East St. Louis Lumber Co. v. Schnipper, 1923, 310 Ill. 150, 141 N.E. 542; School District No. 10 v. Peterson, 1898, 74 Minn. 122, 76 N.W. 1126.

This jurisdiction has never passed directly on the question whether a creditor holding a statutory lien takes preference over an earlier equity incapable of being recorded. In American Savings Bank v. Eisminger, 1910, 35 App. D.C. 51, this court held the lien of a judgment creditor equal to the lien of a bona fide purchaser and thus superior to any secret trust *capable of being recorded*, but not so recorded. This qualification of recordability was carefully and precisely delineated by the court by repetition in these words: "We say, trust capable of being placed upon record, for that is the case here. *Whether* a resulting or constructive trust, *incapable of record*, and in the assertion of which there has been no laches, would yield to the lien also, *we intimate no opinion.*" *Id.* at 55 (emphasis added). The case now before us gives rise to precisely the possible situation envisaged by this court in the *American Savings Bank* case and as to which the court would then "intimate no opinion." We say "possible situation" for it is not the function of this court to resolve whether the facts warrant the imposition of a constructive trust, since appellant failed to point out the possibility of such a course to the District Court. We decide only the question pointedly left open in *American Savings Bank v. Eisminger, supra.* For the reasons indicated above, and in line with the authority cited, we now supply that gap and hold if a new trial discloses (1) a constructive trust inherently incapable of recording and (2) no laches on the part of appellant in the assertion of her rights, that in such case Mrs. Osin's constructive trust will have priority over the judgment creditors of Johnson. But we qualify the above holding to this extent: a judgment creditor who is able to show affirmative reliance on the state of the record without notice of any infirmity should be entitled to the same standing as a bona fide purchaser. See 2 Freeman, Judgments 2043-44 (5th ed. 1925). Thus if a judgment creditor can satisfy the District Court that he, like the trust holders, extended credit on faith of Johnson's record title, he should be entitled to the same priority enjoyed by other bona fide purchasers, unless when the debt arose he had actual or constructive notice of Johnson's fraud on Mrs. Osin. D.C. Code, §45-501 (1951 ed.).

The judgment of the District Court also provided that appellant could elect to take a reconveyance of the property upon her returning to Johnson (for the benefit of Johnson's judgment creditors) the $680 Johnson had paid appellant on his purchase money note. We think that part of the judgment should be vacated and the ultimate disposition of the $680 abide the determination of the equities on a new trial.

The judgment below is affirmed as to the trust holders, Perpetual Building Association, Glorius, et al.; reversed as to the intervenor judgment creditors Hakim and Umbricht; and the case is remanded for further proceedings.

Common-law priority

1. The classic priority contest in restitution, litigated countless times over the centuries, pits a restitution claimant (such as a fraud victim) against a judicial lien creditor of the claimant's transferee. Traditional analysis turns on the analogy discussed in *Osin v. Johnson.* Is a judicial lien creditor enough like a

bona fide purchaser to merit the same protection against latent defects in the transferee/debtor's apparent title? If not, why not? Judge Burger gives a concise statement of an answer that 19th-century courts gave at greater length:

> The well-settled and only ground upon which a person dealing with the holder of the title of real estate subject to a secret trust, of which he has no notice, is permitted to obtain from him a title clear of the trust is that he parts with something of value on the strength of the apparent ownership of the land. This is the very essence of the doctrine of bona fide purchaser. The rule is universal in equity that, in order to constitute a person a bona fide purchaser for value, he must have parted with something either in the way of money or valuable thing, or of a right of action, or have given up some lien which he already had, or assumed some new obligation. He must have altered his position irretrievably in "actual reliance" upon the apparent title of the other party to a particular piece of property.
>
> Now, a mere judgment creditor is not clothed with this armor. He has parted with nothing on the strength of the apparent title of his debtor in any particular parcel of property. Such apparent ownership has not misled him to his injury. He may be disappointed, but mere disappointment does not amount, in legal contemplation, to injury. In the case in hand it appears affirmatively that neither of the creditors knew that the debtor had the title to this land until after they had obtained judgment. But if they had acquired such knowledge previous to the credit, or to bringing suit on their debts, the situation and rights of the parties would not be changed, for the mere giving general credit on the strength of the apparent ownership of the property does not constitute one a bona fide purchaser. Nor does the incurring the expense of a suit at law create an estoppel.

Harney v. First Nat'l Bank of Jersey City, 52 N.J. Eq. 697, 704, 29 A. 221, 224 (Ch. 1894) (Pitney, V.C.).

> If anything is settled by reason and authority, it is, that a judgment-creditor is not entitled to the protection of a purchaser of the legal title against an equitable owner or his creditors, or to any advantage which his debtor had not. . . . Doubtless, a dealer on credit is influenced by the magnitude of the debtor's visible means of payment; but it follows not, that he trusts particularly to the land, for there often is none; nor is it usual, where a mortgage is not taken for a loan, to search the office for incumbrances, or inquire into the solidity of the ostensible ownership. In the ordinary course of dealing, the creditor looks to the debtor's personal ability, and to nothing else. When he looks to real security, he takes a mortgage, which, alone, if the title be not plainly an inchoate one, makes him a purchaser of the beneficial ownership, discharged of all secret trusts or frauds whatever.

Reed's Appeal, 13 Pa. 475, 478 (1850) (Gibson, C.J.).

2. Remember that the creditors primarily involved in these priority contests are *general* (*i.e., unsecured*) creditors. They are called "judicial lien creditors" to distinguish them from the secured creditors who hold "consensual" liens. A voluntary transfer by which one party grants another a security interest is a transaction of purchase, and a secured creditor who acquires that interest for value without notice is a bona fide purchaser.

Because a bona fide purchaser takes the property free of prior equities (like restitution claims), a perfected security interest acquired from the debtor is immune from adverse claims that would have been good against the debtor himself. This basic bfp idea is combined with a basic idea about liens: namely, that a lien can only attach to the property of the debtor, as opposed to property of someone else.

Combining these ideas yields the three levels of priority that we see in *Osin v. Johnson:* (1) the "trust holders" or mortgagees (like Perpetual Building Association), as bona fide purchasers; (2) Mrs. Osin, as equitable owner; (3) unsecured creditors, whose claim is against the "actual estate" of their debtor (Johnson), whatever it might be.

3. *Harney* and *Reed's Appeal* (quoted in Note 1) suggest that an unsecured creditor—in deciding to extend credit to the debtor—is unlikely to have relied on the debtor's apparent ownership of the property subject to judicial lien. But what if a judgment creditor could show that he *had* dealt with the debtor in reliance on record title—or merely on the debtor's ostensible ownership of the asset that is the subject of the adverse claim? According to Vice-Chancellor Pitney, "the mere giving general credit on the strength of the apparent ownership of the property does not constitute one a bona fide purchaser." But it might constitute a change of position, giving that creditor an equivalent defense against prior equities. If the modern tests of bona fide purchase—in particular, the requirement of value—constitute a formal proxy for the harder-to-prove fact of change of position, a defendant who can prove an actual change of position should presumably receive the same protection. See R3RUE §60, Comment *d.*

4. The lien creditors in *Osin v. Johnson* sought protection in the local recording act. (The provisions of these acts vary significantly, but the D.C. statute quoted in a footnote makes a typical example.) At a high-enough level of generality, the attempt is understandable, because the recording act in most jurisdictions allows both lien creditors and bona fide purchasers to enforce rights against property their transferor/debtor did not actually own.

The usual setting in which the recording acts yield that result, however, involves an unrecorded conveyance by the debtor. Debtor owns Blackacre. He sells it to Purchaser, but neither party records the transaction. Debtor stops paying his bills, and Creditor obtains a judgment against him. Entry of this judgment gives Creditor a lien on (let's suppose) all of Debtor's real property within the jurisdiction. Because Blackacre has already been sold, Debtor owns no real property—and this is certainly the result as against Purchaser and anyone else not protected by statute. But the result of the D.C. recording act is that Debtor's unrecorded conveyance is ineffective against Creditor. Creditor's lien attaches to Blackacre, even though it was no longer part of Debtor's "actual estate."

By contrast, the only "deed conveying real property in the District" in *Osin v. Johnson* is the one that Mrs. Osin gave Mr. Johnson. Do the judgment creditors want this deed to be effective or ineffective?

> Although the details of [state recording acts] vary significantly among jurisdictions, they have a common core, to the effect that a conveyance of an interest in real property is not effective against protected third parties until notice has been given by recording in the manner prescribed. The immediate effect of such provisions is to displace the common-law rule of "first in time" by subordinating the interests created by an unrecorded prior conveyance.
>
> Analogous rules are applied to unperfected security interests in personal property by U.C.C. §9-317 (rev. 2000). Comparable provisions appear in statutes requiring the recording or registration of interests in property of particular kinds (such as certificates of title for motor vehicles).
>
> Notwithstanding their evident importance in other contexts, the transaction that underlies a typical restitution claim will frequently be outside the scope of standard recording-act provisions. These provide, in essence, that an unperfected conveyance by Grantor to Grantee is not binding on subsequent purchasers from Grantor or on Grantor's creditors. But when the contest over priority is between a restitution claimant and a lien creditor, the position of the contestants is normally reversed. Thus if the unperfected conveyance from Grantor to Grantee is the result of Grantee's fraud, it is Grantor (the restitution claimant) who seeks to avoid the transaction, while it is Grantee's lien creditors who seek to confirm it. The language of a typical recording act will not accommodate such a claim.

R3RUE §60, Comment *e*.

Restitution in bankruptcy

Issues of priority along the lines discussed will usually arise in bankruptcy—as they did in *Berry*. On one view of the matter, probably the best one, this changes nothing. Bankruptcy tells us how the various claims against the debtor's assets are administered, but state law tells us what the debtor's assets are.

That last observation is merely a truism of bankruptcy law, though a very important one:

> Property interests are created and defined by state law. Unless some federal interests requires a different result, there is no reason why such interests should be analyzed differently simply because an interested party is involved in a bankruptcy proceeding.

Butner v. United States, 440 U.S. 48, 55 (1979). In restitution cases, however, the idea of starting with state-created property law to decide what the debtor owns—in other words, using state law to identify the "bankruptcy estate" in the hands of the bankruptcy trustee—is something that many lawyers find unfamiliar. As a direct result of this professional unfamiliarity, the status of restitution claims in bankruptcy is frequently more precarious than it ought to be.

There are two reasons for this state of affairs. When a restitution claimant like Raborg & Manice asserts an "adverse claim" to assets in the possession of the bankrupt debtor—assets that the trustee wants to use to pay the general creditors—the property interests being asserted tend to be equitable in origin. Equitable interests in property, along with the remedies by which they are vindicated (constructive trust, equitable lien, reformation, and so forth), occupy a part of the legal landscape that largely disappeared from view when the separate equity jurisdiction was abandoned and law schools stopped teaching the subject. Thus when a restitution claimant appears on the scene in a bankruptcy case, the claim he asserts—to take the *Berry* example, "those funds in the debtor's bank account are subject to a constructive trust in my favor"—is often unfamiliar and therefore suspect from the trustee/creditor point of view.

A related reason is the modern role of a statute like the Bankruptcy Code. Lawyers in a complex, predominantly statutory field like bankruptcy come to expect that all the law they need to do their jobs will be set forth in the relevant statute. This is an error leading to an important *non sequitur*: the supposition that a claim not described in the statute is presumptively illegitimate. But the Bankruptcy Code and its direct antecedents made no attempt to codify a great deal of law (meaning "law and equity") that is relevant to bankruptcy cases. In particular, the state law that defines property interests—including the elusive equitable ones—is something that judges and lawyers were supposed to have learned elsewhere. References to equitable interests can be discerned in the Code, but unless the reader already understands what these interests are and how they work, the statutory references can be baffling. This is because the Code and its antecedents were written by and for American lawyers whose legal education was very different from what it is today.

Among the many Code sections potentially relevant to cases of restitution in bankruptcy, two are invoked most frequently. The following excerpts include only the most directly relevant language:

§541. PROPERTY OF THE ESTATE

(a) The commencement of a [bankruptcy case] creates an estate. Such estate is comprised of all the following property, wherever located and by whomever held:

(1) [Subject to exceptions not relevant here], all legal or equitable interests of the debtor in property as of the commencement of the case.

. . .

(d) Property in which the debtor holds, as of the commencement of the case, only legal title and not an equitable interest, such as a mortgage secured by real property, or an interest in such a mortgage, sold by the debtor but as to which the debtor retains legal title to service or supervise the servicing of such mortgage or interest, becomes property of the estate under subsection (a)(1) . . . of this section only to the extent of the debtor's legal title to such property, but not to the extent of any equitable interest in such property that the debtor does not hold.

---

§544. TRUSTEE AS LIEN CREDITOR AND AS SUCCESSOR TO CERTAIN CREDITORS AND PURCHASERS

(a) The trustee shall have, as of the commencement of the case, and without regard to any knowledge of the trustee or of any creditor, the rights and powers of, or may avoid any transfer of property of the debtor or any obligation incurred by the debtor that is voidable by—

(1) a creditor that extends credit to the debtor at the time of the commencement of the case, and that obtains, at such time and with respect to such credit, a judicial lien on all property on which a creditor on a simple contract could have obtained such a judicial lien, whether or not such a creditor exists;

(2) a creditor that extends credit to the debtor at the time of the commencement of the case, and obtains, at such time and with respect to such credit, an execution against the debtor that is returned unsatisfied at such time, whether or not such a creditor exists; or

(3) a bona fide purchaser of real property, other than fixtures, from the debtor, against whom applicable law permits such transfer to be perfected, that obtains the status of a bona fide purchaser and has perfected such transfer at the time of the commencement of the case, whether or not such a purchaser exists.

---

1. What is the relation between these Bankruptcy Code sections and the common-law-and-equity principles previously observed? In particular: How does the language of §541(a) accommodate the results of *Berry* and *Osin v. Johnson*? Does §541(d) add anything to what is already stated in §541(a)? How might we explain the addition of this superfluous language to the Bankruptcy Code of 1978?

2. Section 544, known as the "strong-arm clause," is traditionally described by saying that it gives the trustee the rights of an "ideal lien creditor." (The

standard explanation is that giving the trustee that status on behalf of all unsecured creditors avoids a wasteful "race to the courthouse" between the creditors individually, putting them all on the same footing at the commencement of the bankruptcy case.) Subsections 544(a)(1) & (2) merely describe different ways of obtaining a judicial lien at state law.

Some courts worry about a perceived "tension" between §§541(d) and 544(a), suggesting that §541(d) excludes certain property from the bankruptcy estate while §544(a) brings in property the debtor did not own. What is the clearest example of a situation in which a trustee (as ideal lien creditor) can indeed reach property the debtor did not own at the commencement of the bankruptcy case? Recall the preceding discussion of the recording acts. Compare UCC §9-317(a)(2) (lien creditor takes free of unperfected security interest) and §9-102(52) (bankruptcy trustee is a lien creditor).

Does an ideal lien creditor obtain priority over a restitution claimant in a case like *Berry* or *Osin v. Johnson*?

3. As we have seen in the preceding Chapter, a bona fide purchaser (within traditional equity doctrine) takes property free of "prior equities" generally — in particular, free of asset-based claims in restitution. By contrast, a lien creditor's rights — unless enlarged by statute — reach only what the debtor has. Long before the appearance of the words "bona fide purchaser" in what is now Code §544(a)(3), trustees in bankruptcy sometimes sought the more favorable status of bona fide purchasers in an attempt to avoid valid restitution claims against property in the hands of the debtor. So long as basic equity doctrines were familiar to the legal profession, these attempts were uniformly rejected. In Zartman v. First Nat'l Bank of Waterloo, N.Y., 216 U.S. 134, 135 (1910), a case in which the adverse claimant sought reformation for mistake, the Supreme Court explained:

> The trustee claims that he takes the same kind of title as a bona fide purchaser for value; but the rule applicable to this and all similar cases is that the trustee takes the property of the bankrupt, not as an innocent purchaser, but as the debtor had it at the time of the petition, subject to all valid claims, liens, and equities.

That observation was a commonplace for which the Supreme Court might have cited a wealth of authority:

> [W]e understand it to be the established doctrine, both in England and in this country, that assignees in insolvency or bankruptcy . . . take only the debtor's rights, and, consequently, are affected with all claims, liens, and equities which would affect the debtor if he himself were asserting his interest in the property.

Ryder v. Ryder, 19 R.I. 188, 192, 32 A. 919, 921 (1895). As eventually reformulated by the leading bankruptcy treatise, it was understood that the trustee is not a bona fide purchaser. He stands in the shoes of the bankrupt subject to all the valid liens, claims and equities that existed against the bankrupt, and has no higher or better right except as given him [by statute].

4B Collier on Bankruptcy ¶ 70.62, at 690 (14th ed. 1978).

4. Subsection §544(a)(3) was a new addition to the Bankruptcy Code of 1978, and it has caused trouble ever since—largely because of its poor draftsmanship, but also because lawyers lose sight of the forest for the trees. Does it mean—at least with respect to real property—that the trustee acquires the ownership rights he would have if he had purchased the property from the debtor for value without notice? This would eliminate restitution claims in bankruptcy seeking to recover real (though not personal) property transferred by the debtor's fraud or the claimant's mistake. It would also wipe out the beneficial ownership of real (though not personal) property held by the debtor subject to an express trust. The Restatement describes the problem as follows:

> The scope of the strong-arm power has been more difficult to define since 1978. Bankruptcy Code §544(a)(3) gives the trustee—in addition to the existing status of an ideal lien creditor—certain attributes of "a bona fide purchaser of real property . . . from the debtor." The extent of this protection, or (to put it differently) the purpose for which the trustee is accorded the status of bona fide purchaser, has been disputed, and if the language of the statute is considered out of context the question may appear difficult. The various ramifications of the problem yield two fundamental alternatives.
>
> The more conservative approach reads the trustee's hypothetical status as bona fide purchaser of real property in conjunction with the trustee's power to "avoid any transfer of property of the debtor" (Bankruptcy Code §544(a)). This means that the strong-arm clause must still be primarily understood—insofar as it relates to real property—with reference to the state recording acts. Most (perhaps all) such statutes protect lien creditors against unperfected conveyances of real property by the debtor, but in some states the lien creditor's protection depends on judicial interpretation. By contrast, every recording act gives this protection by its terms to purchasers for value without notice. Because lien creditors are uniformly protected against unperfected security interests in personal property (U.C.C. §9-317(a)(2) (rev. 2000)), the result on this approach is to equalize the treatment of real and personal property in bankruptcy. On this interpretation the post-1978 strong-arm clause is fully consistent with the rules of priority established at state law and described in this section.
>
> The more radical alternative reads §544(a)(3) to give the bankruptcy trustee the status accorded to a bona fide purchaser of real property, not by the recording statutes, but by traditional equity doctrine: in other words, to give the trustee the rights described in §66 of this Restatement. The consequence would be that the trustee takes real (though not personal)

property of the debtor free not only of unperfected conveyances by the debtor, but of all equitable interests to which the property was subject in the debtor's hands. So interpreted, the hypothetical status of bona fide purchaser allows the trustee to claim unencumbered title to real property held by the debtor in express trust; or conveyed to the debtor by a breach of trust in which the debtor was complicit; or obtained as a result of the grantor's mistake or the debtor's fraud. On this reading, the post-1978 strong-arm clause overturns a uniform rule of state property law (though it does so only with respect to real, not personal, property): namely, that the rights of the judgment creditor may not exceed the rights of the judgment debtor, except insofar as the creditor may be protected by statute against unrecorded conveyances by the judgment debtor.

To recapitulate, the first interpretation of §544(a)(3) is fully consistent with state law governing priority between restitution claimants and judgment creditors, and its effect is to ensure uniform treatment of real and personal property. The second interpretation overturns state law on this subject, though as regards real but not personal property. If the Bankruptcy Code is interpreted to be consistent, so far as possible, with property rights created by state law, the trustee's status as a hypothetical bona fide purchaser of real property is explained by reference to the power to "avoid any transfer of property of the debtor."

R3RUE §60, Comment *f*.

B. DISPLACEMENT BY STATUTE: BANKRUPTCY CODE

XL/Datacomp, Inc. v. Wilson (In re Omegas Group, Inc.)
16 F.3d 1443 (6th Cir. 1994)

BATCHELDER, Circuit Judge.

Understandably, creditors of bankrupt debtors often feel like restaurant patrons who not only hate the food, but think the portions are too small. To press the analogy, they also don't like having to wait in line for a table, possibly being seated only to find out the kitchen has just closed. The bankruptcy court is a little like a soup kitchen, ladling out whatever is available in ratable portions to those standing in line; nonetheless, scarcity begets innovation in the hungry creditor's quest to get a little more than the next fellow. This case involves just such an effort. The creditor claimed the debtor defrauded it, and argued before the bankruptcy court, with partial success, that money paid to the debtor in the course of a business transaction was held in constructive trust since the debtor knew bankruptcy was imminent but assured the creditor otherwise. The district court agreed with this disposition. Since we hold that the bankruptcy court erred in applying the law of constructive trust to this bankruptcy situation, we reverse.

[Omegas Group, the debtor in this bankruptcy proceeding, acquired computers from IBM as a "middleman" and resold them to Datacomp, retaining a commission. These resale arrangements may have violated the contractual relationship between Omegas Group and IBM, but Omegas was facing extreme financial difficulties and was apparently ready to cut corners. When Omegas's situation deteriorated still further, accounts between Datacomp and Omegas grew increasingly complex and contentious. In August and September 1990, Datacomp paid Omegas some $1.1 million for computers that were never delivered.]

Omegas filed bankruptcy on October 16, 1990. Datacomp filed its complaint in this adversary proceeding in the bankruptcy court on October 26, 1990, seeking to recover the $1.1 million it paid Omegas by arguing that Omegas's fraud rendered all money it received pursuant to the deal subject to a constructive trust in Datacomp's favor, and thus not part of the bankruptcy estate, citing 11 U.S.C. §541(d).

After an expedited bench trial, the bankruptcy court held that Datacomp could recover $302,142 as held in a constructive trust by Omegas. In short, the bankruptcy court found that Datacomp entered into the agreement described above with Omegas, establishing a relationship which it characterized as "in a sense a joint venture," and that things went more or less according to plan for a while. The court found, however, that on September 12, 1990, Jeffery Sanford, the president of Omegas, "realized he was in serious financial straits with IBM" and that Omegas would not be able to complete the deal. The court concluded that on September 12, "Sanford realized that Omegas was not going to be able to operate in its ordinary course of business with regard to its dealings with Datacomp," and that this development gave rise to an affirmative "duty to disclose its financial problems to Datacomp." The court therefore imposed a constructive trust on "all funds received [by Omegas] after September 12." [The district court affirmed.]

On appeal, Datacomp defends the judgment of the bankruptcy court, but argues that the court should have imposed the constructive trust on the entire amount of funds it tendered to Omegas prior to Omegas's filing for bankruptcy. Under Kentucky law, Datacomp contends, money "wrongfully" appropriated from an innocent party does not become the property of the recipient, but is considered to be held in constructive trust for the benefit of the aggrieved party. Datacomp maintains that it did not have merely a debtor/creditor relationship with Omegas, but a joint venture arrangement that imposed fiduciary duties on Omegas, which Omegas breached. From the start, Omegas misrepresented its financial state and its ability to provide Datacomp with the computers it wanted; as its situation worsened and IBM made it crystal clear that no more computers would be forthcoming, Datacomp asserts, Omegas made no effort to inform Datacomp of the impending disaster, knowing all the while that Datacomp would continue in good faith to send its checks on time. Datacomp points out that the Bankruptcy Code provides that "[p]roperty in which the debtor holds . . . only legal title and not an equitable interest . . . becomes property of the estate . . . only to the extent of the debtor's legal title to such property, but not to the extent of any equitable interest in such property that the debtor does not hold." 11 U.S.C. §541(d). Datacomp argues that since by definition it has an equity interest in any funds held by Omegas in constructive trust, these funds are properly designated as remaining outside the bankrupt estate, and should therefore be returned to Datacomp rather than being incorporated into the estate and divided amongst the creditors.

Omegas, on the other hand, thinks its situation prior to bankruptcy was no different from that of the typical business threatened with insolvency. By the time its principals recognized that Omegas was sinking faster than they could bail, Omegas could not return Datacomp's money or take other action to avoid immediate loss to its other creditors due to the Bankruptcy Code's prohibition of preferential transfers immediately prior to filing for bankruptcy. Omegas denies that its principals committed fraud on Datacomp; instead, it maintains that all its people did was to try, in good faith, to salvage the deal until the last possible moment, and only then take prudent measures, as advised by counsel, to prepare for bankruptcy. To characterize this as fraud giving rise to a constructive trust, Omegas argues, does not comport with the Bankruptcy Code's system of equitable and orderly distribution of the debtor's assets; Omegas claims that Datacomp is not materially different from any other disappointed creditor.

Omegas also argues that the fishy nature of Datacomp's attempt to keep getting IBM computers at a favorable rate [through Omegas] renders Datacomp's hands "unclean," thus preventing it from seeking the equitable remedy of constructive trust. Datacomp also knew about the straits Omegas was in, the Debtor contends; Datacomp took advantage of this knowledge in getting Omegas to agree to this "clandestine relationship," but also knowingly assumed the obvious risk that Omegas might fold before the deal was done.

Nowhere in the Bankruptcy Code does it say, "property held by the debtor subject to a constructive trust is excluded from the debtor's estate." Courts, including the bankruptcy court in this case, which have excluded property from a debtor's estate as being subject to constructive trust, have done so on the authority of §541(d), usually over the protestations of trustees asserting their strongarm powers.

The problem with [this use of §541(d) to accommodate claims based on constructive trust] is that a constructive trust is not really a trust. A constructive trust is a legal fiction, a common-law remedy in equity that may only exist by the grace of judicial action. A debtor that served prior to bankruptcy as trustee of an express trust generally has no right to the assets kept in trust, and the trustee in bankruptcy must fork them over to the beneficiary. However, a claim filed in bankruptcy court asserting rights to certain assets "held" in "constructive trust" for the claimant is nothing more than that: a claim. Unless a court has already impressed a constructive trust upon certain assets or a legislature has created a specific statutory right to have particular kinds of funds held as if in trust, the claimant cannot properly represent to the bankruptcy court that he was, at the time of the commencement of the case, a beneficiary of a constructive trust held by the debtor.

Thus, the essence of the argument put forth by [Datacomp] and similarly situated claimants goes as follows: "Judge, due to debtor's fraud (or whatever), our property rights as beneficiaries of the constructive trust arose prepetition. Therefore, we stand not in the position of unsecured creditors, nor even equal to the trustee in the position of judgment creditors, but as the rightful owner of the *res* held in trust. Oh, and by the way, would you mind conferring on us these ownership rights and declaring that they arose prepetition?" This may seem silly phrased in this manner, but it is exactly the argument that most courts have accepted in holding that, due to some prepetition breach or bad act by the debtor, the claimed property or money is subject to a constructive trust and therefore "did not come into the bankruptcy estate and must be returned to the [debtor]."

Datacomp points out, correctly, that property rights in bankruptcy are determined only by reference to the state law of the jurisdiction. Datacomp further claims that under Kentucky law, Omegas's alleged fraud would give rise to a constructive trust imposed over all the money Omegas took unlawfully from Datacomp. What Datacomp, the bankruptcy court, the district court, and a number of other courts have failed to consider is that just because something is so under state law does not necessarily make it so under the Bankruptcy Code. Ultimately, "state law must be applied in a manner consistent with federal bankruptcy law." Torres v. Eastlick (In re North American Coin & Currency, Ltd.), 767 F.2d 1573, 1575 (9th Cir.1985).

We cannot find a more succinct manner of making our point than did Judge Aspen of the Northern District of Illinois: "[A] constructive trust is fundamentally at odds with the general goals of the Bankruptcy Code." The Oxford Organisation, Ltd. v. Peterson (In re Stotler and Co.),144 B.R. 385, 388 (1992). Quoting a Texas opinion, the judge explained:

> The reluctance of Bankruptcy Courts to impose constructive trusts without a substantial reason to do so stems from the recognition that each unsecured creditor desires to have his particular claim elevated above the others. Imposition of a constructive trust clearly thwarts the policy of ratable distribution and should not be impressed cavalierly.

The equities of bankruptcy are not the equities of the common law. Constructive trusts are anathema to the equities of bankruptcy since they take from the estate, and thus directly from competing creditors, not from the offending debtor. "Ratable distribution among all creditors" justifies the Code's placement of the trustee in the position of a first-in-line judgment creditor and bona fide purchaser for value, empowered to avoid certain competing interests (and even to nullify the debtor's "preferential" prepetition payments to otherwise entitled creditors) so as to maximize the value of the estate. To a party defrauded by the debtor, incorporating the proceeds of fraud in the debtor's estate may seem like allowing the "estate to benefit from property that the debtor did not own." Quality Holstein Leasing, 752 F.2d 1009, 1013 (5th Cir. 1985). But as the Seventh Circuit has pointed out, "allowing the estate to 'benefit from property that the debtor did not own' is exactly what the strong-arm powers are about: they give the trustee the status of a bona fide purchaser for value, so that the estate contains interests to which the debtor lacked good title." Belisle v. Plunkett, 877 F.2d 512, 516 (7th Cir. 1989) (criticizing *Quality Holstein Leasing*). The Code recognizes that each creditor has suffered disappointed expectations at the hands of the debtor; for this reason, it makes maximization of the estate the primary concern and entitlement to shares of the estate secondary. Imposing a constructive trust on the debtor's estate impermissibly subordinates this primary concern to a single claim of entitlement. To permit a creditor, no matter how badly he was "had" by the debtor, to lop off a piece of the estate under a constructive trust theory is to permit that creditor to circumvent completely the Code's equitable system of distribution.

In light of these provisions and in light of the overall purposes of the Code, §541(d) cannot properly be invoked as an equitable panacea whenever the bankruptcy court thinks a claimant has been particularly burdened by a debtor's bad faith or bad acts. Since the bankruptcy court here erred in doing so, the judgment of the district court affirming the bankruptcy court's judgment is REVERSED.

[The concurring opinion of Guy, J., is omitted.]

In re Dow Corning Corp.
192 B.R. 428 (Bankr. E.D. Mich. 1996)

Spector, Bankruptcy Judge.

This dispute requires the interpretation not just of the holding of a recently-decided case, but its *ratio decidendi* as well. Specifically, I must decide *how* the Court of Appeals for the Sixth Circuit decided as it did in XL/Datacomp, Inc. v. Wilson (In re Omegas Group, Inc.), 16 F.3d 1443 (6th Cir. 1994).

No one disputes the facts, which were stated in the movant's original motion. Wilfarm LLC is a customer of Dow Corning Corporation (the "Debtor"). On March 7 and 8, 1995, the Debtor invoiced Wilfarm for an order of Sylgard 309 silicone surfactant which the Debtor delivered in two truck shipments to Wilfarm per its purchase agreement. On April 12, 1995, a Dow Corning employee called Wilfarm inquiring about payment. Wilfarm was only recently formed out of the merger of two other companies. The Debtor mailed the original invoices to an office which no longer handled the accounts payable function, which apparently was the cause for the delay in payment. When this fact was brought to the Debtor's attention, it faxed the two invoices to the new Wilfarm accounts payable office. On April 17, 1995, Wilfarm's payment clerk then mailed the Debtor its check for $304,198.32. The following day, the original invoices arrived from Wilfarm's former accounts payable office. A different Wilfarm payment clerk issued another check covering the same two invoices—this one including sales tax, in the total amount of $329,294.69. The Debtor received both checks and deposited them in its general account. Both checks cleared. Everyone agrees that this is a case of simple clerical mistake as the second payment was made in error. The parties differ greatly however, as to the consequences which flow from this fact.

On May 15, 1995, Dow Corning filed a voluntary petition for relief under chapter 11 of the Bankruptcy Code. On August 11, 1995, Wilfarm filed a "Motion for Relief From the Automatic Stay Pursuant to 11 U.S.C. §362(d)." After reciting the above facts and characterizing its view of the law applicable to them, Wilfarm requested "this Court [to] lift the automatic stay and allow the debtor to send to the movant the amount of $329,294.69." Additionally, in its accompanying brief, "Wilfarm requests that this Court grant Wilfarm's motion for relief from the automatic stay, and *require* Dow Corning to transfer the mistaken payment back to Wilfarm."

Wilfarm put forth two separate grounds for relief, both of which are based upon Michigan law. First, it asserted that a party who mistakenly pays money to another retains "equitable title" in that money. Accordingly, Wilfarm argued that the Debtor obtained no more than bare legal title subject to Wilfarm's equitable interest and that the money should, therefore, be excluded from the bankruptcy estate pursuant to §541(d). As an alternative, Wilfarm claimed that it is entitled to an order "impressing a constructive trust to divide legal title from the equitable interest in the mistaken payment." The Debtor counter-argued that both of Wilfarm's theories are foreclosed by *Omegas, supra.*[3]

A BRIEF HISTORY OF CONSTRUCTIVE TRUST AND ITS EMERGENCE IN BANKRUPTCY

The use of constructive trusts as a form of relief against unjust enrichment has its beginnings in seventeenth century England. 1 George E. Palmer, *The Law of Restitution* §1.3, at 9–12 (1978). Until recently, the remedy remained limited under English law in that it required the presence of a fiduciary relationship. By necessitating such a relationship, English courts retained a connection (or confusion) between constructive trusts and express trusts.[4]

---

3. I have come to accept the view that the alternate forms of relief requested by Wilfarm are the same. That Michigan law may not have expressly said so each time the matter arose does not change its theoretical underpinnings.

4. As is often stated by courts and commentators, a constructive trust is not an express trust. Instead, it is an equitable remedy that developed by analogy to an express trust. In re Omegas Group, Inc., 16 F.3d at 1449 (citing Emily L. Sherwin, *Constructive Trusts in Bankruptcy*, 1989 U. Ill. L. Rev. 297, 301 (1989)).

American courts greatly expanded use of constructive trusts by eliminating the requirement of a fiduciary relationship. This development drew a line of distinction between express and constructive trusts and led to the general view that the circumstances giving rise to a constructive trust are virtually limitless. See McKey v. Paradise, 299 U.S. 119, 122 (1936).

The use of constructive trust in bankruptcy also has a long history in American law.References to this remedy can be found in bankruptcy cases dating back to the 1800's. See Conro v. Crane, 110 U.S. 403, 407 (1884); Graham v. Boston H. & E. R. Co., 118 U.S. 161, 173–74 (1886). Since that time, literally hundreds of bankruptcy cases have recognized the constructive trust doctrine. For example, in In re Berry, 147 Fed. 208, 210–11 (2d Cir. 1906), the court imposed a constructive trust on $1,500 paid under the mistaken impression that a debt was owing when in fact it was not.

On a number of occasions, the United States Supreme Court has at least impliedly recognized the applicability of constructive trusts within the bankruptcy context. In Cunningham v. Brown, 265 U.S. 1 (1924), several creditors who had been defrauded through a financial scheme masterminded by Charles Ponzi (the debtor and namesake of the infamous "Ponzi scheme"), requested imposition of a constructive trust on money in Ponzi's bank account. The Court denied imposition, but only because the creditors were unable to trace their individual payments. In *McKey, supra*, the Court said that "[i]t would be impossible to state all the circumstances in which equity will fasten a constructive trust upon property . . . [b]ut the mere failure to pay a debt does not belong in that category." 299 U.S. at 123. The Court again addressed the issue in Jaffke v. Dunham, 352 U.S. 280 (1957), where it held that whether there was sufficient evidence to establish a constructive trust was a question of state law.

However, there has existed for some time an undercurrent of dissatisfaction concerning the appropriateness of constructive trusts in bankruptcy. See, *e.g.*, Torres v. Eastlick (In re North American Coin and Currency, Ltd.), 767 F.2d 1573, 1575 (9th Cir. 1985) ("We necessarily act very cautiously in exercising such a relatively undefined equitable power in favor of one group of potential creditors at the expense of other creditors, for ratable distribution among all creditors is one of the strongest policies behind the bankruptcy laws"); Neochem Corp. v. Behring Int'l, Inc. (In re Behring Int'l, Inc.), 61 B.R. 896, 902 (Bankr. N.D. Tex.1986) ("Imposition of a constructive trust clearly thwarts the policy of ratable distribution and should not be impressed cavalierly"); The Oxford Organisation, Ltd. v. Peterson (In re Stotler and Co.), 144 B.R. 385, 388 (Bankr. N.D. Ill.1992) ("a constructive trust is fundamentally at odds with the general goals of the Bankruptcy Code").

THE OMEGAS GROUP DECISION

In the Sixth Circuit, it seemed that all questions concerning constructive trusts in bankruptcy were settled by *Omegas* in 1994. In the broadest language, the court held that one who does not have a court judgment declaring that the debtor holds particular property in constructive trust for it, possesses no more than a general claim to a share of the bankruptcy estate. [The court here quotes some of the more dramatic passages from *Omegas Group*.]

These statements surely point to the conclusion that a party in the position of Datacomp (the creditor in *Omegas*) can expect no relief that is different from the mass of other disappointed creditors. Moreover, these statements initially suggest that the court's underlying reasoning stemmed from its interpretation of state law. That is, that under Kentucky law a constructive trust arises only by operation of law and does not relate back to the time of the unjust enrichment. As such, the money could not be excluded from the bankruptcy estate per §541(d), leaving Datacomp with nothing more than a claim. But the opinion has so many broad statements—some of which are clearly in error and others which are simply perplexing—that it is more important than ever for a trial court to attempt to discern the actual rationale and not be lost by the rhetoric. Therefore, the remainder of this opinion is a quest for the reasoning underlying the *Omegas* holding.

WAS THE OMEGAS GROUP DECISION BASED UPON AN INTERPRETATION OF §541?

Most courts imposing constructive trusts in bankruptcy have done so under the general authority of §541. See, *e.g.*, City Nat'l Bank of Miami v. General Coffee Corp. (In re General Coffee Corp.), 828 F.2d 699, 705–06 (11th Cir. 1987); Vineyard v. McKenzie (In re Quality Holstein Leasing), 752 F.2d 1009 (5th Cir. 1985). Section 541(a) expansively defines "property of the estate" to include "all legal or equitable interests of the debtor in property as of the commencement of the case." This broad language is then limited by §541(d) which provides that when the equitable interest in property is possessed by one other than the debtor, such equitable interest does not become part of the estate. Consequently, this approach necessitates a determination of each party's rights with respect to the property in question.

As a general rule, "[p]roperty interests are created and defined by state law." Butner v. United States, 440 U.S. 48, 55 (1979); see also Barnhill v. Johnson, 503 U.S. 393, 398 (1992) ("In the absence of any controlling federal law, 'property' and 'interests in property' are creatures of state law"). Something can conceivably be "property" in one state—in which case the bankruptcy estate of the party owning it also owns it—and not "property" in another state—in which case the bankruptcy estate would not own it. While the *Omegas* majority opinion did not begin there, it acknowledged this point.

Moreover, since the focus of analysis is what state law says about the rights of a party in Datacomp's position, one would have expected any discussion of Kentucky law to have been more centrally placed and less perfunctorily covered. As such, I have concluded that analysis of Kentucky state law on constructive trusts does not provide the reasoning for the majority decision in *Omegas*.

Perhaps, then, notwithstanding its nod to *Butner*, the majority opinion is premised solely on a textual interpretation of §541. Putting aside the fact that §541(a)(1) includes the word "property" which of course, requires an examination of the state's definition of that word, the language of this section is not so clear as to be beyond construction. And the majority did not claim that these words were so plain as to be beyond the need for explication.

Legislative history dealing with these very words shows unmistakably that Congress, the author of the statute, intended that a debtor who holds property subject to a *constructive trust* holds bare legal title only, subject to the rights of the equitable owner. [The court quotes some of this legislative history.] The majority opinion in *Omegas* stated that "nowhere in the Bankruptcy Code does it say, 'property held by the debtor subject to a constructive trust is excluded from the debtor's estate.'" 16 F.3d at 1448. The obvious response is that the Code does say that the estate obtains only bare legal title when that is all the debtor possesses at commencement of the bankruptcy case; and Congress explained that this formula should apply when the debtor has obtained its interest in the property in a manner which would justify the imposition of a constructive trust in favor of the victim. Because this quote from the legislative history is so oft-cited, the court could not have simply missed it. One must speculate, therefore, that textual analysis of §541 is also not the source of the outcome in *Omegas*.

WAS THE OMEGAS GROUP DECISION BASED UPON AN INTERPRETATION OF §544?

Given the majority opinion's unclear reasoning, was Judge Guy's concurring opinion an attempt to provide the rationale? The concurring opinion rested on state law. Instead of addressing the question directly as one of the proper interpretation of §541(a) and (d), it used state law in conjunction with the trustee's strong-arm powers under §544(a). Judge Guy concluded that the trustee, in his persona as a judgment creditor with an execution against property owned by the entity who eventually becomes a debtor under title 11, would prevail under Kentucky law against a party requesting that the asset be impressed with a constructive trust in its favor. Accordingly, in his view, even if under Kentucky law Datacomp would be entitled to a constructive trust against Omegas before bankruptcy, that right would be cut off by a judgment lien creditor, and therefore the bankruptcy trustee. Was this the underlying rationale of the majority, which was lost within the broad rhetoric? And what is the result in this case if the concurring opinion's analysis is applied here?

The way Wilfarm and the Debtor framed the issue, the question is whether, under Michigan law, the equitable title of a "beneficiary" of a constructive trust "relates back" to the time of the events leading to the remedy. As the wording of this question suggests, this step in the analysis typically occurs only after there has been a determination that state law would in fact allow imposition of a constructive trust. It is only at this time that the priority question needs to be addressed. If the equitable title of a constructive trust beneficiary relates back to the time of the events leading to the remedy, then Wilfarm ought to prevail, and vice versa.

There is no Michigan case which pits party A, who would be entitled to the imposition of a constructive trust for the purpose of recovering cash or personal property from party B, who would be unjustly enriched by its retention, and party C, a judgment creditor of party B, who levies an execution on the property, while in party B's possession. There is therefore no answer in Michigan jurisprudence to this priority contest. It is helpful, then, to look to treatises such as restatements of law for direction.

According to Restatement of Restitution §160, Comment *f*:

> The equitable interest of the beneficiary [of a constructive trust] in the property will be protected if the rights of bona fide purchasers do not intervene. The creditors of the constructive trustee are not bona fide purchasers, and take subject to the rights of the beneficiary.

According to Restatement §173(2), a transfer of personalty "in satisfaction of or as security for a pre-existing debt or other obligation is a transfer for value." On the other hand, the Restatement further explains, the creditors of the constructive trustee are not purchasers for value. So if the constructive trustee "becomes bankrupt, the trustee in bankruptcy is not a bona fide purchaser of the property. So also a creditor who attaches the property or obtains and records a judgment or levies execution upon property is not a bona fide purchaser, although he had no notice of the constructive trust. This is true whether the property is land, or a chattel, or a chose in action, whether the chose in action is in the form of a negotiable instrument or not." Restatement §173, Comment *j*.

The Restatement's conclusion that a judicial lien creditor does not prevail over a constructive beneficiary is reflected in the derivative title rule of Michigan law. That rule provides that a judgment lien creditor has no greater rights than would the judgment debtor. Mich. Comp. Laws §§600.6034 and 600.6017(3); Brogdon v. American Automobile Ins. Co., 290 Mich. 130, 134, 287 N.W. 406 (1939); Kidd v. Minnesota Atlantic Transit Co., 261 Mich. 31, 34, 245 N.W. 561 (1932); Kalamazoo Trust Co. v. Merrill, 159 Mich. 649, 656, 124 N.W. 597 (1910); Nall v. Granger, 8 Mich. 449, 453–54 (1860); Powell v. Whirlpool Employees Fed. Credit Union, 42 Mich. App. 228, 231, 201 N.W.2d 683 (1972).

In applying the *Omegas* concurring opinion's analysis, then, under Michigan law, a judgment lien creditor would be defeated by a party entitled to assert a constructive trust upon the property that was in the possession of the judgment debtor, since the lien creditor takes no greater rights in the property than the judgment debtor. As a result, the judgment debtor's trustee in bankruptcy would likewise be defeated when donning the "hat" of this lien creditor. Another way of saying this, of course, is that Michigan law would allow a constructive trust to relate back given the particular circumstances here. Accordingly, I conclude that Wilfarm would prevail if Judge Guy's reasoning supplies the rationale for the *Omegas* majority opinion.

Unfortunately for Wilfarm, I cannot, with intellectual honesty, conclude that the majority used Judge Guy's analysis. To begin with, Judge

Guy prefaced his opinion with this comment: "Although I concur in the result reached by the court, *I would travel a different route to reach that result.*" More importantly, the trustee's strong-arm powers are determined by reference to state law. 4 Collier on Bankruptcy, ¶ 544.02 at 544–6 (15th ed. 1996). While the majority opinion made broad statements concerning the purpose and underlying policy of §544(a), the court failed to mention a single Kentucky case in connection with these comments. The absence of any reference to state law in this regard clearly shows that application of §544(a) does not provide the reasoning for the *Omegas* decision.

THE POLICY BASED APPROACH

What then is *Omegas'* rationale? While several courts have cited, applied, quoted from, followed or even criticized *Omegas*, only one has extensively analyzed it. In Berger, Shapiro & Davis, P.A. v. Haeling (In re Foos), 183 B.R. 149 (Bankr. N.D. Ill. 1995), Judge Barliant criticized *Omegas'* lack of consistent analysis, noting that the opinion's "general conclusion that, absent a specific state statute to the contrary, constructive trusts are not properly invoked to gain super-priority over the trustee in bankruptcy" followed neither state law nor bankruptcy law. He used the classic approach and decided that *under Illinois law*, a party in a position like those of Datacomp's and Wilfarm's, lacking a judicial declaration of constructive trust, have no equitable interest in property of the estate.

How did the majority reach this result if, as Judge Barliant stated, and as I agree, it was not based on state law or the plain meaning of §541 of the Bankruptcy Code? I conclude that the rationale is solely bankruptcy policy. And, although the *Omegas* court's justification for legislating its view of policy is barely stated, it exists and is cited nonetheless.

Butner is better known for the general rule that property rights are fixed by state law. But its lesser known exception limits that general rule as follows: "*Unless some federal interest requires a different result,* there is no reason why [state defined property] interests should be analyzed differently simply because an interested party is involved in a bankruptcy proceeding." 440 U.S. at 55 (emphasis added).

I conclude that *Omegas* found there to be a conflict between the federal bankruptcy policy of ratable distribution and state property law on constructive trusts. The following statements clearly point to this conclusion. "[J]ust because something is so under state law does not necessarily make it so under the Bankruptcy Code." *Omegas*, 16 F.3d at 1450. "Ultimately, 'state law must be applied in a manner consistent with federal bankruptcy law.'" 16 F.3d at 1450–51. "The equities of bankruptcy are not the equities of the common law. Constructive trusts are anathema to the equities of bankruptcy since they take from the estate, and thus directly from competing creditors, not from the offending debtor." 16 F.3d at 1452. "To permit a creditor, no matter how badly he was 'had' by the debtor, to lop off a piece of the estate under a constructive trust theory is to permit that creditor to circumvent completely the Code's equitable system of distribution."16 F.3d at 1453.[5]

I am not unmindful of the hardship this decision may have on Wilfarm. It is for this very reason that a quest for the true holding of *Omegas* was undertaken so earnestly. The quest was made all the more difficult by the fact that Congress and the case law prior to *Omegas* recognized constructive trusts as being appropriate within bankruptcy. However, after much consideration, there is no longer a doubt in my mind that *Omegas*, in reliance on the federal policy exception of *Butner*, held that the bankruptcy policy of ratable distribution trumps state law on constructive trusts. Therefore, under the rule of the *Omegas Group* decision, Wilfarm's motion must be denied. An order consistent with this opinion will be entered.

Anathema

1. The rallying cry of *Omegas Group*, that "constructive trusts are anathema to the equities of bankruptcy," was unnecessary to decide the case before the Sixth Circuit. The fraud claim, brought by a last-minute buyer (Datacomp) who was unhappy at not getting the computers it had paid for, was marginal at best. In fact, it was easier to see that Datacomp itself had unclean hands than that Datacomp had been defrauded, inviting the defense of equitable disqualification. (This is what Judge Spector means in his concluding footnote that "some supplicants, like Datacomp, have only a dubious call on equity.") On a basic technical level, there was no hint that Datacomp would have been able to trace its funds into the debtor's bank accounts (or anywhere else), and no apparent recognition by the Sixth Circuit of the need to do so.

2. The references in *Omegas Group* to "the equities of bankruptcy" carry unorthodox implications. Bankruptcy normally pursues ratable distribution of the *debtor's* property, not that of other people—whose is whose being defined by state law. Even then, "ratable distribution" normally means "between creditors of the same class." For example, there is no ratable distribution to the

---

5. The principle of "ratable distribution" is relevant only with respect to property interests which are subject to distribution—*i.e.*, those interests which the estate owns, whether by virtue of §544(a) or otherwise. *Cf.* Begier v. IRS, 496 U.S. 53, 58 (1990) ("Equality of distribution among creditors is a central policy of the Bankruptcy Code. Of course, if the debtor transfers property that would not have been available for distribution to his creditors in a bankruptcy proceeding, [that] policy is not implicated"). Yet *Omegas* used this *objective* of asset distribution as justification for determining *what* assets the trustee can distribute. Despite this, and the other shortcomings of *Omegas*, its mandate is controlling upon this Court and its effect is nonetheless quite salutary.

Cases in which the remedy of constructive trust are sought can run the gamut: some supplicants, like Datacomp, have a dubious call upon equity; while others like Wilfarm, present far more sympathetic situations. In the middle lie the vast majority of cases, where fine distinctions necessitate extremely subjective determinations. Trial courts are, as a result of *Omegas*, mercifully spared from this onerous task.

general creditors if the assets on hand all go to the secured creditors. Does *In re Dow Corning* end up robbing Peter to pay Paul?

3. The traditional approach to the problem of constructive trust in bankruptcy, as Judge Spector indicates, is to ask who wins the underlying priority contest at state law. Is it the restitution claimant (the party entitled to constructive trust under local law) or the ideal lien creditor (in the person of the bankruptcy trustee)? He mentions two examples of this approach: the concurring opinion in *Omegas Group* and a Bankruptcy Court decision in Illinois. Both judges found that applicable state law (in Kentucky or Illinois) would decide the contest in favor of the lien creditor. Those conclusions are necessarily doubtful, as they would be in any U.S. jurisdiction, given the bedrock premise that a lien creditor is not a bona fide purchaser and that (accordingly) "the judgment creditor stands in the shoes of the judgment debtor."

Keep in mind that the relevant state law governing priorities will not always be found under the same headings. For example, Judge Spector's very careful review finds "no Michigan case" on the priority contest between A (the restitution claimant) and C (the creditor of the transferee/debtor). But a few paragraphs later, he cites two statutes and a handful of cases for Michigan's "derivative title rule," by which "a judgment lien creditor has no greater rights than would the judgment debtor." Isn't this another way of saying the same thing?

C.   DISPLACEMENT BY STATUTE: UNIFORM COMMERCIAL CODE

Introductory note

Rights and duties measured by "equity and good conscience" may be inconsistent with formal legal entitlements. The whole law of restitution and unjust enrichment can be seen as a catalogue of circumstances in which our legal system (definitely including the "equity" side of it) will intervene to bring formal entitlements and the demands of justice into better alignment. A syllabus in Restitution tends to be a guided tour of successful interventions, so it is important to recognize the consistent theme of resistance. No one wants to defend an unjust outcome, but most restitution defendants are arguing that an unjust outcome ought to be left alone. Where the claimant's standard is equity and good conscience, the defendant's watchword is "finality and predictability"—often achieved by adherence to formal rules.

Formal rules are old-fashioned. The old "legal estoppel"—as opposed to the "equitable" kind we now take for granted—meant that the grantor of a deed, or the maker of any promise under seal, could not assert the truth to controvert his own statements:

> The legal estoppel shuts out the truth, and also the equity and justice of the individual case, on account of the supposed paramount importance of rigorously enforcing a certain and unvarying maxim of the law. For reasons of general policy, a record is held to import incontrovertible verity, and for the same reason a party is not permitted to contradict his solemn admission by deed.

Horn v. Cole, 51 N.H. 287, 290 (1868). As a result, "if a man said he was bound, he was bound." Holmes, The Common Law 262 (1881). Naturally, if someone has been prejudiced by reliance on my erroneous statement, that is a reason to hold me to it—this is the whole theory of present-day "equitable" estoppel. If not, our modern and deep-seated respect for substance over form makes it unlikely, in most contexts, that the law will prefer the "incontrovertible verity" of a formal record to the reality of a transaction, if the reality can be known.

Land titles make a useful standard of comparison. It is usually assumed that nothing surpasses the practical importance of certainty in this area, or the formal sanctity of a deed. Title to land is protected not only by the old version of "legal estoppel" but by the Statute of Frauds and the recording acts as well. Yet courts of equity quickly found reasons to grant specific performance of land contracts that were legally unenforceable for want of a signed writing. It has been clear for centuries that—subject always to "intervening equities"—a deed can be reformed for mistake or rescinded for fraud. Adjustment of mortgage priorities by subrogation or by equitable lien (as in *Houston v. Mentelos*, *Gladowski v. Felczak*, or *Equity Savings*) has never been hindered by the recording acts, though the results will sometimes contradict the provisions of these statutes. Even where the recording acts protect the subsequent purchaser over the prior grantee, they usually impose the standard equitable precondition: that the purchaser claiming protection must have acted without notice.

The contrast is dramatic when we turn from real property to personal property and to issues of lien priorities under UCC article 9. A decision to favor formal entitlements over competing equitable interests is evident in the basic structure of the act, notably its "pure race" filing regime. Unlike the usual recording act, article 9 gives priority both to competing secured parties and to lien creditors over prior, unperfected liens of which they have notice (§§9-317(a)(2), 9-322(a)(1)). The same inclination appears in various subordinate provisions, such as the unforgiving attitude toward errors in financing statements—which can be "seriously misleading" as a matter of law, and therefore ineffective, even if no one is misled (§9-506). More controversially, it appears to be reflected in judicial decisions that deny the availability of equitable relief in article 9 cases on the ground that such remedies are inconsistent with the UCC's formal requirements.

The issue as framed by the Code is whether background "principles of law and equity" have been "displaced" by particular Code provisions:

> Unless displaced by the particular provisions of [the UCC], the principles of law and equity, including the law merchant and the law relative to capacity to contract, principal and agent, estoppel, fraud, misrepresentation, duress, coercion, mistake, bankruptcy and other validating or invalidating cause supplement its provisions.

UCC §1-103(b) (2001). In the 50 or 60 years since the Code was first enacted, the extent of UCC "displacement" has manifestly grown. Because neither the relevant Code provisions nor the "principles of law and equity" have changed in the slightest, the explanation appears to be that background legal principles are receding farther into the background.

The starting hypothesis, which would not be hard to prove, is that the law and equity of restitution and unjust enrichment were both more familiar and more important to the lawyers who drafted the original UCC than they are to the lawyers who interpret it today. The relative unfamiliarity of these topics makes the case for their "supplemental" application via §1-103 less obvious than it would have been to the original drafters; by the same token, the argument for their implicit displacement has become easier to make. The same natural phenomenon—simply the shifting content of what constitutes "common knowledge" for the legal profession—would explain why it is these particular "principles of law and equity" whose applicability to supplement Code provisions has been visibly contested, rather than the other topics mentioned in the same sentence of §1-103.

French Lumber Co. v. Commercial Realty & Finance Co.
346 Mass. 716, 195 N.E.2d 507 (1964)

SPALDING, Justice.

This bill in equity seeks to determine the ownership of certain funds derived from the sale of an automobile at a public auction.

The findings and evidence establish these facts: On February 9, 1959, The French Lumber Co. purchased a 1959 Cadillac automobile and financed this purchase through the Ware Trust Company (Ware). French received $4,600 which together with a finance charge of $460 resulted in a total indebtedness by it to Ware in the amount of $5,060 which was to be repaid in twenty-three successive monthly installments of $207 each. French entered into a Uniform Commercial Code security agreement as security for its note, and this agreement was duly recorded.

On July 10, 1959, French pledged its existing equity in the Cadillac to the defendant Commercial Realty and Finance Co., Inc. (Commercial) as collateral security for funds advanced by Commercial. Commercial's security interest was duly recorded. The note to Commercial was in the sum of $8,040 and was payable in sixty monthly installments of $134. In addition to the equity in the Cadillac this note was secured by a real estate mortgage, a chattel mortgage and assignments of life insurance. The note was signed by French, Arthur T. Winters and Charles W. Proctor.

French failed to make payments under its agreement with Ware, and in the latter part of July 1959, Ware turned over the French chattel mortgage and note to its attorney, Mr. Schlosstein, for the purpose of foreclosure. Arrangements to refinance the mortgage having come to naught, Mr. Schlosstein ordered repossession of the Cadillac on August 15, 1959. In September 1959, Winters and Proctor on behalf of French conferred with Associates Discount Corporation (Associates) about refinancing the Cadillac then in Ware's possession. As a result of these negotiations Winters and Proctor entered into a security agreement with Associates, which was duly recorded, covering the refinancing of the Cadillac for the total amount of $5,022. Upon receiving a note in this amount signed by Winters and Proctor, Associates issued its check in the sum of $4,256 payable to Ware, Winters, and Proctor. This check was turned over by Winters to Mr. Schlosstein on September 4, 1959, and he made a notation on the French note that it was paid in full. Subsequently the Ware security agreement and discharge were sent to Associates. On the check given by Associates was a notation over the indorsements of Winters, Proctor, and Ware that it was in payment in full for the Cadillac.

On August 30, 1960, Associates repossessed the Cadillac because of defaults in payments. A public auction followed, and the present controversy has to do with the ownership of the proceeds ($3,200) of the foreclosure sale. Commercial asserts that it is entitled to the proceeds. Associates asserts that it subrogated to the rights of Ware and is therefore entitled to the proceeds. After finding the foregoing facts the trial judge concluded:

> There was nothing to indicate that French, Winters or Proctor ever informed Associates that Commercial held any security interest in the Cadillac over and above the interest held by Ware. I infer from the evidence that Associates had no knowledge of this situation. It is incredible that Associates would not have taken appropriate protective steps by way of an assignment from the bank. If the assumption is made that Associates was negligent in failing to check the records, this negligent act will not necessarily bar Associates from obtaining the relief it seeks through subrogation. Such negligence was as to its own interests and did not affect prejudicially the interests of Commercial. There has been no change of position by Commercial. It is left exactly in the position it originally was in. It had a claim known by it to be subordinated to Ware. Ware was paid by Associates. If Associates had taken an assignment from Ware, Commercial would have had no cause for complaint.

The judge ordered the entry of a decree declaring that Associates is entitled to the $3,200 arising from the proceeds of the auction sale. From a decree accordingly Commercial appealed.

Commercial seeks to establish rights in the proceeds prior to the rights of Associates. That part of the Uniform Commercial Code here pertinent, §9-322(a)(1), provides that the order of filing determines the order of priorities among conflicting interests in the same collateral. [The Court's UCC citations have been updated.] Under this provision the order of priorities would be: Ware, Commercial, and Associates. This establishes Commercial's priority over Associates unless Associates can establish a right to succeed to Ware's priority.

A security interest can be "assigned" to another creditor without loss of its priority even if no filing is made. §9-310(c). Thus Ware could have made an assignment of its security interest to Associates, and Associates would then have acquired Ware's priority over Commercial. But no such assignment was made.

Associates could also acquire Ware's priority through the doctrine of subrogation. For cases analogous to the present where this doctrine has been applied, see Hill v. Wiley, 295 Mass. 396, 3 N.E.2d 1015 (1936); Worcester No. Sav. Inst. v. Farwell, 292 Mass. 568, 198 N.E. 897 (1935); Home Owners' Loan Corp. v. Baker, 299 Mass. 158, 12 N.E.2d 199 (1937).

In Home Owners' Loan Corp. v. Baker, *supra*, where the doctrine of subrogation was discussed, it was said: "The plaintiff, having paid the debts of the defendant out of its funds and taken its mortgage in the mistaken belief that it would have a first lien on the premises, was not officious. In such circumstances equity has given relief by way of subrogation when the interest of intervening lienors were not prejudicially affected." 299 Mass. at 161-62, 12 N.E.2d at 201.

The trial judge, having found that the conduct of Associates did not prejudice Commercial or cause it to change its position, was of opinion that the principle of the cases cited above was applicable and accorded Associates priority over Commercial. Commercial argues that Associates has elected to stand on its own later security interest and should have no rights to Ware's interest. We are of opinion that this argument lacks merit. Associates was seeking to collect its own claim. This was not inconsistent with its present claim for subrogation to Ware's rights.

The decisions on subrogation discussed above are not superseded by the Uniform Commercial Code. Section 1-103 of the Code provides in part, "Unless displaced by the particular provisions of this chapter, the principles of law and equity . . . shall supplement its provisions." No provision of the Code purports to affect the fundamental equitable doctrine of subrogation.

Commercial argues that even if Associates is entitled to subrogation its rights can rise no higher than Ware's. This, of course, is true. The facts establish that Ware received $4,256 from Associates in payment of the balance due on French's debt to Ware. They also show that Associates received $1,297.50 in payments by French on its debt to Associates. Commercial argues that the $1,297.50 in payments made to Associates by French should be allocated as payment on the $4,256 balance owed to Ware at the time Associates paid off the debt to Ware. This could limit Associates' subrogation rights to $2,958.50. We do not agree. Associates had a right to enforce its own claim without displacing its right to subrogation to Ware's security. Associates is entitled to be subrogated to the full $3,200 of the proceeds.

Contrary to the contention of Commercial, the failure of French to disclose to Associates the existence of Commercial's security interest would have no effect on Associates' rights to subrogation.

The decrees are affirmed with costs of appeal.

Knox v. Phoenix Leasing, Inc.
29 Cal. App. 4th 1357, 35 Cal. Rptr. 2d 141 (1994)

POCHÉ, J.

The issue presented is whether a secured creditor who obtains a defaulted debtor's property can be subject to restitution for the amount of the value of goods furnished the debtor by a third party. The answer is no: unless there are unusual circumstances, the equitable remedy of restitution must defer to the rights given a secured creditor by the California Uniform Commercial Code.

BACKGROUND

In March of 1990 as part of a concerted effort to expand the capacity of its plant in Sonoma County, Domaine Laurier Winery contracted with Mel Knox to purchase 200 seasoned oak wine barrels made in France. Four months later Domaine executed an agreement with Phoenix Leasing Incorporated whereby Phoenix undertook to provide financing for the expansion. Phoenix was protected by (among other things) a security agreement covering all personal property, including "all equipment . . . whether now owned or hereafter acquired" by Domaine.

The wine barrels came in two shipments. Upon arrival of the first lot, Knox sent an invoice to Domaine; Domaine forwarded the invoice to Phoenix, which paid it in August of 1990. With the second lot, Knox sent the invoice for $33,011.37 directly to Phoenix. Domaine also requested Phoenix to pay Knox. Approximately two months after the second shipment was delivered, but before any payment for it, Phoenix declared Domaine in default of their agreement. The barrels were included in Phoenix's subsequent liquidation of Domaine's assets. (Phoenix advanced Domaine approximately $1.1 million, but recovered only about $400,000 from the liquidation.)

By the time Knox's complaint came on for trial it had been reduced to a single cause of action for "Restitution—Unjust Enrichment" against Phoenix. The case was tried on the short cause calendar following denial of Phoenix's motion that, because it was a secured creditor while Knox was not, it was entitled to judgment on the pleadings. The trial did not produce a statement of decision, simply the court's announcement that Knox was entitled to judgment for $21,350 (70 percent of the original cost of the barrels, which was essentially their undisputed resale value). Phoenix perfected this timely appeal from the ensuing judgment.

REVIEW

According to the California Uniform Commercial Code, Domaine's execution of a security agreement describing the property covered gave Phoenix a security interest in that collateral (§§9-203(b), 9-204). [The Court's UCC citations have been updated.] Phoenix perfected that security interest when it filed a financing statement with the Secretary of State (§§9-310, 9-501). Phoenix thus acquired priority over other Domaine creditors (§§9-201, 9-317, 9-322, 9-324), including the right to take possession and sell the collateral if Domaine defaulted (§§9-609, 9-610, 9-615). It being undisputed that Phoenix complied with all of these steps, Phoenix maintains that it is immune to Knox's restitution claim.

The opposing argument, which springs from the code's general directive that its provisions are to be supplemented by "principles of law and equity" (§1-103(b)), has divided courts considering whether restitution can be had from a code-protected secured creditor. On the one hand, a decided majority of jurisdictions have disallowed the equitable remedy of restitution (whether termed unjust enrichment, *quantum meruit*, contract implied in law, etc.). They are willing to accept occasionally harsh results as the price to be paid for preserving the integrity of the Uniform Commercial Code's scheme for secured transactions, encouraging compliance with the Code, and thereby ensuring a predictable system of creditor priorities. On the other hand, California and more recently Colorado, while conceding considerable soundness to the majority position, have permitted restitution from a secured creditor. (Producers Cotton Oil Co. v. Amstar Corp. (1988) 197 Cal. App. 3d 638 [242 Cal. Rptr. 914]; Ninth Dist. Prod. Credit v. Ed Duggan (Colo. 1991) 821 P.2d 788 [27 A.L.R.5th 921]; see also Borg-Warner v. Valentine Associates Ltd. (1989) 192 Ga. App. 123 [384 S.E.2d 223].) An examination of these decisions demonstrates that their disagreement with the majority position is one of degree and is not nearly so profound as appears at first glance. Recovery is clearly the exception, not the norm, and is subject to stern limitations.

The first member of the minority camp—and the sole reported California decision in this area—is *Producers Cotton Oil, supra*, 197 Cal. App. 3d 638. The Producers Cotton firm held a security interest in the farm crops of its debtor. Amstar bought the crops and paid to have them harvested. Amstar knew of Producers' security interest, but neglected to obtain Producers' agreement to subordinate that interest. Amstar deducted the harvesting costs before remitting the sale proceeds of the crops to Producers. Producers sued Amstar and obtained a judgment on the theory that the deduction constituted conversion of its secured collateral.

Amstar appealed, arguing that the California code's article 9 governing secured transactions left room for the equitable principle of restitution. It relied on §1-103(b), which provides: "Unless displaced by the particular provisions of this code, the principles of law and equity, including the law merchant and the law relative to capacity to contract, principal and agent, estoppel, fraud, misrepresentation, duress, coercion, mistake, bankruptcy, or other validating or invalidating cause shall supplement its provisions." Producers responded that "in order to give stability and predictability to commercial transactions, the priorities dictated by article 9 must prevail over equitable principles that might otherwise apply." Concluding that "the facts present a classic case for establishing an implied-in-law contract, or quasi-contract," the Court of Appeal tersely concurred with Amstar: "We agree with the position of Amstar and hold that when a party possessing a security interest in a crop and its proceeds has knowledge of and acquiesces in expenditures made which are *necessary* to the development of the crop, and ultimately benefits from the expenditure, a party who, through mistake, pays such costs without first obtaining subordination, is entitled to recover." (*Producers Cotton, supra,* 197 Cal. App. 3d at 658, 660, original italics.)

A considerably more detailed discussion of the problem was developed in *Duggan, supra,* 821 P.2d 788. Like *Producers Cotton,* the context was agricultural. Duggan furnished feed grain to a livestock company whose accounts receivable and personal property were the subject of a perfected security interest held by a credit association. In accordance with its standard practice, the association financed the livestock company's operations by paying sight drafts given creditors by the livestock company. Duggan continued deliveries while an unsuccessful effort to sell the livestock company was overseen by the credit association. Cattle fed with Duggan's grain were sold and the proceeds paid to the credit association, which also received payment for feedlot services given cattle awaiting slaughter. When the livestock company became financially unable to pay Duggan, suit was brought against the association.

The Colorado Supreme Court upheld the lower courts' determination that Duggan could obtain restitution from the credit association notwithstanding the latter's superior statutory priority as a secured creditor. It opened its analysis by noting that the central issue "whether a creditor that holds a perfected security interest in collateral can be held liable to an unsecured creditor based on a theory of unjust enrichment for benefits that enhance the value of the collateral . . . cannot be answered categorically." (*Duggan, supra,* 821 P.2d at 793.) Recognizing that this problem presented "obvious tension between the doctrine of unjust enrichment and the priority system established by Article 9," the court reviewed the relevant decisions and discerned that the "central point of distinction . . . is the extent to which the secured creditor was involved in the transaction by which the unsecured creditor supplied goods or services that enhanced the value of the secured collateral." (*Id.* at 795-797.) Acknowledging that the Uniform Commercial Code's priority system "reflects the legislative judgment that the value of a predictable system of priorities ordinarily outweighs the disadvantage of the system's occasional inequities," the court formulated this rule: "In a situation where a secured creditor initiates or encourages transactions between the debtor and suppliers of goods or services, and benefits from the goods or services supplied to produce such debts, equitable principles require that the secured creditor compensate even an unsecured creditor to avoid being unjustly enriched. The equitable claim is at its strongest when the goods or services are necessary to preserve the security, as in *Producers Cotton Oil*." (*Id.* at 797-798.)

Producers Cotton and *Duggan* have been subjected to critical comment, some of which is unusually hostile.[6] Were we the first California court to consider the issue, we might well agree with the strict position that allowing restitution claims would be incompatible with the code's priority system. But we do not come to this subject with a blank screen. As evidenced by *Producers Cotton*, California has opted to allow restitution claims against a secured creditor. When properly restricted to a very limited class of cases, this principle is sound.

The reasons supporting the primacy of the article 9 scheme are unquestionably weighty. Article 9 has been in place for more than three decades. Its requirements are by now familiar and integrated into commercial practice. The corresponding benefit is the stability that is essential to a healthy business climate. Compliance with the obligations of article 9 should have a positive consequence.

A secured creditor which has complied with all relevant code requirements to perfect its security interest, should therefore start with something like a presumption in its favor. The whole point of article 9 is to establish a comprehensive scheme affording maximum protection to the secured creditor who has followed its provisions. This preference would be reinforced by the failure of the unsecured creditor to use [available means to protect itself]. As courts and commentators have noted, the unsecured creditor could have (1) demanded cash payment on delivery, (2) perfected a purchase money security interest (§9-324),[7] (3) checked with the appropriate governmental office to determine if the debtor had already granted a security interest posing a possible threat to repayment, or (4) obtained a secured creditor's agreement to subordinate its priority (§9-339).

But victory for a secured creditor is not an immutable law of nature. Fraud, for example, is expressly put beyond the pale. (See §1-103(b).) A code may strive for comprehensiveness, but exceptional situations will arise. Equity is ordinarily meant to operate in these situations, but its operation is subject to

---

6. The authors of the leading treatise on the Uniform Commercial Code—who disagree between themselves as to the proper scope for equitable considerations—list *Producers Cotton* and *Duggan* in a section entitled "Weird Cases: The Creeping Infestation of Article Nine Priority Rules by 'Principles of Law and Equity.'" (2 White & Summers, Uniform Commercial Code (3d pract. ed. 1988) §26-20, pp.554-555; *id.* (1993 supp.) pp.160-164; see also Summers, *General Equitable Principles Under Section 1-103 of the Uniform Commercial Code* (1978) 72 Nw. U. L. Rev. 906 [favoring broad application of equity].)

The author of a treatise on secured transactions excoriates *Duggan* in particular as an "aberration" that is not only "flat wrong" but "makes the mind spin," "turns the world upside down," and "should send chills down the backs of secured lenders everywhere." (Clark, The Law of Secured Transactions Under the Uniform Commercial Code (1993 supp.) §3.14, pp.S3-35-39.)

7. A purchase money security interest can be held by a creditor who either sells the collateral to the creditor or finances acquisition of the collateral by the creditor (§9-103). A purchase money security interest can be perfected after the debtor's receipt of the collateral and still have priority over the holder of a general security interest in the same collateral claiming pursuant to an "after acquired" property clause (§§9-204). We have discussed the purchase money security interest because it is what Knox could have obtained to protect his sale to Domaine.

the principle that "equity follows the law." This deference requires that equitable exceptions to statutory law be carefully limited to reduce any possible conflict with an express statutory command. *Producers Cotton* and *Duggan* show how this may be accomplished.

Those decisions begin with the premise that simply pointing to benefit realized by the secured creditor will not suffice. As *Duggan* notes, gain to the creditor is almost universally present. Something more is required to displace the creditor's favored position. That something is either conduct by the secured creditor or the nature of the unsecured creditor's contribution to the collateral.

At one end of the scale is fraud, which in its myriad forms is "the very essence of wrong; conduct that has always been and always will be wrong, according to the common judgment of mankind; conduct that cannot be dressed up or manipulated or associated so as to invest it with any element of right." (Morton v. Petitt (1938) 124 Ohio St. 241 [177 N.E. 591, 593].) The California Uniform Commercial Code gives it no sanction (§1-103(b)), and courts applying the Uniform Commercial Code are equally stern.

Harder to resolve are the less egregious situations "where a secured creditor initiates or encourages transactions between the debtor and suppliers of goods or services, and benefits from the goods or services supplied to produce such debts." (*Duggan, supra,* 821 P.2d at 798.) These situations present a fertile opportunity for trapping the unwary. If what the secured creditor did or failed to do can be reached by the doctrines of estoppel, misrepresentation not amounting to fraud, or mistake, the code allows redress to an innocent supplier (§1-103(b)). Just as contribution among tortfeasors is proportioned by fault, commercial loss allocation responds to the same impulse. If it had an active hand in promoting a transaction that goes bad, a secured creditor should not escape with a victimized supplier left behind holding an empty bag alone. In simple terms, the creditor should not be allowed to profit from the wrong of its own bad faith.

The most difficult factor is the secured creditor's acquiescence when an unsecured creditor provides goods or services to their common debtor. . . . [The court concludes that "acquiescence" (without more) in a transaction by which another party enhances the value of collateral cannot be enough to support unjust enrichment liability on the part of the secured creditor, because it would seriously undermine the creditor's reliance on the Code filing scheme.]

How does the evidence in this case measure up according to this legal template? Nothing in Phoenix's conduct amounted to fraud, actual or virtual, and Knox does not contend otherwise. The transaction between Knox and Domaine owed nothing to Phoenix in its inception. We have already determined that any acquiescence by Phoenix will not support restitution liability. Phoenix had no duty to overcome the failure of Knox, a merchant knowledgeable about article 9 procedures, to acquaint himself with public information concerning the Phoenix-Domaine relationship.

The barrels provided by Knox were not necessary to preserve the collateral covered by Phoenix's security interest in Domaine's "after acquired" property.

The mere fact that the secured collateral was enhanced by the addition of the barrels does not support liability in these circumstances.

The trial court's conclusion has an undeniable common sense allure — Knox provided barrels; Phoenix ended up with the barrels; Phoenix should therefore pay Knox for their value. Ordinarily this would be sound reasoning supporting an equitable result. Article 9, however, compels a different conclusion. Phoenix complied with statutory provisions intended to immunize secured creditors from such claims in all but the rarest of cases. As this is not that sort of case, the equitable impulse for restitution must yield to the Legislature's command.

The judgment is reversed.

Displacement by balancing

1. How would *French Lumber* come out under the balancing approach of *Knox v. Phoenix Leasing?* If the California court had wanted to, it could have given Knox an equitable lien to match the purchase money security interest that Knox should have obtained for himself. Not surprisingly, the court concluded that such relief would be inconsistent with the orderly operation of the statutory scheme. But in the Massachusetts case, doesn't subrogation of Associates — correcting its "inexplicable" failure to discover Commercial's intervening security interest and to take an assignment from Ware — do as much violence to orderly UCC priorities? Then again, does the subrogation in *French Lumber* do any more violence to statutory priorities than does subrogation in the standard real property case — where a claimant's funds have been applied by mistake to discharge a mortgage on someone else's real property? (This was the result in *AmSouth Mortgage, Houston v. Mentelos*, the Massachusetts precedents cited in *French Lumber*, and countless other cases.) Is there something about personal property — or about contemporary law practice — that makes article 9 priorities less robust?

2. The judges who decided *French Lumber* belonged to the "founding generation" in UCC terms. Their familiarity with "principles of law and equity" and their ideas about "displacement" were probably close to those of the reporters. Grant Gilmore, the author of much of article 9, later remarked of *French Lumber* that "The decision seems entirely sound, and so is the court's suggestion that the parties could have simplified the situation by taking advantage of the Article 9 assignment provisions." 1 Gilmore, Security Interests in Personal Property §15.3, n.7 (1965).

3. Feresi v. The Livery, LLC, 182 Cal. Rptr. 3d 169 (Ct. App. 2014), considered conflicting security interests in the same collateral: a one-eighth share in a limited-liability corporation (apparently a real estate venture) called The Livery, LLC. The LLC originally had four members with equal shares, one 25

percent share being the community property of John Mesa and Renee Feresi as husband and wife. Another 25 percent was held by a family trust managed by Mark Hartley, who was president and "managing member" of the LLC. When Mesa and Feresi were divorced in 2006, she was awarded one-half the couple's former interest in the LLC, making her a 12.5 percent owner. As security for Mesa's continuing financial obligations to her, Feresi obtained in addition a security interest in Mesa's remaining 12.5 percent share. Feresi did not file a UCC financing statement to perfect her security interest, but she notified the other members of the LLC of the relevant transactions.

> By 2008, Mesa was struggling financially and fell behind on his obligations to Feresi and other creditors. On October 7, 2008, Hartley made a short-term loan to Mesa of $200,000 from [a pension plan Hartley controlled]. Although Hartley knew that Mesa's membership share in the LLC secured his financial obligations to Feresi, Hartley nevertheless secured the loan from his pension plan by the same 12.5 percent membership share Mesa pledged to Feresi in 2006.

A few weeks later, Feresi notified Hartley that Mesa was in default, and that she had commenced legal action to compel Mesa to convey to her the 12.5 percent interest in which she held a security interest.

> After he was notified of Mesa's failure to meet his obligations to Feresi, Hartley determined that Feresi had not filed a UCC–1 financing statement to perfect her security interest in Mesa's membership share of the LLC. Hartley took advantage of this circumstance to acquire priority for his own, conflicting security interest in the same membership share by filing a UCC–1 financing statement reflecting the subsequent loan to Mesa.

In the ensuing litigation, Feresi and Hartley asserted competing claims to the 12.5 percent share in which each held a valid security interest. Hartley had been "first to file or perfect," giving him priority by the rule of UCC §9-322. The trial court found, however, that by acting as he did to subordinate Feresi's preexisting interest to his own later one, Hartley had breached the fiduciary duties he owed her as a member of the LLC. The trial court concluded "that the security interest created by Mesa and Hartley in October 2008 in favor of Hartley's pension plan was 'null and void.'"

The findings concerning fiduciary duty and knowing breach were affirmed on appeal. Hartley's position, as described by the court, was that "the UCC sets a 'hard line' that requires courts to disregard the equities and accept 'harsh results' to ensure that commercial transactions are simple, clear and uniform." Citing *Knox v. Phoenix Leasing, Inc.*, Hartley argued

> that the statutory priority given to the holder of a perfected security interest must be upheld even if the holder is unjustly enriched at the expense of an unsecured creditor. In *Knox*, the perfected security interest attached

to all equipment owned or later acquired by a winery. The winery's obligation to the seller of the equipment was unsecured. The *Knox* court acknowledged the harsh result of finding the perfected interest had priority over that of the seller, but said it had to be accepted to ensure "a predictable system of creditor priorities."

Does the reasoning of *Knox v. Phoenix Leasing* support Hartley or Feresi? The Court of Appeal thought the latter:

> We conclude that if a fiduciary engages in inequitable conduct with respect to a person to whom a fiduciary duty is owed, then its claim, lien or security interest may be wholly or partially subordinated. The doctrine of equitable subordination has deep common law roots and is based upon the inherent power of a court of equity to do justice as circumstances dictate. While the doctrine is most frequently asserted in bankruptcy court because it has statutory support in §510 of the Bankruptcy Code, it has also been employed, though sparingly, in other contexts.
>
> As the *Knox* court observed, equity and thus equitable subordination should be invoked with caution by the courts. But where, as here, a petitioner has shown: (1) the fiduciary engaged in inequitable conduct; (2) the misconduct resulted in injury to the petitioner or conferred an unfair advantage on the fiduciary; and (3) invocation of the remedy of equitable subordination will not be inconsistent with the Commercial Code, then the remedy has a place.
>
> The UCC itself acknowledges that its provisions are to be supplemented by "principles of law and equity." (§1-103(b).) The UCC filing system provides a mechanism for creditors to establish the priority of security interests they secure from debtors and allows them to determine if others already have a claim on collateral. It sets the priority of valid security interests in the same collateral through a registration system. The statutory scheme is not intended to provide a vehicle for creditors to take advantage of persons with whom they have a fiduciary relationship. The application of equitable principles in this case strengthens the statutory scheme. Not rewarding the product of sharp practices in the creation of a security interest lends stability and security in commercial transactions among fiduciaries.

182 Cal. Rptr. 3d at 175-76.

4. The Code's only explicit reference to the intended relation between common law and statute is the single sentence about "displacement" (§1-103(b))—already quoted in the Introductory Note to this section, in *French Lumber*, and in *Knox v. Phoenix Leasing*). In the traditional conception, statutory provisions constitute an overlay, superimposed on a common-law background, which they modify or displace only to the extent necessary to achieve statutory objectives. The background itself—neither mapped nor explained by the statute,

let alone codified—comprises the vast body of legal and equitable rules with which the judges and lawyers to whom the statute is addressed are presumed to be familiar. The background law underlying the UCC in this conception includes all of common-law contract and much of personal property law, as well as the particular topics that the drafters chose to mention in §1-103(b). Notice that every one of the topics specifically listed—with the exception of "the law merchant" and "bankruptcy"—might be classified somewhere within the law of restitution.

This relation between background and overlay is logically simple but precarious in practice, because the Code leaves the issue of "displacement" to be decided in each instance as a matter of inference. Deciding whether a particular background rule operates to supplement Code provisions requires first that the rule and its potential application be adequately perceived. Because the text of the Code never refers to the common law background against which it operates (though Official Comments sometimes make this relationship explicit), the question to be decided will only be perceived by lawyers for whom the pre-Code rules retain sufficient salience and weight.

On the other side of the coin—because displacement is always implied, never explicit—drawing the proper inference about displacement simultaneously requires a judgment about what the Code is intended to accomplish and the means necessary to those ends. Where "particular provisions" have evidently been written to resolve troublesome issues of pre-Code law, the answer is clear. Thus where article 2 imposes uniform modern solutions to certain well-known problems of common-law contracts, we see the most obvious kind of "displacement." As an example at a higher level of generality, article 9's explicit choice of a "pure race" regime to determine priority between competing security interests (§9-322) plainly displaces some relevant principles of equity—which would subordinate the interests of subsequent lienors to prior liens of which they had notice—to achieve a system of priorities that is easier to administer. Displacement in this context is reasonably clear, because the alternative (the "race-notice" regime of real property recording systems) is so familiar, and because the language of §9-322 leaves no room for it. Yet even in this important context, as the court held in *Feresi v. The Livery*, displacement need not be all or nothing. Mere opportunism in pushing to the front of the line might be tolerated as the price of greater simplicity. But a secured party whose status as "first to file or perfect" is the result of fraud, duress, or breach of duty is not necessarily entitled to the same statutory priority.

Knox v. Phoenix Leasing examines a more difficult aspect of the "displacement" question. The defendant's contention (ultimately accepted by the court in that case) is that equitable considerations of the kind advanced by Knox are inconsistent with the regular functioning of the statutory scheme—not because they contradict explicit policy choices, but because the proper functioning of the system established by article 9 requires more conscientious adherence to its procedures. The conclusion seems reasonable in the context. Still, equitable considerations of the kind advanced by Knox—we might almost say, the rules of unjust enrichment generally—are *always* inconsistent with the regular functioning of some legal scheme, statutory or otherwise. To put it another way: if courts were always "willing to accept occasionally harsh results as the price to be paid for preserving the integrity of the scheme"—whatever the scheme might be—how much of the law of unjust enrichment would ever be tolerated?

In re Motors Liquidation Co.
777 F.3d 100 (2d Cir. 2015)

PER CURIAM (WINTER, WESLEY, and CARNEY, Circuit Judges):

We assume familiarity with our prior certification opinion, *Official Committee of Unsecured Creditors of Motors Liquidation Co. v. JPMorgan Chase Bank, N.A. (In re Motors Liquidation Co.)*, 755 F.3d 78 (2d Cir. 2014), and the resulting decision of the Delaware Supreme Court, *Official Committee of Unsecured Creditors of Motors Liquidation Co. v. JPMorgan Chase Bank, N.A.*, 103 A.3d 1010 (Del. 2014). We restate the most salient facts.

Background

In October 2001, General Motors entered into a synthetic lease financing transaction by which it obtained approximately $300 million in financing from a syndicate of lenders including JPMorgan Chase Bank, N.A. General Motors' obligation to repay the Synthetic Lease was secured by liens on twelve pieces of real estate. JP Morgan served as administrative agent for the Synthetic Lease and was identified on the UCC–1 financing statements as the secured party of record.

Five years later, General Motors entered into a separate term loan facility. The Term Loan was entirely unrelated to the Synthetic Lease and provided General Motors with approximately $1.5 billion in financing from a different syndicate of lenders. To secure the loan, the lenders took security interests in a large number of General Motors' assets, including all of General Motors' equipment and fixtures at forty-two facilities throughout the United States. JPMorgan again served as administrative agent and secured party of record for the Term Loan and caused the filing of twenty-eight UCC–1 financing statements around the country to perfect the lenders' security interests in the collateral. One such financing statement, the "Main Term Loan UCC–1," was filed with the Delaware Secretary of State and bore file number "6416808 4." It "covered, among other things, all of the equipment and fixtures at 42 GM facilities, [and] was by far the most important" of the financing statements filed in connection with the Term Loan. *Official Comm. of Unsecured Creditors of Motors Liquidation Co. v. JPMorgan Chase Bank, N.A. (In re Motors Liquidation Co.)*, 486 B.R. 596, 603 n.6 (Bankr. S.D.N.Y. 2013).

In September 2008, as the Synthetic Lease was nearing maturity, General Motors contacted Mayer Brown LLP, its counsel responsible for the Synthetic Lease, and explained that it planned to repay the amount due. General Motors requested that Mayer Brown prepare the documents necessary for JPMorgan and the lenders to be repaid and to release the interests the lenders held in General Motors' property.

A Mayer Brown partner assigned the work to an associate and instructed him to prepare a closing checklist and drafts of the documents required to pay off the Synthetic Lease and to terminate the lenders' security interests in General Motors' property relating to the Synthetic Lease. One of the steps required to unwind the Synthetic Lease was to create a list of security interests held by General Motors' lenders that would need to be terminated. To prepare the list, the Mayer Brown associate asked a paralegal who was unfamiliar with the transaction or the purpose of the request to perform a search for UCC–1 financing statements that had been recorded against General Motors in Delaware. The paralegal's search identified three UCC–1s, numbered 2092532 5, 2092526 7, and 6416808 4. Neither the paralegal nor the associate realized that only the first two of the UCC–1s were related to the Synthetic Lease. The third, UCC–1 number 6416808 4, related instead to the Term Loan.

When Mayer Brown prepared a Closing Checklist of the actions required to unwind the Synthetic Lease, it identified the Main Term Loan UCC–1 for termination alongside the security interests that actually did need to be terminated. And when Mayer Brown prepared draft UCC–3 statements to terminate the three security interests identified in the Closing Checklist, it prepared a UCC–3 statement to terminate the Main Term Loan UCC–1 as well as those related to the Synthetic Lease.

No one at General Motors, Mayer Brown, JPMorgan, or its counsel, Simpson Thacher & Bartlett LLP, noticed the error, even though copies of the Closing Checklist and draft UCC–3 termination statements were sent to individuals at each organization for review. On October 30, 2008, General Motors repaid the amount due on the Synthetic Lease. All three UCC–3s were filed with the Delaware Secretary of State, including the UCC–3 that erroneously identified for termination the Main Term Loan UCC–1, which was entirely unrelated to the Synthetic Lease.

A. GENERAL MOTORS' CHAPTER 11 BANKRUPTCY FILING

The mistake went unnoticed until General Motors' bankruptcy in 2009. After General Motors filed for chapter 11 reorganization, JPMorgan informed the Committee of Unsecured Creditors (the "Committee") that a UCC–3 termination statement relating to the Term Loan had been inadvertently filed in October 2008. JPMorgan explained that it had intended to terminate only liens related to the Synthetic Lease and stated that the filing was therefore unauthorized and ineffective.

On July 31, 2009, the Committee commenced the underlying action against JPMorgan in the United States Bankruptcy Court for the Southern District of New York. The Committee sought a determination that, despite the error, the

UCC–3 termination statement was effective to terminate the Term Loan security interest and render JPMorgan an unsecured creditor on par with the other General Motors unsecured creditors. JPMorgan disagreed, reasoning that the UCC–3 termination statement was unauthorized and therefore ineffective because no one at JPMorgan, General Motors, or their law firms had intended that the Term Loan security interest be terminated. On cross-motions for summary judgment, the Bankruptcy Court concluded that the UCC–3 filing was unauthorized and therefore not effective to terminate the Term Loan security interest. In re Motors Liquidation Co., 486 B.R. at 647–48.

B. PRIOR CERTIFICATION OPINION

On appeal to this Court, the parties offered competing interpretations of UCC §9–509(d)(1), which provides that a UCC–3 termination statement is effective only if "the secured party of record authorizes the filing." JPMorgan reasoned that it cannot have "authorize[d] the filing" of the UCC–3 that identified the Main Term Loan UCC–1 for termination because JPMorgan neither intended to terminate the security interest nor instructed anyone else to do so on its behalf. In response, the Committee contended that focusing on the parties' goal misses the point. It interpreted UCC §9–509(d)(1) to require only that the secured lender authorize the act of filing a particular UCC–3 termination statement, not that the lender subjectively intend to terminate the particular security interest identified for termination on that UCC–3. The Committee further argued that even if JPMorgan never intentionally instructed anyone to terminate the Main Term Loan UCC–1, JPMorgan did literally "authorize the filing"—even if mistakenly—of a UCC–3 termination statement that had that effect.

In our prior certification opinion we recognized that this appeal presents two closely related questions. First, what precisely must a secured lender of record authorize for a UCC–3 termination statement to be effective: "Must the secured lender authorize the termination of the particular security interest that the UCC–3 identifies for termination, or is it enough that the secured lender authorize the act of filing a UCC–3 statement that has that effect?" In re Motors Liquidation Co., 755 F.3d at 84. Second, "Did JPMorgan grant to Mayer Brown the relevant authority—that is, alternatively, authority either to terminate the Main Term Loan UCC–1 or to file the UCC–3 statement that identified that interest for termination?" Id.

Recognizing that the first question—what is it that the UCC requires a secured lender to authorize—seemed likely to recur and presented a significant issue of Delaware state law, we certified to the Delaware Supreme Court the following question:

> Under UCC Article 9, as adopted into Delaware law by Del. Code Ann. tit. 6, art. 9, for a UCC–3 termination statement to effectively extinguish the perfected nature of a UCC–1 financing statement, is it enough that the secured lender review and knowingly approve for filing a UCC–3 purporting to extinguish the perfected security interest, or must the secured lender intend to terminate the particular security interest that is listed on the UCC–3?

Id. at 86. The second question—whether JPMorgan granted the relevant authority—we reserved for ourselves, explaining that "[t]he Delaware Supreme Court's clarification as to the sense in which a secured party of record must authorize a UCC–3 filing will enable us to address whether JPMorgan in fact provided that authorization." *Id.* at 86–87.

C. THE DELAWARE SUPREME COURT'S ANSWER

In a speedy and thorough reply, the Delaware Supreme Court answered the certified question, explaining that if the secured party of record authorizes the filing of a UCC–3 termination statement, then that filing is effective regardless of whether the secured party subjectively intends or understands the effect of that filing:

> [F]or a termination statement to become effective under §9–509 and thus to have the effect specified in §9–513 of the Delaware UCC, it is enough that the secured party authorizes the filing to be made, which is all that §9–510 requires. The Delaware UCC contains no requirement that a secured party that authorizes a filing subjectively intends or otherwise understands the effect of the plain terms of its own filing.

Official Comm. of Unsecured Creditors of Motors Liquidation Co., 103 A.3d at 1017–18. That conclusion, explained the court, follows both from the unambiguous terms of the UCC and from sound policy considerations:

> JPMorgan's argument that a filing is only effective if the authorizing party understands the filing's substantive terms and intends their effect is contrary to §9–509, which only requires that "the secured party of record authorize the filing."
>
> Even if the statute were ambiguous, we would be reluctant to embrace JPMorgan's proposition. Before a secured party authorizes the filing of a termination statement, it ought to review the statement carefully and understand which security interests it is releasing and why. If parties could be relieved from the legal consequences of their mistaken filings, they would have little incentive to ensure the accuracy of the information contained in their UCC filings.

Id. at 1014–16.

Discussion

The Delaware Supreme Court has explained the sense in which a secured party must "authorize the filing" of a UCC–3 termination statement. What remains is to answer the question we reserved for ourselves in our prior certification opinion: Did JPMorgan authorize the filing of the UCC–3 termination statement that mistakenly identified for termination the Main Term Loan UCC–1?

In JPMorgan's view, it never instructed anyone to file the UCC–3 in question, and the termination statement was therefore unauthorized and ineffective. JPMorgan reasons that it authorized General Motors only to terminate security interests related to the Synthetic Lease; that it instructed Simpson Thacher and Mayer Brown only to take actions to accomplish that objective; and that therefore Mayer Brown must have exceeded the scope of its authority when it filed the UCC–3 purporting to terminate the Main Term Loan UCC–1.

JPMorgan's and General Motors' aims throughout the Synthetic Lease transaction were clear: General Motors would repay the Synthetic Lease, and JPMorgan would terminate its related UCC–1 security interests in General Motors' properties. The Synthetic Lease Termination Agreement provided that, upon General Motors' repayment of the amount due under the Synthetic Lease, General Motors would be authorized "to file a termination of any existing Financing Statement relating to the Properties [of the Synthetic Lease]." And, to represent its interests in the transaction, JPMorgan relied on Simpson Thacher, its counsel for matters related to the Synthetic Lease. No one at JPMorgan, Simpson Thacher, General Motors, or Mayer Brown took action intending to affect the Term Loan.

What JPMorgan intended to accomplish, however, is a distinct question from what actions it authorized to be taken on its behalf. Mayer Brown prepared a Closing Checklist, draft UCC–3 termination statements, and an Escrow Agreement, all aimed at unwinding the Synthetic Lease but tainted by one crucial error: The documents included a UCC–3 termination statement that erroneously identified for termination a security interest related not to the Synthetic Lease but to the Term Loan. The critical question in this case is whether JPMorgan "authorize[d] [Mayer Brown] to file" that termination statement.

After Mayer Brown prepared the Closing Checklist and draft UCC–3 termination statements, copies were sent for review to a Managing Director at JPMorgan who supervised the Synthetic Lease payoff and who had signed the Term Loan documents on JPMorgan's behalf. Mayer Brown also sent copies of the Closing Checklist and draft UCC–3 termination statements to JPMorgan's counsel, Simpson Thacher, to ensure that the parties to the transaction agreed as to the documents required to complete the Synthetic Lease payoff transaction. Neither directly nor through its counsel did JPMorgan express any concerns about the draft UCC–3 termination statements or about the Closing Checklist. A Simpson Thacher attorney responded simply as follows: "Nice job on the documents. My only comment, unless I am missing something, is that all references to JPMorgan Chase Bank, as Administrative Agent for the Investors should not include the reference 'for the Investors.'"

After preparing the closing documents and circulating them for review, Mayer Brown drafted an Escrow Agreement that instructed the parties' escrow agent how to proceed with the closing. Among other things, the Escrow Agreement specified that the parties would deliver to the escrow agent the set of three UCC–3 termination statements (individually identified by UCC–1 financing statement file number) that would be filed to terminate the security interests that General Motors' Synthetic Lease lenders held in its properties. The Escrow Agreement provided that once General Motors repaid the amount due on the Synthetic Lease, the escrow agent would forward copies of the UCC–3 termination statements to General Motors' counsel for filing. When Mayer Brown e-mailed a draft of the Escrow Agreement to JPMorgan's counsel for review, the same Simpson Thacher attorney responded that "it was fine" and signed the agreement.

From these facts it is clear that although JPMorgan never intended to terminate the Main Term Loan UCC–1, it authorized the filing of a UCC–3 termination statement that had that effect. "Actual authority . . . is created by a principal's manifestation to an agent that, as reasonably understood by the agent, expresses the principal's assent that the agent take action on the principal's behalf." Restatement (Third) of Agency §3.01 (2006); *accord* Demarco v. Edens, 390 F.2d 836, 844 (2d Cir. 1968). JPMorgan and Simpson Thacher's repeated manifestations to Mayer Brown show that JPMorgan and its counsel knew that, upon the closing of the Synthetic Lease transaction, Mayer Brown was going to file the termination statement that identified the Main Term Loan UCC–1 for termination and that JPMorgan reviewed and assented to the filing of that statement. Nothing more is needed.

Conclusion

For the foregoing reasons, we REVERSE the Bankruptcy Court's grant of summary judgment for the Defendant and REMAND with instructions to the Bankruptcy Court to enter partial summary judgment for the Plaintiff as to the termination of the Main Term Loan UCC–1.

The dog that didn't bark

1. The outstanding indebtedness under GM's Term Loan was approximately $1.5 billion. The difference to the banks in the value of secured and unsecured loans in this amount will have depended on the circumstances of the GM bankruptcy, but it was presumably in the hundreds of millions of dollars. Have GM's unsecured creditors been unjustly enriched at the expense of the Term Loan syndicate?

2. JPMorgan as agent for the banks may or may not have "authorized" the filing of an erroneous termination statement: that question is a subtle and potentially difficult one. Assuming the filing was authorized and effective, however, the consequence is simply that a security interest has been terminated by mistake. (What if the extraneous UCC-3 had been personally signed

by J. P. Morgan himself?) Just as in cases of mistaken payment, a mistaken termination or discharge is the beginning of the problem in restitution, not the conclusion.

3. The most significant aspect of "displacement" in *Motors Liquidation* is found in the fact that the principles of law and equity most directly relevant to the case were entirely ignored. The real case for the banks depended on the law and equity of *mistake*. Unless what the UCC calls "the law governing mistake and restitution" (see §§3-418(b), 4A-303) has been displaced by something in article 9, JPMorgan and its syndicate were entitled to restitution to avoid the unjust enrichment of GM's unsecured creditors. Equitable relief to the banks would be a simple matter of declaring the erroneous termination ineffective, or reinstating the lien that was erroneously discharged.

To judge from the four published opinions in *Motors Liquidation*, counsel for the banks never made this argument—even as a fallback position, in case their argument about authority was unsuccessful. Nor did the courts involved appear to understand that—from the standpoint of traditional law and equity— the elaborate debate about authority was ultimately a red herring.

4. Because there is no doubt about what the "principles of law and equity" require, the argument for GM's unsecured creditors would necessarily have been that those principles have been "displaced by the particular provisions of the Uniform Commercial Code." UCC §9-513(d) provides that "upon the filing of a termination statement with the filing office, the financing statement to which the termination statement relates ceases to be effective." Does this provision displace the principles of law and equity that would govern the situation in *Motors Liquidation* if the UCC had not been adopted?

5. Section 1-103(b) refers to "*particular provisions* of the UCC," but the more frequent concern of the courts—as illustrated by *Knox v. Phoenix Leasing*—is with structural implications: the threat posed to the "stability" and "predictability" of the article 9 priority scheme by allowing equitable principles to supplement the Code in particular cases. We can probably agree that stability and predictability would be undermined if Knox, the wine-barrel merchant, could ignore the routine UCC procedures available to perfect his purchase-money security interest, then obtain the same protection by an equitable detour. Does the conduct of JPMorgan, whose security interest was fully perfected (and predictable) until it was terminated by a clerical error, pose a similar risk?

6. Are the structural integrity and underlying policies of article 9 better served by restoring the secured creditors to their intended priority (the position everyone thought they occupied), or by permitting the unintended transfer of hundreds of millions of dollars from one set of creditors to another?

7. Is it relevant that in *Motors Liquidation* there were no "intervening equities"—in other words, interests that would be prejudiced if the banks' mistake were corrected? Potential prejudice would typically be to "reliance creditors": creditors that extended credit to GM (or otherwise changed position) in reliance on the erroneous termination statement. In *Motors Liquidation*, nobody

imagined for a moment that the Term Loan had become unsecured. (Indeed, GM's bankruptcy trustee had already repaid the Term Loan before the filing problem came to light.) Does the potential difficulty of identifying "reliance creditors" in other cases justify a refusal to correct the mistake in this one?

8. The Delaware Supreme Court, with the evident approval of the Second Circuit, identified another reason to find displacement: "If parties could be relieved from the legal consequences of their mistaken filings, they would have little incentive to ensure the accuracy of the information contained in their UCC filings." Is the problem in *Motors Liquidation* a lack of proper incentives? Consider how much of the law and equity of restitution and unjust enrichment might be open to the same objection.

TABLE OF CASES

Principal cases in italics

563

INDEX